The HAJJ *and* BRITAIN'S MUSLIM EMPIRE

The HAJJ *and* BRITAIN'S MUSLIM EMPIRE

JOHN SLIGHT

SPEAKING TIGER

SPEAKING TIGER BOOKS LLP
125-A, Ground Floor, Shahpur Jat
New Delhi – 110049

First published by Harvard University Press
This edition first published in India by Speaking Tiger Books 2024

Published by arrangement with Harvard University Press

ISBN: 978-93-5447-895-6

10 9 8 7 6 5 4 3 2 1

Printed at Chaman Enterprises, New Delhi

Contents

Preface to the South Asian Edition

This book examines the relationship between British imperialism and the Hajj, the Muslim pilgrimage to Mecca. It grew out of a long-standing research interest of mine in the interactions between the British empire and Islam, in all its facets.

I decided to focus on the Hajj for a number of reasons, academic and personal. First, the Hajj, being one of the five pillars of Islam, is an extremely important part of most Muslims' faith, and when Muslims pray, they pray towards Mecca, where the main part of the Hajj takes place. Second, I was struck by the importance of this ritual on my first visit to Hyderabad, to meet my soon to be mother-in-law, Mrs. Aparajita Sinha (my then girlfriend, now wife of fourteen years, Dr. Mishka Sinha, was somewhere else, so left me to do this on my own…). When I landed at Hyderabad airport, I was surprised to see it had its own Hajj terminal. And as it was the month of Hajj, the airport was filled with pilgrims. The atmosphere was electric, with a mixture of emotions—spiritual fervour, excitement, and the more banal things like making sure the baggage was not overweight. While in Hyderabad, I spent much time in conversation with Muslims, Sunni and Shi'a, about the Hajj and Islam, which was extremely fruitful—learning about their personal stories of going to Hijaz to perform Hajj, and to Medina to visit Prophet Muhammad's tomb. Some of them also spoke about their experiences as Indians when they were in a sacred, holy, yet foreign land. For me, these were incredible encounters; proof of how the past is always in the present, when something that a scholar studies through old archival documents remains alive—even though, while the rituals of Hajj have not changed, the experiences certainly have, politically, economically, socially and culturally.

While the book covers the main territories in Africa and Asia where Britain ruled over Muslim colonial subjects, it has a particular relevance for South Asian readers. In the book, I put forward the concept of Britain's Muslim empire—an 'inner empire' that comprised territories that contained large numbers of Muslim subjects—as a way of understanding how the British interacted with Islam in a connected way, sharing information between these territories about Islamic practice, and how they thought this should be administered (with varying results). While there were many such territories, from West Africa to the South China Sea, colonial India was of the utmost importance. Not only from its status as the most important colony in the British empire, the 'jewel in the crown', but also because it contained the largest number of Muslim colonial subjects, from virtually all the different interpretations of the Islamic faith. Moreover, Indian Muslims were a major part of the imperial Indian diaspora, living in colonies as far flung as Malaya and Kenya.

As readers will see in the book, colonial India is a central presence throughout, because the largest number of British colonial subjects in Hijaz to perform Hajj were from there (and, indeed, there was a large number of Indians who settled in Hijaz for trade and Islamic scholarship). To give a snapshot of this, in 1912, in Bombay, over 12,000 pilgrims descended on the port for the Hajj season in order to take their passage on boats going to Jidda, the main port closest to Mecca. Many of their journeys were incredible, coming from the high passes of the Himalayas, the villages of Bengal and from even further afield, such as Afghanistan and Chinese Turkestan. This was an annual phenomenon that colonial officials could not but fail to notice, and decided to attempt to administer, with distinctly mixed results, as the book shows. But this is not a simple story of Britishers versus Indians; the growing complexity of what I have termed Britain's Hajj administration involved a very large number of Indians who worked for the British, in places from Calcutta to Bombay to the British consulate in Jidda. Indeed, some of the Indian Vice-Consuls in Jidda, men such as Dr. Abdur Razzack and Munshi Ihsanullah, were instrumental in shaping Britain's policy towards the Hajj.

Colonial India's relationship with the Hajj highlights the variegated, complex and often chaotic nature of British imperialism.

There was the India that was directly administered by the British, where, in places such as Bengal, officials attempted to stop the activities of pilgrim guides (*mutawwifin*) who toured the villages to encourage peasants to perform Hajj, but who also often engaged in nefarious practices designed to take as much money from these pilgrims as possible. Then there was the India of the Princely States, where Muslim rulers such as the Begums of Bhopal and the Nizams of Hyderabad had teams of administrative staff who facilitated the Hajj for their subjects, in many cases subsidising the costs of pilgrimage for them, without any involvement from the British at all. (The Begums of Bhopal went on Hajj themselves, as detailed in the book.) Among my most cherished archival finds, with the help of my mother-in-law and eminent scholars in Hyderabad, were records of the Nizam's government archives in the Andhra Pradesh State Archives, which painted a fascinating portrait of how the Hajj was administered from what was then considered the premier Muslim princely state.

A major change in the socio-economic profile of pilgrims happened during the colonial period. The advent of steamships, and what has been called imperial globalisation, meant that the cost of going from India to Hijaz for the Hajj plummeted. Many pilgrims, then, bought one-way tickets from Indian ports to Hijaz, performed Hajj, but then had no money to return home. This caused an enormous amount of complications for exasperated British colonial and consular officials, who simply couldn't understand the importance of the ritual in the first place. While these so-called 'pauper pilgrims' also came from other places in the empire such as Nigeria and Sudan, Indians made up the largest contingent. The British, in light of the ferment of the post First World War period with Indian nationalism and the Khilafat movement, decided to spend large amounts of money repatriating these pilgrims back to India, thereby inadvertently facilitating the Hajj.

The story of the Hajj during the height of the British empire is a fascinating one, and it shows us, from a new angle, how Islam was a central part of the British imperial experience, and also how colonial India was the most important component of that. And it is not a story that simply ended when freedom began at midnight in 1947. Indian and Pakistani foreign service officials continued to liaise with British consular officials in Jidda regarding their pilgrim citizens. And, during the Suez Crisis of 1956, the Saudi rupture of diplomatic relations with Britain led the British consulate in Jidda to be staffed by Pakistani officials dealing with their own pilgrim citizens as well as those from the remaining parts of the British empire. History is always complex, and perhaps this is no more so than in this case of the South Asian experience of the Hajj during the era of British imperialism. But in order to make sense of our present, and chart our future, we must understand the past, which is what this book tries to do.

Dr. John Slight
Oxford, May 2024

The HAJJ *and* BRITAIN'S MUSLIM EMPIRE

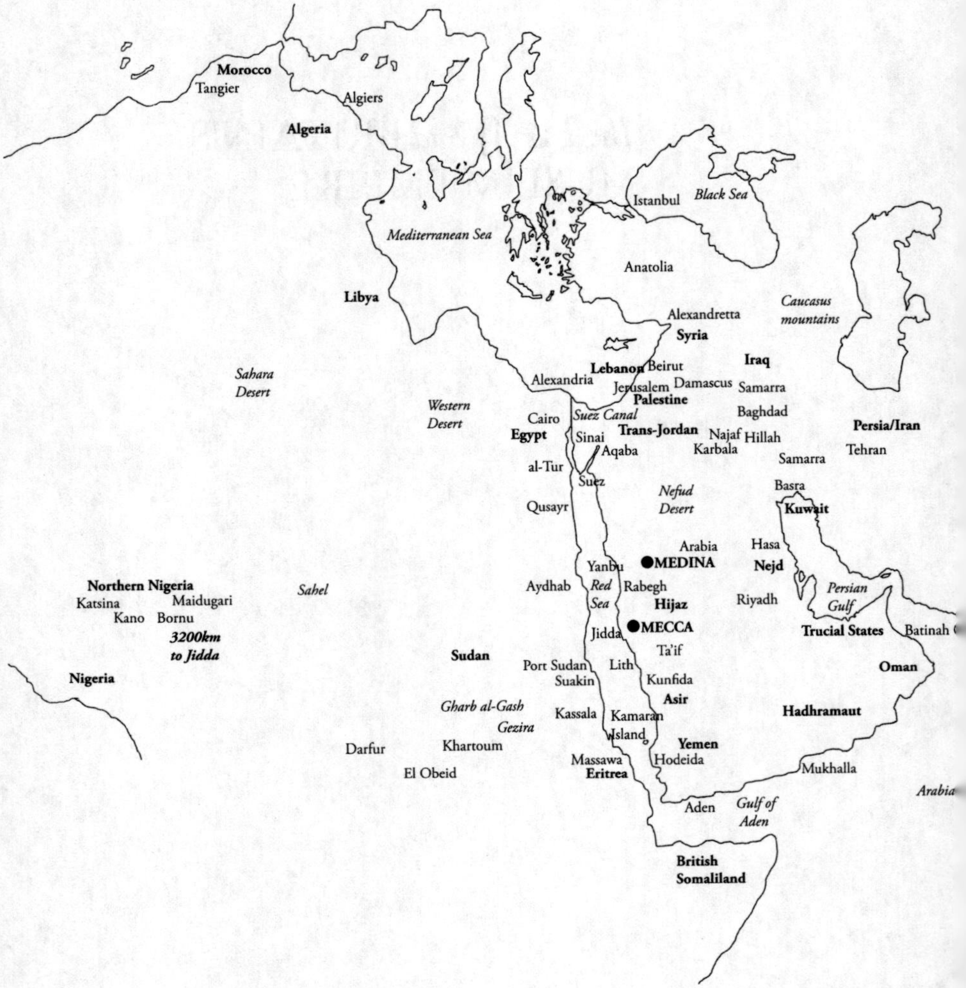

Map of places mentioned in the book

Credit: John O'Connor/John Slight

Kashgar
Kabul
North-West Frontier
Kashmir
Srinagar
Quetta
Lahore
Pakpattan
Wazirabad
Deoband
Delhi
Rampur
Aligarh
Agra
Mahmudabad
Jaipur
Lucknow
Jaunpur
Bengal
Ajmer
United Provinces
Allahabad
Bhagulpoor
Serampore
Karachi
Gujarat
Bhopal
Calcutta
Midnapoor
Kathiawar
Surat
British India and dependent Princely States
24 Pargannahs
Burma
Daman
Diu
Bombay
Rangoon
3500km to Jidda
Hyderabad
Deccan
Bay of Bengal
South China Sea
Philippines
Malabar coast
Mysore
Madras
Aleppy
Ceylon
Zamboanga
Sulu
Penang
Kedah
Kuala Lumpur
Kelantan
Malaya
Seramban
Selangor
Johore
Singapore
Bandar Aceh
Brunei
North Borneo
Sarawak
7350 km to Jidda
Indian Ocean
Netherlands East Indies
Java
Surabaya

Introduction

Britain's Muslim Empire

THIS BOOK IS a study of the British empire's interactions with the Hajj, the Muslim pilgrimage to Mecca, from 1865 to 1956. The crucial events of these dates are the 1865 cholera epidemic, when pilgrims carried this disease from India to Arabia and enabled its spread to Europe, prompting greater British involvement in the ritual, and the 1956 Suez Crisis, which forced Britain to temporarily cede control of its Hajj administration in Saudi Arabia to its Pakistani counterparts. In examining Britain's wide-ranging and complex engagement with the Hajj, this book argues for a fresh angle of vision in viewing the British empire through the conceptualization of a British Muslim empire. Islamic scholar David Margoliouth, writing in 1912, believed that Britain was "the greatest Moslem power in the world," an opinion shared by many British statesmen, politicians, officials, soldiers, academics, and journalists.[1] In 1902, Sir Richard Temple, an official in the government of India, went even further: "It is impossible to distinguish Anglo-Mohamedan power from Britain itself."[2] Significantly, some of Britain's Muslim subjects held similar views. For example, Indian Muslim scholar Cheragh Ali wrote in 1883 that "the British Empire is the greatest Mohamedan power in the world."[3] More recently, Faisal Devji has argued that "such rhetorical forms of religious authority played an important role in formulating British policy, and were often tailored to suit the conveniences of Muslims themselves."[4] This type of rhetoric, extensively employed from the 1870s, was often based on little more than demography and a realization that Britain was steadily expanding its power over what came to be known as the Muslim world. Moving beyond such rhetoric, this book asks: What were the material considerations of Britain's engagement with Islam?

British interactions with the Hajj are an ideal case study for focusing attention on the broader importance of Islam and Muslims to the British empire, and on the concept of Britain as ruler of a Muslim empire. As the fifth pillar of Islam, the pilgrimage to Mecca is an important Islamic practice. The Hajj is simultaneously local and transcontinental, as pilgrims travel from their homes across the world in order to gather in one place in Arabia: the Holy City of Mecca, a location of great religious and geopolitical significance. The pilgrimage is the most significant large-scale movement of people in history for a common religious purpose. In the period covered by this book, a large proportion of pilgrims came from territories under various forms of British control. The Hajj and the pilgrims that performed this ritual became a subject of great interest to imperial powers, Britain first among them. Britain's engagement with the pilgrimage became an established feature of imperial administrations across Africa and Asia. This work argues that as a result of the scope and depth of British involvement in the pilgrimage, Britain's Muslim empire was a tangible political, organizational, and religious entity. This conceptual vision of the British empire provides a valuable new framework for examining Anglo-Muslim interactions in the imperial era and for rethinking the nature of Britain's imperial experience.

In global terms, the British empire's first religion was Islam. Britain ruled over the largest number of Muslims in the world during this period, and its empire contained more Muslims than any other religious group. Across British territories in Africa and Asia, Islam was a common thread. If one reflects on the spatial dimensions of Britain's Muslim empire, Britain possessed what can be termed an "inner empire" of territories that had substantial Muslim populations. Ranging from West Africa to Southeast Asia, this inner empire included the Gambia, Sierra Leone, the Gold Coast, Northern Nigeria, Sudan, Kenya, Tanganyika, Zanzibar, Egypt, Somaliland, Palestine, Trans-Jordan, Iraq, Kuwait, Bahrain, Qatar, the Trucial States, Aden, India, Malaya, Brunei, and Sarawak.[5] This inner empire was a patchwork quilt, like the empire as a whole, and a diverse and interconnected space.[6] The Hajj transcended this empire's arbitrarily imposed colonial boundaries; it was one principal feature that connected the different territories of this inner empire and came to command official attention across this space. The important fact that the British empire contained demographically large and geographically diverse Muslim populations has been noted by only a handful of historians, such as John Darwin, Faisal Devji, Ronald Hyam, and Francis Robinson.[7] This book contributes to these existing studies by examining Britain's relationship with the Muslim world in a much more extended way through analysis of the material considerations of Britain's involvement in the Hajj from a selection of this inner empire's territories. This Islamic inner empire stands in contrast to what could be called an "outer empire" of white settler colonies and dominions, which some historians since the early 2000s have conceptualized as the "British World."[8]

Through analyzing Britain's relationship with the Hajj, this book argues that the governance of religious practices, central to the exercise and legitimation of imperial power, is a vital framework of inquiry in assessing the imperial experience.[9] Therefore, it is important to examine the more practical, quotidian consequences of British rule over millions of people whose faith was Islam. A variety of Islamic religious practices and the peoples intimately associated with them were features of the faith that imperial and colonial authorities engaged with, such as the moral code and religious law called *shari'a;* legal scholars and judges; religious endowments, known as *waqf;* religious celebrations and festivals such as Ramadan and *'Id al-Fitr; mawlid,* celebrations of the Prophet Muhammad's birthday and the birthdays of Sufi saints; mosques; and Sufi orders.[10] Of course, there were many other areas of colonial and imperial engagement where Islam was an important factor, such as the religious education of Muslims, the employment of Muslims in the empire's various armed forces and its numerous colonial, imperial, and consular bureaucracies, the co-option of local Muslim rulers and leaders into the imperial superstructure, and the resistance, armed or otherwise, of Muslims to British rule.[11] British engagement with Islamic practice had enormous implications for everyday imperial governance and for the daily lived experiences of Muslims within the British imperial

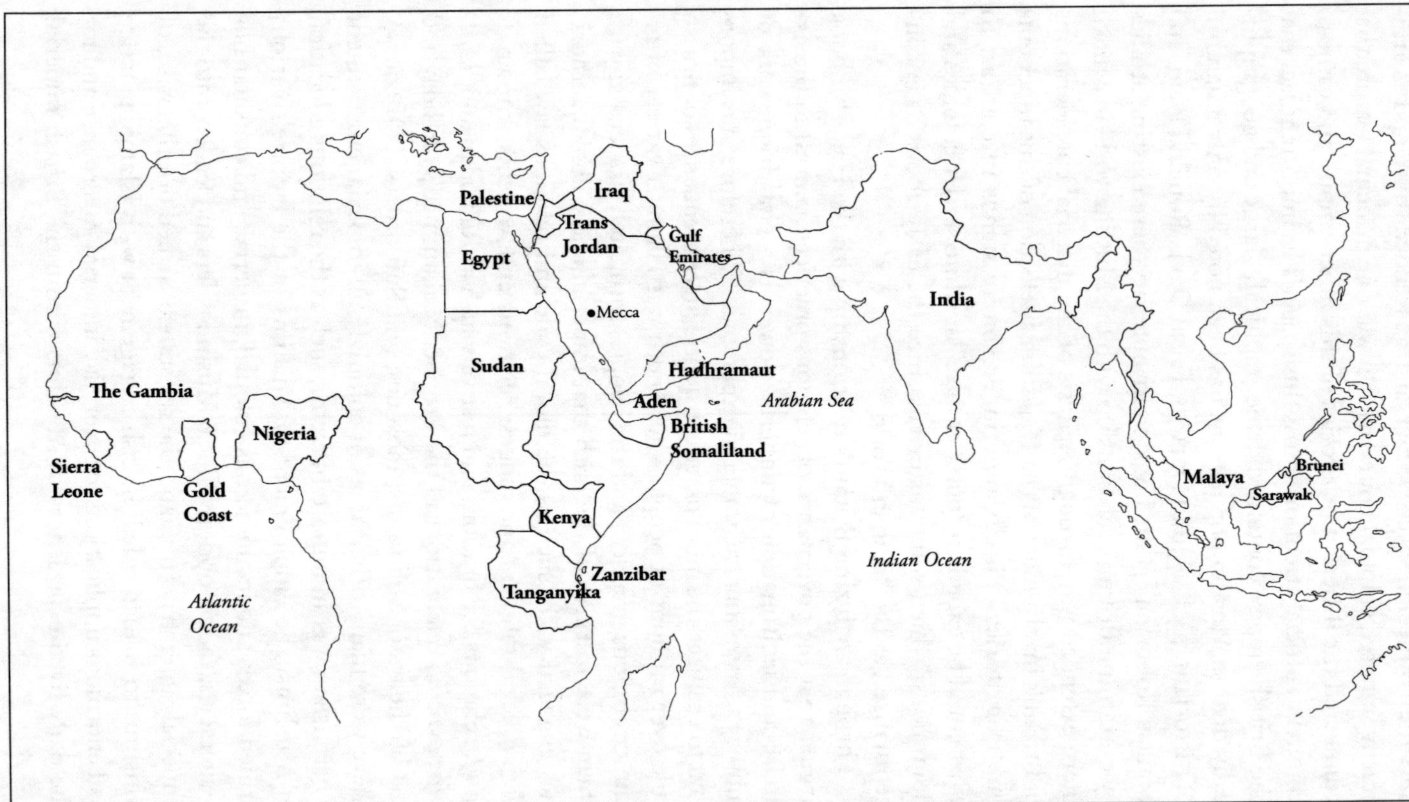

Britain's Muslim empire, c. 1920

Credit: John O'Connor/John Slight

space. Islamic practice could not be ignored or neatly categorized as a tradition that was set in aspic or occurred in a vacuum, whatever the views of some British officials and observers might be. Technology, disease, the movements of people and ideas, politics, ideologies, charity, trade, social relations, law, international relations, and war—all these were entangled with many Islamic religious practices that, in turn, shaped, and were shaped by, British imperial governance. It is this wider landscape of imperial interactions with Islamic practice, outside the scope of this work, that lends further empirical weight to the concept of Britain's Muslim empire, in addition to the case study of the Hajj on which this book focuses.

By the early twentieth century, the Hajj had become an everyday part of imperial administration.[12] Because thousands of subjects left their homes every year to travel to Mecca, it was a movement of people that British officials could hardly fail to notice—an annual phenomenon as familiar to the district officer in Northern Nigeria as it was to the district collector in rural Bengal. For example, the 1932 pilgrimage report compiled by the British consulate at Jidda stated that it should enjoy "the widest possible circulation to British authorities having any interest in the pilgrimage." This report was copied to the Foreign, India, and Colonial Offices in London and to British administrations in Palestine, Iraq, Nigeria, Malaya, India, Egypt, and Sudan.[13] Some historians view the Hajj as a "unique dilemma of empire"—it could not be restricted, given the limited reach of imperial and colonial bureaucracies and concerns about potential unrest, but pilgrims caused a variety of administrative complications within Britain's Muslim empire and the Hijaz itself.[14] Britain had perforce to deal with the Hajj, initially in regard to public health, but imperial engagement with the pilgrimage rapidly encompassed a variety of areas beyond trying to prevent the spread of epidemic diseases. It was not the case, as some have argued, that the British were unconcerned with Islamic rituals such as the Hajj unless they directly threatened imperial rule.[15] Indeed, in the case of the Hajj, the most significant unintended consequence of Britain's involvement was its facilitation of the pilgrimage in an ultimately futile attempt to gain legitimacy among its Muslim subjects. In doing so, it echoed the practices of older Islamic empires, but in the context of subsidized passages on steamships and telegraphed pilgrimage reports. Tracing the lineaments of these developments in detail demonstrates how Britain came to act like a Muslim power, albeit inadvertently. Although studies exist on how the Ottoman, Safavid, and Mughal empires sponsored Islamic practices such as the Hajj to buttress their legitimacy, there has been no comparable wide-ranging work on the British empire.[16]

The Geographies of Britain's "Imperial Hajj"

This book focuses mainly on the territories in Britain's Muslim empire—India, Malaya, Sudan, and Nigeria—that accounted for the vast majority of Britain's pilgrim-subjects who traveled to and from the Hijaz every year. Despite the important differences between the internal dynamics of these disparate societies, as well as their local and regional contexts, each year thousands of people from all these places made the same momentous decision—to leave their homes and set out for the Hijaz to perform the Hajj. Some returned, others settled in the Hijaz, and others died during their journeys or in the Hijaz itself. In any history book, there are limits of coverage, and this list obviously excludes several British territories from which Muslims went on Hajj.[17]

Geographically, the Indian Ocean has been a favored space of inquiry for historians such as Sugata Bose who have studied Britain and the Hajj.[18] Their work has built on studies by scholars such as Michael Pearson, who have viewed maritime spaces such as the Indian Ocean as a unified whole in order to analyze phenomena such as the pilgrimage and long-distance trade.[19] This aspect of the Indian Ocean and the waters connected to it, such as the Red Sea, did not go unnoticed during the period covered by this book. For example, in an 1867 House of Commons debate, Sir Stafford Northcote, secretary of state for India, said that he was "astonished . . . to see how frequent and close are the communications between India and the eastern side of the Red Sea. . . . Indians are not indifferent to what is passing on the eastern side." In Northcote's opinion, pilgrims to Mecca were the most important feature of these connections: "Hundreds and thousands of our subjects go to Mecca year by year, and on their way they gather reports of what is passing in the countries bordering on the Red Sea."[20]

Although the Indian Ocean is an important space in which to examine Britain's interactions with the Hajj, this book uses what Thomas Metcalf terms a "transcolonial framework" in order to encompass a broader space. This includes territories in the Indian Ocean world and those beyond it that had connections to the Hijaz by means of the Hajj. Despite their different histories, considering India and Malaya together because the Hajj from these places was a principally maritime enterprise, and bringing Nigeria and Sudan into this analytical framework, given that pilgrims from these territories crossed the Sahel and the Sahara (a space comparable to the Indian Ocean in the sense that both are vast interconnected spaces over which people, goods, and ideas travel) offers a broad scope for comparative analysis of how these British territories grappled with the pilgrimage. Taken together, these places highlight the immense diversity and interconnectedness of Britain's Muslim empire, which stretched from the Atlantic Ocean to the South China Sea, and provides a new perspective on Britain and the pilgrimage.[21]

Britain's engagement with the pilgrimage was not hermetically sealed within the borders of its inner empire. Other European colonial empires were heavily invested in the administration of the Hajj at the same time as Britain, although none experienced the scale and scope of interaction with the ritual that the British had. Indeed, British officials sometimes cooperated with these imperial powers on the subject of the pilgrimage. Many pilgrims who passed through Britain's Muslim empire, intermingling with British pilgrim-subjects at various transport hubs, often originated from areas under the colonial rule of other European powers. For the majority of this period, borders were permeable—at least for pilgrims. Pilgrims from the Netherlands East Indies often sailed to Jidda from Singapore; Afghans, Chinese, and Russian subjects from central Asia frequently headed to Bombay for the same purpose; pilgrims from French West Africa trekked through Sudan to reach the Red Sea. Similarly, pilgrims from Nigeria crossed some seven hundred kilometers of French territory on their journey across the continent to Mecca. This led to a variety of Anglo-European interactions regarding the pilgrimage, whether among British and European consular officials in the Hijaz or between authorities based in various British and European colonies. British officials often scrutinized the policies of European colonial powers on the Hajj and in some cases sought to emulate them.

Britain was a global power over and above its position in the Muslim world, and the larger political setting of Britain's administration of the Hajj was the imperial rivalries between Britain and the Ottomans, French, Dutch, Germans, Italians, and Russians. Mecca's location near the eastern littoral of the Red Sea, one of the world's most vital strategic and economic arteries, lent the Hajj particular importance in imperial calculations. In studying the Hajj, then, it is important to see beyond the artificial borders drawn by European empires and, indeed, beyond the geographic boundaries of area studies in academia.[22] The Hajj evocatively transcends borders and boundaries, both real and imaginary.

Routes to Mecca

What routes did pilgrims follow to Mecca? By briefly outlining them, we can begin to get a sense of pilgrims' travels, which formed one strand of a web of connections that crisscrossed Britain's Muslim empire and the wider Islamic world in which this empire was situated.[23] Although trade is not a focus of this book, commerce and piety often went hand in hand. Pilgrims often engaged in trading activities, and commercial and pilgrimage routes were invariably the same. Although the Hajj was the most important Muslim pilgrimage, it formed part of the broader context of Muslim religious travel, which, in the Muslim case, included journeys by scholars in search of religious knowledge *(talab al-'ilm)*, other significant Muslim pilgrimages such as those to the Shi'i centers of Najaf and Karbala in Iraq, and trips to numerous shrines of Sufi saints and notables across Asia and Africa. Although the roads to Mecca were infinite, in this period it is possible to discern certain major routes taken by pilgrims and the transport hubs they used along the way. Some had been in existence since the medieval period; others rose to prominence during the colonial era as European empires attempted to channel pilgrims along various routes, with varying degrees of success. Nevertheless, technological change and the policies pursued by the Ottoman empire and European colonial powers had a significant impact on the nature of pilgrims' routes and journeys during the course of the nineteenth century.

From West Africa, pilgrims traveled along paths through the Sahara Desert, the Sahel, and the Sudanic savanna to the Red Sea and then across to Jidda from ports such as Suakin and Massawa. Many pilgrims worked their way across Africa, even settling as laborers in Sudan, before crossing the Red Sea to perform Hajj, and then repeated the same route back home—a journey that, for some, took up to ten years.[24] Colonial authorities attempted to shape this journey's contours; they tried to funnel pilgrims along established land routes toward the Red Sea ports that had grown in this period through involvement with Indian Ocean trade.[25] Even though Suakin declined once the British established Port Sudan in 1909, it still served as an embarkation point for pilgrims traveling to Jidda. From 1925, Sudan's Gezira agricultural scheme was an important source of employment for pilgrims from West Africa. Looking northward, pilgrims traveled from the Maghrib by land and sea from ports such as Algiers and Tangier to meet those from across Egypt who gravitated toward Cairo, the starting point for a pilgrim caravan that, since the thirteenth century, had crossed the Sinai Peninsula and traveled down the Hijaz toward Mecca. The return journey from Mecca to Cairo took just over a month.[26] The Cairo caravan was a largely ceremonial affair by the late nineteenth century, when steamships attracted a larger number of pilgrims on the Suez-Jidda route. Once pilgrims reached Jidda, it was a forty-five-mile journey to Mecca itself, either in unwieldy wooden structures called *shugduf* that sat across camel's humps, on foot, or, from the 1920s, by car.

The Hijaz railway from Damascus to Medina, opened in 1908 to facilitate pilgrims' journeys and consolidate Ottoman control over that empire's Arab provinces, sounded the death knell for the Damascus pilgrim caravan. Pilgrims who gathered in Damascus came from the Caucasus region, Anatolia, southeastern Europe, and the province of Syria itself.[27] Steam power did not affect a route traveled by pilgrims from Iraq, along with those who joined the trail from further afield in central and South Asia, which cut across

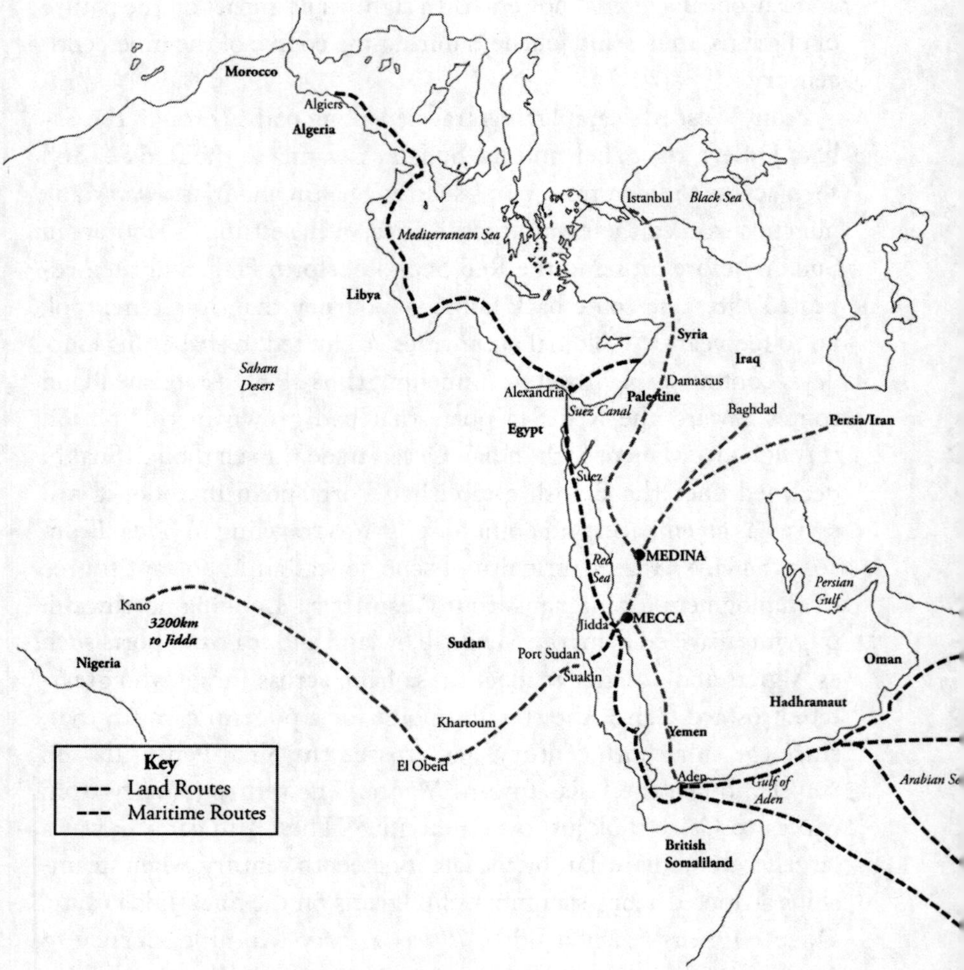

Major Hajj routes in the age of empire

Credit: John O'Connor/John Slight

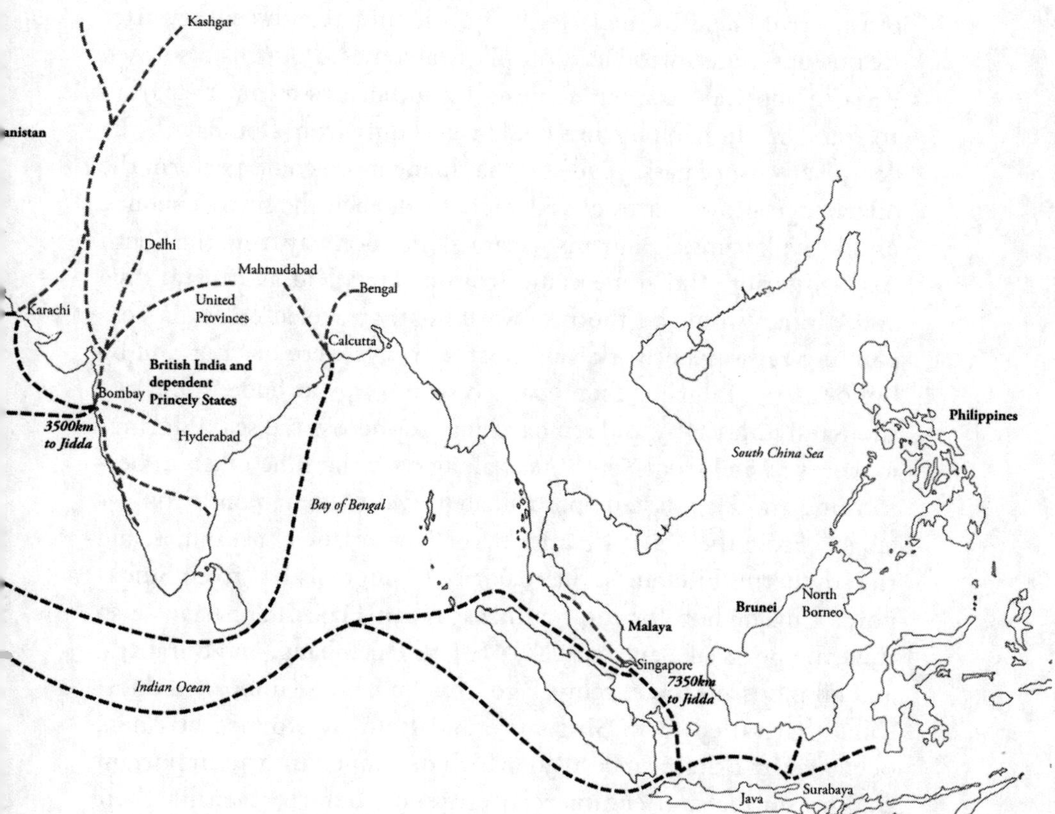
Kashgar
anistan
Delhi
Mahmudabad
Bengal
Karachi
United Provinces
Calcutta
British India and dependent Princely States
Bombay
3500km to Jidda
Hyderabad
Bay of Bengal
South China Sea
Philippines
Brunei
North Borneo
Malaya
Singapore
7350km to Jidda
Indian Ocean
Java
Surabaya

central Arabia's great Nefud Desert. However, by the later 1920s, cars had begun to ply this route and had dramatically slashed the journey time to Mecca to a few days.[28] Along the southern coastline of Arabia, smaller numbers of pilgrims arrived from the coastal littorals of East Africa and western South Asia. As Saudi border controls expanded in the 1930s, being dropped off in one of southern Arabia's small ports was one of the few ways to reach Mecca that avoided any contact with European or Saudi authorities. Further east, the most important embarkation points were the great port cities of Bombay and Singapore, which gained their importance for prospective Hajjis in the latter half of the nineteenth century after steamships were introduced on pilgrim routes. Pilgrims also used Karachi and Calcutta, but a ruling by authorities meant that from 1903 to 1912 Indian pilgrims could travel only from Bombay.[29] The decreased cost of passage meant that many more could perform the pilgrimage. Lower fares considerably broadened the socioeconomic profile of pilgrims.[30] Pilgrims streamed into Bombay from the South Asian interior, and some came from as far afield as central Asia and China. From the 1860s onward, many traveled on India's expanding railway network, but most journeys were on foot and by bullock cart. Pilgrims then boarded steamships to Jidda, some two thousand miles away and ten days' journey across the sea. Pilgrims' journeys to and from South Asia, along with the time taken in performing the Hajj, lasted approximately two to four months on average.[31] From the Malay Peninsula, the Netherlands East Indies, and the southern Philippines, the majority of pilgrims left from Singapore, a major hub for the Southeast Asian Hajj. Indonesians also used the ports of Bandar Aceh, Medan, Palembang, and Surabaya, and Filipinos left their archipelago from Sulu and Zamboanga. Most ships that sailed from Singapore and Bombay stopped at Aden, occupied by Britain since 1839, which developed into an important coaling station and commercial entrepôt, before reaching their destination at Jidda.

All these routes rapidly declined as air travel expanded in the 1950s. Subsequently the number of paths to Mecca increased exponentially, along with pilgrim numbers. But despite the advances in transportation technology in this period, the decision to go on Hajj remained a time-consuming and costly commitment.

Topics of Inquiry

This book asks: How and why did Britain become involved in the Hajj to such a large extent? How and why did this interaction develop from 1865 to 1956? What impact did it have on the pilgrimage itself? In attempting to answer these questions, this work argues that Britain's engagement with the ritual was more complex and multilayered than many existing accounts suggest. Several of these accounts, noting how imperial rule led to Islamic resistance, view the Hajj principally as a catalyst for numerous revivalist anticolonial resistance movements.[32] As Nile Green cogently argues, the actions of Muslims in such movements became "so thoroughly registered in the imagination and archive of empire as to offer historians the double attraction of being automatically 'important' and abundantly documented in colonial records."[33] To be sure, the activities of these figures were important, but they were always only one factor among many related to British involvement in the Hajj. The existing scholarly emphasis on their activities has obscured other, no less significant facets of the pilgrimage. Indeed, the main reason for Britain's initial engagement with the Hajj from 1865 was not concerns about the Hajj as a site of anticolonial activity but a devastating cholera epidemic that killed hundreds of thousands of people worldwide and prompted Britain, alongside other European powers, to take notice of the pilgrimage and the extensive travel networks related to it as a conduit for disease.[34]

In a different vein, several works on Britain and the Hajj have also focused on attempts by British authorities to regulate the pilgrimage on a medical basis, given the threat of epidemic disease posed by the annual movement of large numbers of pilgrims.[35] This was an important sphere of activity and had a great impact on the organization of the pilgrimage, as we shall see. But, couched in a Foucauldian model of surveillance and sanitary control, these studies give the impression that sanitation and security were virtually the sole concerns of

British officials engaged with the ritual. Imperial engagement with the Hajj, in light of the mass of official material on the subject, did not revolve just around these twin axes of sanitation and security that have largely preoccupied historians. Moreover, the effectiveness and impact of British imperial policies regarding these medical and political aspects of the Hajj were not replicated in a vast range of other areas associated with the ritual that Britain engaged with.

Moving beyond these interpretive frameworks, this book examines a series of understudied areas of inquiry, such as Britain's engagement with "pauper" pilgrims, the role of Muslim employees in Britain's Hajj administration, the impact of British policies during the First World War on the Hajj, Saudi-Wahhabi interaction with British pilgrim-subjects, the local administration of the Hajj from places such as Suakin, Jidda, Bombay, Hyderabad, and Singapore, and, finally, Britain's engagement with the Hajj during the Second World War and until the 1956 Suez Crisis. Bringing together these topics, supported with examples from across Britain's Muslim empire, and lengthening the time frame of this topic beyond 1924, which several existing studies take as an endpoint, this book presents a broader and more nuanced picture of Britain's relationship with the Hajj during this period.

Imperial involvement with the pilgrimage developed in great complexity throughout the late nineteenth century as an administrative apparatus was constructed to deal with the annual movement of pilgrims to and from the Hijaz. Bureaucracies related to the pilgrimage were established across British India and several princely states with Muslim rulers, in Malaya and its Sultanates, Sudan, and Nigeria. These complemented the apparent center of Britain's Hajj administration, the British consulate in the Red Sea port of Jidda, the main disembarkation point for most seaborne pilgrims. One of this book's central arguments is that attempts by these bureaucracies to grapple with the administrative challenges posed by the pilgrimage drew Britain into a deeper engagement with institutions and practices in the Islamic world. There were many tensions and paradoxes that informed Britain's relationship with the Hajj, such as a perceived need to appease Muslim religious sentiment through policies of noninterference with religious practices. This policy jostled with an inconsistent desire to exercise varying degrees of control over pilgrims' movements and the increasing need to uphold British prestige in the Hijaz.

The cheaper cost of long-distance travel gave rise to large numbers of British subjects termed "pauper" pilgrims in the Hijaz and port cities such as Bombay. These "subaltern Hajjis," whether from India, Malaya, or Nigeria, who had run out of funds in the course of their quest to perform the Hajj, were rued by officials as a stain on British prestige, especially given that few other Islamic or European powers with Muslim subjects encountered this issue to the same extent. The issue of relief for indigent pilgrims had been a constant preoccupation of Muslim rulers (in Arabia and elsewhere) since the early years of Islam. Britain's engagement with the issue of destitute pilgrims will be analyzed throughout Chapters 2 to 6.[36] These Hajjis were not anticolonial activists or traveling scholars. The only record of their existence is within the imperial archives and some pilgrimage accounts. Largely indistinct or fleetingly referred to in existing narratives, this group of pilgrims held far more agency over their pilgrimage experience, in the face of British administrative practices, than has been previously assumed.[37] British engagement with destitute pilgrims drew Britain deeper into the Muslim world, grappling with multiple issues within Islamic law and customs. From a stance of indifference and dismissal in the early 1850s, British attitudes toward destitute pilgrims evolved into what eventually became, by the 1920s, a series of intercontinental and interoceanic relief, subsidy, and repatriation efforts for this group that spanned Britain's Muslim empire, representing a substantial investment in facilitating the Hajj for its pilgrim-subjects. Yet throughout all this, British officials rarely understood the spiritual attraction of the Hajj for people that made them endure such suffering on a journey that held for them the spiritual reward of seeing Mecca and the Ka'ba, a point made frequently in Hajj narratives.

Attempts to regulate this group of pilgrims from across Britain's Muslim empire were frequently stymied by the actions of indigent pilgrims who did not conform to officials' administrative schemes. There was never any really effective attempt to prevent such people going on Hajj, if such action was ever possible, precisely because of

British concern for Muslim opinion. This is attested by the extensive documentation in various archives that details British consultations on the topic of destitute pilgrims with a variety of Muslim figures across the British empire. However, behind such sensitivity, as in the vast majority of British interactions with the pilgrimage, was pragmatic self-interest. "Pauper pilgrims" were one of several features of the pilgrimage that were at the outer limits of imperial control. In considering the limits of Britain's administration of the Hajj, we might think of its effectiveness and reach in terms of a sliding scale from hegemony to helplessness. Considering the mechanics of imperial administration in this way gives us a more flexible analytical model than simply giving entities labels such as "limited Raj" or "hegemonic state." British interactions with destitute pilgrims can be characterized as largely ad hoc, reactive, and haphazard. Nevertheless, as indicated earlier, these policies and practices led to an unintended facilitation of the pilgrimage for these poor pilgrim-subjects, unconsciously emulating the policies of earlier Islamic empires. However, Britain was not a benevolent "protector of Islam." A concern to sustain imperial rule and a desire to uphold prestige in the Muslim world remained key determinants in British calculations.

Another topic that features throughout this book is the role played by Muslim employees in Britain's Hajj administration, as well as Muslims who were consulted on pilgrimage-related measures. This work argues that they held a degree of agency in influencing, shaping, and executing Britain's policies on the pilgrimage, enhancing the Islamic character of the British empire, and contributes to debates about indigenous collaboration in the practice of imperial rule pioneered by Ronald Robinson, moving beyond studies that have focused on elite Muslim figures such as Sir Syed Ahmad Khan.[38] These Muslims within the colonial and consular bureaucracies were a driving force in the refashioning of Britain's imperial role toward facilitating Islamic practices such as the Hajj. Especially in the Hijaz, Britain's involvement in the Hajj was impossible without recourse to Muslim officials who were able to travel freely in the *haramayn*, the area around Mecca and Medina that was closed to non-Muslims. The frequently short tenure of British consular officials in Jidda meant that they tended to rely heavily on their Muslim subordinates, whose knowledge of the Hajj was far greater. The role of such Muslim officials within the imperial framework highlights the complications of categories of "British" and "Muslim" in opposition to each other.[39] Muslim officials in the British consulate at Jidda, men like Dr. Abdur Razzack, Dr. Abdur Rahman, and Munshi (clerk) Ihsanullah, wrote many reports for their superiors that are preserved in the archives and discussed in Chapters 2, 3, 4, and 5.

These men were not "collaborators" in any pejorative sense; although they were all paid by Britain, from their surviving reports and correspondence it is clear their first allegiance and duty was to Islam and assisting Hajjis to the best of their ability. The fact that they were ensconced in the bureaucracies of a power run by Christians appeared to be uncontroversial for them. British officials gave their Muslim employees tacit acknowledgment and support of their efforts regarding the Hajj. These men incorporated their interpretations of Islamic ideas of governance and welfare into the imperial framework. To illustrate this, it is worth quoting at length the Indian vice-consul Dr. Abdur Rahman's report on the November 1914 Hajj, his last in that post:

> All I wished was an improvement in the condition of affairs prevailing there, bettering the treatment of pilgrims during this sojourn in the Holy Places, and the sure means of their return home after the performance of Hajj. . . . I have to view with great satisfaction that all of my suggestions were favourably received by the Indian Government, and that the same were not a voice in the wilderness, but had a very favourable echo from proper quarters. . . . The formation of the Hajj Committees in the big towns of India as was suggested by me is a step in the right direction.[40]

Although this book emphasizes the agency that Muslim employees in Britain's Hajj administrations possessed, it is important to note that these men had no political power, and they worked in the context of an unequal power relationship between them and their employers. Ultimate decision-making power on Hajj-related matters remained in the hands of the British. Nevertheless, it is significant how often British officials agreed with the ideas and proposals of their Muslim employees, which often flouted Britain's ostensible policy of noninterference with the Hajj. This suggests a more complicated set of interactions and negotiations that demonstrates the capacity of Muslims within the imperial bureaucracies to shape the experience of the Hajj for pilgrims. This was not a coherent, single-minded project with anticolonial intentions, and it developed in an inchoate fashion. Muslim employees were an important part of Britain's association with the Hajj.

Archives and Voices

This study has used a number of archives, and from working through them it became evident that the pilgrimage increasingly attracted the attention of British officials from the late nineteenth century on, given the enormous amount of Hajj-related documentation generated by the authorities.[41] Exploring how this developed is one of this book's central concerns. This book draws on official sources and private papers held at a number of archives, including the National Archives of the United Kingdom, India, and Malaysia; India Office records in the British Library; state archives in Bombay and Hyderabad; the Sudan archive in Durham; the Middle East Centre Archive and Rhodes House Library in Oxford; Thomas Cook's archives in Peterborough; and, finally, the Oral History Archive in Singapore. The use of multiple archives dictated by this study's wide geographic scope led to the methodological necessity of disaggregating these discrete imperial and colonial archives.[42] Although some document collections, such as those of the British consulate in Jidda, hold letters and memos from across Britain's Muslim empire, it is possible to build a fuller picture of Britain's interactions with the Hajj only by following, where possible, the paper trails to their varied places of origin. The information on the Hajj that reached the apex of empire in London represented a very small fraction of the activities undertaken by officials on this subject in Britain's Muslim empire and beyond. The wide range of minor and major archives used enables this work to present a broad and detailed picture of Britain's relationship with the Hajj, from Whitehall to the various localities of

Britain's Muslim empire. Drawing on this variety of archives means that the administration of the flows of pilgrims from across Britain's Muslim empire to and from the Hijaz can be adequately surveyed. These archives give us "a real sense collectively of how the British empire conceptualized the Hajj through the lens of the official mind."[43] As Kim Wagner and Ricardo Roque have argued, a "constructive attitude of critical engagement" toward official archives that remains aware of their limitations and exclusions while also appreciating their heterogeneous, complex nature appears the most productive approach to this set of sources.[44]

This leads to the difficult question of how to interpret these bureaucratic repositories of empire. Caches of documents now preserved for the likes of historians were once, to use Sean Hanretta's term, "technologies of rule."[45] The realities of imperial governance in relation to the Hajj, such as the small number of British officials involved, their short tenure in positions such as consul in Jidda, the multiple competing demands of all these officials' roles, and general preconceptions of Islam and Muslims, meant that they often repeated and reinforced certain prejudices related to pilgrims in their documents. Officials saw pilgrims as swayed by religious zealotry, a group of hapless, helpless people who launched themselves on a journey fraught with danger and the real possibility of death. A common view among officials was that if local circumstances were favorable, effective and efficient British governance, in the form of reforms and regulatory control, could save these pilgrims from themselves. However, merging such discourses of British rule with the messier and more contingent realities of governance creates the falsehood that these archives are proof that colonial states possessed overwhelming power and an all-encompassing gaze.

This picture becomes more complex when we realize that in fact much of the information about the ritual and British pilgrim-subjects came from Muslims themselves. An important point here is that there are numerous Muslim voices within the various colonial and imperial archives, extensively used throughout this book. Although there is reportage and filtering by British officials, as well as bias and omission, there is much material directly authored by Muslims working within the imperial bureaucracies, as well as apparently verbatim reports of what certain Muslims who were not in Britain's employ said and thought. As Aishwary Kumar has argued, the colonial archive was a "field of intersecting narratives."[46] Although these Muslim voices from the archives cannot be considered representative of all Muslims in this period (indeed, no voices can), this does not mean that they should be ignored. The writings of Muslims from within the various colonial archives form a rich corpus of material that offers valuable new perspectives that greatly deepen our understanding of the pilgrimage in this period. Consequently, the official archive "must be approached as a messy product of multiple, contingent and shifting forces."[47] The imperial eyes through which the Hajj was observed were both British and Muslim.

Augmenting these official records is a variety of Hajj accounts in English, Arabic, and Urdu, whose authors are many and varied. They include Muslims in the service of various governments; religious scholars and men from the professional classes; two female rulers of Bhopal, an Indian princely state; male and female British converts to Islam; and non-Muslims who went on Hajj in disguise. These accounts are an invaluable set of mostly Muslim voices that provide an important perspective beyond official sources. In addition, these narratives remind us of the immediacy and power of the pilgrimage as a religious experience.[48]

Chapter Outline

Chapter 1 provides a contextual background for this subject. It first explains the Hajj rituals, moves on to briefly consider the crucial role played by leading Muslim empires, such as the Mughals and the Ottomans, in facilitating the pilgrimage for their subjects in order to enhance the prestige and religious legitimacy of these polities, and then surveys the engagement of other European empires with the Hajj in this period, which forms a comparative backdrop to Britain's interactions with the Hajj. In order to situate the Hajj within a wider geography of religious pilgrimages, the chapter concludes with outlines of other pilgrimages that the British empire engaged with in this period: Shi'i pilgrimages to Najaf and Karbala in Iraq; *ziyara*, visits to shrines and tombs of Sufi holy men and other notable Islamic figures; Christian, Jewish, and Muslim pilgrimages to sites in Palestine; and, finally, the Hindu Kumbh Mela in India.

Chapter 2 charts early British interactions with the Hajj from the 1850s to the close of the nineteenth century. Beginning with Britain's relationship with the Hijaz and early British observers of the Hajj such as Richard Burton, it next considers the pilgrimage narrative of Nawab Sikander Begum of Bhopal. Cholera's role as a catalyst for greater British involvement in the ritual is then surveyed, along with quarantine measures and Muslim reactions to them. The central part of the chapter is concerned with the evolution of British policies in India and the Hijaz on the issue of destitute pilgrims from the 1870s and the role of Muslim consultation in India on this issue. Related to pauper pilgrims is an examination of the important role played by successive Muslim employees as Indian vice-consul in Jidda through their attempts to ameliorate the situation of destitute pilgrims. From the 1870s, the ritual was also perceived by some officials as a site of anticolonial interaction among Muslims, which further enhanced the pilgrimage's importance to British authorities. The remainder of the chapter briefly explores these imperial concerns and questions of surveillance and conspiracies.[49]

Chapter 3 examines the Hajj during the Edwardian era through three case studies. The first is Britain's initial engagement with the pilgrimage from Nigeria and Sudan, which reflects the widening of Britain's Muslim empire in the Edwardian era. The second is a ground-level analysis of the administration of the Hajj from Bombay, the main departure point for most Muslims going on Hajj from South Asia. Given this fact, Bombay's administration was particularly complex and in addition was mostly run by Muslim officials. The third case study is the nizam of Hyderabad's Hajj administration, which complicates the picture of a monolithic British colonial bureaucracy interfering with the pilgrimage from India. Because the nizam was the ruler of India's premier Muslim princely state, some subjects and employees of the wealthy nizam enjoyed a sponsored pilgrimage. The nizam's government possessed a highly sophisticated Hajj administration. Consequently, many features of British India's Hajj administration experience were absent from the Hyderabadi experience. The chapter concludes by considering the continued debate over destitute pilgrims on the eve of the First World War and how this was entangled with Anglo-Ottoman imperial rivalries.

Chapter 4 traces a central narrative of how Britain dealt with rapid politico-religious change in the Muslim world in the early twentieth century. The importance of the Hajj to Britain's Muslim territories sharply increased when it went to war with the Ottoman empire in November 1914. Britain became even more directly involved with the Hijaz through its sponsorship of Sharif Hussein of Mecca's "Arab Revolt" of 1916–1918 against the Ottomans, overturning their nearly four-hundred-year-old suzerainty over the area. Although Britain proclaimed its "noninterference" in the Holy Places of Islam, Hussein's kingdom was, in effect, a British client state. The chapter analyzes how these events affected the pilgrimage. In the postwar period, Britain made various unsuccessful attempts to reform the Hajj's administration. Hashemite control over the Hajj disintegrated into barely disguised extortion of pilgrims in the early 1920s when Britain cut Hussein's subsidy. The chaotic nature of the Hajj in this period and wider disagreements with Hussein over the Middle East's political landscape contributed to Britain's rejection of the "Hashemite solution" in Arabia, and officials became less concerned about the westward expansion of Ibn Saud and the Wahhabis in Najd. Britain's gamble to directly influence the political sovereignty of Arabia through supporting Hussein's Arab Revolt in 1916–1918 and its tacit acceptance of the Saudi-Wahhabi takeover of Mecca and Medina in 1924 were vitally important events that caused the Hajj's character and meaning to change profoundly.

Chapter 5 examines the impact of the imposition of Wahhabi religious policies on the Hajj and Hajjis, how this developed during the initial phases of Saudi rule, how it was tempered in light of the Great Depression, and the concomitant response of British pilgrim-subjects. The Saudis improved the organization of the pilgrimage. British perceptions of Wahhabism became more benign, and officials learned to work with this form of fundamentalist Islam. Significantly, Britain was far from hostile to Saudi-Wahhabi rule over the Hijaz and the pilgrimage and cultivated the Saudis as allies when anticolonial nationalism in its Muslim territories increased from the late 1920s. Despite progress in the Hajj's organization, Muslims, especially from India, reacted strongly against Wahhabi doctrines, which they thought contrary to several Islamic practices. These included acts of devotion that occurred during the pilgrimage, such as *ziyara*, visits to saints' and notables' shrines. The enforcement of Wahhabi religious policies was noted in a neutral fashion by the British, who gradually withdrew from being actively involved in the Hijaz's internal religious affairs.

Chapter 6 examines Britain's administration of the ritual from the far ends of its Muslim empire—Nigeria and Malaya—during the interwar period. From the 1920s, both territories expanded their administrative involvement with their border-crossing pilgrim-subjects, who traveled thousands of miles across savanna and ocean to and from the Hijaz. This expansion was partly dictated by concerns about pilgrims who became destitute at various points of their journeys, whether in the Hijaz or elsewhere. In the Malayan case, the Malay pilgrimage officer played a central role in the colony's engagement with the Hajj, and for Nigerian pilgrims, local leaders living in Sudan who originated from Nigeria occupied a similar role. For colonial authorities, issues of pilgrim relief and repatriation loomed large in both cases, and there was coordination among several authorities in Britain's Muslim empire on ways to control destitute pilgrims. In the Nigerian case, such control was never fully realized. A final area this chapter examines is the means whereby colonial and consular authorities attempted, with little success, to curb the slave trade that accompanied the pilgrimage every year, when Malay and Nigerian pilgrims fell prey to slave traffickers.

The Epilogue surveys Britain's interactions with the Hajj during the Second World War and the postwar era of decolonization. The conflict saw Britain's attempt to use the Hajj as a vehicle for propaganda and efforts to facilitate the pilgrimage as a means of keeping its pilgrim-subjects supportive of the war effort. The contraction of Britain's Muslim empire meant that there was a revival of interest in administering the pilgrimage in colonies such as Nigeria and Malaya. Saudi oil wealth meant that the kingdom's coercive power increased, so destitute pilgrims were quickly apprehended and repatriated. Saudi Arabia's termination of diplomatic relations with Britain as a result of the 1956 Suez Crisis forms an endpoint to this study, marking an effective conclusion to British involvement with the pilgrimage on any meaningful scale.

The Conclusion explores the legacy of Britain's relationship with the Hajj and its Muslim empire, which continues to resonate in the early twenty-first century, as shown, for example, by the reopening of the British consulate in Jidda in 2000 to deal with the increased numbers of British Muslims going on Hajj, and ends with a restatement of the work's main themes and arguments. Britain's wide-ranging interactions with the Hajj highlights the degree to which imperial governance and religious practice became interlinked, the real limits of imperial rule when faced with a group such as border-crossing Muslim pilgrims, and the significance of Islam to the British imperial experience.

1

Contexts

Introduction

The travels of Muslims from across the world to the Holy City of Mecca in the Hijaz to perform the Hajj has been a constant feature in world history since the Prophet Muhammad's Farewell Pilgrimage in AH 11/632 CE. It is the single largest annual gathering of people on the planet for a religious purpose.[1] The Hajj is "unique among religious pilgrimages for its doctrinal centrality, geographic focus, and historical continuity."[2] As one of the five pillars of Islam, the Hajj is obligatory for all Muslims who are financially and physically able to undertake it.[3] Once pilgrims reach Mecca, they can fulfill one of their core religious obligations and participate in a series of deeply profound rituals, the anticipation and subsequent experience of which remain in their memories forever. If the spiritual experience of the Hajj can be summarized, the end of Ikbal Ali Shah's 1928 pilgrimage account seems apt: "From life I need nothing more. I have been to Mecca, the cradle of my faith."[4]

Mecca—and Medina, the location of the Prophet Muhammad's tomb—are powerful religious symbols. In their daily prayers as individuals and as part of the *umma*, the worldwide community of believers, Muslims worship in the direction of the Ka'ba, the large black cubic structure in the center of the Holy Mosque in Mecca and the spiritual center of Islam. But as well as being a profoundly spiritual experience, the Hajj, like other religious pilgrimages, is also a historical and material phenomenon that encompasses a variety of features, such as taxation, commerce, the logistics of travel, official bureaucracy, and the politics surrounding the pilgrimage.[5]

Although the pilgrimage has pre-Islamic roots, the Muslim Hajj is nearly 1,400 years old. Europe's imperial moment in the Muslim world and its impact on the pilgrimage were a significant interlude in the ritual's history. This chapter provides a broad context to the Hajj in order to appropriately situate Britain's involvement in the pilgrimage from 1865 to 1956. It describes the rituals that make up the Hajj and the parts of the Qur'an that discuss the pilgrimage. A survey of Islamic and European empires' engagement with the pilgrimage brings out several themes that contextualize Britain's later involvement in the Hajj, such as how these polities positioned themselves as Islamic empires, how they became patrons or protectors of Islam in relation to the Hajj in order to gain legitimacy for imperial rule, and how multiple imperial regulations regarding the Hajj were evaded or subverted by pilgrims. Finally, this chapter shows how the Hajj, while unique in many respects, was part of a wider religious geography of pilgrimage, and it examines Britain's interactions with these pilgrimages, which highlights how technological change and policies of accommodation were important in shaping the contours of this wide-ranging imperial engagement.

The Hajj as Ritual

The Hajj is notable for the unchanging nature of the rituals that pilgrims must perform.[6] These rites were ordained by the Prophet Muhammad shortly before his death in 632 CE and are a series of ritual reenactments of faith-testing events from the lives of the Prophet Abraham; his wife, Hajar; and his son Ismail. Before commencing the Hajj during *dhu al-hijja*, the twelfth month in the Islamic lunar calendar, male pilgrims don the *ihram*, two white sheets that cover the body. Women are directed only to wear modest clothing. The *ihram* shows the equality and humility of all pilgrims before God, regardless of individual differences in race, nationality, age, gender, or wealth. Once they have donned the *ihram*, pilgrims repeatedly call the *talbiyya*, the pilgrims' invocation, "Here I am,

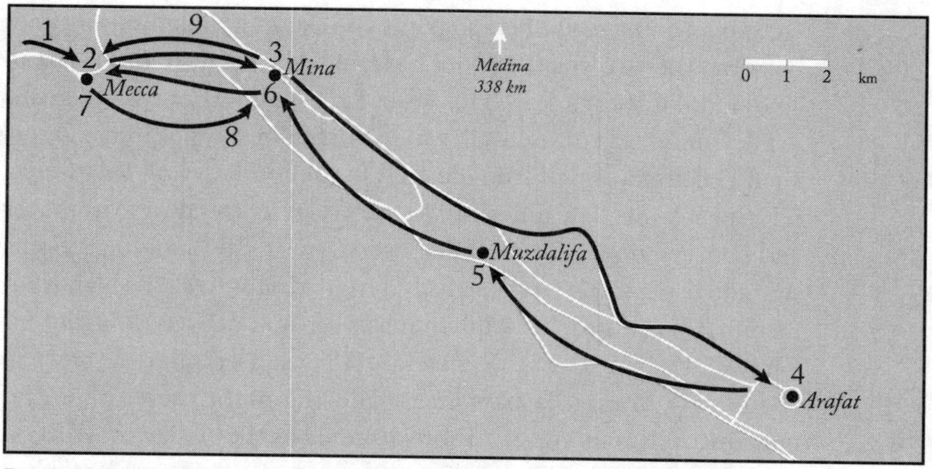

Day 1 (8th Dhu al-Hijja)

1. Miqat
Arrival and change into ihram

2. Mecca
Circling the Ka'ba (tawaf)
Passing between the hills of Safa and Marwa (sa'y)

3. Mecca to Mina
Overnight stay

Day 2 (9th Dhu al-Hijja)

4. Mina to Plain of 'Arafat
Day of vigil (wuquf)

5. 'Arafat to Muzdalifa
Collecting stones and overnight stay

Day 3 (10th Dhu al-Hijja)

6. Muzdalifa to Mina
Stoning largest pillar (Jamrat al-'Aqaba)
The day of 'Eid

7. Mina to Mecca
Circling the Ka'ba
Passing between the hills of Safa and Marwa

8. Mecca to Mina
Stay for two or three nights

Hajj rituals

Credit: Adapted by John O'Connor and John Slight from Venetia Porter (ed.), *Hajj: Journey to the Heart of Islam* (London: British Museum Press, 2012). Reproduced with the permission of the British Museum Press.

Lord, responding to Your call [to perform the Hajj]. Praise belongs to You, all good things come from You, and sovereignty is Yours alone." The first ritual is the *tawaf*, where pilgrims circle seven times around the Ka'ba in the center of the Holy Mosque in Mecca, also called the *Bayt Allah* (House of God), supposedly the equivalent of God's throne in heaven. The Ka'ba is doubly significant because Muslims face in its direction during their *salat*, daily prayers. During this circling, many pilgrims try to approach and touch the Black Stone that is set in the corner of the Ka'ba. The origins and powers of the stone are disputed, but pilgrims who cannot touch the stone salute it from a distance to signal their renewed commitment to God, and others believe that physical contact with it absorbs sin. After the *tawaf* comes the *sa'y*, when pilgrims run back and forth seven times between the two small hills of Safa and Marwa near the Ka'ba in emulation of Hajar's search for water for Ismail.[7] After this, pilgrims drink from the Zamzam well, which miraculously appeared and rescued Hajar and Ismail from death. On the ninth day of *dhu al-hijja*, pilgrims travel a few miles to Mount Arafat to spend time in prayer and conversation, a ritual called *wuquf*, meaning "standing." Some stay and listen to a sermon delivered from Mount Arafat, which commemorates the Prophet Muhammad's sermon delivered during his Farewell Pilgrimage at the same site. After sunset, pilgrims move to the nearby Muzdalifa pass and spend the night there. The next morning, pilgrims travel a short distance to the Valley of Mina; at *Jabal Rahma*, Mount Mercy, they perform the *jamarat*, which involves throwing pebbles at pillars that signify places where Abraham rejected Satan's temptation to disobey God's order to sacrifice Ismail. Once this "Stoning of the Devil" is complete, pilgrims offer an animal sacrifice at Mina to commemorate the sheep God accepted from Abraham in lieu of Ismail. Simultaneously, Muslims who are not on Hajj celebrate the holiday of the *'Id* (also spelled 'Eid) with their own animal sacrifices. Pilgrims are then required to perform six more stonings and one more *tawaf* and *sa'y*. A pilgrimage is valid only if the whole journey is undertaken with the intention of coming closer to God, so every ritual does not have to be performed precisely.[8] There are huge spiritual rewards associated with a successfully completed Hajj—pilgrims are absolved from all previous sins.[9] A further bonus of completing the pilgrimage is the ability to prefix one's name with "Hajji" for men or "Hajja" for women, a distinction that enhances pilgrims' status in their local community. The Hajj's importance in Islam is heightened by the fact that, every day, Muslims pray in the direction of Mecca.

The Qur'an contains various chapters (singular, *sura*; plural, *suwar*) that command Muslims to perform the Hajj.[10] It is important to describe these because they are cited innumerable times in British documents in the archives as justification, or otherwise, for a variety of British and Muslim proposals and responses to the issue of destitute pilgrims that are detailed throughout this book. The first reference to Hajj in the Qur'an states simply, "Perform the pilgrimage

Pilgrims surrounding the Ka'ba, Mecca, c. 1900

Credit: Royal Geographical Society, London

and the visit [to Mecca] for Allah." It goes on to stipulate that those who cannot, whether from ill health or other reasons, should send "such gifts as can be obtained with ease." While Muslims are on Hajj, there should be "no lewdness nor abuse nor angry conversation." A verse of critical importance, "And whatsoever good ye do Allah knoweth it," describes how the performance of good deeds while on Hajj will be known by God and came to be interpreted as requiring the disbursement of *zakat*, or alms-giving, to poor pilgrims and others in the Hijaz.[11] Later in the Qur'an, "Pilgrimage to the House [of Abraham, referring to the Ka'ba] is a duty unto Allah for mankind, for him who can find a way thither," underscores the mandatory nature of Hajj for Muslims except in certain circumstances, such as illness or penury.[12] Another command to pilgrims is "So make pro-

Pilgrim camp at Arafat, 1909, Abbas Hilmi Album

Credit: Mohamed Ali Foundation

vision for yourselves" before going on Hajj. These last two passages from the Qur'an repeatedly appear in British official memorandums and reports as evidence to support restrictions on poor pilgrims who traveled to the Hijaz.[13] The final reference to pilgrimage is the Hajj *sura*, where God ordered Abraham to "proclaim unto mankind the Pilgrimage. They will come unto thee on foot and on every lean camel; they will come from every deep ravine"[14]—and, many centuries later, by steamship and airplane.

Muslim Empires and the Hajj before 1800

Before considering the cases of the Mughal and Ottoman empires that are the principal examples in this section, several antecedents to European interactions with the Hajj before the nineteenth century should be mentioned briefly. The Frankish crusader states controlled the land routes between Syria and Egypt from 1116 to 1187. This forced Egypt to replace Aqaba with Aydhab as the main port for the Red Sea's pilgrimage traffic in this period.[15] In the early modern period, Portuguese expansion into the Indian Ocean disrupted the Hajj in 1541. Spurred by the legacy of the Reconquista, the Portuguese mounted a naval expedition in the Red Sea that blocked pilgrim and merchant ships sailing to the Hijaz.[16] This built on previous attempts by Portuguese commander Alfonso de Alberquerque, who mounted an unsuccessful expedition to secure the Red Sea for Portugal in 1513. One of Alberquerque's aims during the 1513 expedition was to steal the Prophet Muhammad's body from Medina and then demand that Muslims leave the Christian Holy Land as a condition for his returning the body. Compared with the crusader states' limited impact on the Hajj, the Ottoman and Mughal empires' inability to respond adequately to this Portuguese challenge hampered pilgrims' voyages to and from Arabia. Portuguese control over Daman and Diu on South Asia's western seaboard tightened their grip over the region's seaborne traffic, and a Mughal attempt to capture these ports failed in 1582. Mughal court historian Abu'l Fazl referred to the Portuguese resentfully as a "stumbling block" to South Asian pilgrims' travels.[17] This obstructionist activity was not confined to European powers; Shi'i Safavid Iran closed its border to South Asian pilgrims several times during the sixteenth to eighteenth centuries.[18] Conversely, in 1595, the Mughal emperor Akbar (1556–1605) forced European trading companies to assist pilgrims by providing armed naval escorts for pilgrim ships after an upsurge in piracy in the Indian Ocean; England was responsible for India's south coast, France for the Persian Gulf, and the Netherlands for the Red Sea, although these protective measures proved ineffective.[19]

Several Mughal and Ottoman policies on the pilgrimage were echoed in later British actions. This points to the need to transcend what Dane Kennedy has termed the "binary distinction between Islamic and Western empires."[20] The remainder of this section will provide an overview of these policies. Michael Pearson asserts that "the early modern Islamic empires saw it as their duty to ensure that as many of their subjects as possible could go on pilgrimage."[21] This principally took the form of state-sponsored caravans by land and sea, which in practice meant a procession of people who traveled together. Pilgrim numbers from South Asia rose because of state patronage. In the early modern era, there were approximately 15,000 pilgrims every year out of a total South Asian Muslim population of 22.5 million, and an Indian Muslim community emerged in the Hijaz.[22] According to a Mughal official, these pilgrims went on Hajj "at great public expense, with gold and goods and rich presents."[23] Mughal emperors sponsored the pilgrimage to "stand out as defenders of Islam."[24] In Chapter 4, we will see similar rhetoric used by Britain in the context of the Hajj during the First World War.

This sponsorship began after Akbar conquered Gujarat in 1573, which meant that Surat, the South Asian gateway to Mecca, fell under Mughal rule.[25] Akbar's continued search for sources of ideological authority as a means to consolidate his rule made subsidizing the Hajj for his subjects, and the resultant increase in a Mughal presence in Mecca, increasingly attractive.[26] An imperial edict proclaimed that "the travelling expenses of anybody, who might intend to perform the pilgrimage to the Sacred Places, should be paid." The Mughal Hajj caravan left Agra in 1576 with its party of sponsored pilgrims and an enormous donation of 600,000 rupees (R) for the Holy Places. Members of the Mughal royal household, who made up part of the caravan, were delayed in Surat until October 1576 while a *cartez* was secured from the Portuguese so they could cross the Arabian Sea unhindered. The lack of a Mughal navy left pilgrims vulnerable to Portuguese maritime depredations. In 1577, another caravan left for the Hijaz with R 500,000 and R 100,000 for the sharif of Mecca, the ruler of the Hijaz, who had a distinguished lineage as a descendant of the Prophet Muhammad's grandson Hasan ibn 'Ali.[27]

These gargantuan amounts of money caused many poor people from across the Muslim world to flock to the Hijaz in 1577–1578 to share in the alms bonus. This trend caused considerable consternation among the Ottoman authorities in the Hijaz. The large numbers of poor Indian pilgrims led to food-provisioning difficulties in Mecca, and the newly established Indian quarter in Mecca frustrated the plan of Ottoman sultan Murad III (1574–1595) to restructure the city center.[28] By contrast, Akbar apparently received many fulsome letters of thanks from pilgrims for his donations.[29] Mughal involvement in the Hajj drew Ottoman ire because it threatened their role as custodians of the two Holy Cities. Decrees from Murad III and the governor of Egypt to the sharif of Mecca ordered that Mughal subjects should return home directly after performing the Hajj.[30] This affected a party of women from the Mughal royal court and their large number of retainer-pilgrims, who were accused of indulging in activities contrary to *shari'a* law. When this party returned in 1582, Akbar broke off relations with the Hijaz and the Ottomans after hearing of the royal ladies' treatment in the Hijaz. The loss of the huge Mughal charitable donations through corruption also contributed to Akbar's shift in policy on the Hajj. He regarded Meccans—and his own emissaries—as corrupt. No more Hajj caravans were sent in his reign after 1580.[31] Nevertheless, many destitute Indian pilgrims remained in Mecca living in huts near the Holy Mosque or inside the mosque itself at night. The Ottoman sultan ordered his local representatives to destroy the huts and expel these pilgrims.[32] The issue of destitute pilgrims had its roots, albeit in a very different context, in the early modern period.

Emperor Jahangir (1605–1627) and his family reinstituted paying for pilgrims' journeys to the Hijaz. For example, in 1612 a ship with 1,500 pilgrims sailed to Jidda under the patronage of Jahangir's mother, and the Mughal empress sent 1,700 pilgrims on Hajj in 1619. Trade and donations to the Holy Cities continued. In 1622, R 200,000 was sent for trade and to provide alms for poor pilgrims at Mecca and Medina. Lavish gifts were also sent by other notables, such as Mufti Ahmed Saeed in 1650, who dispatched a diamond-studded candlestick and a hundred-carat diamond. Emperor Aurangzeb (1658–1707), known as a *zinda pir*, a living saint, was also prolific in his gifts to the Holy Cities and to Indian religious scholars who studied under their Arab counterparts and established religious schools in the Hijaz, which contributed to the transmission of religious knowledge back to India by traveling scholars. Aurangzeb also gave money to "professional" pilgrims who went on Hajj and *ziyara* to the Prophet Muhammad's tomb on his behalf. The sharif of Mecca's ambassadors traveled to India in 1686, 1690, and 1693 to solicit more donations from the Mughal emperor. Aurangzeb reinstituted the annual Hajj caravan, *ganj-i-sarai*, to the Hijaz, with an *amir al-hajj*, the leader of a pilgrimage caravan, on a more formal basis and paid for the expenses of poor pilgrims.[33] This Mughal facilitation of the Hajj for pilgrims was similar to Britain's actions in the late nineteenth century through its repatriation of destitute pilgrims. Although the British policy was reactive, the effect was the same as Mughal sponsorship: the state effectively underwrote the pilgrimage's cost.

Ottoman involvement in the Hajj began in 1516–1517 when Selim I (1512–1520) conquered the Mamluk empire, which extended over Egypt, Syria, and the Hijaz. In religious terms, control of Medina, Mecca, and the Hajj gave the Ottomans immense prestige in the

Sunni Muslim world.[34] However, Ottoman control over the Hijaz was as nominal as that of their predecessors until late nineteenth-century attempts to consolidate their authority over Arabia, for example, under the Ottoman governor Nuri Pasha in the early 1880s.[35] The sharif of Mecca acknowledged the Ottoman sultan-caliph's suzerainty but remained the Hijaz's effective ruler and was responsible for the administration of the Hajj. This was counterbalanced by the Ottoman governor in the Hijaz, backed up by imperial garrisons in Mecca, Medina, Jidda, and Yanbu. A dual system of government emerged in which the sharif and governor would often plot against each other because their interests and aspirations were invariably different.[36] Despite these practical limitations on exercising their sovereignty over the Hijaz, the Ottoman sultans sought to consolidate their legitimacy as Muslim rulers by assuming the title *khadim al-haramayn al-sharifayn*, the "servant of the Holy Sanctuaries." In this role, the Ottomans, like their forebears, were responsible for providing funds for Mecca and Medina's upkeep and were obliged to ensure that the main pilgrim routes to the Hijaz were secure.[37]

An important component of Ottoman control of the Hajj was the highly sophisticated organization of pilgrim caravans from Cairo and Damascus. The financial administrators of the caravans were vital to their smooth operation; these men were responsible for paying subsidies to Bedouin tribesmen along the route in order to ensure that they did not attack the caravan. Given the poverty of the Bedouins, it made logical sense for them to help themselves to the rich pickings of the pilgrimage caravans, a trend that continued until the late 1920s.[38] Ottoman donations and subsidies to the Hijaz, along with monies from Egyptian *waqf* foundations, enabled the Ottomans to undertake the construction of an extensive network of garrisoned forts along the route from Damascus to Medina and structures in the Holy Cities themselves, such as mosques, hostels, and, critically, infrastructure related to the water supply. The Holy Mosque in Mecca periodically underwent extensive renovation, rebuilding, and decoration throughout the Ottoman period. These initiatives were designed to further enhance the Ottoman sultan's religious legitimacy.[39]

The 1699 Treaty of Karlowitz with Habsburg Austria galvanized the Ottoman empire into exercising greater control over the Hajj, "reinforcing its image as the paramount Islamic state."[40] One example of this was the complexity of the pilgrimage administration run from Damascus in the first half of the eighteenth century, with extensive budget planning, a tax-collecting tour of the city's surrounding areas, the expansion of the fortress network on the route to Mecca, and reorganization of the relief force that accompanied the caravan, which led to some improvements in security. As commander of the Damascus pilgrimage, the city's governor administered a vast economic, social, and military enterprise. Karl Barbir has argued that the road from Damascus to Mecca in this period was as important to the Hajj as Indian Ocean sea routes from the late nineteenth century.[41]

The internal and external challenges faced by the Ottoman and Mughal empires in the late eighteenth century affected the pilgrimage along the Hajj routes. Traveling conditions in the Hijaz became less safe—a large Bedouin attack on the Damascus caravan in 1757 caused the deaths of many pilgrims. State patronage of pilgrim caravans declined. Donations and funding continued to flow from both empires, albeit on a lesser scale.[42] At the turn of the nineteenth century, the Ottoman governor in Jidda had only a few hundred soldiers, as well as those attached to the annual Hajj caravans from Egypt and Syria, to uphold Ottoman power and ensure security for pilgrims.[43] This fragility was exposed when the Najdi Saudi-Wahhabi polity was able to briefly dominate the Hijaz from 1803 to 1818, which considerably disrupted the Hajj, before Saudi-Wahhabi forces were ejected by Egyptian troops.

European Empires and the Hajj

The British empire was one of several with non-Muslim rulers at their apex that ruled over Muslim subjects and engaged with the Hajj. Principally, these were the European empires of the Netherlands in the Indonesian archipelago, called the Netherlands East Indies in the colonial period; France in North and West Africa and, from 1919, Syria and Lebanon; Russia in the Caucasus and central Asia; and Italy in Somalia, Eritrea, and Libya.[44] From the late eighteenth century on, the relentless expansion of the European empires across the

Muslim world meant that by 1920 only a few independent Muslim powers were left, such as Turkey, Persia, Afghanistan, and the Hijaz. Even these polities experienced varying degrees of external pressure by European states.[45] Consequently, the Hijaz, with its Ottoman, Hashemite, and then Saudi rulers, was one of the very few places outside non-Muslim sovereignty. The relationship of the European empires with the Hajj had a wide variety of similarities to and differences from the British experience and will be considered at various points throughout this book. These interactions were variously accommodating and restrictive, dictated by numerous political and economic factors and a desire for information about border-crossing pilgrim-subjects. Eric Tagliacozzo has highlighted the ambivalence of European empires toward the Hajj, arguing that they saw the pilgrimage as "relatively harmless" but also associated the ritual with the "potential of dangerous rebelliousness," along with other negative conceptions that formed a broader discourse on Islam.[46] Many studies of the Hajj and these empires focus on these perceptions. This section considers in turn the Dutch, French, and Russian relationships with the Hajj.

The Netherlands steadily expanded its control over the mainly Muslim Indonesian archipelago from the seventeenth century. In this early period, the Dutch became aware of people called "Hajjis" in this space and gained more knowledge about pilgrims' journeys across the Indian Ocean.[47] The Dutch administration of the pilgrimage was colored by concern that the Hajj was a transmitter of radical ideas, and this led to a concomitant distrust of Hajjis and attempts to regulate pilgrims' journeys. Dutch perceptions of Indonesian Hajjis as potential militants derived from the Padri Revolt in Sumatra. In 1803, three Sumatran pilgrims who returned from Hajj began a jihad against the Dutch that lasted until the 1830s. These pilgrims' experience of fundamentalist Wahhabi rule in Mecca and contact with returned Hajjis were an important factor in their decision to launch a jihad on their return, although the movement also possessed strong local roots.[48] This Dutch experience partly overlaps with Britain's involvement in the Hajj because of its brief occupation of Java from 1811 to 1816. Sir Thomas Stamford Raffles, founder of modern Singapore, wrote in his 1817 *History of Java* that Hajjis were the greatest enemy of the colonial regime; according to him, credulous Indonesians thought that some Hajjis had supernatural powers, which made it easy for these figures to incite rebellion. Hajjis were apparently active in every uprising, in league with Arabs and Indonesians. Dutch policies reflected such prejudices. For example, the son of a *bupati* or regent, a local Indonesian leader, could not hold high office if he had been on Hajj.[49]

From 1799, when the Dutch took over the administration of the East Indies from the Dutch East India Company, there was an extensive and sustained attempt to regulate the Hajj.[50] As early as 1825, the authorities in Batavia laid down regulations that stated that pilgrims had to pay 110 florins for a pilgrim passport, and regents were ordered to discourage Muslims from going on Hajj.[51] However, because the Dutch thought that only a few hundred went on Hajj every year, they relaxed passport regulations in 1852; colonial officials thought that the real enemy was "Arab priests" operating in the East Indies. The Dutch were concerned about the broader effects of events such as the 1857 Indian rebellion and were worried that their pilgrim-subjects might come into contact with Indian rebels who had fled to Mecca. Regulations introduced in 1859 required that Muslims seek permission to go on Hajj from their regent, who stamped their passport and then quizzed pilgrims on their return to check that they had really gone to Mecca, despite the fact that most regents had not traveled there themselves.[52] This absurd exam was dropped in 1902. Pilgrims had to pay a fee to go on Hajj, some 200 guilders in 1873, a fairly large amount of money. Regulations, laws, and statutes formed a legal framework for colonial regulation. From the mid-nineteenth century, a large number of codes, laws, and statutes covered the Hajj; for example, pilgrims had to check in with the Dutch consul in Jidda and also when they returned to ports in the East Indies. A particularly convenient regulation for the Dutch was that they were not legally obliged to give financial assistance to pilgrims in Arabia.[53]

In the 1850s and 1860s, the Dutch knew rather little about the influence of Hajjis or what happened once pilgrims left the East Indies.[54] But lack of knowledge did not mean lack of information. Dutch officials across the Indies at the local level recorded in detail the names of pilgrims and how much money they took with them, creating a huge record of movement from small villages and settlements scattered across Indonesia. In this enterprise, they were assisted by indigenous subordinates. Nevertheless, passenger lists remained imprecise, filled with Muhammads and Ahmads. The Dutch colonial authorities in the East Indies could be bypassed altogether if pilgrims traveled from Singapore to Jidda, and the Dutch consulate in Jidda could be avoided by sailing from Suez to Yanbu, a port north of Jidda. However, this evasion of colonial controls made pilgrims more susceptible to the nefarious activities of some pilgrim brokers in ports such as Singapore, and the Dutch colonial state never possessed the administrative capacity to prevent their subjects being swindled by these men.[55]

Indonesian pilgrim numbers rose in the last two decades of the nineteenth century because of the spread of steamship travel across the Indian Ocean and rising economic prosperity in the East Indies. Nevertheless, Dutch consular officials estimated that almost a third of Indonesian pilgrims became destitute in the Hijaz in the 1870s.[56] Greater numbers of Hajjis greatly concerned the Dutch, who feared their supposedly malign influence.[57] Compulsory return tickets for pilgrims were mandated in 1897 and made legal as part of a pilgrims' ordinance in 1922. In 1898, pilgrims were allowed to travel only by steamship, a boon to European-owned shipping companies whose fleets were largely steam powered. Dutch officials also made money from pilgrims, so Dutch protests to the sharif of Mecca about his extortionate practices in regard to pilgrims were rather hollow. The Dutch consulate in Jidda was established in 1872, and the consul, W. H. Read, an English businessman, made pilgrims pay 2½ guilders to stamp their passports, even after 1875, when the East Indies government abolished the charge. In 1883, Consul J. A. Kruijit and several Muslim businessmen established a monopoly system whereby the sharif of Mecca gave them one guilder per pilgrim transported by them to Malaya. The guild of pilgrim guides also entered the scheme. Steamship ticket prices doubled, enriching all the members of this corrupt syndicate.[58] Traveling to the Hijaz became quicker for Indonesian pilgrims, but in these instances they had to contend with a further drain on their financial resources from the employees of their colonial ruler.

The Netherlands' consular presence in the Hijaz amplified colonial fears about the Hajj. Consul W. H. Read, in close communication with his counterpart at the British consulate, J. N. Zohrab, wrote to his superiors in the late 1870s that it was impossible to stop radical anti-Christian letters being sent from Mecca to Indonesian regents. Dutch concerns about unrest in Mecca meant that local officials in the East Indies were warned to be alert for any repercussions in their districts. Although the consulate was also concerned with protecting its pilgrim-subjects, much information was collected about potential subversion, especially about Sufi orders and the Indonesian community in the Hijaz. The ongoing war between the Muslim Sultanate of Aceh and the Dutch from 1873 to 1914, where *'ulama*, an educated class of Muslim legal scholars, and Hajjis played a prominent role, contributed to Dutch perceptions of Islam as a "pervasive and co-ordinated threat" and Mecca as a focus of colonial anxiety.[59] For example, Dutch colonial administrator K. F. Holle was tasked in 1873 with investigating the social influence of Hajjis in the East Indies and reported back that they were "instigators of fanaticism."[60] Scholars have suggested that fear about the Hajj's insurrectionary potential meant that the colonial state did not enact measures that might have addressed the myriad difficulties faced by pilgrims. In relation to the Hajj, Dutch anxieties centered on worst-case scenarios—although the pilgrimage might be unthreatening, if extremists influenced pilgrims, this would have an impact in the East Indies, where the Dutch were very few in number.[61]

One of the most important figures related to the Dutch colonial Hajj was Christiaan Snouck Hurgronje (1857–1936), pithily described by Eric Tagliacozzo as a "scholar of Islam and servant of a repressive state."[62] Snouck Hurgronje stayed in Mecca for six months in 1885 to study the faith and developed a reputation as an expert on Islam and the links between Arabia and the East Indies. Raden Aboe Bakar Djajadiningrat, an Indonesian who worked in the Dutch consulate in Jidda monitoring Indonesian pilgrims and scholars, played a vital intermediary role for Snouck Hurgronje, arranging meetings for him with Indonesian scholars and Meccan *'ulama*. Snouck Hurgronje successfully lobbied for the Dutch to employ an Indonesian vice-consul in Jidda who could travel to Mecca and check on the Indonesian community there. Dutch consular officials in Jidda were heavily reliant on their Indonesian and Arab subordinate staff, much like British officials in Jidda and across Britain's Muslim empire were on their Muslim officials, as discussed in this book.[63]

In his role as adviser for native and Arab affairs for the East Indies government, Snouck Hurgronje advised his superiors on numerous occasions against interference with the Hajj, such as requiring compulsory return tickets and issuing official warnings against going on Hajj.[64] In relation to return tickets, pilgrims had to pay more toward the cost of their Hajj up front, which boosted the profits of shipping companies that had lobbied for many years for this measure.[65] He sent repeated letters to his superiors that detailed how Dutch policies, especially on pilgrim shipping, caused hatred toward the colonial administration among pilgrims.[66] Snouck Hurgronje engaged in a campaign against colonial misrepresentations of the Hajj and highlighted the lack of historical and linguistic knowledge possessed by consular officials in the Hijaz, which caused them to exaggerate the Hajj's perceived dangers to the Netherlands.[67] The First World War led to a harder Dutch attitude towards the Hajj; against Snouck Hurgronje's advice, it was temporarily banned in 1915, and thousands of Indonesian pilgrims were stranded in the Hijaz.[68] Although his knowledge of Mecca, the Hajj, and Islam in the East Indies meant that his views were often sought, they were also sometimes ignored by his employers.[69] Snouck Hurgronje was resigned that he could do little to ameliorate pilgrims' hardships and change Dutch policy.[70] He viewed pilgrims with faint contempt, was concerned about the transmission of dangerous ideas and pilgrims across the Indian Ocean, and thought it essential for the Dutch to be aware of "irreconcilable elements" among pilgrims. He cultivated a network of informants in Mecca to provide him with intelligence on the Hajj and was immersed in helping the authorities crush Muslim Acehnese resistance to Dutch rule in the late nineteenth century. The Dutch consulate continued this type of intelligence activity in the Hijaz up to the Second World War, with an increased focus on anticolonial Indonesian nationalists.[71] The Hajj from the East Indies was an important component of the overall pilgrimage; in the years before the First World War, around one-quarter of all pilgrims came from the archipelago, and Indonesians were the largest group of pilgrims who arrived from overseas.[72]

In contrast to the Dutch, French officials in Africa discussed and evaluated their policies in their Muslim territories through the prism of France as a *puissance musulmane*, or Muslim power, from Napoleon's invasion of Egypt in 1798 and the subsequent conquest of Algiers in 1830 until decolonization.[73] David Robinson has argued that although France was suspicious of Islam, it extensively accommodated and granted considerable autonomy to Islamic practices.[74] France made a conscious effort throughout North and West Africa to control Islamic societies, establish Muslim leaders and allies, and use Muslim employees. Several scholars have argued that from the 1840s the Hajj became an instrument of religious and social politics in the French Muslim empire; the assertion of control over the Hajj was a political strategy that sought to legitimate France's colonial authority.[75] After the conquest of Algiers, French officials actually banned the Hajj, but this had little effect, given the polity's open borders. From 1840, France's appropriation of *waqf* foundations in Algeria and the colonial state's administrative logic meant that the French took on these foundations' functions, which included organizing and financing the Hajj for its constituents. France also ended up paying for the return journeys of destitute Algerian pilgrims in the Hijaz and Port Said in Egypt, an expensive undertaking at seventy-five francs per person at the turn of the twentieth century. There were various unsuccessful attempts to control the cost of this repatriation. These situations were remarkably similar to the British case charted in this book.[76]

In the late nineteenth century, the authorities in French West Africa contracted French shipping companies to provide cheap transport for the Hajj. These companies then enjoyed a quasi-monopoly, much like Britain's engagement of Thomas Cook as travel agent for the Hajj from India in the same period, discussed in Chapter 2. Indeed, Cook offered its services to Algeria in 1890 but was rebuffed. Pilgrims traveling on French-owned ships were easier to track, and Algerian pilgrims had to travel in groups of twenty with a *shaykh* from their place of origin, who would act as an intermediary throughout the journey and report back to the French authorities.[77]

For pilgrims who traveled to Mecca overland, although European colonial conquest in the late nineteenth century made the Sahara and Sahel unsafe, colonial rule meant that traveling conditions for pilgrims subsequently became less hazardous as routes came to be less blighted by war or slave raiding.[78]

Official support for the pilgrimages of France's elite subjects and employees was one method of promoting France as a patron of Islam. In 1837 and 1842, subjects deemed potentially useful to French rule in Algeria were offered free passage on ships from Algiers to Alexandria.[79] In the mid-nineteenth century, Governor Louis Faidherbe in Senegal inaugurated the practice of sponsored pilgrimages for French allies in order to demonstrate France's respect for Islam. Hamat Ndiaye Anne, Senegal's principal Arabic interpreter in the 1860s and 1870s, was rewarded for his service with a fully paid-for pilgrimage. Bu El Mogdad, Hamat's successor, was sent to Mecca several times on official duties and argued that *marabouts*, religious leaders and teachers, should be allowed to go on Hajj because in his words "it would be known in the country that it was made under French patronage and that this patronage was as valuable as the best-established reputation as a good Muslim."[80]

Like their Dutch counterparts, French administrators largely felt that going on Hajj could create a negative perception of colonial rule among their subjects and that returned pilgrims could challenge French rule. Colonial scholar-administrators in West Africa such as Alfred le Chatelier, Paul Marty, and Xavier Coppolani were instrumental in strengthening French surveillance over many areas of life in France's Muslim territories, including the Hajj. Indeed, French involvement in the Hajj was largely driven by the desire of the colonial state to monitor pilgrims. In Algeria, this led to systematic regulations on the Hajj, such as a travel permit being introduced in 1892 and 1894. Official inspectors on board pilgrim ships noted details such as the sanitary conditions on the vessel and received pilgrims' complaints about conditions on board. Tighter supervision was introduced during events such as Colonel Ahmed 'Urabi's revolt of 1881–1882 in Egypt, when French officials in North Africa thought that this might have a negative effect on their pilgrim-subjects in Mecca. However, officials' views were not monolithic; in

1900, for example, one official wrote in a report that the Hajj was a perfect "breeding ground" for anticolonial ideas, while another argued that the Hajj actually served to highlight the many differences among Muslims across the world, which made pan-Islamic activities in Mecca less likely. The Hajj from Algeria was banned twenty-two times between 1875 and 1915, with officials citing concerns over public health, although this was often a pretext for political concerns.[81]

From 1900 and especially during the First World War, a further French concern that contributed to attempts to increase control over the pilgrimage was the continued movement of pilgrims outside state control, with the implications this had for the transmission of disease and anticolonial ideas. Regulations were introduced in Algeria regarding passports, visas, and permissions that pilgrims needed from the colonial state. The ability of Muslims in French North and West Africa to travel overland to Mecca and the limited resources of these colonial states meant that surveillance was patchy, however, and many Muslims left for Mecca without the correct papers or acquired passports for destinations such as Tripolitania or Malta.[82] Scores of pilgrims made the journey overland to avoid having to deal with the colonial state's Hajj bureaucracy, which involved passports, certificates, and deposits.[83] These journeys often took many years, like those undertaken by pilgrims from Nigeria.[84] Pilgrims forged, lost, or duplicated colonial documentation and used the black market in Jidda to buy the tickets of dead pilgrims or returned as destitute pilgrims under a false name and then reclaimed another pilgrim's deposit. Despite a variety of French measures, attempts to control indigent pilgrims and what officials termed "unauthorized" pilgrims were consistently ineffective throughout the colonial period, a direct parallel to the British failure to stem the flow of destitute pilgrims from across their Muslim empire to and from Mecca.[85]

These trends continued as the twentieth century wore on, when officials in North and West Africa invested huge efforts in sponsoring and controlling the Hajj.[86] One early example of this was the French organization of a group of six hundred Algerian dignitaries to perform the Hajj and meet Sharif Hussein of Mecca in 1916, a French ally. From the 1920s, officials in Algeria and the French

Ministry of Foreign Affairs saw the Hajj as a propaganda opportunity to promote the benefits of French rule to their pilgrim-subjects. Specially equipped pilgrim ships were brought in for the official Algerian Hajj. These maritime convoys continued into the 1950s and were designed to showcase the pilgrimage under French colonial rule as safe and efficient.[87] There were similar efforts in West Africa, where the "official" Hajj began in the early 1930s when state-organized pilgrims traveled from Dakar and Casablanca to Mecca by steamship.[88] This sponsorship of hundreds of pilgrims each year was a form of surveillance intended to contain the spread of anticolonial ideas. Officials were concerned about the rapidity with which their pilgrim-subjects picked up such ideas in Mecca and then transmitted them back to West Africa.

The Hajj was a key element of a "particular discourse on the French colonial presence in the Muslim world."[89] This was the presentation of France as a benevolent, accommodating empire, a paternalistic attempt to persuade Muslims inside and outside their empire that French rule was acceptable. Moreover, French officials developed the idea of a French Muslim world, inhabited by *Musulmans français.* By the early 1950s, the official Hajj using government and commercial airplanes had expanded from aiding high-ranking Muslim loyalists to a much wider section of French West African colonial society. Colonial policies of sponsoring the Hajj for selected groups, such as high-ranking Muslim colonial officials, local leaders, and Muslim soldiers who had served in campaigns such as Indochina, were designed to inculcate a positive vision of France. This selective sponsorship was also used as a means of dividing French Muslim subjects into those who were sponsored and those who were not, in the hope that internal tensions within these Muslim societies generated by this division would lessen the possibility of unified resistance to French rule. Muslim soldier-pilgrims also featured in Britain's imperial experience, detailed in Chapter 4. Gregory Mann and Baz Lecocq have detailed how the post-1945, state-subsidized, official Hajj was a "colonial outpost" of the French welfare state that cost millions of francs a year to aid pilgrims from North and West Africa.[90] Nevertheless, France's impact on the Hajj was limited because pilgrims continued to avoid imperial frameworks and make their own way to Mecca.[91]

Because of France's involvement in the 1956 Suez Crisis, its consular service in the Hijaz was expelled and had to operate from Beirut and Khartoum; it never regained the ability to monitor the Hajj in Arabia.[92] Britain's experience of the Hajj during the Suez Crisis, detailed in the Epilogue, was a similar imperial denouement. The official Hajj by airplane was abandoned to free-market forces in West Africa in 1952 and North Africa in 1956.[93]

Much like their French and Dutch colonial peers, Russian officials tended to mistrust Islam and were concerned about the possibility of Muslim revolts.[94] In relation to the Hajj, tsarist authorities were anxious about their Muslim subjects' contacts with Mecca, seen as a haven of "fanaticism" and subversive ideas. The establishment of Odessa on the Black Sea in 1796 opened a new route to Mecca via Istanbul, making the Hajj easier for Russia's Muslim subjects. Russia's war against the Ottomans and Persia from 1804 to 1813 and its subsequent subjugation of the Muslim areas of the Caucasus led to a more negative official attitude toward the Hajj. Authorities in the Caucasus began to deny permission for people to go on pilgrimage, believing that Hajjis would return and spread their influence in a way unfavorable to Russian rule. In 1842, the War Ministry justified interference with the Hajj, but under a cloak of secrecy; Orenburg's governor was told to deny applications for the Hajj with "plausible pretexts." However, such attitudes and policies coexisted with officials who took Tsarina Catherine's 1773 proclamation of toleration to her Muslim subjects seriously and argued against restricting the pilgrimage. Governor-General of Bessarabia Mikhail Vorontsov discouraged Crimean officials from impeding pilgrims because he thought that this might cause unrest.[95]

Russian expansion into central Asia from the 1860s in fact facilitated the Hajj for Muslims living in this region. Although the subsequent construction of the Trans-Caspian Railway in 1899 and the Tashkent–Orenburg line in 1906 was for strategic and economic purposes, they inadvertently gave central Asian pilgrims a cheap and fast way to reach Mecca. Along with the spread of steamships on Russian shipping routes from the 1870s and the introduction of a direct Odessa–Jidda service in 1903, pilgrim numbers increased rapidly. For example, 20,000 to 50,000 pilgrims arrived in Odessa over one month in 1907, the majority of whom were poor and hailed from the Ferghana Valley in central Asia.[96]

Russian policies toward the Hajj followed a wavering line among ambivalent accommodation, tolerance, and fear about the Hajj's effects on Russian Muslims. Decrees by Konstantin von Kaufman, the governor of newly conquered Turkestan, gave Muslims the right to travel to any Islamic holy place, and in 1870 restrictions on passports to Mecca were lifted. As in the British empire, Russian officials disagreed over the nature of imperial involvement in the Hajj. In 1872, the Ministry of Internal Affairs tried to ban the Hajj because of concerns about the numbers of pilgrims traveling to the Ottoman empire; von Kaufman resisted this move, citing the prospect of disorder. A few years later, the ministry stated that the pilgrims posed no danger to Russia, but by the late nineteenth century the pendulum had swung back—the Hajj was a "scarcely tolerated evil," and returning pilgrims were thought to spread "extremist Islamism."[97] A government memo from St. Petersburg in 1897 sent to all provinces noted that the Hajj was a powerful means of strengthening Muslim "fanaticism."[98] Under Tsar Nicholas II (1894–1917), officials convinced of Ottoman-led pan-Islamic conspiracies sought to limit Russian Muslims' interactions with Mecca and other Islamic centers, such as Istanbul and Delhi.[99] Russian officials had an exaggerated sense of the Ottoman sultan-caliph's power over Muslims.

Overall, however, the Hajj "barely registered in official consciousness" until the 1890s, and measures to regulate or control the movement of pilgrims were not very effective.[100] Police officials in Turkestan were aware that the majority of pilgrims left for Mecca without passports. One potential route central Asian pilgrims might take was to cross into Afghanistan and then India, which took around a month. They would then take a train from Peshawar to Bombay, where charities helped poor pilgrims with their passages to Arabia, and then a steamship to Jidda. Around a quarter of pilgrims leaving Bombay in the 1890s were thought to be Russian subjects.[101] By the mid-1880s, the Russian consul in Jidda reported that destitute Russian pilgrims were given money by local merchants to return home. According to Daniel Brower, "The movement of pilgrims was the domain of communal endeavour beyond the bounds of Tsarist regulations and controls. . . . An unsupervised Hajj undermined Russian claims to be a well-ordered state."[102] The tsarist state's ineffectiveness in tightly regulating pilgrims' travels, most of whom were poor, was somewhat similar to the British experience charted in this book. A 1900 report on the pilgrimage that aimed to regularize tsarist administration was largely in reaction to European pressure in the form of international sanitary and public health conferences in the 1890s. Consequently, the tsarist government adopted a policy of protecting pilgrims in 1901, framed in terms of public health. This policy informed rules introduced in 1903 to assist pilgrims by providing facilities such as special railway coaches, government steamers, and medical assistance, along with sanitary inspections at designated departure ports and the supervision of large pilgrim groups by loyal Muslim figures or civil servants. In effect, Russia had become "a patron of pilgrims."[103] Although officials still viewed the Hajj with suspicion, suppressing it was deemed impossible because of fears of Muslim unrest and the basic inability of the Russian government to do so. Therefore, assistance was deemed the most pragmatic solution.

The Tsarist state sometimes delegated its organization of the pilgrimage to Muslims. Eileen Kane has detailed how in 1907, the authorities gave a Muslim entrepreneur, Said Gani Saidazimbaev, a contract as general agent for the Turkestan pilgrimage, and in 1908 he was named head of Muslim pilgrims in Russia. Saidazimbaev's plans were modeled on Thomas Cook's during that firm's tenure as travel agent for the Hajj from India, detailed in Chapter 2. His ambitious plans for organizing pilgrims were partly realized, with between 7,000 and 10,000 pilgrims using his railway coaches, hostels, and leased ships. But shipping companies and local merchants in Odessa saw the scheme as threatening to their interests. Pilgrims reacted badly to Said's makeshift Odessa "Hajj complex," a former bakery where they were locked up after being escorted there off trains by policemen. Prime Minister Peter Stolypin was appalled to hear about Said's activities, and Said lost the contract, on which he had already made a loss of 60,000 roubles. Competing firms and associations resumed their pilgrimage activities alongside increased government involvement, their combined activities mirroring in many ways the contours of the Hajj from British-ruled Bombay, discussed in Chapter 3.[104] Daniel Brower has argued that Russian tolerance of the Hajj and assistance to pilgrims resulted from the pragmatic decisions required of a multireligious empire and were in a sense a default solution.[105]

The Soviet Union took a harsher stance toward the Hajj, although this oscillated between liberalization and extreme restrictions. The Hajj was banned from the Soviet Union in 1928, although 207 pilgrims made it to Mecca in 1929, and a small number were allowed on Hajj in 1944–1945. Soviet officials saw the ritual as having a negative impact because pilgrims' departures and returns were occasions for unwelcome displays of piety. The ban on the Hajj was relaxed in the postwar era, but restrictive pilgrim quotas remained in place because small pilgrim groups were easier to supervise, and the same approved people went on Hajj repeatedly. The Soviet bureaucracy deliberately made applying for permission to perform the Hajj difficult. Many Hajjis were officials in state directorates, such as the Council for Religious Cults and the Council for Religious Affairs. The secret police vetted all Hajj applicants and rejected many; each pilgrim party often had one person who was either a member of the KGB or an informant. Restrictions on the Hajj meant that the importance of Islamic holy places in Russia was enhanced, a natural response to a situation where Muslims could not fulfill one of the five pillars of Islam. The most popular shrine was the Takht-i-Sulayman in the central Asian town of Osh, which attracted 60,000 pilgrims each year in the 1940s and 100,000 per year in the 1950s. Promoting the shrine as a "second Mecca," Soviet-backed Muslim religious leaders decreed that three visits to it were equivalent to performing the Hajj.[106] Ending this survey of European empires and the Hajj here at the Takht-i-Sulayman shrine, this chapter now moves on to consider the broader canvas of other religious pilgrimages in the British empire.

The Wider Geography of Religious Pilgrimage

Although the Hajj is the most important pilgrimage in Islam doctrinally, it is only one component of a landscape of religious pilgrimages that span the globe and the many diverse interpretations of

Islam. These religious pilgrimages can be imperfectly divided into two classes: (1) Shiʿi pilgrimages to the shrine cities of Najaf and Karbala in Iraq and (2) the practice of *ziyara*, pilgrimages to shrines of Sufi saints or other Muslim notables, including the Prophet Muhammad's tomb at Medina. The nature of pilgrimages to Medina, Najaf, and Karbala was similar in scope to that of the Hajj if the pilgrim was journeying from West Africa or Southeast Asia. Britain's engagement with Shiʿi pilgrimages in Iraq forms an illuminating case study for comparison with its involvement in the Hajj.[107] This section will examine Shiʿi pilgrimages before considering Britain's engagement with pilgrimages to Sufi saints' shrines, then broadening out beyond Islam to discuss the examples of Muslim and Christian pilgrimages in Palestine during the British Mandate period, and finishing with a survey of Britain's administration of the Hindu Kumbh Mela in India.

In Shiʿi Islam, pilgrimages to the tombs of Ali, the Prophet Muhammad's cousin, in Najaf, and Husayn, the Prophet's grandson, in Karbala are undertaken to acknowledge these men's leadership of the Muslim community and renew the bond between the believer and these important figures in Shiʿi Islam. Unlike the Hajj, these pilgrimages can be undertaken at any time of year, although there are some auspicious dates on which to perform these rituals.[108] British involvement in Shiʿi pilgrimage to Najaf and Karbala began earlier than its sustained engagement with the Hajj and was precipitated by the expansion of East India Company influence over Awadh, a great Shiʿi kingdom in North India. In 1849, the company opened relations with the shrine cities in order to distribute the Oudh (Awadh) Bequest of around R 121,000 annually, bequeathed by the kings of Awadh since 1786 for disbursement in Najaf and Karbala. This money was spent on public projects such as the Hindiyya Canal, religious figures such as *mujtahidun*, who were influential figures because of their ability to make pronouncements on religious and political developments, *ʿulama*, and "deserving persons" such as poor pilgrims. The East India Company and later the government of India became the trustees of the bequest. From 1852, it was paid through the British political resident in Baghdad to a *mujtahid* in Najaf and Karbala, respectively. The upheaval caused by Awadh's annexation by the company in 1856 and the 1857 Indian rebellion, coupled with the bequest's reputation, led to a large influx of Indian pilgrims who settled in the shrine cities. Indian pilgrims tended to arrive in Basra by ship and then traveled up-country to Najaf and Karbala.[109] Aggressive British policies in Awadh inadvertently provided a fillip to Indian Shi'i pilgrimage to the shrine cities.

British reforms of the bequest in 1867, 1903, and 1912 were driven by various factors but had the common aim of trying to increase British influence over the *mujtahid* community in the shrine cities and the surrounding Ottoman provinces, which reflected Britain's growing political involvement in the region. A separate Indian Fund, established in 1867 but abolished in 1903, caused a sharp rise in the number of destitute Indian pilgrims and settlers in the shrine cities, and further reform in 1912 was partly intended to marshal funds to repatriate these people. The Ottomans were hostile to the bequest from the early 1900s, seeing it as a vehicle for British influence. Britain's occupation of Iraq during the First World War meant that the bequest was seen as one method of increasing British prestige in the country, although most recipients of the money had either actively resisted the British during the war or were hostile to the British occupation.[110] After 1929, the Indian Muslim protector of pilgrims, a newly created position based in the British Residency, Baghdad, distributed the bequest four times a year in the shrine cities, a duty transferred to the Indian consul in 1933, but payments petered out in the 1950s.[111] Although only a small minority of the monies from the bequest reached pilgrims who were British subjects, this financial vehicle meant that Britain played a uniquely intimate role in the political, social, and religious history of Najaf and Karbala. The bequest was prone to mismanagement and corruption, but for many decades it provided a potential source of funds for Indian pilgrims. The Oudh Bequest was one critical feature that set Britain's engagement with Shi'i pilgrimage in Iraq apart from its involvement in the Hajj.

The second feature that further marks out the difference between British interactions with Shi'i pilgrimage and with the Hajj was Britain's invasion of Iraq in the First World War and the subsequent period when Iraq was a British mandate, during which Britain temporarily exercised direct control over the Shiʿi pilgrimages. Although some *mujtahidun* in the shrine cities supported the 1914 Ottoman jihad proclamation against Britain, France, and Russia, Ottoman war policies, such as requisitioning and conscription, led to an uprising in Najaf and Karbala in 1915, and the cities were essentially autonomous entities by 1916. Sir Percy Cox, chief political officer, was ordered in 1917 to keep the Shiʿi Holy Places outside direct British control, but continued supplies to the Ottoman armies from these cities meant that British political officers were stationed there. Plebiscites conducted in 1918–1919 showed that residents of the cities were unhappy with continued British rule. After the 1920 rebellion in Iraq, when Shiʿi actors united briefly with other Iraqis against Britain, the Shiʿi community became politically marginalized, a trend exacerbated by the establishment of the British Mandate and Faisal's installation as Hashemite king of Iraq.[112] Nevertheless, because the Shiʿa constituted over 55 percent of Iraq's population, Britain could not ignore them and their pilgrimages—a demographic sentiment echoed in other political calculations regarding Sunni Muslims and the Hajj across Britain's Muslim empire.[113]

British attitudes toward the Shiʿa were condescending, but officials thought it vital to recognize the pilgrimage's importance to the shrine cities as part of a wider strategy to gain support from the community. One administrative report described how Iraqi Shiʿa possessed "the tinge of political indocility."[114] The Shiʿa were seen as backward and prone to violence, and Shiʿism was perceived as "a metonym for all that was wrong with Iraq."[115] During the war, pilgrim numbers had collapsed, causing recession and inflation in the shrine cities, but by December 1918 there was a revival, with Indian pilgrim numbers returning to their prewar level of several thousand annually.[116] In 1918, British officials in Najaf reported that they "cannot indefinitely administer a town rotten with abuses that loudly challenge our dignity," a statement that served to justify their belief that British administrative reforms in the town should be continued and intensified. To these political officers, the choice was clear: whether Najaf "is to become a glorious monument to British administration in the eyes of every Shiaʿh Muhammadan, or a hotbed of anti-British intrigues, entirely depends on our early recognition of its [the pilgrimage's] influence and size." This did not extend to the political officers handing several buildings that had previously been used to house pilgrims back to their owners. It was envisaged that Shi'i pilgrim numbers would increase through opening the Euphrates to river traffic and extending Iraq's railway network.[117] Military authorities provided boats from Baghdad for the tens of thousands of pilgrims who wanted to travel to Karbala in 1919. After making the pilgrimage, several Iraqi tribal leaders went on to Mecca by sea after the British civil commissioner assured them that they could travel from Jidda to Mecca without being harassed because they were Shi'a, a pledge that held little weight once these pilgrims reached the Hijaz.[118]

As Yitzhak Nakash has shown, British and Iraqi officials made concerted efforts between 1919 and 1924 to regulate the pilgrimage, introducing mandatory passports, fixing visa fees, setting health and quarantine regulations, reviving quarantine stations, and limiting the length of a pilgrim's visit to not more than three months.[119] This record of activity masks the difficulties British officials had in regulating the pilgrimages during Ramadan, Muharram, and various auspicious days, when thousands of pilgrims visited the shrine cities.[120] During the period of direct British political administration in Karbala, an official report described how "everything possible has been done to show the people that the British Government exercises a wide and benevolent tolerance towards their institutions and beliefs. The Moslem element has been preserved in the administration as far as possible." The political office's staff was Muslim except for the political officer and the treasurer, and all the work was conducted in Arabic.[121] One of the office's main tasks in relation to the 1919 pilgrimage was to help over 1,000 Indian pilgrims return home.[122] After complaints from Indian Shi'a, the government of India appointed a protector of Indian pilgrims in December 1928 who had a range of duties similar to those of his namesake in Bombay; one of his most important duties was repatriating destitute Indian pilgrims stranded in Iraq.[123] This administrative activity was remarkably similar to Bombay's Hajj administration, discussed in Chapter 3. Overall, however, British officials were more concerned about the supposed corruption and anti-British intrigues of the *mujtahidun* in Najaf and Karbala than about the Shi'i pilgrimages.[124]

The official reports offer tantalizing glimpses of extraordinary journeys undertaken to the shrines, which became rarer after the 1921–1923 extension of the Iraqi railway system. A British officer met two men and one woman, all over fifty, on the road from Hillah to Karbala in 1919. They had begun their journey from Karachi eleven months earlier and had walked the entire distance in order to visit Husayn's shrine.[125] Railway development in the form of the Baghdad–Basra and Hindiyya–Karbala lines offered many services to pilgrims. In 1925, Iraqi Railways began selling tickets in Iran and India; over 75,000 tickets were sold in 1928–1929.[126] British officials sent out pamphlets that advertised the ease of traveling in Iraq on pilgrimage. One publication by Iraqi Railways in 1922, in Arabic and Urdu, extolled the "quick" journey at "reasonable" cost, which enabled more time to be spent at shrines. Railway supervisors had the duty of "looking after" pilgrims, and refreshments on board were provided. In addition to a table of fares, one could find out the cost of transporting skeletons or corpses, although only a maximum of seven were allowed per person.[127] Advances in rail and sea transport meant that Indian pilgrims could undertake the whole journey in around three weeks. As with the Hajj, technological change dramatically altered the character of the Shi'i pilgrimage.[128]

The Iranians were the largest group of pilgrims, some 100,000 a year during the peak of Shi'i pilgrimage in the late nineteenth century, but their numbers declined after the First World War because of Iranian government policies. From 1923 to 1925, Iran banned the pilgrimage. Afterward, Iranians stayed in the shrine cities for only a few days, traveling on Iraqi trains and by taxi. Reza Shah, Iran's new ruler from 1925, sought to attack popular Shi'i traditions and introduced new restrictions on pilgrims in 1927–1929, including a ban on traveling via Iraq to perform the Hajj. Consequently, Iranian pilgrims had to travel through the Soviet Union or even via Bombay instead of taking the old Najaf–Medina route. Britain's invasion of Iran in August 1941 led some Iranians to hope that Britain might assist in reviving the practice of pilgrimages to the shrine cities.[129] Iranian government policies were factors as important as any British endeavors in the changing nature of pilgrimage to the shrine cities.

The reduction in Iranian pilgrim numbers meant that the Iraqi government began to focus on eradicating the phenomenon of destitute Indian pilgrims. Measures such as the Iraq Residence and Nationality Laws of 1923 and 1934, the introduction of cheap return tickets that pilgrims were required to purchase in India, efforts by British officials in India to discourage pilgrims from leaving without enough money, and limiting the length of pilgrim's visits to only three months a year in the mid-1930s meant that the figure of the destitute Indian pilgrim became a rarity in the shrine cities.[130] In these policies, Iraqi officials were aided by the Indian Muslim protector of pilgrims, attached to the British Residency in Baghdad.[131]

Britain's involvement in Shiʿi pilgrimage to the shrine cities, either through the Oudh Bequest or British administration, had varying implications for Shiʿi pilgrims. Britain's role was perhaps more visible compared with its association with the Hajj, given the construction of railways, the disbursement of monies in the shrine cities, and the institution of various regulations, even though these elements were present in some shape or form in relation to the Hajj. Other similarities affected Indian pilgrims in particular, such as attempts to remove destitute Indian pilgrims from the shrine cities and the work of Indian Muslim officials in the Baghdad Residency, some of whom, like the protector of pilgrims, held the same title as their Sunni counterparts in Bombay. But in a wider context, Britain was less important to the Shiʿi pilgrimages than the pilgrimage policies of Iran's successive rulers, which affected Iranian pilgrims, who made up the vast majority of those visiting the shrines. Moreover, British policies that attempted to cultivate the loyalty of the Shiʿi community in India from the mid-nineteenth century did not necessarily translate into policies affecting the shrine cities. Britain's relationships with Iraq and Iran ranged over many more areas than the pilgrimage alone, and the Shiʿa population of Britain's Muslim empire was far smaller and less geographically dispersed than its Sunni counterpart. Given the Sunni numerical predominance among the global *umma*, the Shiʿi shrine cities did not hold the same sacred status in the Muslim world as Mecca and Medina. All these factors meant that Shi'i pilgrimage to Najaf and Karbala did not possess the same magnitude of importance to the British as the Hajj.

The vast majority of pilgrimages undertaken by Muslims were, in fact, more localized, to their nearest shrine of a saint or notable, where pilgrims received blessings from the saint or notable—a ritual called *ziyara*, which literally means "visit."[132] Customary Islam is a powerful force in many Muslims' lives, despite reformist and fundamentalist influences. This is evident from records related to the Hajj; many Muslims combined their pilgrimage to Mecca with visits to shrines in the Hijaz and elsewhere on their itinerary.[133] In particular, as the location of the Prophet Muhammad's tomb, Medina's importance as a pilgrimage destination increased as Muslim veneration of the Prophet grew from the nineteenth century.[134] This pilgrimage experience was further spiritualized by Sufi mystics who connected it with the Prophet's life.[135] That this trend affected many Muslims is unsurprising; after all, the spread of Islam to many areas in Africa and Asia occurred not through conquest but through Sufi orders' missionary activity after the ninth century CE.[136] Widespread "saint cults" satisfied the desire for nearby holy places, given that most Muslims live many miles from Mecca. Even for Muslims closer to Mecca, such as tribesmen in southern Iraq, *ziyara* to the shrines of their local saints was seen as an adequate substitute for the Hajj.[137] Over the centuries, despite attacks by Wahhabis and others against saint veneration, the popularity of local shrine visits, in the words of Frederick Denny, "appears to be ineradicable."[138] Terminologies of "official" versus "popular" Islam are misleading; although there are certainly deep conflicts, often such boundaries are more blurred in practice.[139]

In South Asia, *ziyara* to the shrines of such Sufi saints as Sheikh Mu'inuddin Chishti at Ajmer, Sheikh Nizamuddin Auliya in Delhi, and Baba Farid at Pakpattan remained important sources of political and religious authority in the colonial period. Chishti's shrine has been one of the most popular Muslim shrines in India since the late sixteenth century and is also visited by Hindus. Chishti, who died in 1236, was a Sufi who gained recognition for his personal relationship with God. The popularity of the shrine increased when Emperor

Akbar began making an annual pilgrimage there from 1562 to 1579, a patronage continued by his successors. Within the shrine's mosque, there is an inscription that likens the Mughal emperor and the mosque to the Ka'ba. This showed how the emperor "wished to be thought of."[140] For Sufi saints, the Hajj was central to their lives, and many performed the ritual multiple times. Mecca was a natural place for meeting and discussion among them and was the location where many received visions and revelations. Pilgrimage to Mecca was seen as a minimal religious obligation for these saints, "without which all mystical training would be useless."[141] The trustees of Sufi saints' shrines in India that possessed large amounts of land and property tried to avoid appropriation of these assets by "passively supporting" British rule.[142] Britain's administration of pilgrimages to these shrines in the colonial period is a fertile area for future research.[143]

In West Asia, Palestine, the birthplace of Jesus and the site of many events in the Bible, was considered the Holy Land by Christians. Britain's involvement in Christian pilgrimages stretched back to the nineteenth century, when Thomas Cook escorted a tour group of 60 people to Palestine in 1869. Once the Suez Canal opened that same year and India-bound ships stopped in Alexandria for a week, Cook took advantage of this and offered tours of the Holy Land; by the end of the century, these attracted 12,000 people a year.[144] A greater stream of pilgrims visited after the British army pushed Ottoman forces out of the area and took Jerusalem in December 1917.

Pilgrimages to sites in Palestine were also important to Jews and Muslims. On his entry into Jerusalem in 1917, General Edmund Allenby declared "that every sacred building, monument, holy spot, shrine, traditional site, endowment, pious bequest, or customary place of prayer of whatsoever form of the three religions will be maintained and protected according to the existing customs and beliefs of those to whose faith they are sacred."[145] Indian Muslim troops guarded the Dome of the Rock and al-Aqsa Mosque. Hajji Amin al-Husseini, mufti of Jerusalem, considerably raised Jerusalem's status in the Muslim world through fund-raising tours to India, Kuwait, and Bahrain in 1923–1924 to facilitate the restoration of the city's two Muslim holy sites, which led to an increase in Muslim pilgrims.

However, violence was a common feature of the British Mandate, to which these pilgrimages were no stranger. Britain's announcement in February 1920 that it would carry out the 1917 Balfour Declaration led to anti-Jewish riots during the festival of Nabi Musa, the pilgrimage to Moses's alleged tomb that attracted pilgrims from across Palestine. Nabi Musa, previously seen as a folk event, came under the purview of British authorities; banners carried by pilgrims were scrutinized by the district commissioner at Jerusalem's Jaffa Gate to ensure that they were not inflammatory before being allowed through.[147] The close proximity of Muslim and Jewish pilgrimage sites led to confrontation. Conflicts between Jewish and Muslim communities over these, such as the Wailing Wall and the Temple Mount, flared up in 1928 and 1929, which prompted a League of Nations Commission of Enquiry in 1930.[148] Britain left Palestine amid a paroxysm of violence in 1948; its administration of the Palestine pilgrimages remains understudied.

Aside from the Hajj, Hindu pilgrimage in India was probably the largest case of British involvement in religious pilgrimages. Britain's engagement with Hindu pilgrimage in India predated its involvement in the Hajj by several decades; consequently, there were several important parallels between the imperial administrations of these rituals.[149] The various demands of imperial governance created a default engagement with pilgrimages, Hindu and Muslim alike.[150] Kama Maclean has argued that the British administration of the gigantic Kumbh Mela at Allahabad was "heavy-handed and predicated on suspicion rather than benevolence."[151] Suspicion and pragmatism meant that British officials calculated that it was more advantageous to accommodate the mela than restrict it; similar conclusions were drawn in the case of the Hajj.

Another striking point of comparison between Britain's interactions with both Hindu pilgrimage and the Hajj was how Britain's delicate balancing act among intervention, reform, and a concern to adhere to noninterference in religious practices led, under the weight of this bundle of contradictions, to unintentional facilitation. In the case of the Hajj, it was Britain's provision of funding for poor pilgrims' homeward-bound voyages; in that of the Kumbh Mela, it was Britain's wholesale financial support of that pilgrimage from 1900, once the mela had ceased to be profitable.[152] The Kumbh Mela, like the Hajj, was recognized by British officials as a site of and conduit for disease, trade, news, and anticolonial activism. Officials and travelers repeatedly stressed the dangers of the mela, often ascribed to Hindu "fanaticism." This set of perceptions was also shared by some elite Indians and was used to justify British control.[153] In a similar vein, albeit with less success, officials and Muslims alike stressed the "fanatical" element among Muslim pilgrims performing the Hajj as one justification for further involvement.

In deciding the nature and scope of imperial engagement, official reliance on consultation with "reliable natural leaders" in society was important regarding both the Kumbh Mela and the hajj. Official decisions on the mela were often influenced by Indian representations. Kama Maclean has argued that after Queen Victoria's 1858 proclamation of religious tolerance to her subjects in India, "religion was the foremost arena where Indians could contest British power." Indians used the proclamation to agitate against British restrictions on the mela or to argue for increasing Indian participation in its administration.[154] Like their Muslim counterparts, Hindu elites used the proclamation to argue that proposed reforms—in the case of the Kumbh Mela, for example, the potential reintroduction of pilgrim taxes—would be misinterpreted by poorer, less educated pilgrims as an infringement of it. This phenomenon was seen regularly in the case of the Hajj, detailed in Chapter 2.[155] Furthermore, the regular turnover of British personnel involved in the colonial administration of the mela—positions such as collectors, district magistrates, and district commissioners—meant that these men, inexperienced in the details of the mela, often relied on their Indian subordinates and local notables for knowledge and advice.[156] This trend was particularly mirrored in the regular turnover of British consuls in Jidda, who were frequently dependent on their longer-established Muslim subordinates for detailed knowledge about the Hajj.

Political and technological developments in the nineteenth century made both the Hajj and the Kumbh Mela accessible to a larger and broader socioeconomic section of Muslims and Hindus. An improvement in traveling conditions on land and sea occasioned by the rise of British imperial power in South Asia and beyond made pilgrimages more popular. In the case of the Kumbh Mela, safer conditions on roads and Allahabad's connection to the Grand Trunk Road in 1828 and the railway network in the 1870s made it more accessible than ever before. The growth of India's railway network enabled a concomitant growth in the number of Hindu pilgrims to various pilgrimage sites. The journey was much cheaper and was increasingly made by "peasant-pilgrims." Similarly, the rapid expansion of steamships involved in a pilgrim traffic that crisscrossed the Indian Ocean, by this point a British lake, brought the Hajj within the realm of possibility for poorer Muslims from Malaya and India to East Africa. Technology and British imperialism were important foundations for mass participation in Asia's pilgrimages in this period.

However, there were substantial differences in the imperial administration of these rituals, largely rooted in the fact of British sovereignty over Hindu pilgrimage sites, which had occurred incrementally in tandem with the East India Company's expansion across the subcontinent from the late eighteenth century. The company's policy of pragmatic religious tolerance perhaps made it more susceptible to being drawn into the management of Hindu pilgrimage and temples. In 1806, the company committed itself to managing the temple at Jagannath in eastern India and took over the collection of a pilgrim tax at Allahabad, Gaya, and Jagannath from 1812 until 1840.[157] For many pilgrims from remote villages, the mela was the first time they encountered the colonial state. British intervention in the mela ranged far more widely than regulation related to the Hajj. For example, an 1840 act proscribed "extortion of alms" through practices such as public nudity by pilgrims at the Kumbh Mela. British legislation reduced some pilgrims such as *sadhus* (holy men) to begging, which meant that they were subsequently criminalized and seen as anarchic figures.[158] Criminalizing poor Muslim pilgrims was beyond the capacities of the coercive colonial state, although some officials wanted to prevent such people from performing the Hajj.

Although the 1866 International Sanitary Conference in Istanbul focused on the Hajj and epidemic disease, the delegates were also concerned about the threat to public health posed by Hindu pilgrimages and advised the government of India to introduce sanitary police and quarantine measures. This led to a progressive tightening of sanitary regulation, which preoccupied officials from this point onward far more than concerns about anticolonial activity at pilgrimage sites. Intervention was intimate, down to instructing where pilgrims could defecate. The 1867 cholera epidemic led to imposition of quarantine measures on major routes used by pilgrims leaving Haridwar. The epidemic also revived an old debate among officials about how pilgrimage attendance could be restricted, although it was realized that this was unfeasible given the ever-increasing scale of the mela and the 1858 proclamation of religious tolerance. Officials had decided that pilgrims were the main vectors of disease transmission, and the mela was dispersed by sanitary police in 1875, 1882, and 1890.[159] In 1892, the Haridwar mela was dispersed by the police and army because of the presence of cholera, a move that was resisted by pilgrims and led to condemnation from the same elites and local notables whom officials, in an attempt at co-option, had consulted for advice on pilgrimage administration.[160] Intrusive reforms, such as the sanitary policing of latrines on pilgrim sites and clampdowns on overcrowding in pilgrim guesthouses, led to complaints and hostility from pilgrims, although a more common response was for pilgrims to subtly evade regulations. For example, a quarter of pilgrims at the Haridwar mela in 1885 evaded a bridge-crossing tax. British officials justified these types of colonial intervention on the grounds that it did not constitute interference with religious expression.[161] Much of the Hajj's sanitary administration was copied from Hindu pilgrimage administration, although much of this regulation was less enforceable—given the location of the Hajj in Arabia, beyond British sovereignty, it could never have been "dispersed" by Britain or, indeed, the Ottomans, in the event of a cholera outbreak.[162]

The British were aware that the mela played an important role in disseminating nationalist ideas because of its huge number of attendees. At times of crisis, especially during the First World War, officials were fearful of the subversive potential of large gatherings such as the mela. The authorities tried to restrict pilgrim numbers in 1918 because they were concerned that it would be calamitous if most pilgrims at the mela turned against the British, given that most of the Indian army was deployed overseas. Restrictions on the sale of train tickets valid around the time of the mela were unsuccessful—

pilgrims resented the move and traveled instead by road and river. Pilgrim numbers were not reduced at all. But British perceptions of the mela, like those of the Hajj, were multifaceted. The fact that recruiters for the Indian army operated at the mela suggested that the British did not see the mela as populated solely by those opposed to British rule.[163] The multiple views of British officials on the Kumbh Mela and the Hajj perhaps account for the sense of what might be termed an "imperial indecisiveness" that attended discussions of any proposed policies on these rituals.

In many areas aside from sanitary intervention, then, the mela fell beyond the boundaries of British control, a state of affairs rather similar to that of the Hajj, as subsequent chapters will elucidate. Religious pilgrimages had always been an area of human activity that concerned empires and their rulers, but it was only from the nineteenth century that increasingly complex European—and Asian—imperial states were able to substantially expand the ambit of their involvement with such religious rituals, although this ran up against the political and administrative limits of such polities. The Hajj's transcontinental scope and religious status among Muslims meant this ritual received particular attention and engagement, and Chapter 2 analyzes the emergence and development of Britain's involvement in the Hajj in the last third of the nineteenth century.

2

Pilgrimage in the Mid-Victorian Era, c. 1865–1900

Introduction

In the second half of the nineteenth century, Britain's subject Muslim populations were largely concentrated in India and the Indian Ocean's littorals. The southern Arabian port of Aden, occupied in 1839, was ruled from Bombay; Zanzibar became a British protectorate in 1890, and Britain increased its control over Peninsular Malaya's Muslim sultanates. This inner empire of largely Islamic territories broadened considerably with British expansion into Sudan and Nigeria in the late 1890s. Throughout the life span of Britain's Muslim empire, the largest number of its Muslim subjects was Indian. Indians formed the largest numbers of pilgrims from outside Arabia alongside Egyptians and Indonesians. By the end of the nineteenth century, the annual transregional travels of thousands of Indian pilgrims to and from Mecca had become a permanent fixture of British imperial administration across India and its consular administration in Arabia. Consequently, this chapter's geographic focus is the Hijaz and, across the Arabian Sea, India.

The majority of existing works on Britain and the Hajj center on the late nineteenth century.[1] Although this chapter will acknowledge these studies' concerns, which mostly concentrate on British efforts to combat epidemic disease and anticolonial, pan-Islamic activities related to the Hajj, emphasizing these aspects has tended to exaggerate the extent and effectiveness of Britain's overall ability to exercise control over certain aspects of the pilgrimage. This chapter builds on Radhika Singha's pioneering work on "pauper" pilgrims to move beyond other studies that take indigent pilgrims as a given feature of the Hajj and explores the interactions between this group of pilgrims and British officialdom. These pilgrims were often seen by officials and others as incapable—the very attribute that such officials often displayed in their inability to stem the flow of poor pilgrims between India and the Hijaz.[2] Alongside sanitary and quarantine regulations and concerns about pilgrims' potentially subversive sojourns in the Hijaz, destitute pilgrims' travels occupied a substantial amount of time for those officials tasked with engaging with the Hajj.

Before analyzing British interactions with destitute pilgrims in detail, this chapter opens with an appraisal of Britain's relationship with the Hijaz up to the 1850s. It considers accounts from this period that mention poor pilgrims and highlights the initially dismissive British response to this group. Surveying the wider context of British perceptions of Islam—especially in relation to the impact of the 1857 Indian rebellion—shows how these fed into suspicious attitudes toward the pilgrimage. Nevertheless, British views of Islam became more ambivalent and less hostile as the century wore on; the empire's deepened interactions with the Hajj formed part of this shift in attitudes. The chapter continues with a brief examination of the 1865 cholera epidemic, which focused Britain's attention on the pilgrimage, and then provides a Muslim perspective on the Hajj through analyzing the begum of Bhopal's pilgrimage account.

Britain's engagement with destitute pilgrims increased in complexity from the 1870s as authorities in Jidda and India attempted to grapple with the seemingly intractable question of how to deal with the presence of these pilgrims, stranded in Jidda after the conclusion of each Hajj. Officials did not develop a clear-cut policy on this issue. A huge body of information on destitute pilgrims, often contradictory, was produced by a variety of British and Muslim officials and by local Indian Muslim leaders consulted by the British. Muslims significantly influenced an official stance of inaction toward these pilgrims. One area, however, where Britain attempted to supervise pilgrims' travels was Thomas Cook's appointment as travel agent for the Indian Hajj from 1886 to 1893. But Cook's exit from the Hajj travel market further underscored the limits of Britain's capacity to exercise a supervisory role over the flow of pilgrims to and from Mecca. The issue of destitute pilgrims is emblematic of Britain's interactions with the Hajj; Britain was simply unable to exercise control over this group. Britain's relationship with the pilgrimage in this period was characterized by numerous contradictory drives and an underlying uncertainty that was almost disabling in enacting various policies. A desire to exert a degree of control over certain aspects of the Hajj ran in tandem with an almost complete inability to enact certain administrative measures.[3] An important reason for this was British wariness about the consequences of interference in such an important religious practice, reflected in and exacerbated by their assiduous cultivation of local Muslim opinion across India on this issue. In doing so, Britain was drawn deeper into the intricacies of the Islamic faith. By the eve of the First World War, Britain's engagement with this group of pilgrims was transformed into wholesale repatriation of them, effectively underwriting the cost of their Hajj.

The key role played by Muslim employees at Jidda formed another important part of British interactions with the pilgrimage. These men energetically occupied themselves with the thorny issue of destitute pilgrims and helped shape Britain's emergent Hajj administrative apparatus by contributing to official knowledge about the pilgrimage. The work of these men within imperial bureaucracies demonstrates the complexity of Anglo-Muslim relations in this period, which cannot be characterized as being implacably hostile. Nevertheless, in the final analysis, motives of pragmatic self-interest drove British and Muslims alike.

One strand of British thinking about the pilgrimage was tinged with paranoia and suspicion over the Hajj's potential as an occasion for anti-British activity. Because Mecca and Medina were closed to non-Muslims, the idea of these cities and the Hijaz as a menacing, unknown space contributed to this perception. However, these views became gradually more nuanced from the early 1880s as Britain's Muslim employees, especially those in Jidda, provided a fresh channel of information on the Hajj to their employers. This chapter's examination of Islamic "subversion" related to Mecca and the Hajj and directed against Britain reveals the largely ephemeral nature of this phenomenon and shows how some officials who dealt with this topic were prone to exaggeration and hyperbole. Taken together, these themes show how Britain's evolving association with the Hajj was not an aspect of imperial administration that was likely to disappear. If anything, the complexities that surrounded Britain's interactions with the Hajj demonstrate how officials were drawn haphazardly, yet irrevocably, into a deeper engagement with this aspect of Islamic religious practice. Britain's emergent administrative involvement with the Hajj in this period brings into focus some of the material realities of Britain's Muslim empire.

Beginnings: Trade, Politics, Shipping, Travelers, and Poor and Princely Pilgrims

The initial impetus for England's first forays into the Red Sea area during the seventeenth century was trade. However, these efforts were opposed by Indian merchants, the Hijazi authorities, and English pirates operating in the area. A mob massacred several British merchants in Jidda in 1724. British merchants were again put under threat from the local populace in the late eighteenth century because the East India Company authorities refused to continue the Mughal practice of sending annual donations from Surat to the Holy Cities. Nevertheless, the relative profitability of the Jidda trade meant that British merchants remained engaged in commercial activity at the port.[4]

Several events precipitated a more active British connection with the region. In the aftermath of his invasion of Egypt in 1798, Napoleon informed the sharif of Mecca that he would "facilitate" the Hajj, continue to send Egypt's donation to the Holy Places and confirm the appointment of the Egyptian *amir al-hajj*.[5] In response to Napoleon's offensive, Bombay's governor dispatched a small naval force to the Red Sea, which attacked French-held Suez and Qusayr in April and August 1799. Captain Sir Home Popham was dispatched to the Red Sea in 1800 to coordinate forces from Britain and India against the French and ensure the cooperation of local rulers, especially Sharif Ghalib of Mecca. Popham was also ordered to establish a factory in Jidda for trade with India and to secure concessions and treaties with the sharif. Mahdi Ali Khan, an Indian Muslim notable, was Popham's assistant in negotiations with Ghalib. These went nowhere; Ghalib distrusted the British because they were Christians and a potential economic threat to Hijazi trade. Ghalib floated the possibility of acquiescence with British proposals, but only in exchange for a guarantee that Britain would ensure his independence from his Ottoman suzerains. Popham refused; Britain was concerned to preserve the Ottoman empire's territorial integrity. Mahdi Ali Khan became involved in local plots to unseat Ghalib, hoping that another ruler would be more amenable to British requests. Popham's recourse to Ali Khan points to what William Roff calls the "inherent ambivalence" of British attempts to understand and engage in Hijazi affairs—they were in many ways powerless without using men like Ali Khan, a feature seen later in this book.[6] Napoleon's Egyptian misadventure highlighted the strategic and economic importance of the Red Sea and the Hijaz to Britain, and British awareness of the Hijaz was further enhanced by reports of the Egyptian ruler Muhammad 'Ali's campaigns against the Saudi-Wahhabi forces in the Hijaz from 1811 to 1818.[7]

In October 1837, the East India Company appointed British agents—elevated to vice-consuls by the Foreign Office in October 1838—to Suez, Qusayr, and Jidda in order to "facilitate steam communication" between Egypt and India. Alexander Ogilvie was the first vice-consul in Jidda and arrived there to serve in its hot climate at the end of 1838. An economic treaty with the Ottomans that same year led to a large increase in trade with Jidda. Indian Muslims played a key role in this trade—the richest person in Jidda in the 1850s was Faraj Yusr, an Indian who had interests in shipping and banking.[8] The majority of goods imported to Jidda were British, and by the 1880s the value of these was around £1.5 million. By 1897, British subjects in the Hijaz (mainly Indian Muslims) made up approximately one-seventh of the population, with over three hundred families in Jidda alone; over 50 percent of commerce was in Indian hands.[9] Aden's seizure by troops dispatched from the Bombay Presidency in January 1839 was driven by British desires for a suitable port in the region that would protect the route to India and encourage greater trade. Indian pilgrims who briefly transited through the port back and forth between India and the Hijaz formed a substantial portion of Aden's large Indian Muslim community.[10]

The advent of steam-powered ships from the 1830s and the opening of the Suez Canal in 1869 transformed the maritime pilgrimage into a field dominated by European shipping companies. The seminal voyage of the steamship *Hugh Lindsay* on March 20, 1830, from Bombay to Suez, a venture backed by the Bombay Presidency, cut the journey time from many weeks to only twenty-one days.[11] In 1841, the Peninsular and Oriental Steamship Navigation Company secured the concession at Suez for a regular service to Bombay.[12] European shipping companies began buying steamships from the 1840s and from the 1850s began to charter ships for pilgrims. The British India Steam Navigation Company had begun transporting pilgrims from the Persian Gulf to Jidda before 1869.[13] The Suez Canal's opening that same year created a variety of new shipping routes in the Red Sea and Indian Ocean. European shipping companies quickly moved into the pilgrim traffic market, forcing many Muslim-owned businesses to close, and subsequently controlled two key pilgrimage routes from India (Bombay to Jidda) and Southeast Asia (Singapore to Jidda). Many European firms established both scheduled and chartered routes for the pilgrim trade. The government of India's laissez-faire policies to encourage merchant shipping meant that the pilgrim traffic was unrestricted and relatively unregulated until the 1860s. However, increased sanitary regulations for the pilgrimage after the 1860s meant that some shipping companies were reluctant to enter the pilgrim trade. By the 1930s, the Mogul Line, a Parsi firm managed by British agency house Turner Morrison since 1913, carried 70 percent of pilgrims who traveled from Indian ports. In Southeast Asia, the British firm Alfred Holt and Company (the Blue Funnel Line) and the Dutch firms SMN

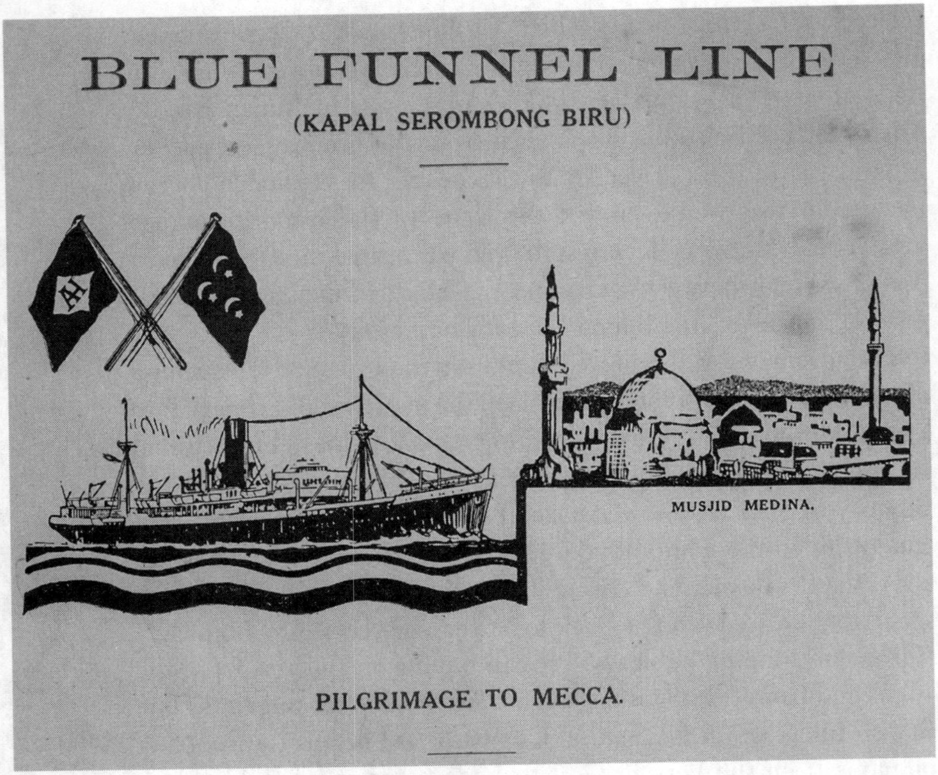

Advertisement for the Blue Funnel Line, c. 1930s

Credit: Ibrahim Tahir

(Stoomvaart Maatschappij Nederland) and RL (Rotterdamsche Lloyd) established a consortium in the late 1920s called Kongsi Tiga to coordinate their majority share of the pilgrim traffic from Singapore and the Netherlands East Indies. There was also a small non-European shipping presence in the Indian Ocean's pilgrim traffic market, for example, the Shustari Line, the Nemazee Line, and, from the 1930s, the Scindia Line. The Khedival Mail Line was the dominant shipping line for Egyptian pilgrims but was bought by British shipping interests in the late nineteenth century.[14] One means whereby Muslim firms could be competitive, especially in India, was a rate war, which pushed down ticket prices and made the journey more feasible for poorer Muslims.

European shipping companies became the dominant players in the pilgrim traffic because they were able to leverage their administrative and logistical experience gained from other markets, such as the transport of migrants from Europe to North America. The pilgrim traffic formed one component of a larger business of migration flows, especially Asian migrant labor, which shipping companies sought to profit from. Steamships had huge advantages over sail. European companies trumped their Asian competitors because they enjoyed government subsidies for mail services and could also deploy various financial and organizational resources—scheduling and route-planning logistics and brokers, recruiters, and agency houses. Overall, though, steamships were cheaper and quicker for passengers than smaller sailing vessels. Steam power made a greater difference in competitive pricing for tickets the farther away the port of origin was from Mecca.[15] Within the broader context of an "imperial maritime order," European shipping companies' dominance of the pilgrim traffic using steamships made the cost of a passage to the Hijaz affordable for a larger number of pilgrims than ever before.[16] The total number of pilgrims leaped from around 100,000 in the 1830s to some 300,000 by the end of the nineteenth century, mainly driven by this increase in maritime activity.[17] However, many were able to afford only a one-way passage; these were the destitute pilgrims who were to prove a bane to British officials from the 1870s to the 1950s.

These indigent pilgrims were noticed by a variety of observers long before the 1870s, when colonial and consular officialdom began to engage directly with this group. One of the first examples appears in Mrs. Hassan Ali's *Observations on the Mussulmauns of India*, published in 1832.[18] She lived in Lucknow from 1816 to 1828 with her husband, Mir Hassan Ali, who had worked as a translator for British employers in both Calcutta and Britain. Her perspective on Islam is rather unusual because she remained a Christian living in a Muslim household.[19] The book's section on Hajj is gleaned from information solicited from her father-in-law, Mir Haji Shah. After a period of military service, Shah went on Hajj three times to Mecca and also went on pilgrimage to Karbala. Shah was himself a poor pilgrim; he had only enough money to travel to Arabia and while there "fell short of funds, but he cured the wife of a rich merchant of a serious disease, who gave him money to continue his journey."[20] He noted that there were few female pilgrims, who tended to come from lower classes "whose expenses are generally paid by rich females" because problems of keeping purdah meant that many wealthy female Muslims did not travel to the Hijaz.[21] Going on Hajj from India was a "formidable undertaking," but many yearned to fulfill their religious obligation.[22] Shah dismissed the journey's difficulties as "mere mortal annoyances," given the spiritual comfort Muslims enjoyed once they reached the Ka'ba.[23] For numerous pilgrims in the period covered by this book, going on Hajj was the first time they had left their villages or towns. Mrs. Ali's father-in-law had a fortuitous combination of skill and luck that saved him from destitution in the Hijaz, unlike many others who went on Hajj before and after him.

Coinciding with the publication of Mrs. Ali's book was Jaffur Shurreff's 1832 work *Qanoon-e-islam; or, The Customs of the Mussalmans of India.* The book's British translator wrote that Indian Muslims were subjects of special interest because of their historical legacy as India's past rulers. Now that the British had displaced them, the translator believed that British "curiosity" about Muslims had "a real practical utility, to understand thoroughly a people with whom we have constant transactions and daily intercourse, in relations of public officers, soldiers and subjects, in administering the government of this country."[24] According to Shurreff, the travels of poor pilgrims to Mecca were apparently made possible by "charitably disposed and opulent natives" who owned *fyz-e-billah*, God's grace or bounty ships, which would take poor pilgrims to the Hijaz from Bombay and provide them with food and drink for the voyage, along with cloth for their *ihram.*[25] This mode of travel for poor pilgrims is seen in a slightly altered form later in this chapter, as is the Qur'anic injunction that people should go on Hajj only if they have sufficient money to do so, although the phrase in question, *istata'a ilayhi sabilan*, although it has various translations, means "able" in a more general sense than just having the requisite financial capability, for example, being physically healthy enough to perform the ritual. This section from the Qur'an was repeated multiple times by British officials throughout this period, as this book will show.[26] Unlike these officials, Shurreff understood why the word of God was no deterrent to poor Muslims: every step a person took "kaabah-wards" meant a sin "blotted out"; once returned, the Hajji would enjoy high status in the community; and finally, if pilgrims died during their journey, they would achieve instant martyrdom, which explained the large numbers of elderly Hajjis. Again, in contrast to British officials, who often painted the pilgrim as a helpless victim embroiled in a journey filled with hardship and viewed as a baffling ordeal, Shurreff highlighted the pilgrimage's importance to Muslims, which negated any material disadvantages: "Many live for years in the joyful anticipation of being one day able to perform the circuit of the kaabah; nay, very many never have the idea of it out of their minds."[27] Despite the vaunted "practical utility" of Shurreff's account, there is no evidence from the archives that officials consulted it.

Accounts by intrepid British travelers in the 1850s were probably more instrumental than Ali's and Shurreff's in contributing to their countrymen's knowledge about the pilgrimage.[28] In the early 1850s, James Hamilton traveled to Cairo via Sinai to Suez, down the Red Sea to Yanbu and Jidda, around the Hijaz, across the Red Sea to Suakin, then to Khartoum, and back up the Nile to Cairo.[29] Hamilton's tour of the Hijaz did not include Mecca because he felt that the city contained no "historically remarkable" monuments, and perhaps because he was wary of entering the city, given that it was closed to non-Muslims.[30] However, he did encounter a wide variety of pilgrims undergoing extraordinary journeys. One group he met in Suez came from Lahore. They had traveled to Mecca via Bushire in Iran, had extended their travels to Cairo, and planned to return home via Baghdad: "At each new halting place they obtained directions how to reach the next; they neither enquired, nor cared about the state of the countries through which they passed."[31] Later in his travels, Hamilton also saw a West African pilgrim (known as *takruri* in Arabic; the plural is *takayrna*), who had come across the Sahel through Bornu, Bagharmi, Wadai, and Darfur; the pilgrim had been traveling on foot for over a year.[32] This was the first mention of *takayrna* pilgrims by a Briton. They would become a category of pilgrims that attracted official attention from the 1920s as Hajj administrations were established in Nigeria and Sudan, covered in Chapter 6.[33]

The destitute pilgrims in Jidda who were British subjects—described by Hamilton as a "most unpleasing sight"—displayed, in his eyes, a need for official action, especially given the British empire's economic and demographic stake in the Hijaz. He mused that British respect for liberty had prevented the government of India from addressing the issue, but he felt that "such English subjects do little honour to our name." As a precursor to his suggestions to the government of India, he cited the Qur'anic injunction that the Hajj was not a mandatory ritual if pilgrims could not afford the journey to and from the Hijaz. Hamilton argued that the government of India should enforce a deposit on pilgrims that covered the cost of a return passage to prevent pilgrims from becoming destitute. The British consul in Jidda, Charles Cole, had apparently given free return passages to 6,000 Indians, and a deposit would ease Cole's financial burdens.[34] According to Hamilton, Britain had the right to take "special interest" in and "exercise a strict surveillance" over the Hijaz because of its dominance of Hijazi trade; because Britain's 25 million Indian Muslim subjects viewed Mecca with "pious veneration" and thousands performed the Hajj every year; and because of the Hijaz's insecurity due to the corrupt Ottoman administration.[35] Hamilton was several years ahead of his time; the Hajj really attracted the interest of British officialdom only from 1865. Given the dates of Hamilton's journey, perhaps he passed Richard Burton on his travels, an explorer whose pilgrimage to Mecca disguised as an Afghan physician and petty trader garnered extensive public attention in Britain.

Richard Burton has been a popular figure for scholarly attention, but his remarks on aspects of Britain's relationship with the Hajj, such as destitute pilgrims, have been little studied.[36] Burton's 1855–1856 account of his audacious travels to Mecca and Medina in 1853 reflected the views of contemporaneous writers who saw Muslims as essentially fanatical; poor Muslims were motivated to perform the Hajj in "a fit of religious enthusiasm, likest to insanity." Like Hamilton, he felt that the government of India should "interfere" with the pilgrimage because he interpreted this flow of Muslims as permanent emigration that would weaken India's labor productivity. Burton thought that there were other negative effects of this phenomenon:

"It sends forth a horde of malcontents that ripen into bigots; it teaches foreign nations to despise our rule."[37] This perception of the Hajj was shared by various British officials in this period, examined later in this chapter. Nevertheless, as Dane Kennedy has pointed out, the overall impression from Burton's account is that he respected Islamic practice and found the religion and Muslim culture "appealing at a deeply emotional level."[38] The ambiguous nature of Burton's engagement with the pilgrimage is well illustrated in the following passage, which marries a profound engagement with Islamic ritual with a self-awareness of his achievement in reaching the heart of Islam:

> I truly may say that, of all the worshippers who clung weeping to the [Ka'ba] curtain, or who pressed their beating hearts to the stone, none felt for the moment a deeper emotion than did the hajji from the far-north [i.e., Burton]. It was as if the poetical legends of the Arab spoke the truth, and that the waving wings of angels, not the sweet breeze of morning, were agitating and swelling the black covering of the shrine. But, to confess the humbling truth, theirs was the high feeling of religious enthusiasm, mine was the ecstasy of gratified pride.[39]

Alongside Burton's suggested reforms of various aspects of Hijazi administration was his idea, similar to Hamilton's, that Britain should use the Qur'anic stipulation that pilgrims did not have to perform Hajj if they lacked the financial means to do so. This, Burton hoped, would prevent poor pilgrims from leaving India. Pilgrims would have to prove that they could afford the journey before receiving a travel permit. Burton felt that through such a permit, Charles Cole, the British consul in Jidda, could assist "our" Indian pilgrims: "Though men die of starvation in the streets, he [the consul] was unable to relieve them. The highways of Meccah abound in pathetic Indian beggars, who affect lank bodies, shrinking frames, whining voices, and all the circumstance of misery, because it supports them in idleness." These pilgrims, coupled with the 1,500 Indians resident in Mecca and Jidda, warranted, in Burton's view, an expansion of Britain's consular representation; any opposition by the sharif of Mecca to a

British Muslim agent in Mecca "would soon fall to the ground."[40] The pugnacious explorer's belief in the necessity of British involvement in the Hajj, primarily to stanch the flow of indigent pilgrims, while echoed by Cole, found little purchase among officials in India.

Cole's exasperated correspondence in 1853 with the Bombay authorities illustrates how unconcerned officials in India were about destitute pilgrims. One part of Cole's duties was to repatriate destitute British subjects, but he thought that Indians were excluded from this category. Consular assistance was given according to notions of identity and subjecthood that were informed by a strict racial and ethnic hierarchy, although this was not explicitly spelled out in regulations. Contrary to Hamilton's account, Cole told his superiors that he had given no financial assistance to pilgrims. He believed that some arrangement was necessary to halt the flow of destitute pilgrims because it was only Indians who were begging and dying in the streets of Jidda, which he felt was a blow to British prestige in Arabia. Ottoman officials operated an ad hoc system whereby pilgrim ships' captains were forced to carry some of these pilgrims home gratis. Cole was concerned that unless action was taken to prevent "absolute paupers" leaving India to go on Hajj, the Indian government would be liable for the financial cost of repatriation.[41] This was of little concern to officials in India. Henry Anderson, secretary to the government of Bombay, wrote to his superiors that the relief of destitute British subjects did not extend to Indians; in any case, the government had no legal means of preventing poor pilgrims from traveling to Mecca. Moreover, Anderson felt that it was an issue for the Ottoman authorities to deal with.[42] India's governor-general, the Earl of Dalhousie, was even more emphatic that the Hajj had nothing to do with the British authorities; he believed that the government had no right to prevent anyone from going on pilgrimage.[43] These responses reflected the prevailing administrative doctrine in India. Liberal reforms undertaken by the colonial state were confined to what officials considered "secular" affairs.[44] However, British views on the Hajj and destitute pilgrims underwent a radical change in this period, driven, in the first instance, by the impact of the 1865 cholera epidemic.[45]

Before examining the disease's effects on Britain and the Hajj, it is instructive to step back and survey the context of British interactions with and perceptions of Islam and Muslims in this period and to show how these formed the backdrop to the empire's association with the pilgrimage. When the East India Company began to rule over Muslims in the late eighteenth century, it initially had to work within the existing framework of Mughal legitimacy. From this perspective, Britain's Muslim empire had long antecedents. The Mughal emperor Shah Alam II (1759–1806) stipulated that when he gave the East India Company the grant of Bengal's *diwani* in 1765, which gave the company the right to administer and collect the province's land revenues, it had to govern "agreeably to the rules of Mahomed and to the law of the empire."[46]

British suspicion of Muslims was exacerbated by the 1857 Indian rebellion.[47] Given the extensive literature on this rebellion, the role of Muslims in these events will be briefly surveyed to contextualize how the rebellion's consequences affected British involvement in the pilgrimage.[48] Initially, Britons in India viewed the rebellion—caused by a combination of conditions in the East India Company's armies, taxation, and the deposition of various Indian rulers—as the result of Muslim resentment at their loss of political power. The speed and scale of events led some to think that it was a Muslim conspiracy that ultimately aimed to resurrect the Mughal empire, a view expounded by various officials, although scant evidence for this interpretation emerged afterward.[49] In 1858, British loyalist Syed Ahmad Khan published *Asbab-e-Baghawat-e-Hind* (Causes of the Indian revolt) to counter British notions of a Muslim conspiracy behind the rebellion, and its English translation in 1873 helped undermine this idea among Anglo-Indian society.[50] Although some *'ulama* called for jihad and issued various *fatawa* against British rule, this element played a minor part.[51] The role of Indian Wahhabis in the rebellion has been debated; some scholars have questioned how far Muslims followed Wahhabi preachers.[52] Islamic socioreligious reform movements opposed to British rule before 1857 were barely involved in the rebellion, and the support given to Britain by the nizam of Hyderabad and other Muslim rulers played an important role in Britain's victory over the rebels. Muslim involvement in the rebellion that took inspiration from Islam was "neither cohesive, extensive nor, ultimately, significant."[53] Britain's response to the rebellion was brutal. According to one chronicler of a later anticolonial struggle, during the rebellion the British acted "in an indescribably barbaric fashion. . . . They left behind a trail of destruction and devastation that even the most devastating earthquake and cyclone would not have caused."[54] In Thomas Metcalf's words, the British after 1857 "became an increasingly suspicious, insular and racist ruling power."[55]

After Queen Victoria's 1858 proclamation of religious tolerance to her subjects in India, a direct consequence of the rebellion, religion was one of the foremost arenas where Indians could legitimately contest British power, a feature evident throughout this book.[56] British ambivalence toward Islam in this period was exemplified by official monitoring for seditious activities, combined with a strategy of cooperation with a wide range of elite Indian Muslim leaders from the 1870s and a degree of sensitivity to what officials termed "Muslim opinion," a strategy repeated in the 1900s in Sudan through the cooption of some *'ulama* and Sufi orders.[57] One example of this cooperative approach can be seen in this chapter's section dealing with Muslim consultation about destitute pilgrims.

Parallel to these efforts sat the lurid prose of journalists, writers, scholars, and officials, who dwelt on Muslim "fanaticism." These tropes have been exhaustively studied, so there is little need to rehearse them here.[58] One example worth citing, however, is former Bengal civil servant W. W. Hunter's 1871 book *The Indian Musalmans*, which posed the controversial question whether Muslims were bound by the Qur'an to rebel against Queen Victoria. Hunter raised the specter of a "rebel colony" of Wahhabis on India's northwest frontier who sent "fanatic swarms" against British India. These men were the architects of an anticolonial conspiracy, energized by returning Hajjis from the Barelvi movement active in the 1820s, preaching a "purified" Islam.[59] This idea of the Hajj as a mechanism for anticolonial agitation cast a long shadow over British perceptions of the pilgrimage.[60] Hunter's book reflected a tendency among the British in India to link anticolonial Muslim movements together under a Wahhabi umbrella. This notion gained currency during the Wahhabi trials of 1865–1871 and after the assassination of Indian viceroy Lord Mayo in 1872 at the Andaman Islands penal colony by Shere Ali Afridi, although he had no links with Wahhabi prisoners.[61] Islam was seen as having the potential to spark insurrection, but British officials had a "respect for the faith which verged between condemnation and admiration."[62] Despite these fears, Britain crushed Islamic uprisings across the empire with relative ease despite the brutal nature of some of these conflicts.[63]

This view of Muslims remained largely unchanged until the 1890s, when the decline of Christian evangelism and new academic developments led to a more positive reappraisal of Islam among Britons.[64] The rise of universalist attitudes to religion and criticism of Christianity mitigated negative interpretations of Islam. Indeed, aspects of Christianity such as the persecution of sects were contrasted with Muslim tolerance of nonbelievers. Orientalist scholarship on Islam in the late nineteenth century praised Islam's capacity for moral reform. The Prophet Muhammad was seen as a moral reformer who introduced monotheism to pagans, and was commended for banning alcohol.[65] The respected Orientalist scholar T. W. Arnold saw the spiritual strength of Islam in its simple credo and stressed that scholars should examine Islam's peaceful spread through the "unobtrusive labours of the preacher and the trader" rather than the "fury of the fanatic."[66] Britain's increased knowledge of the Muslim world also contributed to this reassessment of Islam.[67]

In the postrebellion period, supposed Muslim accountability for the 1857 rebellion created prejudices and misconceptions that influenced British perceptions of the Hajj in the late nineteenth century; these sat alongside less dramatic but perhaps more representative experiences of Anglo-Muslim relations regarding the pilgrimage explored in this chapter. Muslim "conspiracies" and frontier jihads have to be placed in a wider context that includes British interactions with the Hajj. Taken together, they highlight Britain's ultimately ambivalent relationship with Islam. Once British rule in India was secure after the rebellion, "the nature of colonial governance after 1858 changed towards a concern to maintain established social institutions."[68] Although the Hajj was far more than simply a social institution, it also fell under this rubric.

The 1865 cholera epidemic in the Hijaz challenged this status quo and was the main catalyst for Britain's active involvement in the pilgrimage. The disease killed 15,000 out of 90,000 pilgrims in the Hijaz and spread to Europe; 200,000 people died worldwide. This was not the first time cholera had struck—it was first recorded in India in 1817 and Arabia in 1821 and was responsible for the deaths of around 20,000 pilgrims in the Hijaz in 1831. In 1866, Britain's cholera commissioners reported that these epidemics always originated in India.[69] The 1866 International Sanitary Conference convened in Istanbul as a result of the epidemic directed that preventive measures to protect Europe from cholera should be linked to arresting its development in India primarily through maritime quarantine, which played an important and controversial role in British India's medical policy.[70] Anticholera measures would be a "continuance and extension" of hygiene procedures undertaken by the authorities for Hindu pilgrimages, which illustrates how the Hajj was situated in a wider framework of sanitary regulations that affected religious pilgrimages. The Red Sea would require more elaborate quarantine measures, which would affect pilgrim traffic. Muslim pilgrims would receive "especial attention" given the role of the Hajj in spreading cholera in 1865. Quarantine stations were eventually established at al-Tur on the Sinai Peninsula in 1877 and Kamaran Island at the southern end of the Red Sea in 1881. In Mecca itself, the Ottomans would undertake hygiene measures similar to those in place at Hindu pilgrimage sites, mentioned in Chapter 1.[71]

Delegates to the 1866 sanitary conference were worried about pilgrims' travels on steamships; overcrowding and the shortened journey times to the Hijaz had increased the risk of cholera appearing on board ships and then spreading when pilgrims disembarked in the Hijaz. These conditions, combined with outbreaks in the Hijaz during the Hajj, facilitated the transmission of cholera to Europe. However, Britain's policy of noninterference in foreign states' sanitary administrations meant that it voted against the conference's proposal for international institutions in the Red Sea out of fear that this could set a precedent that might lead to India's subjection to international sanitary observation. Although Britain was opposed to sanitary intervention in the pilgrimage, its cholera commissioners pointed out the "pitiable condition of the Indian pilgrims in the Hedjaz during the pilgrimage. Men, women, and children are there exposed to every kind of hardship, to want of shelter, famine, disease, extortion and pillage, and are often forced to sell their liberty, for two or three years, to enable them to procure the means of returning to their homes." Because these destitute pilgrims were British subjects, the commissioners felt that they merited special attention, and they proposed that there should be measures to prevent "such disastrous scenes" in the future.[72] Such sentiments remained in evidence in 1878, when a British official reporting on quarantine in the Red Sea and sanitary regulation in Mecca wrote that one of the "gravest difficulties" related to the Hajj was the "great poverty of the very many persons who enter upon it." The Hajj had become, in his view, "a matter of religious vagrancy, and the Hedjaz a sort of Elysium for vagrants."[73] The destitute pilgrim was an important part of officials' concerns about the pilgrimage.

The cholera commissioner's 1866 report reflected Britain's cautionary attitude toward intrusions in Indian public health in the late nineteenth century, informed by the perceived risk of civil unrest. Any sanitary regulation of the pilgrimage threatened to damage the government of India's strategy of cooperation with Muslim leaders and cost the same parsimonious government money. Regulations were seen as vulnerable to misinterpretation by "lower class" Muslims, who would supposedly view them as interfering with religious practices, a viewpoint also largely held by Muslim leaders. Their ability to travel to the Hijaz for Hajj in relative comfort meant that they had very different concerns from those of the majority of pilgrims, who were chiefly interested in the voyage being as cheap as possible—a contrast analyzed later in this chapter.[74]

The quarantine measures applied to pilgrims were widely resented by those who had to suffer them throughout this period.[75] One example of many came from Irfan Ali Beg, a deputy collector from Manipur, who complained about his enforced stay of ten days at the quarantine camp on Kamaran Island in the Red Sea in his 1896 pilgrimage account: "The quarantine prohibition is trying us much and is especially troublesome for those who are active and men of work."[76] According to the quarantine regulations, pilgrims were generally held in these camps for five to ten days, although there were instances of longer periods of detention. Not all pilgrims uniformly acquiesced to this quarantine regime. At al-Tur in 1877, a group of pilgrims revolted against the camp supervisors, and the Egyptian army was called in.[77] Ali Beg penned some poetry as his ship finally left Kamaran for Jidda:

> Of Kameran they speak so bad
> Disgusted as much as they are sad
> The brackish water of its shore
> No tongue may taste it any more
> Oh Kameran thou didst take our peace
> And every comfort did thou cease
> So did thou kindle glowing fire
> As every heart is full of ire
> What raised thy value so much more
> Its nearness to the Arabian shore
> Now let us thank God that He
> Has by His favour made us free.[78]

Several fine studies have analyzed Britain's involvement in the Hajj in regard to medicine, sanitation, and quarantine in extensive detail, so more need not be said here.[79] Although the 1865 epidemic triggered Britain's initial interest in the Hajj, the empire's engagement with the pilgrimage rapidly encompassed aspects far beyond sanitation and quarantine. However, in Britain's early pilgrimage reports, the future directions of the empire's engagement with the Hajj were not immediately apparent.

The confluence of cholera and the Suez Canal's opening in 1869 prompted the first British pilgrimage report that same year. The canal became a vital communications artery for the empire, and the Red Sea and the eastern Mediterranean became more important to Britain because events in these seas could affect the security of shipping through the canal. The canal meant that the Red Sea became a region for international rivalry among Britain, the Netherlands, France, Italy, the Ottoman empire, and Abyssinia. Consequently, this maritime space evolved from an area of interest mainly to British

India to a wider British imperial concern.[80] Conditions on the coastal littorals and hinterlands of the Red Sea therefore received heightened attention from British officials. The early pilgrimage reports contained little information compared with those compiled in the 1920s and 1930s, which often ran to twenty to forty pages of dense text.[81] For example, in 1869, Arthur Raby, the consul in Jidda, merely wrote that after the pilgrimage, the Hijaz's public health was satisfactory; about 110,000 pilgrims stood at Mount Arafat, and 5,000 to 6,000 pilgrims waited for ships in Jidda after the Hajj's conclusion.[82] The quantity of information did not greatly increase in the following year, except for the observation that 1870 was marked by a "Grand Pilgrimage," a Hajj *akbar*, an event every seven years, when performing the Hajj had greater spiritual benefit for pilgrims.[83] Beyond these patchy reports, other early references to pilgrims tellingly described how they "effectually evade detection and place themselves beyond the reach of British supervision," in this case referring to pilgrims from Singapore in 1869 who stopped over at Alleppey in South India and al-Mukalla in southern Arabia.[84] Britain's involvement in the pilgrimage assumed a more concrete form in 1871, when the consul noted that pilgrim departures on ships were regulated according to the 1870 British Indian Native Passenger Ships Act. However, there are no sources to corroborate the consul's account, so it is unclear whether the note was merely a sop to the government of India to demonstrate the effectiveness of its legislation.[85]

The best sources of information for British officials about the Hajj in this period were Muslims, not consuls. Previous accounts of the pilgrimage had been published without official prompting; Nawab Sikander, begum of Bhopal (1844–1868), wrote hers at the request of Colonel Durand, foreign secretary to the government of India. Durand was anxious to read about her impressions of Arabia, especially Mecca, after she had completed the Hajj in 1864.[86] The account, translated from Urdu by a British officer's wife and published in 1870, was designed to appeal to a British audience in India to further reinforce the begum's image as "a good and loyal Muslim."[87] It was dedicated to Queen Victoria. As Barbara Metcalf has argued, some Indian pilgrimage narratives written in this period demonstrate that these authors had internalized British colonial concerns about governance. Their experiences of Ottoman and Hijazi administration in the Hijaz, which were often contrary to their expectations of how governments should operate in regard to providing order, cleanliness, and assistance to persons such as poor Indian pilgrims, led them to identify more closely with the British colonial administration, cementing their roles as subjects and functionaries of empire.[88] Imperial issues related to the Hajj's administration had a central place in these accounts and suffused the author's expectations of the pilgrimage experience; these works are sprinkled with suggestions for reforming various bureaucratic practices.[89] In the begum's case, her internalization of imperial ideals of the "improving" ruler stemmed from her extensive experience with reforming Bhopal's revenue and judicial systems, police force, transport infrastructure, educational provision, and civil administration. Unimpressed with Ottoman governance of the Holy City, she wrote that despite an annual expenditure of £300,000 on Mecca, the city was dirty and badly administered. Ottoman officials "would see what a state of order and cleanliness I would keep the august cities in, and what arrangements I would make for the proper maintenance of the Holy Shrines"—comments made to people in Mecca that filtered back to the Hijaz's governor and the sharif of Mecca, who took offense at the begum's remarks.[90]

The begum's attitude toward the Ottoman authorities was shaped by her mixed experiences while she was in the Hijaz. After a "prosperous" voyage from Bombay to Jidda in late January 1864, she was immediately embroiled in tortuous negotiations with Ottoman officials in Jidda over customs payments for her vast quantity of luggage: "merely a year's supply of grain and clothes, also cooking vessels, and bales of cloth for the poor at the shrines of the exalted city of Mecca and august Medina," along with jewelry destined for charity.[91] She excoriated the Ottoman and Hijazi authorities for extorting money from poor Indian pilgrims. When her party arrived in Mecca after being overcharged for camels, the city was gripped by cholera, which killed four members of her entourage.[92] One feature of the Hajj that particularly alarmed the begum was the prevalence of poor pilgrims in Mecca who constantly pestered her party for alms. Once she was ensconced in Mecca, her prayers and other

Nawab Sikander Begum of Bhopal and her ministers, 1862

Credit: Science Photo Library

devotions were interrupted by "religious mendicants" who gathered below her lodgings, which she blamed on the dowager begum's "lavish liberality." After the dowager begum presented gifts to the sharif of Mecca and the Hijaz's governor, this news spread rapidly. Nawab Sikander was then "completely mobbed" by poor pilgrims, which prevented her from performing the *tawaf*. The begum lamented that she felt "perfectly helpless, and began to question the utility of having gone to Mecca for devotional ends"—and possibly also the wisdom of taking the dowager begum along with her. In the begum's account, destitute pilgrims were not the hapless victims ubiquitous in official correspondence; they were capable of spoiling the pilgrimage experience for one of the British empire's most prominent and loyal Muslim subjects. The begum also mentioned that Mecca's inhabitants included "almost all the bad characters that have been driven out of India," referring to those who had traveled there after the 1857 rebellion.[93] This was a claim that recurred in official correspondence analyzed later in this chapter. Quite possibly these officials had read the begum's account.

The begum's difficulties during her Hajj, coupled with her decision not to travel to Medina because of her party's inability to speak Arabic (it is not known why they did not hire an interpreter), meant that instead of feeling a sense of belonging to the *umma* in Mecca, she identified more readily with Indian Muslim pilgrims, who she felt were persecuted in the Holy City.[94] The begum's account gives little insight into her inner spiritual reflections on performing the Hajj, in contrast to her daughter's 1909 pilgrimage narrative, analyzed in Chapter 3.[95] Nawab Sikander Begum's travelogue predated by several years a torrent of pilgrimage-related information that flowed to British officials. A significant portion of this concerned destitute pilgrims. British interactions with this aspect of the Hajj were ambiguous and complex, as we shall see, and officials had a limited ability to regulate destitute pilgrims' travels.

Britain's Emerging Engagement with Destitute Pilgrims

The 1875–1876 pilgrimage seasons marked a substantial change in Britain's relationship with the pilgrimage, when officials first seriously grappled with the issue of destitute pilgrims. Three years earlier, the Foreign Office had proposed to abolish the consulate at Jidda, a move opposed by the government of India, but the position of British consul had remained unfilled until George Beyts, a partner in a local shipping firm based in Jidda, assumed the role in 1874.[96] Britain's heightened focus on destitute pilgrims was precipitated by a letter from Beyts to the Indian government in 1876. He was astonished that poor pilgrims were not prevented from leaving India in the first place and saw them as utterly helpless: "These poor ignorant fanatics become doomed to a certain death unless relieved by charity. These unfortunate miserable squalid creatures lay in hundreds before the British Consulate starving and dying, they become a perfect nuisance to the authorities who as a rule send them to the British representative for relief."[97] Charity from local Muslims and Beyts had eased the situation, but when his own funds were exhausted, the consul asked the government of India for help. Its refusal led him to demand a solution. Although he recognized that the Indian authorities were unwilling to impose travel restrictions on their subjects, he suggested that these pilgrims' predicament could be alleviated through using a "respectable, intelligent and unbigoted" Muslim who would warn pilgrims of the dangers in going on Hajj without enough money.[98] As other officials came to realize, any governmental action regarding destitute pilgrims, and the Hajj more widely, could be effective only through employing Muslims.

To press his case, Beyts raised the piquant issue of how "very undesirable it would be if only for the sake of British prestige, leaving humanity aside, that large numbers of human beings should be suffered to die from want of food, water, and transport back to their countries within sight of the British Consulate, or as in fact with its very flag moving over them." The blow to British prestige in Arabia and the wider Islamic world dealt by these starving indigent pilgrims was as much a concern to Beyts as the condition of these people outside the door of his consulate. Aden's political resident also exhorted India to deal with the "evil" situation. The resident was the first of many officials to highlight how Britain's administrative inaction on the pilgrimage compared unfavorably with the actions of other European empires—France and the Netherlands required pilgrims to present evidence that they could afford the journey before they were allowed to go on Hajj.[99]

Beyts's theory that poor pilgrims went on Hajj because wealthy Muslims gave *zakat* in the form of an outward passage to Jidda and food for the voyage, and that these pilgrims were then left penniless in the Hijaz, sparked a lengthy investigation ordered by the India Office to find solutions to the matter.[100] The consul believed that wealthy Muslims were "deporting vagrants as pilgrims by the shipload."[101] These documents illustrate the importance officials placed on soliciting Muslim opinion on this topic. The inquiry generated a large body of knowledge about the Hajj that, for example, debunked Beyts's theory.[102] These documents confirm British officials' reluctance to prevent people from going on Hajj for fear of upsetting Muslim opinion, a fact the Muslims consulted by the British played on. The official view from India differed markedly from those of Beyts and some officials in London. Foreign Secretary Lord Derby, writing from Whitehall, thought it "highly impolitic" for destitute Indian subjects to die on Jidda's streets and believed that they should be repatriated at India's expense, along with measures to prevent poor pilgrims from going on Hajj.[103] The India Office reluctantly accepted repatriation charges on a provisional basis, but only in urgent cases, which did not include taking on responsibility for destitute pilgrims.[104] After two years of silence from Calcutta on the matter, London demanded an immediate response to its original 1875 inquiry.[105]

The Indian authorities' extensive reply exemplifies conflicting official views about the pilgrimage, and it derailed attempts by the foreign secretary and Beyts to stimulate greater activism regarding poor pilgrims. Above all, officials in India were concerned to uphold their policy of noninterference in religious practices and were acutely sensitive to Muslim opinion on destitute pilgrims, reflecting the post-1857 climate. At the local level, officials frequently found strong opposition to any government measures perceived as preventing Muslims from performing the Hajj. Their superiors in Calcutta took a laissez-faire approach: the phenomenon was not serious and should be allowed to adjust itself. The government would simply publish the pilgrimage's cost and emphasize the difficulties pilgrims would face if they failed to take this amount. Nevertheless, the government thought that it was the responsibility of "respectable" Indian Muslims and Islamic associations to disseminate such facts. The official position stemmed from perceptions of destitute pilgrims as "the lowest and most ignorant, as well as the most fanatic of their persuasion," which led to a view that preventive measures would have little effect. Government repatriation of poor pilgrims was rejected because it would encourage more poor pilgrims to go on Hajj. Any restrictions on the pilgrimage would be "impolitic" and "specially inopportune" because of an upsurge in support among Indian Muslims for the Ottoman empire, then at war with Russia.[106]

Nonintervention in the issue of destitute pilgrims did not mean nonengagement, however, as shown by the voluminous replies from local officials throughout India. This particular consultation exercise reflected a wider British readiness to treat "Indian Muslims" as a generalized category and a distinct political group, as well as a broader trend in government policy that sought regular consultation from those whom the British termed society's "natural leaders," a reaction against what officials saw as an overly official government before the 1857 rebellion.[107] We might term this "the consultative Raj." But as C. A. Bayly has argued, these "mechanisms of consultation were only partly successful in bringing information to collectors and magistrates," and British prejudices against indigenous religious institutions "caused them to exclude well-informed people from the process of consultation."[108] Despite these restrictions, at a basic level this corpus of material gathered by officials on the Hajj gave the British far greater knowledge of the nature of poor pilgrims' travels and showcases valuable Muslim views about destitute pilgrims. Such correspondence about poor pilgrims was a "major influence in the formation of colonial ideas about the Hajj."[109] Officials, especially those serving at the provincial and local levels, placed great value on the opinions of Muslims whom they consulted, which lends empirical weight to the argument that Muslims were instrumental in reinforcing Britain's policy of nonintervention in this aspect of the pilgrimage.

Caution was a dominant thread running through these reports. Officials thought it vital to gauge Muslim opinion and seek Muslim approval of potential changes to government policy regarding something as important as the Hajj; similar consultation exercises were carried out in relation to the sanitary regulation of the ritual.[110] However, it is important to remember that the opinions of those who appear in these colonial records were, unsurprisingly, highly unrepresentative. Women were not consulted by the British because of the obvious difficulties of doing so. The Muslim officials and community leaders consulted were generally men who were wealthy and educated at the college level or above. Their closeness to the local British officials who undertook the exercise informed how they couched their views on the Hajj to the British. In light of this, local Muslim notables were also asked to convene meetings at places such as mosques, where a wider cross section of the community was consulted. However, the socioeconomic profile of these group meetings was manipulated by the British as evidence of what they saw as the ill-considered choices of poor and ignorant Muslims. Furthermore, as these reports came in from across the Raj, prejudices held by the British toward certain peoples were reinforced; for example, the opinions of Mappillas and Pathans were dismissed because of their supposed "fanaticism," and those of rural Bengali peasants were castigated because of their supposed ignorance of certain religious matters. The views of the small number of Muslims who were consulted were influential in shaping Britain's policy of inaction toward destitute pilgrims. Evidence of this qualified cooperation between officials and Muslims further undermines interpretations that present Briton and Muslim as implacably opposed to each other in this period. Both groups viewed the issues in terms of pragmatic self-interest. Some officials used Queen Victoria's 1858 proclamation that Britain would not interfere in Indian religious practices to oppose any proposed restrictions on pilgrims' travels, and the investigation did not lead to any curtailment of poor pilgrims' freedom to go on Hajj.

Extracts from these reports offer important insights into how poor pilgrims went on Hajj and official and Muslim responses to the destitute-pilgrim issue. In Alleppey, twenty Muslims were sent annually to Jidda, and their outward journey and food were paid for by richer members of the town's Muslim community. Poorer Muslims in Malabar generally had enough funds to go on Hajj, but those without went from house to house successfully seeking *zakat* because, according to the collector, it was a "fanatical" district. Because of local Muslim Mappilla rebellions, the collector thought it extremely unwise to interfere in the existing Hajj arrangements.[111] Bombay's authorities had more experience of pilgrims than other areas because it was the main departure point for Indian pilgrims traveling to Arabia by sea. Officials there were skeptical of the government's ability to prevent destitute pilgrims from going on Hajj by requiring them to show proof of sufficient funds, a view shared by Punjab's lieutenant-governor.[112] Awadh's junior secretary believed that any measures that prevented Muslims from going on Hajj would be viewed as the first steps toward interference in other Islamic practices.[113] Bengal's lieutenant-governor consulted the Mahomedan Literary Society, established in 1863, a cornerstone of the Calcutta establishment whose members sought government patronage, recognition, and privileged status through their loyalty to British rule, as well as other members of Calcutta's Muslim community, for their views. He concluded that wealthy Muslims were "morally responsible" for destitute pilgrims through *zakat* and learned that poor Muslims went on Hajj because they believed that dying in Mecca would result in admission to paradise. He suggested that the authorities should publicize the financial cost of going on Hajj, register pilgrims and prohibit them from going on Hajj without funding, and form Muslim committees to fund poor pilgrims' homeward passages. A Muslim official pointed out to the lieutenant-governor the problems with these proposals: publicizing the Hajj's cost would be ineffectual since the journey's difficulties were common knowledge and sometimes even acted as an incentive; registration and prohibition would be seen as interfering in a religious duty and would be liable to misinterpretation by Muslims.[114]

Some Muslims' responses to the consultation conflicted with ideas that the pilgrimage rendered all Muslims equal. Throughout these documents, Muslims consulted by the colonial state drew a clear distinction between themselves and the "ignorant masses." Several thought it "improper" that pilgrims begged to fund their travels; others believed that the Qur'an and hadiths prohibited the poor from going on Hajj. Destitute pilgrims were viewed as professional beggars who wanted to die in Mecca to absolve their sins. A few believed that "rich nawabs" used "charity ships" to transport pilgrims to the Hijaz, a feature of the Hajj during the Mughal period but no longer practiced in the nineteenth century. The British official who compiled these views from Bhaugalpur's Muslims thought that "common humanity" demanded some restrictions on destitute pilgrims. He understood that the obligation to perform Hajj was *wajib;* that is, it was spiritually beneficial, but it was not detrimental if Muslims did not go on pilgrimage. Consequently, he thought that measures to prevent destitute pilgrims would be seen by any sensible Muslim as an act of great kindness.[115]

Muslim elites skillfully played up the potential for widespread Muslim unrest if colonial authorities enacted any restrictive travel measures on pilgrims, which poor, uneducated Muslims would see as interference with their Islamic faith. This effectively stymied the activist proposals of some officials in response to the destitute-pilgrim issue and, as Rafiuddin Ahmed has argued in relation to Bengali Muslims, was part of a wider strategy whereby these elites "used the rhetoric of the Muslim masses to achieve their class of community interests."[116] It was not just colonial officials who could manipulate the socioeconomic stratification of India's Muslim population to buttress arguments for maintaining the status quo. For example, in Bengal's Twenty-Four Parganas district, Deputy Magistrate Maulvi Abdul Latif, a member of the Calcutta elite, founder of the Mahomedan Literary Society, and an active member of Calcutta's Anjuman-i-Islami, an association that declared its loyalty to Britain in 1857 and was subsequently regularly called on to advise officials on Muslim opinion, convened a meeting where the subject was discussed. He reported that although wealthy pious Muslims had funded poorer pilgrims to go on Hajj in the past, this trend had declined significantly in the recent past. Latif was in favor of discouraging poor pilgrims, but dissuasion was inadvisable, according to him, because of potential Muslim disaffection, which would arise from their interpreting such preventive measures as interference with Islam. Contrary to British officials who could not grasp why poor Muslims embarked on such a hazardous journey, Latif stressed its meritorious nature and reminded officials that most Muslims were aware of the difficulties from returned Hajjis. Latif thought it unlikely that Muslims who gave *zakat* would give money to the government to assist indigent pilgrims. However, despite such drawbacks, Latif thought that the government should provide a solution "out of the abundance of its wonted humanity and generosity" and suggested a passport fee that would endow a destitute-repatriation fund, which he believed would enjoy "unanimous approbation" from Indian Muslims.[117]

Significantly, Latif advocated that any destitute fund should be managed by a Muslim. He argued that any British consul in Jidda would be unable to speak Indian languages and therefore to distinguish between deserving and undeserving cases, whereas an English-speaking Indian Muslim official of "high character" would be extremely valuable to the Jidda consulate.[118] Latif found support from his colleague, Magistrate R. H. Wilson, who agreed that it was "very desirable" to have an Indian Muslim at the Jidda consulate.[119] Latif's proposals chimed in with those of other Muslims consulted; for example, one suggested that Muslim agents should be employed in Bombay to inquire about pilgrims' financial means when they applied for passports, if these were introduced.[120] Another colleague supported the idea of a "well educated and pious" Muslim agent at ports such as Bombay to collect pilgrims' deposits that would be transferred to Jidda. Those without funds should be persuaded to return home because going on Hajj without sufficient funding was against the "tenets" of Islam; there would be no objection to these measures because they did not interfere with Islamic practice.[121] Chapter 3 details how Bombay's pilgrimage administration was primarily run by Muslims, although they performed different roles from the ones suggested here. The eventual appointment of a Muslim official in Britain's Jidda consulate was not solely due to Latif's suggestion, but it is significant that this was proposed by Muslims as well as British officials. Muslims clearly had some influence in defining the contours of Britain's administrative involvement in the pilgrimage.

British officials did not always agree with the Muslims they consulted, nor were Muslim voices, whether in the colonial archive or in pilgrimage accounts, united in agreement on how to deal with destitute pilgrims. For example, the British magistrate of Midnapor blanched at his Muslim respondents who thought that the government should provide for poor pilgrims' needs. In his view, this would create grievances, and the authorities should instead "rest content" with the status quo.[122] One Muslim gentleman disbelieved reports of poverty among Indian pilgrims in Jidda and the reluctance of those living in the port to assist them, a commonly held viewpoint among Muslims consulted. In any case, the man argued, Muslims would find their own solution because any official intervention to alleviate the phenomenon would be seen as interference with Islamic practice and could cause "serious discontent."[123]

By contrast, Sayyid Amir Ali, a liberal lawyer and university lecturer in Islamic law, believed that the "sensible portion" of India's Muslims would be grateful for any government measures that would reduce poor pilgrims' sufferings.[124] Ali saw any British relief as analogous to the bequest founded by the king of Awadh, which provided funds for poorer pilgrims to visit Shi'i shrines in Iraq.[125] Ali's report quoted at length from Ahmed Hassan's 1871 pilgrimage narrative *Pilgrimage to the Caaba and Charing Cross*, which dwelt on poor pilgrims:

> Thousands who make this trip from religious motives do so without having more money than is barely sufficient to pay their passage to India from Jeddah. . . . On reaching Jeddah they are forced to beg, and they thus become exposed to all sorts of hardships, sufferings, and dangers, besides being a source of distress to others. . . . It would, in my opinion, be well if the Indian Government were to take some steps to prevent poor pilgrims from thus rushing on their own destruction, by allowing none to go who could not show that they had the means of making the trip and returning in safety.[126]

Hassan's suggestions, Ali believed, were open to misinterpretation by the "ignorant mass" of Muslims. Like others consulted by British officials, Ali suggested that committees should be established at Bombay and other ports, composed of "thoroughly upright, intelligent and liberalized Mohammedans who would throw themselves heart and soul into the work," who would issue certificates of travel if pilgrims had enough money and explain to poor pilgrims that the Qur'an enjoined Hajj only on those who could afford it. The committees would also have a fund-raising arm for a destitute-pilgrim fund.[127] Ali's views and suggestions were echoed by Sayyid Mahomed Abu Saleb, a Bengali landowner. In response to the initial British inquiry, Saleb collected funds to assist in destitute-pilgrim repatriation, which demonstrated how British inquiries in fact led one Muslim to facilitate the Hajj for his poorer brethren.[128] The frequency of suggestions that Muslims be involved in administering the flow of pilgrims to and from India within the colonial framework clearly had some effect, because Muslims were employed by the British for various Hajj-related duties from the late 1870s.

Although the insights of these Muslims on the Hajj cannot be accepted uncritically, one man consulted, Maulvi Hamid Bukht Mozumdar, appeared especially knowledgeable about destitute pilgrims. His father had performed the Hajj eight times and on each occasion had paid for poor Muslims to accompany him. Mozumdar had firsthand knowledge of destitute pilgrims from the seven years he had spent in Mecca. He thought that such pilgrims were contravening the prescriptions laid down in the Qur'an and outlined the charitable administrations organized by the Ottomans, the nawab of Rampur, and the begum of Bhopal, all of whom distributed money to poor pilgrims in Mecca, although Indians received only a small share of this. The nizam of Hyderabad's relief efforts were given only to those who had made the Hajj with his permission, and the alms given by the begum and the nawab to poor pilgrims were, in Mozumdar's view, carelessly distributed. There were also hostels in Mecca for poor pilgrims; his father had owned two. Mozumdar believed that the authorities needed a suitable Muslim employee in India to issue passports and inquire into pilgrims' means, and the government of India should enlist the support of the wealthy Muslim princely rulers to ensure that their charitable donations to Mecca were spent on accommodation and aid to poor pilgrims there. Mozumdar had no issue with the colonial authorities working with Muslims to help these destitute pilgrims. However, he thought that cautioning poor Muslims against going on Hajj would have no effect: when his father said the same to poor pilgrims, they did not listen to him.[129] The desire to perform Hajj trumped worldly matters of finance. The British discovered that poorer pilgrims, unsurprisingly, were unlikely to listen to official remonstrations about having sufficient funds for Hajj in published notifications. The destitute pilgrim was a potent image of the empire's inability to control these religious travelers. As Radhika Singha has argued, "Pilgrim mobility could be circumscribed but not cut off."[130]

After the investigation concluded, the Foreign Office believed that repatriating destitute pilgrims at government expense would encourage such people. Chapters 3 and 4 will detail a remarkable shift in policy toward wholesale repatriation of indigent pilgrims. Although Lord Derby in 1878 accepted the difficulties of repatriation, he still felt that a situation where Indian pilgrims starved at the consul's door was unacceptable, and he suggested a private charitable fund under the consul's control. Derby was also concerned about the "rascality" of pilgrim agents in the Hijaz and Bombay who defrauded pilgrims.[131] He went on to suggest appointing "respectable" Muslims as pilgrim agents to give information and assistance to pilgrims.[132] The authorities in Calcutta thought that this was of "doubtful expediency," and those in Bombay believed that this "would only create fresh complications."[133] However, three years after discarding such ideas, and perhaps in response to proposals by Muslims and some British officials, the Bombay authorities planned to employ a Muslim assistant to pilgrims, who would "protect them from extortion, give them information about the voyage, and help them get lodgings in Bombay."[134] The role of Muslims in Bombay's Hajj administration will be examined in Chapter 3. Destitute pilgrims had focused official attention on the complex character of the journeys undertaken by Britain's pilgrim-subjects, which, in turn, led to an increase in the numbers of Muslims employed within the imperial bureaucracy on Hajj-related duties.

Indigent pilgrims from India also contributed to Anglo-Ottoman tensions. Ottoman regulations that required pilgrims to possess passports were introduced in 1881, largely because of the presence of destitute pilgrims in the Hijaz. However, the difficulty of implementing this regulation, combined with the complications it raised in relation to the difficult issue of extraterritorial jurisdiction by European powers in the Ottoman empire (the Capitulations), meant that the requirement for passports was abandoned after only one year.[135] In 1884, the Constantinople Board of Health wanted the British consulate in Jidda to pay for the maintenance of destitute pilgrims during their detention in the Kamaran quarantine camp; because of the British government's opposition to quarantine, this was rejected out of hand.[136] The phenomenon of destitute pilgrims proved remarkably difficult for Britain to resolve satisfactorily, given the variety of conflicting British and Muslim viewpoints on the matter.

In Southeast Asia during this period, by contrast, there was a contested solution to the repatriation of destitute pilgrims. There, the Hajj was connected to more general flows of transregional migrant labor. Many Indonesian Muslims temporarily emigrated to Malaya and Singapore to work on plantations or in other areas of the economy to save up money to embark on Hajj, or they undertook this work after they returned from Hajj to pay back money they had borrowed for this purpose. Some, however, never left Singapore, because they were unable to accumulate the necessary money to make the voyage to the Hijaz.[137] Indonesian Muslims also traveled to the Hijaz via Singapore because by doing so, they could circumvent Dutch passport controls and regulations. The most prominent example of the repatriation of poor pilgrims from the Hijaz to Southeast Asia was the system run by the Alsagoff company in Singapore. The firm, owned by al-Saqqaf, a Hadhrami family, ran plantations on Kukup Island near Singapore that were notorious for their poor working conditions. The company's response to labor shortages on its estates was contracting the labor of Southeast Asian pilgrims in the Hijaz who had run out of money. Sayyid Muhammad bin Alsagoff would pay for these pilgrims' voyages back to Singapore, and the pilgrims would be bound to work on the company's estates for a fixed period, although the cycle of debt often extended the time spent on estates. These contracts were collective, typically involving three to eight pilgrims on one contract.[138]

By the late 1880s, this system had evolved: Alsagoff's labor shortages decreased, and the pilgrim contract ticket became largely a moneylending venture. The firm was one of the largest moneylenders in Jidda. If pilgrims could not pay their debt within a fixed time after their arrival back in Singapore, they would rectify this by working on the estates. Very few did so in practice, however. In 1889, for example, 190 out of 200 pilgrims who entered into these contracts had paid their debts. Those who failed to repay worked on the estates for only two months at most before they paid off the balance, often with assistance from friends. Tellingly, Alsagoff refused to enter into contracts with destitute Indian pilgrims in the Hijaz because they would have been able to repay the debt only by laboring on estates, and this labor was not needed by the end of the nineteenth century.[139] It remains unclear why this type of contract-labor system for pilgrims did not operate in other parts of the world that had similar economic structures. In 1896, concerned that this phenomenon was akin to indentured labor, the Straits Settlements government canceled the Alsagoff contract-ticket system and the next year instituted an obligatory return-ticket system.[140] The Alsagoff contract ticket was a novel and harsh method that enabled destitute pilgrims to perform the Hajj, but it proved to be short-lived.

These early years of Britain's closer engagement with the pilgrimage led to proposals from several quarters on how this interaction should develop, especially regarding indigent pilgrims. One person who contributed to the discussion was Beyts's successor as consul in Jidda, James Napoleon Zohrab, in 1880. Zohrab came from an Armenian Eastern Orthodox family that had fled from Persia in the late eighteenth century. Like his father and brothers, he entered Britain's diplomatic service, and he was unimpressed by Britain's overall position in relation to the Hajj.[141] British subjects in the Hijaz had "ceased to enjoy British protection" and were subject to robbery, cruelty, and ill-treatment. Each year, hundreds of destitute pilgrims were forced to scavenge for scraps among rubbish and starved to death, a fate suffered only by British subjects, according to Zohrab. The consul stridently stated that "the question of protecting the Indian pilgrims . . . [was] no longer optional." Although the Indian government was aware of the situation, the consul thought that its inquiries among Indian Muslims on how to mitigate such scenes were unsatisfactory. Zohrab believed that the Muslims consulted had "vague and obscure opinions" that made the authorities apprehensive that any action would be interpreted by India's Muslims as interference with religion and would cause discontent. Muslims in Jidda had quizzically told Zohrab that if Britain felt compassion for its Muslim subjects and wanted to protect them, it was strange that they received no support from official quarters during their pilgrimages. Having privately consulted elite Indian pilgrims in Jidda, he concluded that they believed that "active British control should be exercised during the whole of that time of trial and suffering," but this would never be aired in public because it was "so subversive of the exclusive conservatism . . . and prejudice which constitutes the foundations of Islam." Zohrab viewed Islam as essentially reactionary; by contrast, in his mind-set, Britain should be a reforming force in relation to the Hajj.[142]

Zohrab's remedy for this state of affairs was that Britain should introduce compulsory return tickets to prevent destitute pilgrims from leaving India, an idea formed after conversations with Hijazi *'ulama*, who told Zohrab about the Qur'anic injunction that Muslims should perform the Hajj only if they were physically and financially able, and about the Dutch example of compulsory return tickets. The Dutch system, which Zohrab wanted Britain to emulate, involved registration at the consulate, where pilgrims would receive the deposit for their return journey and a certificate that attested to their status as Hajjis. After some initial opposition from Indonesian pilgrims, the certificates were now apparently "eagerly sought" as proof of Hajji status in the East Indies. Zohrab thought that if Britain withheld the right for Indians and Malays to call themselves Hajji without a consular certificate, opposition to other administrative changes would be "swept away"—one of the consul's rather naïve assumptions on these topics. The success of the scheme's implementation rested on the participation of Britain's Muslim subjects in the Hijaz, India, and Malaya.[143]

Another voice for reform regarding Britain's broader association with the Hajj came from Zohrab's friend, the writer, traveler, and anti-imperialist Wilfrid Scawen Blunt, who visited Jidda at the end of 1881 to gather material for his book *The Future of Islam*, which proffered a pundit's view of Islam and the Hajj. From his time in Jidda, he concluded that Islam was "convulsed by political portents of ever-growing intensity."[144] Blunt believed that Britain had shown "culpable negligence" to its pilgrim-subjects, which he claimed was an opinion echoed by many people in Jidda, which was probably what Zohrab told him. Zohrab's views, perhaps unsurprisingly, agreed with Blunt's.[145] Astonished that this important matter had been left "entirely in the hands of chance" and drawing a sharp contrast with Dutch pilgrimage policy, Blunt argued that regulating the Hajj was an important part of Britain's duty toward the Muslim world, "one we should be grossly in error to neglect."[146]

Blunt predicted that the inevitable fall of the Ottoman empire would mean that Britain would have a unique opportunity to act as the Muslim world's "adviser and protector," and that the caliphate would move to Mecca under British protection. Because so many pilgrims came from British territories, Blunt hoped that a post-Ottoman Hajj would be "principally under English auspices." Blunt proposed the "systematic development" of the Hajj by the British government, rattling off ideas such as the construction of a railway from Jidda to Mecca, government-chartered pilgrim ships, and the transfer of Indian *waqf* proceeds to Mecca. More immediately, he advocated the appointment of a Muslim agent to look after pilgrims' interests, which would "have a disproportionately beneficial effect on the political feelings of Muhammadans towards British rule."[147] Although Zohrab's private and Blunt's public proposals for more active British intervention were generally disregarded in official circles, they underscored the continued importance of the Hajj and Muslim pilgrims to British imperial interests and the importance of Muslim involvement in Britain's administrative engagement with the ritual. Blunt's and Zohrab's remarks reflected wider concerns that the protection of Britain's Muslim subjects had a role in imperial rivalries being played out at various points across Asia in this period.[148]

A few years after these suggestions from Zohrab and Blunt, a rather different development occurred in relation to Britain's involvement in the Hajj with the appointment of Thomas Cook as the official travel agent for the Indian Hajj from 1886 to 1893. Although this move was not solely due to the issue of destitute pilgrims, poor Indian pilgrims were a significant reason for the company's entry into, and exit from, the Hajj business. The difficulties and tragedies these pilgrims faced on voyages across the Indian Ocean prompted the government of India to attempt to mitigate these problems while simultaneously attempting to uphold a policy of noninterference with the Hajj by engaging a private company.[149] This novel experiment in attempting to manage the transportation of pilgrims, set up between the government of India and a private firm, proved to be short-lived, not least because the company could not make a profit when most of its customers were poor pilgrims.

Thomas Cook's connection with the Hajj was precipitated by several scandals related to voyages on pilgrim ships. The ill-fated voyage of the steamship *Jeddah* in 1880 was used by Joseph Conrad as a template for a scene in his famous novel *Lord Jim*.[150] Pilgrims' voyages also appeared in other popular Victorian literature, such as Sir Arthur Conan Doyle's Sherlock Holmes story *The Sign of Four*. Mr. Small, the story's peg-legged villain, along with his companion Tonga, are adrift in the Indian Ocean, having escaped from prison on the Andaman Islands. After eleven days, as Small explained, "we were picked up by a trader which was going from Singapore to Jiddah with a cargo of Malay pilgrims. They were a rum crowd, and Tonga and I soon managed to settle down among them."[151] The *Jeddah* (owned by the Singapore Steamship Company, run by Sayyid Muhammad bin Alsagoff) set out from Singapore to Jidda on July 17, 1880, and stopped at Penang. Near the Gulf of Aden, the ship sprang a leak. Its European officers abandoned the ship and its pilgrim passengers. However, the pilgrims saved the ship, and it was towed into Aden. This prompted a storm of outrage at the conditions on pilgrim ships—the story made the front page of *The Times* in London—and various official inquiries condemned the conduct of the European crew.[152]

An incendiary article in the *Times of India* in 1885 shed further light on the travel experiences of poor pilgrims. Anonymously authored by a steamship captain on the Bombay–Jidda route, it described how pilgrims from across South and central Asia "tramp the best part of the way to Bombay in poor, miserable conditions." After being duped by pilgrim brokers and examined by doctors from the Preventative Service in Bombay, they boarded overcrowded pilgrim ships. Older steamships were repeatedly resold, which meant that the pilgrim traffic was competitive, with ever-lower prices that encouraged poorer prospective pilgrims to make the voyage. But these steamships were generally in bad repair, cramped, and insanitary. The author felt that pilgrims had little sense of fraternity with their coreligionists during their voyage; several nationalities were "mixed together, and one is growling at the other in his own language." After the pilgrimage's conclusion, he wrote, it was common to see in Jidda many "lying on the beach under the shade of rocks, without money or clothes, without food and water, dying of disease and starvation." The writer also thought that the government's attitude to the Hajj was inconsistent; authorities recommended that pilgrims should have enough money for the journey but simultaneously proclaimed noninterference in religious affairs. Once again, an unfavorable contrast was drawn between French and Dutch pilgrimage policies and the Indian government's laissez-faire approach: "Our government is afraid that if they do not allow our poor old

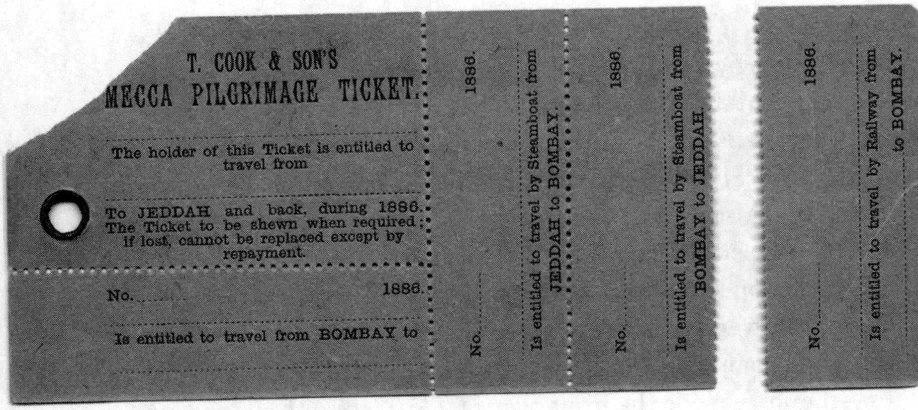

T. COOK & SON'S
MECCA PILGRIMAGE TICKET.
The holder of this Ticket is entitled to travel from
To JEDDAH and back, during 1886. The Ticket to be shewn when required; if lost, cannot be replaced except by repayment.
No. 1886.
Is entitled to travel from BOMBAY to

1886.
No.
Is entitled to travel by Steamboat from JEDDAH to BOMBAY.

1886.
No.
Is entitled to travel by Steamboat from BOMBAY to JEDDAH.

1886.
No.
Is entitled to travel by Railway from to BOMBAY.

Thomas Cook Mecca pilgrimage ticket, 1886

Credit: Thomas Cook Archives, Peterborough

natives of India to go on hajj, they will keep them out of heaven."[153] The government's response to the article was unsurprisingly skeptical; one official described it as full of "exaggerated verbiage and irrelevant matter" and refuted the article's various claims. The official was more strident regarding prohibiting pilgrims from leaving without sufficient funds; this would be easily evaded, impossible to enforce and leading to "serious outcry" over interference with religious liberty. The author's identity was uncovered; Mr. Baldwin was a skipper on a ship owned by a Muslim firm. He was criticized for writing the article instead of approaching the government with his concerns.[154] For Europeans directly involved in the pilgrim trade, pilgrims were often denigrated as a group, with little comprehension of their desire to perform the Hajj.

Despite the dismissive official attitude toward the article, this type of continued criticism about the pilgrim trade in official and non-official circles, along with scandals such as the *Jeddah*, led the viceroy to approach Thomas Cook's son, John Mason Cook, in 1885 to request that the travel firm of Thomas Cook and Sons reform the transportation arrangements for the pilgrimage from India. The government of India's stance on the pilgrimage was clear; it had "no direct concern" with the pilgrim traffic" but wished only to "mitigate the sufferings of the poorer class of Muhammadans who undertake the pilgrimage."[155] This approach came on the heels of repeated overtures since 1881 by British officials to Cook regarding the pilgrimage.[156] Because Cook's business interests in India were well established by this point, the firm felt able to take on this new role. Cook would be the sole travel agent for the Hajj and would receive assistance from government officials; the protector of pilgrims' office established in Bombay in 1882 would be placed under the firm's control; Cook would arrange with railway and steamship companies for pilgrims' travel and publish fare prices, appoint Muslims to positions in the company "in all cases where necessary," and distribute pilgrim passports; and the government would cover losses the firm incurred up to an agreed limit.[157] In the government resolution announcing the scheme, the viceroy of India, the Marquess of Dufferin, confidently stated that "a scheme of this nature . . . cannot fail."[158] Before this experiment formally began in 1886, John Mason Cook wrote more circumspectly that "I know this business is surrounded with more difficulties and prejudices than anything I have hitherto undertaken."[159]

An 1886 report by John's son, Frank Cook, on pilgrim conditions in Jidda gave an indication of the nature of the pilgrimage business the firm had entered into. In conversations with boatmen in Jidda harbor, Frank Cook's group, accompanied by the British consul Thomas Jago and interpreter Yusuf Kudzi, were told that indigent Indian pilgrims "have to be landed for nothing or as much as the boatmen can squeeze out of them."[160] Jago told Cook that when the last pilgrim ship was ready to depart, he unilaterally decided to help a handful of poor pilgrims leave Jidda using a small miscellaneous fund from the consulate.[161] After consultation with "influential" Muslims in Bombay and Calcutta, John Mason Cook sent Frank on an extensive tour of India to publicize and explain the firm's involvement in the Hajj. At each major town, he would ask the local commissioner to call a meeting of Muslim leaders, where arrangements were explained and then opinions were invited from those present.[162] Cook's firm had to deal with the thousands of poor pilgrims who flocked to Bombay every year, who faced unscrupulous pilgrim brokers, interminable waits for steamships, overpriced accommodation, and overcrowding on ships. These conditions prevailed despite legislation such as the

TABLE OF THE MECCA PILGRIMAGE OF 1880.

Nationality of Pilgrims.	Arriving by Sea.	Arriving by Land.	Total of Mussulman population represented.
Ottoman subjects including pilgrims from Syria and Irak, but not from Egypt or Arabia proper	8,500	1,000	22,000,000
Egyptians	5,000	1,000	5,000,000
Mogrebbins ("people of the West"), that is to say Arabic-speaking Mussulmans from the Barbary States, Tripoli, Tunis, Algiers, and Morocco. These are always classed together and are not easily distinguishable from each other	6,000	...	18,000,000
Arabs from Yemen	3,000	...	2,500,000
,, ,, Oman and Hadramaut .	3,000	...	3,000,000
,, ,, Nejd, Assir, and Hasa, most of them Wahhabites .	...	5,000	4,000,000
,, ,, Hejaz, of these perhaps 10,000 Meccans . .	...	22,000	2,000,000
Negroes from Soudan	2,000	...	10,000,000(?)
,, ,, Zanzibar	1,000	...	1,500,000
Malabari from the Cape of Good Hope .	150	...	
Persians	6,000	2,500	8,000,000
Indians (British subjects)	15,000	...	40,000,000
Malays, chiefly from Java and Dutch subjects	12,000	...	30,000,000
Chinese	100	...	15,000,000
Mongols from the Khanates, included in the Ottoman Haj	...	...	6,000,000
Lazis, Circassians, Tartars, etc. (Russian subjects), included in the Ottoman Haj	...	...	5,000,000
Independent Afghans and Beluchis, included in the Indian and Persian Hajs	...	...	3,000,000
Total of Pilgrims present at Arafat .	93,250		
		Total Census of Islam	175,000,000

1880 pilgrimage numbers, by W. S. Blunt

Credit: W. S. Blunt, *The Future of Islam* (London: Kegan Paul, 1882)

Pilgrim Brokers Act 1886 and an updated Native Passenger Ships Act 1887 that were designed to regulate brokers' behavior and improve conditions on board pilgrim ships, which led to greater official surveillance of pilgrim vessels, such as medical inspections of pilgrims before embarkation.[163] The travails faced by Cook showed how the pilgrimage in this period had become an overwhelmingly nonelite activity.

The complexities of pilgrim transportation defeated Cook. Protracted negotiations between the company and shippers, brokers, and railway companies meant that the scheme was not fully operational until 1887. Cook's reports on the Hajj business frequently expressed exasperation at the thousands of Indian pilgrims who departed for the Hijaz without passports, the issuance of which was chaotic—they were given out in a rush before pilgrims boarded their ships in Bombay. More frustrating to Cook was the continued losses the firm incurred on the pilgrim business, which meant that it had to ask the government of India every year for the full subsidy contained in the original agreement. However, this subsidy still did not cover the firm's actual losses. In order to stanch these losses, Cook offered free fares to some pilgrims on occasion to stimulate demand, thereby facilitating the Hajj for a number of poor pilgrims. Perhaps the final straw was the huge failure of the firm's commercial intelligence in 1893. It failed to realize that that year was a Hajj *akbar*, when performing the ritual had particular spiritual merit, and chartered only two instead of four steamers, which meant that its share of pilgrims carried slumped to 9 percent from a healthier 37 percent the previous year.[164]

Cook's management of pilgrim transportation faced significant criticism. For example, the Bombay newspaper *Mauj-i-Nerbudda* carried a critical article that described how the firm oversold tickets for ships. Its eyewitness reporter wrote of crying children left behind on the quayside as their parents departed for the Hijaz.[165] However, the protector of pilgrims argued that there was "not a particle of truth" in the allegations.[166] Similar claims were harder to refute in another case, when twenty-three men with valid tickets were not allowed to board a ship because of lack of space.[167] The government of India wrote to Cook's agent distancing itself from the firm's contract, reiterating that it had no "direct concern" with pilgrim traffic, and that intermittent actions by the government were merely due to a "desire to . . . mitigate the sufferings of the poorer class of Mahomedans who undertake the pilgrimage."[168] Official developments were limited because the government did not want to interfere directly with the Hajj since it was a religious obligation.[169] Although this was rooted in pragmatism, not beneficence, officials' comments demonstrated the centrality of destitute pilgrims to Britain's engagement with the Hajj.

Cook realized as early as 1889 that this aspect of the firm's business would never turn a profit because the vast majority of its Indian pilgrim customers were poor, and pilgrim shipowners were consistently offering lower fares than his firm.[170] Cook had not been supported by Indian Muslims in the endeavor and would continue only if the government paid for future losses.[171] These tensions came to a head; the government decided to discontinue its pilgrim-traffic subsidy to the firm, and Cook's contract was terminated in 1893.[172] As Cook had found to its cost, the complexity and difficulties of pilgrimage transport were beyond its capabilities, a cautionary tale against further official involvement. John Mason Cook's statement that "some government officials said I am powerless to make any improvement. . . . I reminded them that government officials have been to a great extent powerless in relation to the pilgrimage" was a good summation of the whole situation.[173] The brief foray of Thomas Cook and Sons into the business of the Hajj was a colorful episode in Britain's interactions with the Hajj, and it signaled the limits of British attempts to alter the nature of pilgrims' travel experiences.

British attitudes and responses to indigent pilgrims were shaped by a desire to ameliorate the issue because of the negative impact this group had on the British empire's prestige in the Hijaz and the wider Muslim world. The interplay between destitute pilgrims and British imperial prestige occurred within the broader context of intense imperial rivalry among the Ottoman, British, Dutch, and French empires on the issue of the Hajj and control of the Red Sea as a strategic corridor, which in turn was part of a larger competition for power and resources that extended far beyond Arabia. Indeed, Britain's Hajj bureaucracies developed alongside concurrent administrative efforts in other empires that had a stake in the pilgrimage.[174] For the British, this seemingly inexorable impetus for greater engagement with the Hajj sat uneasily with a concurrent wish to uphold noninterference in their subjects' religious practices, a stance influenced by the weight of Muslim opinion on the matter, which authorities were keen to solicit. This resulted in a substantial increase in official understanding of the pilgrimage and of Britain's poorer pilgrim-subjects who went on Hajj. This relatively small amount of Indian Muslim viewpoints, derived from highly selective consultation processes, was a motive force in British inaction and also underscored how the Hajj was not always the equalizing experience that some professed it to be. One vital aspect that emerged from Britain's consideration of destitute pilgrims was the acute need for greater Muslim involvement in Britain's nascent Hajj administration.

Muslim Employees in Britain's Hajj Administration

The expansion of Muslim employment in Britain's growing Hajj administration began in 1878 when the Indian government sent Assistant Surgeon Dr. Abdur Razzack of the Bengal Medical Service on Hajj to monitor the sanitary situation of Indian pilgrims and assess the effects of the quarantine lazaret at al-Tur in the Red Sea, which had been established the previous year.[175] Existing studies have explored Razzack's role in sanitary regulations and the Hajj, so this section will examine his role in shaping Britain's engagement with the issue of destitute pilgrims. Razzack was sent on Hajj by the British annually from 1878 to 1882, and his reports were read by officials in London, Aden, Egypt, India, and Malaya. His employment in the Jidda consulate was formalized in 1882, and he became permanently based there, partly because of growing numbers of destitute Indian pilgrims; his remit was expanded to include providing assistance to Indian pilgrims and concerning himself with their general welfare while they were in the Hijaz.[176]

Razzack's appointment was probably partly due to suggestions by British officials and Indian Muslims consulted in the investigation detailed in the previous section and the requests of Zohrab, the consul in Jidda, for greater Muslim involvement in Britain's Hajj administration.[177] In fact, Zohrab had asked for much more in 1880: an Indian doctor who spoke Arabic, English, and Hindi, two clerks with similar linguistic abilities as well as Malay, and three multilingual interpreters. He hoped that these employees would also administer any destitute-pilgrim repatriation fund that might be established by Muslims.[178] The consul's requests reflected the relatively weak position he and his European peers held in Jidda. As Ulrike Freitag has argued, despite the consuls' positions as representatives of imperial powers, in Jidda they were "exposed and helpless," and their position was "heavily circumscribed" and vulnerable because of their enforced isolation from local society. Consequently, employing Muslims enabled these difficulties to be partly overcome. Men like Razzack could travel to Mecca, although local Ottoman officials were unhappy with an official representative of Britain going to Mecca, and Razzack forged better relations with Hijazis and Indians than with his British superiors.[179]

In an attempt to reinforce his new position, Razzack proposed in 1880 that a Muslim doctor should be sent to Mecca every year to "strengthen British influence among the Moslem population of Asia" and monitor the Hajj. His superiors in India saw this as unnecessary because Razzack already visited the Hijaz annually. They realized that the Ottomans would oppose a doctor employed by Britain traveling to Mecca to report on sanitary regulations in relation to the Hajj there. The doctor's proposals were frostily received by officials in Bombay and Bengal, who knew from consultation with local Muslims that there was general opposition to further governmental involvement in the Hajj. The government of India's view was that "the proposal to intervene more actively on behalf of the Moslem pilgrimage to Mecca must for the present be abandoned. . . . If or when the Muhammadan community evince a desire again to raise the question and are prepared to provide necessary funds we shall be willing to reconsider."[180] However, Razzack's value to the British because of his ability to travel to Mecca and Medina meant that the official policy of no further action was altered in 1882 when Razzack was ensconced in the post of vice-consul in Jidda. Razzack now became a key voice calling for further British intervention in the pilgrimage, while his employers adhered to a stance of noninterference.[181]

Nevertheless, some of Razzack's suggestions met with approval from his colleagues, such as Zohrab's successor in Jidda, Thomas Jago. In 1885, Razzack argued that a fund should be established at Jidda by prominent Indian Muslims to assist indigent pilgrims.[182] In an echo of Beyts's theory that rich Muslims sent their poorer counterparts on Hajj without enough money, Razzack accused the main Muslim princely states of India—Hyderabad, Bhopal, and Rampur—of this practice. The doctor played on his colleague's first-hand experiences to harness his support: "As an instance of the misery which these people suffer from extreme want and penury, it is scarcely necessary for me to repeat what you [Jago] saw the other day when you went to make enquiries regarding the condition of twenty Indian pilgrims lying near the quarantine office, who had made their homes amidst a stinking mass of puddles and dirt." Razzack wanted Muslim princely rulers to contribute to a charity fund controlled by him that would disburse money to pilgrims on a means-tested basis. To sidestep official policy, Razzack wrote that the fund could be operated "without giving any publicity to our intentions, or coming ourselves to the front, which would be in conformity to the decision of the Government of India, declining all responsibility for giving any pecuniary help to the pilgrims."[183] Razzack also wrote separately to the Foreign Office in London advocating a consular officer for Mecca to protect pilgrims "because the pilgrims' present treatment is scandalous and an officer should be present to remonstrate and object in every case of gross illegality."[184] In other areas, the suggestions in Razzack's pilgrimage reports, according to Michael Christopher Low, "formed the practical basis for Government of India efforts to reform and institutionalise the pilgrim traffic." For example, the Indian Native Passenger Ships Act was amended twice in the 1880s as a result of the doctor's proposals.[185] The shibboleth of governmental noninterference in religious practice was being subtly critiqued and eroded by a Muslim employee within the British bureaucracy, a trend that continued and expanded in subsequent decades.

Officials were generally ambivalent about intervention of any kind. Those who did propose greater imperial engagement with the pilgrimage in the shape of administrative measures were largely unsuccessful in pressing their claims. The archival record shows a sense of British impotence. Although officials were anxious about Britain's inability to protect its subjects from robbery and extortion during the Hajj, they felt that little could be done in practice to forcibly change the situation on the ground.[186] Consequently, existing studies perhaps exaggerate the extent of British imperial control over the pilgrimage beyond sanitary measures and sometimes understate the role of Muslim agency in Britain's engagement in the Hajj.[187]

Razzack's reports provide his unique perspective on the pilgrimage's role in facilitating—or preventing—Muslim unity and equality. The doctor was worried that the "timid and ignorant peasantry of East Bengal" who generally made up half the numbers of Indian pilgrims were "under the thumb of their spiritual guides [*mutawwifin*, pilgrim guides] not only from natural pliability, faith and credulity, but their almost complete inability to communicate with the people of this country."[188] Razzack also wrote of "poor Malay pilgrims, ignorant and helpless, unable to understand any other language but their own."[189] Despite the derogatory tone of Razzack's remarks, his observations complicate interpretations that stress the pilgrimage's unifying effect in terms of pilgrims having a wider appreciation of the Islamic world as a whole and, indeed, the power of the Hajj as a catalyst for transmitting ideas. These analyses elide the fact that most pilgrims in this period were often poor and illiterate and had little education. Razzack's final point is also crucial: most pilgrims were not multilingual. They were reliant on the proficiency of their *mutawwif* in Arabic to negotiate the Hajj experience. Consequently, there was little scope for interaction and the exchange of news and ideas with their fellow Muslims from other parts of the Islamic world; this was something enjoyed only by Muslims who had proficiency in the lingua franca of Arabic. Some pilgrims who expected to experience the unity of the *umma* and its equality during the Hajj instead became more aware of the many differences—linguistic, ethnic, and socioeconomic—among this global community of believers.[190]

Destitute pilgrims continued to preoccupy Razzack throughout the duration of his employment in the Hijaz, given that they were a central concern of British authorities involved with the pilgrimage in this period.[191] In 1886, he wrote that their living conditions were "miserable . . . heart-rending to behold." However, Razzack thought that their religiosity "will buoy up the hearts of even the poorest and most destitute and steel them to bear every variety of privation and misery in the hope of a better future thereafter."[192] Improving this group's pilgrimage experience was one of his most important tasks. For example, his 1887 Hajj report opened with an emotional passage on the issue; indigent pilgrims stranded in Jidda suffered from "want, privation and disease." That year's pilgrimage had the highest number of destitute pilgrims on record: over 4,955 from India out of a total of 10,324. The percentage of destitute Indian pilgrims was often near 40 percent, but this year's tally meant that nearly 50 percent of Indian pilgrims were destitute, and the Ottoman authorities complained to Britain about this large influx of indigent pilgrims. There were simply too many that year for Indian Muslim merchants in Jidda and Mecca to assist with repatriating all of them, as they had done in previous years. Although Razzack felt that only the "absolutely helpless" should be assisted, a fund for destitute pilgrims was now urgently needed.[193] This reflected similar social welfare endeavors related to Indians in Britain, such as the financial assistance given by the India Office—grudgingly—toward the repatriations of fifty-seven destitute Indians from London between 1889 and 1915.[194] In India, organizations such as the Mahomedan Literary Society were again consulted and reported back that "impecunious pilgrims" should now have some restrictions placed on them.[195] Razzack thought that only a "slight hint" from the authorities was needed to make rich Muslims in Bombay and Calcutta establish a destitute-pilgrim fund. Razzack drew a telling parallel with the Ottomans' practice of paying to send their poor pilgrims, albeit few in number, back to Anatolia on ships; the doctor felt that Britain should emulate the Ottomans and act more like a Muslim power.[196]

Although Razzack worked within the imperial framework, the record of his work shows how he cooperated with Muslims outside officialdom in a search for solutions to the destitute-pilgrim issue. The case of Sir Syed Ahmad Khan's involvement in the issue of destitute pilgrims, in response to Razzack's ideas, further shows the prominent role Muslims played in Britain's relationship with the Hajj. Khan, a prominent Islamic reformer and modernist and founder of the Anglo-Muhammadan College at Aligarh in 1875, was sent Razzack's reports on indigent pilgrims and the doctor's proposal for a relief fund in 1890 because Khan had apparently been interested in improving pilgrimage conditions for some time. British officials wanted Khan's input on the issue but reiterated their desire to remain detached from the matter because official assistance would "encourage" poor pilgrims. Instead, the British thought that a relief fund would be valuable and hoped that Razzack's idea could be realized through private efforts.[197] Although Khan thought the fund a good idea, he believed that harnessing private efforts in India to send money to Mecca would be "quite useless" because giving *zakat* to poor pilgrims was considered more virtuous during the charitable giver's Hajj. Khan enlisted the help of Hajji Muhammad Ismail Khan from Aligarh; his family was settled in Mecca, and he traveled there frequently. Ismail Khan thought that there were three types of Indians in Mecca aside from expatriates: "professional beggars" who believed that the pecuniary opportunities were greater in Mecca than in India; poor pilgrims who wanted to stay in the Hijaz; and those stranded there because they had no money. Syed Ahmad Khan thought that this last category of pilgrim should be assisted through a fund, but there were three problems: whether public or private, a fund would encourage pilgrims to apply for relief; local fund-raising efforts would need centralized coordination; and without input from the Muslim princely states, there would be "no chance of success." The potential fund's central committee would liaise with Razzack, and the colonial authorities would remain uninvolved.[198]

The government's response to Syed Ahmad Khan's letter demonstrated the role Muslims had in shaping official policy or, rather, inaction. One official thought that Razzack should be consulted further because he had the greatest knowledge of conditions in the Hijaz for pilgrims.[199] Another thought that genuine cases of hardship could be helped if Razzack could decide which poor pilgrims would receive disbursements. The whole issue was postponed because it was felt that further consultation was needed with Muslim leaders, since Syed Ahmad Khan and his modernist movement were not part of the "orthodox class" that constituted the majority of pilgrims.[200] Other officials supported Razzack's earlier proposal: the government should ask a few wealthy Muslims to quietly send money to Razzack to provide relief at his discretion, and "there should be no flourish of trumpets nor public canvassing of native states."[201] Although the government of India informed the consul at Jidda of these conclusions, along with recommendations that Syed Ahmad Khan should coordinate a relief plan with Razzack, there is no further record of the scheme, so it seems that nothing came to pass.[202] This episode from 1890 clearly delineates the complexity and ambiguity of Britain's interactions with the Hajj: a stance of noninterference uneasily juxtaposed with more activist desires. Muslims within and outside the imperial framework contributed to British policy, even if, in this case, it remained in stasis.

Razzack's death at the hands of Bedouins outside Jidda on May 30, 1895, highlighted his importance to the British. While he was walking with the consul, both were shot at by Bedouin tribesmen. The consul was injured, but Razzack was shot in the heart. The consul's report on the incident said that the Bedouins thought that the officials were quarantine doctors, whom they despised; a hospital and a disinfecting machine had recently been attacked in Mecca because the Bedouins thought that these things and the doctors were responsible for cholera. Jidda's panicked European community escaped to vessels in the harbor.[203] French and British gunboats headed to Jidda. A "provisional occupation" of the town was considered, and the Foreign Office advised the viceroy of India that it might be prudent to temporarily stop pilgrims from going to the Hijaz.[204] These actions were mainly in response to the injuries the British consul sustained, as opposed to Razzack's murder. Nevertheless, the doctor's family was not forgotten. Razzack left behind one Hijazi wife, three sons, and one daughter. He possessed three houses and a small amount of land in Serampore, near Calcutta, which were all *waqf*, endowed to a mosque. Bazlul Karim, the district's deputy magistrate, recommended that Razzack's family could be maintained if Abdus Satta, Razzack's nephew, was given a subregistrarship in the local administration, a suitable position because the man knew English, Persian, Hindi, and Bengali.[205] The British consul at Jidda felt that Razzack's death was a "very great, irreparable loss for the Consulate. He was well educated, with a keen intelligence, an upright, straight forward, fearless character. After thirteen years residence here no one was more respected in Jedda. H.M.G. have lost a good faithful public servant. . . . It will be difficult to replace him."[206] As Michael Christopher Low has stated, Razzack's "influence over pilgrimage affairs is unquestionable."[207] Razzack proved that Muslim employees were a vital component of Britain's dealings with the pilgrimage, a fact repeatedly demonstrated in subsequent decades.[208]

The doctor's immediate successor as vice-consul, Dr. Mohammed Hussein, was also highly valued by his employers and played an important part in shaping British knowledge of the Hajj. In his 1896–1897 Hajj report, he began with a detailed account of the pilgrimage's origins in the sixth and seventh centuries CE. Like others before him, Hussein wrote that according to the Qur'an, performing the Hajj was compulsory only for those who could afford it and were physically able. The vice-consul wearily noted the "blind religious zeal of millions of uneducated Moslems," exacerbated by pilgrim guides from the Hijaz who traveled across India to attract pilgrims. These guides, coupled with unrestricted travel and improvements in transportation, "had made them [the pilgrims] look upon the hajj as the only source of salvation open to them." These developments had made the Hajj attain "such magnitude that it has attracted the attention of all the leading powers of the world."[209]

One small but significant example of Britain's relationship with the pilgrimage occurred during Hussein's tenure, when Hussein and the consul made their contribution to the empire-wide celebrations of Queen Victoria's Diamond Jubilee in 1897. A telegram of congratulations was sent to the queen, and a reception was held at the consulate, which was illuminated in lights. Queen Victoria was aware that many of her subjects performed the Hajj—one of her private journal entries noted meeting a party of Indian pilgrims from South Africa's Cape Colony who were delayed in London on their way to Mecca, and in 1898 she lobbied the British ambassador in Istanbul to raise the ill-treatment of Indian pilgrims with Ottoman sultan Abdul Hamid II (1876–1909).[210] The queen's Diamond Jubilee was also commemorated by some British Indians living in Jidda who established a collection to help poor pilgrims return home to India. Placed under the supervision of Dr. Hussein and two resident Indians, the collection was named the Jubilee Indian Pilgrims Relief Fund and was amalgamated with a smaller, similar fund founded by Razzack.[211] Queen Victoria's Diamond Jubilee served to institutionalize Britain's initial forays into the relief and repatriation of its destitute pilgrim-subjects. However, this process was fraught with difficulty from the outset. In Singapore, it was discovered that of the 112 "Malay" pilgrims provided with return passages by the consul in 1897, over 85 were Javanese from the Netherlands East Indies.[212] Official engagement with destitute pilgrims continued to increase in scale and complexity until the postwar period of decolonization.

In this jubilee year, the plague's effect on the pilgrimage provides a further example of how attitudes toward greater Anglo-Muslim cooperation had changed. The disease, which originated in Hong Kong in 1896, spread to India and the Hijaz, which led France and Russia to suspend the Hajj from their empires early in 1897. The government of India, which denied that the plague was in Bombay for ten days after the first cases appeared, opposed a similar prohibition because land quarantine measures such as observation camps were established to stop pilgrims traveling to Bombay. The Hajj from India was severely restricted—departures were suspended from Bombay and Karachi—but not prohibited. Muslims in princely states were informed that it was "useless" to go to Bombay and were told to wait until next year. Officials in India warned London against ordering prohibition if the Ottomans did not place restrictions on the Hajj. Such a move would be "misunderstood and likely to cause grave dissatisfaction" among Indian Muslims. The government of India was fearful that any ban on the Hajj due to the spread of epidemic disease would create a precedent for European powers to pressure it to repeat such a measure during any subsequent cholera outbreak, given international sanitary agreements in place at the time.

Hyderabad's resident reported that Muslim opinion would be unfavorable to a total prohibition of the Hajj, but if this happened, the nizam's government would cooperate. However, India ultimately acquiesced to demands that the Hajj from India be suspended by European powers and the Ottoman government, fearful that the plague might spread. This action, regarded with alarm by the authorities, in fact led to little resentment from Indian Muslims. For example, Mysore's resident explained the reasons for prohibition to the state's Muslim notables, who agreed with the stance and promised to communicate this to their communities. The prohibition was explained by *qadis*, judges, to mosque attendees during Ramadan, and Mysore's

Muslims apparently "fully recognised and appreciated" the ban, which was revoked the following year.[213] Given the grim experience pilgrims had had with epidemic disease over the decades, it is unsurprising that opposition to these restrictions was muted by the late 1890s.

The multifaceted functions of Muslim employees as intercessors between British officials in India and Jidda and pilgrims crucially enhanced Britain's understanding and administration of the pilgrimage. These men had a certain influence over Britain's pilgrimage policies. Employees' suggestions sometimes found their way up the various levels of imperial bureaucracies and coalesced into official policies. Muslim officials frequently complicated Britain's overall stance of noninterference with the Hajj; the views these men expressed, especially regarding destitute pilgrims, were generally more interventionist than those of their employers. Muslim employees possessed a degree of agency that was demonstrated repeatedly in their interactions with the British. Their intimate knowledge of conditions during the Hajj was the polar opposite of the opinions of some of their employers, who viewed the pilgrimage as a harbinger of and catalyst for darker things than spiritual fulfillment.

Muslim "Conspiracies," British Surveillance, and the Hajj

A prominent interpretive strand in existing studies of Britain and the Hajj that cover this period highlights the pilgrimage's importance as a site for anticolonial machinations, sometimes bundled together under the rubric of pan-Islamic activities, from the late 1870s. These had antecedents in earlier British perceptions of the Hajj as an unknown space beyond the reach of imperial authorities, coupled with concerns that Mecca harbored many Muslims who had been involved in the 1857 Indian rebellion. The viceroy of India, Lord Lytton, played a key role in fomenting such conceptions, raising alarms in London in 1876 over a supposed pan-Islamic threat that featured Indian rebels in Mecca.[214] The governor of Bombay, Sir Bartle Frere, writing in 1872, is an illustrative example of this trend; in his words, the Hijaz was "a natural asylum for fanatical Moslem exiles from India, and they may there pass their lives in a congenial atmosphere of fanaticism."[215] The rapid growth of Indian pilgrim numbers after 1857 led to concerns among some officials—which turned out to be largely unfounded—that this development would lead to an increase in anti-British "Wahhabi" and pan-Islamic ideas among pilgrims.[216] Such notions were a potent cocktail that played on official anxieties. Consequently, several scholars have argued that Britain engaged in surveillance of the pilgrimage to monitor activities that threatened the British imperial order.[217] To be sure, pilgrims' reliance mainly on European steamships to travel across the Indian Ocean made the observation and regulation of pilgrims during these voyages possible.[218] Eric Tagliacozzo states that the European empires saw the Hajj as relatively innocuous, but also simultaneously as a site of potential anticolonial rebellion.[219] Moreover, Michael Laffan has argued that Britain, France, and the Netherlands maintained consulates in Jidda to "manage an imagined Islamic threat among their subjects."[220]

This work contends that, in the case of Britain, these interpretations somewhat exaggerate the scope of such developments. Although British officials certainly sought to ensure that they knew a reasonable amount about events that occurred during each pilgrimage season, Seema Alavi has argued that British concern over pan-Islamic conspiracies was "often exaggerated."[221] Imperial surveillance of Muslim anticolonial plots and pan-Islamic activities was certainly not extensive and all-encompassing, partly because such actions appeared rather nebulous and partly because of the difficulties of obtaining concrete information on such goings-on, whether in Arabia or India. One example of this was official concerns that funds were being raised in India for a jihad in the name of Mecca and Medina during the 1870s; it turned out that the fund-raising was actually for a project to improve the water supply to these Holy Places.[222] Official viewpoints were more diverse and nuanced, reflective of a similarly heterogeneous set of attitudes among British officials in India both toward Indian Muslims as a whole and toward more specific groups such as the Wahhabis on India's northwest frontier.[223] The "official mind" was not homogeneous. Some saw the Hajj as a hotbed of conspiracy, subversion, and sedition, but many other officials—generally older and more experienced—were sanguine and, indeed, sometimes skeptical about the extent of the pilgrimage's role as a catalyst for anticolonial movements and Islamic radicalism.[224] The Hajj's function in fostering such movements and British surveillance activities should be balanced with other aspects of Britain's interactions with the pilgrimage, such as destitute pilgrims. Topics such as indigent pilgrims are not as sensational as conspiratorial skulduggery, but they are perhaps more representative of Britain's association with the Hajj in this period.

The concerns of some British officials about the Hajj in this period were driven by the emergent ideology of pan-Islamism from the 1870s and its potential effects on pilgrims who were British subjects. Pan-Islamism was an ideology with multiple versions and visions, but in its simplest form, it was the identification of Muslims with their fellow believers across colonial and national borders and advocated sociopolitical solidarity among all Muslims and a unified resistance to anti-Muslim European imperial aggression. Pan-Islamism emerged in a political form in the 1860s and 1870s, when Turkish and Arab intellectuals and other figures, such as the Iranian-born political activist Jamal ad-Din al-Afghani, began debating this concept as a means to prevent the Ottoman empire's further fragmentation. The ideology was directed against aggressive European imperial expansion in the Muslim world, typified by the French takeover of Tunisia in 1881 and the British occupation of the Ottoman province of Egypt in 1882.[225] Despite the central importance of the Ottoman empire and the figure of the caliph to pan-Islamic ideology, it was never an "officially endorsed" policy but was promoted by the empire's bureaucratic and intellectual elites.[226] Defensive and antagonistic to European political, military, and economic dominance, it emphasized the sultan as caliph, to whom all Muslims supposedly owed allegiance, and was seen as an "alternative vision of world order that would give the Ottomans equality in international relations."[227] The ideology formed part of the Ottoman empire's centralization and self-strengthening efforts in the late nineteenth century, when it tightened central control over its mainly Muslim provinces outside Europe and Anatolia. Pan-Islamism was also designed to increase the Ottoman empire's standing among Muslims across the world, especially those living in European colonial empires. Sultan Abdul Hamid II hoped—forlornly, as it turned out—that pan-Islamism would dissuade European powers from further aggression against the empire. The Hajj became a site for "intensive and direct propaganda"; the Ottoman archives contain pamphlets designed to be distributed as propaganda among pilgrims that "aimed to increase the influence and image of the Sultan-Caliph as the servant of the Holy Places . . . and advocated [Muslim] unity and solidarity."[228] Nevertheless, it remains difficult to accurately gauge the effects of such propaganda on pilgrims who were British subjects. Pan-Islamism largely collapsed after the First World War.[229] Despite the undoubted reality of pan-Islamic sentiment among numerous Muslims in this period, some contemporary European writings on the topic were skeptical. Many British observers believed that pan-Islamism died when Abdul Hamid II was deposed in 1909.[230] For example, a 1919 Foreign Office pamphlet titled *The Pan-Islamic Movement* stated that by 1908 Orientalists believed that Pan-Islamism had "no existence—one defined it as 'a phantasm abstracted from the Moslem profession of religious fraternity and magnified by European imagination.' "[231]

British pilgrimage reports in the mid-nineteenth century seldom use the phrase "Pan-Islam," but some officials raised the specter of transcontinental Muslim conspiracies centered on the Hijaz. Zohrab, Britain's consul in Jidda, struck a particularly alarmist tone in 1879 in the midst of the Second Anglo-Afghan War and after the conclusion of the Russo-Turkish War of 1877–1878. From his correspondence with the sharif of Mecca, he concluded that Muslim "feeling" across Africa and Asia was sufficiently inflamed that a small event might "raise revolt." European governments should avoid "any and every measure which might excite fanaticism." The consul ominously noted that various Muslim nationalities were now in close correspondence with one another: "The organization seems complete and the union perfect, and restless spirits are ever moving in search of pretexts to raise complications."[232] Zohrab believed that the Hijaz was a key fulcrum on which this nebulous organization was based because of the Hajj. His reports to Foreign Secretary Lord Salisbury were framed to lay out for Salisbury "the importance of establishing British influence in the Hejaz on solid bases," an objective predicated on the sharif of Mecca's then-favorable disposition toward Britain.[233] Perhaps the tense international situation prompted Zohrab's agitated reports. He presented no firm evidence to support his statements and singularly failed to increase Britain's influence in the Hijaz. This type of imperial alarm regarding the Hijaz and the Hajj extended to Dutch officials as well, who had greater cause for concern, given their ongoing war against the Muslim Sultanate of Aceh.[234] Nevertheless, Zohrab's idea of employing secret agents to monitor the Hajj was summarily rejected; his superiors had little appetite for this type of surveillance.[235]

British officials held a variety of views about Muslim "intrigues" related to the Hajj. In 1881, an official in India noted that "there will always be Mahomedan dreams and machinations going on, and we cannot prevent them. Long before they can result in any practical danger we shall have notice of what is coming from enquiries in India. It would be a mistake to risk showing in the centre of the Mohamedan religious world that we are dreading and watching." This view, that such machinations were largely ephemeral and easily contained, buttressed wider arguments that the Hajj did not require extensive imperial surveillance.[236]

Elsewhere in the British empire, such as Cape Colony in South Africa, officials had more positive views of pilgrims that formed a stark contrast to the negative examples just described. Such viewpoints were based on location—South Africa was far away from the geopolitical stress points of imperial Asia, and the Muslim population of the Cape Colony was relatively small. Another factor was class; the average cost of the journey to the Hijaz was £300, which meant that most South African pilgrims were affluent.[237] In 1877, Julian Pameilots, a Foreign Office official, noted that Malays (descendants of slaves brought to the Cape by the Dutch after 1658), whom he glowingly described as a "most industrious race," had taken advantage of new steamship services established in the 1860s from the Cape to Zanzibar and Aden to head to Mecca in ever-increasing numbers. According to Pameilots, this development meant that Cape Malays traveling to perform the Hajj would "increase their attachment to the British government and . . . contrast the liberty and justice they enjoy under British rule with the treatment they everywhere else received."[238] Indeed, in 1874, the governor of the Cape, after representations from local imams, gave that year's party of Malay pilgrims a letter asking British officials to give them any assistance they needed during their travels.[239] These examples illustrate the diversity of British official perspectives on pilgrims; the Cape's governor saw pilgrims as respectable subjects, and in Pameilots's opinion, the Hajj had the effect of making these Malay pilgrims more loyal to Britain instead of turning them into anticolonial activists through exposure to anticolonial and pan-Islamic ideas in Mecca.

By contrast, from his desk in Britain's Jidda consulate, Zohrab saw the Hijaz, through the medium of the Hajj, as the "focus of Moslem thought and the nucleus from which radiate ideas, advice, instructions, and dogmatical interpretation." Zohrab thought that some of the thousands of pilgrims who were British subjects went on Hajj for political purposes because Mecca was "free from European intrusion" and a safe area for meetings and exchanging ideas. Because Britain did not monitor who went on Hajj from India, meetings could be convened "at which combinations hostile to us may form without our knowing anything till the shell bursts in our medst [*sic*]." Zohrab argued that a Muslim agent at Mecca would allow Britain to obtain valuable intelligence to preempt "hostile combinations."[240] The dramatic tone of Zohrab's reports and others like his needs to be placed in a wider context and should not be taken as representative of a monolithic imperial viewpoint. Of course, one of Zohrab's roles was to ascertain any threats to British interests that emanated from the Hijaz, but the lack of concrete details on the threats he outlined shows the uncertainty of the information at his disposal. These reports need to be read against his proposal for a Muslim agent and how Britain's ability to acquire further information on the pilgrimage was impossible without recourse to Muslim employees.

Britain's use of Muslim agents to monitor pilgrims has attracted scholarly attention. Michael Christopher Low has concluded that the idea that men such as Razzack were spies, defined in the sense that they obtained information considered secret or confidential without the permission of the person who possessed that information, seems on balance highly unlikely, although Razzack's position enabled him to launch a variety of investigations in Mecca.[241] In October 1885, the doctor sent the consular interpreter and the Indian Muslim vice-consul at Hudayda, who was on Hajj in Mecca, to check on three men from Bhopal who were also performing the pilgrimage. Razzack persuaded the Ottoman authorities to agree to seize these men's papers and to allow the Hudayda vice-consul to examine them. Only the Ottoman authorities were aware of British involvement in this affair, a vital prerequisite given the presence of British consular officials in Mecca. Although police officers in India alleged that the ex-nawab of Bhopal, Siddiq Hassan Khan, one of the founders of the reformist Ahl al-Hadith movement in India, used these men to correspond with the Mahdi in Sudan, nothing was uncovered except a collection of books by Siddiq Hassan Khan. The governor of Mecca ordered *'ulama* to examine the books, which were pronounced "distinctly Wahhabical." The three men left for India without further harassment. It was in fact Razzack who proposed further surveillance of pilgrims: "No doubt there are many disaffected people from India, relics of 1857 and the later Wahhabi movement, residing at Mecca who are in constant correspondence with their friends in India; and if some sort of secret surveillance were kept over these people at Mecca it would perhaps lead to some important discoveries."[242] Despite Razzack raising such specters, his employers did not, in this case, follow up on the doctor's suggestions.

The idea of British-employed Muslim secret agents in the Ottoman empire was raised again in 1896. Although this was never more than a proposal, it reignited debates about the utility of Muslim agents to monitor the Hajj. Officials in the British embassy in Istanbul suggested that secret agents should collect information on relations among certain figures in Istanbul, Jidda, Basra, and Baghdad as a useful way to track Muslim "intrigues." This was scotched because it was impossible to locate a suitable candidate.[243] The suggestion resurrected an idea from 1881 to have "Muslim detectives" at Mecca. At that time, this was seen as impractical because no "suitable" Indian Muslim would go on Hajj as a spy, a view that the Indian government continued to hold in 1896.[244] Furthermore, by 1896, Hussein, the vice-consul at Jidda, was seen as a man of "intelligence and fidelity" who could provide information on the Hajj.[245] Hussein was given money from India's secret-service budget, and Lord Cromer in Egypt was asked to assist with the expenses because of the number of Egyptian pilgrims.[246] So if Muslim officials in the

Jidda consulate received secret-service money, did they spy on pilgrims? The documentary record is inconclusive, but it seems very unlikely. One government of India official's remark that "overactivity in sedition hunting is likely to do a good deal of mischief" is probably the best description of Britain's attitude toward monitoring the pilgrimage.[247]

By the end of the nineteenth century, British officials settled into an acquiescent attitude toward the Hajj's role as a channel for Muslim interaction. In 1896, for example, when the nizam of Hyderabad's brother-in-law wanted to buy a pilgrim hostel in Mecca, Hyderabad's resident asked his superiors for help, and Calcutta agreed to ask the Ottomans to relax an 1867 law that barred foreigners from buying property. One official astutely observed that although measures that would increase connections between Hyderabad and other Muslim states might be "objectionable," the pilgrimage gave ample opportunities for such relationships already; a house in Mecca owned by a Hyderabadi notable would make "little or no difference."[248] Of course, other actions beyond house buying might have provoked British ire. Nevertheless, it appears that British officials had realized that their ability to counter "intrigues" by pilgrims in Mecca during the Hajj was limited. In any case, it seems fair to conclude that the British empire had not been particularly adversely affected by any such plans that were concocted during the Hajj or in Mecca and Medina in this period.[249]

The British example can be compared with the Netherlands through considering the views of Orientalist and colonial official Christiaan Snouck Hurgronje, who lived in Jidda and Mecca from 1884 to 1885. Snouck Hurgronje was probably the most perceptive European observer of the Hajj and its role in regard to anticolonial, pan-Islamic, and conspiratorial endeavors. He was attuned to the multiplicity of official views on the Hajj, writing about how one Dutch official spoke of Hajjis as "the plague of native society" and stated that Hajjis encouraged Indonesians to "sow resistance, sow fanaticism," whereas another official saw this perception "as the invention of clumsy colleagues" and described Hajjis as "sober, orderly people."[250] Snouck Hurgronje thought that "Europeans greatly exaggerated the city's role as a breeding ground for anti-colonial agitation in the Islamic world." He believed that the overwhelming majority of pilgrims returned to their homes "not as rebels but as sheep." However, there were a small number of "conspirators" in Mecca who used the Hajj's "freedom" to spread propaganda to pilgrims, and some pilgrims returned from Mecca with "pan-Islamic tendencies which can easily develop into fanaticism."[251] We cannot discount these interesting and in some cases significant characters, but analyzing Britain's relationship with the pilgrimage primarily through the prism of their activities obscures the fact that most pilgrims were not engaged in anticolonial and pan-Islamic machinations and conspiracies.

Conclusion

Snouck Hurgronje's remarks on the Hajj demonstrate how it had become a more prominent subject of European imperial attention during this period. In Britain's case, initial disinterest and dismissal—especially in relation to the plight of poor Indian pilgrims—were overturned by the 1865 cholera epidemic, which precipitated a much greater British interest and involvement in the Hajj. However, medical and sanitary matters were only one aspect of Britain's burgeoning relationship with the pilgrimage. Destitute pilgrims and Muslims within and outside Britain's emergent Hajj administration also played an important role in shaping the reaches and limits of the empire's association with the Hajj, as this chapter has shown. British attitudes toward the Hajj were ambiguous and complex, as is exemplified by officials' engagement with the destitute-pilgrim issue. The paradoxes inherent in stances that stressed noninterference with religious practice, derived from a fear of potential Muslim unrest, alongside voices that demanded further intervention in the pilgrimage led to a state of indecision. In practice, however, this meant anything but disengagement, as is shown by the large amount of time and effort British officials and Muslim interlocutors and employees spent on the subject, attested to by the capacious volume of Hajj-related documentation. The figure of the destitute pilgrim in the Hijaz demanded, for some, a solution to rescue British prestige, but it was complicated by the shibboleth of noninterference and, critically, the solicitation of Muslim opinion on any potential action on this matter by the colonial state. Muslims were important in reinforcing Britain's noninterventionist policy and, through the employment of Muslims as an integral part of the empire's nascent Hajj bureaucracy, pushed the further evolution of Britain's pilgrimage administration, and called for a more activist approach to the Hajj. These Muslims who worked within the imperial framework were no stooges of empire; they possessed agency, had some influence over Britain's engagement with the Hajj, and greatly complicated the empire's general principle of noninterference in religious practice. Muslim employees and their work in operating Britain's administration of pilgrims, and wider debates within various bureaucracies on matters such as the religious validation for destitute pilgrims' travels, contributed to the increased role of Islamic religious practice in imperial governance. After Queen Victoria's 1897 Diamond Jubilee, marked in Jidda by the formal inauguration of a destitute-pilgrim fund at the British consulate, the horizons of Britain's Muslim empire widened as British forces conquered Sudan and Nigeria; India was no longer the sole focus of Britain's association with the Hajj.

3

Pilgrimage in the Edwardian Era, 1901–1914

Introduction

By the time Queen and Kaisar-i-Hind (Empress of India) Victoria died on January 22, 1901, Britain's inner empire of territories with large Muslim populations included India, Malaya, Egypt, Kenya, Zanzibar, Nigeria, and Sudan. In these areas, British rule or predominance had destroyed, displaced, or subjugated established Muslim regimes within a few short decades: khedival rule in Egypt; the Zanzibar sultanate; the Mahdist state in Sudan; and the Sokoto caliphate in Northern Nigeria. These acquisitions formed part of a dramatic worldwide acceleration of European expansion, exemplified by the partition of Africa. As administrations were established or modified in these new territories of Britain's Muslim empire, it was striking that the pilgrimage received early attention from officials—the Hajj was a ritual that was accorded a certain importance. This chapter will analyze Britain's interactions with the Hajj during the Edwardian period using case studies from Nigeria, Sudan, Hyderabad, and Bombay. These cases highlight the importance of local and regional geographies in studying Britain's interactions with the Hajj and the need to focus on several local examples that provide the necessary empirical detail to support assertions and arguments; otherwise, there is a danger of overgeneralization in a study of this nature that covers broad geographic areas. This chapter also underscores how India was far from a homogeneous administrative entity, and it demonstrates the diversity of the Hajj experience within that colony from multiple perspectives. Hyderabad possessed a sophisticated pilgrimage administration, and it facilitated the Hajj for its subjects and other Muslims with little reference to Britain but took advantage of the princely state's location within the broader imperial framework. The complex administration of the Hajj from the port city of Bombay was largely run by Muslims, coordinated with various elements of the city's Muslim civil society. These case studies are illustrative examples of how Britain's Muslim empire worked in practice. The time span of the archival sources on Hyderabad and Bombay is mainly limited to the Edwardian period, hence their inclusion here. This chapter will conclude with an examination of the destitute-pilgrim issue and its intersection with international politics and imperial prestige on the eve of the First World War, the high-water mark of British attempts to resolve this phenomenon before that conflict radically changed the pilgrimage's political landscape.

The Hajj from Nigeria and Sudan

There are some unexpected parallels when one considers the Hajj from the Sahara and Sahel region of Africa alongside the Indian Ocean world. Reflecting the numerous studies of the Indian Ocean, the Sahara and Sahel can perhaps be viewed as an inland sea, a vast space crisscrossed by multiple routes, along which moved goods, ideas, and a variety of people—pilgrims, scholars, slaves, and economic migrants.[1] Both spaces were characterized by a dense web of connections that spanned the Muslim world, encompassing both the land and the sea.

Considering these two spaces together brings into sharper focus comparative examples of the Hajj from Africa and the Indian Ocean world. In Sudanic Africa and on the Indian Ocean, those with money had easier modes of travel—on camel, the "ship of the desert," and in first-class cabins on pilgrim ships. By contrast, poor pilgrims from Africa walked the route; those from South Asia traveled third class or as stowaways on ships. One important common feature of the Hajj from Nigeria, Sudan, and India was the figure of the destitute pilgrim. However, as will be elucidated in Chapters 4, 5, and 6, the methods whereby various colonial governments perceived and responded to this type of pilgrim differed widely and changed over time. Colonial states were ultimately powerless to prevent poor pilgrims from traveling to Mecca; although Indian pilgrims were required to purchase return tickets for a brief period during the mid-1920s, many circumvented this by traveling overland or avoiding traveling on designated pilgrim ships from Bombay; poor African pilgrims simply avoided all places of colonial authority, such as border posts, during their journey.[2] Such practices were perhaps easier in Africa because colonial states there were skeletal, possessed rudimentary administrative structures with limited European personnel, and were held ultimately by the threat of violence aided by modern weaponry.[3]

In Northern Nigeria, Mecca was central to certain segments of Nigerian Muslim society. In the opening years of the twentieth century, the remnants of the Sokoto caliphate rejected Christian rule and embarked on a *hijra* (migration after the example of the Prophet Muhammad in 622 CE) to Mecca, far beyond British control. This flight of people disintegrated in the savannas when they were attacked by British forces in 1903. The imposition of British rule was seen as an apocalyptic sign and led many who had not joined the initial *hijra* to set off toward Mecca to perform Hajj in the years after 1903. These people were dubbed "irreconcilables" by the colonial authorities.[4] British officials in Nigeria were concerned that the Hajj might act as a transmitter of ideas from anti-British Nigerians and others in Mecca back to the colony, an attitude similar to official conceptions of Indian rebels from 1857 in Mecca. Therefore, Nigerian authorities requested regular reports from the British consul at Jidda. In the words of Northern Nigerian official John Morley, it was thought "important to know what sort of influences they [pilgrims] might be subject to once they were there [in Mecca]."[5]

As alien rulers in an unfamiliar environment, officials were struck by this phenomenon of thousands leaving Nigeria for the long journey to Mecca every year. W. P. Newby, resident in Bornu, near Nigeria's northeastern border, reported a "steady flow" of pilgrims eastward, around 5,000 during 1906–1907, whom he castigated as "malcontents, of whom we are well rid."[6] But the continued outflow of pilgrims, despite their apparent hostility to British rule, was unsettling to officials who saw it as a drain on the colony's labor supply, similar to Richard Burton's conception of the Hajj from India in the early 1850s.[7] In 1907–1908, when another 5,005 pilgrims were recorded as leaving Bornu, only 400 pilgrims were recorded as returning, a trend seen as "not very satisfactory."[8] Officials were evidently unaware of the growing trend of Nigerian pilgrims working along the route to Mecca to fund their journeys, especially in Sudan. This gave rise to *takayrna* communities across Sudanic Africa and to the phenomenon of what Bawa Yamba has termed "permanent pilgrims."[9] As Baz Lecocq has argued, this combination of travel for Hajj and labor migration was possible because it was permitted in the Maliki school of *fiqh*, religious law, which was followed by many West African Muslims. This school also absolved pilgrims of the responsibility of having the means for their return journey.[10] In this period, the increase in the number of Britain's pilgrim-subjects and their increasingly diverse geographic origins coincided with the consolidation of Ottoman imperial control in the Hijaz, most notably through the extension of the Hijaz railway from Damascus to Medina in 1908. This project had an international dimension through the involvement of Muslims in Asia and Africa in fund-raising for the project, and one of its aims was to improve the Ottoman empire's standing among Muslims worldwide, although the extent of its impact on African Muslims remains understudied.[11]

Overall, the rise of a colonial "peace" in this period was beneficial for the security of pilgrims and travelers across Sudanic Africa and, more widely, facilitated the spread of Islam.[12] In Sudan and Nigeria, as in India, Muslims took advantage of the boundaries and infrastructures of colonial states.[13] The initial period of British rule in Sudan was significant because it broke the prohibitions on Hajj by the rulers of the Mahdist state. This revived the main routes through Sudan toward the Red Sea ports of Suakin and Massawa, which were a conduit for pilgrim traffic from across Sudanic Africa. Initially inadvertently and later as a definite policy, British authorities facilitated the Hajj for African Muslims.[14] Although these policies were partly designed to dampen the possibility of resistance due to resentment of non-Muslim rule, British efforts to legitimate their rule over Muslims by facilitating the pilgrimage had similarities to the policies undertaken by the Ottomans and the Mughals, outlined in Chapter 1, which sought to assist pilgrims in order to buttress the political and religious legitimacy of these empires.

The mercurial Sudanese ruler Muhammad Ahmad, known as the Mahdi, prohibited the pilgrimage for his subjects. This policy caused General Charles Gordon in Khartoum to inform the Mahdi in 1884 that he wanted to reopen the pilgrimage route through the country. The Mahdi rejected this, seeing Gordon's idea as an "impropriety" because he was not Muslim; he argued that Gordon should accept Islam first before engaging in discussions related to Islamic practice.[15] Since the Mahdi's emergence as a charismatic millenarian leader and his polity's rapid growth since 1883, the number of pilgrims had nevertheless increased. The Mahdist movement recruited pilgrims into its armies, arguing that the Hajj had been replaced by jihad.[16] The closure of the main pilgrimage route through Sudan had a detrimental economic impact on the Hijaz.[17] Therefore, it was unsurprising that the sharif of Mecca was distressed by news that khalifa Abdullahi, the Mahdi's successor, had reaffirmed the prohibition on Hajj for his subjects. Instead, the Hajj had been replaced by a pilgrimage to the Mahdi's tomb in Omdurman. Abdullahi was concerned about Egyptian and British steamships on the Red Sea, many of which carried pilgrims, and the possibility of pilgrims engaging in espionage against the Mahdist state.[18] An anxiety that pilgrims could be spies was not confined to European officials. The khalifa's decision did not go uncontested in Sudan. In response to this policy, in the late 1880s Abu Jummayza gathered together a large, anti-Mahdist following from the Masalit tribe and African pilgrims who found the route to Mecca blocked in western Sudan. Despite the Mahdist prohibition, many pilgrims still managed to make their way across Sudan to the Hijaz.[19]

In the initial years after Britain established a fragile hold over Sudan, the movements of pilgrims across Sudan on their way to and from the Hijaz caused alarm among officials. This reaction was partly based on the bloody process of "pacification" after the reconquest, when British soldiers and officials in the western Bahr al-Ghazal faced resistance from West African pilgrims who were trying to reach Mecca.[20] Prominent Islamic notables were of particular interest to the British. One example was the proposed itinerary of Muhammad al-Mahdi al-Sanusi, leader of the Sanussiyya Sufi order, who intended to travel from Cyrenaica through Sudan on his way to perform the Hajj in 1901. Governor-General Sir Reginald Wingate wrote to his superior, Lord Cromer, consul-general in Egypt, that al-Sanusi's travels "might probably raise the entire country." In Wingate's view, the Mahdist state's destruction had not diminished Sudanese beliefs that "the 'expected Mahdi' will eventually come and many of them believe the Senussi is the genuine article." Wingate believed that al-Sanusi was capable of sparking instability further afield; his appearance in the Hijaz would "signal" an Arab revolt.[21]

Sufism was a specific concern for imperial authorities in Northeast Africa in this period. Many officials viewed these orders as dangerous to imperial rule, and it became a priority for the colonial state to gather intelligence on them. In remote areas under nominal British control, such as the Western Desert that covered Egypt and northeastern Sudan, Sufi networks were this landscape's predominant feature. Although by 1914 officials in Sudan had co-opted orders such as the Khatmiyya into the apparatus of imperial rule, Sufism was still regarded with some ambivalence.[22] Although Sufi orders adhered to particular interpretations of Islam, the example of al-Sanusi's intention to perform the pilgrimage demonstrated that this Sufi order viewed the Hajj as an important part of Islamic practice.[23] British officials in Sudan, constantly concerned by the prospect of potential turmoil in this newly acquired territory, were quick to see pilgrimage journeys such as al-Sanusi's as a threat.

However, as British rule in Sudan became embedded, officials' reactions to the pilgrimage became more varied. A letter from Sudan's acting governor-general in 1908 reported the governor of Kordofan Province's disturbing news that there was a "pilgrim army on its way to Mecca." On leave in Britain, Wingate, however, found the claim a "gross exaggeration." Like his counterparts in India, Wingate believed that pilgrims' travels were "not a matter on which we can justly interfere" and thought it "impossible for the Government to undertake to give any specific facilities" to pilgrims. Wingate counseled the acting governor-general that "it is not a bad plan to consult some of the well-known and other religious authorities in Sudan. . . . They generally have their own methods of dealing with these questions and very often there is a good deal to commend them."[24] As was the case in India, officials in Sudan sought advice from a small cross section of their Muslim subjects on the pilgrimage.

The results of consultations with Sudanese Muslim notables were a central reason why the colonial state in Sudan suddenly became more engaged with the Hajj. An administrative apparatus was established shortly before the First World War. This was not directed just at Sudanese pilgrims; the majority of pilgrims in the territory were from West Africa, mainly Northern Nigeria. "Pilgrim villages" were built at the main departure port of Suakin in 1908, in response to the phenomenon of temporary settlements appearing every year around pilgrimage time, and the government granted an annual subsidy of 3,000 Egyptian pounds every year from 1911 to 1913 to pay for pilgrims' quarantine fees and their stays in the villages. While there, pilgrims resided under the authority of *shaykhs*, some of whom were from Nigeria, not British officials.[25] Pilgrims were also inadvertently aided by government policies through railway construction in Sudan, which enabled richer pilgrims to take the train to get to the Red Sea ports more quickly, and those who could not afford tickets walked along the train tracks. When the railway line from Suakin to Khartoum was completed, pilgrim numbers from Sudan leaped from 1,227 in 1905 to over 4,000 in 1906.[26] Similar increases in numbers accompanied the construction of the railway line linking Port Sudan on the Red Sea coast with El Obeid in Kordofan between 1906 and 1911.[27]

Initial official ignorance and wariness toward pilgrims in Nigeria and Sudan, alongside a disinclination to involve the colonial state in administering these pilgrims' journeys, gave way to greater official engagement with the Hajj, especially in Sudan. This was precipitated by officials' consultations with Muslim religious leaders. Britain's facilitation of the Hajj in Sudan formed part of a wider project concerned with encouraging what officials termed "orthodox" Islam as a way to gain the support of Sudanese Muslims, many of whom had resented the Mahdist prohibition of the pilgrimage. Equally important, the British administration wanted to encourage *takayrna* pilgrims from West Africa to work as cheap laborers in Sudan on their way to and from the Hijaz, given Sudan's labor shortage.[28] Officials believed that these positive policies on the Hajj enhanced British prestige in Sudan and beyond, especially among pilgrims who traveled through Sudan from French colonial territories.[29] Political stability and labor concerns were the twin markers of Britain's engagement with the Hajj from Sudan and Nigeria. By contrast, British officials in colonial East Africa were "little concerned" about Islam. This viewpoint, combined with the fact that this space was "lightly administered" except in some areas, such as Kenya's so-called White Highlands and Buganda, meant that officials were hardly interested in the small numbers of pilgrims from coastal areas, most of whom were part of Hadhrami networks.[30] Issues of migration, subsidy, and political legitimacy were also evident thousands of miles east in India's Deccan, in the administration of the Hajj from Hyderabad, India's most prominent Muslim princely state.

Hyderabad: Muslim Administration of the Hajj within the Framework of British Paramountcy

Despite its political position, Hyderabad's organization of the pilgrimage under nizam Asaf Jah VI (1867–1911) was notable for the almost nonexistent involvement of his political masters, the British. This highlights the complex variety of Britain's interactions with the pilgrimage within its Muslim empire; in this case, there was overwhelming Muslim agency in the administration of the Hajj from this princely state. Existing studies of the Hajj make virtually no mention of this princely state, although there is a growing body of scholarship on Hyderabad and the princely states that has sought to rehabilitate these polities from their marginal position in South Asian historiography. The 562 princely states constituted 20 percent of the area and population of India as a whole. This section contributes to arguments that some princely states, far from being "museums of a traditional India," should rather be seen as more dynamic polities that were part of a wide range of religious, regional, and imperial networks.[31]

In contrast to British India, Hyderabad sponsored pilgrims to perform the Hajj. In the 1880s, for example, the nizam issued at least 500 to 600 free return tickets for the Bombay–Jidda voyage a year.[32] The files of the nizam's government are filled with petitions requesting funding for journeys to perform the Hajj. Hyderabad was an important nodal point for Indian Muslims who had settled in the Hijaz, had returned to India, and then wished to travel back to Arabia. Hyderabad's Hajj administration, like that of British India, was not immune to complaints and criticism. The role of Muslims as intercessors to facilitate the pilgrimage for their coreligionists was another parallel trend. Although only a small number of Urdu files on the pilgrimage were accessible from the local archives in Hyderabad, they have never been used before and provide a rich new perspective on how the Hajj was administered in this part of Britain's Muslim empire.

The nizam's financial generosity toward pilgrims was one component of his legitimacy as a Muslim ruler, despite his political emasculation under the British. It was an important way of rewarding service by government officials, who were granted leave and six months advance salary before they left for the Hijaz.[33] The pilgrimages of soldiers in Hyderabad's army were also subsidized, a policy mirrored in British actions during the First World War, discussed in Chapter 4. For example, armed with a supporting letter from his commanding officer, Mirza Abdullah Beg had "been intending to go on hajj for many years" and wanted to take his wife and his sister, who also possessed a "deep desire" to perform the pilgrimage, "but poverty and financial crisis [were] a hurdle" to their goal.[34] Mirza Abdullah Beg was given tickets and six months' salary for his family's Hajj.[35] Other letters from men of Hyderabad's First Lancers are also referred to in the correspondence; like Beg, they probably received assistance.[36]

Muslims outside the realm of state administration and the army also sent petitions to the nizam to fund their Hajj.[37] Richer Hyderabadis often recommended poor prospective pilgrims to the nizam for aid.[38] The state's support often extended to ship's tickets and expenses for the round trip to Mecca. Final authorization for the release of tickets and funds for poor pilgrims rested with the nizam.[39] In 1900, R 30,000 was allocated for this religious patronage.[40] However, the government's funds for sending people on Hajj were not limitless. One official wrote in 1901 that "if each [pilgrim] is given 200 rupees the government cannot afford it. The government could manage the extra expenditure if there were one or two persons. . . . It is not possible for the department to help such a large number of people."[41] Nevertheless, in 1908, the nizam's government paid 300 pilgrims' expenses.[42] This number, which was somewhat less than the "thousands of poor people" cited in petitioners' letters as a hopeful indicator that they might receive Hajj expenses, was probably representative for this period.[43] This financial patronage had a complex administrative structure: for example, in 1897, a maulvi named Mubeen was given R 2,000 for his Hajj, which came from the government's "hospitality fund" rather than its "charity fund" because otherwise "many poor hajjis will be deprived of this benefit."[44] The nizam's subjects also requested assistance for other schemes related to the Hajj; Sardar Ali Khan wanted approval and funding to construct a government rest house in Bombay for pilgrims, to be named the Lord Minto Pilgrim Guest House because of Minto's efforts to abolish certain quarantine regulations that affected pilgrims.[45]

The nizam's largesse attracted Muslims from across India and beyond to Hyderabad who hoped to perform the Hajj with his financial assistance. One successful applicant, Sheikh Abdul Baqi, wrote in 1901 that he was "a poor man and a stranger here. . . . It is hoped that provisions for the journey will be provided by the government. . . . The caravan is about to leave today or tomorrow. . . . Now I have come to you and beg you to provide me with the same help and provisions that are given to other people. I would be highly obliged to you and will remember you in my prayers."[46] Another family from Bengal who could barely afford the train fare to Hyderabad arrived "with a noble expectation that the government would provide us with the expenses of the journey. We are empty handed. We are unable to fulfil our desire without the help of the government. So, we kindly request the government to have a sympathetic eye on us and provide us with the ticket to Mecca and provisions for the journey as well."[47] Two families had traveled from Bukhara in central Asia to Hyderabad in the hope of accomplishing their "dream of going to the holy House of Allah."[48] The members of one family who had waited in Hyderabad for over a year in the hope of receiving funds from the nizam's government assured the authorities that if their application was successful, they would "pray for the long life and prosperity of the government."[49] As the departure date for the government of Hyderabad's pilgrim party approached, the number of petitions for assistance increased. Ten "confused and embarrassed" people wrote collectively to the nizam because they were "not able to collect together the means for the journey and other expenses" and hoped that they would benefit, like previous pilgrims, from the government charity fund for performing Hajj.[50] The nizam's support for poor pilgrims meant that Hyderabad became an important transit point for those from South and central Asia en route to Mecca.

Although Hyderabad was part of Britain's Indian empire, it was perceived as an authentically "Islamic state" by some Muslim religious travelers who were originally from India but lived in Mecca and Medina. They then migrated to Hyderabad and, for various reasons, wished to return to the Hijaz. Although some petitions do not directly mention the Hajj, the nizam's distribution of *zakat* to these migrants was a further method of bolstering his legitimacy in the wider Muslim world: recipients would give blessings on the nizam's behalf at the Ka'ba and doubtless inform other pilgrims in Mecca of his generosity. Meccan resident Haji Abdul Latif and his family migrated to Hyderabad, "having heard of this Islamic state," but after a year they wanted to return to Mecca. The government authorized that Latif could receive tickets for his family and a small amount of money for expenses.[51] The nizam's reputation for *zakat* was the reason two men cited for migrating from Mecca; however, they had faced many "difficulties" and wished to return to the Holy City. If the nizam gave them money to journey back, they would pray for him at the Ka'ba.[52] Economic concerns such as Mecca's lack of "natural and economic resources" had caused Abdul Aziz and his family to incur "huge debts" to travel to Hyderabad "with the hope of receiving benefits from the kind generosity of the government that is well known to everyone." Aziz requested money to return to Mecca and stated that "a virtuous deed earns many rewards in comparison to other places."[53] Qadmi al-Hajj Abdul Latif Muhammad Hussein and his family, originally from Mecca, asked for assistance to perform the Hajj and would "visit the holy Ka'ba and pray to Allah for you [the nizam]" if he received *zakat* for this purpose.[54] Hussein's experience of "oppression" from the Hijazi authorities had prompted his migration to Hyderabad, but his twelve-year sojourn in Hyderabad had proved difficult: "I am living a miserable life. I had to sell the basic articles of the house for food. I have three boys, two girls and a wife. Sometimes we have to starve. . . . The climate of this city did not suit us and we fell ill." Officials strongly supported his application, having found Hussein's case "deserving."[55] Hyderabad was an important part of a wider web of connections related to religious—and economic—travel between India and the Hijaz.

Hyderabad's connections to these broad networks of religious travel through the nizam's support for poor pilgrims went even further than the Hajj and also included Shi'i pilgrimage sites in Najaf and Karbala and *ziyara* to the Prophet's tomb at Medina. Sayyedani, a widow, wished to visit Karbala, but because of a "financial crisis" she was unable to afford the travel expenses.[56] The greater prominence the Prophet Muhammad had among Muslims in this period probably accounts for the manner in which petitioners prioritized visiting his tomb above performing Hajj.[57] For example, Muhammad Qasim Ali wrote: "I have been nourishing a great desire for a long time to visit the Holy Tomb of Prophet Muhammad and Mecca and Medina and ultimately perform hajj."[58] A Naqshbandi Sufi successfully applied for funding to travel to Medina, where he would "observe retirement in the mosque." His devotion to the Prophet Muhammad was clear: "I am growing impatient and nothing is here to satisfy my thirst ever since I have been told that the Prophet is calling me to Medina."[59] The nizam was a vital source of religious patronage for the pious across the Muslim world for several religious pilgrimages.

Placing these records in a broader context, we can see how they contributed to Hyderabad's status as "a cosmopolitan centre of migration from many directions."[60] From the late nineteenth century, the state was seen by some Muslims as a haven; the prince of Shihr and al-Mukalla from the Hadhramaut in southern Arabia and many Somalis, known as *habashis*, settled there. Afghans, Arabs, and Africans were employed in the state's army.[61] To travelers such as Wilfrid Scawen Blunt, the city of Hyderabad was "like a great flower bed, crowded with men and women in bright dresses, and with a fine cheerful air of independence, more Arab than Indian. . . . Instead of the squalid back streets and the pauper population of native Madras . . . many men carry swords in their hands, one sees . . . camels in the streets."[62] The policies and proclivities of the nizams forged a variety of close connections between Hyderabad and the Muslim world, constituting a distinctively Islamic geography that existed within the British imperial framework.

Before Hyderabadis and those aided by the nizam arrived in the Hijaz, Bombay was the main city on these pilgrims' itineraries, and praise for the princely state's pilgrimage administration in the port was lacking from some Indian Muslims. This sharply contrasted with the views of some British officials who consistently commented on the well-organized Hyderabadi pilgrimage, lamenting that British India did not follow Hyderabad's example.[63] In 1908, a "well-wisher of the government" sent a complaint about the behavior of the nizam's agents in Bombay. The complainant alleged that Hyderabadi pilgrims had to pay the agents extra to certify their free passage tickets by stamping their chits, and he claimed that "the chits of the poor are seized forcefully" and were sold to shipping agents. The "well-wisher" hoped that the nizam's government would "take actions against this evil deed and help the poor to be free from the clutches of tyranny."[64] Another Hyderabadi, Fazil Muraj, accused the nizam's agents of keeping pilgrims waiting for days outside their office, and two policemen were needed to prevent this group of pilgrims from storming the office. Muraj argued that the poverty of pilgrims allowed people to treat them badly, and he thought that Hyderabad's Hajj administration was unsatisfactory.[65]

The purpose of Muraj's letter, however, was a business proposal to offer himself as an intermediary for organizing the Hyderabadi Hajj from Bombay. His "influence" with a British steamer company meant that he could arrange passages for Hyderabad's pilgrims on favorable terms. This would lead to savings and enable "the great Lord [the nizam] to send more hajjis."[66] One official caustically noted that it was "very bad to complain against honest and able government employees," and that Muraj would have been wise to focus solely on his proposal.[67] Muraj's complaints provoked a lengthy rebuttal by the nizam's official or *madagar* in Bombay, Maulvi Gulam Mustafa, who dismissed the allegations as "hearsay." Mustafa faced many difficulties in the course of his work and had to use policemen to prevent non-Hyderabadi pilgrims from entering his office to acquire free tickets: "I was not authorised to give tickets to every poor person coming to me." He questioned how he could distribute tickets to over 450 people in three hours "in a foreign country." Mustafa's emphasis on Bombay being a foreign country is a telling indicator of how Hyderabadis conceptualized their state's place in the imperial system. In Mustafa's lengthy letter, he mentions the British authorities only once: "I have received a certificate from the Bombay Police Commissioner for good management."[68] Although Mustafa, as a government official, thought that there was no need to respond to Muraj's complaints, he advised that Muraj "must be made a member of the administrative committee for the hajj next year as he assures to arrange the tickets at a cheaper rate and provide hajjis with a more comfortable ship."[69] Furthermore, Muraj's brother, Gulam Ali, a justice of the peace in Bombay, had a role in "looking after those indigent persons who are sent to their homes by the government of Hyderabad."[70] Gulam Ali's position as a figure of some note within the colonial power structure may have accounted for the openness of Hyderabadi officials to his brother's involvement in the state's Hajj administration. Overall, however, Hyderabad appears in several ways as an entirely separate entity from British India within this Hajj-related correspondence.

One of the most significant features of the files that were accessible is the virtual absence of British involvement in Hyderabad's Hajj administration. The only evidence of Britain's presence in these files is the statements made by Maulvi Gulam Mustafa, a copy of British India's notification for the 1906 Hajj that set out arrangements for pilgrims in Bombay, a letter from Hyderabad's British resident about the management of hostels at Mecca and Medina, and a mention by the *madagar* that he liaised with the protector of pilgrims in Bombay on various matters related to pilgrims' departures to the Hijaz.[71] It appears that the Hajj was an important aspect of Hyderabad's administration that could be undertaken with hardly any reference to its British political masters.

How far this assessment can be applied to other Muslim princely states and their rulers can be ascertained through a brief examination of Bhopal, whose ruler Sikander Begum featured in Chapter 2. In 1903, her granddaughter, Sultan Jahan Begum, followed in her grandmother's footsteps and performed the Hajj, publishing her pilgrimage account in 1909. Her first step toward Mecca involved seeking permission from the government of India, a restriction that appears to have been in place since the early nineteenth century during East India Company rule, and one that seems to have applied only to princely rulers.[72] In this sphere, then, such rulers had less freedom in fulfilling their religious obligations than their subjects. Despite the begum's earnest statement that after her eight-month absence for Hajj she would "devote myself to the administration of my state, faithfully serving the government," the government of India ordered her to remain in the country and attend the Coronation Durbar of Edward VII on January 1, 1903. The begum left Bhopal only in November of that year.[73] This restriction must have galled the begum, given her desire since childhood to perform the Hajj—"the most cherished sentiment of my heart"—as well as her profound feelings about visiting the Prophet Muhammad's tomb, which she described as "the angel-cradled portal of the Light of the World, the Master of the Universe, the Intercessor for sinners, the Medium of the Faith, our Prophet (on whom descend the Blessings of God) . . . the heaven-domed shrine at Medina."[74] Perhaps one reason for the British-imposed restriction was the fragile governmental situation in Bhopal, which the begum frankly admitted in her account "resembled a tottering pillar," and she stated that "the condition of helplessness to which it had been reduced haunted me day and night."[75]

Although the timing of Sultan Jahan's pilgrimage was dictated by her British masters, she was able to effectively leverage her status as a princely ruler and faithful ally of the Raj to ensure that she secured special treatment regarding matters such as quarantine for pilgrims. A further letter to the government of India, republished in her account, asked for exemption from the usual quarantine procedures in India or for them to be undertaken in Bhopal. This was duly granted, and her party spent ten days just outside Bhopal in quarantine conditions while she enjoyed a special quarantine camp in Bhopal's royal gardens. A further missive requested exemption from quarantine at Kamaran Island "in consideration of my friendship with and fidelity to the British government."[76] Although the Ottoman authorities agreed to the government of India's request for the party's exemption, the outbreak of plague in Bhopal meant that some form of quarantine had to be observed. Consequently, the ship docked at the island of Bil Said near Jidda, where the begum spent an agreeable time.[77] Other arrangements befitting a princely ruler were also forthcoming. Railway officials were requested to get the royal train as close as possible to the pilgrim ship at Bombay so Jahan Begum and her female companions could exit on a palanquin directly onto the vessel. A guard of honor and a gun salute were also arranged for her arrival in Bombay. Lieutenant-Colonel Lawrence Impey, Bhopal's political agent, whose role now included travel arrangements for his charge, informed the begum that she would be given the same "honors, escort and customs facilities" that the sultan of Zanzibar received from the Ottoman government when he performed the Hajj.[78] Ensuring that the rulers in Britain's Muslim empire were well treated by all and sundry during their pilgrimage travels was yet another prop in reinforcing the attractiveness of being part of Britain's larger imperial realm—one that paid attention to important Islamic religious practices like the Hajj.

Bhopal had a highly developed administrative apparatus to support the pilgrimage caravan that accompanied the begum to the Hijaz. Bhopal, like Hyderabad, provided funds to its poorer Muslim subjects to enable them to go on Hajj—50 poor people were given funds to accompany the caravan. This was no small affair, consisting of around 300 people, strictly organized with its own set of rules that even stipulated how its participants should behave during their journey—"Even if rudeness should be met with, it should be overlooked and borne patiently, the holy object of the blessed journey being kept in mind." The caravan's personnel had strictly delineated roles that ranged from *mir-i-kafila*, head of the caravan, and *safir-i-consul*, responsible for negotiations with consular agencies, to interpreters, accountants, magistrates, postmen, and two muezzins to deliver the daily calls to prayer. The list of duties for the members of the caravan were equally wide ranging, including supervising embarkation and disembarkation, dealing with customs, arranging transport in Arabia, guard duties, running the traveling kitchen, and making purchases. Such was the caravan's scale that a whole ship, the SS *Akbar*, was chartered from Bombay.[79] Sultan Jahan said very little about her time in the Hijaz, perhaps to avoid what she felt would be repetition of her grandmother's account. However, the begum made some significant observations on the Hajj, emphasizing the pilgrimage's role in enabling men to "obtain information relating to the remotest parts of the world, which may be of use to them in their various pursuits," a by-product of the process whereby the pilgrimage drew people "together in a spiritual bond to obtain an insight into one another's social condition, and by comparing notes gather ideas for such social reforms as are necessary."[80] Like her grandmother, Sikander Begum, she presented the Hajj in her account under a reforming rubric. The colonial authorities loom larger in the begum of Bhopal's case than in that of Hyderabad because the begum was traveling as a royal personage beyond the borders of her state, and India, to the most important religious center of a foreign power. Through her status and loyalty to Britain, the begum enjoyed special treatment in some areas, but the power Britain held over her is demonstrated by the colonial authorities dictating when she could leave for Hajj—a clear interference with the performance of her religious practice.

In Hyderabad and beyond the realm of begums and nizams, the experience of a pilgrim from Hyderabad's professional class in this period provides valuable detail unavailable in the official government archives. The Hajj account of Mahomed Ullah ibn Salar Jung, a Cambridge alumnus, barrister, and chief justice at the nizam's court, illustrates his spiritual feelings about performing the pilgrimage, his *ziyarat* to shrines and religious studies in the Hijaz, his perceptions of the Hajj's administration, and the condition of poor pilgrims. Salar

Jung sailed from Bombay on a Peninsular and Oriental steamer in November 1909, changed ship at Aden, and then reached Suez. In Egypt, he "assumed the incognito" of a typical Indian pilgrim.[81] His dress could not disguise his connections; he met his "old friend" D. A. Cameron, consul-general of Alexandria, and the directors of the Khedival Mail Company.[82] Before Salar Jung left Suez for Jidda, he witnessed the departure of Egypt's khedive Abbas Hilmi (1892–1914) and his harem on a private yacht to begin their Hajj, the first by an Egyptian ruler since Muhammad 'Ali in the early nineteenth century.[83]

Despite the absence of epidemic disease at Jidda, Salar Jung's ship was quarantined at al-Tur lazaret for eight days.[84] This prompted harsh criticism of the European powers involved in this process: "Nobody exactly knows who is to blame for these haughty commands; but the pilgrims must put up with the inevitable. European powers treat the poor pilgrims most mercilessly, under the fallacious belief that they are taking sanitary precautions for the safety of Europe. We feel sure that similar treatment would never be tolerated by any non-Moslem people."[85] After his arrival in Jidda, he traveled to Mecca and stayed at a hostel owned by the nizam of Hyderabad.[86] He and his party "could not control our feelings" and immediately went to the Holy Mosque. Here, Salar Jung offered a corrective to Richard Burton's account. Instead of Muslims viewing the Ka'ba for the first time with "fear and awe," as Burton put it, Salar Jung wrote that instead "what true Moslems feel is the satisfaction of having performed *farz*, one's duty, and the satisfaction of standing, not so much in view of a house of stone and mortar, but in the appointed place."[87] Salar Jung was incensed at Burton's prejudiced comments. In response to Burton's remark that "lying to Orientals is meat and drink and the roof that shelters him," Salar Jung commented that "if his own actions can be excused on any ethical ground, the Oriental can plead the same."[88] The barrister used his pilgrimage account to present a new perspective on the pilgrimage for the English-speaking market he was appealing to.

The most spectacular part of Salar Jung's pilgrimage was observing the Egyptian khedive, who led his country's pilgrimage escort (estimated to have cost over £50,000) on the rain-soaked first day of the Hajj.[89] After the sermon at Mount Arafat, pilgrims rushed to their next destination, "singing joyous songs."[90] At the end of his pilgrimage, Salar Jung undertook many *ziyarat*, indicative of how the Hajj often formed only one element, albeit the major one, of pilgrims' religious travels in the Hijaz. His itinerary included the Jamat al-Ma'ala cemetery, where the son of the first caliph, Abu Bakr, and the cupola of Khadija, the Prophet Muhammad's first wife, were located, the *dar al-Khayzaran*, where Muhammad secretly prayed until his companion Umar's conversion to Islam, and the *bayt al-Nabi*, Khadija's house, where the Prophet Muhammad's daughter Fatima was born. In the house's corner was the place where the Prophet Muhammad used to recite his prayers. Salar Jung followed suit, providing further testament to the Prophet's importance to Muslims in this period.[91] The barrister also had time to undertake religious studies and became the pupil of several eminent scholars. He then sailed back to India via Suez.[92] Salar Jung's account demonstrates how pilgrims' experiences in the Hijaz often went beyond just performing the Hajj.

Salar Jung raised the issue of the treatment of poor pilgrims in the Hijaz in his account. He thought that they were a "much maligned and ill-treated class" who traveled to Mecca "at great risk to perform a religious duty and every facility should be afforded to them for the purpose." Salar Jung believed that "unsympathetic restrictions" such as quarantine should be abolished, and the savings should be invested in infrastructural and sanitation improvements in the Hijaz because "a pilgrim's difficulties begin as soon as he reaches Jeddah—he gets a drenching while landing, he drinks bad water, gets indifferent shelter, no proper means of arranging to immediately start on journey to Mecca and his health suffers in consequence." In stark contrast, Salar Jung's only difficulties were sensitive skin due to desert sand and mosquito bites. After his Hajj rituals were complete, he bathed and then called on friends to sympathize with the problems they experienced during their pilgrimages.[93] The barrister's solutions to obviate the tribulations of the majority of pilgrims were a railway to Mecca, which he thought "easy to accomplish" because the Hijaz railway had reached Medina in 1908; giving Bedouins paid work during the Hajj season; and an improved harbor at Jidda.[94] Salar Jung, like his contemporaries, such as the begums of Bhopal, Muslim employees in Britain's colonial and imperial bureaucracies, and British officials and observers, brimmed with ideas for reforming the Hajj experience but remained powerless to enact them in light of Ottoman suzerainty over the Hijaz.

Salar Jung's account provides an important snapshot of the pilgrimage experience of someone from the professional classes in this period. Although his narrative underscores the Hajj's deep spiritual attraction, Salar Jung's recommendations for reforms of the administration of the pilgrimage in order to alleviate the difficulties faced by poorer pilgrims demonstrate this group's centrality to the overall pilgrimage experience.[95] Hyderabad and Britain facilitated the Hajj for their poorer subjects, albeit with different methods and motivations. For Britain, repatriating destitute pilgrims stranded in the Hijaz was a reactive measure. In stark contrast, the nizam's distribution of funds to poor Muslims before they left for the Hijaz was proactive. This policy no doubt enhanced Hyderabad's status as an "Islamic state" and contributed to Hyderabad's attractiveness to Muslim migrants. Britain's dominance over Hyderabad perhaps stimulated such religious patronage from the nizam. Using a range of fresh sources, this case study has illuminated a new dimension of the British empire's interactions with the Hajj in this period and lends further credence to the concept of a British Muslim empire. The case of Hyderabad underlines the power of Muslim agency in the administration of the pilgrimage; the hand of colonial officialdom was largely absent.

The Hajj from Bombay

It is a curious lacuna in existing works on Britain and the Hajj that none have examined Bombay in any extended manner, despite the fact that it was the main port of departure and arrival for pilgrims from India for most of the colonial period. Moreover, the numerous shipping routes that converged on Bombay meant that prospective pilgrims from central Asia, China, Iran, and even Africa, many of whom had no forms of documentation, ended up in the port.[96] Britain's association with the Hajj within its Muslim empire was far from confined to British colonial subjects. This section explores Britain's association with the Hajj through the prism of this major port city, examining Bombay's Hajj administration. It argues that the Bombay authorities and Muslim "civil society" generally worked together in an attempt to manage the enormous task of dealing with the annual influx of pilgrims to the port. This cooperation was underscored by the fact that the city's Hajj administration was mainly staffed by Muslims. An elaborate administrative apparatus was in place by 1914, with a dedicated protector of pilgrims who headed a Pilgrim Department, as well as a Hajj Committee. This apparatus was complemented by pilgrim hostels run by the authorities and private Muslim citizens, in addition to the vital involvement of the city's wider Muslim community, which, for example, provided iced water to pilgrims waiting on the wharves for their ships to Jidda. Although the authorities encouraged such private initiatives, significant amounts of public funds were invested in the city's pilgrimage administration and further afield. For example, in 1912, Bombay provided R 41,000 that year to Karachi when it was opened to pilgrim traffic.[97] The authorities' engagement with the pilgrimage covered innumerable aspects, which ranged from the protector of pilgrims' attempt to make "suitable" arrangements for ladies in purdah waiting to board pilgrim ships to officials drawing up a list of what should be supplied on each ship as part of the revised Pilgrim Ships Act 1895.[98]

Although British officials in Bombay had noted the annual phenomenon of departures and returns related to the Hajj since the 1850s, especially the fact that most pilgrims were poor and received material support from Bombay's Muslim population, the ritual became a subject of sustained official attention only from the mid-1870s onward.[99] One indication of this comes from the correspondence related to a petition by Golam Hussein Roghay for a monopoly over the port's pilgrim traffic. Roghay believed that Bombay's governor was already "undoubtedly aware" of the pilgrimage and its importance in Islam. To support his proposal, Roghay painted an evocative picture of how thousands of "innocent and ignorant" pilgrims newly arrived in Bombay were cheated by brokers of fake pilgrim tickets and boarded ships that deposited them near Bombay, not Jidda.[100] Roghay's petition was rejected, but he was told that administrative measures related to the Hajj were "under consideration" and were partly concerned with protecting pilgrims from brokers' fraudulent practices.[101] As owner of the Mahomedan Pilgrimage Agency, Roghay was interested in the government taking a more active role in pilgrimage administration, although he couched this in terms of pilgrims' interests.[102] In this case, piety and commerce were intertwined. Roghay's business associate unsurprisingly wrote in a supporting letter that government support was "indispensable to eradicate this evil" of dishonest pilgrim brokers and agents and was particularly necessary at railway stations, where pilgrims were met by "gangs of swindlers" who, "being men of low character are always prone to fights," which prevented Mahomedan Pilgrim Agency employees from distributing leaflets advertising the company.[103] These pleas prompted some official action; the authorities decided that the Railway Police should intervene to prevent pilgrims being defrauded by "unscrupulous persons."[104] The commercial concerns of the Mahomedan Pilgrimage Agency were one catalyst for colonial officialdom in the port to act in a less laissez-faire manner toward activities related to the pilgrimage.

Nevertheless, several years passed before Bombay's Hajj administration was placed on a more established footing with the creation of the post of protector of pilgrims in 1887. The protector, a Muslim, reported to Bombay's police commissioner and headed the Pilgrim Department, staffed by Muslims. Bombay's official involvement in the pilgrimage was an overwhelmingly Muslim enterprise on a vast scale. Thousands of pilgrims sailed for the Hijaz from Bombay each year: in 1909, 21,000 in total, of whom 13,000 arrived over seventeen days; the year after, some 18,000; and in 1911, nearly 23,000 because it was a Hajj *akbar.*[105] Consequently, the duties of the protector of pilgrims were wide ranging: coordinating the Pilgrim Department's "great pressure of work" during the season when pilgrims arrived in Bombay; visiting every vessel that returned from Jidda in order to liaise with ship's captains and doctors; receiving complaints from pilgrims; noting the Ottoman authorities' treatment of pilgrims; writing an annual report on the Hajj from Bombay; visiting hostels and other places where destitute pilgrims lodged and arranging repatriation to their homes across India; attending local hospitals to inquire about sick pilgrims; and answering inquiries from people who wanted news of lost relatives who had gone on Hajj. A further duty was answering queries from pilgrims, which entailed dealing with a large number of letters, telegrams, and postcards. These contained questions about sailing dates, railway stations, shipping companies, passage rates, hostels, vaccinations, expenses for the journey, pilgrim brokers, return tickets, passports, the quarantine period, depositing cash, the situation in Jidda, and provisions required for the journey.[106]

The protector of pilgrims was either a government employee or a private individual. From 1887 to 1912, the post was held by, respectively, a "well to do private individual," two police inspectors from the Criminal Investigation Department (CID), a native assistant to the political superintendent in Kathiawar, a managing clerk in a solicitor's office and member of the Hajj Committee, and a translator of Urdu, Arabic, and Persian in the Oriental Translator's Office in Bombay. S. M. Edwardes, Bombay's police commissioner, thought that it was essential that the protector be multilingual, come from a "respectable family," and be robust enough to deal with brokers, shipping agents, and the variety of pilgrims who came from across India and central Asia to Bombay.[107] The authorities sometimes made ill-advised appointments to the position. For example, in 1911 Muhammad Ibrahim Tungekar had to resign because he fell into "considerable public disrepute" due to his involvement in a court case. Edwardes drily noted that "needless to say, there was a woman at the bottom of the matter." Tungekar was prosecuted for adultery but managed initially to avoid censure through "buying off the husband."[108] Those who became the protector of pilgrims were not necessarily the men of piety that their title may have suggested.

The work of Bombay's Pilgrim Department was a complex logistical affair. Its task, condescendingly put by one protector of pilgrims, was to "render embarkation as easy as possible for hordes of helpless and illiterate pilgrims," a statement that demonstrated the centrality of indigent pilgrims to the department's work.[109] By 1912, the department consisted of the protector, a head clerk, three assistants, an interpreter, and a female superintendent. The head clerk dealt with the voluminous correspondence addressed to the protector, accompanied the protector on visits to hostels, hospitals, and docks, and was responsible for managing the assistants. The first assistant kept accounts of the estates of pilgrims who were hospitalized and those who had died in the Hijaz or Bombay, and handled correspondence from heirs of these deceased pilgrims. The second assistant was a typist who dealt with correspondence with pilgrims. The interpreter had the capacious role of reporting to the protector on "all occurrences happening among the pilgrims."[110] The female superintendent attended to the "comforts and well-being of all female pilgrims." In 1910, this was one of the few posts held by a non-Muslim, a Mrs. Currie, who was "very energetic" and fluent in Hindi.[111]

Musafirkhanas (pilgrim hostels), free to their guests and paid for by "trustees of Mahomedan gentlemen," had four police constables and six cleaners working in them, employed by the department.[112] There were also three government-run pilgrim hostels, and in 1910, the authorities further augmented existing arrangements by establishing a semitemporary camp for 2,000 pilgrims costing R 24,000. However, this was not ready in time, so R 10,000 was allocated to pay for pilgrims' rented accommodation. Pilgrims were allowed to stay in hostels for free for fifteen days.[113] Another service was distributing 5,000 free copies of the *Bab-i-mecca* (Gateway to Mecca), an informational handbook for pilgrims that provided guidance such as directions from the docks to pilgrim hostels; numerous requests for the pamphlet came from across India. This official booklet was part of a broader information network about the pilgrimage for the literate, mainly transmitted through Urdu pamphlets and travelogues.[114] Most pilgrims, however, were illiterate and relied on their peers for information about the Hajj. This official record masks a more haphazard working environment; in fact, because the Pilgrim Department was often short-staffed, it was often reliant on pilgrim brokers to distribute passports, ensure that pilgrims were vaccinated, and assist the police in their pilgrimage-related tasks.[115]

Muslim policemen were employed at railway stations to escort pilgrims to hostels, and they guarded these establishments to prevent "unauthorized brokers" mixing with pilgrims. Other policemen superintended the thousands of pilgrims who had to pass through humiliating experiences at the disinfection shed on the wharves, where pilgrims had their bodies stamped to indicate that they had passed medical muster.[116] Inspector Mahomed Taqi from the CID engaged with Bombay's Muslim community by raising funds to pay for poor pilgrims' railway tickets home; in 1911–1913, he raised R 8,130 for 630 of them.[117] Taqi remonstrated with pilgrims who did not have enough money for a ticket to the Hijaz to get them to return to their homes.[118] These policemen were on the front line of attempts to manage the pilgrimage from Bombay, especially in relation to destitute pilgrims, and several, such as Taqi, pursued their own initiatives.

Bombay was a central hub in a web of connections related to the Hajj that encompassed the Indian Ocean and simultaneously reached into India's interior. A variety of local administrations across India contacted Bombay's Pilgrim Department for assistance with the Hajj. After failing to secure a ship to take its pilgrims to Jidda, officials in Hyderabad requested help from Bombay in locating one, at premium cost if necessary. Hyderabadi officials also asked Bombay to ensure that their pilgrims whose passes were not checked by their agent were prevented from boarding ships because it had been discovered that several hundred pilgrims' passes had been fraudulently resold during a previous pilgrimage season.[119] Bombay's Hajj officials attached some importance to assisting Hyderabad's *kafila safar*, the leader of Hyderabad's pilgrimage caravan (not an actual caravan, simply a group of people traveling together) during his time in Bombay, given Hyderabad's status as India's premier Muslim princely state.[120] The working relationship between these officials in Bombay and Hyderabad demonstrates how the mechanics of Hajj administration could be operated entirely by Muslim functionaries within the overarching framework of imperial rule.

Bombay's experience in administering the annual flow of pilgrims to the Hijaz meant that its influence spread to other ports on India's Arabian Sea littoral. The Anjuman-i-Islam, a reformist charitable association involved in many activities, proposed in 1911 that Karachi should be opened to pilgrim traffic after a surge in pilgrim numbers that year because of a Hajj *akbar*.[121] The association's idea was favored by officials, who felt that it would relieve the congestion in Bombay caused by the yearly influx of pilgrims because those from north

India, central Asia, and Afghanistan would be drawn to Karachi instead. In Bombay, Edwardes commented: "As matters stand I suggest the mountain should come to Mohammed." Bombay agreed to provide R 11,000 per annum to fund Karachi's Hajj administration and a one-off grant of R 30,000 to set up infrastructure, staff, and embarkation facilities.[122] However, Karachi's officials were concerned that the port's intended transformation into a pilgrim port would lead to "paupers thronging the streets of the city without shelter." To assuage these doubts, the Bombay authorities emphasized how cooperation with Muslim citizens had ameliorated such scenes because a committee of "influential and wealthy Mahomedans" provided accommodation in pilgrim hostels.[123] Karachi's establishment as a pilgrim port from 1911 was driven by Muslim proposals that officials in Bombay's Hajj administration expediently fixed on to lessen their workload during the pilgrimage season. This was short-lived, however; Karachi was closed to pilgrim traffic when war broke out in 1914.

Karachi's establishment as a pilgrim port was accompanied by unease about the effect its opening would have on the activities of pilgrim guides, *mutawwifin*, which officials were relatively powerless to control. Most guides were Bengalis who had settled in the Hijaz and traveled to India each year to preach the importance of performing the Hajj. Bengalis were a large proportion of Indian pilgrim guides and Hajjis partly because they were the largest Indian Muslim community, alongside Punjabis. Their preponderance was also probably due to the activities undertaken by Islamic revivalist movements in Bengal in the mid-nineteenth century that contributed to the "Islamization" of Bengali Muslim peasants. Revivalist movements generally emphasized the importance of certain obligatory Islamic practices, such as performing the Hajj, while condemning those seen as un-Islamic, such as shrine worship, and led to a greater sense of Bengali Muslims' Islamic identity and connection with the wider *umma*.[124] Official inquiries in 1909–1910 revealed that pilgrim guides would travel from village to village "with tales of cheap passages and an easy journey." They preached at village mosques and saints' tombs about the obligatory nature of pilgrimage. A British official noted that the guides neglected to mention the conditions on the obligation to perform the Hajj in the Qur'an that any potential pilgrims should go only if they were generally able to do so, financially and physically.[125] There was a general view among officials involved in the Hajj that the ignorance and naïveté of pilgrims, combined with the extortionate practices of these guides in India and the Hijaz, were responsible for the many cases of destitute pilgrims that were a constant feature of Britain's Hajj administrations across its Muslim empire.[126]

In their reports, the Bombay authorities presented a picture of concerted action against brokers: one was imprisoned for twenty-one days for cheating pilgrims.[127] The 1911 pilgrim season saw a reduction in the number of Bengali pilgrims, which the protector of pilgrims ascribed to his warnings about "nefarious" guides being transmitted by local administrators to the populace. Guides were monitored on their arrival in Bombay and "warned to be circumspect in their behaviour." Their details were recorded by authorities in Bombay and sent to the consul in Jidda. Such precautions were ineffective because many avoided contact with officialdom. Others simply waited until they had left India with their pilgrim charges and then commenced their strong-arm tactics in the Hijaz.[128] By 1913, guides had become a convenient scapegoat for problems related to the Hajj in Bombay; they were put under police surveillance and "prevented from meddling with pilgrims" because they were supposedly involved in cases of theft and fraud in pilgrim hostels.[129] At least until the First World War, when travel controls were tightened, the authorities were unable to prevent the annual flow of guides between the Hijaz and India. Guides played a vital role in pilgrims' journeys to the Hijaz and were key figures in popularizing the pilgrimage among a broad swath of India's Muslims who were encouraged, despite their poverty, to buy one-way tickets to Jidda.

Relief for destitute pilgrims was one of the roles ostensibly undertaken by Bombay's Hajj Committee, a consultative nonofficial body established in 1908 as a way of formalizing the role of the city's Muslim citizens in pilgrimage administration. The committee's general remit was "to superintend the arrangements and despatch of pilgrims from Bombay," and it met once a week during the Hajj season. It was a socially elite body: from 1912 to 1925, its members included justices of the peace, lawyers, merchants with interests in India and the Hijaz, hostel owners, and a former manager of the Persian Gulf and Steam Navigation Company.[130] Committee members undertook fund-raising efforts for repatriating pilgrims from Bombay to their homes; in 1912, R 3,482 was raised through placing charity boxes in the city's mosques.[131] It also supervised the Indigent Pilgrim Fund, worth R 42,000 by 1922, although disbursements from this were controlled by the police commissioner.[132] The deployment of Western methods of civic charitable philanthropy highlighted a significant shift from more traditional Islamic models, such as *waqf* endowments.

The committee's efficacy came under attack from Bombay police commissioner Lynch Blosse in 1922, when he proposed its abolition. Blosse accused it of having been ineffective for several years; meetings were finished in ten minutes, one member attended only to protect his shipping interests, and the body's sole achievement since 1919 had been organizing shipments of grain to Jidda during a food crisis, although Blosse thought that this had been accompanied by "profiteering."[133] Charges that the committee was superfluous in Bombay's Hajj administration prompted a more general official evaluation.[134] Some officials thought that the government should "gradually withdraw from the direct management of the hajj" and be replaced by a Hajj committee that had real powers, which would mean that members would take a more active role.[135] Others argued that the changing political situation—the 1919 Montagu-Chelmsford reforms had ushered in more local self-government, and the Khilafat movement caused the government in Delhi to exercise more jurisdiction over the administration of the Hajj—meant that the committee should continue without any official supervision.[136] Eventually, the status quo was maintained. The lack of powers invested in the committee by the authorities was the likely cause of official charges of ineffectiveness. Committee members often had a direct interest in various aspects of the pilgrimage and used the body to protect or enhance these interests. Bombay's Muslim citizens who were firmly situated outside officialdom had a more beneficial impact than the Hajj Committee on pilgrims' experiences in Bombay.

There was a marked degree of cooperation between these Muslim citizens and the authorities. One man informed the authorities in 1886 that he was building a hostel that would house 2,000 pilgrims and would gift this to the government. His untimely death delayed the project, but the hostel was finally completed in 1887. Its limited capacity led the government to offer land adjacent to it to expand the hostel, which his executors agreed to pay for.[137] In 1912, Mirza Mohamed Shirazi gave R 3,500 to the government for a temporary shed to provide shelter from the rain for pilgrims while they waited to enter the disinfection shed, and he donated a sum that enabled 800 destitute pilgrims to be shipped from Jidda to Bombay, a gesture publicly acknowledged by the government. Shirazi's reply underscored how his duty as a Muslim was the primary reason for his generosity: "What little I have done is in obedience to a call to duty to my co-religionists."[138] The fact that he was cooperating with a non-Muslim government was irrelevant to this higher calling. This cooperation did not remain confined to Bombay's Muslims. The begum of Bhopal funded repatriation efforts, sending R 2,400 a year from 1909 to 1912 to the Indigent Pilgrim Fund, which enabled hundreds of pilgrims to return to their homes across India by train.[139] Every pilgrim season, a number of Bombay's Muslims paid for poor pilgrims' tickets to Jidda: in 1911, one man paid for 27 pilgrims, and in 1912, Shirazi paid for 800 pilgrims.[140] The Anjuman-i-Islam association took a different tack and tried to persuade poor pilgrims in Bombay to purchase return tickets for their journey to Jidda.[141] These two examples were probably representative of numerous private initiatives to facilitate pilgrims' experiences in Bombay that occurred without government involvement.[142]

A more complex example was the establishment of the Anjuman-i-khuddam-i-kaaba in May 1913 by Shaukat Ali, who later played a significant role in the Khilafat movement, and Abdul Bari. Shaukat Ali acquired a license as a pilgrim broker, and the association's office in Bombay provided services to pilgrims; branches were established across India. Shaukat Ali proposed that a shipping company should be established by Indian Muslims that would initially be supported through financial contributions from Indian Muslim rulers for ships; the profits would be used to repatriate destitute pilgrims from the Hijaz. This plan, however, was never implemented, and the organization's activities were curtailed when Britain and the Ottoman empire went to war in 1914. The viceroy's subsequent declaration that the Holy Places of Mecca and Medina would be immune from the conflict rather negated one part of the organization's rationale, which was defending these cities from foreign intrusion, and the authorities banned the organization from sending money abroad. Because of the Ali brothers' support for the Ottoman empire, they were interned for the war's duration, and the organization's activities ceased.[143]

This section has analyzed the nature and scope of Britain's Hajj administration from this important port city, used by the vast majority of Indian pilgrims to travel to and from the Hijaz. In contrast to the government of India's viewpoint, the Bombay authorities' experience of the Hajj was much more direct, given the large annual influx of pilgrims into the city. Official interaction with the logistics of pilgrims' travels was deepened by multilayered and multifaceted dealings with Muslims—those who worked within the colonial bureaucracy and those outside, who formed part of Bombay's civil society. A large amount of the day-to-day work of Bombay's Hajj administration was undertaken by Muslims, who played a vital role in this corner of Britain's Muslim empire. Despite the fact that the colonial administration's involvement in the Hajj was driven by pragmatism as opposed to altruism, the relationship among British officials, their Muslim employers, and Bombay's Muslim community was intensely collaborative. However, the difficulties faced by officials regarding the Hajj Committee, pilgrim guides, and destitute pilgrims mean that the overall semblance of order presented in the files and reports must be questioned. Even though complex administrative arrangements were established for the Hajj, the effectiveness of official actions was highly contingent and ultimately dependent on Muslims within and outside the bureaucracy. The next section returns to the analysis of the destitute-pilgrim issue, drawing out Britain's confused attempts to ameliorate this phenomenon before these, in turn, were dramatically curtailed by the portentous events that unfolded in Europe over the summer of 1914.

Destitute Pilgrims and Imperial Prestige

The final years before the First World War saw a substantial change in Britain's policy on destitute pilgrims. In Chapter 2, we saw how Britain's initial position of disinterest on this issue evolved during the late nineteenth century as British officials, their Muslim employees, and Muslim leaders engaged in lengthy debates on how to resolve the phenomenon. However, arguments for greater intervention in the form of compulsory return tickets came to nothing, and nonofficial assistance to poor pilgrims largely remained the norm. This section charts how successive Muslim vice-consuls at Jidda drove the government of India to reexamine the issue. These debates took place amid increasingly strained Anglo-Ottoman and Anglo-Muslim relations, exemplified by trends such as Indian Muslim support for the Ottomans during the conflicts in the Balkans and Tripolitania through measures such as aid to the Islamic Red Crescent, and the revivified pan-Islamic policies of the Young Turks in the Ottoman empire from 1908.[144]

Anglo-Ottoman tensions had been rising inexorably since the mid-nineteenth century. Ottoman sultan-caliph Abdul Hamid II (1876–1909) was an Anglophobe. The Ottoman leadership saw Britain as an unscrupulous expanding power, an interpretation borne out by its grabs of Ottoman territory—Cyprus in 1878, Egypt in 1882, Kuwait in 1899–1901, Aden's hinterland in 1901–1904, and the Sinai Peninsula in 1906. These formed part of a series of setbacks for the Ottomans, who also had to contend with chronic debt problems that led to the empire's bankruptcy in 1875. On the other side, British politicians, diplomats, and officials saw the Ottomans as a declining power that was increasingly unstable as it continued on a path of slow but interminable implosion. Crises on imperial frontiers, such as the 1901 al-Darijah incident, when British troops killed thirteen Ottoman soldiers near Aden, and subsequent boundary negotiations punctuated by the occasional dispatch of British warships did nothing to help relations. The ruler of Najd, 'Abd al-'Aziz ibn Sa'ud, who was under Ottoman suzerainty, made contact with Britain in 1904 and asked for protection against his local rivals the Rashidis. The most serious event that marred Anglo-Ottoman relations was the 1906 Aqaba boundary crisis. On May 3, 1906, in response to Ottoman troops occupying Taba, a town on the Gulf of Aqaba, Britain gave the Ottomans ten days to agree to delineate the border in the Sinai Peninsula. Two days before the expiry of the ultimatum, the Committee of Imperial Defence in London considered a naval operation against the Dardanelles but warned that such a move would have "far-reaching military consequences" because the British empire contained so many Muslim subjects who might react adversely to this operation.[145] The Ottomans backed down and agreed to British demands for boundary negotiations. The relationship between the two powers was highly fraught.

These events formed the wider backdrop to Anglo-Ottoman interactions over the Hajj. British consular and diplomatic remonstrations over the sufferings of Indian and Malay pilgrims in Mecca were repeatedly countered by the sharif of Mecca and the Hijaz's Ottoman governor with accusations that Britain had covert designs on the Holy Cities. Ottoman officials were concerned about the Hijaz's growing Indian community, which was fairly independent of the local authorities' control. Furthermore, many Indian settlers retained their status as British subjects for practical reasons and could theoretically appeal for British protection. The Ottomans also suspected Britain of fostering Arab separatism, which centered on a potential Arab caliphate in Mecca. Fearfulness about intrigues in Mecca was not a condition exclusive to the European imperial powers.[146]

British officials in India were more receptive to addressing issues related to the Hajj because of the political changes of this period. The 1909 Morley-Minto reforms established separate electorates for Muslims, and in 1910 the Viceroy's Council had eleven Muslim representatives, 40 percent of the whole body, far outweighing the actual percentage of Muslims in the subcontinent.[147] The extent to which Britain's engagement with the Hajj shaped colonial conceptions of Muslims as a distinct category of person remains difficult to ascertain. There was widespread Indian Muslim support for the Ottoman empire and its pan-Islamic policies, although, as Justin Jones has argued, this was far from monolithic. For example, the most influential Shi'i newspaper, *Akhbar-i-Imaniya,* stated in 1906 that "British rule in Mecca and Medina will be more welcome than that of the Sultan."[148]

In light of this background, India's review of the destitute-pilgrim issue in 1912 was a watershed moment. Issues of imperial prestige came to the fore as officials became acutely concerned that these poor pilgrims could cause negative repercussions for the empire's image. The consequences of the expansion of long-distance travel, which enabled many poorer Muslims to perform the Hajj, had caught up with their colonial rulers. Divergent perspectives among British and Muslim officials and Muslims consulted on the issue created a sense of official inertia and confusion. The appearance, once again, of destitute pilgrims in Jidda in 1912 caused alarm in official circles, which resulted in the allocation of significant funds to repatriate these pilgrims. Although the outbreak of war halted this process, a Rubicon had been crossed. Britain had now actively facilitated the Hajj for its poorer subjects, albeit for pragmatic rather than altruistic reasons related to the circumstances of their travels. Nevertheless, through directly assisting pilgrims by effectively underwriting the cost of their pilgrimage, Britain was acting like a Muslim power, akin to the Ottomans and Mughals who helped their poorer subjects go on pilgrimage.[149]

The question of imperial prestige was particularly acute among Britain's Muslim vice-consuls in Jidda. Dr. Hussein, like his predecessor in Jidda, Dr. Razzack, found it inexcusable that every year Britain had to witness "a large crowd of Indian pauper pilgrims left in the Hedjaz," unlike the French, Dutch, and Egyptian authorities, who enforced compulsory return tickets. The presence of over 500 destitute pilgrims in Jidda after the conclusion of the 1905 Hajj, who Hussein argued could not be treated with "indifference," prompted the vice-consul to propose to his employers that now was an appropriate time to test whether the authorities could introduce a compulsory return-ticket system for pilgrims' travels. The establishment of plague and observation camps in Bombay in 1895, where pilgrims were allowed in only if they could show enough money for a return railway ticket and were permitted to leave for the Hijaz only if they had spent time in the camp, had not aroused "adverse comment" from Muslims. This gave Hussein grounds for optimism that this system could be extended to steamship tickets from Bombay to Jidda.[150]

Hussein's idea was transmitted to local officials in India, who were ordered to gather responses from Muslim associations and notable personages across India, similar to the 1876–1877 consultation process; the response was largely negative.[151] Although a meeting of local Muslims in Srinagar responded positively to the proposal because it echoed Qur'anic stipulations, they held a minority view.[152] A court superintendent in Gwalior thought that it was "unbecoming" for the government to become involved with the issue of destitute pilgrims in the Hijaz.[153] An assistant collector in Hyderabad pointed out that any restrictions would be problematic, given that the "custom of pilgrimage to Mecca has become so universal," coupled with increased Indian Muslim migration to the Hijaz, which led to "large and flourishing Indian colonies in several Arabian towns."[154] Mysore's resident thought that the proposal did not "justify the political risk of alienating" Muslim sympathies. He framed this in the context of the recent deterioration in Anglo-Ottoman relations after the Taba border crisis in 1906, which meant that Indian Muslims were "particularly susceptible" to the idea that Britain was "callous" about Muslim feelings.[155]

A letter from one member of Bombay's Muslim community illustrates how Muslims used the rhetoric of Britain as a Muslim power to argue against governmental intervention in this issue. Rafiuddin Ahmed asserted that because Britain was the "greatest Moslem power upon earth," it had "nothing to learn from other governments regarding the subject of the happiness of the Mahomedan pilgrims." In the same vein, Ahmed continued: "It is most pleasing in the Holy Land to hear the Indian Hajjis relate the blessings of British rule—its liberality and justice—to their brethren under other governance. . . . It is the wish of Mahomedans that the Government . . . will continue to be the justest as it is undoubtedly the greatest Mahomedan power in the world."[156] Britain's prestige as a Muslim power, in Ahmed's view, meant that any form of compulsion regarding pilgrims' journeys to the Hijaz should be rejected.

Many responses from Muslims played on British fears by highlighting the dire consequences of a backlash from "ignorant masses" of Muslims. As a result, the authorities abandoned the proposal.[157] The Muslim vice-consul at Jidda broached the idea of compulsory return tickets, but it was struck down by Muslims who were consulted on the issue. The authorities heavily relied on these men as barometers of what they termed Indian Muslim opinion. Consequently, the 1877 recommendation was resurrected; local administrations and the consul in Jidda were ordered to "adopt such measures as they may find feasible" to inform pilgrims of the danger of performing the Hajj without enough money.[158] The decision to drop such a contentious proposal was in alignment with broader strategies during this period to cultivate Muslim leaders as a "potential bulwark of stability" amid a rise in nationalist activity and disputes between Indian Muslims and the British in this period on a variety of domestic and international issues.[159]

However, these calculations were insufficient to temper the concerns of Britain's Muslim employees in Jidda, who felt that the situation regarding destitute pilgrims was an affront to both imperial and Islamic prestige. From 1909 to 1911, Vice-Consul Dr. Abdur Rahman successfully revived the issue of destitute pilgrims as a matter that warranted urgent attention. He described the situation of Indian destitute pilgrims as "a disgrace to Islam as well as to the British community." After most pilgrims had departed, Indian "disease ridden skeletons" populated Jidda's streets, begging and spreading "ordure." The vice-consul was appalled that British inaction led to censure from the Ottoman authorities. The Hijazi governor wrote to the British consul demanding that Britain take responsibility for the removal of indigent pilgrims.[160] Two competing claims collided in Jidda: the Ottoman empire as the protector of the faithful and the Holy Cities and Britain as the "greatest Mohammedan power," aware of the importance of maintaining its prestige in the Muslim world. The logical conclusion of this, as Radhika Singha has pointed out, was that neither power could restrict the travels of destitute pilgrims.[161]

It was left to nongovernment actors to assist these poor pilgrims. Shipping companies such as the Muslim-owned Bombay and Persia Steam Navigation Company provided free return passages, which resulted in an increase in destitute-pilgrim numbers. For example,

Pilgrims at Jidda harbor, c. 1930s

Credit: Royal Geographical Society, London

after the 1910 Hajj there were over 1,000 Indians "in abject misery" in Jidda, and many died.[162] Initiatives to assist destitute pilgrims, such as the 1897 Jubilee Relief Fund established by Indian merchants and consular officials in Jidda, provided only a small amount of relief for destitute pilgrims. In 1910, the fund spent R 913 to provide food for indigent pilgrims who were repatriated on two ships and R 386 on burials, further repatriation, and feeding orphans of Hajjis.[163] Rahman warned that this piecemeal and ad hoc nature of indigent-pilgrim repatriation was unsustainable.[164]

Rahman pressed the government of India to introduce compulsory return tickets and establish Hajj committees throughout the

Raj. He believed that previous hostility to this ticketing system had been based on "imaginary grounds" because of Indian Muslim "ignorance" of the situation in the Hijaz. Hajj committees would provide crucial information about the Hajj. Such bodies would also alleviate the acute lack of knowledge about the pilgrimage Rahman thought common among Indian Muslims. The vice-consul admitted that he himself had "had no idea" how to reach the Hijaz when he had been appointed to his role.[165] Existing measures, such as press notices that stressed the need for Muslims to possess enough funds for Hajj and exhorted Indian Muslims to recognize their "moral obligation to save their co-religionists from the hardships and miseries," had little practical effect.[166] Indigent pilgrims were not a marginal issue during this period. In the later 1880s, as we have seen, almost 50 percent of Indian pilgrims were destitute. By 1911, Bombay's police commissioner estimated that 75 percent of pilgrims who arrived in Bombay, having paid their passage money and bought provisions, were "almost entirely penniless. . . . An appalling number of them literally beg their way to and from Mecca."[167] This situation led to a growing concern among officials that compulsory return tickets were essential to curtail this signal feature of the Hajj from the British empire.[168]

The vice-consul's exhortations prompted a major review of the destitute-pilgrim issue in 1912, but it was the appearance of more impoverished pilgrims in Jidda during officials' deliberations in Delhi that pushed the government of India into paying for their repatriation, a significant change from the government's previous noninterventionist stance. Within a broader context that included issues of British prestige and domestic and international political tumult, this change ushered in a new phase of Britain's association with the Hajj. Britain was actively assisting poor pilgrims, however grudgingly, a trend that continued after the First World War. Although the reasons for Britain assisting its pilgrims to perform the Hajj differed from Ottoman and Mughal practices, the fact remained that Britain, like these Islamic empires, was facilitating the Hajj for its poorer subjects.

For those officials tasked with the 1912 review, concerns about imperial prestige and British relations with the Ottoman authorities in the Hijaz were paramount.[169] The "scandal" of poor pilgrims was especially humiliating to Britain because other European powers and the nizam of Hyderabad's government did not face the same problem, but emulating their policies would have "little practical effect."[170] The viceroy thought that the status quo was unsustainable but felt that the government, at this point, should avoid compulsory return tickets because this would create the impression that the authorities were preventing people from going on Hajj.[171]

The appearance of 4,000 destitute pilgrims in Jidda after the 1912 pilgrimage changed everything. The consul in Jidda asked Bombay's Hajj Committee to allocate R 25,000 to fund the cost of repatriation.[172] Officials in the Foreign Department in Delhi were forced to apply, grudgingly, to the Finance Department to foot the bill.[173] Because of this, Dr. Abdur Rahman's policies were adopted: Hajj committees would be established, and rulers such as the begum of Bhopal would be asked to establish a relief fund.[174] Governmental policy regarding destitute pilgrims, which laid emphasis on private initiatives, had been swiftly overturned.

In 1913, the last peacetime pilgrimage season saw the final flowering of Britain's attempts to deal definitively with indigent pilgrims before the advent of war led to far-reaching changes to the pilgrimage and Britain's interactions with the Hajj. The years 1913 and 1914 marked the end of the first era of Britain's relationship with the pilgrimage. As in 1912, Jidda saw a growing accumulation of destitute pilgrims after the 1913 Hajj, some 300 when the consul in Jidda wired the government of India in March 1913.[175] Officials in Delhi abrogated responsibility for these pilgrims, but the authorities in Bombay unilaterally decided to implement a return-ticket system to prevent pilgrim destitution and award the Turner Morrison Company a monopoly over pilgrim traffic. However, this required swift approval from Delhi and led to protests from Indian Muslims who still retained a slender slice of the pilgrim traffic.[176] Bombay officials' proposals were based on the knowledge that they could do little to prevent the "extensive exodus" of indigent pilgrims to Mecca who came from outside their jurisdiction; they also reflected resentment that the city bore the "entire burden" of pilgrim traffic, including the cost of repatriating pilgrims to their homes across India. Bombay's Pilgrim Department expanded on Dr. Rahman's suggestions for

Hajj committees across India: these bodies would collect subscriptions to a central repatriation fund, provide accurate information on pilgrimage expenses, and try to prevent poor Muslims from setting off for the Hijaz. Taken together, these plans would ease the city's financial burden of funding repatriation for destitute pilgrims for the whole of India.[177] Ultimately, the government of India spent R 17,000 in 1913 on repatriating destitute pilgrims—a significant amount compared with previous trickles of financial support for pilgrims stranded in the Hijaz.[178] Although the government was disinclined to engage in poor relief in India, the Hijaz was a different matter, given the pressure from the Ottoman authorities to repatriate poor pilgrims and the fact that indigent pilgrims tarnished British prestige.[179] Nor was this issue solely confined to India; according to the consul, a lack of ships plying the route from Jidda to Singapore meant that just over a thousand Malays were stranded in Jidda for over six weeks after the end of the Hajj; some had to sell their clothes for food, and several died from starvation.[180]

Within the context of a charged political atmosphere due to Indian Muslim support for the Ottomans, and in the midst of fighting in the Balkans and the Italian invasion of Cyrenaica, officials in Delhi cited the prospect of "political trouble" to pour cold water on Bombay's proposals for compulsory return tickets. Given the issue's "decided political complexion," Muslim opinion had to be gauged before there were any changes in government policy, but it appears that no consultation occurred.[181] Abdulla Khar, director of the Bombay Jama Masjid and president of the Anjuman-i-Islam, petitioned Viceroy Lord Hardinge to postpone any government decision on return tickets—an issue that affected "seventy million loyal Muslim subjects"—so that Muslims could submit their own solutions. Khar believed Bombay's compulsory return-ticket proposal was "inconsistent with ancient traditions and unsuited to the economic conditions and religious sentiments of Indian Moslems."[182] The tense political atmosphere among many Indian Muslims combined with official caution to cement governmental inaction on this issue.[183]

In these final months of peace, the authorities in Bombay fell back on Rahman's Hajj report, which advocated compulsory return tickets to prevent destitute pilgrims dying every year in "pitiable conditions of starvation."[184] This was a testament not to altruism alone but to the affront these pilgrims caused to imperial prestige. The report was translated into Urdu and sent to *anjumans* and Urdu newspaper editors throughout India.[185] Local administrations were ordered to consult urgently with "leading Muhammadan gentlemen and associations" so that Rahman's measures could be introduced for the 1914 Hajj season. The vice-consul's schemes had attracted the secretary of state for India's attention and support.[186] It appeared that a resolution of sorts might have been instituted by the 1914 pilgrimage season, ending a debate on indigent pilgrims that had lasted for over thirty years. However, the outbreak of war in Europe in August 1914 scotched the implementation of compulsory return tickets.

Muslim employees had substantial agency in pushing for a resolution of the destitute-pilgrim issue and consistently raised the fact that the status quo was damaging to imperial prestige. This was reflected in the concerns of British officials, which increased as tensions rose among Britain, Indian Muslims, and the Ottoman empire in this period. All these factors, along with the contingent and fluid nature of the destitute-pilgrim phenomenon in the Hijaz after the Hajj had concluded, contributed to the swift and significant change in policy on destitute pilgrims in 1912–1913: Britain's facilitation of the Hajj for its poorer subjects. Although the outbreak of the war stopped Britain's repatriation of destitute pilgrims, Chapters 4, 5, and 6 will show how this resumed after only a short hiatus and remained a defining feature of Britain's interactions with the Hajj.

Conclusion

Britain's association with the Hajj evolved significantly during this brief period; the widening of Britain's Muslim empire to incorporate Sudan and Nigeria meant that officials grappled with the pilgrimage in vastly different areas of the Islamic world from South and Southeast Asia. In practice, however, their work partly reflected the attitudes held by officials in India seen in Chapter 2. For example, Sudanese government policy went from ignorance and noninterference to active facilitation and cooperation with Muslim leaders, driven by fear of unrest. Local and regional case studies have delineated the immense variety and commonalities of Britain's interactions with the Hajj across a wide geographic space. Although the characters of these regimes in Africa and India were different, a defining feature was the figure of the poor pilgrim, on foot across the Sahel, on board pilgrim ships in the Arabian Sea, or in the Hijaz, with their meager funds expended.

Miles inland from the Arabian Sea, Hyderabad's Hajj administration is a testament to the concept of a British Muslim empire and the power of Muslim agency in a case where the forces of British colonialism, in this sphere at least, were largely absent. This has shed light on a Muslim administration of the Hajj that had several distinct features: the sponsorship of pilgrims to buttress the nizam's politico-religious legitimacy; Hyderabad's role as a nodal point in a transregional environment of religious emigration from Arabia to India; and Hyderabad as an attractive destination for poorer pilgrims hoping for largesse from a Muslim ruler. In comparison with Bombay, the princely state's Hajj administration appeared to be a form of religious charity, while the port's was more a welfare scheme necessitated by the requirement of administrative control, but the end result was similar: facilitating the Hajj for poorer Muslims. Distinguishing between Muslim and non-Muslim authority in relation to the Hajj was sometimes difficult.

In Bombay's Hajj administration, as in Hyderabad, the role of Muslim employees was of paramount importance. This chapter has illuminated the large degree of Muslim agency exercised within the port's Hajj administration, staffed mostly by Muslims. Their institutional collective experience of dealing with the annual flow of pilgrims meant that the Pilgrim Department was a valuable source of information about Hajj administration. In this period, an increasingly fraught relationship between Indian Muslims and the British on many domestic and international issues perhaps accounted for the efforts of Bombay's pilgrimage administration—it would be heavily criticized by Indian Muslims if it fell short in its duties to pilgrims. The deteriorating international situation and widespread Indian Muslim support for the Ottomans during the Balkan Wars undoubtedly contributed to the muddled official reaction to the destitute-pilgrim issue during this charged period. The changing international climate and the opinions of many Indian Muslims, combined with the administrative pressures of large numbers of destitute pilgrims, precipitated a seismic shift in Britain's policy on these pilgrims. Instead of preaching noninterference with Islamic practice, British authorities now actively facilitated the pilgrimage for their poorer subjects by repatriating them at government expense. Although undertaken in very different circumstances from Ottoman and Mughal aid to pilgrims, the British empire also helped its poorer Muslim subjects perform this important religious ritual. Attempts to resolve this situation came to nothing by August 1914, when war broke out in Europe. Chapter 4 will analyze how the enormous changes wrought in the Hijaz after 1914 made Britain's association with the Hajj vastly more fraught and multifarious.

4

The First World War and the Hashemite Interregnum, 1914–1924

Introduction

The First World War, and its aftermath in the Hijaz, was a period of extraordinary flux and bloodshed, as well as a crucial turning point in British policy toward Islamic practice and the Muslim world. This chapter seeks to reframe conventional narratives that center on the Arab Revolt and the postwar creation of an Anglo-French-dominated Middle East by highlighting the pilgrimage's importance to British calculations and actions in the region and beyond. The war against the Ottoman empire meant that a cluster of British officials based in London, Cairo, Khartoum, Jidda, Aden, Bombay, and Delhi—all specialists on the Muslim world—were elevated to important positions in various bureaucracies; the most prominent example of this was the establishment of the Arab Bureau in Cairo in 1916. Two formal spheres of responsibility for Britain's military operations in the Middle East were established after the Ottoman empire entered the war on the side of the Central Powers under the aegis of the Committee of Union and Progress (CUP), a political organization that had controlled the empire since it came to power in a coup in 1913. In the east, Delhi was tasked with the invasion of the

Basra *vilayet* (province), carried out by the Indian Army's Expeditionary Force D. In the west, Cairo and Khartoum assumed responsibility for encouraging Sharif Hussein of Mecca to revolt against his Ottoman suzerain. Despite the often vehement disagreements among these authorities, the conflict's spread into the Ottoman empire's provinces catalyzed the growing links among the various parts of Britain's Muslim empire, such as Nigeria, Sudan, Egypt, Basra, the Persian Gulf, and India. From the perspective of British officials, the war gave the Middle East a unified political geography for the first time. The western and eastern parts of Britain's Muslim empire were brought together in the heart of the Islamic world, a move precipitated by a "crisis of Islam" whose impact reverberated along the variegated pilgrimage routes to Mecca.

The sometimes troubled interactions among officials stationed in these various areas had an important consequence: the burgeoning realization that Islam was the preponderant thread linking territories from Nigeria and Egypt to India and Malaya together. A huge swath of the Muslim world was under British control. In fact, as many of them observed, Britain ruled over a Muslim empire. Vast amounts of information were exchanged on Islamic topics that affected the various parts of Britain's Muslim empire. Amid this torrent of information, however, the Hajj stood out. The pilgrimage was the religious practice that connected this diverse space together. Mecca had enormous religious and geopolitical significance. Every year, the pilgrimage attracted many thousands of the faithful from across Britain's Muslim empire to the Hijaz. Therefore, the area was vitally important to Britain. The importance of the Hijaz was heightened by the province's status as a potential area of rebellion against the Ottoman empire, which would aid the British war effort but would also affect the pilgrimage. Britain's active engagement in remaking the Hijaz's political landscape through fomenting the Arab Revolt had profound consequences for the pilgrimage and Britain's Muslim empire, as the remainder of this book will chart. The enhanced attention paid by Britain to the newly independent Kingdom of the Hijaz after the revolt's outbreak led various parts of the empire's imperial bureaucracies to realize that a successful Hajj would raise Sharif, later King, Hussein's standing in the Muslim world and, therefore, indirectly also reflect positively on Britain. However, increased British attempts to reform the pilgrimage experience were largely ineffective, and Sharif Hussein's perceived mismanagement of the Hajj was an important factor in the eventual breakdown of the Anglo-Hijazi alliance. British engagement with the Hajj in this period highlights the broader importance of Islamic religious practice in imperial politics and governance.

Numerous existing studies covering this tumultuous period reflect changing geographic conceptualizations of the "Middle East" through incorporating areas beyond the region into their various topics of inquiry, which include the 1914 Ottoman jihad proclamation, the rise of Arab nationalism, pan-Islam, the Khilafat movement, and British imperial strategy and military history.[1] However, few of these studies, with the exception of Timothy Paris's work, pay any sustained attention to the Hajj, a lacuna that this chapter addresses. By doing so, it seeks to push forward the transregional scope of this body of work in a new direction.[2]

Despite the significance of Britain's invasion of Iraq and its eventual assumption of control over the major Shi'i pilgrimage centers of Najaf and Karbala, they have already been mentioned in Chapter 1 and are outside the scope of this chapter, which necessarily focuses on the Hajj and the Hijaz. The British-supported Arab Revolt precipitated the first change of ruler in Mecca and Medina since the Wahhabis had briefly seized them from the Ottomans in 1803. From June 1916, Hussein received a huge financial subsidy from Britain; although it was mainly spent on arms, ammunition, and payments to Bedouin tribes, it also financed the Hijaz's pilgrimage administration. The Hijaz was, in effect, a British client state, although the degree to which Britain could exercise its authority over the mercurial Hussein was highly circumscribed. This chapter will analyze Britain's limited authority in relation to the Hajj, where British officials' attempts to extend their direct control over parts of the pilgrimage administration and even establish a hostel and Muslim agent in Mecca were blunted. The official rhetoric of "noninterference" in Islamic practice, reaffirmed throughout this period, rang increasingly hollow. British interference in Hijazi politics greatly influenced the subsequent shift in the Hijaz's sovereignty from the

Hashemites to the Saudis. The Hijaz's political instability after the successful military conclusion of the Arab Revolt in 1918 sowed the seeds for the Saudi takeover of the kingdom. Postwar fiscal retrenchment policies implemented across the empire meant that Britain's subsidies to both Hussein and Ibn Saud were cut. This galvanized a fresh round of fighting between these Arabian rulers, both of whom were British allies, which ultimately confirmed Saudi dominance over the Hijaz, Arabia, and the Hajj in 1924–1925, the consequences of which are examined in Chapter 5. The Hajj was an important factor in the geopolitical changes that affected the Hijaz during this period, which in turn affected politics and policies in Britain's Muslim empire and the wider Islamic world.

The Sharifian Solution and the Hajj

It is often forgotten that the pretext of the now-notorious meeting in Cairo in 1913 between Sharif Hussein's son amir Abdullah and British Consul-General Herbert Kitchener, while Abdullah was the khedive's guest, was to discuss improving conditions during the pilgrimage.[3] Reexamination of the intensively studied interactions between the Hashemites and the British shows that the pilgrimage was at the forefront of these discussions because it was vitally important to both parties. The two men met again in Cairo on February 4, 1914, when Abdullah, once more the khedive's guest, asked whether Britain could prevent any attempt by Istanbul to depose Sharif Hussein because "his father had always done his best to assist Indian Moslem pilgrims amongst whom he had many friends."[4] Abdullah hoped that if his father were deposed, there would be an uprising by loyal tribes, and Britain would ensure that Ottoman reinforcements could not reach the Hijaz by sea.[5]

According to T. E. Lawrence, Abdullah later related to him that the genesis of the Arab Revolt lay in Abdullah's proposal for a gigantic hostage-taking operation of pilgrims designed to forestall the plan of CUP coleader Talaat Pasha to militarily subdue the Hijaz. Abdullah apparently informed Kitchener that during the 1915 Hajj, he would call out the Bedouin tribes during the *'Id* festival and "lay hold of the pilgrims." These hostages would have included Ottoman officials and "leading Moslems of Egypt, India, Java, Eritrea and Algiers." Abdullah expected that this audacious hostage taking would gain the attention of the European powers whose subjects he had kidnapped, and he believed that subsequent European pressure on a weakened Ottoman state to free the hostages would lead to concessions from Istanbul to the Hashemites in return for the hostages' release.[6] Fortunately, his brother Faisal, horrified at the plan and its consequences for the Hashemites, persuaded his father not to approve it.

Amid these discussions, Kitchener agreed with officials in London and India that the "Arab question" should be approached with "great care" and stressed the Hajj's importance to Britain in the whole equation. In his view, Britain could ill afford to neglect its interests in the Holy Places because of the Hajj, given that thousands of pilgrims from across the British empire traveled to the Hijaz: "The welfare and indeed safety of these pilgrims is intimately bound up with the maintenance of order in the districts in question and of a good relationship between Turks and Arabs."[7] Furthermore, debates within British officialdom over who held the sharifate of Mecca had a long history. In 1881, Zohrab, the British consul in Jidda, had written: "The Sultan should no longer be permitted to act without advice in filling up this post. England, having at least sixty million Mohammedans under her rule must feel deeper interest in the man who is supreme at Mecca than the Sultan who has but sixteen million to support his claim to the independent right of nomination."[8] War against the Ottomans intensified Britain's interest in the Hijaz and the Hajj, as well as the idea of Britain as ruling a Muslim empire.

The Ottoman empire's entry into the war on the side of Germany and Austria-Hungary on October 29, 1914, sparked intense rhetoric and propaganda.[9] In Istanbul on November 14, 1914, the highest-ranking religious official in the empire, the *shaykh al-Islam*, proclaimed a jihad against the empire's enemies and exhorted Muslims ruled by Britain, France, and Russia to heed this call. One immediate hasty reaction to this was the declaration of a British protectorate over Egypt on November 19, 1914. Britain's riposte, in a December 1914 proclamation to Arab peoples, paid close attention to its relationship with Islam and the Holy Places: "Look how the Government of England desires to help the Moslems without distinction of race. Look at this example of how England regards the safety of the Holy Places. Since the declaration of war the English government has supplied the inhabitants of Mecca and Medina with gratuitous corn." Alongside the framing of Britain as a friend of Islam, these statements were leveraged to persuade Arabs to rebel against their Ottoman rulers: "You may join with us the English, your friends that love you, and respect your religion, and join with us as your noble Moslem brethren in India and Africa and throughout the world have."[10]

Britain assiduously developed and disseminated propaganda to try to ensure Muslim loyalty and support within and beyond its empire. These efforts included *al-Haqiqa* (The truth), a propaganda sheet in Arabic, Farsi, and Hindi that was designed to show Britain as a strong military power and supportive of Islam.[11] A further example, a postcard with a picture of the Union Jack, with Arabic underneath, reads as follows in translation:

> Symbol of freedom, truth and right
> Proud underneath your folds our soldiers fight
> Each with his life your cause defends
> And heaven to each its blessing sends.[12]

Rulers across Britain's Muslim empire paraded their support; for example, the sultan of Kelantan in Malaya wrote a public letter to his British adviser in which he stated that "we learn with greatest pleasure that the Holy Places of our religion are being protected . . . by the British government."[13] The impact of this propaganda and related proclamations is difficult to measure. Certainly, the Ottoman jihad had little overall effect in terms of inciting the Allied powers' Muslim subjects to large-scale armed insurrection against their rulers.[14] There were some notable and dramatic exceptions, however. Several hundred Indian pilgrims and some members of the Anjuman-i-khuddam-i-kaaba who were in Mecca joined Ottoman forces after the jihad proclamation, three Muslim regiments of the Indian army mutinied at the prospect of fighting the Ottomans, and there were repeated desertions from Indian Muslim battalions stationed on the Suez Canal.[15] Nevertheless, British moves to encourage the Hashemites to revolt found more success than the efforts of their enemies. What impact did the outbreak of war have on the pilgrimage?

During the war's opening weeks in Arabia, pilgrims were still traveling to the Hijaz because the date for Hajj fell during November. Although the Royal Navy immediately blockaded Ottoman ports, the government of India allowed 2,400 pilgrims to travel from Bombay to Jidda.[16] A Hajj *akbar* led nearly 57,000 pilgrims to land at Jidda, of whom 11,670 were Indian. There was a "general fear" among pilgrims that the Ottomans would join the Germans, according to the vice-consul at Jidda, Dr. Abdur Rahman. Less prescient pilgrims in the Hijaz were "panic stricken" after news broke of the Ottoman attack on Russia's Black Sea fleet on October 29, 1914: "There was a great scare among them and after Arafat everybody hurried to Mecca to catch the first steamer." Shipping companies seized this opportunity to raise ticket prices. A shortage of ships meant that thousands were "resigned" to being stranded in Jidda until the war's end.[17] However, the Ottoman authorities were keen to rid themselves of pilgrims who were now enemy subjects, sending boatloads of them, crewed by armed men, onto an overcrowded Singapore-bound Japanese steamer in December 1914.[18] While Sir Reginald Wingate, governor-general of Sudan, was content to allow African pilgrims to "take their chance" by crossing the Red Sea to the Hijaz, those who returned to Suakin were subjected to what Wingate called "moral disinfection" on their arrival because of fears that the Ottomans might have recruited agents from among pilgrims and infiltrated their own agents into Sudan amid this crowd of newly arrived pilgrims.[19] Officials in India feared that pilgrims who were British subjects in enemy territory might be taken hostage or have their "loyalty tampered with."[20] From October 1914 to July 1915, the authorities in Sudan actually suspended the Hajj from that territory.[21] War had swiftly broken a number of the connections that the Hajj had forged across the Muslim world.

For those pilgrims left in the Hijaz, the war meant that appealing to their governments for assistance was not an option. Britain's consular staff was forced to leave. The Dutch consul Van der Poll was the last European consular official to leave Jidda and was given £40 by the British for his assistance in helping Indian pilgrims escape.[22] British Vice-Consul Rahman deposited the unspent balance of the Jubilee Relief Fund with the government of Bombay.[23] The vice-consul's unplanned departure led him to summarize his work. As vice-consul since 1910, he had reported on several pilgrimages and hoped that he had succeeded in demonstrating to his employers and Indians that the hardships pilgrims faced were caused "partly through their own ignorance and partly through circumstances beyond their control." Although his pilgrimage reports were "not very palatable" to some Indian Muslims, he stressed that it was not disrespectful to the Holy Cities to criticize various aspects of the Ottoman Hajj administration: "All I wished was improvement in the condition of affairs prevailing there, bettering the treatment of pilgrims during this sojourn in the Holy Places and sure means of their return home."[24] Despite criticism from Muslim associations, Rahman thought that his suggestions to the government of India about Hajj-related administration were "not a voice in the wilderness but had a very favourable echo from proper quarters." Rahman believed that the recent interest of Islamic societies such as the Anjuman-i-khuddam-i-kaaba in pilgrimage-related issues was "proof of the awakening caused by my reports on these affairs." It was Rahman who had suggested the establishment of Hajj committees across India, a proposal implemented by the government. According to him, these bodies would be "of great use in removing much of the ignorance among pilgrims and disseminating useful information regarding various questions connected with hajj. . . . Pilgrims will go to the Hejaz better informed as to their responsibility and so be well prepared for the hardships of that peculiar journey."[25] However, the question of repatriating destitute pilgrims from the Hijaz, to which this chapter will return, remained unresolved.

As the British consulate in Jidda wound up its affairs, Kitchener assured Hussein that if he rebelled against the Ottomans, his independence and security against external aggression would be guaranteed. Kitchener suggestively noted that "till now we have defended and befriended Islam in the person of the Turks; henceforward it will be that of the noble Arab. It may be that an Arab of the true race will assume the Caliphate."[26] With extensive service in Britain's

Muslim empire, Kitchener addressed the War Committee in London in February 1915. As he did so, Ottoman forces were moving through the Sinai Peninsula toward the Suez Canal and threatened the pilgrim quarantine station at al-Tur; Parker Pasha, the governor of Sinai, argued that any abandonment of al-Tur "would entail an incalculable loss of [British] prestige among Egyptians and Muhammadans who know Tur as a pilgrim station."[27] Kitchener began his address by arguing that it was in Britain's interest to have an Arab kingdom under British protection containing Mecca, Medina, and Karbala. Controlling Iraq, Egypt, the Persian Gulf, and the Red Sea "would secure all the approaches to the Mahomedan Holy Places. This, in [Britain's] position as the greatest of Moslem states, would greatly enhance our prestige amongst the many millions of our Mahommedan subjects."[28] At the highest levels of government, Britain was viewed as a Muslim power, and the Holy Cities' future was seen as vitally important to imperial security, given Britain's special interest in these cities because of the Hajj. India was central to this viewpoint, because it contained the largest number of Muslim subjects. On November 2, 1914, the viceroy of India, Lord Hardinge, proclaimed that Mecca and Medina would be "immune from attack [from British forces] . . . so long as there is no interference with pilgrims from India." When the war ended, the Holy Places would be guaranteed independence, and Britain "would not annex one foot of land in it nor suffer any other power to do so."[29] This proclamation was originally the idea of an Indian Muslim civil servant and president of one of India's Hajj committees, Ahsanuddin Ahmad.[30] In April 1915, Wingate made it known in Sudan that an essential part of any peace terms with the Ottomans would be an independent sovereign state that contained the Holy Cities.[31] These British proclamations of protection and independence for the Holy Places bear more than a passing resemblance, if only in rhetoric, to the 1917 Balfour Declaration and promises made to the Zionists.[32] The Hajj was a key component of Britain's emerging policy on the Hijaz.

The outbreak of war with the Ottoman empire in October 1914 was a key catalyst that focused the "official mind" on the Middle East and the Muslim world more broadly, and particularly on the opportunities this created for reordering and extending the territories of

Britain's Muslim empire. This was no centrally directed project; many British intermediaries wrestled with this question, whether in London, Cairo, Khartoum, or Delhi. Consequently, the situation thrust people such as Sir Mark Sykes into a position as gatekeepers of information about the Islamic world. Sykes had traveled widely in the region; in Palestine in 1898, he had encountered pilgrims traveling toward Mecca.[33] Sykes "fluttered on the fringes of diplomacy," made Islam and the Middle East his area of expertise, and was enamored with the idea of an exotic, unspoiled Arabia. Sykes was an amateur whose insights were sought by many officials. However, his enhanced role in British calculations about the Ottoman empire's Arab provinces did not pass without criticism. T. E. Lawrence remarked that "he would sketch out in a few dashes a new world, all out of scale, but vivid as a vision of some sides of the things we hoped."[34]

British plans concerning the Ottoman empire's future gave rise to fanciful geopolitical visions that caused friction between officials in Egypt and India. Ronald Storrs, Oriental secretary in Cairo, saw a "North African or Near Eastern Vice-Royalty including Egypt and Sudan and across the way to Aden and Alexandretta that would compare in interest and complexity, if not in actual size, to India itself."[35] Muslims in this new political space would apparently then turn away from the Ottoman caliphate to a new British-backed one in Mecca. Storrs believed that British influence over the Arabian shores of the Red Sea opposite Egypt was vital to secure Britain's interests in the region. In the opening months of 1915, the British Residency in Cairo wanted to publicly promise support for an Arab caliphate to curry favor with Arab leaders. This was opposed by officials in India because "spiritual and temporal claims may become so intermixed, particularly in Arabia, that interference on our part may be imperative on temporal grounds and might be construed as a breach of faith."[36] A further aspect of Cairo's desire for an Arab caliphate that caused disquiet among officials in India, given its large number of Muslim subjects, was that an Egyptian-protected caliphate in Mecca would supposedly increase Cairo's prestige among Muslims throughout the empire, at India's expense.[37]

From March to April 1915 in London, the De Bunsen Committee, composed of officials from various government departments, met to consider the Ottoman empire's dismemberment. Those present believed that this would result in the destruction of "the political power of Islam as represented by Turkey." Contrary to those in Cairo, the committee thought that Britain's role in this process would "have made it clear to all Moslems that any hope of an Arab Khalifate was . . . impossible." However, this was couched as an outcome of Britain's policy to encourage revolt among the Arabs, which would relieve pressure on British forces fighting the Ottomans.[38] Sykes believed that an increased number of Sunni pilgrims had "given rise to the idea that possession of the Holy Places carries the Khalifate along with it, although historically this is not the case," an indication of how such actors mixed the pilgrimage with the caliphate question.[39] In Sudan, Wingate hoped that "if we can only arrange that this political change will be a violent one, we will have abolished the threat of Islam, by dividing it against itself, in its very heart. There will be a Khalifa in Turkey and Arabia, and Islam will be as little formidable as the Papacy when the Popes lived in Avignon."[40] These debates, ruminations, and discussions about the Ottoman empire and the caliphate's future caused some officials, Wingate being a prominent example, to reflect on the Muslim world's importance, especially because Britain ruled over a large swath of it. This had profound consequences for Britain's interactions with the Hajj in this period, which will be considered in subsequent sections.

Egyptian high commissioner Sir Henry McMahon's appointment in autumn 1915 to engage in negotiations with Sharif Hussein in order to induce him to revolt against the Ottomans led Wingate to speculate that McMahon's experience in India meant that his new role "would presage an attempt at co-ordinating British policy as regards to Moslems in India, Arabia and the Near East." However, officials in India complained about McMahon's activities.[41] The numerous British actors engaged in its Muslim empire were propelled into a competition for influence over the future shape of official policy. Nevertheless, among all of them, Wingate was the first to perceive a need for Britain to approach its interactions with the Muslim world in some form of totality. Writing to his superior, Lord Cromer, in 1915, Wingate set out his vision, concerns, and appreciation of this space's diversity:

> I am deeply impressed with the fact that the question of our future relations with the Moslem world will eventually require the exercise of statesmanship of the highest order. The whole subject bristles with difficulty. First, the Moslem of India is not the same as the Moslem of Arabia and the Soudan, and the latter is not the same as the Moslem of Persia, Anatolia, or Egypt. In many respects they have different aspirations.[42]

The complexities of Britain's relationship with Islam—and especially the Hajj—would become increasingly evident during its involvement in the Arab Revolt.

In the months leading up to Hussein's decision to break with his Ottoman suzerains, Wingate's private beliefs found an administrative solution of sorts in Sykes's attempts to place Britain's relations with the Muslim world on a more concrete footing. Sykes privately lobbied Lord Robert Cecil, undersecretary of state for foreign affairs, for a coordinating body for Islamic affairs under his control: "Islam on the one side represents difficulties which will trouble us for long, and one help towards dealing with it is to have the picture in true perspective. Let me have two advisers—one from the Foreign Office, one from the India Office—and establish an Islamic Information Bureau in Egypt—which would be in touch with India, Zanzibar, Iran, Mesopotamia etc.—[Sir Percy] Cox [chief political officer with the Indian Expeditionary Force in Iraq] believes this idea would be of assistance. . . . It should be kept secret."[43] Here was an explicit realization of Britain's breadth of involvement in the Islamic world. Sykes's report to the Nicholson Committee just before Christmas 1915 after touring Egypt, Iraq, and India, communicating de Bunsen's proposals, contained a suggestion to set up an "Islamic Bureau" under his own direction in London. This bureau would keep all the various offices and departments that dealt with the Muslim world informed and "co-ordinate propaganda in favour of Great Britain among non-Indian Moslems." Colonel Parker from the War Office bemoaned the lack of information exchanged between Egypt and India and thought that the bureau would give "a more comprehensive and continuous treatment of the various Islamic problems."[44] These proposals reflected an urgent desire by officials in London to know more about the Muslim world. At a War Committee meeting in December 1915, Sykes was grilled by Britain's most senior statesmen:

Prime Minister Herbert Asquith: "Are Arabs all Sunnis?"
Mark Sykes: "Practically all, except at Karbala."
Earl Kitchener: "Wahhabism, does that still exist?"
Mark Sykes: "It is a dying force."[45]

Such were the shortcomings of relying on a gifted amateur. Renamed the Arab Bureau, Sykes's creation was established in January 1916 to coordinate intelligence, propaganda, and political activities in the Middle East and further afield.[46] Its journal, the *Arab Bulletin*, contained summaries of intelligence about the Hijaz and analysis and information on the Arab world and beyond. Although it was shaped by wartime exigencies and reflected its authors' biases and prejudices, the *Arab Bulletin* contains much valuable material on the Hajj in this period.[47]

The Arab Revolt and the Hajj, 1916–1918

The Arab Revolt broke out in June 1916 because of a combination of Sharif Hussein of Mecca's aspirations for a state of his own in Arabia and British encouragement that he should cast off the shackles of his masters in Istanbul. Hussein loftily proclaimed that "the defence of the Hijaz from this evil and aggression, the observance of the rites of Islam that Allah has commanded, and the guarding of the Arabs and the Arab countries from danger to which the Ottoman Empire is doomed because of the misbehaviour of this wicked society [the Committee of Union and Progress]—all of this will be achieved only by full independence and the cutting of all ties with these bloodthirsty conquerors and robbers."[48] Privately, British officials such as Sykes knew that their support for a figure who rejected the Ottoman sultan's role as *khadim al-haramayn al-sharifayn* was an extremely risky strategy vis-à-vis its Muslim empire: "If . . . [Hussein] is driven out of the Holy Places and they are re-taken by the Turks a terrible ferment will be set up by the Muhammadans—we shall have played with fire and probably set our house in a blaze."[49] During the struggle between the Ottomans and the Hashemites for Mecca, the Ottomans

Sharif Hussein of Mecca (1854–1931), 1924

Credit: Corbis Images

shelled the Holy Mosque, although this did not result in any damage, except to their reputation, which the British seized on in their propaganda campaign. On November 2, 1916, Hussein declared himself king of the Arabs, a title recognized by few, least of all his British backers.

These tumultuous changes in the Hijaz had direct consequences for British interactions with the Hajj. A successful Hajj became a key factor in increasing British prestige and buttressing support for the Hashemite regime, which was distinctly lacking in the wider Muslim world, especially in Britain's Muslim empire. One of the revolt's first successes was the capture of Jidda, which received the vast majority of seaborne pilgrims. The Arab Bureau thought that this was a vital first step in facilitating the Hajj for Britain's Muslim subjects.[50] Anglo-Ottoman hostilities, the Arab Revolt, and concomitantly insecure shipping conditions effectively caused the suspension of the maritime Hajj—for example, there had been no direct sailings from Bombay to Jidda for many months.[51] Any resumption of the pilgrimage under Hashemite control meant that Britain, as Hussein's paymaster, would theoretically hold greater influence over the Hajj's management. Wingate, a key behind-the-scenes player during the Arab Revolt, wrote to Cyril Wilson, governor of Red Sea Province, that "I see no reason why we should not mark the new era by somewhat encouraging the pilgrimage."[52] This desire to assist in fulfilling the religious obligations of Britain's Muslim subjects derived not from benevolence but from the policy's propaganda value, to impress on Muslims that the Ottoman regime, "if not actually over, was on its last legs."[53] The Arab Bureau in particular was determined that the Hajj should be a success, and it dissuaded the Egyptian government from attempting to secure a *fatwa* from al-Azhar's *'ulama* that would discourage pilgrims.[54] The British empire's intense political and military interest in Arabia shifted Britain's involvement in the Hajj to a new phase; the Hajj was to be used to facilitate a wider political project designed to boost Hussein's support in the Muslim world, and it formed an important component of Britain's effort to present itself as a power concerned with its Muslim subjects' spiritual welfare.

The reaction of Britain's Muslim subjects to the Arab Revolt was intricately bound up with the pilgrimage. Harold MacMichael, intelligence officer in the newly conquered province of Darfur, wrote that locals thought that the uprising meant that "the prospects of pilgrimage would be bettered." A Nigerian pilgrim party, previously detained by Darfur's freshly deposed sultan, Ali Dinar, now prepared to move on to Mecca. Their movement "added a touch of actuality to the previous impression and gave specific illustration of the reality of a change in conditions."[55] The governor of adjacent

Sennar Province reported that although "interest in any outside news is very slight . . . the fact that the Arab Revolt will enable pilgrim routes to be re-opened is favourably commented upon."[56]

In India, the news "exploded like a bombshell." Many suspected British involvement. The Anjuman-i-khuddam-i-kaaba condemned Hussein, an act that gave an "unfortunate direction to a large body of opinion."[57] Many leading Muslim figures, such as Abdul Bari, could not understand why Muslims would revolt against their sultan-caliph.[58] Worryingly for Britain, many "loyal and reasonable" Muslims were ambivalent about the revolt. The begum of Bhopal feared that an independent Hijaz would fail to reduce pilgrimage expenses, although Hussein suggested a "radical" reduction in pilgrimage dues to celebrate his newfound independence.[59] Like that of the begum, the first reaction of many was: what would the Hajj under Hussein's rule be like?[60] According to British officials, pro-Ottoman Indian Muslims knew that their only "effective war cry was 'The Holy Places in danger' " because they believed that most Muslims were loyal to Britain. Concerns among some Indian Muslims over the Holy Places led to a meeting in Lucknow on June 27, 1916, which passed a damning resolution that "the Arab rebels . . . and their sympathizers [the British]" had endangered Mecca and Medina.[61] The revolt was seen by some Indian Muslims as further evidence of Britain's nefarious designs on the Ottoman empire.[62] Some Indian Muslims, however, were sympathetic to the revolt and Britain's war against the Ottomans, such as those involved in the Shi'i newspaper *Ittehad* in Lucknow and a variety of Shi'i associations.[63] Nevertheless, the government of India was concerned about the overall reaction. Moreover, the outbreak of the revolt meant a potential "stoppage" of the Hajj from India, which officials feared would provoke further adverse responses from Indian Muslims.[64] After monitoring these reactions, officials across Britain's Muslim empire came to the same conclusion: facilitating the pilgrimage was vital to increase its support among Muslims for the fledgling British-sponsored regime in the Hijaz.

A telling response to Hussein's British-backed revolt from Haidar Ali illustrates the Ottoman conception of Britain's role in the Hijaz, especially in relation to the Holy Places as a conduit to the wider Muslim world. Like Hussein, Haidar Ali could trace his lineage back to the Prophet Muhammad, but through a rival branch, the Zaid. The CUP appointed Haidar Ali the sharif of Mecca immediately after Hussein proclaimed his independence from the Ottoman empire. Significantly, Haidar Ali was fully aware of British rule over millions of Muslims across Africa and Asia. Haidar Ali's August 1916 proclamation, banned in Egypt and India, castigated Hussein as "under the protection of a Christian government . . . doing what it can to subjugate Moslem nations. . . . England would not help him unless she was afterwards to govern him, and . . . the moment she stretches her fingers into the Hejaz she will not relax her efforts until, by degrees, she annexes it to the other countries she has already fraudulently occupied." In Haidar Ali's view, Britain had reduced 150 million Muslims to "poverty and servitude" and "severed India, Egypt, the Sudan, Zanzibar, Somaliland and a part of Arabia from the body of Islam and occupied them."[65] A subsequent report from the Ottoman Legation in Switzerland stated that even Hussein's supporters were convinced that he was "an instrument for the realization of English ambitions in Arabia," which were "to bring the Holy Places of Islam under their control, and to extend their influence throughout the Moslem world."[66]

Haidar Ali had a deep emotional investment in the Holy Cities. When he visited the Prophet's tomb in Medina in 1912, he wrote: "With what joy and exultation we beheld this sacred edifice! . . . I cannot speak of the intense emotion I felt at being in this holy centre, and I thanked God that my sons experienced similar sensations of awe and reverence. . . . The next day I went early to the *haram* and performed service at the tomb in the form of dusting and generally assisting the eunuchs in charge."[67] After his Hajj, Haidar Ali wrote down various schemes that would facilitate the pilgrimage, and he hoped that they might be enacted: "If God would only give the opportunity to do these things! I have planned and thought about them all my life."[68] This reflected the wider late Ottoman involvement in the Hajj, often on a vast scale that ranged from public works in the Holy Cities, such as Mecca's water system and repairs to the Ka'ba, to the construction of the Hijaz railway from Damascus to Medina between 1900 and 1908.[69]

Ottoman rhetoric was not entirely inaccurate. In Cairo, Ronald Storrs outlined what amounted to an extension of Britain's informal empire to Jidda after his personal assessment of the port's administrative arrangements. His report stated that the condition of Jidda's port and quarantine authorities "render some form of external supervision imperative. . . . There should be an Englishman in charge." However, given Hashemite and Allied sensitivity to any assumption of British control over Jidda, he recommended that the putative official possess a neutral title such as "Port and Embarkation Officer." Nevertheless, the official would "at once be recognised as the administrative authority of Jeddah." Storrs suggested that it was "peculiarly undesirable he should show in this capacity during the pilgrimage," a critical caveat given previous British assurances of the inviolate status accorded to the Holy Places and the Hijaz. These administrative measures were seen as vital components of the aim that the first Hajj under Hashemite rule should begin "as brilliantly as possible," according to Storrs.[70] Storrs's report illustrated British awareness of the pilgrimage's power as a conduit for information across the Muslim world and the realization that his recommendations, if implemented, would have to be sensitively addressed: "That universal disseminating news agency [the Hajj] could not fail to distribute into every corner of the Islamic world the picture of Great Britain with one hand already laid on the Hijaz."[71]

The importance attached to the Hajj, heightened by the Arab Revolt, meant that the Foreign Office swiftly picked up Storrs's report and relayed similar views to India. Plans unfolded apace. The primary duty of the official in Jidda was as an unofficial adviser to Hussein. However, it was an "equally important" duty to assist the Hashemite authorities in maintaining Jidda's pilgrimage-related administration. According to Storrs, while people in Jidda were cognizant of the fact that responsibility for the "welfare of the pilgrims" rested with the Hashemite administration, they were supposedly asking for a British official, and Britain was ready to step in to fill the gap. The Foreign Office, aware of the need to avoid "giving colour to the idea of our assumption of control in the Hijaz," suggested a "colourless" title, such as pilgrimage officer. Colonel Cyril Wilson, the governor of Red Sea Province in Sudan, became the colorless officer and took up his post in Jidda in August 1916.[72] Hubert Young, an Indian army officer with experience of India's North-West Frontier Province who became an assistant political officer in Iraq in 1915, was seconded as Wilson's assistant in Jidda. An employee of one of the British shipping companies that dominated the pilgrim traffic acted as a further assistant. Captain Norman Bray of the Bengal Lancers was sent to Jidda by Delhi as a representative for the pilgrimage from India, and he also acted as a counterweight to the Arab Bureau's influence over policy in the Hijaz.[73] The final member of staff was Hussein Ruhi, Wilson's clerk and interpreter, glowingly described by T. E. Lawrence as "Ruhi the ingenious, more a mandrake than a man."[74] The critical presence of Muslim employees in Britain's Hajj administration, seen in Chapters 2 and 3, continued in this period.

Young described Wilson as the British resident in Jidda and wrote of the position's "utmost difficulty and delicacy—he had to look after British and Allied subjects, because the foreign consuls had left. He also had to make arrangements for furthering the pilgrimage, including the safe reception and escort of the Egyptian *mahmal* to Mecca." Wilson advised Hussein on military operations, arms imports, and the payment of the king's subsidy, £150,000 per month initially, which rose to £250,000 by 1918.[75] The multitude of British authorities across its Muslim empire had once again responded to events in Arabia, in this case the Arab Revolt, and had extended their administrative remit in relation to the Hajj. If there had been no such revolt, it seems unlikely that such a situation would have arisen in an Ottoman-controlled Hijaz. This latest set of British officials involved in the pilgrimage grasped the cosmopolitan nature of the Hijaz and how many of the people settled in the Hijaz originated from Britain's Muslim empire.[76]

To use Ronald Storrs's phrase, with "one hand already laid on the Hijaz," British officials realized that the Hajj was a key advertisement to the Muslim world that the Holy Places' new political master was competent to oversee such an important Islamic ritual, which would enhance Hussein's legitimacy and safeguard Britain's stake in backing the new regime in the Hijaz.[77] Consequently, officials across the empire showed heightened concern with the pilgrimage. T. E. Lawrence's report on the Hijaz's general situation in November 1916, written after a weeklong tour of the area, concluded that despite its poor pastoral and agricultural economy, the Hajj meant that the kingdom would have international standing; and because Britain had a large number of Muslim subjects, of whom thousands annually went on pilgrimage, Britain should continue to position itself as the Hijaz's ally.[78] In his famous postwar work *Seven Pillars of Wisdom*, Lawrence later described the Hijaz as "maintained despite economics and geography and climate by the artificial factor of a world religion."[79] Harry St. John Philby, a government of India official who converted to Wahhabi Islam, later asserted that Lawrence had briefly visited Mecca in 1917 but had been removed as soon as his presence was known.[80]

The secretary of state for India, Austen Chamberlain, considered it "most desirable on political grounds that the pilgrimage on a limited scale should again take place."[81] In India, officials in the Political Department fleshed out these grounds: "1) our friend, King Hussein, is largely dependent on it [the pilgrimage] financially, and 2) it is desirable to neglect no means of popularising the Arab Cause with Indian Mohammedans."[82] The pilgrimage was used—unsuccessfully—as a propaganda tool to popularize Hussein's standing and legitimacy throughout Britain's Muslim empire. From July 1916, Indian Muslims were informed that the Arab Revolt had enabled the pilgrimage to resume. This stress on the Hajj made the British hostages to Hashemite fortune. If the Hajj did not continue, officials were concerned that these propaganda efforts in 1916 would be "largely undone."[83] A government of India communiqué emphasized the difficulties of undertaking the pilgrimage because of a shortage of ships during wartime. However, it was the government's "extreme anxiety to assist the Indian Moslem community in the performance of this religious duty that has induced the Government of India to make even such very limited arrangements as are possible."[84] The government also began spending significant sums of money on subsidies to shipping companies in order to keep tickets to Jidda priced at their prewar level of R 125, which benefited both the companies and poor pilgrims.[85]

Propaganda efforts extended to the press in Britain. In December 1916, *The Times* used the Hajj to trumpet the benefits of Egypt's new status as a British protectorate. The paper reported that Egyptian Muslims' religious "desires" were satisfied by the resumption of the pilgrimage, which had been suspended from Egypt since the war's outbreak. This decision had apparently given the Islamic world an opportunity to compare the "terrible state of affairs which reigned when the Turks were supreme in the Holy Places" with the current "peaceful conditions."[86] Facilitating the pilgrimage was an asset of sorts in Britain's Arabian war efforts, and further afield in its Muslim empire, through demonstrating concern for the religious obligation of its Muslim subjects as a means of neutralizing potential discontent. However, this positioning led to political exposure that could be a significant liability, as will become evident in subsequent sections.

The most striking way in which Britain presented itself as a facilitator of the Hajj was through using the Royal Navy for some of the traditional ceremonies associated with the ritual. Foremost among these was the arrival of the *mahmal*, a pyramid-shaped palanquin carried on a camel that was the centerpiece of the Egyptian pilgrimage caravan that traveled to Mecca for each Hajj. The *mahmal* caravan contained the *kiswa*, a series of large cloths made in Egypt, which were draped over the Ka'ba before each pilgrimage began. This rested on older, established Egyptian and Ottoman practices.[87] Egyptian officer Muhammad Sadiq Bey, the first photographer of the Hajj and occasional treasurer of the *mahmal* caravan, described the arrival of the *mahmal* on an Egyptian ship in the 1880s: "The steamer anchored in Jidda's straits and music was played, drums were beaten and cannons were fired."[88] In 1916, as the Ottomans under Sharif Haidar Ali in Medina prepared their own rival *mahmal*, which never reached Mecca, it was the British who took center stage.[89] The ceremonial spectacle described by Sadiq Bey continued after June 1916. The first Hajj under Hashemite rule began at the end of September 1916 with the arrival of Sir Rosslyn Wemyss's HMS *Euryalus* in Jidda, flying the "Green Flag of Islam," along with HMS *Fox* and HMS *Hardinge*. These ships carried the Egyptian *mahmal* and *kiswa*. The French ship *Montcalm* and yacht *Hadj* were also in attendance, and Rear Admiral A. L. M. Huguet told Hussein that "the English and the French were glad to accompany it here with great ceremony to do it honour . . . and to bear witness of our respects for the Mussalman religion which is that of so many peoples in countries ruled by Britain and France."[90] According to Ronald Storrs, Wemyss was invited to ride at the head of the *mahmal* procession composed of Egyptian troops through Jidda, "an honour which we prudently but reluctantly thought fit to decline."[91] All this pomp and ceremony was rather ironic, given that the Royal Navy had severely curtailed the Hajj when it imposed a blockade on the Hijazi coast in November 1914, a measure that also stopped supplies of grain from reaching the area and remained in place until Hashemite and Arab forces had captured its principal ports.[92]

British reports were keen to stress the successful nature of the pilgrimage, with "no untoward incidents," which had been "too frequent" in earlier years under Ottoman rule.[93] The government of India sent four Indian officers to cover the event for Indian newspapers, but in the end there was minimal coverage in the Indian press, much to the disappointment of officials, such as Sykes.[94] The Bedouins' "demeanour" on the road from Jidda to Mecca was "conspicuously friendly," undoubtedly because of Hussein's payments to these tribes. The Hajj was performed by 2,080 pilgrims from India and 1,000 from Egypt, with the total number of pilgrims estimated at 26,000. Prices for lodgings and guides were strictly controlled, and an "effective" police force had been formed. Hussein's audiences with pilgrims were marked by his lavish distribution of 7,000 loaves a day and £10 in cash to each pilgrim.[95] Hashemite largesse would have been impossible without the substantial financial aid provided by Britain and, to a much lesser extent, France.

If the 1916 pilgrimage was a success for the Allies and the Hashemites, the end of that year's Hajj was less pleasant for Mahmudul Hasan, a scholar and teacher at the Deoband madrassa in North India.[96] Britain exercised its greatest influence over Hussein in the revolt's first frenetic months, which enabled Colonel Wilson to pressure Hussein into arresting Hasan and several other Indian Muslim nationalists in the Hijaz. These men were accused of involvement in an anti-British plot called the Silk Letters Conspiracy. The prelude to Hasan's arrest lay in the Arab Bureau's concoction of a declaration based on its dubious understanding of Islamic authority. The

The Egyptian *mahmal* on a Royal Navy ship guarded by Indian sepoys, c. 1916

Credit: Imperial War Museum, London

declaration stated that the Ottomans were infidels and that only an Arab could be caliph; the bureau hoped that it would lend legitimacy to Hussein's revolt. Khan Bahadur Mubarak Ali, a government of India official, arrived in Mecca in 1916 with this declaration of support for Hussein in order to gather signatures of support from religious scholars. He secured the support of the *shaykh al-Islam*, the chief religious official in Mecca, but was mostly interested in getting signatures from Indian religious scholars, especially Hasan. This scholar, who had performed the Hajj in 1915 and had stayed on in the Hijaz with some companions, refused to sign the declaration of support for Hussein, even when a modified version was brought to him, stating that it was contrary to *shari'a* law. Hasan was summoned to see Hussein, and when he arrived, wearing his *ihram*, he was arrested on December 2, 1916. Hussein told Hasan's companions that at this stage in the revolt he could not afford to offend the British.[97] The idea of the Hijaz as a "safe haven" for Muslims was shaken by these arrests.

But the real catalyst for Hasan's arrest was the discovery of the Silk Letters Conspiracy in August 1916 by the government of India's Criminal Investigation Department through its capture of a letter to Hasan from another Deobandi scholar, Obaidullah Sindhi. The letter outlined plans for an independent government in India. The government of India was fearful of Hasan's influence among Indian Muslims, but he lent only moral support to anti-British activity. However, it was later claimed in the 1918 Rowlatt Committee Report that Hasan was involved in securing a signature from Ghalib Pasha, Ottoman governor of the Hijaz, on a declaration of war against the British that would be used to spark rebellion in India.[98] He was held for one month in Jidda and then taken to Cairo, interrogated by British officials, and imprisoned in Malta until 1917 along with several others, including Hussain Ahmad Madani, a prominent Deoband-trained Indian Muslim Islamic scholar who had lived in Medina since 1899.[99] The arrest and incarceration of these religious scholars and pilgrims marked the furthest reach of the British empire's coercive apparatus into the Hijaz. The idea of Britain as the "friend of Islam" was highly contingent on whether Muslims supported

British imperial rule and British power and the dictates of imperial security.

In a significant break with previous policy, the 1917 Hajj saw the introduction of compulsory return tickets for Indian pilgrims. Action on this tortuous issue, which had appeared to be on the verge of resolution before July 1914, was, as we have seen, postponed because of the war. But the Hijaz's changed political landscape, coupled with shipping shortages, led to its swift imposition; an orderly Hajj meant, in British eyes, no destitute pilgrims. However, this policy did not go uncontested, and once again, it was a Muslim official employed by Britain who had the closest involvement in the Hajj in 1917 compared with that of his British colleagues in Jidda. Moreover, the volatile situation in the Hijaz during this period gave such officials significant scope for interpreting their duties regarding the Hajj without the close supervision of their superiors. Hakim Said Hassan, a police officer from India's United Provinces, went on Hajj along with 1,200 other Indians.[100] He recorded over 50,000 pilgrims at Arafat, some 10,000 from Sudan and West Africa, and 15,000 from Najd. Hassan had to contend with Indian pilgrims destroying their return tickets in the belief that they would be treated as *miskeen*, poor pilgrims, and the British authorities would give them free return passage, although this seemed strange, given that they had already paid for the tickets. Nevertheless, through a notice printed in Hussein's newspaper, *al-Qibla*, which warned pilgrims not to dispose of return tickets, and Hassan's efforts to persuade the heads of the *mutawwif* guilds to warn pilgrims against disposing of return tickets, he managed to halt the practice. It appears that Hassan's sojourn in the Hijaz was not particularly happy: although he conceded that Hussein had introduced some reforms, "in spite of all this the moral character of the people is really disgusting. They are given to all sorts of vices and it is not an uncommon sight to see men lying about dead drunk in Jedda. Even in the holy city of Mecca people do not refrain from indulging in intoxicants."[101] The notion that Mecca was the ideal barometer of Islamic practice seems marginally less convincing if Hassan's report is to be believed.

As the Arab Revolt continued through 1917, officials directly involved in the Hijaz became increasingly cognizant that the situation there, especially regarding the pilgrimage, was of interest and importance to their colleagues throughout Britain's Muslim empire. For example, a note on the Hajj from the political resident at Aden was sent to the high commissioner in Cairo, the governor-general of Sudan, the pilgrimage officer in Jidda, the government of Bombay, and the Foreign and Political Department of the government of India. Significantly, the source of this information on the Hajj, like many others, was a Muslim official, J. S. Kadri, whose unique perspective on the pilgrimage could not be replicated by his British employers: "The ways of God are inscrutable and He does what men can never divine. Hussein's overthrow of the Ottomans made it possible for Indians to go to Mecca and perform their most cherished and fundamental duties of the faith."[102] In Kadri's opinion, because pilgrims were "generally illiterate and unacquainted with Arabic and the conditions of Arabia," they were vulnerable to the unscrupulous practices of pilgrim guides and others who made their living from the pilgrimage. To protect pilgrims' interests, Kadri argued that it was desirable for Britain to have a protector of pilgrims in Jidda and Mecca, appointed by the British government, who should know Arabic, as well as Indian languages, and report to the British consul at Jidda.[103] As in examples from Chapters 2 and 3, proposals for expanding Britain's administrative involvement in the Hajj came from Muslim employees as much as from British officials.

One portentously significant feature of the Hashemite takeover of the Hijaz and the Hajj was the renewed tension between Hussein and his enemies in Najd—Ibn Saud and the Wahhabis. The government of India had formally opened relations with Ibn Saud in 1910. An Anglo-Saudi treaty was signed in 1915, and Ibn Saud received a subsidy of £5,000 a month to fight the Rashidis, allied to the Ottomans, although there had been little fighting between the two enemies by 1917.[104] The Arab Bureau marked the 1917 Hajj by lamenting the slow progress of the Arab Revolt, with Medina still in Ottoman hands and no significant victories, and the main feature of the pilgrimage was the large contingent of 12,500 (of whom 7,000 were armed) from Najd, headed by Ibn Saud's father.[105] Colonel Wilson was keen to stress that the pilgrimage was a "great success" because there were no Hijazi-Wahhabi clashes, especially because both Ibn

Saud and Hussein were British allies and received British subsidies. Hashemite officials attempted to prevent Wahhabis from "mixing" with Meccans and pilgrimage guides; this included a ban on Meccans marrying Wahhabis.[106] All this information came from Hussein Ruhi, one of Wilson's staff; this underscores how limited British information on events during the Hajj would have been without using Muslim employees.[107]

Hussein, Faisal, and others in the Hashemite firmament had reason to distrust the Wahhabis. They were firmly opposed to Wahhabism. Faisal recounted how in 1912 Ibn Saud had sent Wahhabi missionaries to Mecca who preached that Meccans were infidels and an "intolerable" presence in the Holy Places.[108] Wahhabi missionaries traveled to the Hijaz again in 1916. Faisal underlined to Lawrence in December 1917 the importance of the struggle with the Wahhabis and what would happen if the Hashemites failed to "strangle" Wahhabism. Their victories over the Ottomans would be worthless; "Great Britain will not profit by the Arab revival, the tomb at Medina and the Haram at Mecca will be destroyed, and the pilgrimage is prevented."[109] Hussein repeatedly returned to the "seriousness" of the Wahhabi threat in conversations with British officials. Ibn Saud was "fanning the flame of fanaticism to further his own ambitions." Hijazi tribes who gathered dates in Ibn Saud's territory were exposed to the "full blast" of Wahhabi influence and were given rifles and money. Wahhabi preachers had "insidious methods." In trying to ensure British support against Ibn Saud, Hussein emphasized how his revolt was not only political, to free himself from the Ottomans, but also to provide the "honourable upkeep" of the Holy Cities in order to facilitate the pilgrimage.[110]

Colonel Wilson fell back on using Britain's policy of noninterference in religious matters in order to avoid further embroilment in the continued friction between Britain's subsidized allies in Arabia.[111] Ibn Saud was bitter that Hussein enjoyed larger British subsidies, which he had used to buy tribal loyalty from those who had previously professed fealty to Ibn Saud. Consequently, Ibn Saud frequently appealed for equal treatment by the British and was fearful that if the Allies won the war, Hussein would be an influential monarch, while he would remain "a mere Bedouin chieftain."[112] Because of strained relations with Hussein, Ibn Saud banned his followers from performing the Hajj in 1918, although 12,000 Najdis still arrived, the Wahhabis among them apparently being "incognito."[113] This "clash of Islams" between Hashemite and Wahhabi over the Hajj would reach a crescendo in the postwar period.

The Hajj, the Arab Revolt, the war against the Ottoman empire, and many other related issues were often bundled together by officials as "the Mohamedan question." Colonel Wilson's experience in Jidda with the Hajj, as well as his time in Sudan, probably contributed to his correspondingly broad view of this: "Issues of first importance to us as an Empire, with our millions of Moslem subjects, depend on how the Mohamedan question is handled now and in the future."[114] Captain Bray, also based in Jidda but with extensive experience in India, grasped that "the whole question is an imperial one. India, Egypt, Aden are but links in the chain of dominion. Yet before the war we were woefully ignorant of conditions prevailing in each other's spheres. A perpetual interchange of views, of intelligence, of affairs, of policy is an absolute necessity, an obligation to our empire as a whole."[115] Similar thoughts were shared at the highest levels of power in London. Edwin Montagu, secretary of state for India, wrote to the War Cabinet in 1917 that because "England, the greatest Mohammedan power in the world, has been forced into hostility to Turkey . . . we shall find ourselves with large Mahomedan interests of great imperial importance stretching right from India to the western boundaries of Egypt."[116] This bringing together of the western and eastern parts of Britain's Muslim empire in the Hijaz as a result of Britain backing Hussein's Arab Revolt, coupled with these British officials' interactions with the pilgrimage, which attracted thousands of Muslims from across the British empire, catalyzed the realization among British officials that the connecting thread among so many of Britain's territories was Islam—and the Hajj.

British interactions with the Hajj until this period had largely been dominated by India, whose pilgrims were, and remained, the most numerous from Britain's Muslim empire. However, the increased exposure British officials had to the Hijaz during the war meant that the broader character of this Muslim empire, seen in microcosm in the Hijaz because of the Hajj, came into sharper focus. A key figure in this regard was David George Hogarth, an Oxford archaeologist who became one of the principal intelligence officers involved in the Arab Revolt. His 1917 handbook on the Hijaz was a timely undertaking, given the increased numbers of Britons involved in that theater, and succinctly summarized the main features of the Hajj for its readers.[117] His observations inculcated an awareness of Mecca, Medina, and Jidda as cosmopolitan centers where British subjects from Asia and Africa lived.[118] Jidda included a "moiety of negroes and Somalis, most of whom live outside the walls. . . . About 300 British-Indian subjects are registered, but the exact number of families are not recorded."[119] On a later mission to "try and persuade the Old Man of Mecca [Hussein] to do things he doesn't want to do," he noted the village of *takayrna* pilgrims outside Jidda, whose inhabitants were "content to stay there for years after taking seven to eight years to get to the Holy Land, marching from the Atlantic to the Sudan."[120] It was only after the war that pilgrims from Nigeria and Sudan received increased and unwanted attention from British officials.

As the war neared its end in the final months of 1918, many strands came together in strengthening a perception among officials and others that Britain was the world's preeminent Muslim power and ruler over a Muslim empire. These strands included the Ottoman empire's collapse, the sense that the peace was an opportunity to reorder the British empire, and the exposure many officials had had to the Hijaz and the pilgrimage.[121] This viewpoint is evident in documents from officials across Britain's Muslim empire and beyond. For example, the British consul-general in Batavia, capital of the Netherlands East Indies, thought that it was "impossible to overestimate the vast prestige which we should get among the faithful if we conducted not later than 1919 a successful pilgrimage. A mixed Javanese-Malay pilgrimage would have added value in that the interchange of views between the two parties would by no means derogate from the high appreciation which most of the natives of the archipelago begin to feel for our administration of Malaya in so far as we respect Islam."[122]

In Egypt, when the new high commissioner, Sir Reginald Wingate, was presented with a memorandum from two officials "on the desirability for co-ordination of our treatment of Moslem questions and peoples in our various dependencies," he commented that "we must do more on this in the future."[123] Among all British officials, Wingate possessed the clearest conception that Britain must consider its Muslim empire as a connected whole in order to ensure the continued security of imperial rule. He communicated this view at length to the viceroy of India, Lord Hardinge:

> I gather . . . that there have been informal discussions in London on the subject of improved organization for collecting, appreciating and disseminating information regarding Moslems within and without the Empire. . . . I have always believed this was necessary. . . . I do feel it incumbent upon us to take careful note of moral and political influences that are being exercised on various populations. . . . As India is very certainly the centre of our Eastern Moslem world, so Cairo will inevitably become the western centre.[124]

Wingate's plans for greater organization among Britain's Muslim territories came to little, as did his plan for Cairo to become the head of a great African viceroyalty to rival India, with himself at its head. But the diverse theaters of operations during the war and the conflict's impact on areas such as the Hijaz, Palestine, Iraq, and Egypt had brought officials together as never before—on the ground and by letter or telegram—and had forced them to consider more closely events beyond their respective territories.[125] Wingate returned to this theme in a letter to Foreign Secretary Arthur Balfour:

> I have for long felt it is desirable to obtain a freer interchange of opinions and information about the progress, moral and material, of the Moslem populations throughout the Empire, and more direct communications between the administrations of the less important dependencies and the principal centres of Islamic thought. At these centres only can the real trend of Moslem opinion be correctly estimated, and the general lines of our Moslem policy, propaganda and counter-propaganda be usefully determined.[126]

The idea that Britain ruled over a Muslim empire was probably given its clearest exposition by Count Leon Ostrorog, former undersecretary at the Ottoman Ministry of Justice before the war who then worked for the British government: "His Britannic Majesty is the greatest ruler of Mohammedans in the world. He controls a much greater number of Mohammedans than did the Sultans of Turkey in their days of extensive power. It is of the most vital and obvious interest for Great Britain that this state of things should be maintained."[127] The official mind had begun to view Islam more clearly as a phenomenon that transcended colonial and imperial boundaries, and each territory had common interests with regard to the faith; the most representative example of this commonality was the Hajj. Indeed, it was Muslims employed by the British who often expressed this most clearly. Indian army captain Ajub Khan, in Mecca to perform the Hajj and supply intelligence in 1919, wrote that "as we are the greatest Moslem ruling power in the world, our share of protecting the interests of our Moslem fellow subjects at these Holy Places is equally greater."[128] The events of the First World War in the Hijaz brought to fruition the idea that Britain had a Muslim empire, and that in some senses it was a Muslim power.

The last wartime pilgrimage was very small: only 44,000 pilgrims were recorded present at Arafat. The relative absence of Indian pilgrims meant that British officials took more notice of *takayrna* pilgrims from Sudan and Nigeria. Some used the Khedival Line day service from Suakin to Jidda. However, many avoided contact with Sudanese and Hijazi authorities by traveling "in small batches by native sailing boats" from Suakin. W. P. Cochrane, author of this Hajj report, thought it impossible to predict the effect of peace on the pilgrimage, but "the general opinion among those most interested in pilgrim traffic is that provided shipping is available, the opening of Medina will undoubtedly have a marked effect on the next season, as to many the pilgrimage is incomplete, and with some of little or no value, unless it includes a visit to the tomb of the Prophet."[129] Despite the armistice signed on October 30, 1918, at Mudros, which ended hostilities in the Ottoman empire, Medina surrendered only on January 10, 1919. Fakhri Pasha, the Ottoman commander who successfully defended the city throughout the war, refused after the armistice to abrogate his sacred duty to protect the Prophet's tomb from the Hashemites.[130] Once Fakhri Pasha and his force left Medina, it finally became possible, for the first time since 1916, for Muslims to perform the Hajj and also travel to Medina to visit the tomb of the Prophet Muhammad. This moment of triumph for the Hashemites (and Britain) was short-lived, however. The following section will analyze Britain's involvement in the pilgrimage as the Hashemite regime unraveled.

"A Monster of Our Own Creation," 1918–1924

The ebullience of officials such as Wingate about the potential for reordering Britain's Muslim empire in the closing months of the war and the possibilities of reforming the Hajj experience for the millions of Muslim subjects in this empire underwent a rapid retreat in the postwar period. Britain was assailed by a series of crises from 1919 to 1924 that spanned the entire empire, from Ireland to India.[131] Within this broader tumult, there was also a set of crises that assailed Britain's Muslim empire, with rebellions and revolutions in Egypt and Iraq, the Third Anglo-Afghan War, and the *hijra* and Khilafat movements in India.[132] Britain's interactions with the Hajj in these volatile years were another feature of the extended crisis, although they have been largely absent from existing works that take a synoptic view of this period, a somewhat surprising omission given Timothy Paris's argument that "after maintaining control of the Red Sea route to India, the integrity of the hajj was perhaps Britain's most vital concern in Arabia."[133] Furthermore, the pilgrimage was one of the principal reasons for the deterioration of Britain's relations with King Hussein in these years.[134] For the king, the Hajj was not only a vital source of income for his impoverished kingdom but also a key prop in his campaign for legitimacy as ruler of the Hijaz and his wider pretensions to be king of the lands of the Arabs, *malik bilad al-'arab*, and, in 1924, caliph.[135] These claims were met with skepticism by his detractors across the Muslim world, who saw him as a British puppet. In discussions with British officials, Hussein himself was uncomfortably aware that the Hijaz's status as an independent state was "somewhat difficult to reconcile with the actual state of affairs."[136] However, Hussein used the Hashemite administration of the pilgrimage to assert his independence from Britain; inconsistent attempts by Britain to extend a supervisory role over aspects of the pilgrimage were repeatedly blunted. Along with factors such as Hussein's refusal to accept the postwar political landscape of an Anglo-French-dominated Middle East in the form of the League of Nations Mandate system, disputes over the Hajj were an important contributing factor to Britain's shift away from Hussein and acceptance of the Saudi invasion of his kingdom in 1924, which had profound consequences for the Hajj.

Far from the turmoil in the postwar Hijaz, the importance Britain attached to the Hajj was underlined by the establishment of an interdepartmental committee on the pilgrimage in Whitehall in 1919. Although quarantine measures were a major part of the committee's remit, it considered Britain's overall engagement with the pilgrimage. Given Britain's support of Hussein's regime, the committee felt that Britain could no longer only guard the interests of British subjects but should now ensure that Hussein managed the Hajj adequately. The Treasury decided that part of Hussein's subsidy should go toward the administration of the Hajj; the British government was now indirectly paying for the costs of the Hijaz's pilgrimage administration.[137] The limits of British aims to hold Hussein's Hajj administration to account are evident in the minutes from subsequent meetings. Major Young, having a frustrating experience serving in Jidda as one of Britain's representatives, argued that threatening to suspend assistance to British subjects who made up the majority of pilgrims "might make him [Hussein] more reasonable on other things." This was unlikely, given that some of this assistance, such as the R 1,150,000 subsidy for Indian pilgrims from 1919 to 1920 that kept steamship ticket prices artificially low, was partly a "form of propaganda for Hussein," who was widely disliked in India. The India Office representative on the committee said that "a badly managed pilgrimage, even if it entailed the death of large numbers of pilgrims, would be preferable politically to any sort of restriction" on pilgrims traveling from India.[138] Amid these discussions, the lives of pilgrims ranked low compared with political and financial considerations.

Finance was a prime factor in the decline of Anglo-Hijazi relations, which had a deleterious impact on the Hajj. Britain's extensive subsidies to the Hijaz were trimmed as part of a global fiscal retrenchment necessitated by Britain's parlous financial situation after the war, which was exacerbated by an economic downturn. The Arab Bureau emphasized that such subsidies were a "burden" in these straitened circumstances, especially because they had been "grossly misspent" by the Hashemites on overpaying soldiers and disseminating Hashemite propaganda in Iraq, Yemen, and Syria.[139] The reduction in Hussein's monthly subsidy from £200,000 to £25,000 over October to December 1919, however, did not entail any retreat from Britain's engagement with the Hijaz. According to the Arab Bureau, the kingdom's future "closely affect[ed] British interests." Britain had "a moral responsibility" for the Hijaz's future. One critical aspect of this was the pilgrimage; its importance had been "dealt with too often to need further emphasis." Britain's continued financial leverage over the Hijaz meant that further British assistance "should be conditional on the king accepting our advice (preferably through the medium of advisers appointed by us) . . . in establishing a proper administration."[140] Britain's increased involvement in the Hajj was evident during the 1919 pilgrimage season, when Major W. E. Marshall was the Hijaz's inspector-general of quarantine and public health, with control over medical and quarantine arrangements.[141] The foothold Britain now held in the pilgrimage administration was a spur for other officials, analyzed later, to argue for extending Britain's engagement with the Hajj. These proposals were based on negative assessments of Hussein's ability to successfully manage the pilgrimage. However, such criticisms, which repeatedly appear in official sources and are largely accepted in scholarly works, must be placed in their wider context. The massive subsidies given to Hussein had dramatically distorted the Hijaz's political economy. Britain's ultimate withdrawal of these subsidies in February 1920 meant that Hussein's previous largesse to Bedouin tribes, for example, became unsustainable, with tragic consequences for pilgrims' travels in the Hijaz.

Alongside these developments, the Indian Khilafat movement of 1919–1922 was probably the most important overarching event that Britain had to factor into its relationship with the pilgrimage, and the movement's power militated against greater imperial involvement in the Hajj. Forged out of Indian Muslim opposition to the 1919

Rowlatt Act (an extension of the 1915 Defence of India Act), Britain's treatment of the Ottoman empire in the Paris peace talks, and the issue of the caliphate's future, this movement has received extensive scholarly attention and so will be considered only briefly regarding its relevance to the pilgrimage.[142] The alliance of Abdul Bari and the Ali brothers with Gandhi in September 1920 led to India's first noncooperation movement, but it had lost its force by 1922, and its grievances related to the Holy Places were rendered irrelevant by postwar peace treaties and Kemal Atatürk's abolition of the caliphate in 1924. The movement's roots partly derived from general Indian Muslim hostility to Hussein's regime.[143] For example, a Deobandi *alim* (scholar) wrote that Muslims had "firmly fixed in their minds" that Hussein was "a puppet of the English," which meant that the Holy Cities were "practically under [British] control."[144] At the Muslim League's annual meeting in 1918, an attendee said that Indian Muslims "take a deep interest in the fate of their co-religionists outside India."[145] The Khilafat movement's gathering force contributed to the stressful atmosphere among the members of the British delegation at the Paris peace talks. Edwin Montagu, secretary of state for India, warned his colleagues about the dangers of alienating Muslims who had been mostly loyal during the war: "Let us not . . . tell the Moslem what he ought to think, let us recognise what they do think."[146] This led Prime Minister Lloyd George to remark that Montagu's attitude during the negotiations was "not so much that of a member of the British cabinet, but of a successor on the throne of Aurangezeb!"[147] In Francis Robinson's phrase, religion was "imported" into Indian politics on an enormous scale, which had ramifications beyond India's shores.[148]

The Khilafat movement was extremely influential in shaping British policy on the Hajj, especially in India.[149] Indeed, from 1919 to 1922, almost every proposal or action undertaken by the various officials involved in the Hajj was colored by the Khilafat movement, as is evident throughout this section; it was often mentioned, implicitly or explicitly, as the reason for supporting or opposing various schemes or policies. In 1919 and 1920, India subsidized return passages for pilgrims at a cost of over R 1,150,000 and maintained a pilgrimage officer at Jidda for Indian pilgrims; after the Khilafat movement subsided in 1923, officials in India were "no longer in favour of subsidising Mahomedans who visited the Holy Places," although this continued in practice.[150] Although such actions were expediently pursued because of the Khilafat movement's intensity, the biggest challenge to British power in India since 1857, in the broader context of this study, it is clear that subsidizing pilgrims' journeys and having an Indian Muslim official at Jidda were familiar features of Britain's engagement with the Hajj.

Upheaval in another strategically vital territory of Britain's Muslim empire manifested itself during the first postwar pilgrimage in 1919. The Egyptian Revolution came as an unexpected shock to some officials; one wrote to the head of the Cairo Residency, Milne Cheetham, that "the extent and violence of the movement in Egypt has evidently come as a complete surprise to you."[151] More alarmingly, revolutionary sentiment was displayed during the Hajj. Some Egyptian officers who made up the escort of the Egyptian *mahmal* caravan demonstrated with a gun salute in favor of independence while they were in the Hijaz.[152] The wider tumult across Britain's Muslim empire, including war with Afghanistan and rebellion in Iraq, led to acute concerns about troop garrison levels across this arc of instability.[153] Such worries were heightened because Muslim soldiers made up a significant proportion of Britain's fighting force, especially in the Indian army, because of Britain's "martial races" theory and the perception that Muslims were reliable subjects. Out of 683,149 troops recruited to the Indian army during the First World War, no fewer than 98,000 were Punjabi Muslims.[154]

Given the context outlined here, it is perhaps unsurprising that British officials used the Hajj for propaganda purposes in 1919, when Britain sponsored the pilgrimage of hundreds of preselected Indian Muslim soldiers stationed in Egypt as they waited to be sent home after a long deployment supporting Britain's war effort in the region.[155] This idea drew on longer antecedents, such as ideas developed after the 1857 Indian rebellion that to preserve military discipline it was necessary that Indian army authorities "understood the religious needs of their men" and incorporate customary religious practices into military life.[156] More specifically, after the start of the Arab Revolt, British commanders of Muslim units had been ordered to discuss the revolt with selected Indian officers to "remove misunderstanding" about government policy. During the war, attention was paid to soldiers' religious sensibilities; for example, the begum of Bhopal donated 900 Qur'ans and 1,400 Islamic religious tracts to soldiers, who seemed to genuinely appreciate such gestures.[157] From the soldiers' viewpoint, as detailed by David Omissi, military service "affected the outward signs of Muslim identity at a fundamental level." For example, the pay of Punjabi Muslim soldiers was spent in the province to build mosques, fund sons' religious education, augment the income of Sufi saints and the upkeep of shrines, and pay for the costs of soldiers and their extended families to perform the Hajj.[158]

This novel scheme, hitherto neglected by scholars, illustrates how Britain was prepared to exploit its soldiers, under the rubric of assisting their spiritual welfare, in the vain hope of improving perceptions of Britain as a supporter of Islamic practice for its Muslim subjects. Two very different people independently conceived this idea. King George V proposed that some of the Indian Muslim soldiers in the Egyptian Expeditionary Force should be allowed to perform the Hajj before returning to India.[159] A few days later, a similar suggestion came across the desk of the secretary of state for India, Edwin Montagu, from Everard Digby, an Indian army reserve officer stationed in Egypt. Digby was convinced that every soldier asked "would . . . jump at the chance."[160] Furthermore, Digby believed that King Hussein would be "flattered" because this would "emphasise his own importance," and that "the dramatic character of the pilgrimage would catch the imagination of the whole Muhammadan world." Britain, "the greatest Muhammadan Empire in the world" after it had defeated the Ottoman empire, "the next greatest Muhammadan power," would provide an unprecedented spectacle if, "solicitous of the spiritual welfare of its Muhammadan citizens," British authorities made "special arrangements for a large proportion of its Muhammadan veterans to perform the hajj." This would "prove to the whole Muhammadan world that the British Empire realises its responsibility as the largest Muhammadan power and can meet those responsibilities in the grand manner." Beyond this grandiose prose, Digby put forward several pragmatic reasons for the scheme. It would, he thought, reduce the risk of British Muslim subjects being influenced by "extreme exponents of nationalism" and "still" anti-British "intrigue" in Afghanistan, Egypt, and Persia. Moreover, the scheme would ensure that British rule in Iraq "would begin under the most favourable auspices."[161] Digby's proposal and Montagu's handwritten response, "The scheme—if at all practicable—is a fascinating one—political effects might be excellent," show that these men had little genuine concern for the spiritual welfare of Muslim soldiers who had paid a heavy price in blood for Britain over the preceding years.[162] Instead, the Hajj was to be cynically used in an attempt to deflate anti-British sentiment throughout the Muslim world.

The scheme was duly put into practice; two batches of soldiers sailed from Suez to Jidda on January 24 and February 12, 1919, each spending over two weeks in Mecca, and the event was regarded as a great success by British officials.[163] Eight thousand soldiers signed up, but the final number of soldier-pilgrims was 166 officers and 4,400 men because of the constrained financial situation.[164] Wingate, now high commissioner in Egypt, believed that it would have a "good effect," and Sir Percy Cox thought that "it should certainly go to prove that allegations as to our intention to destroy the Mussalman faith are unfounded."[165] Captain Salamatulla Khan, leader of the Indian Muslim soldier-pilgrims, proclaimed to Hussein: "Our government takes great care and thought for our religion and religious customs. In spite of transport being so scarce nowadays it has afforded us a ship and given us the opportunity of doing pilgrimage." The report to the War Office further amplified these soldier-pilgrims' positive views: they were "delighted at the arrangements" and expressed their "heartfelt gratitude to the British government."[166] Unfortunately, there are no surviving letters in the archives from these soldiers, unlike their comrades in France, to provide a valuable alternative perspective to official reports.[167] Britain was playing a double game with this exercise: in addition to the use of soldier-pilgrims for propaganda, several Indian officers were tasked with writing intelligence reports on their time in the Hijaz, a unique opportunity for such efforts, which underlines the vital role played by Muslims employed by Britain to further imperial knowledge of the political situation in the Holy Cities.

However, the pilgrimage of these soldiers was not an unqualified success and showed the practical limitations of Britain's attempt to manufacture political capital out of the event. Relations between the soldiers and some of Mecca's inhabitants descended into open conflict. Captain Ajub Khan described how the "usual mulcting and cheating of the poor Indian pilgrims was much resented by our men and on several occasions they resorted to violence and rioting, but timely intervention always checked further developments."[168] For example, there was a fracas at a water halt between the soldiers and some Bedouins after one of the soldiers was insulted. The Bedouins then "generally vilified" all Indians, and one fired on a soldier, just missing him. After the soldiers seized two of these tribesmen, a local Hijazi official demanded that the Bedouins be released but was ignored. When the soldiers reached their destination, the tribesmen were finally handed over to the authorities.[169] Khan perceived that Indians in Mecca were in an unenviable position. Calling someone an Indian was apparently a great insult, and many Indians pretended to be Arabs as a result.[170] The idea of the *umma* as a peaceful community of equals during Hajj rang hollow in this instance. Ethnic tensions bubbled to the surface, exacerbated by these pilgrims' status as soldiers in the British Indian army. The grand objectives of Britain's sponsored soldier pilgrimage fell short in their practical application, a further example of the empire's inability to control aspects of the pilgrimage experience for its subjects.[171]

Nevertheless, these difficulties did not dissuade Captain Ajub Khan from arguing to his superiors that Britain should intervene more deeply in the Hijaz's pilgrimage administration. Khan thought that the Hashemite government was "well-meaning," but its governance was "backward," and although Hussein was "very anxious for the welfare of pilgrims," his officials were corrupt.[172] He was scathingly critical of the Hashemite government's organization; there was "none for practical purposes."[173] By the Hajj's conclusion, the overall situation was a "chaotic state of affairs." Khan had several suggestions for improvements, such as a metaled road from Mecca to Jidda, improved water supplies in the towns, and more experienced government officials. Significantly, Khan believed that there was an "urgent necessity" for a British representative at Mecca and Medina—"a permanent official at these important centres of the Islamic world"—because of the huge number of Britain's pilgrim-subjects and the significant number of British subjects who had settled in the Holy Cities.[174] Other suggestions, such as a hospital and British Muslim officials in Mecca, would enable Britain to "relieve us of our duty to our subjects as well as greatly enhancing our popularity and influence in the Muslim world."[175] The appointment of a British representative in Mecca was seen as an essential preliminary for these proposals to become reality. Colonel C. E. Vickery, Major Marshall's successor, held out little hope of changes in the Hashemite pilgrimage administration because "any suggestion calling for enterprise and innovation of any sort is at once vetoed by a narrow minded and obstinate king."[176] Khan in fact became the British representative at Mecca in 1920, and his work, according to Vickery, was "very valuable," a fact Vickery used to argue for the post becoming permanent.[177] However, Hussein objected to Khan's presence in Mecca, and the position was abolished after only a few months, an event interlinked with the king's opposition to British attempts to establish a pilgrim hostel in Mecca.

Britain's abortive venture into Mecca's hostelry sector was initially prompted by its European allies and was another example of how officials were aware of the breadth of Britain's Muslim empire. In January 1918, France and Italy purchased hostels in Mecca for their poorer Muslim subjects, which led officials in Cairo to argue that Britain should follow suit. Not doing so would attract "adverse comment" from its Muslim subjects. More important, it was argued, a hostel should be established because Britain sent "more pilgrims to Mecca than any other nation. . . . It is due to our prestige that they should be suitably looked after." The Arab Bureau observed that a hostel would attend to pilgrims' comforts, but it would also "ensure they are kept free from all corrupting influences."[178] Wingate recognized that although India's "preponderant interest" in the Hajj meant that it should have the first nomination for a hostel agent, its staff should include members of "other important Moslem communities in the Empire."[179] The authorities in Malaya agreed to pay for a share of the capital and annual expenditure on the hostel.[180] A Muslim Commission consisting of Hussein Ruhi, Hakim Said Hassan (an Indian inspector based in the Hijaz), and a Sudanese engineer was appointed to reconnoiter Mecca for a suitable site.[181] British officials in Jidda stressed to the commission that "a very large proportion of pilgrims visiting Mecca in normal times come from different parts of the British Empire." Therefore, it was "essential . . . that the building selected shall be in all respects worthy of an Empire which comprises such vast numbers of Moslem subjects."[182] Colonel Wilson in Cairo argued to the Foreign Office that "[we] strongly urge that sufficient funds are forthcoming to make the hostel a credit to the British Empire with its millions of Moslem subjects."[183] Ruhi estimated that buying a suitable building would cost £10,000, with operating costs of £11,000 a year.[184] A physical presence in the heart of Islam was seen as vital to Britain's pilgrimage-related interests and emblematic of its status as ruler over millions of Muslims.[185]

However, the pilgrim hostel never materialized because of Hussein's worsening relations with Britain and hostility to it from London and the government of India because of the Khilafat movement. Before the scheme was torpedoed, Wingate sent Captain Nasiruddin Ahmad of the Aden Political Staff to Mecca in April 1920 to prepare the pilgrim hostel, replacing Captain Ajub Khan as the British representative there.[186] In October 1920, the Foreign Office poured cold water on the whole proposal: the "extreme sensitiveness of Indian Moslem opinion rendered the present moment inopportune for the initiation of a scheme in which the hand of the government would be immediately detected." The government of India's recourse to consultation with Muslims about the hostel was a critical factor in this decision. Delhi and the India Office feared that a British hostel "would involve the risk of antagonising Moslem sentiment in India." Facing this opposition and the "uncompromising attitude" of Hussein to the hostel and Britain's representative in Mecca, the plan died.[187] Foreign Secretary Lord Curzon ordered officials in Jidda to inform Hussein of Britain's decision. Furthermore, in response to the king's "unconcealed objection" to any foreign official in Mecca, Britain would withdraw Nasiruddin.[188] British plans to further extend its involvement in the Hajj were once again stymied by the cautious attitude of officials in India, informed by Muslim consultation, with the added disincentive of Hussein's hostility to a more prominent British presence in Mecca.

One of the most important factors in Britain's connection with the pilgrimage in this period, which was central to the empire's deteriorating relationship with Hussein, was the recurrent crisis over destitute pilgrims. As a result of Cairo's intimate involvement in the Hijaz during the war, officials there now devoted greater attention to this phenomenon. Egypt's new high commissioner, General Edmund Allenby, wrote to Curzon in 1920 after reading a report from Colonel Vickery and Captain Ajub Khan in Jidda that the "protection and care of destitute British pilgrims in the Hedjaz is a matter deserving early attention." The wartime requirement of compulsory return tickets for Indian pilgrims had been dropped after the conflict ended. The alarmist nature of these reports probably captured Allenby's attention. For example, one read: "Still a good many pilgrims stranded in Jidda. Persian Gulf Steam Navigation Company seemed to have treated their pilgrims badly, many of whom are dying of hunger."[189] A later report from Jidda was equally doom-laden: "The state of the country is bad. There is in effect no government. King Hussein has no aptitude for governing."[190] Allenby knew that he was wading into an area of Britain's relationship with the Hajj that had a long and troubled history, detailed in Chapters 2 and 3. Because many pilgrims had died "whilst waiting and hoping for assistance," Allenby thought that there was a need to address this issue because it would become larger once the pilgrimage revived fully in peacetime. Allenby echoed the government of India's proposals, such as deposits for return fares, and conveniently sidestepped Egypt taking extra responsibility for pilgrims. The cost of any extra consular staff needed to give "facilities" for sick and destitute pilgrims should be borne by India.[191] The high commissioner thought that each part of Britain's Muslim empire should retain separate responsibility for its pilgrim subjects in the Hijaz. Optimistically, Allenby wrote that "it only remains for Hussein to play his part in safeguarding . . . [these interests]. . . . To assure this we shall no doubt be able to bring pressure upon him if necessary."[192] Such pressure was financial, although Britain appeared powerless to prevent a recurrence of situations featuring destitute pilgrims that had last been seen before the war.

Allenby's high-minded memorandums did little to change Britain's experience of destitute pilgrims, although, because of the tense situation among officials produced by the Khilafat movement, the empire resumed its repatriation of destitute pilgrims, albeit on an ad hoc and reactive basis. The British consulate in Jidda was "besieged by wailing crowds, who were with great difficulty induced to go away, only to be replaced by others," and officials requested R 5,000 from the government of India for "relief work."[193] Major Marshall, the officer in charge, hoped that India would come up with extra funds because relief work cost R 100 every day.[194] In October and November 1921, the government of India paid for the repatriation of over 600 destitute Indian pilgrims.[195] This piecemeal repatriation and the continued presence of destitute pilgrims, over 700 in 1922, meant that the compulsory return-ticket proposal resurfaced.[196] Officials in India remained opposed to this, citing opposition from Muslim members on India's legislative council. Their colleagues in Jidda found it "profoundly discouraging" that despite their repeated calls for return tickets, "shiploads of potential destitutes are again to be allowed to travel from India to the Hedjaz in contravention of the Koranic injunction and apparently for the personal satisfaction of various Moslem gentlemen on Haj Committees and other bodies whose responsibility appears not to extend to the combating or obviation of this nuisance, but to cease with its initiation."[197] A voluntary return-ticket system with a registration and deposit scheme had some success: over 5,500 Indians registered, 581 return tickets were issued from Bombay, 407 were deposited at the consulate, and 222 pilgrims deposited money, which amounted to R 76,744.[198] The entire system was chaotic; some Indians who asked at the consulate for repatriation claimed that they had been told before they left India that there was a specific fund to which they could apply.[199] The Persian Gulf Steam Navigation Company carried 100 Afghan and central Asian pilgrims to India at R 25. The cost of this bureaucratic confusion to Delhi was around R 30,000.[200]

India's financial outlay on facilitating the Hajj for its poorer subjects (and others from outside India) formed part of a wider context in which British officials viewed conditions in the Hijaz as "rapidly becoming intolerable" for pilgrims. Outside the main towns, Bedouins attacked groups of pilgrims on the roads, and some pilgrim guides took a percentage of each raid because Hussein was now heavily taxing their earnings. Both trends were a consequence of Hussein's subsidy from Britain being cut. Those on the ground in Jidda, Major Marshall among them, believed that the only solution to the crisis was the abdication, "forced or otherwise," of Hussein, or measures such as suspending the pilgrimage because the conditions in the Hijaz "expose pilgrims to risks to which it would be inhuman to allow them to take."[201] Marshall's colleague Vickery was aware of the Hajj's importance to Hussein and how it could be used as leverage to further Britain's interests in the region: "It is through the pilgrimage that we can strike at the King." Vickery proposed a draft telegram to Hussein that would say that because of his inability to guarantee pilgrims' safety and comfort, "notices dissuading people from undertaking the pilgrimage this year had been published in our dependencies." Indeed, Britain's French allies frequently asked British officials why this action had not already been taken.[202] However, Marshall realized that London and Delhi would not agree to such dramatic moves because of "certain misrepresentation in India and elsewhere," given the current power of the Khilafat movement.[203]

Despite the very real difficulties faced by the Hashemite government in administering the Hajj, Hussein was adamant that this particular crisis was Britain's fault. The king castigated "the poverty and ignorance of the majority of pilgrims, especially from India, remarking that they were a burden to the country and an anxiety to his administration, and had only themselves to blame for what befell them." Hussein harked back to the presteamship era when pilgrim numbers had been far less, and those who had arrived from overseas invariably came from wealthier classes; but cheap travel had "flooded the Hejaz with the old and infirm, the destitute and the helpless, drawn from the poorest classes."[204] Despite his derogatory words, Hussein recognized that the Hijaz did not possess the requisite institutional and infrastructural capacities and capabilities to effectively manage the large number of pilgrims who visited every year. These tens of thousands of seaborne arrivals and hundreds of thousands of pilgrims in total were a direct consequence of technological and economic changes that had contributed to the comparative ease of travel over the past fifty years. Moreover, British officials in Jidda agreed that Hussein was hardly to blame for the presence of destitute Indian pilgrims in his kingdom; it was seen as reasonable for the king to demand that Britain deal with this group.[205] The descendant of the Prophet Muhammad and guardian of the Holy Cities wanted to limit pilgrim numbers; conversely, the British empire facilitated the Hajj for its Muslim subjects for pragmatic and self-interested reasons arising from the challenging political situation it faced during this period.

During 1923, the worsening situation with destitute pilgrims emphasized the different views held by officials in London, Delhi, and Jidda and underscored the vital importance of having Muslim employees within Britain's Hajj administration. Officials in the Foreign Office were alarmed that the government of India, echoing the view of India's Central Hajj Committee, composed of Indian Muslims, wanted to abolish the post of Indian pilgrimage officer in Jidda "at a time when it is considered increasingly necessary to create an efficient organization for pilgrims from across other parts of the empire" such as Malaya, Sudan, and Nigeria.[206] The post was retained. Muhammad Yasin Khan, former registrar at the Aden Resident's Court, was appointed Indian pilgrimage officer in 1923. Officials in Jidda thought that Khan's services would be "invaluable," especially because it was predicted that there would be "thousands" of indigent pilgrims—now fewer than 2 percent traveled from India with return tickets. British officials were faced with pilgrims who had been repatriated twice who "now turn up smiling to ask that their names may again be noted for return passages." The consul in Jidda, Reader Bullard, lamented that the "prospects of accumulation of Indian pilgrims in Jeddah after the hajj and of widespread destitution are, indeed, somewhat terrifying." These alarming statements meant that officials in India considered the entire question once again in 1923. In Jidda, officials realized that Hussein could easily counter British grievances against him by "complaining of the nuisance . . . constituted by this accumulation of destitutes, for whose presence in that condition in the country the Government of India is entirely responsible."[207] The various parts of Britain's Muslim empire that dealt with the Hajj were anything but united in their attitude toward one of the most vexatious aspects of pilgrimage administration.

One of the most trenchant critics of Britain's administration of the Hajj was Consul Reader Bullard, who faulted the approaches of both the Hijazi and Indian governments toward pilgrims.[208] Bullard felt that the Hijazi government was unable to make "proper provisions" for pilgrims, a situation compounded by its rejection of any "assistance" from Britain, which was seen "as an attempt to encroach on the Hejaz's sovereign rights mainly because it implies criticism of Hussein's government." Bullard debunked Hussein's claim to be a defender of pilgrims: "If he can do anything for them at the expense of, for example, the foreign shipping companies he does it and does his best to ensure his own actions remain concealed." Bullard's chief complaint regarding the government of India was related to destitute pilgrims, "who sit on my doorstep and want a free or assisted passage back to India at the expense of the Indian government." He thought that this state of affairs could be avoided by copying the Dutch and Malayan examples of compulsory return tickets, which would eliminate the phenomenon of "hundreds of Indians who get just enough for the voyage, perhaps cadge it from the pious and are penniless when they leave Bombay and expect to be sent home at government expense." However, Bullard realized the power of Indian Muslim opinion in shaping policy through arguments that any British intervention was interference with Islamic practice. Bullard wryly noted that "those devils," referring to the government of India, would merely quote the parts of the Qur'an that stated that one had to have sufficient funds to go on Hajj. In his opinion, the Indian authorities did little to ensure that their pilgrim-subjects adhered to this religious instruction, and he lamely wrote that "they talk of doing something. I hope they will."[209]

In fact, the government of India was active; it continued to provide a considerable subsidy for repatriating pilgrims, some R 35,000 in 1923.[210] This was despite the fact that some officials in the India Office and Delhi wanted this support to end; the government of India "could not be expected to supply differential treatment in favour of Mahomedan pilgrims," a viewpoint informed by the political complexities that surrounded increasing communal tensions between Muslims and Hindus on the subcontinent.[211] With over 24,000 Indian

Sir Reader Bullard, British consul at Jidda, 1923–1925, 1936–1939

Credit: National Portrait Gallery, London

pilgrims projected to arrive in the Hijaz, officials anticipated that many would be destitute. The consulate in Jidda warned that "the good news that destitution is no bar, in the eyes of the Indian government, to a trip—even an annual trip—to Mecca, is doubtless spreading in India."[212] Bullard sketched an evocative picture of Indian destitute pilgrims at the British consulate in 1923:

> We have lived surrounded by Indian destitutes—real and pretend—this week. Every morning at about 5.30 there starts a hubbub like the buzz that breaks out in a theatre when the curtain falls, only a hundred times louder. For weeks several dozen Indians have lived in the square at the side of the Agency, but the approaching departure of several boats has brought hundreds of others. We reckon there were 1,200 yesterday, pushing, quarrelling, yelling, demanding tickets, trying to push in at the gate, and so on.[213]

Despite these scenes, Bullard was optimistic. The consulate had adopted a "ruthless" policy to "discourage swindling." With the exception of arranging tickets for sick pilgrims, the consulate ignored these indigent pilgrims "until the very last minute," which discouraged those who actually had enough money for a ticket, who went away and bought one. These methods pleased shipping agents "who thought that we should queer their pitch with charity," given that a large number of pilgrims paid for full-price tickets. Typically, shipping firms would sell tickets at lower prices nearer departure time, which was a further incentive for pilgrims with little money to wait in Jidda.[214] At the consulate, Bullard and his staff selected 10 percent of poor pilgrims "at the very last moment" and gave the vast majority of tickets to women, but this process was "not easy to manage." Bullard praised the assistance he received from Jidda's police superintendent but later discovered that "his magic influence consisted in telling the Indians that not only would every one of them get a ticket, they would receive two rupees a head as well! The next time, this lie having been found out, the discipline was less good! However, we managed."[215] Bullard's official report noted that "only time can sift the honest from the dishonest destitute, and meanwhile thousands of Indians are lying about the streets converting the whole of Jeddah not excepting the doorstep of HM Agency, into a latrine." There were 5,600 indigent Indian pilgrims in Jidda at the end of the 1923 Hajj. The consulate estimated that "perhaps 1,500 can pay for their return, and the rest will be or pretend to be destitute. . . . At least 4,000, possibly more will have to be carried for nothing or next to nothing. Even if 10% of transport was allotted [for destitute pilgrims, as decreed by Hussein] this would only be for 900 pilgrims."[216] *The Times* summarized the Bombay protector of pilgrim's report from 1923, filled with "harrowing tales of hardship" of extortion, robbery, and the plight of indigent pilgrims stranded in Jidda, and noted that Hussein "might neutralize the feeling of hostility if he were manifestly anxious to lighten the burden of the pilgrims."[217]

At the same time, however, the Khilafat movement's waning power provided an opportunity for official attempts to resolve the issue of Indian destitute pilgrims, which had proved a constant feature of Britain's association with the Hajj since the 1870s. A revised version of the Indian Merchant Shipping Act 1923 was introduced, and Section 208A made it obligatory for any Indian or foreign pilgrim who sailed from an Indian port to purchase a return ticket or deposit the necessary sum with the government before embarkation. There were some special exemptions: for example, if pilgrims stated that they were traveling to the Hijaz to settle there permanently. A later amendment introduced in 1925 by Muslim legislators specifically discriminated in favor of richer pilgrims—only those traveling in the lowest class on pilgrim ships had to produce a return ticket in order to get an embarkation ticket to board the ship.[218] Shipping companies liaised with the commissioner of police in Bombay in issuing tickets to Jidda only to those whose passports showed that they had deposited R 60 with the police to cover the cost of their return journey. After the Hajj's conclusion, pilgrims went to the shipping company's offices in Jidda with their passport, which showed the R 60 deposit, and received return tickets. Pilgrims who lost their passports were checked against lists sent from India and given emergency passes by the consulate in Jidda.[219] Officials fervently hoped that "any drawbacks will be outweighed by one advantage: the elimination of the destitute Indian pilgrim."[220] In July 1924, the Jidda consulate reported that there were "no emaciated Indians lying at the . . . gate waiting for a passage home" and believed that it would be disastrous if this system were abandoned.[221] This procedure operated only on a trial basis until the act was finally passed into law for the 1926 Hajj season.[222] Although it appeared that Britain's policy on destitute pilgrims had finally been resolved, the repatriation of its pilgrim-subjects continued throughout the interwar period, albeit

Destitute Indian pilgrims outside the British consulate at Jidda, c. 1923

Credit: Sir Reader Bullard and Lady Bullard

on a smaller scale, so the legislation was not totally successful. Indeed, British repatriation efforts were extended in these years to Britain's indigent pilgrim-subjects from Sudan, Nigeria, and Malaya, examined in Chapter 6. Destitute pilgrims remained a part of Britain's relationship with the Hajj.

Britain's engagement with the Hajj in these tumultuous years extended even further when it took on a role as a facilitator in the 1923 *mahmal* dispute between Egypt—independent in 1922 but still under a large degree of British control—and King Hussein. The *mahmal* was, as we have seen, an established tradition over five hundred years old.[223] One British official recalled how he and others lined up on Suez's quayside wearing formal morning coats to witness the arrival of the *mahmal* from Cairo "on a gaily caparisoned elephant" and its departure for Jidda.[224] The Egyptian government recalled the *mahmal* in 1923 while it was on a ship outside Jidda because of Hussein's refusal to allow the accompanying Egyptian medical mission into the Hijaz. Hussein cited the settlement of certain issues regarding donations from Egyptian *waqf* endowments as a condition for giving approval for its landing. Bullard counseled Hussein that "your refusal would expose you to accusations of being indifferent to the welfare of Egyptian pilgrims . . . and would make a painful impression all over the Moslem world."[225] Given Egypt's still-subordinate relationship to Britain, its government requested that Bullard make "strong representations" to Hussein on the issue.[226] High Commissioner Allenby thought Hussein's attitude "intolerable" and reported that Hussein's obstruction of Egypt's medical mission meant that the recall of the *mahmal* was the "only means they have of putting pressure on Hussein."[227] The Egyptian government consulted with Allenby in Cairo before recalling the *mahmal*. The affair "shocked public opinion in Egypt" and was also raised in the House of Commons. Nevertheless, Allenby thought that the issue would be resolved because Egypt had cut off the revenue and supplies that accompanied the *mahmal*, which damaged the Hijaz's economy.[228]

Hussein denounced British intervention in the matter: Britain's "imperialistic aims fostered a quarrel between two Moslem nations which need never have arisen."[229] Relations between Egypt and the Hijaz were repaired by the next Hajj season after the Egyptian government was approached through Britain's Arab agent in Cairo, acting on behalf of Hussein, and the *mahmal* was dispatched.[230] One small difference from previous tradition was that because Egypt now had nominal independence from Britain, the British consul in Jidda no longer gave a reception when the *mahmal* arrived in Jidda.[231] However, the strained relationship between Egypt and the Hijaz continued in 1924. Returning Egyptian pilgrims complained that they had been badly treated because of extortion by the Hijazi authorities and Bedouin tribesmen, and Egypt's *amir al-hajj* reported that the band of text that surrounded the top of the *kiswa* that stated that it was donated by Egypt's King Fuad (r. 1922–1936) was removed. As a result, Egypt considered suspending wheat and oil donations to the Hijaz.[232] Hussein's acute sensitivity to any infringements on his sovereignty was understandable, especially in the realm of the pilgrimage, one of the few areas where he could exercise his kingdom's independence and appeal to a wider Muslim audience. These ructions in Egyptian-Hijazi relations were rendered temporarily irrelevant when Ibn Saud attacked westward from Najd and conquered the Hijaz in 1924–1925.

The British were fully aware of the potential for major conflict between the Hijaz and Najd. At a meeting with Major H. R. P. Dickson in 1920, Ibn Saud said that if his dispute with Hussein was not resolved, "a religious war" would ensue. His Wahhabi followers, the Ikhwan, were "straining at the leash."[233] Ibn Saud raised the prohibition on Hajj for his followers in 1920, and Britain was drawn into this latest move when Ibn Saud asked for an Indian officer to accompany these pilgrims from Najd to "ensure fair play" while they were in the Hijaz.[234] As in the *mahmal* dispute, Britain acted as the interlocutor between the various polities tied to it who had a stake in the pilgrimage.

Britain's position as one of the principal participants in Arabian affairs was put under pressure by Hussein's attitude toward the region's wider political landscape. In July 1921, the king rejected outright an Anglo-Hijazi treaty in initial negotiations conducted by T. E. Lawrence because of his opposition to the new regional political structure, dominated by the Anglo-French Mandate Territories. This led the ever-controversial Lawrence to recommend that Ibn Saud should occupy the Hijaz to overcome Hussein's intransigence. In Lawrence's view, a Wahhabi takeover would present "no real danger" to Britain because Ibn Saud "never possessed Wahhabi fanaticism" and would be able to "restrain" his followers, which would critically guarantee the safety of pilgrims and pilgrimage routes. He continued in a provocative vein that Ibn Saud could then be "ejected easily by a Muslim Indian tank division" of the British army. This extraordinary putative expeditionary force could be deployed "to recover Mecca and break the Wahabi movement," like Egyptian ruler Muhammad 'Ali's early nineteenth-century offensive against them.[235] Lawrence's extraordinary proposal was quickly quashed by officials in Delhi, who stridently restated the government of India's stance of strict noninterference in the Hijaz.[236] The importance of a safe and secure Hajj was appreciated by officials serving in other areas of Britain's Muslim empire. Iraq's high commissioner, Sir Percy Cox, in 1922 wrote that "any violence on hajj would react adversely on British prestige throughout Islam."[237]

Nevertheless, British officials shared a collective exasperation with Hussein's perceived mismanagement of the Hajj, seen as a combination of incompetent administration and extortion of pilgrims. Palestine's high commissioner, Sir Herbert Samuel, wrote in June 1922 that Britain now "felt tired of Hussein and all his works and considers that any change that may come in the Hejaz would be welcome as being an improvement on the existing state of affairs."[238] The Colonial Office viewed any political change in the Hijaz, which meant Ibn Saud removing Hussein from power, as posing no "danger of conflagration," given Ibn Saud's proven pro-British attitude.[239] Sir Arthur Hirtzel at the India Office commented: "The feeling is growing that it would be a good thing if Ibn Saud did establish himself at Mecca, though no doubt we would have one or two bad quarters of an hour before things settle down."[240] Officials in India preferred Ibn Saud, with whom they had established relations since 1910, over Hussein, who had been supported by officials in Cairo and Khartoum.[241] In Jidda, consular official Lawrence Grafftey-Smith colorfully described Hussein as "a monster of our own creation" after a particularly chaotic pilgrimage in October 1923.[242] Foreign Secretary Lord Curzon and the Foreign Office's frustration with Hussein meant that they were willing to consider any remedy that might lessen the burden of Britain's Hajj administration.[243] Hussein's British detractors had not considered that the king lacked the deeper financial resources of the Ottomans to pay off Bedouin tribes and adequately garrison the network of forts along routes used by pilgrims, which had afforded a measure of safety during the Hajj. Nor did Hussein, unlike his Saudi successors, possess the military means to subdue these same Bedouin tribes, who preyed on pilgrims. Perhaps most important, Hussein did not enjoy the subventions and funding that the Ottomans had given to the Hijaz's Hajj administration, which augmented the revenues gathered from pilgrims.[244]

Hussein's proclamation of himself as caliph in March 1924 was perhaps a fatal move, a convenient excuse for Britain to abrogate any of its responsibilities to its erstwhile ally. In the words of Reader Bullard, this move was "exceedingly unpopular, and was one of the reasons why, when he was attacked by the Wahhabis, he found no friends."[245] Ibn Saud's invasion of the Hijaz in 1924 negated the need for Britain to move actively against its erstwhile ally because its other Arabian ally had unilaterally decided to take decisive action. However, it is extremely unlikely that Britain would have made any attempt to remove Hussein itself. The outbreak of open war between Ibn Saud and Hussein in 1924, characterized by British Muslim convert and pilgrim Eldon Rutter as a "wolfish struggle for power," put extra pressure on Britain's Hajj administration in Jidda.[246] Thomas Rapp, a consular official in Suez, was sent there in the summer of 1924 to assist Bullard with the departure of 30,000 pilgrims who were British subjects, fearful of the consequences of Ibn Saud's advance into the Hijaz.[247] Rapp was sanguine about the situation; he thought that Ibn Saud's "religious scruples" had prevented the Wahhabis from attacking Mecca up to this point, even though they had the power to do so. Rapp wrote that the "welfare of tens of thousands of Moslems who arrived from British protected territories was the principal preoccupation of the Consul" who was, however, "powerless . . . to safeguard them against . . . the general abysmal conditions under which they were exposed."[248] Despite this situation, he, and many other officials across Britain's Muslim empire involved in the Hajj, saw the war "as one between Arabs to be settled by them."[249] This reflected the official British line, which was underscored when a delegation of notables from Jidda met with Bullard on September 24, 1924, and asked him to arrange a British protectorate over the Hijaz to save them from Ibn Saud and his Wahhabi followers. Bullard responded that this would be impossible.[250] After Britain's roller-coaster experience with the pilgrimage during the postwar period, the Hashemite-Saudi conflict ushered in a return to a policy of inaction, as Britain's two Arabian allies fought for control of the Hijaz and the Hajj.

Conclusion

The years from 1914 to 1924 saw perhaps the most far-reaching changes to the Hijaz's political landscape since the early nineteenth century. This chapter has sought to reframe the conventional narrative of this period of the Hijaz's history by emphasizing the Hajj's importance to Britain's actions in the region and further afield. The First World War and its consequences for the Hijaz had the extraordinary effect of giving Britain's Muslim empire a degree of coherence as officials dealing with the region came to realize that Islam and British policies on Islamic practice were signal features that connected these territories together. The Hajj was a central part of this realization, given that the site of the ritual was the Holy City of Mecca, and because of the geographic breadth and administrative depth of British involvement with the pilgrimage since the 1860s. The Arab Revolt and Britain's increased role and influence in the Hijaz resulted in moves to reform the pilgrimage experience. Britain's rhetoric of noninterference in religious practice had no relation to administrative practice. But at the point when Britain arguably had its greatest influence over Hussein and his Hashemite kingdom that ruled over the area where the Hajj took place, its sway proved to be limited. For British officials, this was all the more frustrating given that for political and propaganda purposes they believed it vital that Britain should facilitate the Hajj and appear as the friend and protector of Islam. One example of this was the ambivalent experience of Indian Muslim soldier-pilgrims. The sense of opportunity and realization in regard to Britain's Muslim empire and Britain's interactions with the Hajj died a slow death after the end of the war. The unraveling of the Hashemite regime served to define the limited scope of Britain's involvement in the pilgrimage's administrative aspects just as some of the empire's Muslim employees were agitating for further involvement. Intervention such as a British representative at Mecca proved short-lived, and wider-scale proposals for deeper involvement remained stillborn, given the huge influence the Khilafat movement and the general "crisis of Islam" had on Britain's interactions with the Hajj. However, one result of this tumult that surrounded events such as the Khilafat movement was the resumption of large-scale repatriation of destitute pilgrims, which had longer antecedents. This practice of facilitating the Hajj for Britain's poorer pilgrim-subjects had become an embedded part of Britain's interactions with the pilgrimage. By the early 1920s, for many officials the importance of the Hajj to the British empire was so obvious as to not require elaboration; this religious practice, and Islam more widely, had become closely interlinked with imperial politics and governance. But the advent of Saudi-Wahhabi control over the Hijaz had an even greater impact on the Hajj than the period of the Hashemite interregnum. Chapter 5 marks a shift in this book's focus by examining the changing spiritual experience of the Hajj for pilgrims in parallel with analyzing the continuing developments in Britain's engagement with the pilgrimage.

5

Britain and the Hajj under Saudi Control, 1924–1939

Introduction

As British officials came to view their ostensible ally king Hussein as a political liability because of his perceived mismanagement of the Hajj and his refusal to accept the regional political landscape of Anglo-French mandate territories, many of them became more prepared to accept Ibn Saud and his Wahhabi followers as the power controlling the Holy Places of Islam.[1] The necessity for postwar fiscal retrenchment across the British empire also affected Britain's other ally on the Arabian Peninsula. The Treasury warned Ibn Saud that his subsidy would end in March 1924. Ibn Saud astutely observed that the Hajj was the most lucrative source of income in Arabia. Because of Ibn Saud's frustration with Hussein's administration of the Hajj, the king's repeated prohibition on Ibn Saud's Wahhabi soldiers performing Hajj, and finally, Hussein's audacious proclamation of himself as caliph in March 1924, conflict broke out between these two British allies. Ibn Saud's invasion of Hussein's kingdom saw him and his followers gain control of the Hijaz in 1924–1925, a struggle that was a vital foundation for the establishment of the Kingdom of Saudi Arabia in 1932.

This chapter argues that the advent of Saudi-Wahhabi rule over the Hajj had a profound impact on pilgrims' experiences. As Britain came to accept the Wahhabi ascendancy over the Hajj, there was a shift in British policy back toward noninterference in the Hajj, although Britain's Muslim employees remained actively involved throughout this period. Indeed, Britain was also unable to influence Saudi-Wahhabi actions in regard to the Hajj, and explicitly did not seek to, despite representations from a number of Britain's Muslim subjects. The nature and impact of Wahhabism on the Hajj from 1924 to 1939 shifted as Saudi forces conquered and consolidated their control over the Hijaz and responded to the effects of the Great Depression from 1929. A key theme throughout this chapter is the Wahhabi aversion to *ziyara*, pilgrims' visits to the shrines and tombs of saints and notables that pilgrims undertook in addition to performing Hajj.[2] This highlights how pilgrims from across Britain's Muslim empire and beyond challenged Wahhabism in the Holy Places, and it illustrates the continued diversity of Islamic practices among Muslims. Therefore, this interpretation seeks to provide nuance to the prevalent historical orthodoxy that tends to stress a linear trajectory of Islamic modernism and universalism in this period.[3] In the face of the economic pressures the Saudi regime faced as a result of the Great Depression's effect on the Hajj, Wahhabi religious policies were modified into a form of compromise with the continued diversity of Islamic practices demonstrated by pilgrims in the Hijaz. Despite these trends, the cumulative impact of Wahhabi policies on the Hajj meant that pilgrims gradually—and grudgingly—accepted Wahhabi restrictions on various Islamic practices during their sojourns in the Holy Places.

Before the advent of Saudi control, the interpretation of Islam held by the ruler of Mecca was of little concern to Britain, as it did not generally affect pilgrims. But the Wahhabi ascendancy over the Hajj added an extra layer of religious complexity to British interactions with the pilgrimage. British officials and Muslim employees had to grapple with the administrative consequences of Wahhabi policies on pilgrims who were British subjects. Imperial governance and religious practice had always been delicate and rarely uncontroversial, but this was an extraordinary situation that officials now had to navigate. Saudi control and Wahhabi religious policies in the Hijaz would have been less significant were it not for the Hajj, and the thousands of pilgrims from across Britain's Muslim empire who congregated in Mecca each year, which gave this politico-religious landscape a special significance for Britain's local consular administration of the pilgrimage in Jidda, and broader imperial politics. Wahhabi Islam in the Holy Places was of great importance and concern to the subjects of Britain's Muslim empire: what happened in Mecca affected Muslims who lived many thousands of miles away from the Holy City.

Numerous studies recount and analyze the failure of Britain's "Sharifian solution" and Ibn Saud's rise to regional predominance and tend to focus on the Anglo-Saudi diplomatic relationship, which revolved around tortuous negotiations over the thorny issue of fixing the frontiers of Ibn Saud's kingdom in relation to the British-protected amirates and mandated territories that ringed his polity.[4] Historians have also extensively analyzed the beginnings of development in what became Saudi Arabia, presented largely uncritically as the story of how Ibn Saud led his subjects into the modern age.[5] Oil, discovered in Najd in 1939, is the predominant driver of this narrative. However, the Hajj, which was the single most important source of income for Ibn Saud from 1924 until oil royalties began to flow in 1940, has generally been overlooked. Moreover, except for Sugata Bose's work, studies of Britain and the pilgrimage generally take 1924 as their endpoint and pay little attention to the Saudi period of control.[6] Bose argues that the Hajj took on "overtones of resistance to both Saudi orthodoxy and European imperialism" and was "ultimately impervious to boundaries, regulation and the designs of those who sought to manipulate the hajj's sanctity to their own political goals."[7] But substantial scope remains for more detailed consideration of the complex religious changes that affected the Holy Places and the Hajj, especially regarding the responses of British officials and pilgrims who were British subjects to this politico-religious regime change. Wahhabi religious policies were a turbulent force among pilgrims, and they affected how British officials engaged with the Hajj. The fact that the Saudis still control the Holy Cities means that their interpretation of Islam—Wahhabism—is an important context within which pilgrims experience the Hajj in the early twenty-first century. Consequently, this crucial initial period of Saudi-Wahhabi rule demands scholarly attention.

Although Saudi archives on this contentious topic remain closed, two principal sources that shed light on Wahhabi religious policies and the Hajj are British reports from the consulate at Jidda and a limited number of pilgrimage narratives.[8] Muslim employees within the consular bureaucracy were a vital source of British information about the Hajj and conditions in Mecca and Medina.[9] By contrast, their British employers' direct involvement with the Hajj was limited; Consul Sir Andrew Ryan recalled how in the early 1930s he never saw any more of the pilgrimage than "the passage through Jedda of people, many already wearing the *ihram*."[10] A significant contributor to Britain's voluminous consular archive in this period was an Indian Muslim, Munshi Ihsanullah. Born in Punjab, Ihsanullah had forged a career as a merchant and banker in Medina, but the First World War ruined him. He traveled to Damascus, where he worked for British military intelligence at the end of 1918, and then moved to work for Britain's consulate in Jidda. He was proficient in Urdu, Arabic, and English, knew some Bengali and Turkish, and was very well connected to officials, merchants, pilgrim guides, and *'ulama* in Jidda, Mecca, and Medina, as well as Bedouin tribesmen. Consul Reader Bullard wrote that "he enjoys a very high reputation for good sense and integrity."[11] He was appointed Indian pilgrimage officer in 1925 and promoted to Indian vice-consul in 1927. Ihsanullah wrote his reports in Urdu, which were then translated into English by three Indian clerks working in the consulate, Nur Hussein Shah, Hajji Muhammad Sharif, and Shah Jahan Kabir.[12] Many of the views espoused by successive consuls at Jidda regarding Britain's Hajj policies and administration, such as the system whereby Indian pilgrims deposited their steamship tickets with the British consulate, originally came from Ihsanullah, who also exerted great effort to persuade those in the Khilafat movement of the utility of British measures related to the Hajj.[13] These were facts that many officials, such as Reader Bullard, were perfectly willing to admit: "He became invaluable and many suggestions he made were adopted and became law in India to the great advantage of pilgrims."[14] Consequently,

The staff of the British consulate at Jidda, c. 1926, including Malay Pilgrimage Officer Haji Abdul Majid (standing, far left), Indian Pilgrimage Officer Munshi Ihsanullah (standing, wearing dark suit), Dr. Hakim Din, Indian medical doctor (standing to Ihsanullah's immediate left), Consul Francis Stoneweather-Bird (seated, center), and his wife, Norman Mayers Album

Credit: Middle East Centre Archive, St. Anthony's College, Oxford

established conceptions of what has been termed the "official mind" of British imperialism need to be nuanced to incorporate voices such as Ihsanullah's.[15] There was a Muslim element to the "official mind."

In order to appreciate the nature and implications of Wahhabism's impact on the Hajj, it is necessary to briefly summarize the movement's history and beliefs. Wahhabism was formulated and expounded by a religious scholar from Najd, Muhammad ibn 'Abd al-Wahhab (1703–1787). After a religious education at Medina, Basra, and Hasa in the late eighteenth century, upon his return to Najd he preached a fundamentalist and puritanical doctrine that rejected Islam as practiced by his fellow Arabians. Ibn 'Abd al-Wahhab stressed the importance of monotheism. He denounced all forms of mediation between God and believers and believed that the doctrine of the oneness of God, *tawhid*, should be strictly respected. He declared that saints' cults and visiting holy men's tombs, prevalent among Arabia's Muslim oasis dwellers, nomads, and those living in Arabia's sedentary societies, led to *kufr*, or unbelief, and were blasphemous, polytheistic activities. The obligation to undertake jihad against those who did not follow these principles—non-Muslims and Muslims alike—was critical, as was the requirement that Muslims should strictly adhere to *shari'a* law. His overall concern was the purification of Islam from what he viewed as innovations and deviations, *bid'a*, that had developed after the initial Muslim conquests in the seventh century CE. Ibn 'Abd al-Wahhab found a political patron in the figure of a minor chieftain in Najd, Ibn Saud, ancestor of his twentieth-century namesake, who took in ibn 'Abd al-Wahhab after he was expelled from various settlements for his unpopular views. Ibn Saud embraced Wahhabism, and the movement became a tribal confederation energized by a prophetic mission. In 1773, the Saudi-Wahhabi alliance made Riyadh its capital, and the polity expanded swiftly. In 1803 and 1805, the Wahhabis seized the Holy Cities of Mecca and Medina, which had been under Ottoman suzerainty since 1517, and proceeded to destroy the many tombs and shrines dotted about Mecca and Medina, including, most controversially, the Prophet Muhammad's tomb. Sharif Ghalib of Mecca, effectively a Saudi prisoner, agreed to adhere to the imposition of Wahhabism over the Hijaz in 1806. These actions caused outrage across the Muslim world and earned the Wahhabis a long-standing reputation for intolerance, destruction, and fanaticism. In response, Muhammad 'Ali, the ruler of Egypt, invaded the Hijaz in 1811, and by 1818 he had broken the power of the first Saudi-Wahhabi amirate. The Saudis and Wahhabis retreated to their Najdi homeland, where they remained a reduced force until the First World War. Nevertheless, their brief moment of triumph in the Holy Cities meant that Wahhabism stimulated or gave its name to numerous reformist and fundamentalist movements across Asia as Muslims responded to political dislocation caused by European and indigenous rivals.[16] This history, however, was less troubling to Britain by the early 1920s, as the next section will demonstrate.

British Perceptions of Wahhabism

Britain's accommodation of Wahhabism after the First World War highlighted official flexibility in dealing with militant, fundamentalist forms of Islam when Britain was faced with the paramount importance of ensuring, as far as possible, a safe pilgrimage for its subjects across its Muslim empire. Britain's historical aversion to Indian Wahhabis, highlighted by paranoia among some officials in India about their activities, belonged in the nineteenth century. The threat of Indian Wahhabi "fanaticism," however real or chimerical, had disappeared by the early 1900s.[17] The government of India had primary responsibility in relations with Ibn Saud. Captain William Shakespear, Kuwait's political agent, was the first European to meet the Najdi ruler in 1910.[18] British reports repeatedly drew a distinction between Ibn Saud, who was often lauded as an astute, pragmatic ruler, and his more "fanatical" Wahhabi *'ulama* and soldier-followers, the Ikhwan.[19] However, voices from other parts of Britain's Muslim empire sounded a more uneasy note. In 1917, Sir Reginald Wingate, governor-general of Sudan and a key player in the Arab Revolt, wrote to Foreign Secretary Arthur Balfour, describing how Ibn Saud was "fanning the flame of Wahabite [*sic*] zealotry as a necessary counterpoise to Sharifial gold and ordnance. The Wahabites [*sic*] overran the Hedjaz in recent times and might do so again. Ibn Saud, as the sword of a purified Islam . . . might pierce the more secular shield of the Emir of Mecca."[20] Wingate's background in military intelligence during the reconquest of Sudan in 1896–1899 meant that he was acutely sensitive to what he viewed as the danger of Muslim "fanaticism" after his experience fighting the Mahdist state and then, as governor-general, brutally extinguishing "neo-Mahdist" uprisings that occasionally affected parts of Sudan from 1900 to 1914. Wingate highlighted the previous example of Wahhabi rule over Mecca and Medina in the early nineteenth century as a cautionary tale.[21] If the Wahhabis captured the Holy Places and repeated their earlier actions, it would cause outrage across the Muslim world. For Britain, this would be disastrous; by 1919, with the addition of the Middle Eastern mandate territories and the Tanganyika mandate, over half of the world's Muslims were under some form of British control.

Harry St. John Philby, a government of India official who converted to Wahhabi Islam in 1930 and became close to Ibn Saud, was the first to argue for a stance that evolved into Britain's pragmatic policy of religious neutrality toward the Wahhabis.[22] In 1918, Philby asserted that "it is not for us to judge their creed, but the more their hatred for other Muslims intensified the more it converged with our interests." "Other Muslims" referred to the Ottomans and Sharif Hussein. In Philby's view, Ibn Saud should receive British friendship, arms, and money because Ibn Saud believed that there should be peace between Wahhabis and Christians, who were *ahl al-kitab*, People of the Book, and thus occupied a higher status and recognition than "backsliding" Muslims.[23] Philby's increasingly iconoclastic views about Britain's policy of Hashemite support contributed to his resignation from government service. His superior, Sir Percy Cox, found it "very difficult" to find Philby a position because of his anti-Hashemite stance.[24] After Philby converted to Islam and settled in Jidda, he repeatedly criticized Britain in numerous articles and lectures in the 1930s for allowing Ibn Saud to "fade out of the picture" while McMahon, Wingate, and Whitehall "turned" to Hussein because "the very name of Mecca mesmerised the British government."[25] Philby was ahead of his time in championing Ibn Saud. Britain's ambivalent support for Ibn Saud during the First World War did help—in a small way—the fight against the Ottomans and brought pressure to bear on Hussein. However, Philby failed to think through the consequences of a Wahhabi victory in the Hijaz and how it would affect the thousands of pilgrims who traveled from across Britain's Muslim empire every year to Mecca and then returned home with tales of their experiences of the Wahhabis.

Scholar-spy David George Hogarth, a seminal figure in the Arab Revolt, acutely summarized the nature of British interests in Arabia in this period, which were based on ensuring the security of Arabia's surrounding seas and, vitally, were framed around the conception of Britain as a Muslim power:

> The least calculable of British Arabian interests—that which the greatest Mohammedan Power of the world must take in the city and district which is, theoretically, the spiritual centre of Islam,

> and practically, its paramount pilgrimage resort. That the pilgrimage has created in the past, and still maintains, a serious British interest in the Hejaz is obvious. It is of no little concern to us that the Indian pilgrims, who of recent years have constituted a majority of those who resort to Mecca from outside Arabia, should be reasonably safe, healthy and well-treated during the Haj season; further, that the ruling power in the Hejaz should be friendly enough towards the Power responsible for those pilgrims to discourage propaganda unfriendly to our rule.[26]

Overall, British policy dictated assiduous noninterference with Islamic practice. However, in the case of the pilgrimage, this policy had been jettisoned in various ways since the 1870s. With the Ottoman empire's downfall, Britain was uncontestably the most important power in the Muslim world. Consequently, as Hogarth pointed out, the health and safety of its thousands of Muslim subjects who went on Hajj every year could not be ignored for fear of damaging Britain's prestige, that invaluable and intangible commodity.[27] This factor, coupled with King Hussein's intransigent and increasingly anti-British attitude, contributed to Britain's turn toward Ibn Saud, outlined in Chapter 4.

Despite increasing acceptance by officials across Britain's Muslim empire of Saudi-Wahhabi rule over the pilgrimage, there was some concern for pilgrims' welfare during the Hashemite-Saudi conflict. Simultaneously, officials were averse to any sort of overt British intervention to alleviate the situation for pilgrims, a stance symptomatic of underlying British self-interest. Britain privately requested that Ibn Saud ensure that pilgrims who were British subjects were not harassed; the British government attached the "greatest importance" to freedom of access to the Holy Places for its pilgrims and hoped that Ibn Saud would not jeopardize this.[28] Colonial Secretary James Henry Thomas reflected government policy when he wrote to Iraq's high commissioner, Sir Henry Dobbs, that Britain must not be perceived as being involved "in any struggle for possession of the Holy Places of Islam."[29] *The Times* warned the British government "to desist from anything having the remotest resemblance of such an attempt at intervention" in the Hijaz.[30] Views from officials in India strengthened the argument for nonintervention. The viceroy reported that Indian Muslims viewed the war in the Hijaz as furthering Islam's destruction, and that members of the Khilafat movement lauded Ibn Saud's policy and were "raising an outcry at the prospect of Britain giving support to Hussein or otherwise in the civil war in the Holy Land." "Muslims," the viceroy added, "generally favoured the removal of Hussein, but did not regard the Wahhabis very highly."[31] These multiple perspectives affected British policy on the Hajj. Britain accepted Ibn Saud and Wahhabi sovereignty over the Holy Places as a better alternative than Hussein, despite the unknown quantity of Ibn Saud as ruler of Mecca and Medina. However, Reader Bullard, consul at Jidda during the dying days of Hussein's regime in September 1924, presciently foretold that if Ibn Saud took Mecca, there would be "longer-lived complications arising from the difference between the tenets of the Wahhabis and those of the bulk of the pilgrims."[32]

After this shift in policy, Hogarth's aim in a 1925 lecture was to rationalize how Wahhabism was not inimical to British interests. The Wahhabi advance did not mean that the Holy Places and the pilgrimage were "in the hands of heretics. Wahabites [*sic*] are not that, but on the contrary, ultra-orthodox literalists, who accept nothing beyond the original revelation as they understand it, and regard all subsequent accretions of doctrine as impieties."[33] Hogarth's remark was symptomatic of a wider British attitude toward the Wahhabis that was rhetorically defined by Orientalist views about the original "purity" of Islam, which matched uncannily with Wahhabi beliefs. Hogarth went on to claim that Britain had adequately prepared for a Saudi-Wahhabi victory in the Hijaz; in response to the uncontrollable "religious ebullition" of the Ikhwan, officials "took measures" to make Ibn Saud "specially dependent" on Britain.[34] Hogarth believed that Wahhabi rule over the Holy Places and the pilgrimage would not be disastrous because Ibn Saud—"an unusually liberal and far-sighted ruler"—would not have to make any great effort to equal or better the standard of Hussein's Hajj administration. Furthermore, Ibn Saud would be aware that his control would not be "open to unfavourable comparisons with that of Hussein."

Hogarth foresaw that the Wahhabis would "discourage relics of pre-Islamic cult and non-Koranic local associations honoured by the vulgar among the faithful" and might force "Najdean austerities" on Mecca, but "they can hardly be more unpopular than . . . the recent control of King Hussein." In his final analysis, pilgrims' experiences were "little likely to be seriously altered by the present access of Wahhabism."[35] As subsequent sections of this chapter illustrate, Hogarth's last statement was wildly inaccurate.

The Beginnings of Saudi-Wahhabi Control over the Hijaz

Britain's assessments of Saudi-Wahhabi intentions initially seemed to be borne out by Ibn Saud's early conciliatory declaration to the people of Mecca in September 1924. However, such an emollient announcement was vital in light of the recent Wahhabi capture of Ta'if, a town near Mecca, where the Wahhabis had massacred several hundred townspeople. This tragic event, coupled with the memory of Wahhabi actions after their capture of Mecca in 1803, did not prevent British officials in Jidda from optimistically hoping that Ibn Saud would not allow "indiscriminate massacre and pillage in the holy city."[36] However, officials elsewhere, such as Humphrey Bowman in Jerusalem, were more pessimistic, writing privately that Wahhabi raiders "slay and mutilate wherever they go" and that in the "villages they passed through . . . all had been killed, including women and children."[37] Ibn Saud proclaimed to Meccans that King Hussein had "neglected the rights of the Holy Places. In his rashness he even debarred Najdis from fulfilling one of the five Muslim duties, that of performing the pilgrimage—apart from the brutality with which he treated the pilgrims in general." In Ibn Saud's words, "Islamic zeal and Arab patriotism" had forced him and the Wahhabis to "make the religion of God supreme and defend the sacred place."[38] Explaining his stance to the political resident in the Persian Gulf, Ibn Saud wrote that Hussein "has demolished one of the pillars of our faith [Hajj]—a matter in which Najdis cannot continue to give way as they have in the past."[39] Religious considerations were arguably equally as important as political and economic factors in Ibn

Ibn Saud and two of his sons, c. 1930s

Credit: Royal Geographical Society, London

Saud's push for mastery over the Hijaz and the Holy Places. The importance of Hajj to Ibn Saud was exemplified when he entered Mecca in October 1924, clad in the pilgrim's garb of the *ihram*, a highly symbolic gesture.[40]

The first reports that trickled out from Mecca under Saudi-Wahhabi rule appeared less catastrophic than previously feared. Wahhabi practices had chiefly affected the city's many religious schools, where all texts except the Qur'an and hadiths were banned. This resulted in a large number of Malay and Javanese students abandoning their studies and returning home.[41] One British eyewitness in Mecca during this period was Eldon Rutter, a businessman who had worked in government service in the Malay states in 1919 and had converted to Islam.[42] Starting in Cairo in May 1925, Rutter had traveled from Suez to Massawa in Italian Eritrea, where he boarded a dhow for Qahma on the Tihana coast, south of Jidda. In the Hijaz, Rutter managed to dismiss his pilgrim guide, which gave him an unusual amount of freedom.[43] He asked some Meccans about the entry of the Wahhabis: several Ikhwan rode through the city's deserted streets and "cried out the promise of security and that the peoples of Mecca—the Neighbours of God—were under the protection of God and Ibn Saud."[44] Such reassurances probably did little to assuage the fears of the city's inhabitants about what might happen next.

Britain's success in gleaning information about conditions in Mecca under the new regime and its impact on pilgrims would have been impossible without Muslim employees in the consular bureaucracy, who could travel there freely. Ihsanullah went to Mecca in April 1925 to check on British subjects who lived there. He reported that the situation was problematic because Ibn Saud had come under "the influence of religious fanatics." The exuberant Wahhabis had proposed several schemes, such as forcibly converting all pilgrims to Wahhabism and destroying tombs visited by pilgrims because such places "amounted to idolatry." Only Wahhabi imams were allowed to conduct prayers in the Holy Mosque at Mecca. Apparently, few pilgrims attended prayers at the mosque, preferring to recite them in their hostels. These actions, contrary to what Ibn Saud had assured before the occupation of Mecca, had caused "much heart-burning amongst the pilgrims and all orthodox Moslems" according to Ihsanullah. For example, a group of Indian Muslims in Mecca had returned home before the Hajj because they believed that pilgrimage "under such circumstances could not be regarded as lawful." If we are to believe Ihsanullah, one Indian nationalist, Maulvi Mohammed Said, the superintendent of the Southiali madrassa in Mecca, said that the situation demanded a representative of the British government at Mecca to look after the pilgrims.[45] Although it is impossible to verify Ihsanullah's claim, it appears clear that Wahhabi policies had caused friction among Meccans and pilgrims alike.

These tensions among the *umma* were exacerbated by the continued existence of the Hashemite regime under siege in Jidda, where the town's defense was controlled by Hussein's son Ali after the king's abdication. The continuing war between Ali and Ibn Saud was fairly desultory: "A few shells are fired morning and evening and that is all."[46] The conflict and reports of Wahhabi policies in the Holy Places meant that Ibn Saud had to persuade pilgrims to perform the first Hajj under his rule. Ibn Saud invited pilgrims from South and Southeast Asia to arrive via Saudi-controlled ports such as Rabegh instead of Hashemite-held Jidda.[47] When Indian pilgrims arrived at Rabegh, Ibn Saud reiterated that he had occupied the Hijaz in order to "remove from the house of God oppression and misbelievers and their supporters and to extend assistance to Muslim visitors." He assured pilgrims that they would be able to travel in safety, in contrast with conditions under the Hashemite regime, which had treated pilgrims "despotically."[48] Although political control over the Holy Places and the Hajj was ultimately assured, given the ineptitude of Ali's armed forces—his air force consisted of a few planes flown by alcoholic White Russian émigrés—Ibn Saud had to reassure pilgrims that he would be a more competent custodian of the Hajj.[49]

In this strained situation, the Indian Khilafat delegation visited the Hijaz in February 1925 but did not get further than Jidda.[50] The movement had now lost much of its influence, given that the sting had been removed from its supporters' grievances after Mustafa Kemal Atatürk, Turkey's new ruler, and the Turkish National Assembly abolished the caliphate on March 3, 1924. Indeed, Turkish nationalists labeled the Khilafat movement's activities as foreign interference in Turkish affairs. Turkey's abolition of the caliphate flew in the face of the movement's assertion that the risk of this eventuality was due to British machinations. An Indian intelligence report on the delegation remarked dismissively that "nobody seemed to care whether or not they came back at all."[51] In fact, King Ali prevented the delegation from traveling to Mecca because it received a letter from Ibn Saud that dwelt on his desire to free the Hijaz from Ali's "evil domination."[52]

The government of India issued several communiqués that stressed its noninterference in the situation while emphasizing official attempts to facilitate the pilgrimage for its subjects. Unless safety regulations were ignored, the authorities could not stop ships from heading to the Hijaz despite the fact that there were "abnormal" risks in making the pilgrimage, and it was "only [a] reluctance to interfere in the domain of religion that prevented them from taking steps to discourage [the Hajj]."[53] Nevertheless, after the ships sailed, Britain reminded Ibn Saud and Ali that they were responsible for pilgrims' well-being, dispatched Indian Muslim officials and a Royal Navy ship to Rabegh to "observe" pilgrim arrivals.[54] Ali's ships were sporadically bombarding the port, and he abrogated any responsibility if pilgrims were killed. In the event, Indian pilgrims made it to Mecca safely.[55]

In Mecca and Medina, Ibn Saud's rhetoric largely failed to match reality. Ihsanullah, sent there in 1925 during the Hajj, reported that because of ruthless punishments, Saudi territory was far more peaceful than during the Hashemite period. However, religious intolerance by the Wahhabis was apparently rife, especially toward the practice of *ziyara*, visiting saints' and notables' tombs and shrines. For example, Ihsanullah found that two Indian pilgrims had been imprisoned and condemned to death for praying at the tomb of Khadija, the Prophet Muhammad's first wife. Ibn Saud himself said to Ihsanullah that he disapproved of this interference with "harmless religious practices," although in this instance he had to defer to his followers.[56] Eldon Rutter described the Meccan reaction to the destruction of the dome and minaret of the *mawlid al-nabi*, the Prophet's birthplace in Mecca: "Faces grew grave, and here and there among the company a bitter curse would be uttered against the Nejdis." Rutter explained how "it was dangerous to stand and look for long at this or any other sacred site or building, for a passing Wahhabi, seeing one so occupied, would be quite capable of laying about him with his camel stick, calling down curses the while upon those who make supplication to the Prophet."[57] Later in his account, Rutter described a party of Indian pilgrims walking toward the tomb of caliph Uthman (one of the first Four Rightly Guided Caliphs of Islam) in al-Baqi cemetery in Medina, led by an elderly Indian man with a long gray beard: "Straight before him he gazed, and tears fell down from his eyes in a ceaseless stream" when he was confronted with the remains of Uthman's grave, reduced to a piece of wood thrust into the ground, beside which was another Indian reciting from the Qur'an and a further Indian man sitting by them, sobbing.[58] Nevertheless, Rutter broadly approved of Ibn Saud's rule because he governed according to *shari'a* and ensured public security.[59] British officials regarded the 1925 Hajj as a success, despite such incidents, perhaps given their experiences of past Hajj seasons during King Hussein's regime.[60] Ibn Saud had to balance the demands of his more zealous Wahhabi followers and the need to ensure a continual stream of pilgrims, who were the Hijaz's main source of revenue.

The complex dynamics Ibn Saud faced in ruling the Hijaz were further complicated by the pilgrimage's international dimension. The annual flow of Muslims from across the *umma* included pilgrims who held a huge variety of interpretations of Islam at odds with Wahhabism. Indian Muslim pilgrims in particular deplored the policy of tomb demolition. Telegrams were sent to the British consulate at Jidda addressed to Ibn Saud; one from the head of an Islamic association in Bombay stated that during a mass meeting in a mosque, those present considered Wahhabi actions "deserving of the whole of Muslim hatred and curses for irreligious acts." In response, Ibn Saud asked whether Wahhabi agents could travel to India in order to "expound the tenets of the Wahhabi faith and contradict the lying propaganda spread by our enemies who endeavour to gain by words what they cannot by arms."[61] Within India, opinion was divided. The *Muslim Outlook* asserted that stories about tomb destruction were "deliberate lies." Maulvi Muhammad Shaifi, a member of the Legislative Assembly, said that the whole of Arabia was grateful to Ibn Saud. Despite this chorus of approval, Indian intelligence officials felt that the gathering force of complaints against Ibn Saud meant that he could lose the support of many Indian Muslims.[62] The reputation of Ibn Saud and his Wahhabi followers among some Indian Muslims had been damaged. For the first time since the earlier period of Wahhabi rule over the Holy Cities, the ability of pilgrims to perform *ziyara*, an important part of their religious itinerary, was circumscribed by the Wahhabis.

The Hashemite Kingdom of the Hijaz was finally extinguished when Ibn Saud occupied Jidda in December 1925. In the days after the takeover, civil employees were retained in order to undertake reforms to the pilgrimage administration in advance of the next Hajj season. Ibn Saud reaffirmed his hope that "greater comfort and security will be provided for all pilgrims than has ever been provided formerly."[63] Wahhabi policies, however, made their mark in the port city. The Tomb of Eve in Jidda, a long mound with a small mosque in the middle, a popular shrine for "childless wives and languishing maidens," was closed.[64] Wahhabi actions in this first phase of their rule in the Hijaz brought out the continued importance customary Islam held for many pilgrims, especially from India, which were in stark contrast to Wahhabi beliefs. However, British officials had little appetite to deal with the grievances of their pilgrim subjects who were opposed to Wahhabi strictures.

Military success over the Hashemites provided a fillip to Wahhabi activity as the 1926 Hajj approached. A variety of Wahhabi propaganda—"forceful and otherwise"—was directed at pilgrims. The consul at Jidda reported that religious freedom for pilgrims and residents was becoming "increasingly difficult." This included the minutiae of male grooming: barbers were ordered to leave at least fifteen hairs on a man's face, as per the orders of the Prophet.[65] The consular authorities were sanguine about these developments, drawing a distinction between Ibn Saud's "modern ideas" and those of his "fanatical followers" and predicting that religious freedoms would return, although they were mindful that if Ibn Saud refused to implement Wahhabi practices, there would be a rebellion. Officials in Jidda believed that Wahhabi policies would have to be tempered; otherwise, the polity's one source of revenue—pilgrims—would wither away.[66]

The possibility that Wahhabi sovereignty over the Hajj would precipitate a decline in the pilgrimage's popularity appeared real in this period of uncertainty. Given the stories of tomb and shrine destruction that traveled across the Muslim world's religious and trade networks, some pilgrims were wary about performing the Hajj. Officials in other parts of Britain's Muslim empire were also cautious. Sir Henry Dobbs, Iraq's high commissioner, thought it "undesirable" that Iraqis should go on Hajj because "any ill treatment to which fanaticism of Sultan of Nejd's followers might expose them would have most unfortunate effect upon relations between Iraq and Nejd." King Faisal of Iraq, son of the deposed King Hussein, wanted to officially prohibit the Hajj from his kingdom, a move the commissioner averted; instead, Faisal issued a communiqué that advised pilgrims to postpone their departure until the situation in the Hijaz became clearer.[67] Faisal's personal animosity toward Ibn Saud and the Wahhabis and the Shi'i majority in Iraq set this British mandate at odds with the new regime in the Holy Places. In Egypt, British officials informally requested that the Egyptian government not send the *mahmal* caravan to the Hijaz because it was accompanied by a brass band—music being anathema to the Wahhabis.[68] Officials viewed the Hajj under Wahhabi rule as a source of potential strife between Ibn Saud's emergent state—a British ally—and the constituent parts of Britain's Muslim empire, all of which had an interest in the pilgrimage.

It should be emphasized here that Wahhabism was nothing like a monolithic entity, and in the tense atmosphere of 1926, some Wahhabis were opposed to Ibn Saud's more conciliatory policies, such as allowing some worship at tombs. In order to appease these factions, Saud sent the grand *qadi* of Hijaz to Medina to supervise the destruction of the Prophet's family's tombs. British officials in Jidda took a relaxed view: "Unless some fanatical Indians become annoyed at destruction of various tombs the pilgrimage should pass off without any incidents." Ibn Saud had banned Najdis going on Hajj in 1926, precisely because he feared a clash between his Wahhabi followers and pilgrims who held opposing interpretations of the faith.[69]

The Egyptian *mahmal* incident was the biggest example of this "clash of Islams" during the 1926 pilgrimage, which attracted some 58,000 pilgrims from overseas. When the procession halted temporarily, a crowd of Ikhwan gathered, insulted the Egyptian *amir al-hajj,* the leader of the Egyptian pilgrimage caravan, and threw stones at him. In response to this, the *amir al-hajj* ordered his escort to fire on them. Thirty men were killed. Ibn Saud arrived in person "and calmed down both parties avoiding a massacre."[70] The funds traditionally carried with the *mahmal* were returned to Egypt, and diplomatic relations between both countries were severed until 1936.[71] Although this incident caused a storm in official and diplomatic circles, as well as among the Egyptian press, it did not dissuade Egyptians from going on Hajj, as their numbers remained steady throughout this period.[72] Critically, the incident precipitated the end of the pomp and ceremony that surrounded the *mahmal* procession; in 1936, Egypt sent a "pilgrimage mission" to the Holy Places without an *amir al-hajj* or a military escort. Officials in Jidda speculated that Ibn Saud wished to maintain the "rigid simplicity of his convictions, and cleanse the holy places of Islam of the accumulated cobwebs of centuries," such as the Egyptian *mahmal* and worship at tombs, many of which were apparently "lying in a state of neglect, their domes demolished and their walls desolate."[73]

The Wahhabi destruction of tombs continued to create a negative impact among Indian Muslims. There was much outrage among sections of Indian Muslims, especially Shi'i Muslims, when it was confirmed that the Wahhabis had destroyed many tombs in the Hijaz, including those of the Prophet Muhammad's family.[74] Maulana Kutubuddin Abdul Wali, president of the Khuddamal Haramain in Lucknow, said in a press communiqué that all Muslims should "protest against this insult to Islam and adopt all possible means to free the Holy Land from the Nejdis."[75] A Muslim League meeting at Lucknow in June 1926 ended with the demand that tombs should be repaired and that every Muslim, whether Sunni or Shi'i, must be allowed to perform the Hajj and visit Medina to "pay their respects to the memory of the Prophet and other heroes of Islam." If this did not transpire, Muslims should protest by postponing going on Hajj.[76] The Indian Moslem Hejaz Conference at Lucknow that same year, attended by the Shi'i maharajah of Mahmudabad, the Ali brothers, and others, emphasized the need for united action against "Wahhabi excesses and acts of sacrilege." Sympathetic telegrams were received from the Aga Khan and Mohammad Ali Jinnah, the future leader of Pakistan. The concluding resolutions of the conference referred to Wahhabi "excesses . . . in demolishing and desecrating sacred monuments and tombs, burning of sacred books, persecuting *'ulama* and religious heads . . . interfering in the free performance of the rites of haj, increased taxes and conveyance charges for hajis, and treating non-Wahhabis as infidels and heretics." One resolution proposed the postponement of the Hajj.[77] There was further division among Wahhabis, with some Egyptian and Indian Wahhabis splitting with their Najdi counterparts over religious questions. This led Ibn Saud to ban discussions of religion at the 1926 World Islamic Conference, held in Mecca under his patronage, where he declared that because most Muslims lived under colonial rule, which posed the risk of the Holy Cities being controlled by Christian nations through the influence of their Muslim subjects, he alone had the right and duty to rule the Holy Cities because he had conquered them through God's will.[78] The linear trajectory that characterizes Islamic history in the late nineteenth and early twentieth centuries as a story of Islamic reform and universalism sits uneasily with the evidence in these records that attests to the continued emphasis many Muslims placed on customary Islamic practices such as *ziyara*.[79]

However, some accounts reported that Wahhabi policies in the Holy Places were less controversial. For example, Ihsanullah, recently promoted to pilgrimage officer, wrote in his report on the 1926 Hajj that tomb destruction provoked little complaint except from Shi'a. His conversations with pilgrims suggested that Wahhabism was "not now regarded as being so wholly impossible as was at first thought, and many go so far as to say that they represent a perfectly true and literal translation of the Koranic teachings."[80] Perhaps Ihsanullah sought to downplay the divisive effects of Wahhabi religious policy on the Hajj because he believed that the Wahhabis had a much more "reasonable and sensible policy" on the Hajj than King Hussein. Certainly, Ihsanullah received many complaints from British pilgrim-subjects who were admonished, arrested, and fined by Wahhabis in Mecca for various infractions.[81] Resigned acceptance, rather than outright embrace, is perhaps the best description of pilgrims' responses to Wahhabism.

Another aspect of Wahhabi religious policies that affected pilgrims' experiences was the Wahhabi disapproval of pilgrims' recitation of prayers for the intercession of dead saints and notables on their behalf with God. New rules set out that pilgrims could say prayers at these places only as prescribed in the Qur'an. Nor were they allowed to "kiss or rub themselves against the tombs," which caused outcry from Persians and, to a lesser extent, Indians. Guards at the tombs and cemeteries beat pilgrims who did not follow Wahhabi rules and called them *mushrikin wa kuffar*, meaning "idolaters and infidels." However, pilgrims who disobeyed these orders were too numerous for the guards to handle. After negotiations led by Ihsanullah and Muslim pilgrimage officers from other European consulates, some places were opened for a few hours, and pilgrims were allowed into the tombs to say prayers as prescribed by the Wahhabis, "even if they were obliged to think the rest." Despite the guards' presence, "an occasional lucky pilgrim would get in a surreptitious kiss or rub, satisfy his conscience and become the envy of his fellows."[82] Wahhabi restrictions on *ziyara* highlighted the multiple religious objectives of Hajjis. The Hajj formed the most important component of a multistop religious itinerary in the Hijaz, which was threatened by Wahhabi policies. Consequently, the Hajj rituals gained a greater centrality to Muslims in this period, largely because the opportunity to practice *ziyara* in the Hijaz became strictly curtailed. The 1926 pilgrimage season was the most turbulent in recent history, even when set against examples seen in Chapter 4.

Over a decade of ambivalent relations between Ibn Saud and the Ikhwan erupted into open rebellion at the end of the 1920s, although there was only one decisive battle at Sabila in March 1929, which broke the power of the insurrection.[83] Their revolt was in reaction to Ibn Saud's close relations with Britain, the question of how to deal with the practices of pilgrims whom the Ikhwan considered polytheists, and Ibn Saud's curtailment of Ikhwan raiding in British territories such as Iraq and Trans-Jordan—all critical issues that Ibn Saud grappled with as he attempted to balance the demands of competing groups with his desire to establish a more centralized administrative regime and weaken tribal power.[84] It took until early 1930 for Ibn Saud to extinguish the rebellion. The Ikhwan rebellion formed a crucial backdrop for the further imposition of Wahhabi policies on pilgrims.

What impact, if any, did Wahhabi control over the Hajj have on pilgrim numbers? In 1927, the Hajj attracted more than 130,000 pilgrims from overseas. Pilgrim numbers during this period are shown in Table 5.1. However, this number was so huge because the Hajj day was a Friday, and therefore it was a Hajj *akbar*, which increased the merit of performing Hajj sevenfold. In addition, the Hijaz's public security that Ibn Saud had established and maintained undoubtedly attracted the faithful.[85] The sharp increase in pilgrim numbers meant that there were more Indian destitute pilgrims: over 5,000 applied for repatriation. In a surprising development, Abdul Kader Kusuri, a leader of the Khilafat Committee, visited the British consulate to "express his gratitude" for officials' assistance to Indian pilgrims and hoped that an Indian vice-consul would be swiftly appointed to further this work.[86] Destitute pilgrims were less enamored with Brit-

Table 5.1 Estimated pilgrim numbers, 1921–1943

Year[1]	Arrivals by sea (mainly Jidda)	Indians	Malays	West Africans	Sudanese[2]	Egyptians	Estimated numbers at Arafat
1921	57,255	12,065	10,702	4,623		3,957	57,000
1922	56,319	12,849	6,550	4,850		3,000	65,000
1923	75,221	24,459	10,224	5,307		7,040	100,000
1924	92,707	18,432	21,263	3,926		11,231	150,000
1925	2,352[3]						
1926	55,725	18,937	3,073	1,377		16,094	120,000
1927	132,109	26,514	12,184	957	589	15,547	220,000
1928	100,767	14,022	4,418	2,014	2,051	14,099	180,000
1929	88,538	15,146	1,455	2,338	1,371	18,522	200,000
1930	84,821	11,061	2,590	3,525	1,065	17,127	100,000
1931	39,346	7,276	506	1,558	588	4,967	50,000
1932	29,065	9,634	80	780	527	2,312	60,000
1933	20,705	7,093	101	509	420	1,698	50,000
1934	25,291	7,399	173	891	534	4,302	50,000
1935	33,898	11,113	617	1,164	866	5,361	70,000
1936	32,423	8,439	906	1,196	2,559	5,724	60,000
1937	49,957	10,588	2,524	4,787	1,658	10,226	80,000
1938	63,788	15,238	4,725	6,046	2,054	10,096	125,000

(*continued*)

Table 5.1 (Continued)

Year[1]	Arrivals by sea (mainly Jidda)	Indians	Malays	West Africans	Sudanese[2]	Egyptians	Estimated numbers at Arafat
1939	57,602	17,669	2,059	4,217	1,238	8,314	100,000
1940	32,152	6,179	61	3,734	851	6,879	60,000
1941	9,664	4,891	0	1,818	156	2,096	75,000
1942	23,863	10,444	0	7,048	1,396	3,613	80,000
1943	20,909	67	0	5,129	2,512	13,135	80,000

1. Pilgrim numbers are drawn from the annual pilgrimage reports of the British consulate at Jidda, in Alan Rush (ed.), *Records of the Hajj: A Documentary History of the Pilgrimage to Mecca* (Gerrards Cross: Archive Editions, 1993), vols. 5, 6, and 7. Michael Laffan rightly cautions that "pilgrim statistics are more an indication than a hard fact." Michael Laffan, *Islamic Nationhood and Colonial Indonesia: The Umma below the Winds* (London: Routledge Curzon, 2003), 53. Note on classifications of nationality and ethnicity: until roughly the outbreak of the First World War, the category "Indians" generally referred to all those who arrived in the Hijaz from Indian ports. Consequently, this number included people from Afghanistan and central Asia. Until 1921, pilgrims from British Malaya were counted in the same category as pilgrims from the Netherlands East Indies. Finally, "West Africans" was a catchall term for any African pilgrims. The largest number of pilgrims in this period generally came from the Netherlands East Indies, and a large proportion of pilgrims were often from the Arabian Peninsula.

2. Recorded separately from West Africans only after 1927.

3. Landed at Rabegh, a town north of Jidda controlled by Ibn Saud. There was no detailed British report on the Hajj this year, which contained pilgrim numbers because of the Hashemite-Saudi conflict. Jidda was under the control of King Ali, and Mecca was under the control of Ibn Saud.

ain's Hajj administration, and they organized daily protest meetings against the government of India, the consulate, the Indian pilgrimage officer, and the shipping companies.[87]

In contrast to the large number of Indian pilgrims, the predominantly Shi'i Persians boycotted the Hajj for religious reasons. Indian Shi'i Muslims were also angered by Saudi-Wahhabi religious policies. The Shi'i maharajah of Mahmudabad appealed to the viceroy of India to support a deputation to Mecca to arrange for tomb reconstruction and "remonstrate" with Ibn Saud. However, this plan was denounced by some, such as Mohamed Irfan, secretary of the Indian 'Ulama Society, who believed that Britain should not become involved because this would breach its "promise" to remain aloof from Hijazi politics.[88] Of course, Britain, as the predominant power in the Middle East, was deeply involved, but it did not intervene on such issues as the intricacies of religious practices in the Hijaz. British officials were more preoccupied with the need to delineate the boundaries between Ibn Saud's domains and territories under British control or protection—Iraq, Trans-Jordan, Kuwait, and the Persian Gulf amirates—a task made all the more difficult by Ikhwan raiders who refused to recognize the tentatively demarcated borders in their area of operations.

The impact of the Ikhwan rebellion became evident during the 1928 pilgrimage. Although the Hijazi authorities were more mindful of pilgrims' welfare, there was much "interference in the performance of special rites by different sects." The British consul ascribed this to Ibn Saud's political need to placate more "fanatical" Najdi elements.[89] In 1927, Ibn Saud apparently promised that "Muslims from all parts and beliefs would be permitted to perform hajj according to their own special rites." This move might have been related to the recent conclusion of a friendship treaty with Britain. However, because of unrest on the Iraq-Najd border related to the Ikhwan rebellion, Ibn Saud now had to bow to the demands of Najdi Wahhabis "even at the expense of losing favour in the eyes of the Islamic world."[90] Although pilgrim numbers in 1928 were predictably smaller than during the 1927 Hajj *akbar*, with only some 14,000 from India compared with some 26,000 from 1927, it is difficult to ascertain how much this decline was due to a general disinclination to perform Hajj under Wahhabi parameters.[91]

Alongside Wahhabi religious policies, the Saudi authorities sometimes took drastic measures to counteract Britain's failure to stem the flow of destitute pilgrims from across its Muslim empire to the Hijaz. In 1928, poor pilgrims were detained if they remained in the Hijaz twenty-five days after the end of the pilgrimage, and the cost of imprisonment was recouped from shipping agents.[92] The frustration of officials in Jidda tasked with dealing with destitute pilgrims is apparent in their derogatory language: "The roads and all open spaces in town are packed with humanity, and an overpowering stench proclaims to high heaven the incapacity of the Hejaz government to provide for the elementary needs of the pilgrims, and to deal with a situation which each year seems to become progressively more offensive."[93] Blaming the Hijazi authorities was unfair. Although India's Hajj Enquiry Committee, which sat from 1929 to 1930, partly acknowledged Britain's culpability for the situation, there was no further attempt to tighten existing legislation to curb destitute pilgrims.[94]

In regard to the issue of Wahhabi religious policies, not all non-Wahhabi Muslims on Hajj accepted the new status quo. An illuminating example of this was the case of Maulvi Mushtaq Ahmad, a Sunni preacher from Delhi, in 1928. According to Ihsanullah, Ahmad was taunted by Indian Wahhabis to proclaim his beliefs in the Hijaz, and he "allowed his religious zeal to outrun all prudence and addressed a gathering in the mosque in Mecca, loudly proclaiming that all Wahhabis were infidels." Ahmed was arrested and jailed, and his friends exhorted Ihsanullah to help. Despite Britain's policy of nonintervention in religious matters where "official representations were out of place," Ihsanullah pointed out to Ibn Saud that his treatment of this religious leader might affect his popularity in India and result in fewer Indian pilgrims next year. This ensured Ahmad's release and an audience with an apologetic Ibn Saud. Afterward, Ahmad's bitterness against the king subsided, and he said effusively to Ihsanullah that "Ibn Saud had listened to him most patiently and had been at pains to show that his beliefs as a Wahhabi were not as incompatible with those of the Sunnis as is generally believed."[95] Ahmad's initial speech was bound to provoke a reaction. His treatment is an example of the constraints imposed by the Wahhabis that affected the ability of pilgrims from across the *umma* to engage in religious debates while on Hajj.

The relative lenience with which acts of *ziyara* were viewed by the Saudi authorities disappeared in 1929, a development that undoubtedly caused dismay among many pilgrims. Indian pilgrim and modernist scholar 'Abd al-Majid Daryabadi described the situation around Muhammad's tomb: "They [soldiers] push the pilgrims and sometimes they flog them with their willow and club. They do not hesitate to even drag women. Thus they seek to impose the 'Nejdi Shariah.' But some of the soldiers are very mild and they neglect or overlook the violation of the rules and regulations by the pilgrims."[96] Daryabadi sent a letter to Ibn Saud in which he argued "that every Muslim had equal rights to the holy sites of Mecca and Medina," and that "in the interests of unity, even the persuasions considered wayward or false should be granted space in which to engage in their rituals."[97] In his travelogue, Daryabadi also highlighted how most of the pilgrims with whom he traveled on the outbound journey were "elderly, weak, sick, poor, illiterate, and . . . anonymous."[98] The overall pilgrimage experience was mixed and uncertain.

A drawback of the official archive is the lack of insight into pilgrims' inner spiritual feelings.[99] Maulvi Sayyed Ahmad Husain Saheb Amjad, a pilgrim from Hyderabad, recorded his experiences of the 1928 Hajj in poetry, a common form of expression in Urdu Hajj narratives. Although he refers to the impact of Wahhabi policies in his prose, the poetry encapsulates a profound spiritual experience. After he slept outside the Holy Mosque in Mecca, he wrote:

> I have come to you on my head
> Sacrificed everything in your path
> I will ever meet you as Allah wills
> I have already seen your house.[100]

After praying with thousands of other pilgrims at Mount Arafat, one of the culminating points of the Hajj, he wrote:

> I am indigent and you are rich
> I am meek and you are the Supreme Being

I am helpless and you are powerful
I am a slave and you are the Lord
I am a man of all sorts of needs
You are the purveyor of all needs.[101]

These expressions of pilgrims' exaltations during their Hajj in this period illustrate that however much Wahhabism affected the pilgrimage, the inner spiritual feelings felt by pilgrims toward God while they were fulfilling this pillar of their faith remained as critical as ever to their overall experience. Amjad was also part of a broader poetic tradition; the Holy Mosque and the Ka'ba were consistently popular topics in poetry across the Islamic world. In 1880, Sadiq Bey, Egyptian officer and photographer of the Hajj, penned his own poetry within a broader account that described the Egyptian pilgrimage caravan's route from Cairo to Mecca:

In the Ka'ba's grace and radiance
Parting from You burns my heart
Yet are not photographers destined to burn in fire?
I have You drawn on paper
In friendship and recollection.[102]

This section concludes with an extended consideration of Amir Ahmad Alawi's account of his 1929 pilgrimage, *Safar-i-Sa'adat* (Propitious journey). His account has a candid nature and contains incisive assessments of Britain's engagement with the ritual, the experience of performing the Hajj from India in this period, and, importantly, the Hajj under Saudi-Wahhabi rule. Written as a *roznamcha*, or daily diary, and translated by Mushirul Hasan and Rakshanda Jalil, it is an invaluable historical source.[103] Amir Ahmad Alawi was part of the Indian Muslim gentry and served as a deputy collector in various parts of the United Provinces in North India. He left his hometown of Kakori, in the United Provinces, on January 31, 1929, and was driven to Lucknow, where he caught the train to Bombay. Shortly after he arrived, Alawi booked a first-class ticket for R 450 (second class cost only R 195) but had to wait twelve days before his ship, the SS *Rehmani*, departed. Alawi was inoculated against cholera, although a friend suggested that if he paid a couple of rupees, he could obtain a false vaccination certificate. This information suggests that pilgrims with sufficient funds could circumvent British medical regulations in force for pilgrims' voyages. In his guest house, Alawi met a water carrier who, having paid for his ticket, had only 200 rupees left for his journey and intended to walk from Mecca to Medina—an evocative example of a poor pilgrim's determination to perform the Hajj and visit the Prophet Muhammad's tomb. Indeed, Alawi met the same water carrier later in Medina, his pious wishes fulfilled.

The departure of Alawi's ship was delayed by communal riots, but when the appointed day arrived, the sight of many pilgrims making for the docks heightened Alawi's sense of Muslim solidarity: "Pride in the unity of Islam surged within me."[104] Amid this melee of boarding, a British police sergeant stood by the ship's gangway, and, according to Alawi, "beat several hajjis with his cane and kicked others. . . . I was shocked and dismayed by this brutish behaviour; I found it revolting." With 1,900 pilgrims trying to board, along with Alawi and three other passengers in first class, he speculated that if the sergeant's behavior had provoked a riot, the consequences would have been tragic. Pilgrims complained about the British sergeant's behavior to members of the Bombay Hajj Committee who were at the docks, but it remains uncertain whether this protest was noted and acted on.[105] This type of detail in Alawi's account is a necessary corrective to the official record, which says little about the mistreatment of pilgrims by British officials.

The experience of boarding and traveling on a pilgrim ship during this period brought home to Alawi the unfavorable manner in which pilgrims were treated during quarantine procedures and the voyage itself. As part of the quarantine regulations, pilgrims went through a fumigation procedure and a medical check. Alawi lamented that his fellow passengers, "steeped in their passion to see your Exalted House [the Kaʿba], . . . are willing to undergo every manner of humiliation and not a word of protest escapes from their lips. They are treated no better than goats and sheep in a slaughterhouse; yet they do not pollute their tongue with grievance or complaint."[106] After setting sail from Bombay, the ship stopped at Karachi to load wheat, which meant that pilgrims in the hold had to make way for the new cargo. This prompted Alawi to reflect that "had Muslims been owners of ships, they would never have put innocent hajjis to such hardship. . . . The revenue earned through profit on transporting goods is given greater premium than the comfort of pilgrims."[107]

As more pilgrims embarked at Karachi, Alawi praised the quiet demeanor of British officials and the efficient manner in which members of the Karachi Hajj Committee supervised the embarkation of pilgrims, compared with the experience in Bombay—a pilgrim's embarkation experience in British India was far from uniform, as were the journeys pilgrims had undertaken to get to their chosen ports. Alawi met one family on board who had ridden on horseback for forty days from Kashgar in southwestern China to Karachi. Some Afghan pilgrims who had boarded at Karachi seized control of the ship's deck and scared away the ship's British and Indian officers, who had previously shouted at the other pilgrims on board. However, the young British officers repeatedly kicked pilgrims as they dispensed water to them three times a day during the voyage.[108] Despite this mistreatment, the example of the Afghan pilgrims illustrates how some pilgrims were far from the picture painted of them in various colonial records as hapless and helpless persons.[109]

In the Red Sea and Jidda, Alawi was again confronted with and frustrated by the bureaucracy that attended the Hajj. When the ship docked at Kamaran Island, Alawi described the pilgrims as "prisoners" as they were checked by doctors, hosed down, and their clothes fumigated, although he thought that the quarantine camp was orderly.[110] Complaints by pilgrims to the government of India about the quarantine procedures led to the abolition of mandatory quarantine in 1931.[111] This underlined an important shift regarding sanitary regulation, the threat of epidemic disease, and the pilgrimage; the last reported outbreak of cholera during the Hajj was in 1912.[112] Once he had landed in Jidda, Alawi and other Indians had to deposit their return tickets at the British consulate, a regulation that pilgrims were angry with, although this was a temporary measure because of the large pilgrim numbers from India, and the British authorities worked in cooperation with their Hijazi counterparts and the Indian pilgrim guides.[113] Alawi believed that the British wanted to reduce pilgrim numbers by imposing petty regulations such as this; he wanted to avoid depositing his ticket but was warned by a fellow pilgrim not to. The Afghan pilgrims were told that they could not leave Jidda unless they had deposited their tickets, and they duly complied with the procedure.[114] This British regulation, designed to reduce the number of destitute pilgrims, served as a grating reminder to those like Alawi and the Afghans how colonial bureaucracy still reached them in the Hijaz.

Alawi had a mixed experience in Mecca, colored as it was by repeated disputes with his pilgrim guide and a pessimistic reflection on the extent of British power in the Hijaz.[115] Alawi's wealth meant that he was able to travel by car to Mecca, which took only two hours—by camel, the trip took two days.[116] On sighting Mecca, he and his companions were "like moths to a flame, we raced towards that light with abandon. The tongue and the pen cannot describe the state of our mind at that instant."[117] Alawi's exhilaration was deflated by the manner in which his Indian *mutawwif* passed him to a Meccan colleague who did not know how to perform the *tawaf* correctly and asked for money after Alawi had performed the ritual. This, along with other incidents, caused Alawi to castigate the pilgrim guides as a profession and bemoan the power they had over pilgrims at various points in his account.[118] While reading the Qur'an in Mecca's Holy Mosque, Alawi was repeatedly asked for alms by Indian and Sudanese pilgrims.[119] He was scathing about the economic situation in the Hijaz, noting how markets were "flooded" with British goods: "The wealth of the world of Islam finds its way to Europe through Mecca."[120] Alawi believed that although the Holy Cities were protected by God, the poor quality of the Najdi soldiers meant that Britain could occupy them in minutes, even though this scenario was a virtual impossibility.[121]

A poor opinion of Najdis was a sentiment apparently shared by pilgrims and Meccans alike, mainly because of the imposition of Wahhabi policies. Alawi thought that "every Meccan . . . is an inveterate enemy of the Nejdi" and had not met a single person during his time in the Hijaz who favored Wahhabi rule.[122] Alawi traveled to Medina by car, and his experiences there made him ill disposed to the Hijaz's new rulers. At the Prophet Muhammad's tomb, "the yearning of a lifetime wells up. . . . A strange state was upon me. Tears coursed down my face"—a reflection of the profound spiritual exultation that this *ziyara* had on him and many other pilgrims.[123] These feeling were shattered, however, when he visited al-Baqi cemetery in Medina. Alawi called Najdis "barbarians" for their destruction of various tombs there, and he and his companions left "carrying the burden of longing and pity in our hearts."[124]

At the Friday sermon in the Prophet's Muhammad's mosque, pilgrims were ordered by the imam to make their prayers to the Prophet with their backs to the Prophet's tomb; otherwise it would be considered *shirk*, idolatry.[125] In reaction to his experience of Wahhabi policies, Alawi wrote that "I never used to speak ill of the Saudis before this hajj travel but now it has become impossible to keep one's tongue silent after having witnessed their barbaric actions. May Allah give them better counsel!"[126] At the Prophet Muhammad's tomb chamber, Alawi described how Wahhabi guards were employed to ensure that no one touched the screen around the tomb or stood with clasped hands in supplication. These restrictions did not go uncontested—Alawi described Punjabi pilgrims arguing with the guards and Egyptian women who shouted "the choicest abuses" when they were prevented from offering prayers.[127] As he left Medina, "I felt as though I was leaving my heart behind in that holy compound. . . . After I lost sight of [the] green dome . . . my life suddenly seemed a waste."[128] Alawi's unflinching description of and reactions to Wahhabi policies in Medina are a testament to the difficulties pilgrims faced there, but also to their determination to defy such proscriptions.

Returning to Mecca in time for Hajj, Alawi performed the rituals, but after the Hajj, he again had the frustrating experience of dealing with the bureaucracy of the British consulate in Jidda. Alawi traveled to Jidda to collect his return ticket, and in order to expedite this collection, he met several times with Munshi Ihsanullah, who apparently had the power to decide who left on which ship. Ihsanullah promised him a place on the SS *Rehmani*, but in a later confrontation at the consulate, Alawi was told that departures were on a first-come, first-served basis.[129] Ihsanullah's power over pilgrims was underscored in a scene described by Alawi. At Ihsanullah's home, surrounded by pilgrims, he gave "each one the same answer: 'you will be given your ticket when your number comes.' An old man fell at his feet and began to cry piteously and asked for his ticket, and received the same response. The poor man was forcibly evicted from the spot."[130] Alawi contrasted this treatment with the Dutch consulate, which did not follow this procedure. He wrote that the British consular staff "could not care less for our welfare. . . . How can I possibly narrate the troubles faced by those poor illiterate souls who are lying by the roadside and don't even have the courage to approach their rulers?"[131] However, in one instance, Ihsanullah's power did not extend far beyond the Hijazi coastline. When Alawi and his fellow pilgrims boarded the SS *Rehmani*, Ihsanullah was unable to get the Afghan pilgrims to move from their position on the ship's deck, which they had reoccupied.[132]

Regulations and documentation continued to be a source of anxiety for Alawi on the return voyage because his passport had not been returned when he collected his ticket from the consulate, but he was informed by a British employee of the SS *Rehmani* that a passport check was not carried out when the ship docked in India.[133] After a little over four months away, Alawi arrived back home in Kakori on June 8, 1929.[134] Alawi's account remains without equal in its unflinching description of and commentary on the twin trials of British bureaucracy and Wahhabi policies that pilgrims from South Asia and elsewhere in Britain's Muslim empire faced in this period. Alawi performed the Hajj at an opportune moment because it was evident that the Hijaz's financial prospects were not reassuring in the closing months of 1929. This situation worsened substantially in the 1930s and had significant consequences for the Hajj.[135]

The Hajj during the Great Depression, 1930–1939

The Wall Street crash in October 1929 and the ensuing Great Depression had global consequences, and the impact it had on the pilgrimage illustrated its far-reaching effects. The severe economic downturn prevented many Muslims from performing Hajj. The Jidda consulate reported that "the heart of Islam is now beginning to feel the reflex action of world conditions."[136] Economic pressure affected the Hajj in two ways.[137] First, the issue of Indian destitute pilgrims was complicated by the appearance of pilgrims who attempted to reach Mecca by avoiding the Bombay–Jidda steamship route. Britain remained powerless to prevent poor Indian pilgrims from reaching their goal and continued to facilitate these pilgrims' journeys by repatriating them to India. Second, because the Depression led to a slump in pilgrim numbers, Saudi-Wahhabi policies moved toward a cautious form of religious compromise with pilgrims.

Sir Andrew Ryan, consul at Jidda from 1930 to 1936, wrote that of all the "administrative problems which this great annual movement created" for Britain, he and his staff's primary concern was to "ensure as far as possible that [pilgrims] should not set out without having the means to return." However, "this was not as simple as it sounds" because although many governments operated return-ticket systems, "Moslem opinion was divided as to the lawfulness of attaching such a condition to the performance of a religious obligation." Ryan was cognizant that African pilgrims especially felt that the obligation to perform Hajj was "paramount, and that the rest lay with God."[138] The issue of African destitute pilgrims will be analyzed in Chapter 6; Ryan's general point underlines the central importance of the destitute-pilgrim issue to Britain's overall interactions with the pilgrimage, which only increased in complexity with the onset of the Great Depression.

The Depression led to the rise of a new type of destitute pilgrim from India because greater numbers were unable to afford the return ticket from India but had the tenacity to set out on foot for Mecca to perform the Hajj. These pilgrims traveled overland to Mecca via Persia and Iraq or landed on the Persian Gulf coast before striking out across the desert.[139] Overland pilgrims were the abiding feature of the Hajj from Britain's Muslim territories in Africa, whose mostly poor pilgrims walked across the continent on their way to Mecca. Because of the Depression, some Indian pilgrims made equally extraordinary journeys, crossing the Persian Gulf and then walking hundreds of miles across Arabia to Mecca. The Jidda consulate conceded that in light of this new overland route, destitute pilgrims would continue to be a feature of the Hajj, "however strict the control in India may be," and that the yearly phenomenon continued to be "damaging to British prestige."[140] British authorities in the Persian Gulf attempted to stanch the flow of hundreds of pilgrims crossing the Gulf by trying to prevent pilgrims leaving from the Indian port of Gwadur, a mere two hundred miles from Arabia, and mounting surveillance on the Batinah coastline, where pilgrims who sailed from Gwadur disembarked.[141] Reader Bullard realized the ultimate futility of Britain's—and Saudi Arabia's—preventive measures: "Nothing could prevent a penniless Indian Moslem from begging his way across northern India and Baluchistan, getting a lift in a dhow across the Gulf, and setting out to walk to Mecca."[142] Writing to his family, Bullard was even more pessimistic, lamenting that "nothing seems to be able to deter the destitute from India from coming to Mecca," but he noted that the phenomenon "was worse when I was here before, for if a man could find the money for his ticket to Jeddah he could come, even though he would certainly arrive penniless." Saudi attempts to stop poor pilgrims from taking this route led to alternative routes springing up, for example taking a dhow to other Arabian ports such as al-Mukalla, on Arabia's southern coast, or to various inlets south of Jidda beyond the control of officialdom.[143] Britain and Saudi Arabia had limited ability to prevent these people from performing the Hajj.

Bullard's perceptions, however, had their limitations, and it was Lal Shah, a Muslim official at the British consulate in Jidda, who was able to gain a unique insight into the world of overland destitute Indian pilgrims in 1938. While he was stranded at a coffee shop on the road to Mecca after his car broke down, Shah spoke to several poor pilgrims who told him tales of the routes they took to the Hijaz that evaded all administrative formalities and payments. These pilgrims, unaware of Shah's occupation, cheerfully told him that the government of India would repatriate them; some explained that the cost of the government-sponsored return journey could never be recovered from them because they would give the authorities false names and addresses on the IOU forms that the consulate issued to pilgrims who received money for repatriation.[144] Demonstrating imperial impotence on the issue and dependence on their Muslim subjects and employees, British officials in Jidda lamented that destitute pilgrims were a "considerable embarrassment" and thought that the issue should be taken up by "some influential Indian" so the Indian vice-consul would "no longer have to work with destitute lady pilgrims lying on the floor of his office or pulling his hair."[145] The zeal of poor pilgrims to perform the Hajj continued to triumph over British and Saudi attempts to halt this group's travels to Mecca. Indeed, it seems clear that British repatriation efforts encouraged such people to attempt the journey.

Destitute pilgrims' government-paid return journeys to India meant that Bombay was forced to deal with this group as well. For example, in 1933, over 100 pilgrims remained stranded in hostels there at the end of the pilgrimage season. That year, the Pilgrim Department spent just under R 4,000 from the Indigent Pilgrim Fund to repatriate pilgrims stranded in Bombay after they arrived back from the Hijaz; what might be termed official "sponsorship" of destitute pilgrims extended across the Indian Ocean. After an allegation in 1930 by the shipping company Turner Morrison that poor pilgrims in Jidda had "concealed their resources," the British consul at Jidda recommended police intervention at Bombay. Consequently, the authorities boarded returned ships to find out whether alleged destitute pilgrims had funds. Charities and individuals who usually issued "charity tickets" to poor pilgrims were instructed to ensure that pilgrims who intended to return to India had sufficient funds for the entire journey. Despite such interventions, the long history of government-funded repatriation undoubtedly continued to encourage poorer Muslims to go on Hajj in the expectation of official financial assistance.

Anglo-Muslim cooperation in Bombay over pilgrims' travels reinforced the perception that poorer Muslims could attempt the journey and receive help from various quarters. Bombay's civil society continued to assist with the flow of pilgrims into the city. For example, one Islamic association sent iced water for pilgrims' outward journeys; Bombay's Memon Association Relief Committee sent three lorries to transport destitute pilgrims, accompanied by thirty volunteers, when a ship returned during communal rioting in May 1932; poor pilgrims in the Carnac Road *musafirkhana* were fed at the expense of private charities for a few days before their repatriation; and the Fatmabai Rogay Charitable Trust spent R 3,090 to send 17 pilgrims to Mecca in 1932.[146] The work undertaken by these organizations eased parts of some poor pilgrims' journeys to Mecca.

In 1939, the chairmen and executive officers of Hajj committees in Bombay and Karachi visited the Hijaz, the first time people involved in Britain's Hajj administration in India had met their colleagues in Jidda in a formal capacity and observed firsthand Britain's Hajj administration in the Hijaz. Their encounters with Indians begging in the Hijaz, "which they realise brings the whole of India into disrepute," made them argue for the imposition of measures to prevent such scenes. However, the political climate among Indian Muslims, who were "already critical of the disproportion between the dues charged and the services rendered by the Saudi government," coupled with the complication that any changes would require legislation, meant that nothing was done. Significantly, Indian Muslim criticism of Hajj-related administration had shifted from the British to the Saudis.[147] Furthermore, concerns of these representatives about the loss of prestige posed by destitute Indian pilgrims were now focused on the Indian nation instead of the British Raj. This presaged a wider shift toward Muslim officials in Britain's Hajj administrations viewing destitute Indian pilgrims in national rather than imperial terms, a trend that accelerated after the Second World War.

The Great Depression affected Wahhabi religious policies on the Hajj and Britain's reaction to them. The government of India's *Confidential Report of the Hajj Enquiry Committee* in 1930 confirmed the continued official policy of noninterference in religious practices in the Hijaz. The committee had consulted various bodies, including Britain's Jidda consulate, on Britain's administration of the Hajj and Saudi administrative efforts. The report's first page drew attention to complaints from pilgrims that arose from "the fact that Nejdis are reactionary and intolerant in matters of religion and are at pains to interfere with certain observances and practices, which have been customary as part of the pilgrimage among Indian and other pilgrims." It was considered "undesirable" to address these concerns because the committee believed that Indian Muslim opinion would be against any official representation to Ibn Saud on this topic. Sensitivity to Muslim opinion went hand in hand with British self-interest: "If even diplomatic representations on any of these points are made which are in the least likely to prejudice the harmonious relations that exist at present between both governments, we would certainly prefer that no action be taken."[148] This stance rested on earlier wide-ranging negotiations with Ibn Saud on a variety of political issues but nevertheless reflected a British priority of ensuring that its pilgrim-subjects would be "safe as regards their property and person" while in the Hijaz.[149] Although Wahhabi religious policy clearly caused concern, such worries were trumped by the need to maintain good relations with Ibn Saud. After all, Ibn Saud was perceived as a reliable British ally in the Hijaz and Arabia, certainly more so than his predecessor, King Hussein.

Britain's accommodation of Wahhabi Islam was underlined by the efforts of officials such as Ihsanullah in Jidda when pilgrims landed—he warned pilgrim guides to "avoid leading pilgrims to such places as might react un-favourably on their susceptibilities" and stressed to anyone listening on the quayside that pilgrims should comply with Wahhabi regulations. Consequently, many pilgrims, though not all, remained in the environs of Mecca and did not travel to Medina to visit the Prophet Muhammad's tomb. But the acute economic pressure on Ibn Saud's kingdom meant that the application of Wahhabi practice was relaxed. Pilgrims were able to take advantage of the Najdi soldiers' lack of pay and bribed them so they could kiss the Prophet's tomb "to their heart's content."[150] The intensification of the worldwide Depression in 1931 meant that the Hajj that year "justified poor expectations," and only around 40,000 pilgrims arrived from overseas.[151] Philby estimated that in a good year, when around 100,000 pilgrims would arrive, the government would earn £5.5 million from taxes and pilgrimage and customs dues. But the slump, he calculated, had caused a calamitous 75 percent drop in revenue.[152] One way in which this shortfall was made up, complained a retired Shiʿi Indian government official to the British consul, was the requirement that Shiʿa had to pay more in pilgrimage-related taxes than Sunnis. However, Britain steadfastly adhered to its policy of religious neutrality on this matter, and no representations were made on this issue to the Saudi authorities.[153] Economic depression had led to Wahhabi compromise, but the freer religious atmosphere that marked the pilgrimage experience of pre-Wahhabi times had now disappeared forever.

Ihsanullah made a critically important observation in March 1931 when he reported that "now pilgrims are giving up on the idea of visiting several holy shrines and sacred tombs, and at present remain contented with performing the paramount duty of hajj only."[154] It appeared that pilgrims in the main had accepted certain Wahhabi conceptions of religious practice. Nevertheless, laxer enforcement of Wahhabi policies due to the Depression perhaps boosted pilgrims' determination to continue with customary Islamic devotional practices despite the risks. In 1931, a venerated well at the Prophet's tomb, closed by the Wahhabis, was broken open by pilgrims at night. The next day, many came to draw the sacred water; one man was arrested and flogged.[155] These examples of confrontation and compromise highlight a regime beset by contradictions in its religio-political economy. Tombs at Medina were being repaired before the Najdi *'ulama* protested to Ibn Saud, and work stopped. The Saudi government charged a road tax for pilgrims to go to Medina; but in order to generate much-needed extra revenue, the authorities had to allow Hajjis to visit the Prophet's tomb and other shrines in the first place. Ihsanullah observed that Ibn Saud's policy "remains as strongly Wahhabi as is consistent with economic and financial necessity of not choking off pilgrims."[156] The kingdom's parlous financial situation led Ibn Saud to seek financial help from the nizam of Hyderabad, the world's richest Muslim. In exchange for the nizam's generosity, a fact withheld from the Najdi *'ulama,* Ibn Saud gave the nizam permission to refurbish the Prophet's tomb at Medina.[157]

The Kingdom of Saudi Arabia's dire financial straits, exacerbated by economic crises that resulted in its king asking other non-Wahhabi Muslim rulers for money, probably contributed to a more tolerant religious policy on pilgrims.[158] The Saudis' maintenance of official parity with gold, coupled with the pound sterling's and the rupee's break with the gold standard in 1932, meant that prices in the Hijaz were 40 percent higher than in 1931. Therefore, most pilgrims became impoverished. In Jidda, the British consulate's transmission of this information to the government of India, which revised its estimate of the pilgrimage's costs upward, led the Saudis and others with a commercial interest in the Hajj to use the Indian press to discredit British announcements. These parties claimed that R 500 to 750 would be sufficient funds for performing the Hajj, in contrast to the amount cited by the British, which was 100 percent higher. After pilgrims discovered the true cost of the Hajj after they arrived in the Hijaz, many went to the British consulate and "clamour[ed] for redress and help . . . but were told they were largely to blame for trusting the Hejazi government and its agencies rather than their own government."[159] The Depression was making performing the Hajj, and making money from it, increasingly challenging.

The Saudis' need for a more lenient religious policy was underscored by the extremely low numbers of pilgrims by historical standards that came on Hajj in 1933: only some 20,000 from overseas and a mere 7,000 from India.[160] Ihsanullah reported "a marked tendency in direction of more liberal policy towards non-Wahhabi Muslims." The influence of more devout Wahhabi elements had diminished. One example of this was the appointment of Faisal, son of Ibn Saud, as viceroy of the Hijaz during Ibn Saud's absences on tour in other parts of the kingdom. According to Ihsanullah, Faisal was "disposed towards liberalism by his personal tastes" and had curbed the punishments of religious offenses. Another official, the minister of finance, quoted from the Qur'an to Ihsanullah: "Let your religion be yours and mine be mine." As a way of ensuring revenue from pilgrims, the minister wanted to restore the shrines and tombs at Medina. At these places, pilgrims now reported the ease with which devotional practices at shrines and tombs could be carried out. The English translation of an official Saudi pilgrimage guide spoke of a visit to Medina as though it were obligatory, a far cry from the practices and actions of the Wahhabis in their first years of rule over the Holy Places.[161]

At this point it is instructive to contrast the official British reports on Wahhabi policies with the accounts of two pilgrims from Britain's Muslim empire who traveled to the Hijaz for Hajj in 1933. Lady Evelyn Cobbold was born into a family of Scottish aristocrats and visited North Africa with her family regularly as a child.[162] By 1914–1916, letters from her Arab friends referred to her as Lady Zainab, which suggests that she had already converted to Islam. Indeed, she states in her pilgrimage account that she "does not know the precise point when the truth of Islam dawned on me. It seems that I have always been a Moslem."[163] In 1933, at the age of sixty-five, she became the first British Muslim woman to reach Mecca, although the strain of the journey meant that she did not complete all the Hajj rituals. Traveling by boat and train from Southampton to Port Said in Egypt, she took a boat to Jidda. She was received there with some skepticism by both the British consul, Sir Andrew Ryan, and her host in Jidda, fellow convert Harry St. John Philby. Her journeys to Mecca and Medina were made in the company of Mustafa Nadhir, an employee of Philby's, and an old Sudanese pilgrim whom she had befriended.[164] Reflecting on her observations of Wahhabi policies, Cobbold hoped that "time will lessen the scowl of the Ikhwan and soften their hearts towards their brother Moslem and teach them tolerance; at the same time we can but admire in the Wahhabi the purity of his faith and his strict adherence to his convictions."[165] Cobbold's admiration and support for the Wahhabis were partly tempered by her reaction to their antishrine policies: "Khadijah's tomb in common with all others has been razed to the ground by the Wahhabis. . . . These Puritans wish to clean Islam of all the superstitious growth of centuries and restore it to the simple faith taught by the Koran, and are no doubt in the right, but one cannot but regret the disappearance of so much beauty."[166] Although Cobbold's interpretation of Islam was fiercely individual—for example, she did not perform the five daily prayers—her ambivalent reaction to Wahhabi actions echoed that of many other pilgrims.

Gulam al-Hasnain Panipati, a Shi'i Indian Muslim, took a harsher view than Cobbold. Although he was not an aristocrat like Lady Evelyn, he was by all accounts a respected personage, given letters from the Saudi finance minister that stated that he "should be provided with all sorts of comfort."[167] He was met by Ihsanullah on the deck of his ship in Jidda and was invited to the pilgrimage officer's house.[168] In the al-Baqi cemetery in Medina, he observed the "cruel" behavior of the Najdi guards, who beat and punched a scholar who made some of his clothing touch one of the graves, despite other pilgrims pleading with the guard to stop.[169] Panipati wrote that "these Nejdi think the whole world is involved in the act of polytheism."[170] On another occasion in the cemetery, Panipati saw a pilgrim pay a guard who then allowed him to touch and kiss the graves.[171] He observed an Indian imam delivering a sermon in the mosque by the al-Baqi cemetery "in order to propagate Wahhabi beliefs only. . . .

Nobody is allowed to give sermons, whether he belongs to the Hanafi or Shafi'i or any other school of law. Everybody has to follow Wahhabi imams."[172] His dissatisfaction with Wahhabism highlights the depth of Shi'a feelings about the death of Islamic pluralism in the Hijaz. The impact of Wahhabi religious policies generated conflicting responses from these two pilgrims, who spanned the broad spectrum of Muslims who made up Britain's Muslim empire. The Wahhabis' fundamentalist conception of Islam was seen as damaging to the unity and diversity of Islam.

By the mid-1930s, the religious temper of the Holy Places had calmed. Nevertheless, Ihsanullah advised Indian pilgrims to avoid visits to shrines that might "lead to unpleasant incidents."[173] A more lenient Wahhabi stance toward Islamic practice continued into the 1934 Hajj season, characterized by a more peaceful atmosphere. One pilgrim was even allowed to visit the tomb of Khadija, the Prophet's first wife.[174] Even Philby, whose conversion to Wahhabi Islam made him one of its most fervent advocates, wrote that a visit to the shrine and tomb of the Prophet in Medina had returned to being part of pilgrims' "ritual programme."[175] Only a few events reported by Ihsanullah showed the divisions that simmered below the surface among the *umma* on Hajj. One was a speech delivered in the Holy Mosque by Maulvi Ahmad Dehlavi, who denounced all non-Wahhabis. He was "severely assaulted" by several pilgrims and had to be rescued by the police, who arrested his assailants. The other was the expulsion of two West Africans for "witchcraft," which was a lucky escape for them considering that the penalty for "sorcery" was death.[176] Ihsanullah's 1935 summary best sums up the character of pilgrims' experiences in the late 1930s: "Usual restrictions on visits to tombs and shrines were officially maintained, but unofficially circumvented."[177]

The wider context of Britain's Muslim empire in this period informed Britain's policy of studied neutrality toward Saudi-Wahhabi practices in relation to the Hajj. The rising nationalist tide in India, Iraq, Egypt, and especially Palestine, where British forces engaged in violent suppression of the 1936–1939 Arab Revolt, meant that Saudi Arabia was increasingly seen as a trusted conservative Muslim ally. Consequently, any misgivings Britain may have harbored regarding

Saudi policies on the Hajj were minimized; the thought of causing any further friction in the Middle East was anathema. In 1937, Bullard wrote to Foreign Secretary Anthony Eden in response to reports that Ibn Saud had refused to hold a general Arab Congress out of deference to Britain, alluding to the Palestinian situation: "It is fitting that an Arab Moslem government and a country where the divine inspiration was revealed and Islam originated should take anxious thought for all matters affecting the Arabs. . . . On the other hand it is fitting that the country which contains the two Holy Sanctuaries and is based on piety and divine worship alone should be left to itself in such matters and safeguarded from suspicion, so that the will of God alone may be done."[178] The Saudi authorities took pains to suppress any mention of the Palestinian situation throughout the kingdom because this would have caused tension among pilgrims as well as Saudi subjects.[179] This was no special favor to the British; Ibn Saud placed severe restrictions on nationalist and anticolonial activities in the Holy Cities, especially during the Hajj. These restrictions were generally effective, which explains why nationalist and anticolonial activities are hardly discussed in this book. Officially, this was because Ibn Saud thought that the Hajj should be a time for worship and not politics, but given that the kingdom was dependent on the Hajj as a source of income, it was vital to ensure that the ritual was not marred by any disturbances from nationalists and anticolonial activists or, indeed, any form of "agitators" as defined by Ibn Saud.[180] Nevertheless, consular officials such as Ihsanullah did note the presence of several nationalist figures from India during the 1936 Hajj, which he surmised "resulted in a fairly extensive exchange of views." Significantly, however, Ihsanullah's observation did not cause British authorities any notable alarm.[181]

The retirement in 1937 of Ihsanullah, recently awarded an MBE and previously granted the title of Khan Bahadur, further underscores the importance of Muslim employees within Britain's Hajj administration to the empire's overall engagement with the Hajj. Sir Reader Bullard attested to his importance and the problems Ihsanullah's high profile created: "Ibn Saud, who in the first years of his reign used . . . Ihsanullah a great deal, probably regretted that he had to confide in so small a man, and began to show hostility to him."[182]

According to Bullard, Ihsanullah knew the administrative work related to the pilgrimage "better than anyone else" and had "a great and salutary influence" on British India's pilgrimage policies.[183] Bullard noted dolefully that "now he has retired, leaving to his successors to carry on the hard struggle."[184] This referred to Ihsanullah's efforts on behalf of Indian pilgrims, especially those who were destitute: "The slightest injustice done to an Indian . . . fills him with indignation, and he has worn himself out trying to make Indian pilgrims safer from exploitation in the Hejaz than Wigan cotton operatives on holiday in Blackpool."[185] Ihsanullah's position in the consular bureaucracy at Jidda, his work with pilgrims from across Britain's Muslim empire, such as Nigerians, Sudanese, and Malays, and his role as a crucial source of information regarding the imposition of Wahhabi policies on the Holy Places further highlight the complexity, breadth, and depth of Britain's relationship with the pilgrimage and Islam.

Conclusion

The onset of Wahhabi rule changed the meaning of the Hajj. Pilgrims who came on Hajj also visited saints' and notables' tombs, and these practices were directly opposed to Wahhabi policies and actions. But because the Depression led to a slump in pilgrim numbers to the Hijaz, these devotional acts were allowed to continue, albeit under restricted circumstances, in order not to discourage pilgrims from coming to the Hijaz. These restrictions and the Saudi government's attempts to popularize the Hajj among the *umma* meant that the Hajj became an even more important part of Islamic religious practice. Throughout this period, Wahhabi religious policy was contested by pilgrims who held interpretations of Islam at variance with those of the new rulers of the Holy Places. This had important implications for Britain's association with the Hajj. British nonintervention in these Wahhabi actions highlighted its reluctance to influence these events that were part of the Wahhabi-era Hajj, a shift from previous British policies, proposals, and actions in regard to the pilgrimage. British concerns to accommodate this form of fundamentalist Islam, precisely because it held sway over the Holy Places and the Hajj, gave imperial interactions with the pilgrimage and pilgrims a greater complexity, especially because most of Britain's Muslim subjects viewed the new rulers of the Hajj as heretics. Although Britain continued to try to resolve the issue of destitute pilgrims, this chapter has demonstrated continued British helplessness when confronted with the determination of these poor Muslims to undertake extraordinary journeys to perform the Hajj. Britain's repatriation of destitute pilgrims continued as it had for many years. Having evaded various forms of regulation and control, indigent pilgrims returning to their homes with British help were one defining feature of the imperial administration of the Hajj. Muslims within the colonial bureaucracy, especially Munshi Ihsanullah, played a key role in assisting pilgrims in navigating the vicissitudes of the Hajj under Saudi-Wahhabi rule and remained important transmitters of information and advice on the pilgrimage to their British employers.

Seen through the prism of the pilgrimage, Islam in this period experienced a sustained contest between universalism and localism, between Wahhabi policies and the continued vitality and diversity of Islamic devotional and customary practices. In the middle of this contest, often literally, were those employed by Britain to engage with the Hajj, and pilgrims themselves, many of whom were British subjects. British officials sought to delink imperial governance from the Hajj, with varying degrees of success. Wahhabi policies on the Hajj meant that the ritual—and Islam more widely—retained a continued significance to imperial rule across Britain's Muslim empire. In September 1939, the outbreak of war in Europe hindered Saudi attempts to attract pilgrims from overseas. Ibn Saud continued to encourage "agents in India to carry on religious propaganda for them with the object of attracting the faithful to spend their money in the holy land" and extended the system to Muslims in South Africa—Wahhabi proselytizing reached out across Britain's Muslim empire and beyond.[186] But the widening of the conflict into a global conflagration and the insecurity of sea routes led to a drop in pilgrimage numbers. It was not until the vast growth in Saudi Arabia's oil wealth and the rise in air travel after 1945 that Wahhabi proselytizing resumed on a far greater, global scale.

6

Hajj from the Far Ends of Britain's Muslim Empire, 1924–1939

Introduction

Moving on from the internal dynamics of the pilgrimage under Saudi-Wahhabi rule, this chapter focuses on Britain's interactions with the Hajj from Sudan, Nigeria, and Malaya during the interwar period. From the 1920s, all three territories expanded their administrative dealings with the Hajj and gained greater prominence in Britain's overall relationship with the pilgrimage. Nigeria and Malaya constituted the far ends of Britain's Muslim empire. Sudan is also included in this analysis because Nigerian pilgrims walked and worked across Sudan on their way to and from Mecca. The vast majority of pilgrims who arrived in the Hijaz from Sudan hailed from West Africa.[1] Although the British authorities in these territories expressed concerns about issues of public health and security in relation to their pilgrim-subjects, this chapter will focus on other issues that loomed large, namely, slavery, destitute pilgrims, and colonial attempts to control the movements of pilgrims.

What is the utility of placing together these two case studies from Africa and Asia? Malay and Nigerian pilgrims undertook the longest journeys to Mecca in Britain's Muslim empire. One was largely maritime, the other mainly overland. Malay pilgrims voyaged across the expanse of the Indian Ocean, and Nigerians embarked on a "great trek . . . always going on" across the Sahel to the Red Sea.[2] Considering these case studies together highlights the overall importance of the Hajj to British imperial rule—it was a religious practice that colonial authorities, in places as different and far-flung as Nigeria and Malaya, engaged with and invested significant time, money, and energy on. Studying Britain's interactions with the Hajj from these territories in a single framework of analysis allows us to see how this imperial engagement was not hermetically sealed within each colonial territory. Due to the border-crossing nature of pilgrims' travels to and from the Hijaz, Britain's engagement with the Hajj from these territories alternated among local, regional, and transcontinental foci. Viewing these case studies together brings into focus the wider importance of Islam and Muslims to the British imperial experience, and it lends empirical weight to the concept of Britain as ruler of a Muslim empire. Despite the numerous differences between these territories, there are some striking and unexpected similarities regarding the Hajj.

Officials in Malaya borrowed concepts and regulations regarding the administration of the pilgrimage from India, and their counterparts in Sudan and Nigeria adapted practices from both India and Malaya in turn. There was extensive cooperation among officials from these territories and their colleagues in Jidda. Colonial efforts to curb the traffic in slaves from West Africa and Southeast Asia to the Hijaz and the enslavement of African pilgrims in the Hijaz were consistently unsuccessful. Many Nigerians and Malays worked at various points on their routes to fund their Hajj.

Pilgrims who fell into destitution in the Hijaz and elsewhere along their journeys were a key reason that colonial authorities in both Nigeria and Malaya increased their engagement with the Hajj in the interwar period—one component of wider colonial "welfare" projects. The net result of this involvement, much of which was expedient and reactive, facilitated the spiritual journeys of these poor pilgrims and, in the Malay case, led to the employment of a Malay pilgrimage officer, who played a significant role in the colony's administration of the Hajj. Local leaders in Sudan were an integral part of the territory's interactions with pilgrims. Nigerian destitute pilgrims were particularly successful in circumventing regulations imposed by British authorities designed to control pilgrims' travels to and from the Hijaz. Although Malay pilgrims were generally richer, and the maritime route they took enabled the colonial state to exercise closer regulation of pilgrims, a variety of factors rendered many of them indigent. Consistent difficulties in establishing the identity of pilgrims from Malaya and Nigeria meant that British repatriation efforts often benefited poor pilgrims from French and Dutch colonies as well. Taken together, Nigerian and Malay indigent pilgrims attest to the limits of Britain's ability to prevent this poorer class of Muslims from fulfilling their spiritual goal, and indeed show how Britain enabled the Hajj for this group of pilgrims. Viewing these groups together demonstrates that destitute pilgrims were not solely an Indian phenomenon and were an important issue across Britain's Muslim empire. The imperial administration of the Hajj was consistently faced with the determination and success of poor Muslims in getting to Mecca to perform the Hajj. This chapter begins with the cases of Nigeria and Sudan and concludes with Malaya.

Nigeria and Sudan: Slavery and Destitute Pilgrims

After the First World War, British officials in Jidda became increasingly aware of the presence of pilgrims from Nigeria and Sudan in the Hijaz. At the same time, British authorities in these territories were becoming more deeply involved in areas of Islamic practice, such as *shari'a* law, and paid greater attention to the pilgrimage. This shift was initially prompted by concerns over the Hajj as a conduit for slave trafficking and a transmitter of Mahdist ideas.[3] Official apprehension about the latter had been evident since the early 1900s but gained greater currency during the pilgrimage of the emir of Katsina from Northern Nigeria in 1921–1922. The emir was accompanied along part of the route by a colonial official, G. W. Webster, and reported to Webster that he had received information that there were several active anticolonial plots in progress in Mecca led by Nigerians. Webster's report back to his superiors in Nigeria fed into broader anxieties about Islamic uprisings in the colony after the 1923 conviction of Said bin Hayatu, a descendant of Uthman dan Fodio, founder of the Sokoto caliphate, for plotting a Mahdist uprising. As Jonathan Reynolds has argued, colonial officials in Nigeria were rarely experts on Islam and relied on academic materials from their French counterparts in West Africa, an unedifying combination that undoubtedly served to fuel colonial anxieties.[4] Pilgrims picking up Mahdist ideas while on Hajj, however, were arguably never the dominant factor in the imperial engagement with the pilgrimage from Nigeria and Sudan.

The nature of Nigerians' journeys to Mecca, combined with economic and political developments along the route, created a set of circumstances where phenomena such as slavery came to exercise the attention of British officials in this period. The journeys of these *takayrna* pilgrims were rather different from those of their counterparts from India, Egypt, and Malaya. The main difference was time. It was not uncommon for a pilgrim to spend at least five to seven years, if not longer, to get to Mecca, perform the Hajj, and return home.[5] The journey from Northern Nigeria to Red Sea ports such as Port Sudan and Suakin in Sudan was approximately 1,800 miles, of which 700 miles was in French territory. Pilgrims spent years working their way across Sudanic Africa to pay for their onward journey. Sudan's Gezira cotton scheme, established in 1925, gave labor opportunities to Nigerian pilgrims to pay for their travels and ensured a ready supply of labor for the scheme.[6] After performing the Hajj, pilgrims often spent a year doing menial labor in the Hijaz to enable them to afford the journey home. In the course of these epic journeys, Nigerian pilgrims faced a different set of difficulties from their Indian counterparts. Perhaps the most terrifying was enslavement.[7]

Despite the decline of slavery in the Islamic world from the 1880s, pilgrims who traveled along routes in Africa to the Red Sea remained vulnerable to being captured and sold into slavery.[8] The increase in pilgrim numbers during this period meant greater economic activity in Jidda and the Holy Cities; slaves were in demand for various tasks, such as transportation, construction, and domestic work in households.[9] The risk of enslavement for African pilgrims remained high in the Hijaz itself. Children were particularly at risk. In 1910,

German missionary and traveler Hermann Kumm described the children and young women who accompanied male pilgrims as "easily transported coinage" to Mecca, where they could be sold for cash.[10] After the First World War, H. R. Palmer, resident in Bornu in northeastern Nigeria, accompanied the emir of Katsina on his journey to Mecca as far as Jidda, traveling by pony cart. His 1919 report on the journey highlighted this fact that West African children were sold in Mecca, and he recommended that the Hajj from Nigeria should be restricted to those over twenty-one, a measure that was never enacted because of the impossibility of enforcement, although it was echoed by the British consul in Jidda in 1924.[11] In 1926, C. A. Willis, former director of the Intelligence Department in Khartoum and newly appointed governor of the Upper Nile Province, wrote an extensive report on slavery and the pilgrimage in which he noted that enslaving children was particularly attractive for traffickers because they were more easily controlled, especially since traffickers often married the girls.[12] Officials repeatedly focused on this particularly emotional topic, given the assumed preponderance of child pilgrim-slaves in the wider pilgrim-slave traffic.

Slavery in the Hijaz was closely associated with the Hajj because the majority of slave trading occurred during the pilgrimage season, when the potential market for buyers and sellers became much wider. British reports from the interwar period outlined several typical examples of sales in the Hijaz, but pilgrims were also captured as they walked across the Sahel and were subsequently smuggled across the Red Sea for sale. British officials cited various cases: a Sudanese village chief persuaded people to let their young sons accompany him on Hajj and then sold the boys in Mecca; a Nigerian who married a widow with a young daughter in Nigeria took both of them on the pilgrimage and then sold them; when a pilgrim died after having performed the Hajj, his child who accompanied him was captured and sold. Bedouins raided parties of African pilgrims walking between Mecca, Medina, and Jidda for slaves, a trend that fluctuated according to the relative stability of the Hijaz. This type of slave raiding occurred especially during the 1924–1925 Hijazi-Saudi conflict, when the routes in the Hijaz were essentially unprotected.[13]

From as early as the 1870s, when Britain attempted to interdict the slave trade into Arabia, Royal Navy officers repeatedly stressed to their superiors how it was "very difficult to obtain any information about the slave trade" and complained that much of the information they did gather was "merely the result of hearsay."[14] Despite British pressure on the Ottoman authorities from the 1860s, resulting in various laws, conventions, and *firmans* against the slave trade, these were usually unenforceable in areas far from the imperial center, such as the Hijaz.[15] The Hashemite regime did not attempt to stop the slave trade, and King Hussein taxed it as a source of revenue. Some local leaders in Sudan and Nigeria criticized British antislavery efforts. When the emir of Katsina visited London after performing the Hajj in 1922, he said that although the indirect-rule system in Nigeria meant that the British had a "better understanding" of Muslim laws and practices, he resented the British-imposed abolition of slavery.[16] One of the few ways European consuls could free slaves in the Hijaz was if a slave was a subject of one of the European powers and was able to escape his or her owner and take refuge in the relevant consulate in Jidda. Once the slave was inside the consulate, the authorities could use their extraterritorial privileges (the Capitulations) to manumit slaves, a system that continued long after the collapse of Ottoman power in the region.[17]

The resilience of Arabia's slave trade made British authorities in the Red Sea region vulnerable to criticism of their ineffective antislavery efforts. In 1921, Sudan's governor-general, Sir Lee Stack, wrote to the *Journal of the Royal Central Asian Society* in London in response to a critical article by Harry St. John Philby on the slave traffic between Sudan and Arabia, which underlined the central role of pilgrims' travels in aiding this parallel and clandestine flow of people. Stung by the allegations, Stack retorted that pilgrims engaged in "very little slave-trading indeed" but did not deny the existence of the phenomenon in Sudan during the pilgrimage season. Stack detailed the various regulations in place that he believed deterred slave trafficking through the port of Suakin. Before embarking for Jidda, pilgrims were issued passports at Suakin that were checked by British officials, who were assisted by government-appointed and paid *takayrna shaykhs* based in the port. If there were discrepancies in the number of family members on a passport when pilgrims returned from the Hijaz, officials cross-examined the pilgrim with the aid of these "trustworthy" *shaykhs*. Given that everyone who embarked on pilgrim ships was seen by "competent officials," Stack thought that it was extremely difficult for any slave to be smuggled on board and, more tenuously, believed that even a small child who had been enslaved would tell an official about his or her situation.[18] Given the lack of a response to Stack's rejoinder from Philby or antislavery campaigners, it remains unclear how effective it was in silencing British criticism of imperial antislavery efforts in relation to the Hajj.

Slavery and the pilgrimage remained a major concern for the Sudanese authorities throughout the 1920s, as is underlined by the voluminous 1926 report on the topic written by the director of the Intelligence Department in Khartoum from 1915 to 1926, C. A. Willis. A meeting of Sudanese government officials in June 1924 called for further regulation of the pilgrimage precisely in order to check the slave traffic. Pilgrims were supposed to travel only on the Suakin–Jidda route, and, in order to avoid overt imperial coercion, this route was meant to be made attractive to pilgrims by making it a cheap option through the Sudanese government paying for pilgrims' quarantine charges.[19] Willis sketched out the various suggestions that the Hijaz's successive rulers had made to British officials regarding pilgrim-slaves. King Hussein had said that if the European powers were worried about pilgrims being enslaved, they should stop their subjects from going on Hajj. By contrast, Ibn Saud proposed to ban the buying and selling of pilgrims in the Hijaz from outside the region if the British consul agreed to give up the right to manumit slaves, an agreement the British were not prepared to countenance.[20] One section of Willis's report detailed the measures British authorities took against slavery among their pilgrim-subjects in the Hijaz. The Sudanese government gave the British consul in Jidda £50 a year to repatriate destitute pilgrims who might be at risk of enslavement, especially if these pilgrims could not prove their Nigerian nationality, which excluded them from receiving help from the Nigerian Repatriation Fund. Willis argued that this sum should be increased.[21] The British consul manumitted twenty slaves a month, and the Sudanese government had constructed a few huts in Port

Sudan to receive these ex-slaves. However, there was a strict limit on the numbers manumitted because any more would cause "difficulty and expense."[22] Despite official concern over the enslavement of British pilgrim-subjects, Willis's report demonstrated the clear fiscal limits to imperial altruism.

Pilgrim-slaves in the Hijaz were an important segment of a larger slave market that resisted attempts by European and local authorities to curb its practices. Colonial officials, such as the secretary of the Northern Provinces in Nigeria, were certain that the traffic in pilgrim-slaves between Nigeria, Sudan, and the Hijaz was considerable.[23] British and Dutch consuls reported how Hijazis saw slavery as a vital institution, and although Britain's 1927 Treaty of Jidda with Ibn Saud committed him to repress the traffic, he continued to levy import duties on slaves and believed that these people were better off as slaves in Arabia than as free persons in their homes in Africa. Nevertheless, Ibn Saud did make pilgrim guides responsible for ensuring that their charges were not enslaved, and in the case of a woman from Malaya who disappeared, the pilgrim guide who had responsibility for her was severely beaten, fined, and imprisoned by the Saudi authorities. Abolitionists in Britain repeatedly pressured colonial administrators on the issue of "Arab slavery." British officials in Jidda manumitted slaves from their consulate in Jidda as a means to blunt Ibn Saud's continued acceptance of slavery until the 1936 Treaty of Jidda, when the right of manumission was renounced in exchange for Ibn Saud prohibiting the importation of slaves by sea. This resolved a long-standing source of diplomatic tension between Ibn Saud and Britain that occurred whenever a fugitive slave appeared in the consulate requesting manumission (209 times between 1926 and 1933), because Ibn Saud viewed the British right of manumission as an infringement of his sovereignty.[24] In the 1930s, the League of Nations, which had passed a convention on slavery in 1926, lamented that the Hajj remained a major source of the slave trade, but further international regulations in 1936 were intermittently enforced.[25]

Slavery was an important part of broader imperial concerns about the Hajj in this period—specifically that there was little control over pilgrims' travels across the Sahel. Officials felt that only an elaborate system of control over the West African pilgrimage would curb slavery, but they recognized that there was "no means of effectually stopping these sales altogether."[26] By the early 1930s, Sudanese pilgrims had pilgrim passes and were directed to proceed to Suakin, and officials hoped that Nigerians who "formerly roamed almost unchecked on foot" across Africa would be more closely controlled by the Nigerian pilgrim-passport system, which was intended to regulate the Nigerian pilgrimage and prevent these pilgrims from crossing the Red Sea by dhow from Massawa in Italian Eritrea. The number of slavery cases British officials were aware of in the early 1930s was small, only four in three years in the Hijaz, of which two were Nigerian women and children. However, this was probably due to the effects of the Depression, which meant that people had less money to spend on slaves, rather than emblematic of a long-term decline in the slave trade or a reduced appetite among some Hijazis and pilgrims alike to own slaves.[27] Slavery was a feature of the Hajj that Britain remained unable to eliminate but was less visible than destitute pilgrims, to whom this section now turns.

Although officials in Northern Nigeria had been aware of thousands of pilgrims leaving the colony to travel to Mecca since the early 1900s, estimates that some 50,000 were on the move in 1919 prompted the report on the pilgrimage by H. R. Palmer, resident in Bornu, that year. These numbers had jumped from 30,000 in 1912, and nowhere near these numbers returned to Nigeria, prompting official concerns over this substantial drain of labor.[28] Despite the geographic distance between Nigeria and Sudan, Palmer found that the flow of pilgrims provided a strong connective thread between the territories.[29] One feature that characterized this connection was the flow of information. Palmer stressed that there was "annually filtering into the Northern Provinces through returning pilgrims . . . a much greater knowledge of modern oriental politics . . . than has ever been the case in the past."[30] Along the route he traveled, Palmer passed through *takayrna* colonies ruled by *shaykhs*, most of whom had left Northern Nigeria after fighting the British in the early 1900s. In Suakin and Port Sudan, Palmer spoke to *shaykhs* of similar communities who were supporters of the Sokoto caliphate destroyed by Britain in 1903.

Nevertheless, some of these *shaykhs* received salaries from the government and served as vital intermediaries between the authorities and pilgrims, supervising pilgrim registers in the ports.[31]

The attraction of the Hajj, along with Sudan's policies on Islamic practice and economic development schemes, acted as a magnet for West African pilgrims. Palmer fretted that Sudan's "fostering and protection" of a variety of Islamic institutions, especially Sufi orders, would continue to "drain away" people from Nigeria.[32] While the Sudanese government courted the friendship of leaders of Sufi orders, officials in Nigeria wanted to prevent the growth of Sufi influence in the colony.[33] Nigeria's system of indirect rule, whereby indigenous authorities and administrations were incorporated into the colonial system, made it difficult for officials to establish policies on Islamic practice that complemented those operating in nearby British-controlled territories, such as Sudan.[34] In Sudan, many West African pilgrims lived in an area called the Gharb al-Gash near the town of Kassala in the Red Sea Province and worked in the cotton fields of the nearby Gash delta in order to fund their journeys to Mecca or back home. C. A. Willis saw the *takayrna* communities in Kassala as generally "industrious and useful people."[35] Another British observer praised the pilgrims as a "most law-abiding people, whose aim it is to pass through the country with as little trouble as possible. . . . Their presence is a God-send."[36] These examples demonstrate that British views toward West African pilgrims were not uniformly negative and freighted with anxiety over their potential role as transmitters of Mahdist ideas. Despite the efforts of pilgrims who labored in the Sudan for months or years, they were often unable to save very much money beyond a small amount to pay for food, water, and a one-way ticket across the Red Sea to the Hijaz.[37]

Pilgrims who traveled along the routes from West Africa to the Red Sea were generally poor, but their indigence often increased once they arrived in the Hijaz. In Jidda, Palmer reported how Hijazis treated *takayrna* pilgrims with "utmost scorn," given their poverty and race. When he visited the *takayrna* settlement outside the town, some of its inhabitants complained to him that they had no money to return home.[38] Palmer's 1919 report was one of the first by British officials in Sudan and Nigeria that highlighted the plight of destitute pilgrims and also the first to make several recommendations for closer control of the Hajj that would serve to prevent destitution. Palmer advocated that British authorities should coordinate the administration of pilgrims' travels with their French counterparts, given pilgrims' crossing of French territory; pilgrims should be allowed to leave for Mecca only after they gained the approval of their local emir or chief and should deposit £10 in their local province's capital to be returned to them at Suakin after their Hajj to fund their return journey.[39] Palmer's recommendations were seemingly uninfluential, and the issue of destitute pilgrims only gained further prominence, given the deteriorating situation in the Hijaz in 1924.

The general collapse of the Hijazi economy due to the Hashemite-Saudi conflict, combined with news of the Wahhabi massacre after the fall of Ta'if in 1924, meant that many West African pilgrim-laborers applied to the British consulate for repatriation.[40] These men performed a variety of roles, including the carrying of pilgrims' luggage, making other transportation arrangements, and carrying water for pilgrims.[41] The desperate predicament of these pilgrims was compounded by the forcible conscription of some into Hussein's army, who subsequently deserted when they were posted to Mount Arafat. This event also prompted many Nigerians to abandon their pilgrimage and flee to Jidda.[42] In the early 1920s, Nigeria had established a specific repatriation fund for this purpose, funded from the revenue of Nigeria's Northern Provinces, but these events meant that it was drawn on far more than usual. In 1923–1924, 1,293 Nigerians, many of whom were able to escape from conditions of slavery given the Hijaz's instability, were sent by dhow across the Red Sea to Suakin for only a few shillings per head, which cost £679 in total. These measures drew on the examples of British repatriation of Indian pilgrims and also the private initiatives of Muslim rulers. The emir of Katsina, for example, repatriated 400 destitute pilgrims from his emirate at his own expense in 1921–1922. The extraordinary circumstances in the Hijaz led officials in the Jidda consulate to change their tactics on repatriation. Nigerians were now fast-tracked for repatriation. Previously, such applicants had been ignored for a month or two, which would lead those who pretended to be destitute to leave.[43] As with the example cited in Chapter 3 of destitute Indian pilgrims in 1912–1913, British officials facilitated pilgrims' return journeys expediently and reactively, prompted by a fluid situation rather than a considered altruistic concern with pilgrims' welfare.

Although C. A. Willis, governor of the Upper Nile Province in 1926, reported on slavery and the pilgrimage, his report also dwelt on the lack of control that the Sudanese government could exercise over West African pilgrims, who were "almost entirely of the poorest class."[44] Sudan's lengthy and porous western border, with its small number of border posts, combined with the fact that there were four main routes through Darfur, meant that pilgrims were often able to avoid any contact with the authorities.[45] In Darfur, the supervision of pilgrims was largely delegated to local leaders, who were told to move parties of pilgrims along to the nearest district headquarters; some were reluctant to do so, however, because they believed that *takayrna* were "wizards."[46] Pilgrims who entered Sudan without any documentation and who came into contact with British officialdom were given a pilgrim's certificate, but by the time pilgrims reached Suakin, most of them had lost the document.[47] East of El Obeid, near Darfur's border and a railhead from where pilgrims could follow the tracks to Port Sudan, there was no attempt to control the movement of *takayrna* pilgrims because doing so would affect the flow of labor to the Gezira cotton fields.[48] The limited reach of the Sudanese state and the Sudanese economy's need for pilgrim labor served to inhibit any closer control over pilgrims, at least until they reached Suakin and Port Sudan.

However, destitute pilgrims from West Africa, like their fellow pilgrims from India, confounded British authorities by traveling to the Hijaz through areas far beyond Britain's control. Because of the poverty of pilgrims, the Hajj-related administrative apparatus in Suakin and Port Sudan and its costs for pilgrims meant that many traveled to the Hijaz by avoiding British-administered territory.[49] The International Sanitary Convention of 1926 instituted new sanitary and quarantine restrictions that mandated that pilgrims possess return steamship tickets and be vaccinated in Suakin. What happened in practice was that pilgrims paid a compulsory return deposit of 154 piastres before embarking on a ship to the Hijaz. Unclaimed deposits were used to pay the expenses of destitute pilgrims to assist their onward journeys home from Suakin.[50] The quarantine system in place at these ports was seen as vitally important by officials in Sudan, who were concerned that pilgrims might spread epidemic disease. This would threaten the labor force of the Gezira cotton plantations, a vital part of the territory's economy. However, from his investigations, C. A. Willis was convinced that quarantine charges and poor conditions in quarantine camps meant that pilgrims specifically tried to avoid them, which increased the risk of an epidemic. In his words, pilgrims saw the quarantine system as a "piece of oppression if not an interference with the will of God."[51] Furthermore, restrictions on the number of pilgrims that boats of the local Khedival Mail Company could carry because of sanitary rules led the firm to increase its ticket prices, in addition to deposits and quarantine dues. This had the effect of making West African pilgrims travel southward to Italian Eritrea. Once they reached the capital, Massawa, they could cross the Red Sea to Arabia more cheaply by *sambuq* and faced little in the way of colonial administrative measures or pilgrimage-related fees. Willis believed that the only way to ameliorate these trends was to decrease the various fees and charges that pilgrims had to pay in Sudan and turn "a blind eye" to overcrowding on steamers so that ticket prices could go down.[52] In order to expand controls over pilgrims' movements, Sudan's authorities had to facilitate the Hajj for them.

Willis drew on arguments by officials in other parts of Britain's Muslim empire when he advocated the introduction of various measures, none of which were instituted. Like his Indian counterparts, Willis wanted pilgrims to remain at home unless they had money for the entirety of their journey, and he advocated a return-ticket system for the Suakin–Jidda route to ensure that pilgrims possessed sufficient funds for their journey. He pointed out that such a system was in place in Malaya, Egypt, and the Netherlands East Indies, but he realized that an increase in ticket prices would further dissuade pilgrims from using this route.[53] A further difficulty was the necessity of communicating any new measures through the *shaykhs* of *takayrna* settlements because he knew that pilgrims tended not to heed government notices.[54] Perhaps most important, Willis realized that in order to be effective, administrative measures related

African pilgrims on board a ship at Suakin bound for Jidda, c. 1930s

Credit: Dr. J. E. F. Blosse and Mrs. Gillian Kingham

to the Hajj in Sudan needed to be similar to those in operation in British-controlled Nigeria, as well as in the French and Italian empires—a desire that required a level of imperial cooperation and coordination that unsurprisingly remained unrealized throughout this period.[55]

Sudan's governor-general, Sir John Maffey, called for further regulation of the pilgrim route in 1927, although he was aware that the porous borders of colonial states in Africa, coupled with the limited number of government posts in Sudan, meant that this was an ambitious hope.[56] The Saudis, who disliked destitute Africans in the Hijaz because of their begging and lack of any documentation, assisted British attempts at further control by trying to prevent "surreptitious" landings from dhows on the Hijazi coast. In 1927 and 1928, Saudi authorities deported around 1,000 destitute West African pilgrims to Suakin. Saudi officials, like their Ottoman predecessors described in Chapter 2, were critical of Britain's lack of control over these pilgrims. British officials in Jidda recommended "close cooperation" between Nigeria and Sudan to ensure that new regulations that pilgrims would travel via Suakin alone would be enforced, an almost impossible task given that in 1927 alone it was estimated that there were around 56,000 Africans walking along the route to and from Mecca at any one time.[57]

As mentioned earlier, the lack of quarantine and administrative controls in Italian Eritrea until 1934–1935 benefited poorer pilgrims but caused consternation among British officials in Jidda and Sudan, who found it "distressing" that most Nigerian pilgrims arrived from Massawa precisely because they would avoid any official British supervision in the form of the return-deposit system instituted by the Sudanese government. The Jidda consulate plaintively tried to persuade the Italian authorities to adopt a similar deposit scheme for pilgrims, which would reduce the Nigerian government's repatriation bill, and suggested that pilgrims could be "deflected" away from Eritrea to Suakin.[58] The Italians were reluctant to collect fees from pilgrims because of their poverty and sometimes sent them on to Asir, just south of the Hijaz. Two thousand African pilgrims ignored the Saudi proclamation on October 18, 1928, that pilgrims from outside the Arabian Peninsula could arrive only in Jidda and proceeded to travel via Massawa in *sambuqs*, landed on the Hijaz coast at Qunfida and Lith, and then walked on to Mecca. New British and Italian legislative measures in 1929 stipulated that pilgrims had to return via their outward route, which led to a large number of African pilgrims applying for repatriation at considerable expense to the Nigerian and Sudanese authorities.[59]

Measures to control the flow of African pilgrims proposed by both the Sudanese and Nigerian authorities after 1926 forged new connections between them and the British consulate in Jidda and reflected the extensive communication and cooperation of all three bodies.[60] Palmer's successor as resident in Bornu, G. J. Lethem, traveled a similar route in 1927 in order to investigate the role of the pilgrimage and *takayrna* settlements in the transmission of religious and political ideas to Nigeria.[61] Lethem recommended that a Nigerian official should regularly visit Sudan and Jidda to work on pilgrimage-related matters. During his stay in Jidda, Lethem was effusive about Munshi Ihsanullah, of whom he had the "highest opinion." Ihsanullah assured Lethem that he would now endeavor to keep himself regularly informed of events in the *takayrna* community in the Hijaz. However, Lethem was critical of the Sudanese government, accusing it of paying little attention to Nigerian pilgrims in Sudan.[62] In March 1931, the commissioner of Port Sudan, Major Douglas Thompson, visited Jidda to discuss the regulation of pilgrims' travels from Sudan with British officials at the consulate.[63] By 1932, these various consultations resulted in the conclusion of an agreement between the Sudanese government and the Khedival Mail Company, which ran the Suakin–Jidda route: the firm would now issue only return tickets to pilgrims, valid for two years.[64]

Major Thompson traveled to Jidda again for further discussions with his British colleagues in April 1934 to discuss the Nigerian pilgrimage "control scheme," due to come into force later that year. This scheme was adapted from various regulations that had been used in India, Malaya, and the Netherlands East Indies and was partly designed to make Nigeria comply with various international sanitary regulations that had been laid down after the International Sanitary Conference of 1926.[65] According to the scheme, pilgrims would apply to their local administration for a passport and pay a deposit of £5 to cover their quarantine and other fees and transport costs. At Maiduguri, near Nigeria's northeastern border, they would receive a metal disc to identify them as Nigerian. In Suakin, pilgrims would be received by a *takayrna shaykh*, get vaccinated, and be given some money from their deposit to pay for quarantine fees and the return ticket to Jidda. In Jidda, after performing the Hajj, they would receive their return ticket and the remainder of their deposit. Nigerian pilgrims, therefore, had to present themselves to British officialdom at various stages. The scheme was designed to shorten the time pilgrims spent on their journeys, prevent destitution, stem the loss of labor from Nigeria, and reduce the workload of colonial officials. However, the scheme was hampered by its voluntary nature, a feature adapted from various Indian examples in order to dampen any potential protests from Nigerian Muslims. Therefore, it had little impact on pilgrims—only 190 pilgrims out of thousands adhered to the scheme in its first year of operation. For the many pilgrims who wanted to work at places along the route, such as the Gezira cotton scheme, it made little sense to submit to this cumbersome method of regulation with its many bureaucratic minutiae.[66] Although the Nigerian pilgrimage scheme became mandatory in 1938–1939, it was impossible to enforce because of the limited reach of the colonial state within and beyond Nigeria regarding this practice.[67]

The Great Depression's disastrous impact on African pilgrims' employment opportunities in the Hijaz, combined with the nature of their journeys to the Hijaz, underscored how British officials and travelers viewed them as having the lowest status among all pilgrims. On April 5, 1934, a huge fire destroyed Jidda's *takayrna* settlement, an event that led nearly 1,500 African pilgrim-laborers to apply for repatriation. This exacerbated a growing trend driven by the lack of employment opportunities in the Hijaz for African pilgrims as a result of the Depression.[68] Officials in Nigeria and Sudan were concerned about the continued demands placed on the repatriation fund and the effect of sudden influxes of labor into the Sudanese market. Furthermore, African pilgrims were seen as the group furthest beyond the realm of official control. Compared with Indian pilgrims, Sudanese and Nigerians were impossible to trace in the Hijaz, and the voluntary Nigerian pilgrimage control scheme had little effect: "The various ways in which they reach the Hejaz is not conducive to control on their number." African pilgrims were perceived as "generally much poorer and regarded as carrion to be hunted only when the richer game [Malays and Indians] gives out." Officials conjectured that many died because they lived in "indescribable filth and squalor" in Mecca.[69] British convert to Islam Eldon Rutter described with disdain how many West Africans lived in a quarter of Mecca that was a collection of huts made of bushes, camel grass, animal skins, and petrol tins.[70] These dismissive perceptions were reinforced by further comments by officials that West African pilgrims were "notoriously impecunious, and . . . not really welcome" in the Hijaz.[71] Like Indian destitute pilgrims, their West African counterparts in the Hijaz were seen as diminishing British imperial prestige in the heart of Islam. Nevertheless, like the measures put in place by Indian authorities, Nigeria's Repatriation Fund facilitated these pilgrims' journeys.

Although Saudi proposals to regulate destitute pilgrims in 1939 were never enacted because of the outbreak of war, they underscored the shift in British attitudes toward this group and demonstrated how the attitude of Nigerian and Sudanese Hajjis transcended the temporal concerns of bureaucracy. The Saudis decided that certain pilgrimage dues should be collected by shipping agents from pilgrims at ports of departure. In a reversal of roles, the British consul in Jidda counseled the Saudis that their proposal was "open to objection on religious, political and practical grounds"—which virtually echoed the points made by Muslim notables in consultations on pilgrimage administration in British India in the late nineteenth century discussed in Chapter 2. The consulate also accused the Saudis of lacking the "moral courage to deal with [destitute pilgrims] in the proper way by refusing to allow those who do not pay the dues to perform the pilgrimage," a surprising remark given the history of British dealings with destitute pilgrims considered in Chapters 2, 3, 4, and 5.[72]

These disputes and the threat of war meant little to African pilgrims trekking through the Sahel and savannas on their way to Mecca. The immense distances of such journeys meant that the consulate thought—accurately—that the pilgrimage from Africa would be "little affected" by the war. Any disruption would take several years to percolate through to these pilgrims, given the length of their journeys.[73] One of the final reports by the consulate in October 1939, before the war truncated these missives, noted the continued ability of African pilgrims to avoid the authorities by landing on the Arabian coast in dhows from Massawa and limply stated that "the Sudan government has been requested to do whatever is possible to guide all West African pilgrims to Suakin instead of Massawa."[74]

This section has provided a singularly telling example of the British empire's consistent inability to control various aspects of the Hajj from Nigeria and Sudan. Britain's suppression of slavery connected to the Hajj remained a hope rather than a reality. A desire for closer regulation of pilgrims' travels was partly blunted by their value as laborers, and the limited reach of imperial and colonial authorities across the vast areas where pilgrims traveled, especially those places not under British rule, meant that officials were mostly unable to craft and enforce effective regulations. Because of expediency and reacting to events such as the 1924–1925 Hashemite-Saudi war, rather than altruism, Britain came to facilitate poor pilgrims' travels through various repatriation schemes. Destitute pilgrims remained beyond effective British control. This chapter now moves from the Sahel across the Indian Ocean to offer a comparative example of imperial engagement with the Hajj from Malaya, at the eastern end of Britain's Muslim empire.

Malaya: "Colonial Welfare," Destitute Pilgrims, and Slavery

From the early nineteenth century, the transmission of Islamic revivalist and reformist currents to Malaya meant that the obligation to perform the Hajj played a more important part in the religious experience of Malay Muslims.[75] At the same time, the expansion of British power and influence in Peninsular Malaya produced a variety of reactions from Malays, who reflected on the impact of British imperialism on Islam in Malaya. Munshi Abdullah, whose 1854 account of his journey to the Hijaz for Hajj was cut short by his premature death in Jidda before he performed the ritual, believed that Islam was "on a better footing" in British-administered Malaya than in the peninsula's independent kingdoms *(kerajaan)*.[76] Hajji Abdul Majid bin

Zainuddin, the first Malay pilgrimage officer, wrote in 1928 that British rule over Muslims was analogous to the Prophet Muhammad's time in Medina, when the first Muslim community lived there under non-Muslim rule.[77] The various treaties that Malay rulers concluded with the British from the late nineteenth to the early twentieth centuries generally stated that the realm of religion remained under the jurisdiction of these rulers. However, as this section demonstrates, from the 1920s the colonial authorities became deeply involved in the administration of the pilgrimage from Malaya and sought to facilitate the Hajj in order to improve the welfare of their pilgrim-subjects as a means of bolstering support for British rule; their success remains difficult to assess.

Until the First World War, however, British officials considered the pilgrimage a component of the colony's trade, and legislation from the mid-nineteenth century was largely related to shipping conditions, along with a requirement for pilgrims to purchase return tickets. These measures were due to political and commercial interests rather than altruism—some 70 percent of Malay pilgrims sailed in British ships in the 1890s.[78] Like their counterparts in India, British officials in Malaya thought that the issue of pilgrims' health was an unwanted burden on the colonial administration.[79] A Malay messenger was appointed to the British consulate in Jidda in 1896 to assist pilgrims, and another Malay official was appointed to serve a similar function at the Kamaran Island quarantine station in 1904. At the turn of the twentieth century, around 2,000 Malays went on Hajj every year, making up 10 to 15 percent of all pilgrims and spending around six months in the Hijaz.[80]

Pilgrims from Malaya and the Netherlands East Indies congregated in the key port city of Singapore. Britain's Malay pilgrim-subjects were one part of the Hajj from the Malay world of Southeast Asia, which was largely under Dutch control in this period. Indonesian pilgrims were attracted to Singapore by laboring opportunities, the proliferation of new and cheap shipping routes out of Singapore sparked by opening of the Suez Canal, the city's status as the headquarters of several Sufi orders, and pilgrims' desire to avoid various Dutch-imposed restrictive regulations of the pilgrimage.[81] Indonesian and Malay pilgrims, many of whom in the latter case came from Johore in southern Malaya and were sometimes accompanied by their relatives, who wished them good-bye, tended to stay for one to two weeks in Singapore. They were accommodated in crowded boarding-houses in Kampong Haji, the city's Javanese quarter, although in 1920, thousands of pilgrims stayed in government schools in Singapore because of a shortage of accommodation. Pilgrims carried with them three months' supplies for their journey, which added to pressures on accommodation space. The sea voyage to Jidda on *kapal haji*, pilgrim ships, generally took just under three weeks, and the total journey some four to five months.[82]

Many intending pilgrims who arrived in Singapore stayed there for many years before they traveled to Mecca, and some, dubbed *hajji Singapura*, never fulfilled their spiritual goal. People in this group worked in the city to earn enough money for the journey and were similar in some ways to the "permanent pilgrims" who settled across Sudan. Pilgrims who had performed their Hajj with a loan from Hadhrami Arabs worked on Hadhrami-owned pepper, clove, and tea plantations as repayment when they returned to Southeast Asia, as detailed in Chapter 2.[83] Along with Bombay, Singapore was one of the most important port cities for the Hajj in Britain's Muslim empire and the Indian Ocean world.

In contrast to their peers in the Netherlands East Indies and some British officials across Britain's Muslim empire, the authorities in Malaya were not particularly concerned about the Hajj as an enabler of anticolonial activities. As William Roff has argued, officials did not view Hajjis as potential sources of unrest and sought to facilitate the pilgrimage.[84] Colonial officials mostly subscribed to the perception that Malays were "placid" on religious matters, despite concerns that events such as the 1881–1882 'Urabi revolt in Egypt, the victories of the Mahdist state in Sudan, and the Singapore Mutiny of Indian Muslim soldiers on February 15, 1915, might provoke disturbances in Malaya, which they did not. Furthermore, many officials thought that Malays were not as invested in pan-Islamism and events in the Ottoman empire as some Indian Muslims, although there was some fund-raising activity in Penang in 1912 for the Ottoman Red Crescent organization. The main public reaction to the outbreak of war between Britain and the Ottomans in 1914 was, in fact, the various declarations of loyalty to Britain by Malay rulers.[85] British policy on Islam in Malaya, then, was rather different from that in India, which has often stood in for British interactions with Islam as a whole in existing scholarship.

The First World War caused severe financial hardship for Malay pilgrims and prompted the first British intervention into supporting the homeward journeys of destitute pilgrims from Malaya. A sophisticated remittance network between the Hijaz and Southeast Asia supported Malay pilgrims, students, and settlers during their sojourns in Arabia. In 1916, over 800 destitute Malay pilgrims and temporary residents in Mecca left the city once the Arab Revolt erupted, but they became stranded in Bombay after they ran out of funds and were shipped back to Malaya at government expense.[86] The difficulty of sending remittances to the Hijaz during the war meant that many Malay pilgrims suffered a similar predicament there. For example, several Malay Hajjis from Kelantan successfully petitioned the authorities to repatriate destitute Malay pilgrims, arguing that government inaction reflected badly on British prestige. Although fewer than those from India, Malay destitute pilgrims were more expensive to repatriate, given their lengthier homeward journey. For example, Kelantan State spent the sizeable sum of 8,300 Malayan (M) dollars on repatriating destitute pilgrims between 1918 and 1923.[87] Both the colonial authorities and the Malay states supported the pilgrimage through facilitating these return journeys, an unintended policy that was entirely a reaction to the turbulent situation in the Hijaz during the war.

The unsettled nature of Sharif Hussein's administration of the Hajj and the British experience with Malay destitute pilgrims sparked greater interest in the Hajj from colonial officials in the postwar period, which led to greater administrative involvement in the ritual. A 1920 memo on the pilgrimage suggested various measures, most notably that the colonial authorities and the Malay states should fund free passages every year for a fixed number of poor Muslims and Malay civil servants.[88] In February 1921, the Inter-Departmental Pilgrimage Quarantine Committee in London recommended that Malaya should assume sole responsibility for the maintenance and repatriation of Malay destitute pilgrims in Jidda and take a more active role in pilgrimage administration. Officials in Malaya accepted this, and when the colony's Political Intelligence Bureau of the CID was established in 1922, one of its roles was to manage the pilgrimage.[89] The governor of the Straits Settlements argued "how entirely necessary it now is to endeavour to meet the interests of our Muslim subjects wherever and whenever possible," and assisting Malay pilgrims in the Hijaz was one component of this strategy. Colonial Office officials in London blamed the colonial government's lack of arrangements for pilgrims as one reason that this group faced difficulties in the Hijaz and suggested that the government-appointed Muhammadan Advisory Board (established after the 1915 Singapore Mutiny) should copy the Egyptian system of appointing an *amir al-hajj* who would accompany Malay pilgrims every year and liaise with British officials in Jidda. This eventually evolved into the position of Malay pilgrimage officer. Despite British concerns, most Malay pilgrims seemed not to need assistance from their colonial rulers; many of them simply avoided the British consulate in Jidda.[90]

A Pilgrim Committee was formed in late 1922 that included figures such as the director of political intelligence, the chairman of the Muhammadan Advisory Board, and two leading Malays from the Federated Malay States. Their deliberations on issues such as the practicality of compelling pilgrims to travel along certain routes to Mecca and mandatory passports echoed similar discussions held at various points in India, Sudan, and Nigeria: it was seen as "impracticable . . . to introduce any form of compulsion" regarding the Hajj. Restrictive legislation "would savour of grand-motherly interference with the liberty of the subject." The committee pointed out the impossibility of preventing poor pilgrims from attempting to travel via Bombay: "If a person says he is going to Bombay on business it is impossible to contradict this." Any existing problems related to the pilgrimage were cheerily envisaged to be assuaged by the appointment of a Malay pilgrimage officer and introducing a pilgrim pass. Destitute pilgrims were a central concern of these discussions.[91]

The Malay pilgrimage officer became a key part of Malaya's interactions with the Hajj. Hajji Abdul Majid bin Zainuddin, an assistant inspector of schools in the Education Service in Perak and writer of popular didactic texts, was appointed in 1924 to live in Jidda for seven months every year, alongside a clerk, Wan Yussuf bin Wan Husein Temenggong.[92] Abdul Majid's duties in Jidda included registering pilgrims at the British consulate, holding their return tickets, investigating pilgrims' complaints, advising the consul on the Malay pilgrimage, and dealing with deceased pilgrims' estates. He was also tasked with gathering intelligence on pilgrims' activities that might damage the colonial government; significantly, however, this was given a low priority—number nine of his ten duties.[93] In 1923, Abdul Majid had performed the Hajj at government expense as part of his official leave and had been asked to prepare a report on the pilgrimage. One of his findings was that none of the Malay pilgrims he observed seemed "eager to . . . talk politics, all being thoroughly engrossed in the adventure of the pilgrimage itself."[94] Abdul Majid's first report in his post did not mention political discussions among Malay pilgrims at all, an absence that greatly pleased the director of political intelligence.[95] His employers saw his first months on the job as a success; one official wrote that Abdul Majid "should be a permanency; there is no doubt he would be of great help to pilgrims and to us."[96] The working environment in the consulate was not harmonious, however: the British consul criticized Abdul Majid in 1926 for avoiding "as much as possible co-operation with the . . . staff."[97] A popular figure among pilgrims during his tenure, which lasted until 1939–1940, Abdul Majid sometimes paid for the food and drink of destitute pilgrims, a group that featured prominently in his efforts as pilgrimage officer.[98]

Abdul Majid was instrumental in expanding the scope of official assistance to destitute pilgrims. Shortly after his tenure as pilgrimage officer began, he pointed out that aside from a small fund in the consulate, designed to supply destitute pilgrims with food for two days, there was no other aid for destitute Malay pilgrims. Abdul Majid persuaded the director of the Political Intelligence Bureau to lobby his superiors to establish a Malayan Pilgrim Relief Fund in 1927. The colonial government agreed to this and allocated £25 a year for the fund, an amount that increased during the Depression. However, for the most part, destitute Malay pilgrims were helped by their families, who sent remittances to the Hijaz. Malay pilgrims generally did not set out for the Hijaz without sufficient funds; destitution was partly a consequence of fluctuations in the various Hajj-related fees pilgrims had to pay during their stay in Hijaz, and Abdul Majid drew up a list of pilgrimage expenses for circulation, although how much effect this had on pilgrims' budgeting is unknown.[99] Abdul Majid also consistently lobbied for pilgrim ships to supply food for their passengers, a measure that was eventually passed into legislation in 1930 and was especially helpful for poor pilgrims.[100]

Destitution among Malay pilgrims also increased during times of political and economic crisis in the Hijaz in this interwar period. In the midst of the Hashemite-Saudi conflict in 1924–1925, when the Malayan government attempted to discourage pilgrims from going on Hajj, Munshi Ihsanullah acted as a communications lifeline for 300 to 400 Malays in Mecca who wanted to return home, carrying telegrams and letters requesting money (in one overoptimistic case, for over M$5,000) from their relatives back with him to Jidda.[101] In 1925, in the aftermath of the Saudi-Hashemite war, some seventy-one Kelantanese pilgrims were repatriated, and it is likely that this pattern of assistance was replicated across the Malay States.[102] Although 1927 was a relatively peaceful year in the Hijaz and an economically prosperous one in Malaya because of high rubber prices, Abdul Majid reported "much poverty if not actual destitution" among a record 12,184 Malay pilgrims and disbursed £200 from the Pilgrim Relief Fund.[103] Fluctuations in pilgrim numbers were partly dictated by economic conditions, a situation largely shaped by the integration of territories such as Malaya into a Western-dominated world economic system. In Malaya, perhaps more than in most other parts of Britain's Muslim empire, pilgrims' financial ability to perform the Hajj was to a large degree subject to the vagaries of global demand for commodities such as rubber and tin.

During the Depression, when Malay pilgrim numbers collapsed to a low of 80 arrivals in 1932, those who wanted to avoid having to buy a return ticket traveled to India, but many of those who followed this route ran out of money when they reached the Hijaz and became indigent. In 1933, because of "prevalent distress" among Malay pilgrims, the Pilgrim Relief Fund spent £320 on repatriating 40 pilgrims, who signed papers promising to repay this expenditure. This IOU system was the same as India's, and in both cases, repayment was a forlorn hope for the authorities.[104] Because overall pilgrim numbers remained low, with only 617 Malay pilgrims in 1935, repatriation was a small affair, with only 12 pilgrims shipped back to Singapore.[105] Credit for the colonial state's financial contribution to repatriation efforts for destitute pilgrims in this period was due in large part to the sustained efforts of a Muslim employee—Malay pilgrimage officer Haji Abdul Majid.

The Malay states and ordinary people also assisted poor pilgrims. Selangor State, for example, made grants to destitute pilgrims; the pilgrim's family applied to the district officer, and the final decision rested with the State Council. With around M$500 to M$2,000 disbursed per annum, the grant scheme was well known and drawn on, mainly by those who were loyal to the government and had links with religious and educational establishments.[106] Assistance to pilgrims also came from nonofficial quarters. In 1935, Sugei Ujong from Seramban donated £152 to the British consulate in Jidda for distribution to poor pilgrims in Medina, but officials felt that this would infringe Saudi sovereignty, so the money was handed over to the Saudi Ministry of Foreign Affairs.[107] The colonial government in Malaya was an important financial facilitator of the Hajj for poorer Malay pilgrims, but it was only one part of a larger and complex aid structure consisting of the Malay pilgrimage officer in Jidda, the Malay states, private individuals and families, and those involved in the remittance business.

Eric Tagliacozzo has highlighted the fact that despite Islamic teachings, many Malay pilgrims slid into destitution and debt in order to fund their Hajj.[108] The total estimated cost of the Hajj for Malays was some M$400 in the early 1930s, a significant sum.[109] A substantial number of Malay pilgrims in this period came from the west coast of Malaya because this area enjoyed more economic prosperity than the Muslim-majority east coast. Significant numbers of west coast pilgrims sold their property to raise funds for their journey to the Hijaz, borrowed money while they were there, and were reliant on family remittances or repatriation by the colonial government.[110] Many pilgrims spent their lifetime's savings on performing the Hajj, sometimes making themselves indigent in the process.

Another important source of money and credit for prospective pilgrims was *waqf* endowments in Singapore. To die on the Hajj had special merit, so sometimes pilgrims did not amass the requisite funds.[111] Although Malay pilgrims were generally richer than their Indian and African counterparts, destitute pilgrims were equally a feature of the pilgrimage from Malaya.

Identifying where pilgrims came from was an integral part of British attempts to regulate the pilgrimage from Malaya, as in Nigeria and Sudan, but also a vital means whereby funds could be distributed to destitute pilgrims who were actually British subjects. Pilgrim passports had been introduced in Malaya in 1899 but remained optional and were issued by the colonial government and the Malay states with no uniformity in design or content.[112] In 1924, the British consul in Jidda complained that without proper documentation it was virtually impossible to decide which Malay pilgrims to assist and which were from the Netherlands East Indies and therefore needed to be sent to the Dutch consulate.[113] Abdul Majid recommended that compulsory passports should be issued by local district officers for pilgrims, a proposal supported by various colonial officials and the sultan of Kedah.[114] In 1924, a *pas haji*, or pilgrim pass (shown on this book's front cover), was introduced, and in 1926 pilgrims were required to acquire this pass before they were allowed to buy a ticket, although there remained difficulties in distinguishing whether pilgrims were from Malaya, the Netherlands East Indies, or further afield.[115] This led to complications, such as a 1926 case when Chinese Muslims who settled in Malaya were placed with groups of Chinese pilgrims under a Chinese *mutawwif* in Jidda.[116] These issues persisted into the 1930s. Abdul Majid argued that district officers should institute stricter measures to determine the nationality of pilgrims before they issued pilgrim passes; during the 1934 Hajj, he had encountered Siamese and Javanese pilgrims with Malay passes.[117] For some pilgrims, such as Ahmad Sonhadji bin Mohammed Milatu, a Malay who performed the Hajj in 1949, this intermingling of populations meant that during the pilgrimage, the colonial boundaries between Malaya and the Netherlands East Indies that divided Malays dissolved.[118] Colonial administrative attempts to ascertain pilgrims' identities remained incomplete, and peoples from the wider Malay world were able to take advantage of British assistance to indigent pilgrims.

Issues of identity in relation to the Hajj from Southeast Asia become even more blurred if one considers the examples of several Britons who engaged with the ritual in this period. A. W. Hamilton, the director of the Political Intelligence Bureau and protector of pilgrims, traveled on a ship with just under 1,000 pilgrims to Jidda in 1927 to report on the pilgrimage. He recommended that the Malay pilgrim officer should be permanently based in the Hijaz, a move supported by the British consul, especially because many Malays remained in Mecca to study. Hamilton also advocated for an expanded administrative apparatus to engage with the pilgrimage in the form of a small department in Singapore headed by a protector of pilgrims, a proposal influenced by the administration of the pilgrimage in Bombay, detailed in Chapter 3. It seems likely that Hamilton's experiences with pilgrims played a role in his subsequent conversion to Islam, and he performed the Hajj. Known as Haji Hamilton in Malaya, he remained a police officer until his retirement in 1930.[119]

In May 1924, T. H. Bamber arrived in the office of the British consul in Jidda. Bamber, described by the consul as "a fresh faced young man of about 25—dressed as a Malay," was born in India, educated in London, and spent the First World War as a machine-gun instructor. He then traveled to Kedah, one of the Malay states, to seek his fortune after his parents died. His experience there was instrumental in his decision to convert to Islam in 1921. Unfortunately, Sharif Hussein's suspicion that Bamber was a spy meant that the young convert had to return to Kedah without the title of Hajji.[120] Another British convert to Islam based in Southeast Asia who enjoyed more success was Abdur Rahman MacBryan. Intermittently employed in the government of Sarawak from 1920, MacBryan was the sometime private secretary of the rajah of Sarawak, Vyner Brooke. He converted to Islam in 1935 and married Sa'erah, a Malay who worked on one of the rajah's rubber plantations; in 1936, the couple traveled to the Hijaz.[121] Ibn Saud had grown more suspicious of this trickle of European converts and had introduced new restrictions, such as a certificate attesting to converts' pious living for at least four years.[122] MacBryan was apparently "kept on tenterhooks until the last moment" but then was given permission to travel to Mecca.[123] Notions of Briton and Muslim as entirely separate categories break down in these cases of aspiring and actual Hajjis; for these Britons, the Hajj was an immediate and important part of their lives as Muslims. Indeed, considering a "British Hajj" that focuses only on converts based in Great Britain leaves out this wider group, of which a few examples have been given here, who spent much of their lives living and working in Britain's Muslim empire.[124] These men are one evocative example of how Islam shaped the British imperial experience.

One group involved in the Hajj from Malaya that contributed to pilgrim destitution was *shaykh hajis*, or pilgrim guides, and brokers. These men were Hadhramis or Malays who had settled in the Hijaz and traveled around Malaya looking to recruit pilgrims. They had a poor reputation, like their counterparts who operated in India, for cheating pilgrims through various means, such as taking pilgrims' money and then sending them onto a local passenger ship. Guides had to register with the police when they arrived in Singapore.[125] Abdul Majid was a central figure in pressing for legislation that strictly regulated pilgrim guides and pilgrimage brokers in Malaya's ports from 1929 to 1930.[126] British officials in Jidda, along with their Dutch counterparts, issued a blacklist of undesirable pilgrim guides who were banned from entering Malaya or the Netherlands East Indies.[127] Warnings were distributed to mosques and local Malay officials, and the district officers who issued pilgrim passes urged pilgrims not to make any advance payments to pilgrim guides and circulated the announcement that the Saudi government had ordered these men back to the Hijaz.[128] Roderick MacLean, a colonial official who moved to Singapore from India in the 1950s, recalled how he inspected pilgrim ships with the assistance of a Malay clerk and had to "get to know [pilgrim brokers] . . . and make sure they weren't doing anything naughty."[129] However, as William Roff has argued, many of these men were respectable and performed a vital service for pilgrims.[130] Pilgrim guides and brokers occupied an ambiguous role—for pilgrims, they were vital but sometimes ruinous to a pilgrim's finances, and officials saw them as scoundrels whose more unscrupulous activities were difficult to eradicate.

Pilgrim guides were only one transmitter of (sometimes misleading) information about the pilgrimage to prospective pilgrims; for Malaya's colonial society and government officials, information about the Hajj came from a variety of sources. One key intermediary in this period was Malay Pilgrimage Officer Abdul Majid, who wrote a lengthy article on the Hajj in a Malayan journal in 1926. In his piece, he reflected the disdain held by some British officials toward pilgrims, who tended to be elderly—a reflection of the length of time it took to save for the journey.[131] Abdul Majid castigated the "obvious foolhardiness" of these frail and aged people who went on Hajj because of the common expectation that death on Hajj was meritorious—*besar pahala-nya*.[132] He went on to describe how anxious Malays were to see the Prophet Muhammad's tomb because of one of the Prophet's hadiths, in which he stated that people who saw him during their lives would get intercession from him on the Day of Judgment, an undoubtedly powerful incentive. Abdul Majid's own reaction to his first sight of the Prophet's tomb was no less moving: "Tears of delight, starting to my eyes from a sense of being brought back as if it were from death to life and an indescribable lump in the throat rendering speech difficult."[133] Abdul Majid believed that ultimately, only a pious Muslim would understand the incentives for performing the Hajj and visiting the Prophet Muhammad's tomb at such great material and physical costs, thus delineating the limits of colonial understanding regarding the Malay Hajj to a readership largely drawn from Malaya's Anglophone colonial society.[134]

British officials in Malaya who read about the Hajj through Abdul Majid's regular pilgrimage reports were struck by the myriad difficulties faced by pilgrims; one official's marginal note on a 1931 report described that it "discloses an almost incredible state of affairs. . . . [Pilgrims are] swindled, robbed, insanitary, lashed by soldiers for trying to kiss the tomb of the Prophet."[135] This last indignity did not apply so much to Malay pilgrims, given their adherence to the Shafi'i *madhab*, or religious school of law. Colonial officials received information about the Hajj from their Malay pilgrimage officer, whose limited Arabic meant that he relied on translators in the Hijaz for some of his information. This reflected a wider process of dissemination from the British consulate in Jidda across Britain's Muslim empire. A further chain of transmission was the translations of pilgrimage reports ordered by British residents and advisers that were sent on to the rulers of Malay states.[136] Of course, the rulers already knew much of what was presented to them through stories relayed by returned Hajjis. There was no lack of information on the Hajj available to the British in this period, although the archival records show that there was less appreciation of why pilgrims went through such travails to perform the ritual.

A lack of sympathy toward pilgrims as a group did not stop the colonial government from sponsoring the pilgrimages of certain Malays supportive of British rule. This policy was designed to further inculcate loyalty to the colonial government; it also acted as a means of preferment and another method of control. In many ways, this mirrored the policy in place in French West Africa outlined in Chapter 1. Sponsored pilgrimages were introduced from Selangor in 1921 for long-serving, pro-British *penghulus* (local chiefs). This sponsorship was expanded across Malaya during this period. Employees of the colonial government who had been in service for six years could accumulate seven to eight months' leave and were then allowed to go on Hajj.[137] Employees had to request permission to perform the Hajj from their superiors; hundreds of these requests are scattered throughout the colonial archive. The usual approval given by their colonial employers was another means by which to instill support for British rule. In 1931, the colony's General Orders were changed to allow the extension of civil service employees' vacations to permit them to perform the Hajj.[138] Government employees going on Hajj were warned by their superiors to take their leave certificates with them to Saudi Arabia to ensure that they received "preferential treatment."[139] A convoluted financial system facilitated the travels of these employees who went on Hajj. For example, Mohamed Jaafar bin Manjoor of the Kedah Civil Service was advanced four months' salary to help with the cost of his journey to the Hijaz in 1934; the money was available for him to draw from the British consulate in Jidda. This amount was charged to the Crown Agents in London, the body that oversaw the colony's financial transactions, and was recouped from the Straits Settlements government, which in turn took that amount from the government of Kedah.[140] Several of these men retired and settled in Mecca, and their pensions were paid to them from the British consulate in Jidda.[141] A sponsored Hajj was an important reason why Muslim men were attracted to serving the colonial state.

This system also operated in the Malay states, and in the sultanate of Pahang the authorities decided that teachers of the Qur'an were eligible for leave on full pay to go on Hajj as well.[142] It appears that Malay rulers regularly ignored regulations laid down by the British that set out the conditions of pilgrimage leave for government officials.[143] Perhaps this was one example where rulers could show themselves to be more supportive of Islamic practice than the British. Malay rulers also loaned their subjects money to perform the Hajj, like the rulers of Muslim princely states in India detailed in Chapter 3. This was one method of enhancing their religious standing in Malay society and entrenching loyalty and fealty among subjects who benefited from this munificence. For civil servants, this often meant drawing their salary in advance or receiving a loan.[144] For example, Haji Abdul Hamid of Kuala Lumpur received a loan of M$200 from the sultan of Selangor for his pilgrimage in 1893. However, Malay rulers were as keenly aware as British officials of the risk that pilgrims might run out of money in the Hijaz, and Hamid's official form contained the condition that the loan would be void if Hamid asked Selangor for assistance toward his return voyage home or further maintenance.[145] As the balance of power tilted ever further away from Malay rulers, Malays took to petitioning the British residents and advisers who wielded real power in the Malay states. Che Kulu binti Pakeh Nagah's appeal in 1928 for help toward going on Hajj was prompted by a local Malay official's response to her that only men were given assistance toward the cost of the journey. She believed—wrongly—that a petition to a British official might have a greater chance of success.[146] Malay rulers had to balance issues similar to those of the British on sponsored pilgrimages for their employees, but this practice was one way in which they could present themselves as having freedom in administering their state's religious affairs.

The final part of this section examines the pilgrimage from Southeast Asia and slavery. Although pilgrim enslavement was largely an African phenomenon, it also affected Malay pilgrims and was conducted using a similar modus operandi during the pilgrimage season. An early observer of this was Dutch Orientalist Snouck Hurgronje in 1885, who described how the Mecca slave market received occasional "small consignments" from Southeast Asia, and the scholar also saw many young "slave boys from Hindustan."[147] Officials in Malaya recognized that it was "practically impossible" to try to detect whether Malay girls were taken to the Hijaz to be sold; moreover, it was difficult to identify traffickers, generally Malays, Indians, or Hadhrami Arabs, among crowds of pilgrims in bustling ports, such as Singapore. One proposed remedy for this trend was to enforce the compulsory possession of pilgrim passports, a measure that the Dutch colonial government also wished to implement for Indonesian pilgrims who left for the Hajj from ports in British Malaya, and for these passports to be checked against pilgrims' tickets. Until 1924, only tickets were examined.[148] This laxity gave slave traffickers substantial latitude in conducting their business between Southeast Asia and the Hijaz.

More troubling for British officials was the discovery that some of Singapore's prominent merchant families were alleged to be involved in slave trafficking. In 1920, three women of the Alsagoff family took nineteen Chinese girls aged between five and eight from Singapore to Mecca, where they were used as slaves. Chinese girls apparently fetched high prices in Arabia, and traffickers tended to buy the girls in Singapore and then return to Arabia when pilgrims were leaving for Jidda, posing as pilgrims with young daughters.[149] The strict seclusion of women in the Hijaz made it extremely difficult to discover whether there were female slaves in households. It was only the Hashemite-Saudi conflict in 1924–1925 that brought the Alsagoff family's slave ownership to light; the unsettled situation caused the Alsagoffs to send a large group from their household in the Hijaz back to Singapore. The group had to apply for visas, and the authorities in Singapore suspected that most in the party were slaves.[150] In response to questions from British legislators about Indian and Southeast Asian slavery and the Hajj in 1926, colonial officials stressed that the traffic was only "sporadic" but admitted that regarding occasional cases of children being sold into slavery by their parents while on Hajj, it was "quite impossible to carry the matter further."[151] By the late 1920s, officials recognized that even instituting detailed police investigations of pilgrims' circumstances in Malaya would not entirely eradicate the practice.[152] The slave trade that existed in relation to the Hajj threw into stark focus the limited capacity of the colonial state to enforce control over its subjects' activities.

Given that Malay and especially Indonesian pilgrims often crossed multiple colonial and imperial boundaries on their journeys, slavery and the Hajj was an issue that produced some cooperation and coordination between Britain and the Netherlands. In 1924, Dutch officials believed that the optional possession of passports to leave Singapore encouraged the slave traffic during pilgrimage season, and they wanted to know whether the British authorities intended to address this issue. The catalyst for this entreaty was a case of two Christian girls from Java who were kidnapped by a Hadhrami Arab in Singapore and sold to the Bani Shayba family in Mecca, the hereditary keepers of the keys to the Holy Mosque. The girls were finally released after protests by the Dutch consul and Javanese agent in Jidda. The case was a further trigger for calls to coordinate antislavery action among European imperial powers involved in the Hajj, but also for greater control over pilgrims traveling from Singapore. Laissez-faire travel arrangements were incompatible with combating slavery, and the Dutch focus on the slave traffic from Singapore was one reason that pilgrim passes became compulsory in 1926.[153] The interwar period was a particularly fertile moment for antislavery efforts among European powers, although in the case of the slave trade and the Hajj, as this chapter has demonstrated, suppressing it was monumentally difficult.

Colonial interactions with the Hajj from Malaya developed significantly from viewing it as a feature of the colony's trading life to an extensive administrative engagement. This was a multilayered and complex enterprise that involved Malay and British officials in Jidda and all levels of Malaya's bureaucracy, from the High Commission and Malay rulers to district officers and Malay civil servants. Destitution among Malay pilgrims was an important reason for this expansion of the colony's pilgrimage administration. Aiding poor Malay pilgrims was seen as a key plank of a wider policy of support for various areas associated with the pilgrimage. Here, as elsewhere, the role of Muslim employees, Hajji Abdul Majid being the paramount example, was crucial. But as in the case of Nigeria and Sudan, the limits of British control were starkly apparent, whether in relation to ascertaining pilgrims' identities, preventing pilgrim destitution, or restricting the slave trade.

Conclusion

The interwar period marked a high-water mark, in a sense, of the British empire's association with the pilgrimage. Nigeria, Sudan, and Malaya expanded their respective Hajj administrations, propelled by the tumult that the First World War and the Hashemite-Saudi conflict wrought on their pilgrim-subjects, as well as factors such as slavery, destitute pilgrims, and questions over how to regulate and control the flow of pilgrims. Consequently this aspect of imperial administration had now become an established part of the landscape across the entire breadth of Britain's Muslim empire, on a truly intercontinental scale, characterized by pilgrims' epic journeys across savannas and oceans. Imperial governance and religious practice were intertwined at local, regional, and intercontinental levels, characterized by the lateral connections that the Hajj forged among pilgrims and imperial officials, which subsequently shaped the contours of Britain's association with the pilgrimage. In the administration of this important Islamic ritual, Muslim employees and local rulers and community leaders played vital roles in the running of these Hajj bureaucracies. Political concerns about the Hajj from these areas were not paramount in the calculations of British officials; instead, the pages of colonial documents in the various archives are crowded with figures of pilgrim-slaves, sponsored pilgrims, indigent and indebted pilgrims, pilgrims of uncertain subjecthood, and the ever-present issue of repatriation that unintentionally facilitated pilgrims' travels. Efforts to regulate and reduce this tide of destitute pilgrims, especially from Nigeria and Sudan, remained a work in progress once the war in Europe began in September 1939. Religious zeal triumphed over official bureaucracy. Indeed, it was perhaps the last time in recent history that desperately poor Muslims who lived thousands of miles away from Mecca were able to perform the Hajj.

British engagement with the Hajj from these far ends of its Muslim empire was the product of cumulative years of reactive and somewhat haphazard imperial policies and bureaucracy, which nevertheless demonstrate the continued significance of Islam and Muslims to imperial governance. The Second World War and decolonization saw this imperial administration of the Hajj placed under various pressures as Britain's Muslim empire unraveled.

Epilogue: Hajj in the Time of War and Decolonization, 1939–1956

This brief epilogue surveys the ending of Britain's engagement with the Hajj during the Second World War and the era of decolonization. Several key trends characterized this period: the increased focus on pilgrims from Africa and Malaya after Indian independence, the rise of American influence over Saudi Arabia, and, finally, the dramatic change in Britain's involvement in the Hajj during the 1956 Suez Crisis, which marked an effective endpoint of the empire's relationship with the pilgrimage. As enormous as events such as the Second World War and decolonization were, the Hajj remained far from peripheral. The pilgrimage became a site for wartime propaganda, part of bids to win over Muslims to each combatant's cause. British support for the Hajj formed one component of its policies on the Muslim League during the war and in the run-up to Indian independence. Reforming the colonial administration of the Hajj from territories such as Nigeria and Malaya formed part of revivified governance schemes in postwar colonial states, with even greater Muslim involvement. Many thousands of Britain's Muslim subjects still traveled to Mecca to perform the pilgrimage, so British authorities continued to be committed to and engaged with their various Hajj administrations. In the atomic age, Britain remained the ruler of a Muslim empire, and the imperial governance of Islamic practice remained relevant and important—that is, until the later 1950s. This period has not been considered in any existing works on Britain and the Hajj.[1] Despite significant changes, there were also some noteworthy continuities in Britain's Hajj administration during these years in which the global forces of war and decolonization hastened the denouement of this remarkable aspect of Anglo-Muslim interaction.

The conflagration of the Second World War differed from the First World War, when the Arab Revolt meant that the Hijaz experienced active military operations. The conflict's impact on Britain's global position became evident after the war's conclusion, and one part of this was the unraveling of its Muslim empire and the decline of Britain's almost century-old interaction with the Hajj. Nevertheless, in several spheres, the empire's approach to the Hajj in this period had several similarities to the policies pursued during 1914–1918. For example, the pilgrimage was seen as a potential site to spread British propaganda.[2] Just after the war began, the governor of Aden proposed that a statement of Allied war aims "and Moslem interests therein" should be supplied as propaganda to pilgrims who briefly stopped at Kamaran Island, which was seen as "an excellent centre" for this purpose.[3] Officials in India were divided on this proposal; some thought it "ludicrous," whereas others argued that Britain should copy the example of other European powers that paid agents to perform the Hajj and thereby "influence pilgrims by personal contact."[4] Consultation with London resulted in the governor's idea being quashed, although in 1940, pilgrimage souvenir booklets that contained pro-British propaganda were eventually distributed on pilgrim ships docked in Aden.[5] The Hajj was also an arena for propaganda for the Axis powers. Japan's Asian wartime empire contained many Muslim subjects, and news broadcasts assured Muslims that Japan was doing everything possible to secure shipping for pilgrims despite wartime conditions.[6] Britain countered with propaganda of its own, such as a lavishly produced commemorative Hajj brochure given to notable Muslim leaders when they boarded ships in Jidda for their return journey.[7] British fears of Axis propaganda circulating during the Hajj led to Indian soldiers being banned from performing the ritual during the war.[8]

A further area that contained echoes of earlier British wartime interventions was organizing ships for Indian pilgrims. An official in

Delhi presciently wrote that because of the war, Britain would have to "regiment" the Hajj "a great deal more than we ordinarily do."[9] The government of India commandeered ships from companies and fixed pilgrims' fares at prewar prices, heavily subsidizing the Hajj to the tune of tens of thousands of pounds a year for those who wished to brave the journey.[10] Having considered it inadvisable to facilitate the pilgrimage during wartime, Malaya belatedly followed India's lead in seeking to provide shipping facilities and subsidizing the cost of the pilgrimage, but one of the Muslim Malay state councils remarked that these decisions had come too late for the 1940 pilgrimage.[11] Wartime shipping shortages meant that Indian pilgrim numbers dropped to a mere 6,100 in 1940. The Saudi ambassador to London, Hafiz Wahba, wrote of his gratitude to Britain for its attempts to facilitate the Hajj under wartime conditions; he optimistically believed that these moves, which were emblematic of Britain's "traditional wise policy" toward its Muslim subjects, would be "deeply appreciated" among Indian Muslims.[12] However, Italy's entry into the war in June 1940 made the Red Sea unsafe for shipping because Italian-held Eritrea and Somalia commanded the maritime approaches to Jidda.[13] This failed to dissuade the government of India's reckless encouragement for pilgrims "to brave the Italian menace." The authorities continued to subsidize the cost of the sea passage, and 5,000 Indian pilgrims made the journey in 1941. British actions found some favor with their enemies in the Hijaz. Ismail Ghuznavi, a "critical opponent of the Government," recorded his and a hundred other pilgrims' gratitude to Britain. General Archibald Wavell's successful campaign against the Italians in Egypt made it possible for 2,000 Egyptians to go on Hajj as well.[14] Britain managed the limited resources it could deploy for the Hajj to gain favor among a tiny proportion of its Muslim subjects. This mildly promising trend was strengthened by the collapse of Italian power in East Africa in 1941, which made the Red Sea safer for maritime traffic, although the threat of war in Southeast Asia meant that no Malays arrived in Arabia.[15]

However, the rapid gains made by Japan in Southeast Asia in 1941–1942 decisively ended the flow of pilgrims from Malaya and India. Islamic societies advised against pilgrims traveling across a now very dangerous Indian Ocean. More than 1,200 pilgrims from Peninsular Malaya, stranded in Mecca after the Japanese invasion of the colony in late 1941, became the "first refugees of the war" from that colony.[16] Those who held Malay pilgrim passes were given a modest amount of financial assistance disbursed by British officials in Jidda.[17] Britain opposed Dutch proposals to provide safe passage for pilgrims from Japanese-occupied Southeast Asia because of the risk of infiltration of Japanese agents among the pilgrims who would then be able to operate in Saudi Arabia, a concern that echoed similar British concerns for pilgrims arriving in Sudan from the Ottoman-held Hijaz in 1914, detailed in Chapter 4.[18] Ibn Saud's regime, increasingly cut off from the wider Muslim world, heavily relied on Britain to maintain the pilgrimage in a truncated state through supplies of food to the Hijaz and rerouting Indian ships to carry Egyptian pilgrims to Jidda.[19] Ibn Saud notably failed to mention in speeches to his subjects the increasing British—and American—subsidy to Saudi Arabia, which reached £4 million per year by 1943.[20] The dangers to pilgrims who traveled by sea across the Indian Ocean became apparent when an Indian passenger ship was sunk by an Axis submarine off the Yemeni coast in 1943. The government of India was interested in facilitating the pilgrimage partly because one of its main sources of Indian support in this period came from the Muslim League. The league put pressure on the authorities to ensure that people could go on Hajj; for example, its local organization in Jaunpur urged the government in 1944 to "procure all necessary facilities" because Muslims were "anxious to fulfil" their religious obligation.[21] This reflected a wider groundswell of desire across India for the government to facilitate the Hajj because it was suspended from 1942 to 1944 after the War Office advised canceling special shipping arrangements in place because of enemy action; this caused "great disappointment" among Indian Muslims. Consequently, after extended lobbying from various persons, including several Muslim members of the Indian civil service, the government allocated a limited number of ships in 1944 with quotas—3,948 for British India, 592 from princely states, and 205 from other countries, a total of 4,745—but stressed to pilgrims that "possible enemy action cannot be discounted."[23] Pilgrims traveled at their own risk. Officials were aware that the uncertainty of the sea route meant that pilgrims might decide to travel overland from India, a source of great consternation in the past, as seen earlier in Chapter 5, so there was an explicit policy not to publicize the overland route that took pilgrims through British-occupied southern Iran.[24]

How much did Britain's involvement in the pilgrimage and the Muslim world change after the end of the war, given the disruption the conflict caused to the Hajj and the effect it had in ushering in enormous political, economic, and social changes worldwide? Ronald Hyam has observed that Labour foreign secretary Ernest Bevin could have been mistaken for Lord Curzon because of his acute awareness that Britain ruled over more than half of the world's Muslim population. Bevin saw a need for Britain to "widen the vision of itself as an Islamic power." This was juxtaposed to more immediate problems, such as the disastrous postwar situation in Palestine. Bevin counseled that Britain had to "guard against the dangers of aligning the whole of Islam against us."[25] Britain remained committed to being a great power globally and the predominant power in the Muslim world, but this was undermined by the war's corrosive effects, a combination of international, domestic, and colonial pressures.[26] William Roger Louis has detailed Britain's attempts to sustain its influence in the Middle East in the postwar period, an unsuccessful effort to create a new relationship of equal partners to maintain its position. But older views continued to prevail; for example, the British consul at Jidda, Lawrence Grafftey-Smith, described Ibn Saud as a "museum piece Oriental potentate in a desert setting."[27] Although Grafftey-Smith's long experience in the region led him to bemoan the United States' economic influence "in the spiritual metropolis of hundreds of millions of British Moslems," Britain's attitude was to allow and even encourage American economic penetration of Saudi Arabia, not least because Britain's weakened financial situation meant that Ibn Saud's subsidy was reduced by 50 percent in 1945.[28] The British also sought to encourage more pilgrims from across their empire to perform the Hajj because this would further boost Ibn Saud's pilgrimage revenues. American intrusion into what had previously been a British sphere of influence foreshadowed a shift in geopolitical fortune that left the "greatest Muhammadan power" playing a much-reduced role in the kingdom containing Islam's Holy Cities.

Although the pilgrimage had never been devoid of political activity, opposition to British imperialism during the Hajj was a notable feature of the postwar period. Several anti-British pamphlets circulated at Mecca and Medina. One by the Egyptian Muslim Brotherhood condemned Britain "as the root of the malady and the cause of the misery which has befallen the Moslem world." Officials dismissed these pamphlets as not having a "very enduring effect."[29] Egyptian anticolonialism had Islamic and transnational aspects in addition to the important role played by secular Egyptian nationalists.[30] There is ample scope for further investigation of the pilgrimage's role in facilitating anticolonial struggles and ideologies in this period of decolonization. The violent end of British rule in Palestine was keenly felt during the Hajj as well. Philby, who performed the pilgrimage in 1948, noted that although it was the largest since 1929, with over 93,000 pilgrims—which to him "meant the will of Muslims to make the pilgrimage is as strong as ever"—the ritual was overshadowed by the Palestinian situation, which created a "general gloom" and caused a "marked absence of the festive spirit."[31] The appalling situation in one corner of Britain's Muslim empire clearly concerned many pilgrims as they performed the Hajj rituals.

A key shift in the role of Muslims within and outside Britain's Hajj administrations occurred in 1946, when the Muslim League sent a deputation to Ibn Saud to lobby for a reduction in Saudi pilgrimage tariffs. Although this group was unsuccessful in its mission, it "represented the feelings of Indian Moslems," according to Britain's Hajj report. This deputation was the most recent in a growing trend of organizations claiming such legitimacy and acting without imperial sanction or backing in directly engaging with the Saudis on pilgrimage-related issues. Previously, British consular authorities in Jidda had ostensibly represented Indian Muslims' views to Ibn Saud. The new leaders of India's Muslims had supplanted British consular and colonial officialdom.[32]

India and Pakistan gained their independence amid communal violence on an unprecedented scale in 1947; however, in relation to the Hajj, the newly independent government in Delhi appeared rather similar to its British predecessor. In the governmental records on either side of the stroke of midnight, it is difficult to discern that an enormous political change had taken place. In 1948, the government circulated a blacklist of pilgrim guides and asked the British ambassador in Jidda for the latest list. The foreign secretary in Delhi wrote to embassies in Jidda, Bahrain, and Baghdad to request that Indian visas for pilgrim guides from the Hijaz who traveled from India to Jidda with their charges be "severely restricted" because of past complaints about their exploitation of pilgrims.[33] In 1949, the British ambassador in Jidda reported that "considerable numbers of Indian and Pakistani pilgrims were repatriated at their government's expense after the pilgrimage."[34] During these immediate postindependence years, India had the same concerns, priorities, and policies in regard to the Hajj as the British Raj. A similar trend was evident in Singapore. Hajji Sidek Siraj was Singapore's last pilgrimage officer under British rule and continued in this position, with the same duties, serving under the Majlis Ugama Islam Singapura, the body established after independence that advised Singapore's president on Islamic matters.[35] The transition from colonial to postcolonial in the case of the pilgrimage in Britain's Muslim empire was anything but clear cut. Britain's involvement in the Hajj from India has a continuing legacy. Indeed, pilgrimage policies conceptualized by Indian Muslim employees and instituted by the British, such as subsidizing the cost of the Hajj for some, are still enshrined in Indian law today and remain a contentious issue, fiercely debated in the newspapers every Hajj season.[36]

India's independence completely changed the character of Britain's Muslim empire. The broader landscape of Britain's changing strategic and economic priorities meant that there was a greater focus on Malaya, the Middle East, and Africa.[37] Britain's various Hajj bureaucracies in colonies such as Malaya and Nigeria were reconstituted and expanded. A common impulse for this was the desire to reform various aspects of colonial administration after the war's disruption, but the circumstances in each colony were extremely different, given the demands placed on Nigeria's economy and labor market during the war, and the brutal occupation of Malaya by Japan.

After three years and eight months under Japanese occupation, the appeal of performing the Hajj had increased for many Malays, although few could afford it—only 146 pilgrims arrived in the Hijaz in 1946. During these difficult postwar years, the colonial authorities repatriated many destitute Malay pilgrims from the Hijaz between 1945 and 1948. District officers were charged with the seemingly futile task of trying to track down these pilgrims to recover money loaned to them by the government. This led to the financial screening of prospective pilgrims by the authorities.[38] Stringent capital controls imposed during the war remained in place, and pilgrims were allowed to take only 560 Malayan (M) dollars for their expenses, designed to cover a four-month stay in the Hijaz.[39] The pent-up demand to perform the Hajj was evident in the explosion in pilgrim numbers to just under 4,000 in 1948 and the fact that these pilgrims spent the colossal sum of M$10 million on performing the ritual, a trend seen by Sheikh Ahmad bin Mohamed Hashim, chair of the Pilgrimage Advisory Committee, as "a serious drain on the resources of Malays who may finally find themselves on the brink of ruin and bankruptcy."[40]

The rapid recovery of pilgrim numbers from Malaya led to renewed efforts to reform the colony's pilgrimage administration, probably because this apparatus was costing the colonial administration some M$87,000 a year by 1948.[41] Controls were tightened in many areas other than the export of currency. Pilgrims could not receive their tickets to Jidda unless their pilgrim passes had been stamped by the authorities. Following government requirements, shipping companies would not release tickets unless the pilgrim had paid the Saudi government pilgrimage fees up front. Someone who decided to go on Hajj had to visit his or her district officer to get a pilgrim pass and then procure traveler's checks from a local bank, passport photos, and inoculations. When the prospective pilgrim returned to the district officer with documentary proof of these activities, the pass would be stamped and signed.[42] This was a considerable administrative undertaking, as is shown by the hundreds of letters in the archives between district officers and their superiors, although it had an internal logic—pilgrim passes cost M$20 in 1952, and 940 passes issued in Perak that year generated M$18,880 in revenue for the government.[43] Members of Malaya's Pilgrimage Advisory Committee, which included ten Muslim representatives of the Malay states and Singapore, thought that this administration should be handled by Muslim officials instead of the British district officers.[44]

Consequently, as a result of Malay pressure, a Malay pilgrimage commissioner was appointed, and a Pilgrimage Department in Penang was established in 1952, headed by a Muslim pilgrimage control officer whose role was to coordinate with all the local bureaucracies in the Malay states, Singapore, and North Borneo.[45] Malay officials in the colonial government wanted to "promote the Hajj as a marker of Malay Muslim identity," and pilgrimage administration moved to "within the sphere of Malay bureaucracy."[46] The Malay staff in Jidda grew to include the pilgrimage commissioner, Haji Ali Rouse, along with two clerks and extra assistance from the British vice-consul at Jidda, Cyril Ousman, who had previously served in Sudan.[47] In 1949, the Pilgrimage Advisory Committee asked district officers to inquire whether anyone owned *waqf* houses in Mecca that could be used as the headquarters for the Malay pilgrimage officer, now restyled as a commissioner. Had there been any positive answers, it would have been a potentially unique situation for a British colonial official to have his office in a *waqf* property.[48] In 1955, like their Indian and Nigerian counterparts, a delegation of prominent Malay officials visited Mecca, which inspired doctors and nurses from across Malaya to volunteer their services in port cities, on board pilgrim ships, and in the Hijaz during the Hajj season.[49] Despite this Malay involvement and decades of legislation and regulation, conditions on board pilgrim ships in this period were still far from ideal. Dr. Mohamed Baboo, medical officer for Malay pilgrims in 1948, wrote of how, with very few medical items, he treated 1,000 cases, and he compared his setup with the "grand affairs" of the Egyptian Medical Mission, which had surgeons, physicians, opticians, nurses, ambulances, and a dispensary.[50] By the early 1950s, because the pilgrimage had become such an ingrained part of colonial administration in Malaya, especially given the extensive involvement of Muslims in the whole enterprise, many of the mysteries and anxieties that colonial officials had appended to the ritual in the late nineteenth and early twentieth centuries had disappeared.

At the western end of Britain's Muslim empire, Britain's involvement in the Hajj from Nigeria and Sudan in this period illustrates the pervasive nature of the "second colonial occupation."[51] The work of one official on the pilgrimage was a prime example of the late colonial state in action. Stationed in Nigeria, M. Philips was instructed to travel to Khartoum and Jidda in 1949 "to discuss in a general way the details of pilgrimage arrangements and see whether any amendments or improvements could be recommended." At each stop, Philips explained the existing Nigerian Pilgrimage Scheme for those who wished to go on Hajj. Because it was extremely convoluted and confusing, it was unsurprising that the majority of Nigerians did not avail themselves of it. In the postwar period, it was estimated that over 100,000 Nigerians were working in Sudan as agricultural laborers in order to be able to afford to go on Hajj, which illustrates the scale of Philips's task. Philips flagged an enduring paradox of Britain's involvement in the pilgrimage while he traveled around Britain's Muslim empire in Africa discussing schemes to reform the pilgrimage administration: "It is to my mind out of place for Christian governments to endeavour to take up this matter with the Saudi government. . . . The question is one with which Moslems themselves must deal." He formulated recommendations that emphasized greater coordination with Nigerian and Sudanese authorities, facilitated by the new air routes across Africa, a telling example that attests to the connections the Hajj continued to forge across Britain's Muslim empire.[52]

The continued British drive to reform the pilgrimage experience for Nigerians was unsurprising. After all, once the new Nigerian constitution was passed in 1951, Governor John MacPherson believed that Britain would still rule there for another thirty years.[53] The character of the Hajj from Nigeria had changed dramatically from that before the war; 1952 was the first year pilgrims in large numbers traveled by air to Mecca.[54] The resident in Kano had to sign at least 700 passports, many of whose holders possessed airplane tickets.[55] This was a far cry from the long and arduous overland journeys undertaken by pilgrims earlier in the century. Nigeria's Hajj administration appeared to be in the process of extension, but here again, the main people driving developments were Muslims. However, in Nigeria during the early 1950s, they were political players, not subordinate employees. For example, Abubakr Imam, a member of the House of Representatives, recommended to the minister for local government and community development after performing Hajj in 1953 that a Nigerian pilgrimage commissioner should be appointed to represent pilgrims' interests in the Hijaz.[56] This proposal was enthusiastically endorsed by the Colonial Office because the approximately 1,800 Nigerians who went on Hajj every year "justif[y] special arrangements given the difficulties which they face."[57] The emir of Kano and other Muslim leaders went to Saudi Arabia in 1955 to discuss Nigerian pilgrims' difficulties, amid concern by British officials that they had shown potential signs of nationalism. The Foreign Office tellingly recorded that "owing to increasing importance of rulers CO ask that they be given help they might wish and made to feel that the British are friendly and useful to them."[58] Malay representatives made similar visits, facilitated by the Colonial Office and British officials in Jidda, although these were lower-key; one in 1955 was led by Enche Mustapha Albakri bin Haji Hasan, OBE, minister for industrial and social relations, who was described as "a very good man of moderate views."[59] Britain had always assiduously cultivated the image that it was a benevolent friend of Islam; one key example of this was the arrangements that facilitated the Hajj for its Muslim subjects. In a period when policy shifted toward partnership with the probable leaders of colonies that were barreling toward independence, this older concern with Britain's image in the Muslim world remained but was shaped to fit new exigencies.

At the eastern tip of Britain's Muslim empire in Southeast Asia, however, Anglo-Muslim relations steadily deteriorated after the war's end. From December 1950 through 1951, Singapore was beset by rioting and violence by Muslims because of disaffection with various policies of the colonial government. *'Ulama* and students traveling to Mecca were placed under surveillance, and mistrust between Singaporean Muslims and their British rulers ran deep. Many Muslims were convinced that the government would continue to deny them religious rights. The unrest overturned colonial notions of the community as peaceful and loyal, and there was considerable disruption of pilgrims' travels to and from Singapore.[60] Ideas of Britain in partnership with Muslims seemed fanciful in Singapore's fraught atmosphere during this period.

Ibn Saud's abolition of all pilgrimage taxes in 1952 heralded a new phase in the history of the Hajj. The loss in revenue mattered little to the Saudis because of the new riches flowing in from oil royalties.[61] Only one month before this announcement, the Sudanese government asked the British ambassador in Jidda to press the Saudis to reduce the pilgrimage fee for Africans as a means of diminishing the incentive for pilgrims to enter the Hijaz illegally.[62] The Saudi policy appeared to cause a decline in destitute pilgrims because pilgrims now needed less money to perform the Hajj. Consequently, this feature of the imperial-era Hajj that had emerged with the rise of steamship travel to the Hijaz in the 1850s and had been a perennial problem for the British empire's Hajj administrations now seemed to be resolved.[63] However, the pilgrimage circular from the British embassy at Jidda in 1955, sent across Britain's Muslim empire, from Gambia to Malaya, stridently stated that "all possible efforts will be made to prevent . . . [pilgrims] . . . setting out on pilgrimage if they do not have enough money to pay necessary expenses in Saudi Arabia and to get home."[64] The figure of the "pauper pilgrim" had not completely disappeared, but this group was now a marginal issue in contrast to earlier decades, when discussions about destitute pilgrims had filled volumes of Hajj-related documents.

The British empire's long-standing concern with destitute pilgrims was distinctly different from the United States of America's involvement in the Hajj in this period, indicating how British predominance in the region was giving way to that of the United States. In 1952, the Lebanese government requested that the United States airlift hundreds of pilgrims from Beirut to Jidda who were stranded by the inability of Lebanese and Saudi airlines to take a larger-than-expected influx of pilgrims. One U.S. transport plane left every hour from Beirut airport to Jidda for two days running.[65] The U.S. ambassador wrote to the secretary of state outlining the scheme's success: "1. It was a purely humanitarian effort which helped to raise our prestige. 2. Helped to bring home to Middle East the nearness and realness of American power which can only impress area favourably. 3. Dramatizes Middle East to American public, thus rallying support for our policy."[66] This dramatic application of the United States' global power projection and financial resources overshadowed Britain's role as a facilitator of the pilgrimage. Previous British efforts to facilitate the pilgrimage, such as repatriating destitute pilgrims or requisitioning ships to sail from India to the Hijaz in wartime, could not compete for dramatic effect with the sight of the U.S. Air Force transporter fleet. However, this air bridge to Mecca was a short-lived exercise. As the 1953 Hajj season commenced, Secretary of State John Foster Dulles vetoed any repeat of the "Mecca flying bridge" because he thought that America would be blamed if any stranded pilgrims were left behind during such an exercise.[67] It is not impossible that Dulles may have known about the many and varied criticisms leveled at Britain in the past regarding its treatment of pilgrims.

More broadly, the global spread of air transport, like the steamship in the nineteenth century, transformed the nature of the Hajj. In the early 1950s, around 75 percent of pilgrims arrived in Saudi Arabia by ship; twenty years later, over 80 percent arrived by airplane. This trend coincided with the Saudi policy of limiting the time foreign pilgrims stayed in Saudi Arabia—long sojourns in the Holy Cities were consigned to history. Mirroring the exit of European companies from former colonial markets, iconic shipping companies connected to the pilgrim traffic, like Alfred Holt and Company and the Mogul Line, stopped their Hajj services in the 1950s.[68]

The 1956 Suez Crisis is an apposite final example of the limits of British power in relation to the Hajj.[69] The governor of Nigeria feared that Saudi Arabia's termination of diplomatic relations with Britain as a result of the crisis would "adversely affect and perhaps even put a stop to the pilgrimage."[70] Although this did not happen, the burning issue was how Britain's Hajj administration would function after the British embassy in Jidda had shut down because of the diplomatic rupture between Britain and Saudi Arabia. Fifteen thousand Nigerians, along with the Nigerian Pilgrimage Mission, now went on Hajj every year. Before the British embassy staff left Jidda, they asked the Pakistani embassy to assist the Nigerian Pilgrimage Mission. The mission was led by a Northern Nigerian, Mohammed Effendi al-Awin Saleh. When Saleh arrived on the eve of the 1957

Hajj, he ended up giving orders to the local staff from the empty British embassy.[71] The Colonial Office was concerned with the wider context because 22,000 pilgrims from across Britain's Muslim empire were going on Hajj, and the administration of and assistance to all these pilgrims were going to be provided by the Pakistani embassy and Saleh.[72] Although Muslims had played a vital role in Britain's Hajj administration since the mid-nineteenth century, this scene of Pakistanis supervising Nigerians in the British embassy, with British officials entirely absent, is a potent image. The effect of the Suez crisis was symbolic rather than practical; it was an enormous loss of British prestige, which in turn meant a real loss of power.[73] This example illuminates, from a fresh angle, the effect of Britain's Suez misadventure and the broader decline of the British empire.

The events of 1956 presaged the dissolution of Britain's Muslim empire. Its constituent parts gained their independence shortly afterward: Malaya in 1957, Nigeria and Somaliland in 1960, Kuwait and Tanzania in 1961, Zanzibar and Kenya in 1963, Aden in 1967, and the Gulf States in 1971. Although Britain's Hajj administration limped on in some areas after 1956, such as the Gulf States, where British officials made forlorn representations to Pakistan to stop poor pilgrims from making the short journey from Pakistan to the Gulf Coast, that tumultuous year marked the end of Britain's long association with the pilgrimage in any significant way. The complex bureaucratic apparatus involved in the annual flow of pilgrims to Mecca from across the breadth of Britain's Muslim empire—from the Atlantic to the South China Sea—passed into the control of newly independent nations. Just under a century after the British empire began to concern itself with the Hajj, its engagement with this fifth pillar of Islam and, indeed, its status as ruler of a Muslim empire faded into the twilight of history.

Conclusion

Despite the end of Britain's status as a "Mohammadan power," the legacy of Britain as a power with Muslim subjects continues to resonate in the twenty-first century, particularly in relation to the Hajj.[1] The British government continues to recognize the pilgrimage's importance, albeit in a vastly different geopolitical landscape from that in the period covered by this book. In 2008, for example, Foreign Secretary David Miliband firmly emphasized that "the site of the two Holy Places makes Saudi Arabia a very important country in the modern world."[2] The Foreign and Commonwealth Office reopened its Jidda consulate in 2000 and established a British Hajj delegation, whose role was to "supervise" the growing number of British Muslims going on Hajj, some of whom undoubtedly had grandparents who had performed the pilgrimage as British subjects in the colonial era.[3] In 2011, the British *amir al-hajj* was Lord Adam Patel of Blackburn. Although the transportation revolutions of the last two centuries, in the shape of the steamship and the airplane, have meant that many more Muslims have been able to go on Hajj, a key catalyst for changes to the Hajj in the early twenty-first century is the revolution in communications. The growth of the Internet and ever-increasing access to this unprecedented resource mean that many more Muslims can find out more about the rituals and meaning of the Hajj, debate its significance in Islamic practice, and book Hajj package tours online without recourse to more traditional interlocutors of religious authority.[4] Muslims across the world now have more information and access to Saudi pilgrimage policies, actions, and, in the case of tragedies that have befallen pilgrims on Hajj, inaction.[5] The British authorities involved in the Hajj in the early twenty-first century also use the Internet, running blogs and YouTube channels, to demonstrate its "supportive" policies on Islam.[6] British interactions with the issue of destitute pilgrims, which illustrate the intertwined nature of the Anglo-Muslim relationship, have faint parallels with examples from the early twenty-first century.[7] The Internet has enabled some British Muslims to facilitate the Hajj for poorer prospective pilgrims in Britain's former Muslim empire. In 2003, the BBC News website published several reports about Jaipur resident Habib Miyan. He had drawn his pension since 1948 and was supposedly 132 years old. He wished to perform the Hajj but could not afford it. These stories were read by a British Muslim company chairman and a taxi driver, who both gave Miyan the necessary funds to perform the Hajj; the taxi driver gave up his and his son's upcoming Hajj in favor of helping Miyan perform the pilgrimage.[8] Although this brief treatment shows that Britain's current relationship with the Hajj is very different from that in the imperial era, the echoes from the past in the present are compelling.

Using the prism of Britain's relationship with the Hajj, this book has demonstrated that the idea of a British Muslim empire, spatially imagined as an "inner empire" of largely Islamic territories, is a useful and productive conceptualization for the study of British imperial history. Britain's Muslim empire offers us a different vision of the British empire as a political, organizational, and religious entity. Examining the component territories of this space in a single analytical framework enables us to trace out, in multilateral and multilayered detail, the material considerations of Britain's engagement with Islam and Muslims, who made their faith a living phenomenon, and argue for the significance of Islam and Muslims to imperial history. The Hajj is an important area of Islamic practice to examine in terms of imperial interactions, due to its role as a key connecting factor across Britain's Muslim empire. Thousands of pilgrims left their locales every year in a significant movement of people across land and sea (and borders), heading to Mecca to fulfill a common religious purpose. Imperial interactions with the Hajj became an established feature of imperial administration and a catalyst for British officials and Muslims alike to reflect on the British empire's Islamic character. Using the broad geographic canvas of Britain's Muslim empire, drawing together territories such as India, Malaya, Nigeria, and

Sudan, along with focusing on Britain's Jidda consulate in the Hijaz, has allowed this work to construct a broad picture of Britain's interactions with the pilgrimage and to trace connections and comparisons in Britain's administration of the Hajj across its Muslim empire. Through studying Britain's engagement with the Hajj, one of the five pillars of Islam, this book has shown that imperial governance and Islamic religious practice became interlinked and that this combination formed an important component of Britain's imperial experience.

Although the beginnings of Britain's interest in the Hajj lay in the threat of epidemic disease, the empire's relationship with the pilgrimage expanded into a variety of areas. One of these was the idea of the Hajj as an enabler of anticolonial movements. This work has broken away from existing interpretive frameworks that emphasize the primacy of disease, quarantine, Islamic "conspiracies," and British attempts to surveill the Hajj. British officials in the mid-nineteenth century sought to appease Muslim opinion by noninterference in religious rituals to mitigate potential unrest, but in relation to the pilgrimage, such calculations evolved significantly over the period covered by this work. Indeed, by the early twentieth century, imperial involvement in the administration of the annual flow of pilgrims to and from Mecca was considered an established feature of the practice of imperial rule. This book has demonstrated that Britain's interactions with the Hajj were more complex than simply viewing the Hajj as a catalyst for anticolonial movements. Through analyzing topics such as destitute pilgrims, Muslim employees in Britain's Hajj administration, and the impact of Wahhabism on pilgrims, it has shown how Britain's interactions with the pilgrimage were far broader and more nuanced. Moreover, this work has detailed how the faltering attempts by British authorities to exercise greater control over the pilgrimage were frequently thwarted by pilgrims themselves.

One group in particular this book has focused on is destitute pilgrims and the repeated and failed attempts of Britain to regulate this group, which firmly remained at the outer limits of imperial control. Destitute pilgrims were a significant and important feature of Britain's relationship with the Hajj. Officials saw the existence of indigent pilgrims as an affront to imperial prestige. But Britain's engagement with poor pilgrims drew officials deeper into the intricacies of Islamic religious practice, although these officials never grasped the profound spiritual attraction the Hajj had for poor Muslims. The British empire's eventual response to this group demonstrates the validity of the concept of a British Muslim empire. The evolution of a policy of repatriating destitute pilgrims at government expense, a practice that expanded across this inner empire, attests to how Britain inadvertently acted like an Islamic power, facilitating the pilgrimage for its subjects and acting as an unintentional patron of Islamic religious practice. Imperial prestige was an important aspect that underlay many of Britain's actions in relation to the Hajj. Officials were concerned that Britain's administration of its pilgrim-subjects was viewed unfavorably when it was compared with that of its European counterparts and the Ottoman empire, and that Muslim perceptions of British shortcomings would lead to a loss of imperial prestige in the eyes of Britain's Muslim subjects.

The agency displayed by destitute pilgrims in shaping Britain's policies on the Hajj was reflected in another group—those Muslims who worked within Britain's pilgrimage administrations. These men, along with Muslims consulted by the British on Hajj-related matters, held a degree of agency in shaping Britain's Hajj policies. Their employers often agreed with these men's ideas and proposals, despite the fact that these proposals sometimes went against the grain of the official policy of noninterference. Anglo-Muslim cooperation and collaboration on the Hajj were an undeniably important aspect of Britain's relationship with the pilgrimage. This relationship was a complex set of interactions in which Britain's Muslim employees were instrumental in drawing the British into an ever-deeper engagement with their Muslim subjects. These employees possessed the capacity to shape Britain's Hajj administrations. Agency, whether of Muslims in consular or municipal Hajj bureaucracies or of destitute pilgrims, played a role in British calculations, concerns, actions, and indecision regarding the empire's interaction with the pilgrimage.

This multilevel Muslim agency is well illustrated by the example analyzed in this work of the Hyderabadi government's administration of the Hajj, which further complicates the idea of Britain as a monolithic imperial power, seeking to impose its control over the pilgrimage. Beyond the picture this book has detailed of the nizam's administration of the pilgrimage, one of the most significant features of this case study is the virtual absence of any British presence. Where Britain was more directly involved, as in Bombay, the overwhelming reliance of the authorities on the effectively Muslim-run Pilgrim Department and Bombay's Muslim civil society further attests to the role of Muslim agency in this imperial administrative enterprise.

This work's focus on Britain and the Hajj during the years surrounding the Arab Revolt of 1916–1918 has complicated more conventional narratives that cover this tumultuous period by arguing that Britain's interactions with the pilgrimage were an important component of British policy and strategic calculations. Britain's role in fomenting geopolitical upheaval in the Hijaz was quickly followed by a retreat from attempts to extend its control over the Hajj. This book has demonstrated how the Hajj was a key factor in the deteriorating relationship between Britain and its client, King Hussein, and it examined the Khilafat movement's effect on the Hajj. Through these case studies, this work has contributed to a more general understanding of Britain's crisis of empire—and crisis of Islam—from 1918 to 1924.

Most studies of Britain and the Hajj end around 1924 and rarely discuss the period of Saudi-Wahhabi rule over the Hajj. By contrast, this work has detailed the imposition and evolution of a more austere religious climate for the Hajj and Hajjis. Although the impact of Wahhabi policies was tempered somewhat during the Great Depression, they engendered a strong reaction from pilgrims who contested Wahhabi doctrines, which were fiercely opposed to acts of customary devotion surrounding the pilgrimage, such as *ziyara.* This work has demonstrated how pilgrims' reactions to Saudi-Wahhabi rule showed the continuing power of customary Islam, arguing for a revised interpretation of the decline of pluralist practices in Islam when faced with fundamentalist interpretations of the faith in this period.

During the interwar period, concerns over destitute pilgrims, slavery, and the nature of pilgrims' travels caused the expansion of colonial administrative involvement in the Hajj from Nigeria and Malaya, the far ends of Britain's Muslim empire. Bringing these case studies together shows the different means whereby these colonial states sought, largely unsuccessfully, to curb the slave trade in pilgrims and regulate the journeys of their destitute pilgrim-subjects, thereby further demonstrating the limits of Britain's ability to control this group of border-crossing pilgrim-subjects, which came from across the breadth of Britain's Muslim empire.

Britain's engagement with the Hajj after the Second World War also changed dramatically because the shrinking of Britain's Muslim empire led to an increased focus on pilgrims from African colonies, such as Nigeria, and Malaya. Through briefly considering the last phase of Britain's engagement with the pilgrimage from 1945 to 1956, this work sheds new light on the workings of the late colonial state and decolonization and especially on the Suez Crisis, a seminal event in imperial and world history.

The British empire's long association with the Hajj was an extraordinary episode in the history of British imperialism, a complex interaction marked by religious, political, and economic change, conflict, contestation, and collaboration. Ruling over a Muslim empire and engaging with the Hajj were integral parts of the British imperial experience.

Abbreviations

AN	Arkib Negara, Kuala Lumpur, Malaysia
APSA	Andhra Pradesh State Archives, Hyderabad, India
IOR, APAC, BL	India Office Records, Asia, Pacific and Africa Collections, British Library, London, United Kingdom
Jedda Diaries	Robert Jarman (ed.), *The Jedda Diaries, 1919–1940.* Volumes 1–4 (Gerrards Cross: Archive Editions, 1993)
MECA	Middle East Centre Archive, St. Anthony's College, Oxford University, Oxford, United Kingdom
MSA	Maharashtra State Archives, Mumbai, India
NAI	National Archives of India, New Delhi, India
RoH	Alan Rush (ed.), *Records of the Hajj: A Documentary History of the Pilgrimage to Mecca.* Volumes 1–10 (Gerrards Cross: Archive Editions, 1993)
SAD	Sudan Archive, University Library, Durham University, Durham, United Kingdom
Slave Trade	Anita Burdett (ed.), *The Slave Trade into Arabia, 1820–1973.* Volumes 1–9 (Gerrards Cross: Archive Editions, 2006)
SNA	Oral History Archive, Singapore National Archives, Singapore
TCA	Thomas Cook Archives, Peterborough, United Kingdom
TNA	The National Archives, Kew, London, United Kingdom

Notes

Introduction

1. D. S. Margoliouth, *Mohammedanism* (London: Williams and Norgate, 1912), 23. A small selection of similar quotes: "There is no getting over the fact that the British Empire is a Mahomedan power," Viceroy Lord Lytton to Lord Salisbury, May 21, 1877, Lytton Papers, Letters Despatched, 1877, vol. 2, 519, quoted in Peter Hardy, *Muslims of British India* (Cambridge: Cambridge University Press, 1972), 119; "His Britannic Majesty is the greatest ruler of Mohammedans in the world. He controls a much greater number of Mohammedans than did the Sultans of Turkey in their days of extensive power," Count Leon Ostrorog, The British Empire and the Mohammedans, 1, sent to British Residency, Cairo, July 12, 1918, FO 141/786, the National Archives, London (hereafter referred to as TNA); "From the point of view of . . . the position of the British Empire as a great Mohamedan power," Lord Curzon, Conclusions of a Conference at No. 10 Downing Street, January 5, 1920, CAB 23/27, TNA; "We are the greatest Mohamedan power in the world. It is our duty . . . to study policies which are in harmony with Mohammedan feeling," Winston Churchill, Memo to the Cabinet on Situation in the Middle East, December 16, 1920, CAB 24/117, TNA; "The fact is that you cannot run the Empire in watertight compartments, and as the largest Mohammedan power in the world you cannot afford to ignore Mohammedan opinion in formulating your policy," Lord Chelmsford, ex-viceroy of India, Annual Dinner of the Royal Central Asian Society, Imperial Restaurant, Regent Street, London, June 15, 1921, "Annual Dinner," *Journal of the Royal Central Asian Society*, 8:4 (1921), 219–224, 223; "The least calculable of British Arabian interests—that which the greatest Mohammedan Power of the world must take in the city and district which is, theoretically, the spiritual centre of Islam, and practically, its paramount pilgrimage resort," D. G. Hogarth, "Wahabism and British Interests," *Journal of the British Institute of International Affairs*, 4:2 (1925), 70–81, 75. See also imperial histo-

rian J. R. Seeley, *The Expansion of England* (Cambridge: Cambridge University Press, 2010), 141. This type of phrase was employed hundreds of times by officials, statesmen, journalists, and soldiers privately and publicly during this period.

2. Quoted in R. G. Corbett, *Mohammedanism and the British Empire* (London: Wyman and Sons, 1902), 4.

3. Cheragh Ali, *The Proposed Political, Legal and Social Reforms in the Ottoman Empire and other Mohamedan States* (Bombay: Education Society Press, 1883), i. See also Rafiuddin Ahmed: "It is the wish of Mahomedans that the Government . . . will continue to be the justest as it is undoubtedly the greatest Mahomedan power in the world"; Rafiuddin Ahmed to Commissioner of Police Bombay, January 29, 1906, General Department, 1912, Vol. 132, File 768, Maharashtra State Archives, Mumbai (hereafter referred to as MSA).

4. Faisal Devji, "Britain's Muslim Empire and Its Indian Future," *Seminar*, no. 601, September 2009, http://www.indiaseminar.com/2009/601/601_faisal_devji.htm; Faisal Devji, "Islam in British Imperial Thought," in David Motadel (ed.), *Islam and the European Empires* (Oxford: Oxford University Press, 2014), 256–270.

5. India (1765), Sierra Leone (1787), Gambia (1821), Gold Coast (1821), Aden (1839), Sarawak (1841), Malaya (1874), Egypt (1882), Somaliland (1884), the Trucial States (1887), Brunei (1888), Zanzibar (1890), Sudan (1899), Kuwait (1899), Northern Nigeria (1900), Iraq (1914), Palestine (1918), and Trans-Jordan (1921). However, these dates of acquisition are inevitably imprecise, given the complex and sometimes lengthy processes of British conquest and expansion.

6. The best exposition of the Islamic world in geographic and world-historical terms is Marshall G. S. Hodgson, *The Venture of Islam: Conscience and History in a World Civilization*, vols. 1–3 (Chicago: University of Chicago Press, 1974). See also Marshall G. S. Hodgson and Edmund Burke III (eds.), *Rethinking World History: Essays on Europe, Islam and World History* (Cambridge: Cambridge University Press 1993); Marshall G. S. Hodgson, "The Role of Islam in World History," *International Journal of Middle East Studies*, 1:2 (1970), 99–123; and Marshall G. S. Hodgson, "The Inter-relations of Societies in History," *Comparative Studies in Society and History*, 5:2 (1963), 227–250.

7. John Darwin, *The Empire Project: The Rise and Fall of the British World-System, 1830–1970* (Cambridge: Cambridge University Press, 2009), 295–297; Ronald Hyam, *Britain's Declining Empire: The Road to Decolonisation, 1918–1968* (Cambridge: Cambridge University Press, 2006), 154–162; Devji, "Britain's Muslim Empire and Its Indian Future"; Devji, "Islam in British Imperial Thought"; Francis Robinson, "The British Empire and the Muslim World," in W. R. Louis and J. M. Brown (eds.), *The Oxford History of the British Empire*, vol. 4, *The Twentieth Century* (Oxford: Oxford University Press, 1999), 398–420. For similar ideas regarding other European empires, see Chapter 1, "European Empires and the Hajj."

8. Andrew S. Thompson and Kent Fedorowich (eds.), *Empire, Migration and Identity in the British World* (Manchester: Manchester University Press,

2013); Andrew S. Thompson, *Empire and Globalisation: Networks of People, Goods and Capital in the British World, c. 1850–1914* (Cambridge: Cambridge University Press, 2010); Philip A. Buckner and R. Douglas Francis (eds.), *Re-discovering the British World* (Calgary: University of Calgary Press, 2005); Carl Bridge and Kent Fedorowich (eds.), *The British World: Diaspora, Culture and Identity* (London: Frank Cass, 2003).

9. The centrality of religion and its practice to empires, such as Byzantium, the Carolingians, the Mughals, the Ottomans, and Iran's various imperial rulers, has been emphasized in Jane Burbank and Frederick Cooper, *Empires in World History: Power and the Politics of Difference* (Princeton, NJ: Princeton University Press, 2010), 2, 4, 15, 332; C. A. Bayly, *The Birth of the Modern World, 1780–1914: Global Connections and Comparisons* (London: Blackwell, 2004), 325, 363–364; and, most relevant for Britain and the Hajj, David Motadel, "Islam and the European Empires," *Historical Journal*, 55:3 (2012), 831–856.

10. Motadel, "Islam and the European Empires," has an extensive relevant bibliography in the notes. However, see particularly Iza Hussin, *The Politics of Islamic Law: Local Elites, Colonial Authority, and the Making of the Muslim State* (Chicago: University of Chicago Press, 2015); Wael B. Hallaq, *An Introduction to Islamic Law* (Cambridge: Cambridge University Press, 2009), 85–89; Wael B. Hallaq, *Shari'a: Theory, Practice, Transformations* (Cambridge: Cambridge University Press, 2009), 371–384; Iza Hussin, "The Making of Islamic Law: Local Elites and Colonial Authority in British Malaya," in Thomas Dubois (ed.), *Casting Faiths: Technology and the Creation of Religion in East and Southeast Asia* (Basingstoke: Palgrave Macmillan, 2008), 155–174; Gabriel Warburg, *Islam, Sectarianism, and Politics in Sudan since the Mahdiyya* (Madison: University of Wisconsin Press, 2003), 57–103; Jonathan Reynolds, "Good and Bad Muslims: Islam and Indirect Rule in Northern Nigeria," *International Journal of African Historical Studies*, 34 (2001), 601–618; Scott Alan Kugle, "Framed, Blamed and Renamed: The Recasting of Islamic Jurisprudence in Colonial South Asia," *Modern Asian Studies*, 35 (2001), 257–313; C. N. Ubah, "Colonial Administration and the Spread of Islam in Northern Nigeria," *Muslim World*, 81 (1991), 133–148; Auwalu Hamsxu Yadudu, "Colonialism and the Transformation of the Substance and Form of Islamic Law in the Northern States of Nigeria," *Journal of Law and Religion*, 9 (1991), 17–47; Uri Kupferschmidt, *The Supreme Muslim Council: Islam under the British Mandate for Palestine* (Leiden: Brill, 1987), 1–14, is particularly useful; Gregory C. Kozlowski, *Muslim Endowments and Society in British India* (Cambridge: Cambridge University Press, 1985); and Gabriel Warburg, "Religious Policy in Northern Sudan: Ulama and Sufism, 1899–1918," *Asian and African Studies*, 7 (1971), 89–119.

11. Motadel, "Islam and the European Empires," contains an excellent overview of these topics with references to further relevant works. See also Nile Green, *Islam and the Army in Colonial India: Sepoy Religion in the Service of Empire* (Cambridge: Cambridge University Press, 2009).

12. Robert Irwin, "Pilgrimage to Mecca—A History (2)," in Venetia Porter (ed.), *Hajj: Journey to the Heart of Islam* (London: British Museum Press, 2012), 136–219, 204.

13. 1932 Pilgrimage Report, 1, IOR/R/20/A/3524, India Office Records, Asia, Pacific and Africa Collections, British Library, London (hereafter referred to as IOR, APAC, BL).

14. Jonathan Reynolds, "'Stealing the Road': Colonial Rule and the Hajj from Nigeria in the Early 20th Century," *Working Papers in African Studies*, no. 246 (African Studies Center, Boston University, 2003), 1–15, 1.

15. John Darwin, *Unfinished Empire: The Global Expansion of Britain* (London: Penguin, 2012), 295–296.

16. See Stephen F. Dale, *The Muslim Empires of the Ottomans, Safavids and Mughals* (Cambridge: Cambridge University Press, 2010); Suraiya Faroqhi, *The Ottoman Empire and the World around It* (London: I. B. Tauris, 2004); Suraiya Faroqhi, *Pilgrims and Sultans: The Hajj under the Ottomans, 1517–1683* (London: I. B. Tauris, 1996); M. N. Pearson, *Pilgrimage to Mecca: The Indian Experience, 1500–1800* (Princeton, NJ: Markus Wiener, 1996); Naimur Farooqi, *Mughal-Ottoman Relations: A Study of Political and Diplomatic Relations between Mughal India and the Ottoman Empire, 1556–1748* (Delhi: Idarah-i Adabiyat-i Delli, 1989); William Ochsenwald, *Religion, Society, and the State in Arabia: The Hijaz under Ottoman Control, 1840–1908* (Columbus: Ohio State University Press, 1984); and Karl K. Barbir, *Ottoman Rule in Damascus, 1708–1758* (Princeton, NJ: Princeton University Press, 1980).

17. Furthermore, within some of the aforementioned territories, safety concerns, conditions of access, local bureaucracy, and limitations of time meant that some local archives could not be used. These archives include the State Archive in Kaduna, Nigeria; the Public Records Office, Khartoum; the Dar al-Watha'iq, Cairo, Egypt; state archives in Bhopal, Chandigarh, and Kolkata in India; the National Archives in Dhaka, Bangladesh; the National Archives of Kenya and Tanzania; and the Zanzibar National Archives. I hope that scholars of South Asian and African history will conduct future research on the Hajj drawing on the records in these repositories.

18. M. C. Low, "Empire and the Hajj: Pilgrims, Plagues and Pan-Islam, 1865–1908," *International Journal of Middle Eastern Studies*, 40 (2008), 269–290; Michael Miller, "Pilgrim's Progress: The Business of the Hajj," *Past and Present*, 191 (2006), 189–228; Sugata Bose, *A Hundred Horizons: The Indian Ocean in the Age of Global Empire* (Cambridge, MA: Harvard University Press, 2006), chap. 6, "Pilgrim's Progress under Colonial Rules," 193–233; Takashi Oishi, "Friction and Rivalry over Pious Mobility: British Colonial Management of the Hajj and the Reaction to It by Indian Muslims, 1870–1920," in K. Hidemitsu (ed.), *The Influence of Human Mobility in Muslim Societies* (London: Kegan Paul, 2003), 151–179. More recent work, while not focused solely on the Hajj, has emphasized the importance of Muslim transnational connections across the Indian Ocean; see Seema Alavi, "'Fugitive Mullahs and Outlawed Fanatics': Indian Muslims in Nineteenth-Century Trans-Asiatic Imperial Rivalries," *Modern Asian Studies*, 45:6 (2011), 1337–1382.

19. See Pearson, *Pilgrimage to Mecca;* and also Shanti Moorthy and Ashraf Jamal (eds.), *Indian Ocean Studies: Cultural, Social and Political Perspectives* (London: Routledge, 2009); Thomas R. Metcalf, *Imperial Connections: India in*

the Indian Ocean Arena, 1860–1920 (Berkeley: University of California Press, 2007); Rainer F. Buschmann, *Oceans in World History* (New York: McGraw-Hill, 2007); M. N. Pearson, *The World of the Indian Ocean, 1500–1800: Studies in Economic, Social, and Cultural History* (Burlington, VT: Ashgate, 2005); Engseng Ho, *The Graves of Tarim: Genealogy and Mobility across the Indian Ocean* (Berkeley: University of California Press, 2006); Bose, *Hundred Horizons;* M. N. Pearson, *The Indian Ocean* (London: Routledge, 2003); and Kenneth McPherson, *The Indian Ocean: A History of the People and the Sea* (Delhi: Oxford University Press, 1993). Earlier seminal works are K. N. Chaudhuri, *Asia before Europe: Economy and Civilisation of the Indian Ocean from the Rise of Islam to 1750* (Cambridge: Cambridge University Press, 1990); and K. N. Chaudhuri, *Trade and Civilisation in the Indian Ocean* (Cambridge: Cambridge University Press, 1985). Michael Christopher Low makes a valuable point of emphasizing the Hajj in Indian Ocean history and the importance of taking a transregional scope; Low, "Empire and the Hajj," 271.

20. Column 372, House of Commons Debate on East India, Troops and Vessels (Abyssinian Expedition) Considered in Committee, November 28, 1867, *Hansard*, vol. 190, columns 359–407.

21. Metcalf, *Imperial Connections*, 1–16. See also Durba Ghosh and Dane Kennedy (eds.), *Decentring Empire: Britain, India, and the Transcolonial World* (Hyderabad: Orient Longman, 2006). This book does not use the term "transnational," despite its current popularity, because it does not adequately describe the movement of goods, peoples, and ideas across boundaries during the European colonial era. Britain's Muslim empire was not a nation-state, nor were its constituent parts, consisting as they did of colonies, protectorates, sultanates, and emirates. Nation-states began to appear in this space only toward the end of this period. Therefore, "transcolonial" seems the most appropriate term to use for this study. A useful discussion of transnational history is C. A. Bayly, Sven Beckert, Matthew Connelly, Isabel Hofmeyr, Wendy Kozol, and Patricia Seed, "AHR Conversation: On Transnational History," *American Historical Review*, 111:5 (2006), 1440–1465. See also Kevin Grant, Philippa Levine, and Frank Trentmann (eds.), *Beyond Sovereignty: Britain, Empire and Transnationalism, c. 1880–1950* (Basingstoke: Palgrave Macmillan, 2007); Akira Iriye, "Transnational History," *Contemporary European History*, 13:2 (2004), 211–222; and Michael McGerr, "The Price of the 'New Transnational History,'" *American Historical Review*, 96:4 (1991), 1056.

22. Regarding area studies, the phrase "Middle East" was coined by an American naval strategist, Alfred Thayer Mahan, in 1902, in his article "The Persian Gulf and International Relations" in the September 1902 issue of the *National Review*. See James Renton, "Changing Languages of Empire and the Orient: Britain and the Invention of the Middle East, 1917–1918," *Historical Journal*, 50:3 (2007), 645–667.

23. Tony Ballantyne, *Orientalism and Race: Aryanism in the British Empire* (Basingstoke: Palgrave Macmillan, 2002), 1, 13–16.

24. See Bawa Yamba, *Permanent Pilgrims: The Role of Pilgrimage in the Lives of West African Muslims in the Sudan* (Edinburgh: Edinburgh University Press,

1995); J. S. Birks, *Across the Savannas to Mecca: The Overland Pilgrimage Route from West Africa* (London: C. Hurst and Co., 1978); J. S. Birks, "The Mecca Pilgrimage by West African Pastoral Nomads," *Journal of Modern African Studies,* 15:1 (1977), 47–58; and Umar Naqar, *The Pilgrimage Tradition in West Africa: An Historical Study with Special Reference to the Nineteenth Century* (Khartoum: Khartoum University Press, 1972).

25. On Massawa, see Jonathan Miran, *Red Sea Citizens: Cosmopolitan Society and Cultural Change in Massawa* (Bloomington: Indiana University Press, 2009).

26. F. E. Peters, *The Hajj: The Muslim Pilgrimage to Mecca and the Holy Places* (Princeton, NJ: Princeton University Press 1994), 86–98.

27. Ibid., 79–86.

28. By 1930, there were 1,200 cars and lorries carrying pilgrims in the Hijaz. Report for April 1930, in Robert Jarman (ed.), *The Jedda Diaries, 1919–1940*, vols. 1–4 (Gerrards Cross: Archive Editions, 1990), 3:124 (hereafter referred to as *Jedda Diaries*).

29. Karachi was opened to pilgrim traffic in 1912. Government of Bombay Resolution, April 26, 1912, General Department, 1912, Vol. 130, File 916, MSA; Radhika Singha, "Passport, Ticket and India-Rubber Stamp: 'The Problem of the Pauper Pilgrim' in Colonial India, c. 1882–1925," in Ashwini Tambe and Harald Fischer-Tiné (eds.), *The Limits of British Colonial Control in South Asia: Spaces of Disorder in the Indian Ocean Region* (London: Routledge, 2009), 49–84, 54.

30. See Saurabh Mishra, *Pilgrims, Politics and Pestilence: The Hajj from the Indian Sub-continent, 1860–1920* (Delhi: Oxford University Press, 2011).

31. Ikbal Ali Shah was one of thousands of pilgrims who took the Indian Ocean sea route, traveling on the pilgrim steamship *Gurgistan* from Bombay to Jidda in 1927. Ikbal Ali Shah, *Westward to Mecca: A Journey of Adventure through Afghanistan, Bolshevik Asia, Persia, Iraq and Hijaz to the Cradle of Islam* (London: Witherby, 1928), 211–213.

32. Such as Bengal's Fara'izi movement, Sheikh Ahmed of Rae Bareilly and the frontier "Wahhabis" in British India, Sahiliyya Sufi leader Muhammad Abdullah Hassan in Somaliland, and many other examples from the Netherlands East Indies, West Africa, Russia, and China. All these movements attest to the power of reformist and revivalist ideas, generated in the Hijaz by men on Hajj and *rihla* (literally "journey," referring to travels in search of Islamic religious knowledge), in spurring Islamic resistance to non-Muslim power. For a selection of studies reflecting this viewpoint, see Francis Robinson, "Islamic Reform and Modernities in South Asia," *Modern Asian Studies*, 42:2–3 (2008), 259–281; Julia A. Clancy-Smith, *Rebel and Saint: Muslim Notables, Populist Protest, Colonial Encounters* (Berkeley: University of California Press, 1997); Nikki R. Keddie, "The Revolt of Islam, 1700 to 1993: Comparative Considerations and Relations to Imperialism," *Comparative Studies in Society and History*, 36:3 (1994), 463–487; Ali Abdullatif Ahmida, *The Making of Modern Libya: State Formation, Colonization, and Resistance, 1830–1932* (Albany: State University of New York Press, 1994); Fred Von der Mehden, *Two Worlds of Islam: Interaction between Southeast Asia and the Middle East* (Gainesville: University Press of Florida, 1993); Annemarie Schimmel, "Sacred Geography in Islam," in Jamie

Scott and Paul Simpson-Housley (eds.), *Sacred Places and Profane Spaces: Essays in the Geographics of Judaism, Christianity, and Islam* (New York: Greenwood Press, 1991), 163–175; Kenneth W. Jones, *Socio-religious Reform Movements in British India* (Cambridge: Cambridge University Press, 1989); Christopher Harrison, *France and Islam in West Africa, 1860–1960* (Cambridge: Cambridge University Press, 1988); William Roff, "Islamic Movements: One or Many?," in William Roff (ed.), *Islam and the Political Economy of Meaning* (Berkeley: University of California Press, 1987), 31–52; J. O. Voll, *Islam: Continuity and Change in the Modern World* (Boulder, CO: Westview, 1982); Michael Adas, *Prophets of Rebellion: Millenarian Protest Movements against the European Colonial Order* (Chapel Hill: University of North Carolina Press, 1979); Rudolph Peters, *Islam and Colonialism: The Doctrine of Jihad in Modern History* (New York: Mouton, 1979); B. G. Martin, *Muslim Brotherhoods in Nineteenth-Century Africa* (Cambridge: Cambridge University Press, 1977); Nikki R. Keddie, *Scholars, Saints, and Sufis: Muslim Religious Institutions in the Middle East since 1500* (Berkeley: University of California Press, 1972); Fazlur Rahman, "Revival and Reform in Islam," in P. M. Holt, Ann K. S. Lambton, and Bernard Lewis (eds.), *The Cambridge History of Islam*, vol. 2B, *Islamic Society and Civilization* (Cambridge: Cambridge University Press, 1970), 632–656; Nikki R. Keddie, *An Islamic Response to Imperialism: Political and Religious Writings of Sayyid Jamal ad-Din al-Afghani* (Berkeley: University of California Press, 1968); Norman Daniel, *Islam, Europe and Empire* (Edinburgh: Edinburgh University Press, 1966); M. Ahmed, *Saiyid Ahmad Shahid* (Lucknow: Academy of Islamic Research and Publications, 1965); Q. Ahmad, *A History of the Fara'idi Movement in Bengal, 1818–1906* (Karachi: Pakistan Historical Society, 1965); Robert L. Hess, "The Mad Mullah and Northern Somalia," *Journal of African History*, 5:3 (1964), 415–433; and Nicola A. Ziadeh, *Sanusiyah: A Study of a Revivalist Movement in Islam* (Leiden: Brill, 1958). More broadly, the experience of the Hajj highlights doctrinal differences and local variations in religious tradition, which have caused some Muslims to attempt to "purify" Islamic practice in their locality after returning from Hajj, such as members of the revivalist movements mentioned earlier. Scholars such as Michael Pearson have concluded that although some Muslims accepted Mecca as the source of correct Islamic doctrine and conduct and attempted to practice a "purer" form of Islam when they returned, others who returned after performing the Hajj did not instigate changes to their religious practices. M. N. Pearson, *Pious Passengers: The Hajj in Earlier Times* (London: C. Hurst and Co., 1994), 67–70, 72–79.

33. Nile Green, *Bombay Islam: The Religious Economy of the West Indian Ocean, 1840–1915* (Cambridge: Cambridge University Press, 2011), 7.

34. F. E. Peters, *Hajj*, 301.

35. See Low, "Empire and the Hajj"; Mishra, *Pilgrims, Politics and Pestilence;* M. C. Low, "Empire of the Hajj: Pilgrims, Plagues and Pan-Islam under British Surveillance, 1865–1926" (MA thesis, University of Georgia, 2007); Mark Harrison, *Public Health in British India: Anglo-Indian Preventative Medicine, 1859–1914* (Cambridge: Cambridge University Press, 1994); and William Roff, "Sanitation and Security: The Imperial Powers and the Nineteenth Century Hajj," *Arabian Studies*, 6 (1982), 143–161. Michael Christopher Low has

asserted that this led to the Hajj being "colonised"; see Low, "Empire of the Hajj," 150, 180, 189; Low, "Empire and the Hajj," 285–286.

36. The only detailed treatment of this topic is Singha, "Passport, Ticket and India-Rubber Stamp."

37. Ashwini Tambe and Harald Fischer-Tiné, "Introduction," in Tambe and Fischer-Tiné, *Limits of British Colonial Control in South Asia*, 5.

38. See Ronald E. Robinson, "Non-European Foundations of European Imperialism: Sketch for a Theory of Collaboration," in Roger Owen and B. Sutcliffe (eds.), *Studies in the Theory of Imperialism* (London: Longman, 1972), 117–142. On the issue of collaboration, see also James Onley, *The Arabian Frontier of the British Raj: Merchants, Rulers and British in the Nineteenth-Century Gulf* (Oxford: Oxford University Press, 2007); James Onley, "Britain's Native Agents in Arabia and Persia in the Nineteenth Century," *Comparative Studies of South Asia, Africa and the Middle East*, 24:1 (2005), 129–137; Heather J. Sharkey, *Living with Colonialism: Nationalism and Culture in the Anglo-Egyptian Sudan* (Berkeley: University of California Press, 2003); Sarah Ansari, *Sufi Saints and State Power: The Pirs of Sind, 1843–1947* (Cambridge: Cambridge University Press, 1992); G. R. Warbury, "British Rule in the Nile Valley, 1882–1956, and Robinson's Theory of Collaboration," *Asian and African Studies*, 15 (1981), 287–322; and Christian W. Troll, *Sayyid Ahmad Khan: A Reinterpretation of Muslim Theology* (Delhi: Vikas, 1978). See Chapter 2 for Sir Syed Ahmad Khan's correspondence with the government of India on the Hajj.

39. See, for example, the pilgrimage accounts of Irfan Ali Beg, *A Pilgrimage to Mecca by Mirza Irfan Ali Beg, Deputy Collector, Mainpuri* (Benares: Chandraprabha Press, 1896); and Mahomed Ullah ibn Salar Jung, *A Pilgrimage to Mecca and the Near East* (Secunderabad: Bulletin Press, 1912).

40. Report on the Hajj 1915/1333 A.H., IOR/L/PS/10/523, IOR, APAC, BL. For the effects of this policy, see Foreign and Political, Secret—General, May 1916, No. 10, National Archives of India, Delhi (hereafter referred to as NAI).

41. For example, the Archive Editions documentary collection on the Hajj, which mainly uses Foreign Office records, runs to some 6,000 pages. See Alan Rush (ed.), *Records of the Hajj: A Documentary History of the Pilgrimage to Mecca*, vols. 1–10 (Gerrards Cross: Archive Editions, 1993) (hereafter referred to as *RoH*).

42. The usefulness of this approach has been highlighted in Metcalf, *Imperial Connections*, 1–16.

43. Eric Tagliacozzo, *The Longest Journey: Southeast Asians and the Pilgrimage to Mecca* (Oxford: Oxford University Press, 2013), 11.

44. Kim Wagner and Ricardo Roque, "Introduction: Engaging Colonial Knowledge," in Kim Wagner and Ricardo Roque (eds.), *Engaging Colonial Knowledge: Reading European Archives in World History* (Basingstoke: Palgrave Macmillan, 2012), 1–34, 1–6. A good overview of the debate on colonial knowledge and the key literature is Tony Ballantyne, "Colonial Knowledge," in Sarah Stockwell (ed.), *The British Empire: Themes and Perspectives* (Oxford: Blackwell, 2008), 177–198.

45. In relation to French West Africa, see Sean Hanretta, *Islam and Social Change in French West Africa* (Cambridge: Cambridge University Press, 2009), 123–125.

46. Aishwary Kumar, "The Idea of the 'Tribal' in British India: Law, Archive and Memory in Santal Parganas" (PhD dissertation, Cambridge University, 2007), 5–8. See also Ann Laura Stoler, "Colonial Archives and the Arts of Governance: On the Content in the Form," in Carolyn Hamilton (ed.), *Refiguring the Archive* (Dordrecht: Kluwer Academic, 2002), 82–101; and Ann Laura Stoler, *Along the Archival Grain: Epistemic Anxieties and Colonial Common Sense* (Princeton, NJ: Princeton University Press, 2009).

47. Hanretta, *Islam and Social Change*, 125.

48. Mishra, *Pilgrims, Politics and Pestilence*, 9, 98–100.

49. See Roff, "Sanitation and Security"; and Low, "Empire and the Hajj."

CHAPTER 1 *Contexts*

1. Pearson, *Pious Passengers*, 1–3. Pilgrim numbers for the Hajj in the early twenty-first century hover around approximately 2 million per annum. The other major pilgrimages in numerical terms are the various Kumbh Melas that take place (at six- and twelve-year intervals) at Haridwar, Allahabad, Ujjain, and Nashik in India. The 2001 Maha Kumbh Mela in Allahabad attracted 60 million pilgrims.

2. Robert Bianchi, "Hajj," in John Esposito (ed.), *The Oxford Encyclopedia of the Modern Islamic World*, vol. 2 (New York: Oxford University Press, 1995), 88–92. Cooke and Lawrence have argued that the Hajj and other Muslim networks are "under-studied and under-valued"; Miriam Cooke and Bruce B. Lawrence (eds.), *Muslim Networks from Hajj to Hip-Hop* (Chapel Hill: University of North Carolina Press, 2005), xii.

3. The other pillars of Islam are the *shahada* (profession of faith), *salat* (prayers), *zakat* (giving of alms), and *sawm* (fasting, especially during Ramadan). These apply to Sunni Muslims. Sevener Shiʿi Muslims have eight practices, of which five are the same as the pillars, and the Twelver Shiʿi have five principles. The annual and cumulative numbers of pilgrims who made it to Mecca in this period were always a small proportion of the *umma*. Most Muslims did not go on Hajj and remained in their locales. Their experience of the Hajj came through stories told by returning pilgrims.

4. Shah, *Westward to Mecca*, 222.

5. See Robert Bianchi, *Guests of God: Pilgrimage and Politics in the Islamic World* (New York: Oxford University Press, 2004), 37; and, in relation to the Hindu Kumbh Mela, Kama Maclean, *Pilgrimage and Power: The Kumbh Mela in Allahabad, 1765–1954* (New York: Oxford University Press, 2008), 1.

6. Pearson, *Pious Passengers*, 9.

7. The hills are now enclosed within a corridor of the Holy Mosque.

8. Vincent J. Cornell, "Fruit of the Tree of Knowledge: The Relationship between Faith and Practice in Islam," in John Esposito (ed.), *The Oxford*

History of Islam (New York: Oxford University Press, 1999), 63–105, 84–87; and Bianchi, "Hajj," 88–92.

9. Marion Katz, "The Hajj and the Study of Islamic Ritual," *Studia Islamica*, 98/99 (2004), 95–129, 111.

10. Suras 2:196, 3:97, and 22:27–30, in M. Pickthall (trans.), *The Koran* (London: Alfred Knopf, 1930). Marmaduke Pickthall (1875–1936) was a British convert to Islam and gained notoriety for his position that he would refuse to serve if he was ordered to fight against the Ottoman empire, although he was ready to fight for Britain in any other circumstance. After the First World War, Pickthall worked for the nizam of Hyderabad. See Peter Clark, *Marmaduke Pickthall: British Muslim* (London: Quartet, 1986). There are several firsthand accounts by British converts to Islam, some of which cover their pilgrimage experiences. See Harry St. John Bridger Philby, *A Pilgrim in Arabia* (London: R. Hale, 1946); Evelyn Cobbold, *Pilgrimage to Mecca* (London: John Murray, 1934); Eldon Rutter, *The Holy Cities of Arabia* (London: Putnam, 1928); and Joseph Pitts, *Narrative of the Captivity of Joseph Pitts among the Algerines, and of His Fortunate Escape from the Mahometans* (London: Hardt and Cross, 1815).

11. *Sura* 2:196, in Pickthall, *Koran*, 49.

12. *Sura* 3:97, in Pickthall, *Koran*, 78.

13. *Sura* 2:197, in Pickthall, *Koran*, 49.

14. *Sura* 22:27, in Pickthall, *Koran*, 341.

15. F. E. Peters, *Hajj*, 90–91.

16. Pearson, *Pious Passengers*, 93.

17. Quoted in Simon Digby, "Bayazid Beg Turkman's Pilgrimage to Makka and Return to Gujarat: A Sixteenth Century Narrative," *Iran*, 42 (2004), 159–177, 160.

18. Pearson, *Pious Passengers*, 93; Farooqi, *Mughal-Ottoman Relations*, 146.

19. Farooqi, *Mughal-Ottoman Relations*, 153.

20. Dane Kennedy and Dina Rizk Khoury, "Comparing Empires: The Ottoman Domains and the British Raj in the Long Nineteenth Century," *Comparative Studies of South Asia, Africa and the Middle East*, 27:3 (2007), 233–244, 235. See also Karen Barkey, *Empire of Difference: The Ottomans in Comparative Perspective* (Cambridge: Cambridge University Press, 2008); and C. A. Bayly, "Distorted Development: The Ottoman Empire and British India, circa 1780–1916," *Comparative Studies of South Asia, Africa and the Middle East*, 27:2 (2007), 332–344. For an overview of the religious policies of the great early modern Islamic empires, see Dale, *Muslim Empires*.

21. Pearson, *Pious Passengers*, 24.

22. Ibid., 52, 58; Terenjit S. Sevea, "The Indian Muslim Presence in the Hijaz," 229–230, in Brij V. Lal (ed.), *Encyclopaedia of the Indian Diaspora* (Honolulu: University of Hawaii Press, 2006).

23. Abd al-Qadir Bada'uni, *Muntakhab Al-Tawatrik*, 2:214 (1595), quoted in Digby, "Bayazid Beg Turkman's Pilgrimage," 161.

24. Farooqi, *Mughal-Ottoman Relations*, 113.

25. Ibid.

26. Akbar wished to go on Hajj, but his advisers counseled against it.

27. Farooqi, *Mughal-Ottoman Relations*, 114–115; Faroqhi, *Pilgrims and Sultans*, 131. *Cartez* is derived from the Arabic for "paper," *qurtas*.

28. Faroqhi, *Pilgrims and Sultans*, 131–133.

29. Farooqi, *Mughal-Ottoman Relations*, 114–115.

30. Digby, "Bayazid Beg Turkman's Pilgrimage," 162.

31. Farooqi, *Mughal-Ottoman Relations*, 116.

32. Ibid., 118–119.

33. Ibid., 120–126. See also the French traveler Jean-Baptiste Tavernier's late seventeenth-century account quoted in Tagliacozzo, *Longest Journey*, 65–66.

34. Dale, *Muslim Empires*, 178–179.

35. Farooqi, *Mughal-Ottoman Relations*, 109; M. Abir, "The 'Arab Rebellion' of Amir Ghalib of Mecca (1788–1813)," *Middle Eastern Studies*, 7:2 (1971), 185–200, 185; Pearson, *Pious Passengers*, 23.

36. Abir, "'Arab Rebellion,'" 185.

37. Farooqi, *Mughal-Ottoman Relations*, 109; Faroqhi, *Pilgrims and Sultans*, 9.

38. Faroqhi, *Pilgrims and Sultans*, 47–54; F. E. Peters, *Hajj*, 147–148, 152.

39. Faroqhi, *Pilgrims and Sultans*, 78, 81, 93, 103, 109; F. E. Peters, *Hajj*, 154.

40. Barbir, *Ottoman Rule in Damascus*, 10.

41. Ibid., 10, 109, 151.

42. Pearson, *Pious Passengers*, 26.

43. Abir, "'Arab Rebellion,'" 186.

44. China ruled Muslim subjects in Xinjiang and Yunnan and likewise Ethiopia in Somalia, but a consideration of their policies on the Hajj is outside the scope of this book.

45. Sarah Ansari, "The Islamic World in the Era of Western Domination, 1800 to the Present," in Francis Robinson (ed.), *The Cambridge Illustrated History of the Islamic World* (Cambridge: Cambridge University Press, 1996), 90–123.

46. Tagliacozzo, *Longest Journey*, 194–195.

47. Eric Tagliacozzo, "The Dutch Empire and the Hajj," in Motadel, *Islam and the European Empires*, 73–89.

48. William Gervase Clarence-Smith, *Islam and the Abolition of Slavery* (New York: Oxford University Press), 180. See also Keddie, "Revolt of Islam."

49. Karel A. Steenbrink, *Dutch Colonialism and Indonesian Islam: Contacts and Conflicts, 1596–1950* (Leiden: Brill, 1993), 73–74.

50. Tagliacozzo, "Dutch Empire and the Hajj," 6.

51. M. C. Ricklefs, "The Middle East Connection and Reform and Revival Movements among the Puithen in Nineteenth Century Java," in Eric Tagliacozzo (ed.), *Southeast Asia and the Middle East: Islam, Movement, and the Longue Durée* (Stanford, CA: Stanford University Press, 2009), 111–134, 114.

52. Ibid., 111–134; Michael Laffan, *Islamic Nationhood and Colonial Indonesia: The Umma below the Winds* (London: Routledge Curzon, 2003), 38.

53. Tagliacozzo, "Dutch Empire and the Hajj," 7, 15–16.

54. Tagliacozzo, *Longest Journey*, 76, 187; Laffan, *Islamic Nationhood*, 37–38. In fact, according to Laffan, in the late 1870s and 1880s many Indonesians studied at the Sawlattya madrassa in Mecca that was established in 1874 by an Indian involved in the 1857 rebellion.

55. Tagliacozzo, *Longest Journey*, 75–77, 182; Laffan, *Islamic Nationhood*, 54; Tagliacozzo, "Dutch Empire and the Hajj," 12.

56. Tagliacozzo, "Dutch Empire and the Hajj," 8, 18.

57. See also William Roff, "Indonesian and Malay Students in Cairo in the 1920's," *Indonesia*, 9 (1970), 73–87; and Laffan, *Islamic Nationhood*, 39.

58. Laffan, *Islamic Nationhood*, 49–51.

59. Ibid., 41–45; Tagliacozzo, *Longest Journey*, 187–188; Tagliacozzo, "Dutch Empire and the Hajj," 14.

60. Steenbrink, *Dutch Colonialism and Indonesian Islam*, 79.

61. Tagliacozzo, *Longest Journey*, 78, 185.

62. Eric Tagliacozzo, "The Skeptic's Eye: Snouck Hurgronje and the Politics of the Pilgrimage from the Indies," 135–155, in Tagliacozzo, *Southeast Asia and the Middle East*, 135.

63. Laffan, *Islamic Nationhood*, 59, 63.

64. Tagliacozzo, "Skeptic's Eye," 137–140; Tagliacozzo, *Longest Journey*, 161.

65. Tagliacozzo, "Skeptic's Eye," 147; Tagliacozzo, *Longest Journey*, 171.

66. Tagliacozzo, "Skeptic's Eye," 143–146; Tagliacozzo, *Longest Journey*, 166–169; Laffan, *Islamic Nationhood*, 73.

67. Tagliacozzo, *Longest Journey*, 161.

68. Tagliacozzo, "Skeptic's Eye," 140–141.

69. Ibid., 136; Laffan, *Islamic Nationhood*, 55.

70. Tagliacozzo, *Longest Journey*, 165.

71. Tagliacozzo, "Skeptic's Eye," 148–149; Tagliacozzo, *Longest Journey*, 172; Tagliacozzo, "Dutch Empire and the Hajj," 17.

72. Tagliacozzo, "Dutch Empire and the Hajj," 11.

73. David Robinson, "France as a Muslim Power in West Africa," *Africa Today*, 46:3–4 (Special Issue: Islam in Africa, 1999), 105–127, 105. See also A. S. Kanya-Forstner, *Pilgrims, Interpreters, and Agents: French Reconnaissance Reports on the Sokoto Caliphate and Borno, 1891–1895* (Madison: University of Wisconsin–Madison Press, 1997); Laurent Escande, "D'Alger à la Mecque: L'administration française et le contrôle du pèlerinage, 1894–1962," *Revue d'histoire maghrébine*, 26 (1999), 277–292; Vincent Joly, "Un aspect de la politique musulmane de la France: L'administration et le pèlerinage de la Mecque, 1930–1950," *Annales du Levant*, 5 (1992), 37–58; George R. Trumbull, *An Empire of Facts: Colonial Power, Cultural Knowledge, and Islam in Algeria, 1870–1914* (Cambridge: Cambridge University Press, 2009); and Benjamin C. Brower, "The Hajj from Algeria," in Venetia Porter and Liana Saif (eds.), *Hajj: Collected Essays* (London: British Museum Press, 2013), 108–114.

74. D. Robinson, "France as a Muslim Power," 118–122.

75. Baz Lecocq, "The Hajj from West Africa from a Global Historical Perspective (19th and 20th Centuries)," *African Diaspora*, 5:2 (2012), 187–214, 191; B. Brower, "Hajj from Algeria," 108.

76. Lecocq, "Hajj from West Africa," 196–198; Valeska Huber, *Channelling Mobilities: Migration and Globalisation in the Suez Canal Region and Beyond, 1869–1914* (Cambridge: Cambridge University Press, 2013), 233–235.

77. Huber, *Channelling Mobilities*, 209, 222, 225.

78. Lecocq, "Hajj from West Africa," 196–198.

79. B. Brower, "Hajj from Algeria," 110.

80. D. Robinson, "France as a Muslim Power," 106–111.

81. Huber, *Channelling Mobilities*, 217–219.

82. Lecocq, "Hajj from West Africa," 196–198; B. Brower, "Hajj from Algeria," 111; Huber, *Channelling Mobilities*, 211–212, 223.

83. D. Robinson, "France as a Muslim Power," 172.

84. See examples in Chapters 3, 4, and 5. See also Naqar, *Pilgrimage Tradition in West Africa*.

85. Huber, *Channelling Mobilities*, 234–237.

86. Gregory Mann and Baz Lecocq, "Between Empire, Umma, and the Muslim Third World: The French Union and African Pilgrims to Mecca, 1946–58," *Comparative Studies of South Asia, Africa and the Middle East*, 27:2 (2007), 167–181, 167.

87. B. Brower, "Hajj from Algeria," 111–112.

88. Lecocq, "Hajj from West Africa," 196–198.

89. Mann and Lecocq, "Between Empire," 167.

90. Mann and Lecocq, "Between Empire," 168, 171; Lecocq, "Hajj from West Africa," 196–198; B. Brower, "Hajj from Algeria," 112.

91. Mann and Lecocq, "Between Empire," 177–179.

92. Ibid., 182.

93. Lecocq, "Hajj from West Africa," 199. On the Algerian Front de Libération Nationale (FLN) and the Hajj after 1956, see B. Brower, "Hajj from Algeria," 112–113.

94. Daniel Brower, "Russian Roads to Mecca: Religious Tolerance and Muslim Pilgrimage in the Russian Empire," *Slavic Review*, 55:3 (1996), 567–584, 567.

95. Robert D. Crews, *For Prophet and Tsar: Islam and Empire in Russia and Central Asia* (Cambridge, MA: Harvard University Press, 2006), 71–74.

96. Ibid., 289; D. Brower, "Russian Roads to Mecca," 579–580; Eileen Kane, "Odessa as a Hajj Hub: 1880s to 1920s" (National Council for Eurasian and East European Research Working Paper, 2011), 7.

97. D. Brower, "Russian Roads to Mecca," 568–571.

98. Alexander Morrison, *Russian Rule in Samarkand, 1869–1910: A Comparison with British India* (Oxford: Oxford University Press, 2008), 63–64.

99. Crews, *For Prophet and Tsar*, 330.

100. Morrison, *Russian Rule in Samarkand*, 63–64.

101. See files in Pilgrim Traffic, Vol. 14, 1897, FO 78/4882, TNA.

102. D. Brower, "Russian Roads to Mecca," 572–573; Morrison, *Russian Rule in Samarkand*, 63–64.

103. D. Brower, "Russian Roads to Mecca," 576–578; Morrison, *Russian Rule in Samarkand*, 65–66.

104. Kane, "Odessa as a Hajj Hub," 11–22; D. Brower, "Russian Roads to Mecca," 581–583.

105. D. Brower, "Russian Roads to Mecca," 583.

106. Yaacov Ro'i, *Islam in the Soviet Union: From the Second World War to Gorbachev* (London: C. Hurst and Co., 2000), 10, 171–175, 371–372, 454, 575.

107. Peter Sluglett, *Britain in Iraq: Contriving King and Country* (London: I. B. Tauris, 2007), appendix 1, "A Note on Shi'i Politics," 219–232; and Yitzhak Nakash, *The Shi'is of Iraq* (Princeton, NJ: Princeton University Press, 2003).

108. Nakash, *Shi'is of Iraq*, 163.

109. Review of the Civil Administration of Mesopotamia for 1920, 28, IOR/L/PS/10/752, IOR, APAC, BL. See also Meir Litvak, "Money, Religion and Politics: The Oudh Bequest in Najaf and Karbala," *International Journal of Middle Eastern Studies*, 33:1 (2001), 1–21; Juan Cole, *The Roots of North Indian Shi'ism in Iran and Iraq: Religion and State in Awadh, 1722–1859* (Berkeley: University of California Press, 1988); Juan Cole, "Indian Money and the Shi'a Shrine Cities of Iraq, 1786–1850," *Middle East Studies*, 22:4 (1986), 461–580; and Nakash, *Shi'is of Iraq*, 211–229.

110. Meir Litvak, "A Failed Manipulation: The British, the Oudh Bequest, and the Shi'a *Ulama* of Najaf and Karbala," *British Journal of Middle Eastern Studies*, 27:1 (2000), 69–89.

111. Nakash, *Shi'is of Iraq*, 227–228.

112. Sluglett, *Britain in Iraq*, 220–223. See also Percy Cox to Secretary to the Government of India, Foreign and Political Department, May 17, 1915, IOR/L/PS/11/93/P2279, IOR, APAC, BL.

113. Sluglett, *Britain in Iraq*, 219.

114. Administration Report of Baghdad Wilayet for the Year 1917, 125, CO 696/1, TNA. See also E. S. Stevens, *By Tigris and Euphrates* (London: Hurst and Blackett, 1923), 18; and Maj.-Gen. S. S. Butler, "Journey into Unknown Arabia," 1908, 7, unpublished memoirs, Mss. Afr.r.195, Rhodes House Library, University of Oxford.

115. Toby Dodge, *Inventing Iraq* (New York: Columbia University Press, 2003), 64, 67.

116. Reports of Administration for 1918 of Divisions and Districts in the Occupied Territories in Mesopotamia, 9, IOR/L/PS/11/165, IOR, APAC, BL; Nakash, *Shi'is of Iraq*, 167.

117. Reports of Administration for 1918 of Divisions and Districts in the Occupied Territories in Mesopotamia, 9, IOR/L/PS/11/165, 85, IOR, APAC, BL; Monthly Reports of Political Officers of Occupied Territories, March 1919, Kufah-Najaf, IOR/L/PS/11/93/P6265, IOR, APAC, BL.

118. Administration Report of the 'Amarah Division for the Year 1919, 28, CO 696/2, TNA; Civil Commissioner Baghdad to Secretary of State for India, September 12, 1919, IOR/L/PS/11/93/P2699, IOR, APAC, BL.

119. Nakash, *Shi'is of Iraq*, 169.

120. Administration Report of the 'Amarah Division for the Year 1919, 102, CO 696/2, TNA.

121. Administration Report of Baghdad Wilayet for the Year 1917, 125, CO 696/1, TNA.

122. Ibid. See also Proposal of the Government of Bombay for a provision of R 2,000 being made in the budget for the year 1931–32 on the repatriation of destitute Indian pilgrims from Iraq to India, Foreign and Political Department, 1932, 414-N/30, Nos. 1–15, NAI.

123. Report for 1929 on the work of the Protector of British Indian Pilgrims attached to the Secretariat of H.E. High Commissioner of Baghdad, CO 730/159/2, TNA.

124. Administration Report of the Hillah Division for the Year 1919, 16–17, CO 696/2, TNA.

125. Administration Report of the Hillah Division for the Year 1919, 18, CO 696/2, TNA. Also quoted in Nakash, *Shi'is of Iraq*, 165.

126. Nakash, *Shi'is of Iraq*, 169.

127. Travel to Shrines in Mesopotamia by Iraq Railways for Indian Pilgrims 1922 (in Arabic and Urdu), General Department, 1922, File 3442, MSA. On the wider phenomenon of "corpse traffic" to the shrine cities, see Nakash, *Shi'is of Iraq*, 184–201.

128. Nakash, *Shi'is of Iraq*, 172–173.

129. Ibid., 166–173.

130. Ibid., 172–173.

131. See files related to the Indian protector of pilgrims' work in Iraq in CO 730/143/8, CO 730/159/2, TNA.

132. Schimmel, "Sacred Geography in Islam," 169. See also Carl W. Ernst and Bruce B. Lawrence, *Sufi Martyrs of Love: The Chishti Order in South Asia and Beyond* (New York: Palgrave Macmillan, 2002); Christian W. Troll, *Muslim Shrines in India: Their Character, History and Significance* (Delhi: Oxford University Press, 1989); Susan Bayly, *Saints, Goddesses and Kings: Muslims and Christians in South Indian Society, 1700–1900* (Cambridge: Cambridge University Press, 1989); Nile Green, *Sufism: A Global History* (Malden, MA: Wiley-Blackwell, 2012); and Surinder Bhardwaj, "Non-Hajj Pilgrimage in Islam: A Neglected Dimension of Religious Circulation," *Journal of Cultural Geography*, 17:2 (1998), 69–87.

133. For example, Sikander Begum of Bhopal in Chapter 2, and numerous examples in Chapter 5.

134. Schimmel, "Sacred Geography in Islam," 169.

135. Ibid., 165.

136. Green, *Islam and the Army*, 17.

137. Nakash, *Shi'is of Iraq*, 179.

138. F. Denny, "Islamic Ritual: Perspectives and Theories," in Richard Martin (ed.), *Approaches to Islam in Religious Studies* (Oxford: Oxford University Press, 2001), 63–77, 74.

139. Ibid., 77. See also Green, *Sufism*.

140. Catherine B. Asher, "Pilgrim Shrines in Ajmer," in Barbara Metcalf (ed.), *Islam in South Asia in Practice* (Princeton, NJ: Princeton University Press, 2009), 77–87, 77–79.

141. Annemarie Schimmel, *Mystical Dimensions of Islam* (Chapel Hill: University of North Carolina Press, 1975), 106–107.

142. Ansari, *Sufi Saints and State Power;* Moin Ahmad Nizami, "Reform and Renewal in South-Asian Islam: The Chishti-Sabris in 18th–19th Century North India" (PhD dissertation, Cambridge University, 2011), 32–33.

143. See Green, *Sufism.*

144. Hunt Janin, *Four Paths to Jerusalem: Jewish, Christian, Muslim, and Secular Pilgrimages, 1000 BCE–2001* (Jefferson, NC: McFarland, 2002), 174–175.

145. Quoted in ibid., 192.

146. Ibid., 191–193. See also Philip Mattar, "The Role of the Mufti of Jerusalem in the Political Struggle over the Western Wall, 1928–29," *Middle Eastern Studies,* 19:1 (1983), 104–118.

147. See Awad Halabi, "Symbols of Hegemony and Resistance: Banners and Flags in British-ruled Palestine," *Jerusalem Quarterly,* 36 (2009), 66–78; and Awad Halabi, "The Transformation of the Prophet Moses Festival in Jerusalem, 1917–1937: From Local and Islamic to Modern and Nationalist Celebration" (PhD dissertation, University of Toronto, 2006).

148. Naomi Shepherd, *Ploughing Sand: British Rule in Palestine, 1917–1948* (New Brunswick, NJ: Rutgers University Press, 2000), 41, 181. See also Roza I. M. El-Eini, *Mandated Landscape: British Imperial Rule in Palestine, 1929–48* (New York: Routledge, 2006).

149. The major works are Maclean, *Pilgrimage and Power;* and Katherine Prior, "The British Administration of Hinduism in North India, 1780–1900" (PhD dissertation, Cambridge University, 1990). See also Peter Van der Veer, *Gods on Earth: The Management of Religious Experience and Identity in a North Indian Pilgrimage Centre* (Delhi: Oxford University Press, 1988); I. J. Kerr, "British Relationships with the Golden Temple, 1849–90," *Indian Economic and Social History Review,* 21:2 (1984), 139–151; and Arjun Appadurai, *Worship and Conflict under Colonial Rule: A South Indian Case* (Cambridge: Cambridge University Press, 1981).

150. Maclean, *Pilgrimage and Power,* 220.

151. Ibid., 2, 56, 188, 219.

152. Ibid., 155.

153. Ibid., 25–27, 59, 81, 103.

154. Ibid., 111, and examples of Indian agitation related to the mela on 131, 149, 166, 189.

155. Prior, "British Administration of Hinduism," 227–228; Maclean, *Pilgrimage and Power,* 117, 132, 152.

156. Maclean, *Pilgrimage and Power,* 103.

157. Prior, "British Administration of Hinduism," 76–78.

158. Ibid., 57–58.

159. Maclean, *Pilgrimage and Power,* 29, 103–107, 118, 135–138; Prior, "British Administration of Hinduism," 245.

160. Prior, "British Administration of Hinduism," 203–205, 217; Maclean, *Pilgrimage and Power,* 16.

161. Prior, "British Administration of Hinduism," 182, 187, 190, 193–197, 231.

162. British Cholera Commissioners (Edward Goodeve and E. D. Dickson) to Lord Stanley, October 3, 1866, 4–7, PC 1/2672, TNA.

163. Maclean, *Pilgrimage and Power,* 173–175.

CHAPTER 2 *Pilgrimage in the Mid-Victorian Era*

1. See Mishra, *Pilgrims, Politics and Pestilence;* Saurabh Mishra, "Beyond the Bounds of Time? The Haj Pilgrimage from the Indian Subcontinent, 1865–1920," in Mark Harrison and Biswamoy Pati (eds.), *The Social History of Health and Medicine in Colonial India* (Basingstoke: Palgrave Macmillan, 2009), 31–44; Low, "Empire and the Hajj"; Low, "Empire of the Hajj"; Miller, "Pilgrim's Progress"; Bose, *Hundred Horizons;* Oishi, "Friction and Rivalry"; F. E. Peters, *Hajj;* M. Harrison, *Public Health in British India,* chapter 5, "Quarantine, Pilgrimage and Colonial Trade: India, 1866–1900," 117–138; and Roff, "Sanitation and Security."

2. See Singha, "Passport, Ticket and India-Rubber Stamp,"49–84, especially 50; and also Low, "Empire of the Hajj."

3. Mishra, *Pilgrims, Politics and Pestilence,* 124.

4. Abir, "'Arab Rebellion,'" 189–191.

5. Ibid., 191–193. See also Juan Cole, *Napoleon's Egypt: Invading the Middle East* (New York: Palgrave Macmillan, 2007); and Efraim Karsh and Inari Karsh, *Empires of the Sand: The Struggle for Mastery in the Middle East, 1789–1923* (Cambridge, MA: Harvard University Press, 1999).

6. Roff, "Sanitation and Security," 144.

7. Abir, "'Arab Rebellion,'" 194–196; Saleh Muhammad al-Amr, *The Hijaz under Ottoman Rule, 1869–1914: Ottoman Vali, the Sharif of Mecca, and the Growth of British Influence* (Riyadh: Riyad University Publications, 1978), 170.

8. William Ochsenwald, "The Jidda Massacre of 1858," *Middle Eastern Studies,* 13:3 (1977), 314–326, 315.

9. Roff, "Sanitation and Security," 145; al-Amr, *Hijaz under Ottoman Rule,* 169, 175–176; Ochsenwald, *Religion, Society, and the State in Arabia,* 96–97.

10. Al-Amr, *Hijaz under Ottoman Rule,* 144–145.

11. Low, "Empire and the Hajj," 273.

12. Dane Kennedy, *The Highly Civilized Man: Richard Burton and the Victorian World* (Cambridge, MA: Harvard University Press, 2005), 61.

13. Ochsenwald, *Religion, Society, and the State in Arabia,* 201; Miller, "Pilgrim's Progress," 98. Mrs. Hassan Ali, writing in 1832, was informed that pilgrims who left India from Bombay and Calcutta sailed on Arab ships that carried pilgrims to and from the Hijaz and also carried Arabian goods such as coffee, fruit, and drugs to India. Mrs. Hassan Ali, *Observations on the Mussulmauns of India* (1832; Oxford: Oxford University Press, 1917), 114.

14. The remainder of this paragraph is based on Miller, "Pilgrim's Progress," 189–228. See, however, the example of Sayyid Fadl Alawi, who tried to dent British commercial interests by attempting to influence Indian pilgrims not to use British ships in this period, detailed in Alavi, "'Fugitive Mullahs and Outlawed Fanatics,'" 1352–1353.

15. This paragraph is based on Miller, "Pilgrim's Progress," 198–228.

16. C. A. Bayly, *Birth of the Modern World*, 354–355; Low, "Empire and the Hajj," 270.

17. Roff, "Sanitation and Security," 143; Low, "Empire and the Hajj," 274.

18. Probably the first European observer of destitute pilgrims was Johann Lewis Burckhardt in 1814, pointed out in Low, "Empire and the Hajj," 274.

19. W. Crooke, introduction to Ali, *Observations on the Mussulmauns of India*, ix, xi–x.

20. Ibid., ix, xv–xvii; Ali, *Observations on the Mussulmauns of India*, 117.

21. Ali, *Observations on the Mussulmauns of India*, 118.

22. Ibid., 117–118.

23. Ibid., 114–115.

24. G. A. Herklots, translator's preface to Jaffur Shurreff, *Qanoon-e-islam, or the Customs of the Mussalmans of India* (London: Parbury, Allen and Co., 1832), v.

25. Shurreff, *Qanoon-e-islam*, 41.

26. One example that is representative is the Government of Bombay Circular, November 11, 1910, detailing various *suras* from the Qu'ran and hadiths, Foreign Department, General—B, 59–60, February 1911, NAI.

27. Shurreff, *Qanoon-e-islam*, 48.

28. Earlier pilgrimage accounts by Europeans include Carsten Niebuhr, *Travels through Arabia and Other Countries in the East* (Edinburgh: R. Morrison and Son, 1792); and Johann Lewis Burckhardt, *Travels in Arabia, Comprehending an Account of Those Territories in Hedjaz Which the Mohammedans Regard as Sacred* (London: Henry Colburn, 1829). The first English pilgrimage account was Joseph Pitts's *Narrative of the Captivity of Joseph Pitts*, first published in 1704.

29. Alexander Hamilton, *Sinai, the Hedjaz, and Soudan* (London: R. Bentley, 1857), 73.

30. Ibid., 186.

31. Ibid., 7–8.

32. Ibid., 229–230.

33. H. R. Palmer, Resident, Bornu, Nigeria, Report on a Journey from Maidugurai, Nigeria to Jeddah in Arabia, June 16, 1919, CO 879/119, TNA; C. A. Willis, Report on Slavery and the Pilgrimage, 1926, SAD Willis 212/2/3, Sudan Archive, University Library, Durham University (hereafter referred to as SAD); John Morley, *Colonial Postscript: Diary of a District Officer, 1935–56* (London: Radcliffe Press, 1992), 59–61; Reynolds, "'Stealing the Road.'" See also Hermann Karl Wilhelm Kumm, *From Hausaland to Egypt, through the Sudan* (London: Constable and Co., 1910), 262–265.

34. Hamilton, *Sinai, the Hedjaz, and Soudan*, 54–56.

35. Ibid., 73, 79.

36. The best recent study of Burton is Kennedy, *Civilized Man*. Kennedy's bibliography contains an exhaustive list of works about Burton. Low covers Burton and the Hajj in more detail in "Empire of the Hajj" and "Empire and the Hajj."

37. Richard Burton, *Personal Narrative of a Pilgrimage to Al-Madinah and Meccah* (London: Longmans and Co., 1855–1856), 2:185–186.

38. Kennedy, *Civilized Man*, 69–70, 79.

39. Burton, *Personal Narrative*, 2:161.

40. Ibid., 2:185–186. Hamilton, whom Burton perhaps copied, cited 1,500 Indians living in the Hijaz, a figure that included many wealthy merchants in Jidda, who dominated the port's trade. Hamilton, *Sinai, the Hedjaz, and Soudan*, 57.

41. Charles Cole to Arthur Malet, Chief Secretary to the Foreign Department, Government of Bombay, December 7, 1853, Foreign Department, Political—External Affairs—A, May 5, 1854, NAI.

42. H. L. Anderson, Secretary Government of Bombay to Secretary, Foreign Department, Government of India, April 17, 1854, Foreign Department, Political—External Affairs—A, May 5, 1854, NAI.

43. Secretary, Foreign Department, Government of India, to H. L. Anderson, Secretary Government of Bombay, May 5, 1854, Foreign Department, Political—External Affairs—A, May 5, 1854, NAI.

44. Thomas R. Metcalf, *Ideologies of the Raj* (Cambridge: Cambridge University Press, 1994), 36.

45. A particularly striking contrast can be found in the section "'A Monster of Our Own Creation,' 1918–1924" in Chapter 4.

46. Quoted in Rajat Kanta Ray, "Indian Society and British Supremacy," in P. J. Marshall (ed.), *The Oxford History of the British Empire*, vol. 2, *The Eighteenth Century* (Oxford: Oxford University Press, 1999), 508–529, 510. See also Robert Travers, *Ideology and Empire in Eighteenth-Century India: The British in Bengal, 1757–93* (Cambridge: Cambridge University Press, 2007). One by-product of this experience of governance was an appreciation by some administrators of Islamic culture and the taking of Indian women as wives and concubines; see Durba Ghosh, *Sex and the Family in Colonial India: The Making of Empire* (Cambridge: Cambridge University Press, 2006).

47. Hardy, *Muslims of British India*, 60, 62, 81.

48. See Kim Wagner, *The Great Fear of 1857* (Oxford: Peter Land, 2010); Biswamoy Pati (ed.), *The Great Rebellion of 1857* (London: Routledge, 2010); Biswamoy Pati (ed.), *The 1857 Rebellion* (Delhi: Oxford University Press, 2007); Clare Anderson, *The Indian Uprising of 1857–58: Prisons, Prisoners and Rebellion* (London: Anthem, 2007); Rosie Llewellyn-Jones, *The Great Uprising in India, 1857–58: Untold Stories, Indian and British* (Woodbridge: Boydell, 2007); Gautam Chakravarty, *The Indian Revolt and the British Imagination* (Cambridge: Cambridge University Press, 2005); Rajat Kanta Ray, "Race, Religion and Realm: The Political Theory of 'the Reigning Indian Crusade,' 1857," in M. Hasan and N. Gupta (eds.), *India's Colonial Encounter: Essays in Memory of Eric Stokes* (Delhi: Manohar, 1993), 133–182; Eric Stokes, *The Peasant Armed*, ed. C. A. Bayly (Oxford: Clarendon, 1986); Gautam Bhadra, "Four Rebels of 1857," in Ranajit Guha (ed.), *Subaltern Studies IV* (Delhi: Oxford University Press, 1985), 229–275; Rudrangshu Mukherjee, *Awadh in Revolt, 1857–58: A Study of Popular Resistance* (Delhi: Oxford University Press, 1984); and Thomas R. Metcalf, *Aftermath of Revolt: India, 1857–1870* (Princeton, NJ: Princeton University Press, 1964). Crispin Bates and Marina Carter, "Empire and Locality: A Global

Dimension to the 1857 Uprising," *Journal of Global History*, 5 (2010), 51–73, reflects recent historiographical trends in world history but does not mention Mecca as a destination for those who left India after the rebellion.

49. Biswamoy Pati, "Introduction: The Nature of 1857," in Pati, *1857 Rebellion*, xiii–xxi; Pati, *Great Rebellion of 1857;* Alex Padamsee, *Representations of Indian Muslims in British Colonial Discourse* (Basingstoke: Palgrave Macmillan, 2005), 50–53; Thomas Metcalf, *Aftermath of Revolt*, 55–56; Thomas Metcalf, *Ideologies of the Raj*, 139–140. See also Salahuddin Ahmad, *Mutiny, Revolution or Muslim Rebellion? British Public Reaction to the Indian Crisis of 1857* (Oxford: Oxford University Press, 2008).

50. Morrison, *Russian Rule in Samarkand*, 84.

51. Barbara Metcalf, "Introduction—A Historical Overview of Islam in South Asia," in Barbara Metcalf (ed.), *Islam in South Asia in Practice* (Princeton, NJ: Princeton University Press, 2009), 1–27, 22. See also William Dalrymple, *The Last Mughal: The Fall of a Dynasty; Delhi, 1857* (London: Bloomsbury, 2007).

52. Pati, *1857 Rebellion*, xxxviii; K. M. Ashraf, "Muslim Revivalists and the Revolt of 1857," excerpt reprinted in Pati, *1857 Rebellion*, 151–157.

53. Padamsee, *Representations of Indian Muslims*, 51.

54. Sayyid Miyan, *Asira'n-e-Malta* (Delhi: Jamiat Ulama-i-Hind, 2005), 12.

55. Thomas Metcalf, *Aftermath of Revolt*, 289, 291.

56. Maclean, *Pilgrimage and Power*, 111.

57. M. Harrison, *Public Health in British India*, 79, 118, 125. M. W. Daly, *Empire on the Nile: The Anglo-Egyptian Sudan, 1898–1934* (Cambridge: Cambridge University Press, 1986), 122, explains Britain's religious policy in Sudan.

58. A selection of scholarly works includes Gerald Maclean and Nabil Matar, *Britain and the Islamic World, 1558–1713* (Oxford: Oxford University Press, 2011); Shahin Kuli Khan Khattak, *Islam and the Victorians: Nineteenth-Century Perceptions of Muslim Practices and Beliefs* (London: I. B. Tauris, 2008); Diane Robinson-Dunn, *The Harem, Slavery and British Imperial Culture: Anglo-Muslim Relations in the Late Nineteenth Century* (Manchester: Manchester University Press, 2006); David Blanks (ed.), *Images of the Other: Europe and the Muslim World before 1700* (Cairo: American University in Cairo Press, 2006); Geoffrey Nash, *From Empire to Orient: Travellers to the Middle East, 1830–1926* (London: I. B. Tauris, 2005); Padamsee, *Representations of Indian Muslims;* Linda Colley, *Captives* (New York: Pantheon, 2002); Nabil Matar, *Islam in Britain, 1558–1685* (Cambridge: Cambridge University Press, 1999); Nabil Matar, *Turks, Moors, and Englishmen in the Age of Discovery* (New York: Columbia University Press, 1999); Alain Grosrichard, *The Sultan's Court: European Fantasies of the East* (London: Verso, 1998); Paul Fregosi, *Jihad in the West: Muslim Conquests from the 7th to the 21st Centuries* (Amherst, NY: Prometheus, 1998); Ahmad Gunny, *Images of Islam in Eighteenth-Century Writings* (London: Grey Seal, 1996); Jabal Muhammad Buaben, *Image of the Prophet Muhammad in the West: A Study of Muir, Margoliouth and Watt* (Leicester: Islamic Foundation, 1996); Avril A. Powell, *Muslims and Missionaries in Pre-mutiny India* (Richmond, VA: Curzon, 1993); Clinton Bennett, *Victorian Images of Islam* (London: Grey Seal, 1992); Albert Hourani, *Islam in European Thought* (Cambridge: Cambridge University

Press, 1991); W. Montgomery Watt, *Muslim-Christian Encounters: Perceptions and Misperceptions* (London: Routledge, 1991); John Kelsay and James Turner Johnson, *Just War and Jihad: Historical and Theoretical Perspectives on War and Peace in Western and Islamic Traditions* (New York: Greenwood, 1991); Philip C. Almond, *Heretic and Hero: Muhammad and the Victorians* (Wiesbaden: O. Harrassowitz, 1989); Rana Kabbani, *Europe's Myths of the Orient: Devise and Rule* (London: Macmillan, 1988); Maxime Rodinson, *Europe and the Mystique of Islam* (Seattle: University of Washington Press, 1987); Ann Thomson, *Barbary and Enlightenment: European Attitudes towards the Maghreb in the 18th Century* (Leiden: Brill, 1987); Emmanuel Sivan, *Interpretations of Islam: Past and Present* (Princeton, NJ: Princeton University Press, 1985); Kathryn Tidrick, *Heart-Beguiling Araby* (Cambridge: Cambridge University Press, 1981); Rudolph Peters, *Islam and Colonialism;* Edward W. Said, *Orientalism* (New York: Vintage, 1978); Byron Porter Smith, *Islam in English Literature* (Delmar, NY: Caravan, 1977); Samuel Claggett Chew, *The Crescent and the Rose: Islam and England during the Renaissance* (New York: Octagon, 1974); Daniel, *Islam, Europe and Empire;* R. W. Southern, *Western Views of Islam in the Middle Ages* (Cambridge, MA: Harvard University Press, 1962); and Norman Daniel, *Islam and the West: The Making of an Image* (Edinburgh: Edinburgh University Press, 1960).

59. W. W. Hunter, *The Indian Musalmans* (London: Trübner and Co., 1871), 1. Simultaneously, Hunter exhorted the government of India to take a less hostile attitude toward Islam, although this was based on a clear distinction between elite groups, such as landlords and *'ulama,* who could be allies, and the "masses." Ibid., 15–52. Hunter also stated that he was best acquainted with conditions among Muslims in East Bengal, but his use of interchangeable terms in the book meant that the impression he gave was of Indian Muslims as a whole. See also M. Mohar Ali, "Hunter's Indian Musulmans—A Re-examination of Its Background," *Journal of the Royal Asiatic Society,* 1 (1980), 30–51, who argues that the work was a development of decades of official thought rather than a novel thesis.

60. Thomas Metcalf, *Ideologies of the Raj,* 141–142. See also Qeyamuddin Ahmad, *The Wahabi Movement in India* (Calcutta: Firma K. L. Mukhopadhyay, 1994); and Benjamin D. Hopkins, "Sitana and Swat: Patterns of Revolt along the Frontier," in Benjamin D. Hopkins and Magnus Marsden, *Fragments of the Afghan Frontier* (London: C. Hurst and Co., 2012), 75–100.

61. Hopkins, "Sitana and Swat," 77, 81–82; Padamsee, *Representations of Indian Muslims,* 59.

62. Thomas Metcalf, *Ideologies of the Raj,* 143–144. Metcalf uses the example of British Indian Civil Service official Charles Lyall to illustrate this point. See also Hopkins, "Sitana and Swat," 82–83.

63. See F. Robinson, "The British Empire and the Muslim World."

64. See Katherine Watt, "T. W. Arnold and the British Re-evaluation of Islam," *Modern Asian Studies,* 36:1 (2002), 1–98; and Almond, *Heretic and Hero.*

65. T. W. Arnold, *The Preaching of Islam* (London: Constable and Co., 1896), 43; R. Bosworth-Smith, *Mohammed and Mohammedanism* (London: J. Murray, 1889), 108.

66. Arnold, *Preaching of Islam,* 5.

67. Daniel, *Islam, Europe and Empire*, 39. Some contemporaneous writings that reflected this reassessment are Arnold, *Preaching of Islam*, 292; W. H. T. Gardiner, "Notes on Present Day Movements in the Muslim World," *Moslem World*, 1 (1911), 74–77; and Bosworth-Smith, *Mohammed and Mohammedanism*, 218, 259.

68. Thomas Metcalf, *Ideologies of the Raj*, 116.

69. British Cholera Commissioners (Edward Goodeve and E. D. Dickson) to Lord Stanley, October 3, 1866, 2, PC 1/2672, TNA.

70. M. Harrison, *Public Health in British India*, 117.

71. British Cholera Commissioners (Edward Goodeve and E. D. Dickson) to Lord Stanley, October 3, 1866, 4–7, PC 1/2672, TNA.

72. Ibid.

73. Memorandum by Mr. Netten Radcliffe on Quarantine in the Red Sea, and on the Sanitary Regulation of the Pilgrimage to Mecca, June 1879, 52, PC 1/2674, TNA.

74. M. Harrison, *Public Health in British India*, 118, 130.

75. Although the measures were not uniformly resented; see Mishra, *Pilgrims, Politics and Pestilence*, 89.

76. Beg, *Pilgrimage to Mecca*, 48. Snouck Hurgronje thought that the whole quarantine enterprise was corrupt and exploitative and enriched local Ottoman officials. Christiaan Snouck Hurgronje, *Mekka in the Latter Part of the 19th Century: Daily Life, Customs and Learning, the Moslims of the East-Indian-Archipelago* (Leiden: Brill, 2007), 234. See also the report of Ottoman soldiers being sent into the Kamaran camp to make pilgrims pay quarantine fees, in Ata Mohamed, Vice-Consul Hodeida, Report on Kamaran Quarantine Station, October 3, 1891, FO 78/4406, TNA; "The Quarantine of Pilgrims—Protest by the Aga Khan," in *The Pioneer*, April 19, 1906, in Foreign Department, External—B, September 1907, No. 111–140, NAI; and Mishra's discussions of writings about quarantine in Urdu pilgrimage travelogues in Mishra, "Beyond the Bounds of Time?," 33, and Mishra, *Pilgrims, Politics and Pestilence*.

77. Roff, "Sanitation and Security," 153; Mishra, "Beyond the Bounds of Time?," 34.

78. Beg, *Pilgrimage to Mecca*, 70–71.

79. See Huber, *Channelling Mobilities;* Mishra, *Pilgrims, Politics and Pestilence;* Low, "Empire and the Hajj"; Low, "Empire of the Hajj"; M. Harrison, *Public Health in British India;* and Roff, "Sanitation and Security."

80. Tagliacozzo, *Longest Journey*, 177–200; Robert J. Blyth, *The Empire of the Raj: India, Eastern Africa and the Middle East, 1858–1947* (Basingstoke: Palgrave Macmillan, 2003), 66–70. See also Huber, *Channelling Mobilities.*

81. See references to these in Chapter 5.

82. Report on the Conclusion of the Hajj, March 29, 1869, FO 195/956, TNA.

83. Report on the Conclusion of the Hajj, March 18, 1870, FO 195/956, TNA.

84. Papers Laid before the Legislative Council by the Command of the Governor of the Straits Settlements, May 17, 1869, File 8371, CO 273/30, TNA.

85. Report on the Conclusion of the Hajj, March 11, 1871, FO 195/956, TNA.

86. Nawab Sikander Begum, *Narrative of a Pilgrimage to Mecca* (Calcutta: Thacker and Spink, 1870), 2.

87. Dale Eickelmann and James Piscatori (eds.), *Muslim Travellers: Migration, Pilgrimage and the Religious Imagination* (Berkeley: University of California Press, 1990), 6. Sikander Begum did not rebel in 1857, despite pressure from her mother and Bhopal's *'ulama*, because she believed that the revolt was led by the Marathas, Bhopal's former enemies. Her loyalty to the British resulted in her being granted the title of nawab, the return of territory previously lost to a neighboring state, and being awarded the GCSI (Grand Commander of the Order of the Star of India. Siobhan Lambert-Hurley, introduction to Nawab Sikander Begum, *A Princess's Pilgrimage: Sikander Begum's "A Pilgrimage to Mecca,"* ed. Siobhan Lambert-Hurley (Bloomington: Indiana University Press, 2008), xi–lxii, xix–xxi.

88. Barbara Metcalf, "The Pilgrimage Remembered: South Asian Accounts of the *Hajj*," in Eickelmann and Piscatori, *Muslim Travellers*, 85–107, 300–301.

89. See Salar Jung, *Pilgrimage to Mecca and the Near East;* Sultan Jahan Begum, *The Story of a Pilgrimage to the Hejaz* (Calcutta: Thacker and Spink, 1909); Beg, *Pilgrimage to Mecca;* Kalb 'Ali Khan, *Qindil-i Haram* (Rampur: Ra'is al-Matabi, 1873); Ahmed Hassan, *Pilgrimage to the Caaba and Charing Cross* (London: W. H. Allen and Co., 1871); and Barbara Metcalf, "Pilgrimage Remembered," 300.

90. Nawab Sikander Begum, *Princess's Pilgrimage*, 127–128; Barbara Metcalf, "Pilgrimage Remembered," 301.

91. Nawab Sikander Begum, *Princess's Pilgrimage*, 4–5, 8.

92. Ibid., 41, 44, 64–65.

93. Ibid., 29, 41, 44, 64–65, 71–72, 81, 84.

94. Lambert-Hurley, introduction to Sikander Begum, *Princess's Pilgrimage*, xi–lxii, li. Dale Eickelmann and James Piscatori have noted how the experience of Hajj heightens pilgrims' "consciousness of locality and difference." Eickelmann and Piscatori, *Muslim Travellers*, xii–xv; Carol Delaney, "The 'Hajj': Sacred and Secular," *American Ethnologist*, 17:3 (1990), 513–530, 520–521. See also Bose, *Hundred Horizons*, 231.

95. See Jahan Begum, *Story of a Pilgrimage to the Hejaz*, 9–10.

96. Roff, "Sanitation and Security," 147.

97. Capt. G. Beyts, Consul, Jeddah, to Earl of Derby, Secretary of State for Foreign Affairs, December 1, 1876, Foreign Department, General—A, 1877, No. 125–192, NAI.

98. Capt. G. Beyts, Consul, Jeddah, to Brig. Gen. J. W. Schneider, Political Resident, Aden, May 27, 1875, Foreign Department, General—A, 1877, No. 125–192, NAI.

99. Capt. G. Beyts, Consul, Jeddah, to Earl of Derby, Secretary of State for Foreign Affairs, December 1, 1876; Brig. Gen. J. W. Schneider, Political Resident, Aden, to Capt. G. Beyts, Consul, Jeddah, May 15, 1875, Foreign Department, General—A, 1877, No. 125–192, NAI.

100. Capt. G. Beyts, Consul, Jeddah, to Brig. Gen. J. W. Schneider, Political Resident, Aden, May 27, 1875; Secretary of State for India to Government of India, July 8, 1875, Foreign Department, General—A, 1877, No. 125–192, NAI.

101. Capt. G. Beyts, Consul, Jeddah, to Brig. Gen. J. W. Schneider, Political Resident, Aden, May 27, 1875, Foreign Department, General—A, 1877, No. 125–192, NAI.

102. B. W. Colvin, Secretary to Government, North Western Provinces to Secretary to the Government of India, Home Department, July 26, 1876; Lindsay Neill, Assistant Secretary to Chief Commissioner, Central Provinces to Secretary to the Government of India, Home Department, April 5, 1876; E. J. Sinkinson, Junior Secretary to Chief Commissioner, British Burmah to Secretary to the Government of India, Home Department, December 17, 1875, Foreign Department, General—A, 1877, No. 125–192, NAI.

103. Sir Julian Pauncefote, Under-Secretary of State for Foreign Affairs to Sir Louis Mallet, Under-Secretary of State for India, January 1, 1877, Foreign Department, General—A, 1877, No. 125–192, NAI.

104. Sir Louis Mallet, Under-Secretary of State for India, to Lord Tenterden, Under-Secretary of State for Foreign Affairs, February 20, 1877, Foreign Department, General—A, 1877, No. 125–192, NAI.

105. Secretary of State for India to Government of India, January 25, 1877, Foreign Department, General—A, 1877, No. 125–192, NAI.

106. Government of India to Secretary of State for India, July 2, 1877, Foreign Department, General—A, 1877, No. 125–192, NAI. On Indian Muslim relations with the Ottomans in this period, see Azmi Özcan, *Pan-Islamism: Indian Muslims, the Ottomans and Britain, 1877–1924* (Leiden: Brill, 1997).

107. Hardy, *Muslims of British India*, 118–119, 125; Mishra, *Pilgrims, Politics and Pestilence*, 23.

108. C. A. Bayly, *Empire and Information: Intelligence Gathering and Social Communication in India, 1780–1870* (Cambridge: Cambridge University Press, 1996), 339.

109. Mishra, *Pilgrims, Politics and Pestilence*, 20.

110. Sandhya Polu, *Infectious Disease in India, 1892–1940* (Basingstoke: Palgrave Macmillan, 2012), 21; Mishra, *Pilgrims, Politics and Pestilence*, 20–24.

111. W. Hudleston, Chief Secretary to the Government of Fort St. George, to Secretary to the Government of India, Home Department, February 28, 1876; W. Logan, Acting Collector, Malabar, to W. Hudleston, Chief Secretary to the Government of Fort St. George, February 7, 1876, Foreign Department, General—A, 1877, No. 125–192, NAI. On the Muslim Mappilla rebellions, see Conrad Wood, *The Moplah Rebellion and Its Genesis* (Delhi: People's Publishing House, 1987); Stephen F. Dale, *Islamic Society on the South Asian Frontier: The Mappilas of Malabar, 1498–1922* (Oxford: Clarendon, 1980); and Sukhbir Choudhary, *Moplah Uprising, 1921–23* (Delhi: Agam Prakashan, 1977).

112. E. W. Ravenscroft, Chief Secretary to the Government of Bombay to Secretary to the Government of India, Home Department, March 1, 1877; L. Griffin, Secretary to the Government of the Punjab, to Secretary to the Gov-

ernment of India, Home Department, March 9, 1876; L. Griffin, Secretary to the Government of the Punjab, to Secretary to the Government of India, Home Department, March 9, 1876, Foreign Department, General—A, 1877, No. 125–192, NAI.

113. Major A. Murray, Junior Secretary to Chief Commissioner, Oudh to Secretary to the Government of India, Home Department, February 12, 1876, Foreign Department, General—A, 1877, No. 125–192, NAI.

114. R. L. Mangles, Secretary to the Government of Bengal to Secretary to Government of India, Home Department, December 6, 1876, Foreign Department, General—A, 1877, No. 125–192, NAI; Farzana Shaikh, *Community and Consensus in Islam* (Cambridge: Cambridge University Press, 1989), 86.

115. V. T. Taylor, Magistrate of Bhaugulpoor to Commissioner of Bhaugulpoor Division, January 13, 1876, Foreign Department, General—A, 1877, No. 125–192, NAI.

116. Rafiuddin Ahmed, *The Bengal Muslims, 1871–1906: A Quest for Identity* (Delhi: Oxford University Press, 1981), 161.

117. Moulvie Abdool Luteef, Khan Bahadoor, Deputy Magistrate of 24 Pergunnahs, to R. H. Wilson, Magistrate, 24 Pergunnahs, February 14, 1876, Foreign Department, General—A, 1877, No. 125–192, NAI. Latif tried to persuade Bengali *'ulama* such as Maulvi Karamat Ali to issue a fatwa in support of British rule. Shaikh, *Community and Consensus in Islam*, 85–86.

118. Moulvie Abdool Luteef, Khan Bahadoor, Deputy Magistrate of 24 Pergunnahs, to R. H. Wilson, Magistrate, 24 Pergunnahs, February 14, 1876, Foreign Department, General—A, 1877, No. 125–192, NAI.

119. Moulvie Abdool Luteef, Khan Bahadur, Secretary to the Mahomedan Literary Society of Calcutta to Under-Secretary to the Government of Bengal, Political Department, August 5, 1876; R. H. Wilson, Magistrate, 24 Pergunnahs to C. T. Buckland, Commissioner of Presidency Division, February 22, 1876, Foreign Department, General—A, 1877, No. 125–192, NAI.

120. Moulvie Syed Obedoollah Khan, Deputy Magistrate of Magoorah to Magistrate of Jessore, November 22, 1876, Foreign Department, General—A, 1877, No. 125–192, NAI.

121. Meer Mahomed Ali to Under-Secretary to the Government of Bengal, Political Department, September 15, 1876, Foreign Department, General—A, 1877, No. 125–192, NAI.

122. H. A. Cockerell, Commissioner of Burdwan Division, to Secretary to the Government of Bengal, April 22, 1876, Foreign Department, General—A, 1877, No. 125–192, NAI.

123. Syed Moazzum Hosein, Judge of Court of Small Causes, to Under-Secretary to the Government of Bengal, Judicial Department, September 15, 1876, Foreign Department, General—A, 1877, No. 125–192, NAI.

124. Syed Ameer Ali to Under-Secretary of the Government of Bengal, Political Department, October 1, 1876, Foreign Department, General—A, 1877, No. 125–192, NAI.

125. See the section "The Wider Geography of Religious Pilgrimage" in Chapter 1.

126. Hassan, *Pilgrimage to the Caaba*, 119–120, quoted in Syed Ameer Ali to Under-Secretary of the Government of Bengal, Political Department, October 1, 1876, Foreign Department, General—A, 1877, No. 125–192, NAI. This type of account was similar to those describing the journeys of Indian indentured laborers in this period.

127. Syed Ameer Ali to Under-Secretary of the Government of Bengal, Political Department, October 1, 1876, Foreign Department, General—A, 1877, No. 125–192, NAI.

128. Syed Mahomed Aboo Saleb, Zemindar of Gaya, to Under-Secretary of the Government of Bengal, Political Department, November 4, 1876, Foreign Department, General—A, 1877, No. 125–192, NAI.

129. Moulvi Hamid Bukht Mozumdar, Deputy Collector, Sylhet to Deputy Commissioner of Sylhet, November 25, 1876, Foreign Department, General—A, 1877, No. 125–192, NAI.

130. Singha, "Passport, Ticket and India-Rubber Stamp," 71.

131. A further example is the extensive consultation exercise across India regarding the benefits of pilgrim guides being British subjects, whether British subjects should register at the Jidda consulate, and the utility of pilgrim passports and return tickets. The responses fill forty closely typed pages, many from Muslims who had performed the Hajj. The end result was another government of India resolution that was an extended note of advice to pilgrims; see files in FO 78/4778, TNA; and Low, "Empire and the Hajj," 284.

132. Foreign Office to Under-Secretary of State for India, September 24, 1877, General Department, 1878, Vol. 51, File 360, MSA.

133. Secretary, Government of India, to Secretary, Government of Bombay, March 28, 1878; Government of Bombay to Government of India, Home Department, April 23, 1878, General Department, 1878, Vol. 51, File 360, MSA.

134. Secretary, Government of Bombay, to Frank Souter, Commissioner of Police, Bombay, September 17, 1881, General Department, 1881, Vol. 79, File 12, MSA.

135. Singha, "Passport, Ticket and India-Rubber Stamp," 55; M. Harrison, *Public Health in British India*, 121.

136. IO to FO, March 6, 1884, FO 78/4093, TNA.

137. J. Vredenbregt, "The Haddj: Some of Its Features and Functions in Indonesia," *Bijdragen tot de Taal- Land- en Volkenkunde*, 118:1 (1962), 91–154, 118. See also Sunil S. Amrith, *Migration and Diaspora in Modern Asia* (Cambridge: Cambridge University Press, 2011), 67. Amrith analyzes the Hajj and Muslim migration more generally on 65–72. Taking out loans to finance one's pilgrimage was far from exceptional, given the cost of the journey relative to most pilgrims' incomes. For example, Indonesian pilgrims would regularly borrow the necessary amount before they left for the Hijaz and pledge their property as security; Vredenbregt, "Haddj," 135.

138. Vredenbregt, "Haddj," 126–129; Laffan, *Islamic Nationhood*, 47; Tagliacozzo, *Longest Journey*, 47, 73, 77. On the role of Hadhrami merchants and scholars in the Indian Ocean more generally, see Ulrike Freitag, *Indian Ocean Migrants and State Formation in Hadhramaut* (Leiden: Brill, 2003).

139. Vredenbregt, "Haddj," 126–129; Laffan, *Islamic Nationhood*, 47; Tagliacozzo, *Longest Journey*, 47, 73, 77; Freitag, *Indian Ocean Migrants*.

140. See files in FO 78/4778, TNA; and Vredenbregt, "Haddj," 130.

141. See Descendants of Zohrab of the Manuchariants, http://zohrabfamily.atwebpages.com/jamesenz.html. This appears to be a family-tree website that contains extensive archival references.

142. Zohrab to Earl Granville, FO, September 10, 1880, General Department, 1881, Vol. 79, File 12, MSA.

143. Ibid.

144. W. S. Blunt, *The Future of Islam* (London: Kegan Paul, 1882), 3–7.

145. Ibid., 20.

146. Ibid., 20, 110.

147. Ibid., 110–112.

148. Alavi, "'Fugitive Mullahs and Outlawed Fanatics,'" 1351.

149. Low, "Empire of the Hajj," 65–71.

150. See Norman Sherry, *Conrad's Eastern World* (Cambridge: Cambridge University Press, 1966). Joseph Conrad, *Lord Jim* (London: W. Blackwood and Sons, 1900), 7.

151. Arthur Conan Doyle, *The Sign of Four* (London: Penguin, 2001), 162; first published in 1890.

152. W. Fraser Rae, *The Business of Travel: A Fifty Years' Record of Progress* (London: T. Cook and Son, 1891), 208–219, quoted in Low, "Empire of the Hajj," 69; On *Lord Jim* as a historical text, see Tagliacozzo, *Longest Journey*, 109–128. Question by Sir George Campbell MP in House of Commons, August 24, 1880, Straits Settlements Correspondence, 1880, CO 273/106, TNA.

153. *Times of India*, October 31, 1885, 5. On secondhand steamships, see Green, *Bombay Islam*, 113. There are numerous subsequent articles and letters in a wide range of newspapers regarding pilgrim ships throughout the period. See, for example, W. S. Blunt, "Wreck of a Pilgrim Ship in the Red Sea," a letter to the editor, in which Blunt's telling opening sentence is "Mahomedan interests are so largely English interests that I feel sure *The Times* will help to give publicity to the circumstances of the recent wreck of the pilgrim ship *Chebine* in the Red Sea," *The Times*, April 14, 1900, 5; and "Pilgrim Ship on Fire on Red Sea: Several Lives Feared Lost," *The Times*, May 23, 1930, 15.

154. John Nugent, Secretary, Government of Bombay to Mackenzie, Secretary, Government of India, January 21, 1886, General Department, 1885, Vol. 124, File 138, MSA. John Mason Cook called it a "highly coloured statement." *The Mecca Pilgrimage*, Appendix, "Museum" item 163 F, Thomas Cook Archives, Peterborough (hereafter referred to as TCA).

155. Secretary, Government of India to Agent to Thomas Cook in India, December 10, 1884, FO 78/4093, TNA.

156. *The Mecca Pilgrimage*, 4–5, "Museum" item 163 F, TCA; Low, "Empire of the Hajj," 65–71; M. Harrison, *Public Health in British India*, 132–133.

157. Low, "Empire of the Hajj," 69. See also Oishi, "Friction and Rivalry," 165–168.

158. *The Mecca Pilgrimage*, Appendix, Government of India Resolution 1886, "Museum" item 163 F, TCA; *The Mecca Pilgrimage*, 4–5, "Museum" item 163 F, TCA.

159. *The Mecca Pilgrimage*, 12, "Museum" item 163 F, TCA; also Low, "Empire of the Hajj," 69, quoting Rae, *Business of Travel*, 211–212. See also *Papers relating to the arrangements made with Messrs. Cook & Son for the conduct of the pilgrim traffic to and from the Red Sea during the years 1884–95*, Series: Selections from the Records of the Government of India, Home Department, No. 330 (Calcutta, 1896), IND Ind R 1/330, Bodleian Library, Oxford University.

160. "Report of Information Obtained in Jeddah Regarding the Mecca Pilgrimage," October 1886, Folio 161 D, TCA.

161. Ibid.

162. *The Mecca Pilgrimage*, 9, 12, "Museum" item 163 F, TCA; "The Mecca Pilgrimage," cutting from *Civil and Military Gazette*, undated, TCA.

163. Roff, "Sanitation and Security," 151.

164. *Government of India: Report of Arrangements Carried Out by Thomas Cook and Sons in Connection with the Movement of Pilgrims for the Hadj of 1888*, and subsequent reports for 1889, 1890, 1891, 1892, 1893, TCA; Singha, "Passport, Ticket and India-Rubber Stamp," 52, 57.

165. Extract from Vernacular Newspapers, July 31, 1888, General Department, 1885, Vol. 124, File 138, MSA.

166. Protector of Pilgrims to Commissioner of Police, September 4, 1888, General Department, 1885, Vol. 124, File 138, MSA.

167. Memo by Commissioner of Police with Report on Allegations in Extract from *Akbar-i-Churiar*, October 18, 1888, General Department 1885, Vol. 124, File 138, MSA.

168. Secretary, Political Department, Government of India to Agent for Thomas Cook in India, December 10, 1884, General Department, 1885, Vol. 124, File 82, MSA.

169. Extract of Proceedings of the Government of India, Home Department, Sanitary, January 4, 1886, Foreign Department, September 1886, No. 197–199, NAI.

170. M. Harrison, *Public Health in British India*, 130.

171. *Government of India: Report of Arrangements Carried out by Thomas Cook and Sons in Connection with the Movement of Pilgrims for the Hadj of 1888*, TCA.

172. Government of India Resolution, January 11, 1895, TCA; M. Harrison, *Public Health in British India*, 133.

173. *The Mecca Pilgrimage*, 12, "Museum" item 163 F, TCA.

174. See Tagliacozzo, *Longest Journey*, 177–200, 299–300.

175. Medico-Sanitary Report on the Pilgrimage to Mecca by Dr. Abdur Razzack, Indian Medical Service, Appendix L, 99–103, in Memorandum by Mr. Netten Radcliffe on Quarantine in the Red Sea, and on the Sanitary Regulation of the Pilgrimage to Mecca, June 1879, 52, PC 1/2674, TNA.

176. Roff, "Sanitation and Security," 147–148; Low, "Empire and the Hajj," 283.

177. Low, "Empire and the Hajj," 281.

178. Zohrab to Earl Granville, FO, September 10, 1880, General Department, 1881, Vol. 79, File 12, MSA. Beyond officialdom, Yussuf Kudzi, interpreter at the British consulate, served as the vital link connecting Wilfrid Scawen Blunt with Muslim notables in Jidda who hailed from Mecca, Najd, Morocco, Hyderabad, and Somalia during Blunt's fact-finding trip that resulted in his book *The Future of Islam* in 1882. W. S. Blunt, *Secret History of the English Occupation of Egypt: Being a Personal Narrative of Events* (London: Fisher Unwin, 1907), 81; and W. S. Blunt, *Diaries*, pt. 1, *1888–1900* (London: Martin Secker, 1920), 353, 356–358, 360–363.

179. Ulrike Freitag, "Helpless Representatives of the Great Powers? Western Consuls in Jeddah, 1830s to 1914," *Journal of Imperial and Commonwealth History*, 40:3 (2012), 357–381, 359, 362, 365, 374–375.

180. Government of India to Secretary of State for India, June 15, 1880, Foreign Department, Secret, June 1881, No. 425–426, NAI; Low, "Empire and the Hajj," 281.

181. Dr. Abdur Razzack, Assistant Surgeon and Vice-Consul, Jeddah, Report on the "Haj," 1882, FO 881/4762, TNA.

182. Consul Jago to Secretary to the Government of India, Foreign Department, January 21, 1885, 1, FO 881/5113, TNA, in *RoH*, 3:585.

183. Dr. Abdur Razzack, Report on the 1884 Hajj, Inclosure 2, January 10, 1885, within Consul Jago to Secretary to the Government of India, Foreign Department, January 21, 1885, FO 881/5113, TNA, in *RoH*, 3:588.

184. Razzack to FO, August 21, 1894, FO 78/460/1, TNA.

185. Low, "Empire and the Hajj," 283.

186. Dr. Abdur Razzack, Report on the 1885 Hajj, February 27, 1886, FO 78/4094, TNA, in *RoH*, 3:663–670.

187. See Low, "Empire and the Hajj"; Mishra, *Pilgrims, Politics and Pestilence;* M. Harrison, *Public Health in British India;* and Roff, "Sanitation and Security."

188. Dr. Abdur Razzack, Report on the 1885 Hajj, February 27, 1886, FO 78/4094, TNA, in *RoH*, 3:675.

189. Dr. Abdur Razzack to Secretary, Governor of the Straits Settlements, August 17, 1893, FO 78/4533, TNA.

190. This point relates to anthropologist Victor Turner's important concept regarding pilgrimages in general, *communitas*, defined as "a spontaneously or normatively generated relationship between levelled and equal, total and individuated human beings, stripped of structural attributes." Turner, *Dramas, Fields, and Metaphors: Symbolic Action in Human Society* (Ithaca, NY: Cornell University Press, 1974), 202. Equality generated a heightened sense of community and solidarity among pilgrims, alongside an increased piety, derived through the shared experience of participation in the pilgrimage, a process that transcended social differences. See Victor Turner, "The Center Out There: Pilgrim's Goal," *History of Religions*, 12:3 (1973), 191–230; Victor Turner, "Pilgrimage and *Communitas*," *Studia Missionalia*, 23 (1974), 305–327; and Victor Turner and Edith Turner, *Image and Pilgrimage in Christian Culture: Anthropological Perspectives* (New York: Columbia University Press, 1978). Turner's

theories have been criticized by historians, who through individual studies of pilgrimages have not found his theories applicable. See, for example, Pearson, *Pious Passengers;* Bianchi, *Guests of God;* and Alan E. Morinis, *Pilgrimage in the Hindu Tradition* (Delhi: Oxford University Press, 1984). William Roff has constructed a theoretical framework that specifically focuses on the Hajj and Mecca as a sacred space, using Islamic texts, and argues that the collective rituals that make up the Hajj, such as the *tawaf,* alongside evidence from pilgrimage accounts, clearly show "the emotional power of absorption in acts of worship in undifferentiated association with all Muslims," a fact that lends credence to the idea of *communitas.* See William Roff, "Pilgrimage and the History of Religions: Theoretical Approaches to the Hajj," in Martin, *Approaches to Islam in Religious Studies,* 78–86. Although Turner's theories and concepts have their limitations, Roff has shown, through specific examples during the pilgrim's journey and the rituals performed in Mecca, how they have some applicability to the Hajj. Nevertheless, the credibility of the *communitas* concept is undermined by the fact that although all pilgrims are clad in the *ihram,* they remain divided by language, nationality, race, and socioeconomic status.

191. Low, "Empire and the Hajj," 274.

192. Dr. Abdur Razzack, Report on the 1886 Hajj, undated, FO 195/1583, TNA, in *RoH,* 3:747–748.

193. Dr. Abdur Razzack, Report on the 1887 Hajj, February 15, 1888, FO 195/1610, TNA, in *RoH,* 3:761, 783–785.

194. See A. M. Wainwright, *"The Better Class" of Indians: Social Rank, Imperial Identity and South Asians in Britain, 1858–1914* (Manchester: Manchester University Press, 2008), 69–95, 124–156.

195. Chief Secretary Government of Bengal to Secretary, Government of India, Home Department, January 12, 1887, FO 78/4094, TNA.

196. Dr. Abdur Razzack, Report on the 1887 Hajj, February 15, 1888, FO 195/1610, TNA, in *RoH,* 3:784–785. On the Ottoman example, see also files in FO 78/4532, TNA.

197. MacDonnell, Secretary to Home Department, Government of India to Honourable Maulvi Sir Syed Ahmad Khan Bahadur KCSI LLD, February 8, 1890, Foreign Department, External—A, August 1890, No. 149–152, NAI.

198. Sir Syed Ahmad Khan to Government of India, March 9, 1890, Foreign Department, External—A, August 1890, No. 149–152, NAI.

199. Note by W.J.S., March 17, 1890, Foreign Department, External—A, August 1890, No. 149–152, NAI.

200. Note by B.S., March 17, 1890, Foreign Department, External—A, August 1890, No. 149–152, NAI.

201. Note by F.P.H., March 22, 1890, Foreign Department, External—A, August 1890, No. 149–152, NAI.

202. C. J. Lyall, Secretary, Home Department, Government of India to Sir Syed Ahmad Khan, April 9, 1890; H. S. Barnes, Under-Secretary, Foreign Department to Consul Jeddah, undated, Foreign Department, External—A, August 1890, 149–152, NAI.

203. W. S. Richards, Consul Jedda, to Secretary, Foreign Department, Government of India, June 23, 1895, Foreign Department, Secret—E, September 1895, No. 44–64, NAI.

204. Foreign Office to Viceroy of India, June 6, 1895, Foreign Department, Secret—E, September 1895, No. 44–64, NAI. Ochsenwald, "Jidda Massacre," examines a similar episode involving the murder of the British vice-consul and an actual British bombardment of Jidda in June 1858.

205. Bazlul Karim, Deputy Magistrate to Secretary, Government of Bengal, June 23, 1895, Foreign Department, Secret—E, September 1895, No. 44–64, NAI. See also the file The Murder of Dr. Abdur Razzack, FO 78/4789, TNA.

206. W. S. Richards, Consul Jedda, to Secretary, Foreign Department, Government of India, June 17, 1895, Foreign Department, Secret—E, September 1895, No. 44–64, NAI.

207. Low, "Empire and the Hajj," 283.

208. His colleague, Yusuf Kudzi, described as "clever, intelligent, versatile," was reprimanded for trying to establish a monopoly company to sell steamship tickets to Indian pilgrims in Mecca; see files in FO 78/4263, TNA.

209. Jeddah Vice-Consul Dr. Mohamed Hussein, Report on the Mecca Pilgrimage 1896–7, 1–2, Foreign Department, External—A, March 1898, No. 206–215, NAI.

210. Journal entry, March 4, 1891, Buckingham Palace, London, *Queen Victoria's Journals* (Princess Beatrice's copies), vol. 93, p. 71, http://www.queenvictoriasjournals.org/; John Burman, *Britain's Relations with the Ottoman Empire during the Embassy of Sir Nicholas O'Conor to the Porte* (Istanbul: Isis, 2010), 178.

211. George Devey, Consul Jeddah, to Ambassador, Constantinople, June 25, 1897, FO 195/1987, TNA.

212. Governor of the Straits Settlements to Colonial Office, September 29, 1897, File 22924, CO 273/227, TNA. Notably, the Ottoman government and the sharif of Mecca provided little in the way of charity to poor pilgrims; the majority of Ottoman expenditure in the Hijaz predictably went to the military. Ochsenwald, *Religion, Society, and the State in Arabia*, 173–174.

213. Untitled and undated, Foreign Department, Internal—A, April 1897, No. 140–175, NAI. See also files in FO 78/4981, TNA; and Mishra, "Beyond the Bounds of Time?," 37.

214. Özcan, *Pan-Islamism*, 90; Low, "Empire and the Hajj," 281. Austen Henry Layard, British ambassador at Istanbul, propagated similar views.

215. Quoted in William R. Roff, "The Conduct of the Hajj from Malaya, and the First Malay Pilgrimage Officer," *Sari Terbitan Tak Berkala*, no. 1, Occasional Papers no. 1, Institute for Malay Language, Literature and Culture, Kuala Lumpur, 1975, 81–111, 82; and in Low, "Empire and the Hajj," 277.

216. Green, *Bombay Islam*, 105–106. See also Hopkins, "Sitana and Swat," 75–100.

217. See Low, "Empire and the Hajj"; Low, "Empire of the Hajj"; Oishi, "Friction and Rivalry"; Roff, "Sanitation and Security"; and Tagliacozzo, *Longest Journey*, 177–200. On 177–178, Tagliacozzo states that European powers

were ultimately successful in their attempts to surveil and control the Hajj, and that control of the Hajj was seen as fundamental to ensuring the bedrock of European rule. However, as I argue, this control was not total and was repeatedly circumvented and subverted by Hajjis.

218. I am grateful to Professor Ulrike Freitag for this point.

219. Tagliacozzo, *Longest Journey*, 194–195.

220. Laffan, *Islamic Nationhood*, 54.

221. Alavi, "'Fugitive Mullahs and Outlawed Fanatics,'" 1381–1382.

222. Özcan, *Pan-Islamism*, 93.

223. Hopkins, "Sitana and Swat," 77, 84; Morrison, *Russian Rule in Samarkand*, 85–86.

224. This argument is similar to Bayly's in relation to pilgrimages in India. C. A. Bayly, *Empire and Information*, 147–148.

225. "Pan-Islamism," entry in Oxford Islamic Studies Online, from *Oxford Dictionary of Islam*, www.oxfordislamicstudies.com.

226. Cemil Aydin, *The Politics of Anti-Westernism in Asia: Visions of World Order in Pan-Islamic and Pan-Asian Thought* (New York: Columbia University Press, 2007), 10.

227. Ibid., 60.

228. Özcan, *Pan-Islamism*, 53–54; Low, "Empire and the Hajj," 279.

229. For an overview of this phenomenon, see Jacob Landau, *The Politics of Pan-Islam: Ideology and Organization* (Oxford: Clarendon, 1990); and see also Özcan, *Pan-Islamism*. Note also Seema Alavi's point that some scholars have argued that pan-Islamism was centered in Cairo and Ayesha Jalal's argument that "Muslim universalisms" is a more appropriate term. See Jalal, *Partisans of Allah: Jihad in South Asia* (Cambridge, MA: Harvard University Press, 2008); and Alavi, "'Fugitive Mullahs and Outlawed Fanatics,'" 1354. A more appropriate term might be "Islamic union" from the Arabic *Ittihad Islamiyya*.

230. Özcan, *Pan-Islamism*, 130.

231. The Pan-Islamic Movement, FO 373/5/6, TNA. See also Louis Massignon, "What Moslems Expect: An Introductory Study of Moslem Demands," *Moslem World*, 12 (1922), 7–24, 8–10; and Aydin, *Politics of Anti-Westernism in Asia*, 61.

232. Zohrab, Consul Jedda, to Marquis of Salisbury, March 12, 1879, HD 3/55, TNA.

233. Zohrab, Consul Jedda, to Marquis of Salisbury, January 9, 1880, HD 3/55, TNA.

234. In 1881, the Netherlands foreign minister reported that the Dutch consul in Istanbul had witnessed a conversation between two men from Mecca who discussed a plan to incite Muslims in India and the Dutch East Indies to rebellion. The Dutch proposed combining with Britain to undertake "some sort of political surveillance over pilgrims going from their [the Dutch and British] possessions to Mecca, under the cover of the necessity of adopting sanitary precautions in pilgrim ships." Sir Julian Pauncefote, Under-Secretary of State for Foreign Affairs to Sir Louis Mallet, Under-Secretary of State for India, January 6, 1881, enclosing copy of letter from Netherlands Foreign Minister to

Earl Granville, Foreign Department, Secret, March 1881, No. 156–160, NAI. On the links between the Hajj and the Aceh War, see Von der Mehden, *Two Worlds of Islam*, 3–8.

235. Under-Secretary of State for India to Under-Secretary of State for Foreign Affairs, January 28, 1881, Foreign Department, Secret, March 1881, No. 156–160, NAI; see also Roff, "Sanitation and Security."

236. Note by H.M.D., March 2, 1881, Foreign Department, Secret, March 1881, No. 156–160, NAI.

237. Gabeba Baderoon, "'The Seas inside Us': Narrating Self, Gender, Place and History in South African Memories of the Hajj," *Social Dynamics: A Journal of African Studies*, 38:2 (2012), 237–252, 239–240; Mogamat Hoosain Ebrahim, "The Transformation in the Management and Traditions of Hajj at the Cape" (PhD dissertation, University of Kwazulu-Natal, 2007), 20–30. See also Robert C.-H. Shell, "Islam in Southern Africa, 1652–1998," in Nehemia Levtzion and Randal L. Pouwels (eds.), *History of Islam in Africa* (Athens: Ohio University Press, 2000), 327–348; Green, *Bombay Islam;* and Eric Rosenthal and Hedley Churchward, *From Drury Lane to Mecca—Being an Account of the Strange Life and Adventures of Hedley Churchward* (London: Sampson Low and Co., 1931).

238. Pameilots to CO, April 20, 1877, quoted in Ebrahim, "Transformation," 30.

239. Ebrahim, "Transformation," 31.

240. Zohrab, Report on the Necessity of a Consular Establishment in the Red Sea, June 1, 1881, FO 195/1375, TNA, quoted in al-Amr, *Hijaz under Ottoman Rule*, 171.

241. Low, "Empire and the Hajj," 283–284; Roff, "Sanitation and Security," 154.

242. Dr. Abdur Razzack to Secretary, Government of India, Foreign Department, October 12, 1885, Foreign Department, Secret—Internal, August 1886, Nos. 22–28, NAI. See also Foreign Department—Secret—Internal, October 1887, No. 136–143, NAI; Durand, Secretary, Foreign Department, India to Jago, Consul, Jedda, July 27, 1888, FO 685/2, TNA; Secretary to N.W.P., India to Secretary Government of India, Foreign Department, September 3, 1882, FO 685/2, TNA. See Roff, "Sanitation and Security"; Alavi, "'Fugitive Mullahs and Outlawed Fanatics,'" 1340, 1360–1366; and Mishra, "Beyond the Bounds of Time?," 125–126.

243. Mr. Block, Memo, May 11, 1896, Constantinople; R.W.S., Note, June 30, 1896, Foreign Department, Secret—E, January 1897, No. 138–142, NAI. See also Roff, "Sanitation and Security," 156.

244. Under-Secretary of State for India to Under-Secretary of State for Foreign Office, September 24, 1896, Foreign Department, Secret—E, January 1897, No. 138–142, NAI. An idea from 1888 for the vice-consul to supply quarterly reports on seditious papers, Wahhabi propaganda, and the caliphate appears not to have been followed up. Roff, "Conduct of the Hajj from Malaya," 85.

245. G. V. Bosanquet, Note, July 2, 1896, referring to Colonel Tweedie, No. 89, Foreign Department, Secret, March 1881, No. 45–90, in Foreign Department, Secret—E, January 1897, No. 138–142, NAI.

246. C. S. Bayley, Note, July 18, 1896, Foreign Department, Secret—E, January 1897, No. 138–142, NAI. Apparently, Dr. Razzack was paid R 1,250 of secret-service money; Foreign Department, Secret—Internal, October 1889, No. 39–42, NAI.

247. H. S. Barnes, Note, August 13, 1896, Foreign Department, Secret—E, January 1897, No. 138–142, NAI.

248. C. S. Bayley, Note, September 28, 1896, Foreign Department, External—A, October 1896, No. 210–213, NAI.

249. This can be contrasted with the earlier nineteenth century, with the Fara'izi movement in Bengal, for example, and the case of the Padri movement in Sumatra, in the Netherlands East Indies.

250. Snouck Hurgronje, *Mekka*, 258.

251. Bianchi, *Guests of God*, 290–291, 310; Roff, "Sanitation and Security," 156; Low, "Empire and the Hajj," 285–286.

CHAPTER 3 *Pilgrimage in the Edwardian Era*

1. Ralph A. Austen, *Trans-Saharan Africa in World History* (New York: Oxford University Press, 2010), 78–97.

2. Birks, *Across the Savannas to Mecca*, 22. See also Reynolds, "'Stealing the Road.'"

3. John Iliffe, *Africans: The History of a Continent* (Cambridge: Cambridge University Press, 1995), 187, 196.

4. Muhammad Khalid Masud, "The Obligation to Migrate: The Doctrine of *Hijra* in Islamic Law," in Eickelmann and Piscatori, *Muslim Travellers*, 29–49, 38–39; Gordon Lethem, "Report: Journey to Sudan, Jeddah and Cairo," 1925, 64–65, Lethem, Box 8/1, Mss.Brit.Emp.s.276, Rhodes House Library, Oxford University.

5. Morley, *Colonial Postscript*, 59.

6. Northern Nigeria 1906–7 Annual Report, 11, http://libsysdigi.library.illinois.edu/ilharvest/Africana/Books2011-05/3064634/.

7. See Burton, *Personal Narrative*, vol. 2.

8. Northern Nigeria 1907–8 Annual Report, 6, 42, http://libsysdigi.library.illinois.edu/ilharvest/Africana/Books2011-05/3064634/. German missionary Hermann Kumm estimated that at least 10,000 pilgrims were traveling at any one time across the Sahel in 1909. Kumm, *From Hausaland to Egypt*, 262.

9. This concept comes from Yamba, *Permanent Pilgrims*.

10. Lecocq, "Hajj from West Africa," 191.

11. See Muhammad 'Arif ibn Ahmad Munayyir and Jacob M. Landau, *The Hejaz Railway and the Muslim Pilgrimage: A Case of Ottoman Political Propaganda* (Detroit, MI: Wayne State University Press, 1971); and Low, "Empire and the Hajj," 280.

12. Birks, *Across the Savannas to Mecca*, 18; J. Spencer Trimingham, *Islam in West Africa* (Oxford: Clarendon, 1959), 224.

13. Cooke and Lawrence, *Muslim Networks*, 16.

14. Gabriel Warburg, *The Sudan under Wingate: Administration in the Anglo-Egyptian Sudan, 1899–1916* (London: Cass, 1971), 96–98.

15. P. M. Holt, *The Mahdist State in Sudan, 1881–1898* (Oxford: Clarendon, 1958), 111.

16. Lecocq, "Hajj from West Africa," 193.

17. Jago, Consul Jeddah, to Embassy, Constantinople, November 24, 1887, FO 195/1583, TNA, in *RoH*, 3:755–757.

18. Heather J. Sharkey, "Globalization, Migration and Identity: Sudan, 1800–2000," in Birgit Schaebler and Leif Stenberg (eds.), *Globalization and the Muslim World: Culture, Religion and Modernity* (Syracuse, NY: Syracuse University Press, 2004), 113–137, 120.

19. Holt, *Mahdist State in Sudan*, 158.

20. Ahmad Alawad Sikangia, *The Western Bahr al-Ghazal under British Rule, 1898–1956* (Athens: Ohio University Center for International Studies, 1991), 48.

21. Wingate to Cromer, January 24, 1901, SAD Wingate 271/6/11–12, SAD.

22. Daly, *Empire on the Nile*, 122–123.

23. On the Sanussiyya, see Knut S. Vikør, *Sufi and Scholar on the Desert Edge: Muhammad b. 'Ali al-Sanusi and His Brotherhood* (Evanston, IL: Northwestern University Press, 1995).

24. Wingate to Colonel J. J. Asser, Acting Governor-General, August 2, 1908, SAD Wingate 283/3/12–23, SAD.

25. Warburg, *Sudan under Wingate*, 98; Warburg, *Islam, Sectarianism, and Politics*, 74. See also the Kassala Province files 1/056/208, 1/067/275, 1/067/276, 2/010/039, 2/010/040, 2/010/040/B, 2/011/041, 2/011/042, 2/092/410, 2/155/632, 3/035/171, 3/093/398, 2/093/399, 3/096/426, and 5.1.A.39/003/007, National Records Office, Khartoum, Sudan, identified using the Équipe Réseaux, Savoirs and Territoires online database, http://barthes.ens.fr/outils/nro/.

26. D. Roden, "The Twentieth Century Decline of Suakin," *Sudan Notes and Records*, 60 (1970), 1–22, 7. The rise in air transport, the closure of the railway in 1954, and the closing of postcolonial state borders led to the decline of Suakin and Port Sudan as transit hubs for the Hajj.

27. Lecocq, "Hajj from West Africa," 204.

28. Warburg, *Sudan under Wingate*, 97–98.

29. Warburg, *Islam, Sectarianism, and Politics*, 74.

30. Felicitas Becker, "Islam and Imperialism in East Africa," in Motadel, *Islam and the European Empires*, 112–130. Becker also states that there was "limited official interest in East African Islam during the inter-war period"; ibid., 114. John Iliffe states that the Hajj remained too expensive for most Muslims except merchants and *waalimu* (teachers) up to the 1960s in Tanganyika; John Iliffe, *A Modern History of Tanganyika* (Cambridge: Cambridge University Press, 1979), 550. See also Anne K. Bang, *Sufis and Scholars of the Sea: Family Networks in East Africa, 1860–1925* (London: Routledge Curzon, 2003).

31. See Aya Ikegame and Andrea Major, "Introduction: Princely Spaces and Domestic Voices: New Perspectives on the Indian Princely States," *Indian*

Economic and Social History Review, 46:3 (2009), 293–300; C. Zutshi, "Re-envisioning Princely States in South Asian Historiography: A Review," *Indian Economic and Social History Review*, 46:3 (2009), 301–313; Green, *Islam and the Army;* Taylor Sherman, "The Integration of the Princely State of Hyderabad and the Making of the Postcolonial State in India, 1948–1956," *Indian Economic and Social History Review*, 44:4 (2007), 489–516; Waltraud Ernst and Biswamoy Pati (eds.), *India's Princely States: People, Princes and Colonialism* (London: Routledge, 2007); Benjamin B. Cohen, *Kingship and Colonialism in India's Deccan, 1850–1948* (New York: Palgrave Macmillan, 2007); Eric Lewis Beverley, "Muslim Modern: Hyderabad State, 1883–1948" (PhD dissertation, Harvard University, 2007); B. N. Ramusack, *The Indian Princes and Their States* (Cambridge: Cambridge University Press, 2007); Margrit Pernau, *The Passing of Patrimonialism: Politics and Political Culture in Hyderabad, 1911–1948* (Delhi: Manohar, 2000); Michael Fisher, *Indirect Rule in India: Residents and Residency System, 1764–1858* (Delhi: Oxford University Press, 1998); Ian Copland, *The Princes of India in the Endgame of Empire, 1917–1947* (Cambridge: Cambridge University Press, 1997); V. K. Bawa, *Hyderabad under Salar Jung I* (Delhi: S. Chand, 1996); V. K. Bawa, *The Last Nizam: Life and Times of Osman Ali Khan* (Delhi: Viking, 1992); Bharati Ray, *Hyderabad and British Paramountcy, 1858–1883* (Delhi: Oxford University Press, 1988); Sheela Raj, *Mediaevalism to Modernism: Socio-economic and Cultural History of Hyderabad, 1869–1911* (Bombay: Popular Prakashan Pvt., 1987); Zubaida Yazdani, *The Seventh Nizam: The Fallen Empire* (Cambridge: Cambridge University Press, 1985); Shamim Aleem, *Developments in Administration under H.E.H. the Nizam VII* (Hyderabad: Osmania University Press, 1984); Ian Copland, *The British Raj and the Indian Princes: Paramountcy in Western India, 1857–1930* (Bombay: Orient Longman, 1982); B. N. Ramusack, *The Princes of India in the Twilight of Empire: Dissolution of a Patron-Client System, 1914–1939* (Columbus: Published for the University of Cincinnati by the Ohio State University Press, 1978); and Robin Jeffrey, *People, Princes, and Paramount Power: Society and Politics in the Indian Princely States* (Delhi: Oxford University Press, 1978). These works do not mention the nizam's administration of the Hajj. Eric Lewis Beverley, *Hyderabad, British India, and the World: Muslim Networks and Minor Sovereignty, c. 1850–1950* (Cambridge: Cambridge University Press, 2015), will be an important addition to this historiography.

32. Private Secretary, Salar Jung, to Agent, Rubattens and Company, Bombay, September 5, 1881, General Department, Vol. 79, File 635, 1881, MSA. See also Vice-Consul Hussein to Consul Devey, Jedda, July 13, 1898, Foreign Department, External—A, September 1898, No. 107–110, NAI.

33. File 350, Muhafiz No. 169, 1318F, Andhra Pradesh State Archives, Hyderabad, India (hereafter referred to as APSA).

34. File 8, 153–155, Muhafiz No. 8, 1319F, APSA. Nile Green discusses some of the Hyderabadi army's holy men who performed miracles for their adherents during their sea voyages to the Hijaz for Hajj in *Islam and the Army*, 129; see also Green, *Bombay Islam*, 111.

35. File 8, 156–157, Muhafiz No. 8, 1319F, APSA.

36. File 8, 158, Muhafiz No. 8, 1319F, APSA.

37. The majority of files are related to petitioners who requested financial assistance to go on Hajj, and to the administrative processing of these disbursements. See Part I, File 2, Muhafiz No. 3, 1312F; File 34, Muhafiz No. 2, 1311F; File 306, Muhafiz No. 365, 1312F; File 6, Muhafiz No. 9, 1319F; File 8, Muhafiz No. 8, 1319F, File 121, Muhafiz No. 113, undated, APSA.

38. File 8, 108, Muhafiz No. 8, 1319F, APSA.

39. File 11, 42, RC No. 10, APSA.

40. File 3, Muhafiz No. 12, 1318F, APSA.

41. File 8, 107, Muhafiz No. 8, 1319F, APSA.

42. File No. 11, 36, RC No. 10, APSA; File 3, 1316F, APSA.

43. File 8, 149, Muhafiz No. 8, 1319F, APSA. See also the petition of Mir Qadrat Ali, File 8, 151, Muhafiz No. 8, 1319F, APSA.

44. File 46, 48–49, Muhafiz No. 234, undated, APSA. The progress of the money being issued to Mubeen is detailed in File 46, 50–88, Muhafiz No. 234, undated, APSA.

45. File 4, Muhafiz No. 1, 1314F, APSA.

46. Sheikh Abdul Baqi to the Nizam, 5 Shawwal 1319, File 8, 90, Muhafiz No. 8, 1319F, APSA.

47. File 8, 120–121, Muhafiz No. 8, 1319F, APSA.

48. File 8, 139, Muhafiz No. 8, 1319F, APSA.

49. File 8, 142–144, 146, Muhafiz No. 8, 1319F, APSA.

50. File 8, 160, Muhafiz No. 8, 1319F, APSA.

51. File 8, 100–103, Muhafiz No. 8, 1319F, APSA.

52. File 8, 99, Muhafiz No. 8, 1319F, APSA.

53. File 8, 162, Muhafiz No. 8, 1319F, APSA.

54. File 8, 98–99, Muhafiz No. 8, 1319F, APSA.

55. File 8, 133–134, Muhafiz No. 8, 1319F, APSA.

56. File 8, 131, Muhafiz No. 8, 1319F, APSA.

57. Schimmel, "Sacred Geography in Islam," 169.

58. File 8, 149, Muhafiz No. 8, 1319F, APSA. See also the petition of Mir Qadrat Ali, File 8, 151, Muhafiz No. 8, 1319F, APSA.

59. File 8, 159–161, Muhafiz No. 8, 1319F, APSA.

60. Green, *Islam and the Army*, 100. See also Taylor Sherman, "Migration, Citizenship and Belonging in Hyderabad (Deccan), 1948–1956," *Modern Asian Studies*, 45:1 (2011), 81–107, 85–86; Omar Khalidi, "Sayyids of Hadhramout in Early Modern India," *Asian Journal of Social Science*, 32:3 (2004), 329–345; and Omar Khalidi, "The Hadhrami Role in the Politics and Society of Colonial India, 1750s–1950s," in Ulrike Freitag and William G. Clarence-Smith (eds.), *Hadhrami Traders, Scholars and Statesmen in the Indian Ocean, 1750s–1960s* (Leiden: Brill, 1997), 67–81.

61. Ikegame and Major, "Introduction: Princely Spaces," 311.

62. W. S. Blunt, *India under Ripon—A Private Diary* (London: Fisher Unwin, 1910), 172.

63. "The State of Hyderabad takes great trouble with its pilgrims. Every year they come in a state managed caravan, all travelling together with a caravan leader to look after them. . . . The leader this year has done the pilgrimage six times before . . . and knows the ropes. . . . I wish that all the pilgrims from

India could travel in such caravans." Sir Reader Bullard, Consul in Jidda, to his family, April 4, 1937, in Reader Bullard, *Two Kings in Arabia: Letters from Jeddah, 1923–5 and 1936–9* ed. E. C. Hodgkin (Reading: Ithaca, 1993), 150–151.

64. File 11, 1–2, RC No. 10, APSA.

65. File 11, 7–9, RC No. 10, APSA.

66. Ibid.

67. File 11, 11, RC No. 10, APSA.

68. File 11, 12–17, RC No. 10, APSA.

69. File 11, 24, RC No. 10, APSA.

70. File 11, 30, RC No. 10, APSA.

71. File 3, 1316F; File 290, Muhafiz No. 263, 1313F; File 3, Muhafiz No. 3, 1317F, APSA.

72. See, for example, the 1808 application of Begum Shams-i-Nissa, IOR/L/F/4/248/5593, IOR, APAC, BL.

73. Jahan Begum, *Story of a Pilgrimage to the Hejaz*, 130, 144–147. See also Siobhan Lambert-Hurley, *Muslim Women Reform and Princely Patronage: Nawab Sultan Jahan Begam of Bhopal* (London: Routledge, 2007), although it does not examine Bhopal's administration of the Hajj under her reign.

74. Jahan Begum, *Story of a Pilgrimage to the Hejaz*, 9–10, 161.

75. Ibid., 9–10.

76. Ibid., 150–152, 214, 224.

77. Ibid., 191, 214.

78. Ibid., 181, 187, 222.

79. Ibid., 165, 169, 174–176, 179.

80. Ibid., 4–5.

81. Salar Jung, *Pilgrimage to Mecca and the Near East*, 1.

82. Ibid., 31, 43.

83. Ibid., 12–14.

84. Ibid.

85. Ibid., 15–16.

86. Ibid., 51–52.

87. Ibid., 55–56.

88. Ibid., 72–73.

89. Ibid., 66. Interestingly, Salar Jung saw that one of the khedive's officials carried a camera, a reference to Muhammad 'Ali Effendi Sa'udi. See Farid Kioumgi and Robert Graham, *A Photographer on the Hajj: The Travels of Muhammad 'Ali Effendi Sa'udi (1904–1908)* (Cairo: American University in Cairo Press, 2009).

90. Salar Jung, *Pilgrimage to Mecca and the Near East*, 67–68.

91. Ibid., 72–73.

92. Ibid., 75.

93. Ibid., 71.

94. Ibid., 79–80.

95. Barbara Metcalf, "Pilgrimage Remembered," 300–301.

96. Prashant Kidambi, *The Making of an Indian Metropolis: Colonial Governance and Public Culture in Bombay, 1890–1920* (Aldershot: Ashgate, 2007), ex-

amines Bombay's civil society but does not cover the Hajj. Two exceptions to this are Bose's very brief survey of Bombay's Hajj administration in *Hundred Horizons*, 207–208; and Green, *Bombay Islam*, 3, 126, 132.

97. Government of Bombay Resolution, April 26, 1912, General Department, 1912, Vol. 130, File 916, MSA.

98. Large iron ladles for rice, small iron ladles for dal, 4 iron spoons, 4 curry stones, 11 pounds of soap per pilgrim, 12 tin pots for the latrine, 12 tin pots for seasick pilgrims, 2 canvas bathing screens for women, 18 squeegees, and 50 country brooms. Untitled and undated, General Department, 1910, Vol. 133, File 459, MSA; Protector of Pilgrims, Report on 1911 Hajj Season, July 15, 1912, General Department, 1912, Vol. 131, File 992, MSA.

99. Green, *Bombay Islam*, 106.

100. Golam Hussein Roghay to Sir Philip Wodehouse, Governor-in-Council Bombay, August 16, 1875, General Department, 1875, Vol. 63, File 794, MSA.

101. Note by Secretary to Government of Bombay, General Department, September 29, 1875, 1875, Vol. 63, File 794, MSA; Frank Souter to Under-Secretary to Government of Bombay, July 22, 1876; Resolution by Government of Bombay, August 8, 1876, General Department, 1875, Vol. 77, File 574, MSA.

102. Roghay to Wodehouse, July 8, 1876, General Department, 1875, Vol. 77, File 574, MSA.

103. Hajji Sheikh Ismail bin Shaikh Hussein to Sir Richard Temple, Governor of Bombay, August 26, 1878, General Department, 1878, Vol. 51, File 637, MSA.

104. Commissioner of Police, Memo, September 27, 1878, General Department, 1878, Vol. 51, File 637, MSA.

105. Protector of Pilgrims, Report on Pilgrim Season Ending November 30, 1909, April 9, 1910, General Department, 1910, Vol. 134, File 615, MSA; Protector of Pilgrims, Report on Pilgrim Season 1910, May 10, 1911, General Department, 1911, Vol. 158, File 992, MSA; Moulvi Abdulla Ahmed, Protector of Pilgrims Bombay to Commissioner of Police, Report of Pilgrim Season 1911, June 10, 1912, General Department, 1912, Vol. 131, File 992, MSA; Protector of Pilgrims Bombay to Commissioner of Police, April 28, 1913, General Department, 1913, Vol. 141, File 992, MSA.

106. Protector of Pilgrims, Report on Pilgrim Season 1910, May 10, 1911, General Department, 1911, Vol. 158, File 992, MSA.

107. Edwardes to Robertson, April 13, 1911, General Department, 1911, Vol. 158, File 112, MSA.

108. Edwardes to Robertson, April 11, 1911, General Department, 1911, Vol. 158, File 112, MSA.

109. Protector of Pilgrims, Report on Pilgrim Season Ending November 30, 1909, April 9, 1910, General Department, 1910, Vol. 134, File 615, MSA. Reports by the department reflect the scope of the pilgrimage from Bombay and areas the department dealt with: repatriation of destitute pilgrims, pilgrim vessels, numbers of pilgrims and steamers, passage rates, pilgrim accommodation,

pilgrim vaccination, pilgrim inquiries, pilgrim brokers, unauthorized brokers, medical inspection of pilgrims, heavy baggage, temporary police force, passports, female pilgrims' embarkation, ill and deceased pilgrims, pilgrims' effects, infectious diseases, Hajj committees, "coolie" hire, prosecution for cheating pilgrims, assistance from police, medical aid, and tables of pilgrim departures. Protector of Pilgrims Bombay to Commissioner of Police, April 28, 1913, General Department, 1913, Vol. 141, File 992, MSA.

110. Answers to Dr. Venis's [port health officer, Karachi] Questions by S. M. Edwardes, Commissioner of Police, Bombay, undated, probably 1910–1911, General Department, 1912, Vol. 130, File 916, MSA.

111. Protector of Pilgrims, Report on Pilgrim Season Season Ending November 30, 1909, April 9, 1910, General Department, 1910, Vol. 134, File 615, MSA.

112. Ibid.

113. Protector of Pilgrims, Report on Pilgrim Season 1910, May 10, 1911, General Department, 1911, Vol. 158, File 992, MSA.

114. See Green, *Bombay Islam*, 107, for the example of Hafiz 'Abd al-Rahman's travelogue, which gave extensive details on the practicalities of what pilgrims should do in Bombay to prepare for their Hajj. Protector of Pilgrims, Report on Pilgrim Season Ending November 30, 1909, April 9, 1910, General Department, 1910, Vol. 134, File 615, MSA. There was also a similar handbook in Bengali distributed to all the province's Hajj committees for circulation, Report of the Bengal Pilgrim Department, 1933, Foreign and Political Department, 105-N, 1934, NAI.

115. Singha, "Passport, Ticket and India-Rubber Stamp," 52.

116. Protector of Pilgrims, Report on Pilgrim Season Ending November 30, 1909, April 9, 1910, General Department, 1910, Vol. 134, File 615, MSA; Singha, "Passport, Ticket and India-Rubber Stamp," 70.

117. Moulvi Abdulla Ahmed, Protector of Pilgrims, Bombay to Commissioner of Police, Report on Pilgrim Season, 1911, June 10, 1912, General Department, 1912, Vol. 131, File 992, MSA; Protector of Pilgrims Bombay to Commissioner of Police, April 28, 1913, General Department, 1913, Vol. 141, File 992, MSA.

118. Protector of Pilgrims, Report on Pilgrim Season Ending November 30, 1909, April 9, 1910, General Department, 1910, Vol. 134, File 615, MSA. Mahomed Taqi's intimate involvement in the pilgrimage extended to taking charge of two orphans. One was the child of a Pathan who threatened to kill the child, who had a swelling on its neck and so was denied entry onto a pilgrim ship. Moulvi Abdulla Ahmed, Protector of Pilgrims, Bombay to Commissioner of Police, Report of Pilgrim Season 1911, June 10, 1912, General Department, 1912, Vol. 131, File 992, MSA.

119. Assistant Resident, Hyderabad to Secretary, Government of Bombay, September 22, 1881; Sir Salar Jung, Nizam's Minister, to Assistant Resident, Hyderabad, Private Secretary of the Nizam to Sir Salar Jung, September 5, 1881, both in General Department, 1881, Vol. 79, File 635, MSA.

120. The use of the Mughal and Ottoman term was misleading. The "caravan" consisted merely of a group of several hundred Hyderabadi pilgrims,

under the charge of one of the nizam's officials, who traveled together by train to Bombay and then by ship to Jidda. Lieut.-Col. A. F. Pinhey, Resident, Hyderabad, to Secretary, Government of Bombay, October 4, 1912, General Department, 1912, Vol. 128, File 1487, MSA. See also, for example, Lieut.-Col. A. F. Pinhey, Resident, Hyderabad, to Secretary, Government of Bombay, October 20, 1911, General Department, 1911, Vol. 158, File 1213, MSA.

121. Karachi had been open in 1897 and 1900–1901 because of plague in Bombay.

122. Protector of Pilgrims, Report on 1911 Pilgrim Season, July 15, 1912, General Department, 1912, Vol. 131, File 992, MSA; Notes on Proposal to Open Karachi to Pilgrim Traffic, May 1, 1911; Edwardes to Robertson, April 26, 1912; Government of Bombay Resolution and Edwardes to Collector of Customs, Bombay, September 21, 1910, General Department, 1912, Vol. 130, File 916, MSA.

123. Lawrence, Collector of Karachi to Commissioner, Sindh, October 27, 1910, General Department, 1912, Vol. 130, File 916, MSA.

124. Ahmed, *Bengal Muslims*, 1, 49, 82–84, 104, 111, 184; K. W. Jones, *Socio-religious Reform Movements in British India*, 17–25.

125. S. M. Edwardes, Commissioner of Police, Bombay, to Collector of Customs, Bombay, September 21, 1910, General Department, 1912, Vol. 130, File 916, MSA. See also Moulvi Abdulla Ahmed, Protector of Pilgrims, Bombay to Commissioner of Police, Bombay, Report of Pilgrim Season 1911, June 10, 1912, General Department, 1912, Vol. 131, File 992, MSA. On pilgrim guides in Bengal, see Mushirul Hasan and Rakshanda Jalil, "Introduction," in Amir Ahmad Alawi, *Journey to the Holy Land: A Pilgrim's Diary*, trans. Mushirul Hasan and Rakshanda Jalil (Delhi: Oxford University Press, 2009), 21–22.

126. Protector of Pilgrims to Commissioner of Police, Bombay, July 8, 1909, General Department, 1910, Vol. 134, File 615, MSA.

127. Protector of Pilgrims, Report on Pilgrim Season Ending November 30, 1909, April 9, 1910, General Department, 1910, Vol. 134, File 615, MSA.

128. Protector of Pilgrims, Report on Pilgrim Season 1910, May 10, 1911, General Department, 1911, Vol. 158, File 992, MSA.

129. Protector of Pilgrims Bombay to Commissioner of Police, April 28, 1913, General Department, 1913, Vol. 141, File 992, MSA.

130. Haj Committee Rules and Regulations, Government Resolution No. 5497, September 5, 1908, General Department, 1913, Vol. 143, File 1088, MSA; Resolution on Re-appointment of Hajj Committee Members, October 4, 1912, General Department, 1912, Vol. 128, File 1368, MSA; Kelly Commissioner of Police to Government of Bombay, December 23, 1926, General Department, 1922, File 3542, MSA.

131. Triennial Report of the Haj Committee, July 15, 1912, General Department, 1912, Vol. 132, File 618, MSA.

132. C.R.K., Margin Note, January 8, 1923, General Department, 1922, File 3542, MSA.

133. Blosse, Commissioner of Police, to Knight, November 16, 1922, November 20, 1922, General Department, 1922, File 3542, MSA.

134. Blosse, Commissioner of Police, to Knight, November 20, 1922, General Department, 1922, File 3542, MSA.

135. C.R.K., Margin Note, January 8, 1923, General Department, 1922, File 3542, MSA.

136. J.S., Margin Note, January 10, 1923, General Department, 1922, File 3542, MSA.

137. Cumoo Suleiman to G. E. Hourse c/o T. Cook, February 14, 1886; General Department to Commissioner of Police Bombay, June 25, 1886; General Department to Commissioner of Police and Director of Public Works, December 21, 1886, General Department, 1885, Vol. 124, File 82, MSA. However, an official noted that over 2,000 pilgrims in the projected hostel would not be "at all desirable," intimating that their collective odor was far from pleasant. J.R., Margin Note, March 17, 1887, General Department, 1887, Vol. 110, File 912, MSA. Suleiman's plans for pilgrim hostels ran aground on lawsuits filed against his will in court; there were also misgivings about the sites selected by the authorities for the *musafirkhana*. Sir Frank Souter, Commissioner of Police, Bombay, to Under-Secretary, Government of Bombay, February 28, 1887; Secretary to Trustees Haramasji Sohabji to Commissioner of Police, Bombay, November 15, 1888, General Department, 1887, Vol. 110, File 912, MSA.

138. Secretary, Government of Bombay to Mirza Mahomed Shirazi, May 6, 1912; Mirza Mahomed Shirazi to Secretary, Government of Bombay, May 28, 1912, General Department, 1912, Vol. 130, File 691, MSA.

139. Edwardes, President of Hajj Committee, Bombay to Secretary, Government of Bombay, February 28, 1912; M. F. O'Dwyer, Agent to Governor-General of Central India, Indore, to Secretary, Government of Bombay, April 22, 1912, General Department, 1912, Vol. 133, File 682, MSA.

140. Protector of Pilgrims, Report on Pilgrim Season Ending November 30, 1909, April 9, 1910, General Department, 1910, Vol. 134, File 615, MSA; Protector of Pilgrims, Report on Pilgrim Season 1910, May 10, 1911, General Department, 1911, Vol. 158, File 992, MSA; Protector of Pilgrims, Bombay, to Commissioner of Police, April 28, 1913, General Department, 1913, Vol. 141, File 992, MSA.

141. Green, *Bombay Islam*, 36.

142. For details of these, see ibid., 177.

143. David Page, *Prelude to Partition: The Indian Muslims and the Imperial System of Control* (Delhi: Oxford University Press, 1982), 24; Francis Robinson, *Separatism among Indian Muslims: The Politics of the United Provinces' Muslims, 1860–1923* (Cambridge: Cambridge University Press, 1974), 208–209; Hasan and Jalil, "Introduction," 8–9.

144. See Özcan, *Pan-Islamism*.

145. Committee of Imperial Defence Paper 92B, Possibility of a Joint Naval and Military Attack upon the Dardanelles, 1906, quoted in David French, "The Dardanelles, Mecca, and Kut: Prestige as a Factor in British Eastern Strategy, 1914–1916," *War and Society*, 5:1 (1987), 45–61, 50.

146. See Burman, *Britain's Relations with the Ottoman Empire;* al-Amr, *Hijaz under Ottoman Rule*, 173–174; and Ochsenswald, *Religion, Society, and the State in Arabia*, 87–88.

147. Shaikh, *Community and Consensus in Islam*, 152.

148. Justin Jones, *Shi'a Islam in Colonial India: Religion, Community and Sectarianism* (Cambridge: Cambridge University Press, 2011), 175.

149. Officials had articulated this policy in the 1890s. "The Government of India have for years deemed it a matter of high political importance to cheapen and facilitate the journey to Mecca"; Government of India to Secretary of State for India, September 11, 1895, quoted in Singha, "Passport, Ticket and India-Rubber Stamp," 59.

150. Secretary, Government of India, Home Department, to Madras, Bombay, Bengal, United Provinces, Punjab, Burma, Eastern Bengal and Assam, Central Provinces, Coorg, North West Frontier Province, November 27, 1905, Foreign Department, External—B, September 1907, No. 111–140, NAI.

151. Lieut.-Col. P. J. Melvill, Commissioner, Ajmer-Merwan to C. C. Watson, Assistant to Agent Governor-General Rajputana, March 24, 1906; Mr. A. L. P. Tucker, Agent to Governor-General Baluchistan, to Secretary, Government of India, Foreign Department, April 12, 1906; General Secretary Anjuman-i-Islam, Quetta, to Assistant Political Agent, Quetta, February 13, 1906; Her Highness the Begum of Bhopal to Political Agent, Bhopal, March 7, 1906; Report from Maulvi Saiyid Ali Hasan, Revenue Member of the Council of Regency, Indore State, April 18, 1906; Major H. Daly, Agent to Governor-General in Central India to Secretary, Government of India, Foreign Department, November 17, 1906; Sultan Ahmed Khan, BA, LLB, Barrister-at-Law, Chief Justice, Gwalior State, April 13, 1906; Report by Syed Ali Bahadur Bilgrami, Sar Suba of Marwa, May 25, 1906, Foreign Department, External—B, September 1907, No. 111–140, NAI; Secretary, Government of Bombay to Secretary, Government of India, July 9, 1906, General Department, 1912, Vol. 132, File 768, MSA; G. E. Colvin, Agent to the Governor-General of Rajputana to Secretary to the Government of India, Foreign Department, July 10, 1906, Foreign Department, External—B, September 1907, No. 111–140, NAI.

152. Translation of Statement of Different Classes of Muhammadan Gentlemen of Srinagar, enclosed in Lieut.-Col. T. C. Pears, Resident, Kashmir to Secretary, Government of India, Foreign Department, March 14, 1906, Foreign Department, External—B, September 1907, No. 111–140, NAI.

153. Rai Itbar-ul-Mulk Sayyid Muhammad Iftikhar Husein Muztir, Superintendent Court of Wards, Gwalior State, Translation of Note, February 28, 1906, Foreign Department, External—B, September 1907, No. 111–140, NAI.

154. Hamid Ali, Assistant Collector, Hala, to Collector of Hyderabad, March 15, 1906, General Department, 1912, Vol. 132, File 768, MSA.

155. S. M. Fraser, Resident, Mysore to Secretary, Government of India, Foreign Department, June 20, 1906, Foreign Department, External—B, September 1907, No. 111–140, NAI.

156. Rafiuddin Ahmed to Commissioner of Police, Bombay, January 29, 1906, General Department, 1912, Vol. 132, File 768, MSA. Also quoted in Singha, "Passport, Ticket and India-Rubber Stamp," 64. There are many similar responses in this file.

157. Lieut.-Col. P. J. Melvill, Commissioner, Ajmer-Merwan to C. C. Watson, Assistant to Agent Governor-General Rajputana, March 24, 1906; Mr. A. L. P. Tucker, Agent to Governor-General Baluchistan to Secretary of Government of India, Foreign Department, April 12, 1906; General Secretary, Anjuman-i-Islam, Quetta, to Assistant Political Agent, Quetta, February 13, 1906; Her Highness the Begum of Bhopal to Political Agent in Bhopal, March 7, 1906; Report from Maulvi Saiyid Ali Hasan, Revenue Member of the Council of Regency, Indore State, April 18, 1906; Major H. Daly, Agent to Governor-General in Central India to Secretary to Government of India in Foreign Department, November 17, 1906; Sultan Ahmed Khan, BA, LLB, Barrister-at-Law, Chief Justice, Gwalior State, April 13, 1906; Report by Syed Ali Bahadur Bilgrami, Sar Suba of Marwa, May 25, 1906, Foreign Department, External—B, September 1907, No. 111–140, NAI; Secretary, Government of Bombay to Secretary, Government of India, July 9, 1906, General Department, 1912, Vol. 132, File 768, MSA.

158. J. C. Ferguson, Under-Secretary, Government of India, Home Department to Madras, Bombay, Bengal, United Provinces, Punjab, Burma, Eastern Bengal and Assam, Central Provinces, North West Frontier Province, Coorg, and forwarded to Residents and Agents in Hyderabad, Mysore, Central India, Rajputana, Baluchistan, Ajmer-Merwara, Baroda, Kashmir, May 18, 1907, Foreign Department, External—B, September 1907, No. 111–140, NAI.

159. Barbara Daly Metcalf and Thomas R. Metcalf, *A Concise History of India* (Cambridge: Cambridge University Press, 2002), 134.

160. Government of Bombay to Government of India, March 15, 1912, Foreign Department, Internal—B, August 1913, No. 349–352, NAI; Dr. S. Abdurrahman, Vice-Consul Jeddah, Hajj Report 1910–11, General Department, 1911, Vol. 160, File 678, MSA. Singha, "Passport, Ticket and India-Rubber Stamp," 61.

161. Singha, "Passport, Ticket and India-Rubber Stamp," 61.

162. Dr. S. Abdurrahman, Vice-Consul Jeddah, Haj Report 1911–12, Foreign Department, Internal—B, August 1913, No. 349–352, NAI.

163. Author unknown, Note, July 22, 1910, General Department, 1910, Vol. 134, File 44, MSA; Dr. S. Abdurrahman, Vice-Consul Jeddah, Haj Report 1911–12, Foreign Department, Internal—B, August 1913, No. 349–352, NAI.

164. Dr. S. Abdurrahman, Vice-Consul Jeddah, Haj Report 1911–12, Foreign Department, Internal—B, August 1913, No. 349–352, NAI.

165. Author unknown, Note, July 22, 1910, General Department, 1910, Vol. 134, File 44, MSA; Dr. S. Abdurrahman, Vice-Consul Jeddah, Haj Report 1911–12, Foreign Department, Internal—B, August 1913, No. 349–352, NAI.

166. Press Note, May 13, 1912, General Department, 1912, Vol. 130, File 122, MSA.

167. Edwardes, Commissioner of Police, Bombay to Secretary, Government of Bombay, July 24, 1911, General Department, 1911, Vol. 159, File 62A, MSA.

168. India Office to Government of India, June 21, 1912, Foreign Department, Internal—B, August 1913, No. 349–352, NAI.

169. Maharaj Singh, Note, July 11, 1912, Foreign Department, Internal—B, August 1913, No. 349–352, NAI.

170. L. Porter, Note, June 27, 1912, Foreign Department, Internal—B, August 1913, No. 349–352, NAI.

171. L. Porter, Note, August 6, 1912, Foreign Department, Internal—B, August 1913, No. 349–352, NAI.

172. British Consul Jedda to Government of India, undated, Foreign Department, Internal—B, August 1913, No. 349–352, NAI.

173. L.M.R., Note, December 18, 1912; L. Porter, Note, December 20, 1912, Foreign Department, Internal—B, August 1913, No. 349–352, NAI. This request was presented to the Finance Department with the limp note that before the next Hajj "we may hope that this very thorny question will be put upon a more satisfactory basis. The grant will not in any case be taken as a precedent for future action without a fuller consideration of the whole question." Maharaj Singh, Note, January 7, 1913, Foreign Department, Internal—B, August 1913, No. 349–352, NAI.

174. L.M.R. and P.A.C., Note, January 7, 1913, Foreign Department, Internal—B, August 1913, No. 349–352, NAI.

175. Consul Jeddah to Government of India, March 5, 1913, Foreign Department, Internal—B, August 1913, No. 349–352, NAI.

176. L.M.R. and P.A.C., Note, March 8, 1913, Foreign Department, Internal—B, August 1913, No. 349–352, NAI; Claude Hill, Member of Council, Bombay, to Sir Harcourt Butler, Member of Council, April 11, 1913, Foreign Department, Internal—B, August 1913, No. 349–352, NAI; Singha, "Passport, Ticket and India-Rubber Stamp," 64.

177. J. L. Rieu, Secretary, Government of Bombay to Secretary, Government of India, Department of Education, February 4, 1913, Foreign Department, Internal—B, August 1913, No. 349–352, NAI.

178. Sir Harcourt Butler, Pilgrims to the Hedjaz, March 20, 1913, General Department, Vol. 141, File 993, 1913, MSA; Singha, "Passport, Ticket and India-Rubber Stamp," 63.

179. Singha, "Passport, Ticket and India-Rubber Stamp," 60.

180. Consul Jedda to British Ambassador Constantinople, December 12, 1913, CO 273/414, TNA.

181. Sir Harcourt Butler, Member of Council, to Claude Hill, Member of Council, Bombay, April 19, 1913, Foreign Department, Internal—B, August 1913, No. 349–352, NAI; Mahraj Singh, Note, April 15, 1913; Draft Telegram (plus margin note) from Sir Harcourt Butler, Education Department, to Secretary, Government of India, Home Department, April 25, 1913; Claude Hill, Member of Council, Bombay to Sir Harcourt Butler, Member of Council, April 11, 1913, Foreign Department, Internal—B, August 1913, No. 349–352, NAI.

182. Abdulla Khar to Lord Hardinge, May 20, 1913, General Department, 1913, Vol. 140, File 485, MSA.

183. See Saurabh Mishra, "The Politicization of a Holy Act: The Haj from the Indian Subcontinent during Colonial Times," *Journal of the Royal Asiatic*

Society of Bangladesh, 50:1–2 (2005), http://www.asiaticsociety.org.bd/journals/Golden_jubilee_vol/.

184. Bombay Government Resolution, December 11, 1913, General Department, 1913, Vol. 140, File 768, MSA.

185. Ibid.

186. L. C. Porter, Secretary, Government of India to Madras, Bengal, United Provinces, Punjab, Burma, Bihar and Orissa, Central Provinces, Assam, North West Frontier Province, and Coorg, May 16, 1913, Foreign Department, Internal—B, August 1913, No. 349–352, NAI.

CHAPTER 4 *The First World War and the Hashemite Interregnum*

1. Two insightful contemporaneous responses to events in this period are Christiaan Snouck Hurgronje and R. J. H. Gottheil, *The Revolt in Arabia* (London: G. P. Putnam's Sons, 1917); and Christiaan Snouck Hurgronje and R. J. H. Gottheil, *The Holy War "Made in Germany"* (London: G. P. Putnam's Sons, 1915). For the main works dealing with this period, see Askar al-Enazy, *The Creation of Saudi Arabia: Ibn Saud and British Imperial Policy, 1914–1927* (New York: Routledge, 2010); Mustafa Aksakal, *The Ottoman Road to War in 1914: The Ottoman Empire and the First World War* (Cambridge: Cambridge University Press, 2008); Polly Mohs, *Military Intelligence and the Arab Revolt: The First Modern Intelligence War* (London: Routledge, 2008); Priya Satia, *Spies in Arabia: The Great War and the Cultural Foundations of Britain's Covert Empire in the Middle East* (Oxford: Oxford University Press, 2008); Martin Thomas, *Empires of Intelligence: Security Services and Colonial Disorder after 1914* (Berkeley: University of California Press, 2007); James Barr, *Setting the Desert on Fire: T. E. Lawrence and Britain's Secret War in Arabia, 1916–1918* (London: Bloomsbury, 2006); David Fieldhouse, *Western Imperialism in the Middle East, 1914–1958* (Oxford: Oxford University Press, 2006); Timothy J. Paris, *Britain, the Hashemites, and Arab Rule, 1920–1925: The Sherifian Solution* (London: Frank Cass, 2003); Joshua Teitelbaum, *The Rise and Fall of the Hashemite Kingdom of Arabia* (London: Hurst and Co., 2001); David Fromkin, *A Peace to End All Peace: The Fall of the Ottoman Empire and the Creation of the Modern Middle East* (New York: H. Holt, 2000); John Fisher, *Curzon and British Imperialism in the Middle East, 1916–1919* (London: Cass, 1999); Karsh and Karsh, *Empires of the Sand;* Timothy J. Paris, "British Middle East Policy-Making after the First World War: The Lawrentian and Wilsonian Schools," *Historical Journal*, 41:3 (1998), 773–793; Donald M. McKale, *War by Revolution: Germany and Great Britain in the Middle East in the Era of World War I* (Kent, OH: Kent State University Press, 1998); Haifa Alangari, *The Struggle for Power in Arabia: Ibn Saud, Hussein and Great Britain, 1914–1924* (Reading: Ithaca, 1998); Hasan Kayali, *Arabs and Young Turks: Ottomanism, Arabism, and Islamism in the Ottoman Empire, 1908–1918* (Berkeley: University of California Press, 1997); Efraim Karsh and Inari Karsh, "Reflections on Arab Nationalism: Review Article," *Middle Eastern Studies*, 32:4 (1996), 367–392; Roger Adelson, *London and the Invention of the Middle East: Money, Power, and War, 1902–1922* (New Haven, CT: Yale Univer-

sity Press, 1995); Eliezer Tauber, *The Emergence of the Arab Movements* (London: Cass, 1993); Bruce Westrate, *The Arab Bureau: British Policy in the Middle East, 1916–1920* (University Park: Pennsylvania State University Press, 1992); Albert Hourani, "How Should We Write the History of the Middle East?," *International Journal of Middle East Studies*, 23:2 (1991), 125–136; Albert Hourani, *A History of the Arab Peoples* (Cambridge, MA: Harvard University Press, 1991); Rashid Khalidi, *The Origins of Arab Nationalism* (New York: Columbia University Press, 1991); Dan Eldar, "French Policy towards Husayn, Sharif of Mecca," *Middle Eastern Studies*, 26:2 (1990), 329–350; Landau, *Politics of Pan-Islam;* Abdulaziz Shebl, "The Emergence and Demise of an Independent Arab State: The Kingdom of the Hejaz, 1916–1925" (PhD dissertation, University of California at Los Angeles, 1988); M. E. Yapp, *The Making of the Modern Near East, 1792–1923* (London: Longman, 1987); H. V. F. Winstone, *The Illicit Adventure: The Story of Political and Military Intelligence in the Middle East from 1898 to 1926* (London: J. Cape, 1982); Randall Baker, *King Husain and the Kingdom of Hejaz* (Cambridge: Cambridge University Press, 1979); Suleyman Mousa, "A Matter of Principle: King Hussein of the Hijaz and the Arabs of Palestine," *International Journal of Middle Eastern Studies*, 9:2 (1978), 183–194; Elie Kedourie, "The Surrender of Medina, January 1919," *Middle Eastern Studies*, 13:1 (1977), 124–143; Briton Cooper Busch, *Britain, India, and the Arabs, 1914–1921* (Berkeley: University of California Press, 1971); Ulrich Trumpener, *Germany and the Ottoman Empire, 1914–1918* (Princeton, NJ: Princeton University Press, 1968); George Antonius, *The Arab Awakening: The Story of the Arab National Movement* (New York: Capricorn, 1965); and Elie Kedourie, *England and the Middle East: The Vital Years 1914–1921* (London: Bowes and Bowes, 1956). On the Khilafat movement, see Mishra, "Politicization of a Holy Act"; M. Naeem Qureshi, *Pan-Islam in British Indian Politics: A Study of the Khilafat Movement, 1918–1924* (Leiden: Brill, 1999); Özcan, *Pan-Islamism;* Gail Minault, *The Khilafat Movement: Religious Symbolism and Political Mobilization in India* (New York: Oxford University Press, 1982); and F. Robinson, *Separatism among Indian Muslims.*

2. Only Paris's book has a chapter on the hajj, and Satia's work mentions the hajj briefly, describing how British officials saw the ritual as "curious but innocuous" and then detailing how officials such as D. G. Hogarth saw the Hajj as having the "potentiality of being an armed conspiracy" and that the Holy Cities possessed limitless subversive potential, arguing that the British saw Mecca and the Hajj as sites for potential subversion. Satia, *Spies in Arabia*, 204, 214, 216; Paris, *Britain, the Hashemites, and Arab Rule*, 299–319.

3. Westrate, *Arab Bureau*, 14.

4. Kitchener to Grey, February 6, 1914, FO 6672/14/44, reproduced at British Imperial Connexions to the Arab Movement, http://wwi.lib.byu.edu/index.php/British_Imperial_Connexions_to_the_Arab_National_Movement, from G. P. Gooch and Harold Temperley (eds.), *The Last Years of Peace (British Documents on the Origins of the War, 1898–1914), Volume 10, Part 2* (London: Her Majesty's Stationary Office, 1938), 824–838.

5. Ibid.

6. T. E. Lawrence, *Seven Pillars of Wisdom* (London: Wordsworth Classics, 1997), 59.

7. Kitchener to Grey, April 4, 1914, FO 15883/4588/14/44, reproduced at British Imperial Connexions to the Arab Movement, accessed at http://wwi.lib.byu.edu/index.php/British_Imperial_Connexions_to_the_Arab_National_Movement, from Gooch and Temperley, *Last Years of Peace*, 824–838.

8. Zohrab to Goschen, No. 23, Jedda, April 23, 1881, FO 195/1375, TNA.

9. This date of entry is chosen because that was when the Ottoman fleet began sinking Russian ships and shelling Russian forts on the Black Sea. On October 31, the majority of the CUP voted for war allied to the Central Powers, but the die had already been cast. On November 1, Russia declared war and invaded the Ottoman empire. This was swiftly followed by the formal Ottoman declaration of war on Russia on November 2, which led, in turn, to Britain and France declaring war on the Ottomans on November 5. The Ottomans responded with a declaration of war on Britain and France on November 11. I am grateful to Professor William Gervase Clarence-Smith for this clarification.

10. Official Proclamation to the Arab People, December 3, 1914, FO 141/710, TNA.

11. Westrate, *Arab Bureau*, 107.

12. Untitled and undated, CO 323/732/8, TNA. For examples of wartime propaganda by the Ottomans and Germans aimed at the Muslim subjects of the Allied powers, see Landau, *Politics of Pan-Islam*, 103–142, especially 105–121.

13. Translation of letter from Sultan of Kelantan to British Adviser, February 11, 1915, File 147–6, CO 273/425, TNA.

14. Landau, *Politics of Pan-Islam*, 100–103.

15. Özcan, *Pan-Islamism*, 180; David Omissi, *The Sepoy and the Raj: The Indian Army, 1860–1940* (Basingstoke: Palgrave Macmillan, 1998), 238; French, "Dardanelles, Mecca, and Kut," 52. See also Note by Cleveland, Director C.I.D., February 25, 1915; and G.O.C. Army of Occupation, Egypt to C-in-C, India, January 23, 1915, Foreign and Political Department, War—Secret, July 1915, No. 245-251, NAI.

16. Singha, "Passport, Ticket and India-Rubber Stamp," 65.

17. Hajj Report 1333 AH 1915, IOR/L/PS/10/523, IOR, APAC, BL.

18. McMahon to Grey, December 4, 1914, File 52042, CO 273/415, TNA.

19. McMahon to Grey, April 12, 1915, File 17373, CO 273/430, TNA; Westrate, *Arab Bureau*, 68; Daly, *Empire on the Nile*, 164.

20. Secretary of State for India to Viceroy of India, June 7, 1915, File 26724, CO 273/433, TNA.

21. Warburg, *Islam, Sectarianism, and Politics*, 74.

22. Admiralty to Secretary of State for India, March 2, 1915, File 19402, CO 273/433, TNA.

23. Hajj Report 1333 AH 1915, IOR/L/PS/10/523, IOR, APAC, BL.

24. Ibid.

25. Ibid.

26. Kitchener to Sharif Hussein, November 1914, quoted in Sykes, Note on Arabia, April 25, 1915, DS.42.1, File 1, Box 1, Sykes GB-0165–0275, Middle

East Centre Archive, St. Anthony's College, Oxford (hereafter referred to as MECA).

27. H. V. F. Winstone (ed.), *The Diaries of Parker Pasha* (New York: Quartet, 1983), 77.

28. Chairman Maurice de Bunsen, Report of the Committee on Asiatic Turkey, June 30, 1915, Appendix X (fols. 100–105), CAB 27/1, TNA, quoted in Mohs, *Military Intelligence*, 15.

29. Proclamation by the Viceroy, May 27, 1915, FO 141/710, TNA, quoted in Singha, "Passport, Ticket and India-Rubber Stamp," 65; Westrate, *Arab Bureau*, 93.

30. Özcan, *Pan-Islamism*, 179. Former Egyptian proconsul Lord Cromer penned a similar proposal; see Memo by Cromer Respecting Steps to be Taken in the Event of War with Turkey, October 16, 1914, CAB 37/121/124, TNA; Mishra, "Beyond the Bounds of Time?," 37.

31. Ronald Storrs, *Orientations* (London: Nicholson and Watson, 1937), 152.

32. I am grateful to Dr. Faisal Devji for this insight.

33. Roger Adelson, *Mark Sykes: Portrait of an Amateur* (London: Cape, 1975), 60.

34. Quoted in Margaret Macmillan, *The Peacemakers* (London: J. Murray, 2001), 394.

35. Storrs to Fitzgerald, August 3, 1915, quoted in Mohs, *Military Intelligence*, 15.

36. Viceroy of India, January 17, 1915, FO 371/2482, TNA, quoted in Mohs, *Military Intelligence*, 28.

37. In India, there were 66.6 million Muslims; this number is approximately one-fifth of the colony's total population. Mark Sykes, Memorandum on Indian Moslems, submitted to the India Office, File 1, Box 1, Sykes GB-0165–0275, MECA.

38. Chairman Maurice de Bunsen, Report of the Committee on Asiatic Turkey, April 8, 1915, CAB 42/2, TNA.

39. Mark Sykes, Note on the Khalifate, May 25, 1915, File 1, Box 1, Sykes GB-0165–0275, MECA.

40. Wingate, Note on the Politics of Mecca, undated but between April and August 1915, SAD Wingate 135/1/1–5, SAD.

41. Wingate to Clayton, undated but probably January to March 1915, SAD Clayton 469/8/14, SAD.

42. Wingate to Cromer, March 18, 1915, SAD Wingate 134/6/35–36, SAD.

43. Mark Sykes to Bob (Lord Cecil), October 4, 1915, DS.42.1, File 1, Box 1, Sykes GB-0165–0275, MECA.

44. Recounted by Wingate in letter to Clayton, December 4, 1915, FO 882/2/AP/15/12, TNA.

45. War Committee Meeting, No. 10 Downing Street, Evidence Given by Sir Mark Sykes on the Arab Question, December 16, 1915, DR.588, File 1, Box 1, Sykes GB-0165–0275, MECA. Another example of Sykes's questionable expertise on Islam is his Memorandum on Indian Moslems submitted to the India Office, April 25, 1915, File 1, Box 1, Sykes GB-0165–0275, MECA.

46. Westrate, *Arab Bureau*, 31.

47. D. G. Hogarth, "Reflections on the *Arab Bulletin*," *Arab Bulletin*, no. 100, August 20, 1918. The *Arab Bulletins* are reprinted sequentially in Robin Bidwell (ed.), *The Arab Bulletin, 1916–1919*, vols. 1–4 (Gerrards Cross: Archive Editions, 1986).

48. Sharif Hussein, Proclamation, quoted in Tauber, *Emergence of the Arab Movements*, 251.

49. Mark Sykes, "Secret—The Problem of the Near East," June 20, 1916, DR.588, File 1, Box 1, Sykes GB-0165–0275, MECA.

50. *Arab Bulletin*, no. 5, June 18, 1916. The Ottoman response to the revolt in Mecca, which involved a pitched defense of the fort there, led to the Kaʿba being shelled, a fact that Britain used later in its propaganda efforts. *Arab Bulletin*, no. 6, June 23, 1916.

51. Government of Bombay to Government of India, April 26, 1915, Foreign and Political Department, War—Secret, June 1916, No. 223–314, NAI. The war also suspended the flow of remittances from persons such as the nizam of Hyderabad to various public welfare projects and religious tasks in Mecca and Medina, given the concern that the monies might fall into Ottoman hands. Viceroy to Secretary of State for India, April 23, 1915; High Commissioner Egypt to Viceroy, April 27, 1915, Foreign and Political Department, War—Secret, July 1915, No. 245–251, NAI.

52. Wingate to Wilson, June 19, 1916, SAD Wingate 137/4/29–30, SAD.

53. Ibid.

54. Westrate, *Arab Bureau*, 69–70.

55. MacMichael to Wingate, July 16, 1916, SAD Wingate 138/16/50, SAD.

56. Angus Cameron, Governor of Sennar Province, to Wingate, July 24, 1916, SAD Wingate 138/16/52, SAD.

57. *Arab Bulletin*, no. 9, July 9, 1916.

58. Ayesha Jalal, *Self and Sovereignty: Individual and Community in South Asian Islam* (New York: Routledge, 2002), 198.

59. *Arab Bulletin*, no. 9, July 9, 1916.

60. *Arab Bulletin*, no. 15, August 10, 1916.

61. Ibid.

62. Shaikh, *Community and Consensus in Islam*, 167; F. Robinson, *Separatism among Indian Muslims*, 204; Minault, *Khilafat Movement*, 52.

63. J. Jones, *Shiʿa Islam in Colonial India*, 176.

64. Storrs, *Orientations*, 156.

65. Haidar Ali, Translation of Proclamation issued in Hijaz, August 9, 1916, reproduced in *Arab Bulletin*, no. 20, September 14, 1916.

66. Ottoman Legation Berne, September 2, 1916, in *Arab Bulletin*, no. 25, October 7, 1916.

67. George Stitt, *A Prince of Arabia: Emir Shereef Haidar Ali* (London: G. Allen and Unwin, 1948), 119–120. Stitt compiled the memoir from Haidar Ali's diaries, which were translated from Turkish and sent to Stitt by Haidar Ali's widow, Isobel Dunn, now known as Princess Fatima, a British woman who converted to Islam when she married Ali.

68. Ibid., 125. On Haidar Ali's postwar dealings with the British government, see FO 141/740/1, TNA.

69. See Ochsenwald, *Religion, Society, and the State in Arabia;* William Ochsenwald, *The Hijaz Railroad* (Charlottesville: University Press of Virginia, 1980); al-Amr, *Hijaz under Ottoman Rule;* William Ochsenwald, "Ottoman Subsidies to the Hijaz, 1877–1886," *International Journal of Middle East Studies*, 6:3 (1975), 300–307; and Munayyir and Landau, *Hejaz Railway.*

70. Storrs, *Orientations*, 160.

71. Note on the Present Position at Jedda, by "R.S.," June 30, 1916, FO 141/803, TNA, and Reel 5, Box Number II/4, Private Letters and Diaries of Sir Ronald Storrs, Pembroke College, Cambridge. See also Storrs, *Orientations*, 160, 164. Mohs incorrectly states that it was Kinahan Cornwallis who first came up with the idea that a British official should be appointed in Jidda to assist with certain aspects of the pilgrimage but should have an "unpretentious title, so as to avoid drawing attention to his real functions." Mohs, *Military Intelligence*, 44.

72. Foreign Office to Government of India, July 10, 1916, FO 141/803, TNA. The *Arab Bulletin* described Wilson as the "British Representative" to Hussein. *Arab Bulletin*, no. 14, August 7, 1916. Report by Kinahan Cornwallis, July 8, 1916, Foreign and Political Department, War—Secret, March 1917, No. 67-69, NAI.

73. Thomas, *Empires of Intelligence*, 129.

74. Lawrence, *Seven Pillars of Wisdom*, 50.

75. Young, "A Little to the East—Memoirs of an Anglo-Egyptian Official," 137–138, Young GB-0165–0310, MECA.

76. For example, Young noted that the Indian "colony" in Mecca was so large that it had its own school. Young, "A Little to the East—Memoirs of an Anglo-Egyptian Official," 157–158, Young GB-0165–0310, MECA.

77. Note on the Present Position at Jedda, by "R.S.," June 30, 1916, FO 141/803, TNA, and Reel 5, Box Number II/4, Private Letters and Diaries of Sir Ronald Storrs, Pembroke College, Cambridge.

78. Feisal's Operations, October 30, 1916, FO 882/5, TNA.

79. Lawrence, *Seven Pillars of Wisdom*, 18.

80. Philby, Mecca 1939, 1/4/9/3/25, Box 18, Philby GB-0165–0229, MECA.

81. Shuckburgh, India Office, to Foreign Office, April 9, 1917, IOR/PS/11/122/P1670, IOR, APAC, BL.

82. Minute paper, Political Department, Government of India, April 9 & 10, 1917, IOR/PS/11/122/P1670, IOR, APAC, BL.

83. Ibid. See also propaganda suggestions by Risaldar-Major Mataz Khan related to the Arab Revolt in FO 141/682/1, TNA.

84. Viceroy to India Office, April 27, 1917, IOR/PS/11/122/P1670, IOR, APAC, BL.

85. Singha, "Passport, Ticket and India-Rubber Stamp," 66.

86. *The Times*, December 19, 1916.

87. See Kioumgi, *Photographer on the Hajj;* Jacques Jomier, *Le mahmal et la caravanne égyptienne des pèlerins de la Mecque (xiii–xx siècles)* (Cairo: L'Institut

Français d'Archéologie Orientale, 1953); Ibrahim Rif'at Basha, *Mir'at al-Haramayn* (Cairo: Dar al-Kutub al-Misriyya, 1925); Muhammad Labib Batanuni, *Rihla al-Hijaziyya* (Cairo: Matba'at al-Jamaliyya, 1911); and Edward William Lane, *Manners and Customs of the Modern Egyptians* (London: Ward, Lock and Co., 1890), 448.

88. Muhammad Sadiq Bay, *Kawkab al-Hajj fi safar al-Mahmal bahran wa sirat barran* (Cairo, 1884), 11–12. See also Bay, *Mash'al al-Mahmal, Risala fi sir al-Hajj al-Misri bira min yaum khuruja min Misr* (Cairo, 1880); and Bey, *Dalil al-Hajj* (Cairo, 1895). Bay was awarded a gold medal at the Venice Exposition Géographique in 1881 for his photographs of the Holy Cities and the Hajj.

89. Parker report to GHQ, September 10, 1916, in Winstone, *Diaries of Parker Pasha*, 123.

90. Admiralty to W. F. Nicholson, Under-Secretary of State, Foreign Office, October 29, 1916, enclosing report from Admiral Huguet, October 12, 1916; FO to Secret Department, Government of India, November 5, 1916, IOR/L/PS/11/97/P3540, IOR, APAC, BL. It is significant that the French were also at pains to stress their status as a ruler of Muslims; see also British concerns about Mustafa Cherchali, sent by France to act as its representative in Mecca in 1917, High Commissioner for Egypt to FO, May 27, 1917; FO to High Commissioner Egypt, May 29, 1917, FO 141/671/4, TNA; *Arab Bulletin*, no. 24, October 5, 1916; Baker, *King Husain and the Kingdom of Hejaz*, 122. No exact date in September is given because there is substantial confusion among both primary and secondary sources on the exact arrival dates of the Royal Navy ships to Jidda, and which ship carried the *mahmal* and the *kiswa*. Amid the panoply, one official privately noted that the hereditary keeper of the keys to the Ka'ba had died of alcohol poisoning. Young, "Three Months in Jedda," September 26, 1916, DS.244.4, Young GB-0165-0310, MECA. In the 1930s, a "Hajj regatta" had become a custom in Jidda Harbor, with Royal Navy ships taking part. Report on the Hajj of 1932, in *RoH*, 6:493.

91. Storrs, *Orientations*, 168.

92. Westrate, *Arab Bureau*, 68.

93. *Arab Bulletin*, no. 28, November 1, 1916.

94. Westrate, *Arab Bureau*, 70.

95. *Arab Bulletin*, no. 28, November 1, 1916.

96. Barbara D. Metcalf, *Hussain Ahmad Madani: The Jihad for Islam and India's Freedom* (London: Oneworld, 2008), 13.

97. Ibid., 16.

98. Ibid., 23–25.

99. Ibid., 11–12, 29–30. While he was incarcerated in Malta, Madani heard that his family had died of malnutrition in Medina; ibid., 42. See also Miyan, *Asira'n-e-Malta*.

100. Hassan was subsequently appointed Indian pilgrimage officer and performed the Hajj in this role every year until 1922.

101. Notes on Hajj 1917, FO 371/3408, TNA.

102. Mr. J. S. Kadri, Educational Inspector, deputed from Aden, Note on His Experiences of the Haj 1916, Foreign and Political Department, War—Secret, March 1917, No. 67–69, NAI.

103. Mr. J. S. Kadri, "A Pilgrim's Experiences," *Arab Bulletin*, no. 34, December 11, 1916.

104. See Jacob Goldberg, "The Origins of British-Saudi Relations: The 1915 Anglo-Saudi Treaty Revisited," *Historical Journal*, 28:3 (1985), 693–703.

105. *Arab Bulletin*, no. 65, October 8, 1917; *Arab Bulletin*, no. 66, November 30, 1917. Sixty thousand to seventy thousand pilgrims stood at Mount Arafat.

106. *Arab Bulletin*, no. 66, November 30, 1917; *Arab Bulletin*, no. 67, December 16, 1917.

107. *Arab Bulletin*, no. 66, November 30, 1917.

108. *Arab Bulletin*, no. 41, February 6, 1917.

109. *Arab Bulletin*, no. 74, December 24, 1917, quoted in Kedourie, "Surrender of Medina," 127.

110. T. E. Lawrence, "The Sharif's Religious Views," *Arab Bulletin*, no. 59, August 12, 1917.

111. *Arab Bulletin*, no. 76, January 13, 1918.

112. *Arab Bulletin*, no. 92, June 11, 1918.

113. *Arab Bulletin*, no. 104, September 24, 1918. A total of 44,000 pilgrims stood at Mount Arafat. Only 7,000 pilgrims arrived by sea, mainly Indians (1,450) and Sudanese (4,065). *Arab Bulletin*, no. 106, December 6, 1918.

114. Capt. Wilson, Jedda to Wingate, High Commissioner, Egypt, March 29, 1917, FO 141/773, TNA.

115. Capt. Bray, 18th K.G.O. Lancers, Indian Army, Note on the Mohammedan Question, its bearing on events in India and Arabia, and the future of the great Islamic revival now Turkey is no longer the power on which the hopes of the Moslem world are placed. Sent to Capt. Wilson, Jedda, forwarded to Sir R. Wingate, High Commissioner, Egypt, March 25, 1917, FO 141/773, TNA. Another example of such thinking was the suggestion of Percy Cox, political officer at Basra, to T. E. Lawrence, after the British military failure at Kut al-Amara in 1916, that a conference of representatives from across Britain's Muslim empire should be convened to discuss common issues. Cox thought that this would improve consultation among Egypt, Aden, Iraq, and India on policies related to Islam. Quoted in Mohs, *Military Intelligence*, 23.

116. Montagu to Hankey, War Cabinet Memo, November 4, 1917, CAB 24/34, TNA.

117. D. G. Hogarth, *Hejaz before World War I: A Handbook* (Cambridge: Oleander, 1978), 75–77. First published in 1917.

118. Ibid., 28. Hogarth also wrote a history of European exploration and knowledge of Arabia; see D. G. Hogarth, *The Penetration of Arabia* (London: Lawrence and Bullen, 1904).

119. Hogarth, *Hejaz before World War I*, 29.

120. D. G. Hogarth to Billy Hogarth, January 10, 1918, File 3/1, Hogarth GB-0165–0147, MECA.

121. A more general discussion of Britain's postwar strategy in the area is John Fisher, *Curzon and British Imperialism*. However, this sense of "opportunity" must be placed in the context of the wider unrest that had affected the empire during the war, including such events as the Ghadar Conspiracy, the Silk

Letters Conspiracy, the more general Indo-German Conspiracy, and the 1915 Singapore Mutiny.

122. Consul-General, Batavia, to India Office, October 11, 1918, IOR/L/PS/11/150, IOR, APAC, BL.

123. Wingate to Sykes, February 10, 1918, SAD Wingate 167/1/430–434, SAD.

124. Wingate to Lord Hardinge, January 25, 1918, SAD Wingate 167/1/357–361, SAD.

125. Hew Strachan, *World War One*, vol. 1, *To Arms* (Oxford: Oxford University Press, 2001), puts forward a convincing argument for the global nature of the conflict.

126. Wingate to Balfour, February 20, 1918, SAD Wingate 195/1/163, SAD.

127. Count Leon Ostrorog, The British Empire and the Mohammedans, 1, sent to British Residency, Cairo, July 12, 1918, FO 141/786, TNA.

128. Captain Ajub Khan, Observations of Mecca, October 2, 1919, IOR/L/MIL/7/18619, IOR, APAC, BL.

129. Report on Hajj 1336 AH/1918, FO 371/4194, TNA, in *RoH*, 5:105–107.

130. Fakhri's headquarters during the war was in a *kuttab* (elementary school) attached to the Prophet's Mosque. Kedourie, "Surrender of Medina," 133. Kedourie argues that Fakhri's position was justified in light of subsequent events; in contrast to the orderly and organized Ottoman administration, once Hashemite forces entered the city on January 13 and 15, 1919, it was reported that there was looting, pillaging, and disorder that continued for months after their takeover. Ibid., 135–137.

131. John Gallagher, "The Decline, Revival and Fall of the British Empire," in John Gallagher, *The Decline, Revival and Fall of the British Empire: The Ford Lectures and Other Essays* ed. Anil Seal (Cambridge: Cambridge University Press, 1982), 73–153, 90–103.

132. For an example of the close communication between British intelligence officials in Egypt and India during this period, see FO 141/521/2, TNA.

133. Paris, *Britain, the Hashemites, and Arab Rule*, 299. Paris's book is a rare exception to this lacuna.

134. Ibid., 311.

135. In June 1916, at the beginning of the Arab Revolt, Hussein simultaneously declared himself king of the Hijaz and king of the lands of the Arabs. He declared himself caliph in March 1924 and continued to call himself caliph after he abdicated as king of the Hijaz in October 1924 until his death in 1931 in exile in Trans-Jordan, his son Abdullah's kingdom.

136. Report for July 1–11, 1920, in *Jedda Diaries*, 1:271.

137. Minutes of the Interdepartmental Pilgrimage and Quarantine Committee, March 18, 1919, File 22168, CO 273/491, TNA. See also minutes of the committee's meetings in FO 608/101, TNA.

138. Minutes of the Interdepartmental Pilgrimage and Quarantine Committee, December 31, 1920, File 2345, CO 273/512, TNA. See also internal debates among government of India officials about this subsidy in Foreign and Political Department, Secret—External, May 1921, No. 4–14, NAI; and Foreign and Political, Secret—External, November 1919, No. 1–139, NAI.

139. Officers had inflated pay lists and had sold government stores. In early 1918, Amir Abdullah's army of 250 men cost £4,000 per month in salaries alone. Bedouin tribesmen had been overpaid, receiving £3 per month for personal services and double for those who had camels.

140. *Notes on the Middle East*, no. 1, December 7, 1919 (new title of *Arab Bulletin*).

141. Hussein Ruhi estimated that there were 70,000 pilgrims at Mount Arafat; 4,100 arrived from Sudan and 12,500 arrived from India, out of a total of 22,150 arrivals by sea. Report on Hajj 1337 AH/1919, 1–4, FO 371/4195, TNA, in *RoH*, 5:159–162; *Notes on the Middle East*, no. 1, December 7, 1919; Suggestions from Major Thompson, May 8, 1919, FO 608/101, TNA; Lieut.-Col. E. Wilkinson, Report on Inquiries into the Measures for the Sanitary Control of the Hejaz Pilgrimage, 1919, CO 732/39/9, TNA.

142. See Qureshi, *Pan-Islam in British Indian Politics;* Özcan, *Pan-Islamism;* Landau, *Politics of Pan-Islam;* Minault, *Khilafat Movement;* and F. Robinson, *Separatism among Indian Muslims.* Mishra, "Politicization of a Holy Act," focuses more directly on the Khilafat movement and the hajj.

143. Busch, *Britain, India, and the Arabs*, 166–168; Low, "Empire of the Hajj," 156. An example of Indian reactions to the abolition is in Foreign and Political Department, Secret—External, No. 34—X, 1924, NAI.

144. Quoted in Paris, *Britain, the Hashemites, and Arab Rule*, 326.

145. Quoted in Minault, *Khilafat Movement*, 62.

146. Quoted in Macmillan, *Peacemakers*, 391.

147. Quoted in ibid., 390.

148. See F. Robinson, *Separatism among Indian Muslims.*

149. Paris, *Britain, the Hashemites, and Arab Rule*, 302; Qureshi, *Pan-Islam in British Indian Politics*, 423–424. Francis Robinson, *Separatism among Indian Muslims*, 208–211, mentions the Hajj only in relation to the establishment of the Anjuman-i-khuddam-i-kaaba.

150. Paris, *Britain, the Hashemites, and Arab Rule*, 306–307.

151. Sir R. Graham to Milne Cheetham, Cairo, April 16, 1919, DT 52.5.EGY, File 5, Cheetham GB-0165-0055, MECA.

152. *Notes on the Middle East*, no. 1, December 7, 1919.

153. Gallagher, "Decline, Revival and Fall," 90–103.

154. Page, *Prelude to Partition*, 52.

155. For more general works on Indian soldiers in this period, see David Omissi, "Europe through Indian Eyes: Indian Soldiers Encounter England and France, 1914–1918," *English Historical Review*, 122:496 (2007), 371–396; David Omissi, *Indian Voices of the Great War: Soldiers' Letters, 1914–1918* (London: Macmillan, 1999); and Omissi, *Sepoy and the Raj.*

156. Omissi, *Sepoy and the Raj*, 99–100, see also Green, *Islam and the Army.*

157. Omissi, *Sepoy and the Raj*, 100–101.

158. Ibid., 98.

159. General Cox to War Office, October 30, 1918; and Colonel Wigram, King's Private Secretary, to India Office, November 19, 1918, IOR/L/MIL/7/18619, IOR, APAC, BL. These men perhaps knew that seventy French

Muslim soldiers had performed the Hajj sponsored by the French in 1917; see F. E. Peters, *Hajj*, 328.

160. Everard Digby to Edwin Montagu, Secretary of State for India, November 9, 1918, IOR/L/MIL/7/18619, IOR, APAC, BL.

161. Ibid.

162. Montagu's note on Everard Digby to Edwin Montagu, Secretary of State for India, November 9, 1918, IOR/L/MIL/7/18619, IOR, APAC, BL.

163. *Arab Bulletin*, no. 109, February 6, 1919. In 1920, Britain sent a further batch of soldier-pilgrims on Hajj, 54 officers and 970 other ranks. See also *The Times*, September 25, 1920.

164. General Headquarters Egypt to War Office, December 30, 1918, IOR/L/MIL/7/18619, IOR, APAC, BL; *Arab Bulletin*, no. 109, February 6, 1919.

165. War Office to General Headquarters, December 8, 1918, IOR/L/MIL/7/18619, IOR, APAC, BL; Minute by General Cox, Political Department Government of India, July 11, 1919, IOR/L/MIL/7/18619, IOR, APAC, BL.

166. Report of Commander-in-Chief, Egyptian Expeditionary Force to War Office January 31, 1919, IOR/L/MIL/7/18619, IOR, APAC, BL.

167. Communication from Dr. David Omissi, June 4, 2008. See Omissi, *Indian Voices of the Great War*; and Omissi, "Europe through Indian Eyes."

168. Report of General Officer Commanding Egyptian Expeditionary Force to War Office, December 11, 1919, IOR/L/MIL/7/18619, IOR, APAC, BL.

169. Report for September 1–10, 1920, in *Jedda Diaries*, 1:360–363.

170. *Notes from the Middle East*, no. 4, May 24, 1920. The soldier-pilgrims gave rise to a rumor in India that Britain had militarily occupied the Hijaz; see Foreign and Political Department, External—B, Secret, 10–16, 1921, NAI.

171. This type of exercise continued in the 1930s. For example, when HMS *Hastings* visited Jidda in 1931 and 1932, the ship's Somali naval ratings were allowed to perform the Hajj while the ship was in port. Report on the Hajj of 1932, in *RoH*, 6:493.

172. *Notes on the Middle East*, no. 1, December 7, 1919, 11–14.

173. Captain Ajub Khan, Observations of Mecca, October 2, 1919, attached to Report of General Officer Commanding Egyptian Expeditionary Force to War Office, December 11, 1919, IOR/L/MIL/7/18619, IOR, APAC, BL.

174. *Notes on the Middle East*, no. 1, December 7, 1919, 11–14.

175. Captain Ajub Khan, Observations of Mecca, October 2, 1919, attached to Report of General Officer Commanding, Egyptian Expeditionary Force to War Office, December 11, 1919, IOR/L/MIL/7/18619, IOR, APAC, BL.

176. *Notes on the Middle East*, no. 1, December 7, 1919, 11–14.

177. *Notes on the Middle East*, no. 4, May 25, 1920.

178. Director of Arab Bureau to Colonel Bassett, February 2, 1918, FO 686/31, TNA.

179. High Commissioner, Cairo, to FO, April 21, 1918, FO 686/31, TNA; High Commissioner, Cairo, to FO, May 21, 1918, FO 686/31, TNA.

180. Roff, "Conduct of the Hajj from Malaya," 87.

181. Colonel Wilson to Ruhi, June 13, 1918, FO 686/31, TNA; High Commissioner, Cairo, to Stack, Khartoum, June 19, 1918, FO 686/31, TNA.

182. Bassett to Ruhi, July 24, 1918, FO 686/31, TNA.

183. Col. Wilson, Cairo, to unknown, September 11, 1918, FO 686/31, TNA.

184. Telephone message from Ruhi, undated, FO 686/31, TNA; Bassett to Director of Arab Bureau, April 10, 1918, FO 686/31, TNA.

185. See also the later suggestion in Director of Intelligence, Nigeria to Muir, March 29, 1925, proposing that the Sudanese and Nigerian governments should buy the house of a Sudanese religious notable in Mecca "in someone else's name" as a pilgrim hostel staffed by a Sudanese person; Lethem papers, Box 12, File 3, 46–47, Mss. Brit. Emp.s.276, Rhodes House Library, Oxford.

186. Aden to High Commissioner, Cairo, February 24, 1919, FO 686/31, TNA; Cairo to Vickery, Jedda, January 24, 1920, FO 686/31, TNA; Arab Bureau to unknown, March 5, 1919, FO 686/31, TNA. G. Wyman Bury, a British intelligence agent who worked across the Middle East before and during the war and had particular experience of Yemen, argued in a book published in 1919 that Britain should employ "a responsible consular agent (Moslem of course) to reside at Medina, also another to understudy the Jeddah vice-consul when he went to Mecca and to look after the Yenbo pilgrim traffic, would safeguard the interests of our nationals, who enormously outnumber the pilgrims of any other nation. Further interference with the Hejaz, unless invited, would be unjustifiable." G. Wyman Bury, *Pan-Islam* (London: Macmillan, 1919), 102.

187. FO to R. S. Scott, October 21, 1920, FO 686/31, TNA.

188. Curzon to British Agent Jedda, February 14, 1921, FO 686/31, TNA.

189. Report for November 21–December 1, 1919, *Jedda Diaries*, 1:63–64.

190. Report for December 21–31, *Jedda Diaries*, 1:75.

191. Allenby to Curzon, May 22, 1920, FO 371/5092, TNA.

192. Ibid.

193. Report for August 20–31, 1920, *Jedda Diaries*, 1:360–363.

194. Report for September 10–20, 1920, *Jedda Diaries*, 1:381.

195. Report for October 11–30, 1921, *Jedda Diaries*, 1:575–576; Report for October 31–November 30, 1922, *Jedda Diaries*, 1:579–580.

196. Report for October 1922, *Jedda Diaries*, 2:82–83.

197. Report for March 11–31, 1922, *Jedda Diaries*, 2:28, 30. See also Minutes of Inter-Departmental Pilgrimage Committee, February 7, 1922, which resolved to point out to the government of India "the relevant passage in the Koran" that pilgrims should be "self-supporting," IOR/L/E/7/1146, IOR, APAC, BL.

198. Report for April 21–May 10, 1922, *Jedda Diaries*, 2:44. "No Bengalis or Malabaris deposited money . . . only Punjabis and Sindhis appear to carry out this . . . preparation." Report for June 21 –July 10, 1922, *Jedda Diaries*, 2:57.

199. Report for June 1–20, *Jedda Diaries*, 2:53–54.

200. Report for November 1922, *Jedda Diaries*, 2:88.

201. Secret appendix to Report for September 20, 1920, *Jedda Diaries*, 1:383–384. A further report set out the situation more starkly, albeit fancifully; Britain's only course was to "either leave Arabia and the Arabs alone or to take them over under a mandate or protectorate." Report for July 1–11, 1920, *Jedda Diaries*, 1:271.

202. Report for June 1–12, 1920, *Jedda Diaries*, 1:244–248.

203. Secret appendix to Report for September 20, 1920, *Jedda Diaries*, 1:383–384.

204. Report for January 1–10, 1921, *Jedda Diaries*, 1:474–475.

205. British Agent Jedda to FO, February 22, 1923, IOR/L/E/7/1146, IOR, APAC, BL.

206. FO to Under-Secretary of State India Office, January 8, 1923, IOR/L/E/7/1146, IOR, APAC, BL. It was thought that the "greater attention being paid to the pilgrimage in British Malaya and elsewhere in the empire tends to widen the scope of the work. . . . It is probable that Indians only constitute half of our pilgrims." Reader Bullard to Secretary Government of India Foreign and Political Department, June 23, 1926, IOR/L/E/7/1146, IOR, APAC, BL.

207. Report for June 1923, *Jedda Diaries*, 2:134–135. See also British Agent Jedda to FO, February 22, 1923, IOR/L/E/7/1146, IOR, APAC, BL.

208. Bullard's view of Hussein was also derogatory: "Imagine a cunning, lying, credulous, suspicious, obstinate, vain, conceited, ignorant, greedy, cruel Arab sheikh suddenly thrust into a position where he has to deal with all sorts of questions he doesn't understand and where there is no human power to restrain him." Bullard, "Notes for Memoirs—1923," File 4, Box 3, Bullard GB-0165–0042, MECA.

209. Ibid.

210. Turner Morison Company to Government of India Education and Health Department, August 15, 1923, Foreign and Political Department, 1033-M, 1923, NAI; Paris, *Britain, the Hashemites, and Arab Rule*, 307.

211. Minutes of the Inter-Departmental Pilgrimage Committee, Foreign Office, December 18, 1922, L/E/7/1146, IOR, APAC, BL.

212. Report for July 1923, *Jedda Diaries*, 2:139–141, 144–145.

213. Reader Bullard to his family, September 16, 1923, in Bullard, *Two Kings in Arabia*, 14. The consulate was upgraded to an agency in 1923 and a legation in 1930, but for purposes of clarity it will be referred to as a consulate in the text, and the chief British representative as consul.

214. Oishi, "Friction and Rivalry," 164; Singha, "Passport, Ticket, and India-Rubber Stamp," 53.

215. Bullard, *Two Kings in Arabia*, 14–15.

216. Report for August 1923, *Jedda Diaries*, 2:147–149, 154–155.

217. *The Times*, May 12, 1924. Its correspondent in Peshawar two years earlier reported how Hussein was viewed locally as an "infidel interloper" who would not have been in power without British support, and that the "strength and extent of the hostility of ordinary pilgrims is a new feature." *The Times*, September 14, 1922.

218. Singha, "Passport, Ticket and India-Rubber Stamp," 50, 66.

219. Report for July 1924, *Jedda Diaries*, 2:226–228.

220. Report for February 1924, *Jedda Diaries*, 2:195; General Department, 1924, File 5247, MSA.

221. Report for July 1924, *Jedda Diaries*, 2:226–228; Report for August 1924, *Jedda Diaries*, 2:233–234.

222. Report for April 12–30, 1925, *Jedda Diaries*, 2:301.

223. See Doris Behrens Abouseif, "The Mahmal Legend and the Pilgrimage of the Ladies of the Mamluk Court," *Mamluk Studies Review*, 1 (1997), 87–96; F. E. Peters, *Hajj*, 93–94, 165–166; Ibn Battuta, *The Travels of Ibn Battuta*, ed. H. A. R. Gibb, vol. 1 (Cambridge: Cambridge University Press, 1956), 58–59; and Jomier, *Mahmal*.

224. Rapp, "Memoirs, Suez 1924–5," 52, Rapp GB-0165–0234, MECA.

225. Bullard to Hussein, June 27, 1923, FO 686/62, TNA.

226. Allenby to British Agent Jedda, June 26, 1923, FO 686/62, TNA.

227. Allenby to British Agent Jedda, July 4, 1923, FO 686/62, TNA; Allenby to British Agent Jedda, July 6, 1923, FO 686/62, TNA.

228. Allenby to British Agent Jedda, July 4, 1923, FO 686/62, TNA; Allenby to British Agent Jedda, July 6, 1923, FO 686/62, TNA.

229. Scott, Acting High Commissioner, Egypt to Curzon, September 22, 1923, FO 686/62, TNA.

230. Allenby to Ramsay MacDonald, June 21, 1924, FO 686/62, TNA.

231. British Agent Jedda to High Commissioner Alexandria, June 24, 1924, FO 686/62, TNA.

232. *The Times*, August 8, 1924, and August 13, 1924.

233. *Notes on the Middle East*, no. 4, May 25, 1920.

234. Political Agent, Bahrain, to Civil Commissioner Baghdad, Cairo, and Simla, June 8, 1920, DS 247.N48, File 3, Box 15, Philby GB-0165–0229, MECA.

235. FO 371/608/80, TNA, quoted in Baker, *King Husain*, 204.

236. Madawi al-Rasheed, *A History of Saudi Arabia* (Cambridge: Cambridge University Press, 2002), 44–49.

237. Cox to Colonial Office, May 27, 1922, FO 371/7713, TNA, quoted in Paris, *Britain, the Hashemites, and Arab Rule*, 305.

238. High Commissioner, Palestine, to Colonial Office, June 5, 1922, IOR/L/PS/10/936, IOR, APAC, BL.

239. Colonial Office to High Commissioner, Palestine, June 8, 1922, IOR/L/PS/10/936, IOR, APAC, BL.

240. Minutes by Arthur Hirtzel, June 10, 1922, IOR/L/PS/10/936, IOR, APAC, BL.

241. Askar al-Enazy, "Ibn Saud's Early Foreign Policy towards the Rashidi Emirate and the Kingdom of Hijaz, in Light of British Imperial Policy, 1914–1927" (PhD dissertation, Cambridge University, 2006), 195.

242. Bullard to Foreign Office, October 19, 1923, with enclosed Note by Grafftey-Smith, October 17, 1923, FO 800/253, quoted in Paris, *Britain, the Hashemites, and Arab Rule*, 309.

243. Paris, *Britain, the Hashemites, and Arab Rule*, 313.

244. This argument is derived from Mark Sedgwick, "Saudi Sufis: Compromise in the Hejaz, 1925–40," *Die Welt des Islams*, 37:3 (1997), 349–368, 358.

245. Bullard, "Notes for Memoirs—1924," File 4, Box 3, Bullard GB-0165–0034, MECA. See also reports on the negative reactions of Indian Muslims to Hussein's proclamation of himself as caliph in Foreign and Political, Secret—External, 34-X, 1924, NAI.

246. Eldon Rutter, "The Hejaz," *Geographical Journal*, 77:2 (1931), 97–108, 97.

247. Rapp thought that Jidda was an "unutterably sordid town" and that Hashemite defensive preparations in Mecca were "pathetic in the extreme." Rapp, "Memoirs, Suez 1924–5," 53–54, Rapp GB-0165-0234, MECA.

248. Ibid., 53.

249. Ibid., 55.

250. Sultan Ghalib al-Qu'aiti, *The Holy Cities, the Pilgrimage and the World of Islam: A History from the Earliest Traditions until 1925 (1344H)* (Louisville, KY: Fons Vitae, 2007), 518.

CHAPTER 5 *Britain and the Hajj under Saudi Control*

1. The followers of this interpretation of Islam call themselves *al-muwahhidun*, believers in the oneness of God *(tawhid)*. The terms "Wahhabi" and "Wahhabism" are used in this chapter because they are the ones most commonly used in existing scholarly works. Wahhabi revivalism in the Hijaz was called *Mutadayana*, the restrengthening of religion, and was generally referred to by the British as "militant Wahhabism."

2. On the Hajj and its role in the production of orthopraxy and "orthodoxy" in Islam, see Pearson, *Pious Passengers*, 8, 67–68, 72–76; Nehemia Levtzion, *Eighteenth-Century Renewal and Reform in Islam* (Syracuse, NY: Syracuse University Press, 1987); Roff, "Islamic Movements"; Voll, *Islam;* and Rahman, "Revival and Reform in Islam."

3. A selection of examples of this includes F. Robinson, "Islamic Reform and Modernities in South Asia"; Amira K. Bennison, "Muslim Universalism and Western Globalization," in A. G. Hopkins (ed.), *Globalization in World History* (London: Pimlico, 2002), 74–97; F. Robinson, *Islam and Muslim History in South Asia;* Armando Salvatore, *Islam and the Political Discourse of Modernity* (Reading: Ithaca, 1999); Elizabeth Sirriyeh, *Sufis and Anti-Sufis: The Defense, Rethinking and Rejection of Sufism in the Modern World* (Richmond, VA: Curzon, 1999); Voll, *Islam;* Fazlur Rahman, *Islam and Modernity: Transformation of an Intellectual Tradition* (Chicago: University of Chicago Press, 1974); Albert Hourani, *Arabic Thought in the Liberal Age: 1798–1939* (Oxford: Oxford University Press, 1970); Rahman, "Revival and Reform in Islam"; Charles C. Adams, *Islam and Modernism in Egypt: A Study of the Modern Reform Movement Inaugurated by Muhammad 'Abduh* (New York: Russell and Russell, 1968); Aziz Ahmad, *Islamic Modernism in India and Pakistan, 1857–1964* (Oxford: Oxford University Press, 1967); and Malcolm Kerr, *Islamic Reform: The Political and Legal Theories of Muhammad 'Abduh and Rashid Rida* (Berkeley: University of California Press, 1966).

4. See al-Enazy, *Creation of Saudi Arabia;* Hamadi Redissi, "Refutation of Wahhabism in Arabic Sources, 1745–1932," in Madawi Al-Rasheed (ed.), *Kingdom without Borders* (New York: Columbia University Press, 2008), 157–181; Natana J. De-Long Bas, *Wahhabi Islam: From Revival and Reform to Global Jihad* (Oxford: Oxford University Press, 2004); Paris, *Britain, the Hashemites, and Arab Rule;* Al-Rasheed, *History of Saudi Arabia;* Teitelbaum, *Rise and Fall of the Hashemite Kingdom;* Alexei Vassiliev, *The History of Saudi Arabia* (New York:

New York University Press, 1998); Haifa Alangari, *The Struggle for Power in Arabia: Ibn Saud, Hussein and Great Britain, 1914–1924* (Reading: Ithaca, 1998); Joseph Kostiner, *The Making of Saudi Arabia, 1916–1936: From Chieftaincy to Monarchical State* (New York: Oxford University Press, 1994); Shebl, "Emergence and Demise of an Independent Arab State"; Joseph Kostiner, "On Instruments and Their Designers: The Ikhwan of Nejd and the Emergence of the Saudi State," *Middle Eastern Studies*, 21:3 (1985), 298–323; C. Leatherdale, *Britain and Saudi Arabia, 1925–1939: The Imperial Oasis* (London: Cass, 1983); Daniel Silverfarb, "Britain and Saudi Arabia on the Eve of the Second World War," *Middle Eastern Studies*, 19:4 (1981), 403–411; Baker, *King Husain;* M. A. Tayeb, "The Relations of Ibn Saud with Great Britain, 1902–1953" (MA thesis, University of Michigan, 1979); John S. Habib, *Ibn Saud's Warriors of Islam: The Ikhwan of Nejd and Their Role in the Creation of the Saudi Kingdom, 1910–1930* (Leiden: Brill, 1978); Gary Troeller, *The Birth of Saudi Arabia: Britain and the Rise of the House of Sa'ud* (London: Cass, 1976); Daniel Silverfarb, "British Relations with Ibn Saud of Najd, 1914–1919" (PhD dissertation, University of Wisconsin, 1972); and George Linabury, "British-Saudi Relations 1902–1927: A Revisionist Interpretation" (PhD dissertation, Columbia University, 1970).

5. See Leslie McLoughlin, *Ibn Saud: Founder of a Kingdom* (London: Macmillan, 1993); M. Almana, *Arabia Unified: A Portrait of Ibn Saud* (London: Hutchinson Benham, 1980); M. C. Iqbal, *The Emergence of Saudi Arabia* (Delhi: Idarah-i Adabiyat-i Delli, 1977); David Howarth, *The Desert King: A Life of Ibn Saud* (London: Collins, 1964); H. St. John Philby, *Saudi Arabia* (London: E. Benn, 1955); Gerald De Gaury, *Rulers of Mecca* (London: Harrap, 1951); H. C. Armstrong, *Lord of Arabia: Ibn Saud, an Intimate Study of a King* (London: A. Barker, 1934); H. St. J. B. Philby, *Arabia of the Wahhabis* (London: Constable, 1928); and H. St. J. B. Philby, *The Triumph of the Wahhabis* (London: Constable, 1926). On the American role in the development of Saudi Arabia, see Robert Vitalis, *America's Kingdom: Mythmaking on the Saudi Oil Frontier* (Stanford, CA: Stanford University Press, 2006).

6. Bose, *Hundred Horizons*, 212–219.

7. Ibid., 195, 215.

8. See S. L. Dening (ed.), *King Abdul Aziz: Political Correspondence, 1904–53*, vols. 1–4 (Gerrards Cross: Archive Editions, 1996); Rush, *Records of the Hajj;* Jarman, *Jeddah Diaries;* Cobbold, *Pilgrimage to Mecca* (1933); Al-Hajj Khaja Gulam al-Hasnain Panipati, *Safar Nama-e-Hajj* (Delhi, 1934); Maulvi Sayyed Ahmad Husain Saheb Amjad, *Hajj-e-Amjad* (Hyderabad, 1928); and Rutter, *Holy Cities of Arabia*.

9. Onley, *Arabian Frontier of the British Raj*, covers this phenomenon on the eastern side of the Arabian Peninsula.

10. Sir Andrew Ryan, *The Last of the Dragomans* (London: Geoffrey Bles, 1951), 268.

11. Note by Bullard on Indian Clerk, June 17, 1925, IOR/L/E/7/1146, IOR, APAC, BL.

12. Report on the Hajj of 1931, in *RoH*, 6:349, 396.

13. Note by Bullard on Indian Clerk, June 17, 1925, IOR/L/E/7/1146, IOR, APAC, BL.

14. Sir Reader Bullard to FO, July 28, 1937, in Bullard, *Two Kings in Arabia*, 165.

15. See Ronald Robinson and John Gallagher, with Alice Denny, *Africa and the Victorians: The Official Mind of Imperialism* (London: Macmillan, 1961).

16. G. Rentz, "Wahhabism and Saudi Arabia," in G. Hopwood (ed.), *The Arabian Peninsula* (London: Allen and Unwin, 1972), 54–66; Francis Robinson, *Atlas of the Islamic World since 1500* (Oxford: Phaidon, 1982), 120–129.

17. See Jalal, *Partisans of Allah;* Alavi, "'Fugitive Mullahs and Outlawed Fanatics'"; and Hopkins, "Sitana and Swat."

18. H. V. F. Winstone, *Captain Shakespear: William Henry Shakespear* (London: J. Cape, 1976), 84–85.

19. One example of this is "Notes on the 'Akhwan' Movement" by Major H. R. P. Dickson, undated, FO 141/477/4, TNA.

20. Wingate to Balfour, repeated to Baghdad, Delhi and Aden, December 25, 1917, No. 315, FO 371/3380 E146/12076, TNA, quoted in al-Enazy, "Ibn Saud's Early Foreign Policy," 161.

21. This first period of Saudi rule over the Holy Places is detailed in al-Rasheed, *History of Saudi Arabia*, 15–25; and De-Long Bas, *Wahhabi Islam*, 7–40.

22. Philby's peers were critical of his relationship with Saud; one caustically noted that "there is nothing in his [Saud's] manner towards Philby of real friendship. . . . Saud is telling the truth when he says he likes the English and that the more English they are the better he likes them. It is no recommendation to him to become a Muslim . . . or to be wearing sandals when the King himself is wearing socks with 'pure wool made in England' on them." Report on dinner with Saud, Philby and Lord Belhaven [political officer in Kuwait and Iraq who was sent on a mission to Saud during the First World War], Bullard to FO, January 19, 1938, 3/6, Box 3, Bullard, GB-0165–0034, MECA. See also Activities of Philby, 1930, CO 732/45/7, TNA. The best overview of Philby's life is Elizabeth Monroe, *Philby of Arabia* (London: Faber and Faber, 1973).

23. Philby in Najd to Sir Percy Cox, June 2, 1918. Letter 1 of 18 by Philby auctioned at Sotheby's, May 2001, from *Jerusalem Post*, May 6, 2001, quoted in al-Enazy, "Ibn Saud's Early Foreign Policy," 291.

24. Cox to Bray, undated, forwarded to Foreign Secretary, Government of India, File 5/39, Box 2, Cox GB-0165–0341, MECA. Churchill wrote to Sir Percy Cox in 1921 that he was right to dismiss Philby, who was "clearly unsuitable" for official work in the region. Churchill to Cox, August 6, 1921, File 5/37, Box 2, Cox GB-0165–0341, MECA.

25. Philby, "King Ibn Saud of Arabia," undated but probably 1930s, 1/4/9/1/5, Box 18, Philby GB-0165–0229, MECA.

26. Hogarth, "Wahabism and British Interests," 75.

27. Paris, *Britain, the Hashemites, and Arab Rule*, 311.

28. Troeller, *Birth of Saudi Arabia*, 219.

29. Colonial Secretary to High Commissioner, Iraq, September 30, 1924, IOR/L/PS/10/1124, IOR, APAC, BL.

30. *The Times*, October 4, 1924.

31. Viceroy to Secretary of State for India, September 25, 1924, Telegram No. 3890, IOR/L/PS/10/1124, File 3665, Pt. 1, IOR, APAC, BL, quoted in Troeller, *Birth of Saudi Arabia*, 219.

32. Reader Bullard, Consul Jeddah, to FO, September 21, 1924, Foreign and Political Department, External, 1924, No. 4(2), NAI.

33. Hogarth, "Wahabism and British Interests," 71.

34. Ibid.

35. Ibid., 77–79.

36. Report for August 1924, *Jedda Diaries*, 2:247–248.

37. Bowman, Jerusalem, September 24, 1924, Journal Notebook No. 4 (August 1924–October 1926), Confidential Journal, Box 3, Bowman GB-0165-0034, MECA. See also Humphrey Ernest Bowman, *Middle-East Window* (London: Longmans, Green, 1942).

38. English Summary of Proclamation, September 20, 1924, in Dening, *King Abdul Aziz*, 2:628–629.

39. Ibn Saud to Political Resident, Persian Gulf, September 23, 1924, in Dening, *King Abdul Aziz*, 2:633.

40. Mai Yamani, *Cradle of Islam: The Hijaz and the Quest for an Arabian Identity* (London: I. B. Tauris, 2004), 8.

41. Report for October 21–30, 1924, *Jedda Diaries*, 2:256.

42. William Facey, "Pilgrim Pioneers: Britons on Hajj before 1940," in Porter and Saif, *Hajj*, 122–130, 127–128; Michael Wolfe, "Eldon Rutter and the Modern Hajj Narrative," in Porter and Saif, *Hajj*, 131–135, 133.

43. Rutter, *Holy Cities of Arabia*, v–vi, 3, 17, 40–44.

44. Ibid., 142–143.

45. Extracts from précis of Munshi Ihsanullah's Report, April 1925, FO 371/11436, TNA.

46. Report for March 20–April 11, 1925, *Jedda Diaries*, 2:296–297.

47. Report for March 1–11, 1925, *Jedda Diaries*, 2:290.

48. Report for July 21–August 10, 1925, *Jedda Diaries*, 2:335.

49. Report for November 20–December 11, 1924; Report for January 9–19, 1925, in Bullard, *Two Kings in Arabia*, 76–77. It was feared that one pilot, Shirokoff, who drank more than a bottle of whisky a day, which was part of his pay, might "one day reach the point of exhilaration at which the prospect of dropping explosives on Mecca will cease to appear objectionable." His plane exploded in midair on January 18, 1925, a calamity he did not survive. Also quoted in Sedgwick, "Saudi Sufis," 357n41.

50. *Times of India*, February 21, 1925, enclosed in IOR/L/PJ/12/111, IOR, APAC, BL.

51. Extract from Weekly Report of Director of Intelligence, Home Department, February 25, 1925, IOR/L/PJ/12/111, IOR, APAC, BL.

52. Extract from Weekly Report of Director of Intelligence, Home Department, March 11, 1925, IOR/L/PJ/12/111, IOR, APAC, BL.

53. Government of India Communiqué, May 15, 1925, General Department, 1925, File 5748-C Pt. II, MSA.

54. Government of India Communiqué, June 2, 1925, General Department, 1925, File 5748-C Pt. II, MSA.

55. Government of India Communiqué, June 18, 1925; Government of India Communique, June 20, 1925; Government of India Communiqué, June 27, 1925; Government of India Communique, June 29, 1925; General Department, 1925, File 5748-C Pt. II, MSA.

56. Report for May 1–21, 1925, *Jedda Diaries*, 2:303–305.

57. Rutter, *Holy Cities of Arabia*, 270–271.

58. Ibid., 564.

59. Rutter, "Hejaz," 102; Rutter, *Holy Cities of Arabia*, 172.

60. Report for July 21–August 10, 1925, *Jedda Diaries*, 2:325.

61. Ibid., 2:346.

62. Extract from Weekly Report of Director of Intelligence, Home Department, August 13, 1925, IOR/L/PJ/12/111, IOR, APAC, BL.

63. Report for November 28–December 31, 1925, *Jedda Diaries*, 2:368.

64. Report for February 1926, *Jedda Diaries*, 2:377.

65. Extract from Report for March 1926, Jeddah Consulate, FO 371/11442, TNA.

66. Ibid.

67. High Commissioner, Baghdad, to British Agent, Jeddah, April 28, 1926, FO 967/3, TNA. See also the reaction in Persia, Proclamation by the Prime Minister, extract from Tehran newspaper *Iran*, June 25, 1926, FO 141/688/4, TNA.

68. British Agent Jeddah to Foreign Office, Baghdad, India, Egypt, Jerusalem and Singapore, May 25, 1926, FO 967/3, TNA.

69. Report for May 1926, *Jedda Diaries*, 2:387–389.

70. Report for June 1926, *Jedda Diaries*, 2:393–394.

71. Report for July 1926, *Jedda Diaries*, 2:399.

72. See various June 1926 issues from *Al-Balagh*, *Kawkab Al-Sharq*, *Al-Siyasa*, and *Al-Ittihad*, copies held in Dar al-Kutub (the National Library), Cairo.

73. Report for August 1926, in *Jedda Diaries*, 2:422, 427.

74. Extract from Weekly Report of Director of Intelligence, Home Department, May 20, 1926, IOR/L/PJ/12/111, IOR, APAC, BL.

75. Extract from Weekly Report of Director of Intelligence, Home Department, June 17, 1926, IOR/L/PJ/12/111, IOR, APAC, BL.

76. Extract from Lucknow daily newspaper, June 15, 1926, FO 967/3, TNA, in *RoH*, 6:12.

77. Extract from *Pioneer Mail*, October 1, 1926, September 25–28, 1926, IOR/L/PJ/12/110, IOR, APAC, BL.

78. Jedda to India [not specified which person or department], June 8, 1926, FO 371/11433, TNA. See also al-Qu'aiti, *Holy Cities of Islam*, 544.

79. Green, *Bombay Islam*, 1–23, is the best exposition of this argument.

80. Report on the Hajj 1344 AH/1926, 3, FO 371/11436, TNA, in *RoH*, 6:41.

81. Report on the Hajj 1344 AH/1926, 11, FO 371/11436, TNA, in *RoH*, 6:49.

82. Report on the Hajj 1344 AH/1926, 15–17, FO 371/11436, TNA, in *RoH*, 6:53–55. Also quoted in Bose, *Hundred Horizons*, 212.

83. Kostiner, "On Instruments and Their Designers," 309, 317.

84. Ibid., 319. See Habib, *Ibn Saud's Warriors of Islam;* and Robert Fletcher, "Running the Corridor: Nomadic Societies and Imperial Rule in the Inter-war Syrian Desert," *Past and Present*, 220:1 (2013), 185–215. For a contemporary British view of the Ikhwan, see "Notes on the 'Akhwan' Movement" by Major H. R. P. Dickson, undated, FO 141/477/4, TNA.

85. Report for April 1928, *Jedda Diaries*, 3:17.

86. Report for June 1927, *Jedda Diaries*, 2:461–462; Report for July 1927, *Jedda Diaries*, 2:465.

87. Report for August 1927, *Jedda Diaries*, 2:470–471.

88. Report for April 1927, *Jedda Diaries*, 2:453–456.

89. Report for August 1928, *Jedda Diaries*, 3:32–33.

90. Report on Hajj 1928/1346, 11–12, CO 732/31/9, TNA.

91. Report for April 1928, *Jedda Diaries*, 3:17.

92. Report for June 1928, *Jedda Diaries*, 3:24.

93. Report for June 1929, *Jedda Diaries*, 3:76.

94. Confidential Report of Hajj Enquiry Committee on Arrangements in the Hejaz, FO 371/15290, TNA, in *RoH*, 6:313–325.

95. Report for July 1928, *Jedda Diaries*, 3:28–29; Report on Hajj 1928/1346, 11–12, CO 732/31/9, TNA.

96. Abdul Majid Daryabadi, *Safar-e-Hijaz* (Azamgarh, U.P., India, 1929), 121–122, quoted in Bose, *Hundred Horizons*, 227.

97. Homayra Ziad, "The Return of Gog: Politics and Pan-Islamism in the Hajj Travelogue of 'Abd al-Majid Daryabadi," in James Gelvin and Nile Green (eds.), *Global Muslims in the Age of Steam and Print* (Berkeley: University of California Press, 2014), 227–248, 241.

98. Ibid., 234.

99. Bose, *Hundred Horizons*, 207, 220; Mishra, *Pilgrims, Politics and Pestilence*, 9, 98–100.

100. Amjad, *Hajj-e-Amjad*, 28.

101. Ibid., 148.

102. Muhammad Sadiq Bey, *Mash'al al-Mahmal, Risala fi sir al-Hajj al-Misri bira min yaum khuruja min Misr* (Cairo, 1880), 28.

103. Alawi, *Journey to the Holy Land.*

104. Ibid., 90–97.

105. Ibid., 100.

106. Ibid.

107. Ibid., 103.

108. Ibid., 105–108, 118–119.

109. See also the recommendation by Commander Powlett of HMS *Black Swan,* on patrol in the Red Sea in 1877, who reported after a visit to Jidda to inspect pilgrim ships for suspected slave trafficking that pilgrims should be "disarmed before going on board ships; cases have occurred where they have drawn knives to intimidate the officers of the ships." Reports from Naval Officers, Cmdr. Powlett to Rear-Admiral Corbett, December 20, 1877, in Anita Burdett (ed.), *The Slave Trade into Arabia, 1820–1973*, vols. 1–9 (Gerrards Cross: Archive Editions, 2006), 3:346 (hereafter referred to as *Slave Trade*).

110. Alawi, *Journey to the Holy Land*, 116–118. See also Daryabadi, *Safar-e-Hijaz*, 69–76, quoted in Ziad, "Return of Gog," 239.

111. Ziad, "Return of Gog," 247.

112. Roff, "Sanitation and Security," 155. However, there has been no investigation of the pilgrimage's role in spreading Spanish influenza in 1918–1919 and of attempts by European powers to prevent the spread of influenza by pilgrims. Mishra, *Pilgrims, Politics and Pestilence*, 113.

113. Report on the Hajj of 1927, CO 273/535/5, TNA.

114. Alawi, *Journey to the Holy Land*, 124–126.

115. See also Ziad's discussion of Daryabadi's reflections on British political, military, and economic power in Ziad, "Return of Gog," 236–238.

116. Alawi, *Journey to the Holy Land*, 124–126.

117. Ibid., 122–124.

118. Ibid., 127–128, and other examples on 151, 224, 245, 248.

119. Ibid., 133.

120. Ibid., 140, 177.

121. Ibid., 141–142.

122. Ibid.

123. Ibid., 163.

124. Ibid., 166–167.

125. Ibid., 173.

126. Ibid., 174.

127. Ibid., 180.

128. Ibid., 203.

129. Ibid., 232–235.

130. Ibid., 235.

131. Ibid., 236.

132. Ibid., 238.

133. Ibid., 237, 253–254.

134. Ibid., 257.

135. Report for April 1928, *Jedda Diaries*, 3:67.

136. Report for September–December 1929, *Jedda Diaries*, 3:153.

137. See also Bose, *Hundred Horizons*, 214–219.

138. Ryan, *Last of the Dragomans*, 267–268.

139. Report for August–September 1930, *Jedda Diaries*, 3:148–149.

140. Report for May–June 1931, *Jedda Diaries*, 3:267; Report on the Pilgrimage of 1930, May 13, 1931, FO 141/730/5, TNA. The consulate was upgraded to a legation in 1930, and the consul was restyled as minister. However, for the sake of clarity, the terms "consulate" and "consul" will continue to be used.

141. Report for September 1936, *Jedda Diaries*, 4:124. See internal discussions among Government of India officials about the overland route, External Affairs, 1936, 94-N, NAI.

142. Sir Reader Bullard, *The Camels Must Go: An Autobiography* (London: Faber and Faber, 1961), 202–203. See also files in Overland Route, Foreign and Political Department, 1934, 410-N, NAI.

143. Reader Bullard to his family, April 4, 1937, in Bullard, *Two Kings in Arabia*, 150–151.

144. Report for April 1938, *Jedda Diaries*, 4:289–290.

145. Report for February 1939, *Jedda Diaries*, 4:402–403; Legation, Jeddah to Viceroy of India, June 30, 1938, IOR/R/20/B/1456, IOR, APAC, BL.

146. Protector of Pilgrims, Bombay, Report for Pilgrim Season, 1932, 1–4, June 19, 1933, Foreign and Political Department, 1932, No. 213-N, NAI.

147. Report for February 1939, *Jedda Diaries*, 4:402–403.

148. Confidential Report of Hajj Enquiry Committee on Arrangements in the Hejaz, 1, FO371/15290, TNA, in *RoH*, 6:313.

149. Article Three, Treaty with the King of the Hejaz and of Nejd, May 20, 1927, CO 732/26/2, TNA. Articles 3–5 of the treaty dealt with the Hajj.

150. Report on the Hajj of 1348 AH/1930, 16–17, FO 371/14456, TNA, in *RoH*, 6:270–271.

151. Report for March–April 1931, *Jedda Diaries*, 3:212–213.

152. Notes on Saudi Arabia for Dr. Hugh Scott, 1944, 1/4/9/3/28, Box 18, Philby GB-0165-0229, MECA. See also Philby, *Pilgrim in Arabia*.

153. Report on the Hajj of 1349 AH/1931, 28–31, FO 371/15290, TNA, in *RoH*, 6:376–379.

154. Report on the Hajj of 1349 AH/1931, 28–31, FO 371/15290, TNA, in *RoH*, 6:376–379.

155. Report on the Hajj of 1932/1350, 23–25, IOR/R/20/A/3524, IOR, APAC, BL.

156. Ibid.

157. Report for February 1933, *Jedda Diaries*, 3:412.

158. Literally translated as "the Saudi Arab Kingdom," the kingdom was named by royal decree on September 23, 1932.

159. Report for May–June 1932, *Jedda Diaries*, 3:371–372.

160. Report for March 1933, *Jedda Diaries*, 3:418.

161. Ibid.; Bose, *Hundred Horizons*, 216–217. I was unable to locate the Arabic translation for comparison.

162. William Facey, "Introduction," in Evelyn Cobbold, *A Pilgrimage to Mecca* (1933; London: Arabian Publishing, 2008), 4.

163. Facey, "Introduction," 26; Cobbold, *Pilgrimage to Mecca* (2008), 89.

164. Facey, "Introduction," 38–45; Cobbold, *Pilgrimage to Mecca* (2008), 261.

165. Cobbold, *Pilgrimage to Mecca* (2008), 110.

166. Ibid., 209.

167. Panipati, *Safar Nama-e-Hajj*, 61.

168. Ibid., 47–48.

169. Ibid., 71–72.

170. Ibid., 73.

171. Ibid., 74.

172. Ibid., 106.

173. Report on the Hajj of 1933/1351, 18, FO 371/16857, TNA, in *RoH*, 6:559.

174. Report on the Hajj of 1934/1352, 4, FO 371/17932, TNA, in *RoH*, 6:544.

175. Philby, "The Mecca Pilgrimage 1934," 6/1/8, Box 6, Philby GB-0165–0229, MECA.

176. Report on the Hajj of 1934/1352, 16, FO 371/17932, TNA, in *RoH*, 6:647.

177. Report on the Hajj of 1935/1353, 19, FO 371/19002, TNA, in *RoH*, 7:36.

178. Bullard to Eden, FO, copied to Palestine, Cairo, and Baghdad, December 7, 1937, FO 371/20786, TNA.

179. Trott to Eden, FO, copied to Palestine and Cairo, September 26, 1937, FO 371/20817, TNA; J. V. Kelly to Eden, undated, FO 371/20817, TNA. Newspapers in Saudi Arabia were bereft of references to the revolt and instead contained propaganda that emphasized the ease and importance of performing the pilgrimage.

180. Vredenbregt, "Haddj," 108.

181. Report on the Hajj of 1936, in *RoH*, 7:107.

182. Reader Bullard to FO, July 28, 1937, in Bullard, *Two Kings in Arabia*, 165.

183. Reader Bullard to Foreign Secretary, Government of India, July 24, 1937, IOR/L/PS/12/2155, IOR, APAC, BL.

184. Report on the Hajj 1937/1355, 1, IOR/L/PJ/7/789, IOR, APAC, BL.

185. Reader Bullard to FO, April 26, 1937, in Bullard, *Two Kings in Arabia*, 153.

186. Report for March 1940, *Jedda Diaries*, 4:520–521.

CHAPTER 6 *Hajj from the Far Ends of Britain's Muslim Empire*

1. C. A. Willis, Report on Slavery and the Pilgrimage, 1926, 12, SAD Willis 212/2/3, SAD (hereafter cited as C. A. Willis, Report).

2. Eldon Rutter, "The Muslim Pilgrimage," *Geographical Journal*, 74:3 (1930), 271–273.

3. See especially Gordon Lethem, "Report on a Journey to Sudan, Jeddah and Cairo," 1927, 18, 64–70, Box 8, 8/1, Mss. Brit. Emp.s.276, Rhodes House Library, Oxford (hereafter cited as Lethem, "Report"). Lethem also authored a report in the same year, "History of Islamic Political Propaganda in Nigeria," also held in Mss. Brit. Emp.s.276, Rhodes House Library, Oxford. See also H. R. Palmer, Resident, Bornu, Nigeria, Report on a Journey from Maidugurai, Nigeria to Jeddah in Arabia, June 16, 1919, CO 879/119/10, TNA (hereafter cited as Palmer, Report); C. A. Willis, Report; and Reynolds, "'Stealing the Road.'"

4. Reynolds, "Good and Bad Muslims"; Reynolds, "'Stealing the Road,'" 2, 4–5.

5. Lethem, "Report," 12.

6. Reynolds, "'Stealing the Road," 3.

7. Report for June 1923, *Jedda Diaries*, 2:134–135. On slavery in the Islamic world in this period, see Clarence-Smith, *Islam and the Abolition of Slavery*. For a more specific case study of slavery in the Red Sea, see Huber, *Channelling Mobilities*, 172–203. William Ochsenwald touches on the pilgrimage's connection with slavery for an earlier period in "Muslim-European Conflict in the Hijaz:

The Slave Trade Controversy," *Middle Eastern Studies*, 16:1 (1980), 115–126. Other relevant works include Robert W. Harms, Bernard K. Freamon, and David W. Blight, *Indian Ocean Slavery in the Age of Abolition* (New Haven, CT: Yale University Press, 2013); Gwyn Campbell, *Abolition and Its Aftermath in the Indian Ocean, Africa and Asia* (London: Routledge, 2005); Kevin Grant, *A Civilised Savagery: Britain and the New Slaveries in Africa, 1884–1926* (New York: Routledge, 2005); Gwyn Campbell, *The Structure of Slavery in the Indian Ocean, Africa and Asia* (London: Frank Cass, 2004); Ronald Segal, *Islam's Black Slaves: The Other Black Diaspora* (New York: Farrar, Strauss and Giroux, 2001); and John Ralph Willis, *Slaves and Slavery in Muslim Africa* (London: Frank Cass, 1985).

8. Clarence-Smith, *Islam and the Abolition of Slavery*, 76–77.

9. William Gervase Clarence-Smith, "The Economics of the Indian Ocean and Red Sea Slave Trades in the 19th Century: An Overview," *Slavery and Abolition: A Journal of Slave and Post-slave Studies*, 9:3 (1988), 1–20, 8.

10. Kumm, *From Hausaland to Egypt*, 264.

11. Palmer, Report, 1–15; Suzanne Miers, "Diplomacy versus Humanitarianism: Britain and Consular Manumission in Hijaz, 1921–1936," *Slavery and Abolition*, 10:3 (1989), 102–128, 116.

12. C. A. Willis, Report, 10.

13. Bullard to Ibn Saud, 3rd June 1925, in *Slave Trade*, 5:563, 567–568.

14. Reports from Naval Officers, Cmdr. Powlett to Rear-Admiral Corbett, December 20, 1877, in *Slave Trade*, 3:347. On the continued resilience of the slave trade despite repeated Ottoman proclamations banning the practice and British efforts from 1840 to 1895, see Ochsenwald, "Muslim-European Conflict in the Hijaz," 120–124.

15. Miers, "Diplomacy versus Humanitarianism," 102–105.

16. "Nigerian Emir's Visit to Mecca. Britain's Help to Moslems," *The Times*, October 24, 1921.

17. Palmer, Report, 15; Report on the Pilgrimage 1924, Selangor. 3971–1925, 1957/0237768, Arkib Negara, Kuala Lumpur, Malaysia (hereafter referred to as AN). On the issue of manumission in Arabia, see Jerzy Zdanowski, "The Right to Manumit and British Relations with Ibn Saud and Persia in the 1920s," *Journal of Contemporary History*, 2014, doi:10.1177/0022009414538475; Jerzy Zdanowski, *Slavery and Manumission: British Policy in the Red Sea and the Persian Gulf in the First Half of the 20th Century* (Ithaca, NY: Ithaca, 2012); Jerzy Zdanowski, "The Manumission Movement in the Gulf in the First Half of the Twentieth Century," *Middle Eastern Studies*, 47:6 (2011), 863–883; Alaine S. Hutson, "Enslavement and Manumission in Saudi Arabia, 1926–38," *Critique: Critical Middle Eastern Studies*, 11:1 (2002), 49–70; and Miers, "Diplomacy versus Humanitarianism."

18. Sir Lee Stack, "Appendix—Slave Trade between the Sudan and Arabia," *Journal of the Royal Central Asian Society*, 8:3 (1921), 163–164.

19. C. A. Willis, Report, 31.

20. Ibid., 44.

21. Ibid., 46.

22. Ibid., 61.

23. Secretary Northern Provinces, Kaduna to Chief Secretariat Lagos, 1922, quoted in Matthew M. Heaton, "Globalization, Health, and the Hajj: The West African Pilgrimage Scheme, 1919–38," in Toyin Falola and Matthew M. Heaton (eds.), *HIV/AIDS, Illness, and African Well-Being* (Rochester, NY: University of Rochester Press, 2007), 243–261, 251.

24. C. A. Willis, Report, 45; Clarence-Smith, *Islam and the Abolition of Slavery*, 76–77; Miers, "Diplomacy versus Humanitarianism," 120–122; Zdanowski, "Manumission Movement in the Gulf," 866.

25. Clarence-Smith, *Islam and the Abolition of Slavery*, 181–182. See also Report of the Advisory Committee of Experts on Slavery, Second Session of the Committee, April 1–10, 1935, 24–25, CO 732/70/7, TNA.

26. Bullard, Consul Jedda, to Ibn Saud, June 3, 1925, in *Slave Trade*, 6:410.

27. Ryan, Consul Jedda, to FO, June 1, 1934, in *Slave Trade*, 6:668.

28. Palmer, Report, 14–15.

29. Ibid., 11.

30. Ibid., 21. See also Lethem, "Report," 18, 64–70.

31. Palmer, Report, 11–13.

32. Ibid., 13.

33. Ibid., 23.

34. Reynolds, "'Stealing the Road,'" 2.

35. C. A. Willis, Report, 1.

36. G. J. Fleming, "Kassala," *Sudan Notes and Records*, 5:2 (1922), 66–77, 66–67; Palmer, Report, 9.

37. Palmer, Report, 14–15.

38. Ibid., 9; C. A. Willis, Report, 40.

39. Palmer, Report, 15.

40. Report on the Hajj 1342 AH/1924, FO 371/10812, TNA, in *RoH*, 5:579.

41. C. A. Willis, Report, 43. On the same page, Willis was scathing about morals in the Hijaz: "Venereal disease is rampant, and perversion is the rule rather than the exception." Reynolds, "'Stealing the Road,'" 8–9.

42. Report for July 1924, in *Jedda Diaries*, 2:226–228.

43. Report on the Hajj 1342 AH/1924, FO 371/10812, TNA, in *RoH*, 5:579. Reynolds, "'Stealing the Road,'" 8.

44. C. A. Willis, Report, 19.

45. Ibid., 2, 6.

46. Ibid., 9.

47. Ibid., 13.

48. Ibid., 7.

49. Ibid., 10–12; FO to High Commissioner, Egypt, December 10, 1925, FO 141/531/4, TNA.

50. C. A. Willis, Report, 30–34; Heaton, "Globalization, Health, and the Hajj," 253–255, 258.

51. C. A. Willis, Report, 20–23.

52. Ibid., 20–23, 59. See examples of the journeys of Mohamed Sambo Wad Osman and Osman Bagi Wad Abukr in Governor-General, Sudan to High Commissioner, Egypt, December 27, 1930, FO 141/720/4, TNA.

53. C. A. Willis, Report, 25–27.

54. Ibid., 28.

55. Ibid., 60.

56. Heaton, "Globalization, Health, and the Hajj," 253–255, 258.

57. Report on the Hajj 1344 AH/1926, 25, FO 371/11436, TNA, in *RoH*, 6:63; Report on the Hajj 1928, in *RoH*, 6:208. Britain paid £320 for repatriation in 1928; Reynolds, "'Stealing the Road,'" 8; Lethem, "Report," 18.

58. Report on the Hajj 1345 AH/1927, 25–26, FO 371/12248, TNA, in *RoH*, 6:147–148; Report for July 1927, *Jedda Diaries*, 2:465. In 1934, Italian cooperation regarding *takayrna* pilgrims was "promised" but remained nebulous. Report for July 1934, *Jedda Diaries*, 3:504.

59. Report on the Hajj 1347 AH/1929, 31–32, FO 371/13728, TNA, in *RoH*, 6:247–248; Heaton, "Globalization, Health, and the Hajj," 259.

60. Report for December 1930, *Jedda Diaries*, 3:173; Heaton, "Globalization, Health, and the Hajj," 250; Governor of Nigeria to Lethem, November 29, 1924, CO 583/143/6, TNA; Jedda to FO, September 10, 1929, CO 583/167/7, TNA.

61. Governor of Nigeria to Lethem, November 29, 1924; Governor of Nigeria to CO, December 3, 1924, CO 583/143/6, TNA; Lethem, "Report," 18.

62. Gordon Lethem, Appendices to Report, Box 8, 8/2, Mss. Brit. Emp.s.276, Rhodes House Library, Oxford; Governor of Nigeria to CO, October 19, 1926, CO 583/143/6, TNA.

63. Report for January–February 1931, *Jedda Diaries*, 3:194–195; Report for March–April 1931, *Jedda Diaries*, 3:212–213.

64. Report for May-June 1932, *Jedda Diaries*, 3:371–372.

65. Heaton, "Globalization, Health, and the Hajj," 243.

66. Governor of Nigeria to CO, August 20, 1928, CO 583/155/10, TNA; Governor-General, Sudan to High Commissioner, Egypt, May 28, 1929, CO 583/167/7, TNA; Governor of Nigeria to CO, May 20, 1930, CO 583/174/8, TNA. See also discussions among British officials in FO 141/730/5, TNA; Heaton, "Globalization, Health, and the Hajj," 255–257; and Reynolds, "'Stealing the Road,'" 10–13.

67. Heaton, "Globalization, Health, and the Hajj," 253–254, 260.

68. Report for April 1934, *Jedda Diaries*, 3:488–489; Report for May 1934, *Jedda Diaries*, 3:494.

69. Report on the Hajj 1926/1344 AH, 24–25, FO 371/11436, TNA, in *RoH*, 6:62–63.

70. Rutter, "Muslim Pilgrimage," 271–273.

71. Report on the Hajj 1926/1344 AH, 24–25, FO 371/11436, TNA, in *RoH*, 6:62–63.

72. Report for May 1939, *Jedda Diaries*, 4:429–430; Heaton, "Globalization, Health, and the Hajj," 253–254, 260.

73. Report for September 1939, *Jedda Diaries*, 4:462.

74. Report for October 1939, *Jedda Diaries*, 4:473.

75. Virginia Matheson and A. C. Milner (eds.), *Perceptions of the Haj: Five Malay Texts* (Singapore: Institute of Southeast Asian Studies, 1984), 19, 23.

76. Abdullah worked closely with British administrators and missionaries. See Munshi Abdullah, *Pelayaran Ka-Judah* [Journey to Jedda] (1854), in

Matheson and Milner, *Five Malay Texts*, 21. See also Raimy Che-Ross, "Munshi Abdullah's Voyage to Mecca: A Preliminary Introduction and Annotated Translation," *Indonesia and the Malay World*, 28:81 (2000), 173–212. Unfortunately, as William Roff has noted, "Malay pilgrims were not in the habit of writing about themselves or their fellows." Roff, "Conduct of the Hajj from Malaya," 81.

77. Abdul Majid bin Zainuddin, *The Malays in Malaya*, 1928, 96–97, quoted in Moshe Yegar, *Islam and Islamic Institutions in British Malaya: Policies and Implementation* (Jerusalem: Magnes, 1979), 115.

78. Yegar, *Islam and Islamic Institutions*, 230.

79. Tagliacozzo, *Longest Journey*, 144–145.

80. Mary Byrne MacDonnell, "The Conduct of Hajj from Malaysia and Its Socio-economic Impact on Malay Society: A Descriptive and Analytical Study, 1860–1981" (PhD dissertation, Columbia University, 1986), 71–72; Roff, "Conduct of the Hajj from Malaya," 84–85; Tagliacozzo, *Longest Journey*, 189.

81. William Roff, *The Origins of Malay Nationalism* (Oxford: Oxford University Press, 1984), 38.

82. Anthony Green, *Our Journey: 30 Years of Haj Services in Singapore* (Singapore: Majlis Ugama Islam Singapura, 2006), 21, 29–30; Yegar, *Islam and Islamic Institutions*, 228.

83. Roff, *Origins of Malay Nationalism*, 39–42; Yegar, *Islam and Islamic Institutions*, 223–224.

84. Roff, *Origins of Malay Nationalism*, 71; Roff, "Conduct of the Hajj from Malaya," 85.

85. Yegar, *Islam and Malay Nationalism*, 109–112. Islam played a role only in the small Pahang Rebellion, 1891–1895.

86. Roff, "Conduct of the Hajj from Malaya," 86–87.

87. Tagliacozzo, *Longest Journey*, 75.

88. Farrer and Lee-Warner memo, November 24, 1920, quoted in Roff, "Conduct of the Hajj from Malaya," 88.

89. Roff, "Conduct of the Hajj from Malaya," 88–89; MacDonnell, "Conduct of Hajj from Malaysia," 228, 231.

90. Governor of Straits Settlements Sir Laurence Guillemard to CO, October 24, 1922; Note by G.I.M.C., November 28, 1922, File 57483, CO 273/517, TNA; Haji Abdul Majid, Malay Pilgrimage Report for 1927, 843–1346, 1957/0400522, AN; Roff, "Conduct of the Hajj from Malaya," 89, 103–104.

91. Governor of Straits Settlements to CO, April 16, 1924, File 22554, CO 273/525, TNA; Report of the Pilgrim Committee, 1924, 1957/0387494, 1672/1342, AN; MacDonnell, "Conduct of Hajj from Malaysia," 172, 313, 565. The problem of destitute Malay pilgrims stranded in Bombay continued into the 1930s; see files in CO 273/581/9, TNA.

92. Haji Abdul Majid bin Zainuddin, *The Wandering Thoughts of a Dying Man*, ed. William Roff (New York: Oxford University Press, 1978). Unfortunately, Majid's account contains frustratingly little on his experiences as pilgrimage officer in Jidda.

93. Haji Abdul Majid, Malay Pilgrimage Report for 1924, 938–1343, 1957/0389750, AN; Comments on Abdul Majid's report on the 1924 pilgrimage,

938–1343, 1957/0389750, AN; MacDonnell, "Conduct of Hajj from Malaysia," 148–152, 229; Yegar, *Islam and Malay Nationalism*, 236; Tagliacozzo, *Longest Journey*, 147; Roff, "Conduct of the Hajj from Malaya," 91–94; on Abdul Majid's life, see Abdul Majid, *Wandering Thoughts*.

94. Quoted in Roff, "Conduct of the Hajj from Malaya," 94.

95. Ibid., 97.

96. Director of the Political Intelligence Bureau comment on Abdul Majid's report on the 1924 pilgrimage, 938–1343, 1957/0389750, AN.

97. Quoted in Roff, "Conduct of the Hajj from Malaya," 100.

98. Comments on Abdul Majid's report on the 1924 pilgrimage, 938–1343, 1957/0389750, AN; Roff, "Conduct of the Hajj from Malaya," 101; MacDonnell, "Conduct of Hajj from Malaysia," 231.

99. MacDonnell, "Conduct of Hajj from Malaysia," 244–245.

100. Roff, "Conduct of the Hajj from Malaya," 104–105; Article 6.c. of 59 in Federated Malay States Enactment No. 7 of 1930, Assented to by Sultans of Perak, Selangor, Pahang and Yang di per Tuan Besar of Negri Sembilan, CO 273/567/6, TNA.

101. Consul Jeddah to Colonial Secretary, Straits Settlements, Singapore, May 18, 1925, Difficulties in Sending Remittances, 1964–1343, 1957/00181, AN.

102. MacDonnell, "Conduct of Hajj from Malaysia," 225.

103. Haji Abdul Majid, Malay Pilgrimage Report for 1927, 843–1346, 1957/0400522, AN; Roff, "Conduct of the Hajj from Malaya," 101.

104. Haji Abdul Majid, Malay Pilgrimage Report for 1933, 2236–52, 1957/00190, AN; Haji Abdul Majid, Malay Pilgrimage Report for 1934, 2337–1353, 1957/0420237, AN; Roff, "Conduct of the Hajj from Malaya," 101. On the Indian example and the virtual impossibility of getting repayment, see Foreign and Political Department, 1933, Near East Department, 1–24, NAI; Government of India External Affairs Department—General Branch 390(9)G, 1936, NAI.

105. Haji Abdul Majid, Malay Pilgrimage Report for 1935, Kelantan, 872–1934, 1957/0520541, AN.

106. MacDonnell, "Conduct of Hajj from Malaysia," 244–245.

107. Haji Abdul Majid, Malay Pilgrimage Report for 1935, Kelantan, 872–1934, 1957/0520541, AN.

108. Tagliacozzo, *Longest Journey*, 73.

109. Report on the Hajj of 1931, *RoH*, 6:400; Haji Abdul Majid, Malay Pilgrimage Report 1934, 2337–1353, 1957/0420237, AN.

110. District Officer Ulu Selangor to Secretary, Resident Singapore, December 13, 1927, Selangor Secretariat, 5649–1927, 1957/0251119, AN; MacDonnell, "Conduct of Hajj from Malaysia," 249.

111. Tagliacozzo, *Longest Journey*, 72–73.

112. Yegar, *Islam and Malay Nationalism*, 227; Haji Abdul Majid, Malay Pilgrimage Report for 1924, 938–1343, 1957/0389750, AN.

113. Report of the Pilgrim Committee, 1924, 1957/0387494, 1672/1342, AN.

114. British Adviser Kedah Government to High Commissioner Singapore, November 19, 1924; Director, Political Intelligence Bureau to Colonial Secretary, Straits Settlements, Singapore, December 10, 1924, 938–1343, 1957/0389750, AN.

115. See "Pass for Mecca," April 15, 1924, CO 273/525, TNA; MacDonnell, "Conduct of Hajj from Malaysia," 233; Yegar, *Islam and Malay Nationalism*, 236; Roff, "Conduct of the Hajj from Malaya," 101.

116. Director of Political Intelligence Bureau to British Adviser, Perlis, November 21, 1927, enclosing Report on the Pilgrimage 1926/7, A.P. 222–1346, 1957/0479437, AN.

117. Haji Abdul Majid, Malay Pilgrimage Report 1934, 2337–1353, 1957/0420237, AN.

118. Ahmad Sonhadji bin Mohammed Milatu, Reels 20–21, 000201, Oral History Archive, Singapore National Archives, Singapore (hereafter referred to as SNA).

119. A. W. Hamilton, Report on Pilgrimage Conditions 1927, 843–1346, 1957/0400522, AN; Roff, "Conduct of the Hajj from Malaya," 101–102; Tim Harper, "The British 'Malayans,'" in Robert Bickers (ed.), *Settlers and Expatriates: Britons over the Seas* (Oxford: Oxford University Press, 2012), 233–268.

120. Bullard to Mrs. Bullard, May 9, 1924, in Bullard, *Two Kings in Arabia*, 37–38. See also the example of Claude Lewis Miller, also known as Abdel Fattah Miller, in FO 141/480/6, TNA.

121. Steven Runciman, *The White Rajahs* (Cambridge: Cambridge University Press, 1960), 246–247; Bob Reece, *The Name of Brooke* (New York: Oxford University Press, 1982), 20.

122. Report for January 1936, *Jedda Diaries*, 4:82–84.

123. Report for February 1936, *Jedda Diaries*, 4:88–89. His romanticized 1938 travel account, *Triumphant Pilgrimage*, ghostwritten and strangely using a pseudonym, David Chale, accompanied by MacBryan's photo, is a highly unreliable historical source and therefore is not discussed here.

124. On converts to Islam in Britain itself, see Jamie Gilham, *Loyal Enemies: British Converts to Islam, 1850–1950* (London: Hurst and Co., 2014).

125. Omar Bin Haji Abdul Rahim, Reel 21, 000595, SNA; Hasnah Binte Sahlan, Reel 2, 000560, SNA; Taha Bin Haji Abdullah, Reel 1, 000608, SNA; Ahmad Sonhadji bin Mohammed Milatu, Reel 20–21, 000201, SNA; Yegar, *Islam and Malay Nationalism*, 228.

126. Notice by Malay Pilgrimage Officer warning against persons being swindled by persons pretending to be *mutawwifin*, 1927 (in Jawi), 1957/0401691, 1623–1346, AN; Straits Settlements Ordinance to amend Ordinance No. 125 (Merchant Shipping), October 25, 1929, CO 273/559/14, TNA; Roff, "Conduct of the Hajj from Malaya," 107.

127. Roff, "Conduct of the Hajj from Malaya," 107.

128. Warnings to Intending Pilgrims, Kelantan, 42–1931, 1957/0516381, AN.

129. Roderick MacLean, Reel 19, 000301, SNA.

130. Roff, *Origins of Malay Nationalism*, 39; Roff, "Conduct of the Hajj from Malaya," 107.

131. Mohammed Amin Bin Abdul Wahhab, Reel 22, 001597, SNA; Yuhanis Binte Haji Yusof, Reel 2, 000459, SNA; Fatimah Binte Ismail, Reel 7, 001905, SNA; Roderick MacLean, Reel 19, 000301, SNA.

132. Abdul Majid, "A Malay's Pilgrimage to Mecca," *Journal of the Malay Branch of the Royal Asiatic Society*, 4:2 (1926), 269–287, 269.

133. Ibid., 277, 280.

134. Ibid., 287.

135. Note by H.G.R.L., August 1, 1931, Negri Sembilan Secretariat, General 1510–1931, 1957/0454803, AN.

136. See minutes in Negri Sembilan Secretariat, General 1510–1931, 1957/0454803, AN.

137. Haji Abdul Majid, Report on the Malay Pilgrimage 1935, Kelantan 872–1934, 1957/0520541, AN; MacDonnell, "Conduct of Hajj from Malaysia," 152–153, 159; Tagliacozzo, *Longest Journey*, 275.

138. MacDonnell, "Conduct of Hajj from Malaysia," 246. See the examples of Che Abdul Samad bin Haji Hasan, Headteacher, Negri Sembilan, Negri Sembilan Secretariat, 1761–1936, 1957/0456147, AN; Che Abdullah bin Haji Mohammed Salleh, Assistant Registrar in Kelantan's High Court, Kelantan, 680–1938, 1957/0524970, AN; and Buang Haji Siraj, 000715 (Reel 3), SNA.

139. General Circular, Perak Secretariat to State Forest Department, August 11, 1938, 383–38, 1938, 1971/0001358, AN.

140. British Adviser Kedah to Secretary to High Commissioner, Malay States, September 17, 1938, 511–1353, 1934, 1957/0349945, AN.

141. Haji Abdul Majid, Report on the Malay Pilgrimage 1935, Kelantan 872–1934, 1957/0520541, AN; MacDonnell, "Conduct of Hajj from Malaysia," 152–153, 159; Tagliacozzo, *Longest Journey*, 275.

142. See Pahang Federal Secretariat, 1503–1938, 1957/00267, AN.

143. District Officer Batang Padang, Tapah to Secretary to Resident Commissioner, Perak, June 2, 1947, Perak Secretariat, 1632/1947, 1957/0304552, AN.

144. Yegar, *Islam and Malay Nationalism*, 232. See the example of Ahmad Azhari bin Ahmad Naib, Perak Secretariat, 1632/1947. 1957/0304552, AN.

145. Form signed by Haji Abdul Hamid, February 22, 1893, Selangor. Native. 1295–93, 1957/0037810, AN. See also Negri Sembilan. Miscellaneous, 218–1923, 1957/044840, AN; Haji Abdul Majid, Malay Pilgrimage Report 1938–39, and Che Jusoh, Malay Pilgrimage Report 1939–40, Kelantan, 453/1939, 1957/0525835, AN.

146. Memo from British Resident to unknown, November 19, 1928; Appeal to British Resident, Negri Sembilan, 1928, Negri Sembilan Secretariat, 3164/1928, 1957/0453237, AN.

147. Snouck Hurgronje, *Mekka*, 17.

148. Female Slavery in the Hejaz, memorandum by R. Onraet, Director of Criminal Intelligence, Straits Settlements, October 20, 1924, in *Slave Trade*, 5:551–552.

149. Sub-enclosure to Female Slavery memo by R. Onraet, Director of Criminal Intelligence, Straits Settlements, October 20, 1924, in *Slave Trade*, 5:553.

150. Bullard to Colonial Secretary, Straits Settlements, February 27, 1925, in *Slave Trade*, 5:554.

151. IO to FO, August 4, 1927; Enclosure, Legislative Assembly Debates, February 2, 1926, 590, in *Slave Trade*, 6:98–99.

152. Bond, Jedda Consul, to FO, March 6, 1930, Memorandum on Slavery and the Slave Traffic in the Kingdom of the Hejaz, *Slave Trade*, 6:410. The

case of the Jidda consulate's Indian medical assistant owning a slave was a "humiliating discovery" for Consul Reader Bullard. Bullard to FO, May 21, 1924, in *Slave Trade*, 5:464; and Bullard to FO, June 30, 1924, in *Slave Trade*, 5:470–471.

153. Aide Memoire on British-Dutch Discussions about Slave Traffic in the Hejaz, September 1924; Jedda Consul to FO, August 7, 1924, File 42872, CO 273/527, TNA; FO to CO, September 15, 1924; Van Der Plas, Jedda Consul to Bullard, Jedda Consul, August 5, 1924, File 44040, CO 273/527, TNA.

Epilogue

1. See Mishra, *Pilgrimage, Politics and Pestilence;* Low, "Empire and the Hajj"; Miller, "Pilgrim's Progress"; Bose, *Hundred Horizons;* Oishi, "Friction and Rivalry"; F. E. Peters, *Hajj;* M. Harrison, *Public Health in British India;* and Roff, "Sanitation and Security."

2. This took place within the context of German use of Islamic propaganda in the Muslim world. See David Motadel, *Islam and Nazi Germany's War* (Cambridge, MA: Harvard University Press, 2014).

3. Note, undated but probably October 1939, External Affairs, 1939, No. 463-N, NAI; Governor of Aden to Foreign Department Delhi, October 14, 1939, External Affairs, 1939, No. 463-N, NAI.

4. A.S., Note, October 26, 1939, External Affairs, 1939, No. 463-N, NAI; Unknown author, Note, November 21, 1939, External Affairs, 1939, No. 463-N, NAI; Unknown author, Note, December 2, 1939, External Affairs, 1939, No. 463-N, NAI.

5. Secretary of State for India to Delhi and Aden, October 23, 1939, External Affairs, 1939, No. 463-N, NAI; Secretary of State for India to Aden, January 26, 1940, External Affairs, 1939, No. 463-N, NAI.

6. Proclamation in FO 371/35929, TNA, quoted in Tagliacozzo, *Longest Journey*, 137. See also Motadel, *Islam and Nazi Germany's War.*

7. Tagliacozzo, *Longest Journey*, 193; Hajj Propaganda Leaflet 1943, CO 732/87/18, TNA.

8. Report on the Hajj of 1940, *RoH*, 7:412.

9. Note by A.S., October 26, 1939, External Affairs, 1939, No. 463-N, NAI

10. Report on the Hajj of 1358 AH/1940, FO 371/24585, TNA, in *RoH*, 7:381; Proposed Subsidy for the Mecca Pilgrimage, October 4, 1940, T 161/1086, TNA.

11. Secretary Straits Settlements to CO, July 4, 1940; Straits Settlements Circular, November 5, 1940; Meeting of Majlis of Negri Sembilan, December 4, 1940; Negri Sembilan Secretariat, Pilgrimage to Mecca, 1940, 1957/0457829, AN.

12. Hafiz Wahba to Sir Horace Seymour, November 1, 1940, FO 371/24585, TNA, in *RoH*, 7:417.

13. For an overview of Italy's interactions with its Muslim colonies and subjects, see Nir Arielli, *Fascist Italy and the Middle East, 1933–40* (Basingstoke: Palgrave Macmillan, 2010).

14. Report on the Hajj of 1359 AH/1941, FO 371/27259, TNA, in *RoH*, 7:423, 431.

15. Report on the Hajj of 1360 AH/1941, IOR/R/15/1/576, IOR, APAC, BL, in *RoH*, 7:453.

16. Christopher Bayly and Tim Harper, *Forgotten Armies: The Fall of British Asia, 1941–5* (London: Penguin, 2004), 47; Government of India, Indians Overseas Department to Secretary of State for India, September 28, 1942, T 161/1086, TNA; "I find these Malay hajjis the most baffling problem that has come my way since Singapore fell"; undated margin note by unknown author, in CO 273/671/4, TNA.

17. Stoneweather-Bird, Jedda, to FO, June 10, 1942, CO 273/671/4, TNA.

18. Secret Memorandum, FO, June 16, 1943, FO 371/35929, TNA.

19. J. Harold Shullaw, American Legation, Jeddah to Secretary of State, Washington, DC, January 11, 1943, enclosing text of speech from *Umm al-Qura*, no. 938, December 19, 1942, 890.F.00/79, U.S. National Archives, Washington, DC, in *RoH*, 7:481–482.

20. Wm. Roger Louis, *The British Empire in the Middle East, 1945–51: Arab Nationalism, the United States and Postwar Imperialism* (Oxford: Oxford University Press, 1984), 179.

21. District Muslim League Office, Jaunpur, to Secretary, Foreign Department, Government of India, August 1944, External Affairs, 1944, No. 369-ME, NAI.

22. Memorandum on Wartime Hajj, September 18, 1944, External Affairs, 1944, No. 369-ME, NAI.

23. Government of India Press Communique, August 23, 1944, External Affairs, 1944, No. 369-ME, NAI; Khan Bahadur Haji Wahiduddin, MBE, War-time Report on the Hajj Traffic, 1940–45, IOR/L/PJ/125/1/J, IOR, APAC, BL.

24. G.R.J., Note, May 17, 1944, External Affairs, 1944, No. 369-ME, NAI.

25. Quoted in Hyam, *Britain's Declining Empire*, 154.

26. John Darwin, *Britain and Decolonisation: The Retreat from Empire in the Post-war World* (London: Macmillan, 1988), 120.

27. Louis, *British Empire in the Middle East*, 173.

28. Ibid., 180, 193.

29. Report on the Hajj of 1365 AH/1946, FO 371/62089, TNA, in *RoH*, 7:697.

30. British Legation Jeddah to FO, January 5, 1947, FO 371/62089, TNA, in *RoH*, 7:721.

31. News from Mecca, *Muslim Review*, November 1948, Woking, 6/1/21, Box 6, Philby GB-0165-0229, MECA.

32. Report on the Hajj of 1365 AH/1946, IOR/L/PJ/125/1/J; Haj, 1946–1947, Arrangements for Indian Pilgrims, IOR/L/PJ/8/764, IOR, APAC, BL.

33. Foreign Secretary, Delhi, to Jedda, Bahrain, and Baghdad, July 9, 1948, External Affairs, 1948, No. F.13–3, NAI. See also Report on the Hajj of 1365 AH/1946, IOR/L/PJ/125/1/J, IOR, APAC, BL.

34. Report on the Hajj of 1368 AH/1949, 8, FO 371/82698, TNA, in *RoH*, 7:774. For a preindependence example of the continued arrival of Indian destitute pilgrims in the Hijaz, see Grafftey-Smith to FO, August 10, 1946, IOR/L/PJ/125/1/J, IOR, APAC, BL.

35. Green, *Our Journey*, 30.

36. Examples are too numerous to include here, but a search for "Haj subsidy" at the *Times of India* website, http://timesofindia.indiatimes.com/, will yield a lengthy list of articles related to this contentious issue. One example is B. N. Shukla, petitioner against Haj subsidy, "Sunday Debate: Should the Subsidy on Haj Be Withdrawn? Yes," September 9, 2006, http://articles.timesofindia.indiatimes.com/2006-09-09/all-that-matters/27830370_1_haj-subsidy-b-n-shukla-special-flights.

37. Hyam, *Britain's Declining Empire*, 131–137.

38. MacDonnell, "Conduct of Hajj from Malaysia," 387.

39. Federal Secretariat, Kuala Lumpur, Notice on the Mecca Pilgrimage 1949, DRCPW/182/48, AN.

40. Sheikh Ahmad bin Mohamed Hashim, Chair of Pilgrimage Advisory Committee, Memo, undated, Pt I, Pilgrimage Advisory Committee, Federal Secretariat 13907–1949, 1957/0575505, AN.

41. Ibid.

42. Federal Secretariat, Kuala Lumpur, Notice on the Mecca Pilgrimage 1949, DRCPW/182/48, AN.

43. Allocation of pilgrim passes for the Mecca pilgrimage, State Secretary Perak to Secretary to Member for Home Affairs, Kuala Lumpur, undated but probably 1952, Perak Secretariat, 1957/0000407, AN. See also Mecca Pilgrimage 1954, Selangor Secretariat, 1447–1953, 1957/0303225, AN.

44. First Meeting of Pilgrimage Advisory Committee August 20–21, 1949, Pt I, Pilgrimage Advisory Committee, Federal Secretariat 13907–1949, 1957/0575505, AN.

45. Secretary to Member for Home Affairs, Kuala Lumpur to All Authorities in Malaya, November 12, 1952, Mecca Pilgrimage 1953, Selangor Secretariat, 2474–1952, 1957/0302350, AN.

46. MacDonnell, "Conduct of Hajj from Malaysia," 400, 409–410.

47. Haji Ali Rouse, Report on Mecca Pilgrimage 1950, S.U.K. TR 1643/1950, 1957/0345880, AN. Cyril Ousman was killed by Prince Mishari al-Saud on November 16, 1951, and as a result Ibn Saud banned all alcohol from the Kingdom of Saudi Arabia: see PREM 11/249, TNA.

48. Federal Secretariat to Selangor State Secretariat, September 7, 1949, Selangor Secretariat, 2225–1949, 1957/0297913, AN; Negri Sembilan State Secretariat, 1128–1949, 1957/0467439.

49. Tagliacozzo, *Longest Journey*, 207.

50. Dr. S. Mohamed Baboo, Medical Officer in Charge of Malay Pilgrims, 1948, Medical Report, January 19, 1949, Pt I, Pilgrimage Advisory Committee, Federal Secretariat 13907–1949, 1957/0575505, AN.

51. J. M. Lonsdale and D. A. Low, "Towards the New Order, 1945–63," in D. A. Low and A. Smith (eds.), *The Oxford History of East Africa*, vol. 3 (Oxford: Oxford University Press, 1976), 1–64, 12–16.

52. Mr. M. Phillips, CO to FO October 21, 1950, enclosing Confidential Report on the Hajj from Nigeria, FO 371/82698, TNA, in *RoH*, 7:796, 800–802, 805–806, 813–814.

53. Martin Shipway, *Decolonization and Its Impact: A Comparative Approach to the End of the Colonial Empires* (London: Blackwell, 2008), 178.

54. Report on the Hajj of 1950, *RoH*, 7:848.

55. A. T. Weatherhead, "The Possession of Power," undated, 171, unpublished manuscript memoir, Mss. Afr.s.232, Rhodes House Library, University of Oxford.

56. Al Haji Abubakr Imam, Gaskiya Corporation, Zaria to Minister for Local Government, Northern Region, Kaduna, October 6, 1953, CO 554/1318, TNA, in *RoH*, 8:191–197.

57. CO to Hillier-Fry, African Department, FO, August 5, 1954, FO 371/110130, TNA, in *RoH*, 8:198–199.

58. FO to British Embassy, Jedda, March 18, 1955, FO 371/114903, TNA, in *RoH*, 8:236.

59. FO to British Embassy, Jedda, May 16, 1955, FO 371/114903, TNA, in *RoH*, 8:275.

60. Syed Muhammad Khairudin Aljunied, *Colonialism, Violence and Muslims in Southeast Asia: The Maria Hertogh Controversy* (London: Routledge, 2009), 45–49, 65, 127.

61. D. H. M. Riches, Jeddah to FO, June 4, 1952, FO 371/98848, TNA, in *RoH*, 8:15.

62. G. C. Pelham, Jeddah to FO, May 4, 1952, FO 371/98847, TNA, in *RoH*, 8:34.

63. Report on the Hajj 1372 AH/1953, FO 371/110130, TNA, in *RoH*, 8:172.

64. Circular from British Embassy, Jedda to FO, April 24, 1955, FO 371/127150, TNA, in *RoH*, 8:305–306.

65. Mr. Minor, Beirut to Secretary of State, Washington, DC, August 25, 1952, Nos. 344 and 369, US National Archives Series 886A. 413/8, in *RoH*, 8:53.

66. Mr. Minor, Beirut to Secretary of State, Washington, DC, December 11, 1952, US National Archives Series 886A. 413/10, 4–7, 9, 10, 12, in *RoH*, 8:70.

67. Circular airgram issued by Department of State, Washington, DC, June 5, 1953, US National Archives Series 886A. 413/10, 4–7, 9, 10, 12, in *RoH*, 8:71.

68. Miller, "Pilgrim's Progress," 218–226.

69. See Simon C. Smith (ed.), *Reassessing Suez 1956: New Perspectives on the Crisis and Its Aftermath* (London: Routledge, 2008); Afaf Lutfi al-Sayyid Marsot, *A Short History of Modern Egypt* (Cambridge: Cambridge University Press, 2007); Wm. Roger Louis (ed.), *Ends of British Imperialism: The Scramble for Empire, Suez and Decolonization; Collected Essays* (London: I. B. Tauris, 2006); Michael T. Thornhill, *Road to Suez: The Battle for the Canal Zone* (Stroud: Sutton, 2006); Barry Turner, *Suez 1956* (London: Hodder and Stoughton, 2006); M. W. Daly, *The Cambridge History of Egypt*, vol. 2 (Cambridge: Cambridge University Press, 1998); P. J. Vatikiotis, *The History of Modern Egypt from Muhammad Ali to Mubarak* (Baltimore, MD: Johns Hopkins University Press, 1991); Keith

Kyle, *Suez: Britain's End of Empire in the Middle East* (London: I. B. Tauris, 1991); Wm. Roger Louis and Roger Owen (eds.), *Suez: The Crisis and Its Consequences* (Oxford: Clarendon, 1989); Mohamed M. Heikal, *Cutting the Lion's Tail: Suez through Egyptian Eyes* (New York: Arbor House, 1986); Mahmoud Fawzi, *Suez 1956: An Egyptian Perspective* (London: Shorouk International, 1986); John Waterbury, *The Egypt of Nasser and Sadat* (Princeton, NJ: Princeton University Press, 1983); P. J. Vatikiotis, *Nasser and His Generation* (New York: St. Martin's, 1978); Raymond Baker, *Egypt's Uncertain Revolution under Nasser and Sadat* (Cambridge, MA: Harvard University Press, 1978); Jacques Berque, *Egypt: Imperialism and Revolution* (New York: Praeger, 1972); Sa'd Zaghlul Fu'ad, *Al-Qital fi al-Qawl* (Cairo, 1969); and Kamil Isma'il al-Sharif, *Al-Muqawama al-Sirriyya fi Qanat al-Suwais* (Beirut, 1957).

70. Acting Governor, Northern Region of Nigeria, to Secretary of State for the Colonies, November 23, 1956, CO 554/1318, TNA, in *RoH*, 8:335. The diplomatic rupture with the Saudis was also exacerbated by the dispute over the Buraimi Oasis, claimed by Saudi Arabia, Oman, and Abu Dhabi. Britain retook the oasis from the Saudis in 1955.

71. Acting Governor, Northern Region of Nigeria, to Secretary of State for the Colonies, November 23, 1956, CO 554/1318, TNA, in *RoH*, 8:335; Commonwealth Relations Office, London, to Molyneux, Karachi, December 31, 1956; Molyneux, Karachi, to CRO, London, February 5, 1957; CO to FO, February 25, 1957; FO to CO, March 1, 1957, CO 371/127173, TNA, in *RoH*, 8:337–341.

72. CO to FO, February 25, 1957, CO 371/127173, TNA, in *RoH*, 8:339.

73. Darwin, *Britain and Decolonisation*, 72. See also Darwin, *Empire Project;* and Darwin, *Unfinished Empire.*

Conclusion

1. Ali, *Proposed Political, Legal and Social Reforms*, i.

2. Joint press conference with United Kingdom Foreign Secretary and Saudi Foreign Minister Prince Saud al-Faisal, April 23, 2008, www.fco.gov.uk.

3. "Advice to British Hajjis Pilgrimage 2009," http://ukinsaudiarabia.fco.gov.uk/en/help-for-british-nationals/postsa-na-link-k-british-hajj.

4. See Francis Robinson, "Technology and Religious Change: Islam and the Impact of Print," *Modern Asian Studies*, 27:1 (1993), 229–251, which covers this topic for the pre-Internet age.

5. For example, see these BBC News website reports: "Hundreds Killed in Hajj Stampede," January 12, 2006, http://news.bbc.co.uk/1/hi/world/Middle_east/4606002.stm; and "History of Deaths on the Hajj," December 17, 2007, http://news.bbc.co.uk/1/hi/world/Middle_east/4607304.stm.

6. Ahmed Patel, Siddiqa Hassa, and Majid Ahmed, "British Hajj Delegation," http://blogs.fco.gov.uk/roller/thehajj/; launch of British Hajj delegation 2009 on YouTube, http://www.youtube.com/watch?v=A7QMIHnf8Ek; Dr. Abdul Halem, British Foreign and Commonwealth Office, "Hajj Blogger," 2009, http://comment.fco.gov.uk/roller2/halem/.

7. "Mecca Dream for Aged Pilgrim," February 10, 2004, http://news.bbc.co.uk/1/hi/world/south_asia/3455781.stm; "Ancient Pilgrim Prepares for Hajj," October 8, 2003, http://news.bbc.co.uk/1/hi/world/south_asia/3161680.stm; "Ancient Indian's Mecca Dream," October 7, 2003, http://news.bbc.co.uk/1/hi/in_depth/photo_gallery/3172230.stm; "Ancient Man's Prayers Answered," June 6, 2003, http://news.bbc.co.uk/1/hi/england/2970614.stm.

8. "Ancient Man's Prayers Answered."

Glossary

ahl al-kitab People of the Book—Jews and Christians

akbar great; large

'alim a learned person in Islam; a scholar

amir al-hajj officially appointed leader of a country's pilgrimage caravan or group; also called emir al-hajj

anjuman organization; association

dhu al-hijja twelfth and final month in the Islamic calendar; the month in which the Hajj takes place

farz one's duty

fatwa religious opinion concerning Islamic law issued by an Islamic scholar; the plural is *fatawa*

fiqh the understanding of *shari'a*, as developed by interpretation of the Qur'an and Sunna (the Prophet's teachings and practices) by *'ulama*

firman decree issued by an Islamic ruler

fyz-e-billah bounty ships

ganj-i-sarai caravan

hadith words, actions, or characteristics associated with the Prophet Muhammad

haramayn the Holy Mosque at Mecca and the Mosque of the Prophet at Medina

hijra migration; also refers to the Prophet Muhammad's migration from Mecca to Medina in 622 CE

ihram a sacred state Muslims must enter before performing Hajj; commonly refers to the two pieces of white cloth worn by men while performing the Hajj rituals

kafila safar leader of the Hyderabadi pilgrimage caravan

khadim al-haramayn al-sharifayn servant of the Two Holy Sanctuaries; protector of the Two Holy Sites in Islam; a title often held by whoever rules Mecca and Medina

kiswa richly decorated cloths that cover the Ka'ba in Mecca

madagar literal meaning "assistant"; lower-level official in the nizam of Hyderabad's government

madrassa educational institution

Mahdi the rightly guided one; according to Sunnis, he is yet to appear; according to the Shi'a, he is alive but not yet known; he will accompany Jesus to rid the world of evil and bring peace and harmony

mahmal a pyramid-shaped palanquin carried on a camel that was the centerpiece of the Egyptian pilgrimage caravan that traveled to Mecca for each Hajj. The *mahmal* caravan contained the *kiswa*, a set of richly decorated cloths to cover the Ka'ba

masjid literal meaning "place of prostration"; a mosque

maulvi honorific religious title given to Sunni Muslim religious scholars; a highly qualified Islamic scholar

mawlid celebration of the birthday of the Prophet Muhammad or of Sufi saints; the plural is *mawalid*

miskeen poor person; another phrase applied to destitute pilgrims

mujtahid a scholar who is qualified to interpret *shari'a* law through independent reasoning; the plural is *mujtahidun*

munshi clerk; secretary in British government service, generally associated with India

musafirkhana pilgrim hostel

mutawwif guide for pilgrims during the Hajj; the plural is *mutawwifin*

nizam king; ruler; commonly refers to the nizam of Hyderabad

purdah practice of concealing women from men, either through physical separation or the requirement for women to cover their bodies and conceal their form

qadi judge ruling in accordance with *shari'a* law

rihla a quest, travels undertaken to increase a scholar's religious knowledge; also a term for a book recounting such travels

safar nama pilgrimage narrative

salat practice of formal prayers in Islam; one of the five pillars of Islam

sambuq small ship traditionally used to collect pearls or carry passengers

sawm a form of fasting regulated by Islamic jurisprudence, generally to abstain from eating and drinking during daylight hours, and generally associated with Ramadan; one of the five pillars of Islam

sa'y one of the rituals of Hajj; walking between the hills of Safa and Marwa in Mecca

shahada Muslim declaration of belief in the oneness of God and the acceptance of Muhammad as God's Prophet; one of the five pillars of Islam

sura a division of the Qur'an, often referred to as a chapter

takayrna pilgrims from West Africa or sub-Saharan Africa; non-Arab African Muslims; also referred to as *takarir*, *takruni*, or *takarna*. The singular is *takruri*. From the verb *takurrar*, to renew, purify, invigorate religious piety

talab al-'ilm a search for religious knowledge by traveling scholars

talbiyya verbal formula repeated during rituals related to the Hajj

tawaf the circumambulation of the Ka'ba; one of the rituals of the Hajj

'ulama educated class of Muslim legal scholars

umma the worldwide community of Muslims

wajib one's religious duty

waqf religious endowment in Islamic law, usually land or a building for Islamic religious or charitable purposes

wuquf a period of prayer and conversation at Mount Arafat during the Hajj

zakat giving a fixed portion of one's wealth to charity; one of the five pillars of Islam

zinda pir living saint

ziyara literally "visit"; pilgrimage to sites associated with the Prophet Muhammad, his family members and descendants, or other venerated figures in Islam, such as Sufi saints, notables, and scholars

Archival Sources

Cambridge University, United Kingdom
Pembroke College Library

PRIVATE PAPERS

Storrs, Sir Ronald

Centre of South Asian Studies

PRIVATE PAPERS

Darling, M. L.

Plunkett, E. Lawrence

Durham University, United Kingdom
University Library, Sudan Archive

PRIVATE PAPERS

Clayton, Sir Gilbert	280/2; 301/4; 469/8; 471/9
Willis, C. A.	212/2; 212/8
Wingate, Sir Reginald	134/4; 134/5; 134/6; 135/1; 135/4; 137/4; 137/7; 138/5; 138/8; 138/12; 138/14; 138/15; 138/16; 157/3; 158/3; 158/6; 160/1; 160/2; 160/3; 164/5; 165/2; 167/1; 167/2;

University Library, Sudan Archive, continued

169/3; 172/5; 172/7; 176/1; 185/1; 187/1; 187/2; 187/3; 188/3; 189/2; 190/1; 190/3; 192/3; 195/1; 197/2; 201/7; 202/1; 270/1; 271/6; 272/5; 273/8; 273/9; 276/1; 281/2; 282/2; 283/1; 283/3; 284/1; 284/3; 284/4; 284/9; 285/1; 296/1; 297/2; 300/1

British Library, United Kingdom

INDIA OFFICE RECORDS, ASIA, PACIFIC, AND AFRICA COLLECTIONS

IOR/L/F/4/248/5593	Request of Shamsu Nisa Begam to be allowed to go on a pilgrimage to the cities of Mecca and Medina	1807–1808
IOR/L/MIL/7/18619	Collection 425/1449, Pilgrimage to Mecca (Haj): proposed grant of leave to certain Mahomedan officers on termination of hostilities and conveyance of Indian Army details from Egypt Mecca	1931–1939
IOR/L/PJ/12/110	File 6748/22, Khilafat Movement	1925–1928
IOR/L/PJ/12/111	File 6478(d)/22, Indian Muslim Khilafat delegation to Turkey, Hedjaz and Nejd [Saudi Arabia]	1923–1925
IOR/L/PJ/125/1/J	Report on the Hajj of 1365 AH/1946	1946
IOR/L/PJ/8/764	Haj, 1946–1947, Arrangements for Indian Pilgrims	1946–1947
IOR/L/PS/10/523	File 53/1915, Pt 1, German War: the Caliphate and Pan-Arab movement	1914–1915
IOR/L/PS/10/752	File 3156/1918, Pt 4, Mesopotamia: administration; publication of a Blue Book	1919–1920
IOR/L/PS/10/936	File 7251/1920, Pt 1, Arabia: general situation; Hedjaz-Nejd relations	1920–1924

IOR/L/PS/11/97	File P3540/1915, Arabia: the pilgrimage; question of the Sacred Caravan from Constantinople	1915–1919
IOR/L/PS/11/122	P1670/1917, Arabia: proposed communiqué regarding annual pilgrimage to Mecca; Foreign Office concur, with a suggestion	1917–1918
IOR/L/PS/11/150	P1584/1919, Quarantine precautions in connection with the Hedjaz Pilgrimage	1918–1919
IOR/L/PS/11/165	P7523/1919, Reports of the Administration for 1918 of Divisions and Districts of the Occupied Territories in Mesopotamia	1918–1919
IOR/L/PS/12/2155	Coll 6/82, Saudi Arabia: removal from Jidda of Khan Bahadur Ihsanullah	1936–1937
IOR/R/A/3898	File 1449, Annual Report on the Haj Pilgrimage	1937
IOR/R/15/1/576	File 61/13 [III] (D 167), Pilgrimage to Hijaz	1936–1944
IOR/R/20/A/3524	File 1004, Report on the pilgrimage to the Hejaz in 1932	1933
IOR/R/20/B/1456	File C.27/3, Pilgrimage: measure for the prevention of destitution among Indian pilgrims proceeding to Hejaz by devious and unauthorised routes	1939

The National Archives, United Kingdom

CABINET OFFICE

CAB 23/27	Papers nos. 74 (21)–93 (21)	1921
CAB 24/34	Papers nos. 2801–2900	1917
CAB 24/117	Papers nos. 2301–2403	1920
CAB 27/1	British Desiderata in Turkey in Asia	1915

The National Archives, United Kingdom, continued

CAB 37/121/124	Memorandum by Lord Cromer respecting the steps to be taken in the event of war with Turkey	1914
CAB 42/2	War Council	1915

COLONIAL OFFICE

CO 273/30	Despatches	1869
CO 273/106	Straits Settlements Correspondence	1880
CO 273/227	Despatches. Straits.	1897
CO 273/414	Offices. Foreign.	1914
CO 273/415	Offices. Foreign.	1914
CO 273/425	Despatches. High Commissioner.	1915
CO 273/430	Offices: Admiralty, Crown Agents and Council	1915
CO 273/433	Offices: home.	1915
CO 273/491	Offices: foreign	1919
CO 273/512	Straits Settlements Original Correspondence	1921
CO 273/517	Despatches	1922
CO 273/525	Despatches	1924
CO 273/527	Offices and individuals	1924
CO 273/535/5	Pilgrims to Mecca and Medina	1927
CO 273/567/6	Pilgrims to Jeddah	1930–1931
CO 273/559/14	Pilgrim-carrying ships	1929
CO 273/581/9	HM Legation at Jedda	1932
CO 273/671/4	Malayan residents in Middle East: financial relief	1942–1943
CO 276/106	Government Gazettes	1927
CO 323/732/8	Pamphlets for the colonies	1916
CO 554/1318	Appointment of a Pilgrim Commissioner in Jedda for the welfare of Nigerian pilgrims to Mecca	1953–1957

CO 583/143/6	Mahdism in North Africa	1924–1926
CO 583/146/8	Mohammedan Pilgrimage to Mecca and Medina, 1926	1926–1957
CO 583/155/10	Mohammedan Pilgrimages	1928–1929
CO 583/167/7	Control of Mohammedan Pilgrimages to Hedjaz	1929
CO 583/174/3	Pilgrimage to Mecca and visit to England by attaché of Igbirra	1930
CO 583/174/8	Control of Mohammedan Pilgrimage to Hedjaz	1930
CO 696/1	Iraq Administration Reports	1917–1918
CO 696/2	Iraq Administration Reports	1919
CO 732/26/2	Haramain waqfs	1927
CO 732/31/9	Pilgrimage to Mecca, 1928	1928
CO 732/39/9	Report on Inquiries into the Measures for the Sanitary Control of the Hejaz Pilgrimage	1919
CO 732/45/7	Activities of Philby	1930
CO 732/70/7	Slavery in the Middle East	1935
CO 732/87/18	Propaganda during the war: Moslem pilgrimage	1943
CO 879/119/10	Journey from Maidugari, Nigeria, to Jeddah in Arabia; report by H.R. Palmer, Resident Bornu	1919

FOREIGN OFFICE

FO 78/4093	Pilgrim Traffic. Vol. 1	1884–1885
FO 78/4094	Pilgrim Traffic. Vol. 2	1886–1887
FO 78/4263	Pilgrim Traffic. Vol. 3	1888–1889
FO 78/4406	Ata Mohamed, Vice-Consul Hodeida, Report on Kamaran Quarantine Station	1891
FO 78/4532	Pilgrim Traffic. Vol. 6	1893
FO 78/4533	Pilgrim Traffic. Vol. 7	1893
FO 78/4601	Pilgrim Traffic. Vol. 9	1894

The National Archives, United Kingdom, continued

FO 78/4778	Pilgrim Traffic. Vol. 13	1896
FO 78/4882	Pilgrim Traffic. Vol. 14	1897
FO 78/4789	Disturbances at Jeddah	1895–1896
FO 78/4981	Pilgrim Traffic. Vol. 65	1898
FO 141/477	General correspondence	1912–1929
FO 141/480/6	Claude Lewis Miller, refused permission to make pilgrimage	1921
FO 141/521	General correspondence	1919–1929
FO 141/531	General correspondence	1912–1927
FO 141/671	General correspondence	1917–1927
FO 141/682	General correspondence	1916–1929
FO 141/688	General correspondence	1917–1929
FO 141/710	General correspondence	1914–1937
FO 141/720	General correspondence	1930–1931
FO 141/740	General correspondence	1919–1926
FO 141/730	General correspondence	1931
FO 141/773	General correspondence	1915–1932
FO 141/786	General correspondence	1917–1938
FO 141/803	General correspondence	1916–1918
FO 195/956	From Jeddah	1869–1872
FO 195/1375	Egypt, Jeddah, Tripoli, Barbary	1881
FO 195/1583	Damascus, Aleppo, Jeddah, Benghazi, Tripoli	1887
FO 195/1610	Adana, Aleppo, Benghazi, Jeddah, Tripoli	1888
FO 195/1987	From Jeddah	1897
FO 371/2482	Turkey (War)	1915
FO 371/3408	Turkey	1918
FO 371/35929	Pilgrimage of Mohammedans from Japanese-occupied territories to Mecca	1943
FO 371/4194	Turkey	1919

FO 371/4195	Turkey	1919
FO 371/5092	Turkey	1920
FO 371/7713	Arabia	1922
FO 371/10812	Arabia	1925
FO 371/11433	Arabia	1926
FO 371/11436	Arabia	1926
FO 371/11442	Arabia	1926
FO 371/12248	Arabia	1927
FO 371/13728	Arabia	1929
FO 371/14456	Arabia	1930
FO 371/15290	Hejaz and Nejd	1931
FO 371/16857	Hejaz and Nejd	1933
FO 371/17932	Saudi Arabia	1934
FO 371/19002	Saudi Arabia	1935
FO 371/20786	Eastern: General	1937
FO 371/20817	Palestine and Transjordan	1937
FO 371/24585	Organisation of pilgrim transport for 1940 pilgrimage to Mecca	1940
FO 371/27259	Pilgrims to Mecca	1941
FO 371/62089	Transport of pilgrims to the Holy Cities	1947
FO 371/82698	Chartering of ships for the 1950 Mecca pilgrimage	1950
FO 371/98847	Arrangements for pilgrims to Mecca and the Hejaz; abolition of Saudi tax on pilgrims; problems of illegal entrants and destitute pilgrims in transit	1952
FO 371/98848	Arrangements for pilgrims to Mecca and the Hejaz; abolition of Saudi tax on pilgrims; problems of illegal entrants and destitute pilgrims in transit	1952
FO 371/110130	Arrangements for the pilgrimage of Moslems to the Hejaz in 1954	1954

The National Archives, United Kingdom, continued

FO 371/114903	Report on Haj pilgrimage to Moslem Holy Places in Hejaz: arrangements for pilgrims from Nigeria and Malaya	1955
FO 371/127150	Internal political situation in Saudi Arabia	1957
FO 373/5/6	The Rise of Islam and the Caliphate; The Pan-Islamic Movement	1919
FO 608/101	British delegation, correspondence and papers relating to Middle East (political)	1919
FO 685/2	Consulate, Jedda, Ottoman Empire: general correspondence	1883–1886
FO 686/31	Pilgrims' hostel, Mecca	1918–1921
FO 686/62	Egyptian Mahmal; despatch to Mecca and its recall in 1923	1923–1924
FO 800/253	Miscellaneous correspondence. Volume 2	1921–1928
FO 881/4762	TURKEY: Report. The Haj (Pilgrimage), 1882. (Dr. Abdur Razzack)	1882
FO 881/5113	TURKEY: Report. Pilgrim Season, 1884. (Dr. Razzack)	1885
FO 882/2	Arab Bureau: Miscellaneous correspondence	1914
FO 882/5	Arab Bureau: Miscellaneous correspondence	1916
FO 967/3	Hejaz: internal situation	1926

Note: Several of these Foreign Office files are reproduced in Alan Rush (ed.), *Records of the Hajj: A Documentary History of the Pilgrimage to Mecca*, vols. 1–10 (Gerrards Cross: Archive Editions, 1993).

OTHER GOVERNMENT DEPARTMENTS

HD 3/55	Printed FO correspondence on Asia	1880
PC 1/2672	International Sanitary Conference on Cholera: Protocols of Proceedings and Reports, etc.	1866

PC 1/2674	Memorandum by Mr. Netten Radcliffe on Quarantine in the Red Sea and on the Sanitary Regulation of the Pilgrimage to Mecca	1880
T 161/1086	Proposed Subsidy for the Mecca Pilgrimage	1940

Oxford University, United Kingdom
Bodleian Library

Papers Relating to the Arrangements Made with Messrs. Cook & Son for the Conduct of the Pilgrim Traffic to and from the Red Sea during the Years 1884–95
Series: Selections from the records of the Government of India, Home Department, No. 330 (Calcutta, 1896), IND Ind R 1/330

Middle East Centre Archive, St. Anthony's College

PRIVATE PAPERS

Bowman, Humphrey Ernest	GB-0165–0034
Bullard, Sir Reader William	GB-0165–0042
Cheetham, Sir Milne	GB-0165–0055
Cox, Sir Percy Zachariah	GB-0165–0341
Hogarth, David George	GB-0165–0147
Philby, Harry St. John Bridger	GB-0165–0229
Sykes, Sir Mark, 6th Baronet	GB-0165–0275
Rapp, Sir Thomas Cecil	GB-0165–0234
Young, J. W. A.	GB-0165–0310

Rhodes House Library

PRIVATE PAPERS

Butler, Maj-Gen. S.S. Butler	Mss. Afr.r.195
Lethem, Sir Gordon James	Mss. Brit.Emp.s.276
Weatherhead, A. T.	Mss. Afr.s.232

Thomas Cook Archives, Peterborough, United Kingdom

"Report of Information Obtained in Jeddah Regarding the Mecca Pilgrimage," October 1886, Folio 161 D

The Mecca Pilgrimage, "Museum" item 163 F

Government of India: Report of Arrangements Carried Out by Thomas Cook and Sons in Connection with the Movement of Pilgrims for the Hadj of 1888; and subsequent reports for 1889, 1890, 1891, 1892, 1893

Government of India Resolution, January 11, 1895

Andhra Pradesh State Archives, Hyderabad, India

File 4, Muhafiz No. 1, 1314F

File 34, Muhafiz No. 2, 1311F

File 3, Muhafiz No. 3, 1317F

Part I, File 2, Muhafiz No. 3, 1312F

File 8, Muhafiz No. 8, 1319F

File 6, Muhafiz No. 9, 1319F

File 3, Muhafiz No. 12, 1318F

File 121, Muhafiz No. 113, undated

File 350, Muhafiz No. 169, 1318F

File 46, Muhafiz No. 234, undated

File 290, Muhafiz No. 263, 1313F

File 306, Muhafiz No. 365, 1312F

File 11, RC No.10, undated

File 2, RL No. 3, 1312F

File 3, 1316F

Maharashtra State Archives, Mumbai, India
General Department

1875	Vol. 63: File 794
	Vol. 77: File 574
1878	Vol. 51: File 360; File 637

1881	Vol. 79: File 12; File 615; File 635
1885	Vol. 124: File 82; File 138
1887	Vol. 110: File 912
1910	Vol. 133: File 459
	Vol. 134: File 44; File 615
1911	Vol. 158: File 112; File 992; File 1213
	Vol. 159: File 62A
	Vol. 160: File 678
1912	Vol. 128: File 1368; File 1487
	Vol. 130: File 122; File 691; File 916
	Vol. 131: File 992
	Vol. 132: File 618; File 768
	Vol. 133: File 682
1913	Vol. 140: File 485; File 768
	Vol. 141: File 992; File 993
	Vol. 143: File 1088
1922	File 3442; File 3542
1924	File 5247
1925	File 5748-C Pt. II

National Archives of India, New Delhi
Foreign Department

Political—External Affairs—A, May 5, 1854

General—A, 1877, No. 125–192

Political—B, August 1879, Programme No. 144

Secret, March 1881, No. 156–160

Secret, June 1881, No. 425–426

Secret—Internal, August 1886, No. 22–28

September 1886, No. 197–199

Secret—Internal, October 1887, No. 136–143

Secret—Internal, October 1889, No. 39–42

Foreign Department, continued

External—A, August 1890, No. 149–152

Secret—E, September 1895, No. 44–64

External—A, October 1896, No. 210–213

Secret—E, January 1897, No. 138–142

Internal—A, April 1897, No. 140–175

External—A, March 1898, No. 206–215

External—A, September 1898, No. 107–110

External—B, September 1907, No. 111–140

General—B, February 1911, No. 59–60

Internal—B, August 1913, No. 349–352

Foreign and Political Department

War—Secret, July 1915, No. 245–251

Secret—General, May 1916, No. 10

War—Secret, June 1916, No. 223–314

War—Secret, March 1917, No. 67–69

Secret—External, November 1919, No. 1–139

Secret—External, May 1921, No. 4–14

External—B, Secret, 10–16, 1921

1033-M, 1923

Secret—External, No. 34—X, 1924

External, 1924, No. 4(2)

1931, No. 414-N/30, Nos. 1-15

1932, No.213-N

1933, Near East Department, 1-24

1934, No. 410-N

External Affairs

1936, 94-N

1936, 390(9)G

1939, No. 463-N

1944, No. 369-ME

1948, No. F.13–3

Arkib Negara, Kuala Lumpur, Malaysia

1957/00181	Difficulties in Sending Remittances, 1964–1343
1957/00190	Haji Abdul Majid, Malay Pilgrimage Report for 1933, 2236–52
1957/00267	Pahang Federal Secretariat, 1503–1938
1957/0000407	Perak Secretariat, 1952
1957/0237768	Report on the Pilgrimage 1924, Selangor. 3971–1925
1957/0251119	Selangor Secretariat, 5649–1927
1957/0297913	Selangor Secretariat, 2225–1949
1957/0302350	Mecca Pilgrimage 1953, Selangor Secretariat, 2474–1952
1957/0303225	Mecca Pilgrimage 1954, Selangor Secretariat, 1447–1953
1957/0304552	Perak Secretariat, 1632/1947
1957/0345880	Haji Ali Rouse, Report on Mecca Pilgrimage 1950, S.U.K. TR 1643/1950
1957/0349945	511–1353, 1934
1957/0037810	Selangor. Native. 1295–93
1957/0387494	Report of the Pilgrim Committee, 1924, 1672/1342
1957/0389750	Haji Abdul Majid, Malay Pilgrimage Report for 1924, 938–1343
1957/0400522	Haji Abdul Majid, Malay Pilgrimage Report for 1927, 843–1346
1957/0400522	A. W. Hamilton, Report on Pilgrimage Conditions 1927, 843–1346
1957/0401691	Notice by Malay Pilgrimage Officer, 1927, 1623–1346
1957/0420237	Haji Abdul Majid, Malay Pilgrimage Report for 1934, 2337–1353
1957/044840	Negri Sembilan, Miscellaneous, 218–1923
1957/0453237	Negri Sembilan Secretariat, 3164/1928

Arkib Negara, Kuala Lumpur, Malaysia, continued

1957/0454803	Negri Sembilan Secretariat, General, 1510–1931
1957/0456147	Negri Sembilan Secretariat, 1761–1936
1957/0457829	Negri Sembilan Secretariat, Pilgrimage to Mecca, 1940
1957/0467439	Negri Sembilan State Secretariat, 1128–1949
1957/0479437	Report on the Pilgrimage 1926/7, A.P. 222–1346
1957/0516381	Warnings to Intending Pilgrims, Kelantan, 42–1931
1957/0520541	Haji Abdul Majid, Malay Pilgrimage Report for 1935, Kelantan, 872–1934
1957/0524970	Kelantan, 680–1938
1957/0525835	Haji Abdul Majid, Malay Pilgrimage Report 1938–39; Che Jusoh, Malay Pilgrimage Report 1939–40, Kelantan 453/1939
1957/0575505	Pt I, Pilgrimage Advisory Committee, Federal Secretariat 13907–1949
1971/0001358	General Circular, Perak Secretariat, 383–38, 1938
DRCPW/182/48	Notice on the Mecca Pilgrimage 1949

National Archives of Singapore, Oral History Archive

Ahmad Sonhadji bin Mohammed Milatu	000201 (Reels 20–21)
Roderick MacLean	000301 (Reel 19)
Yuhanis Binte Haji Yusof	000459 (Reel 2)
Hasnah Binte Sahlan	000560 (Reel 2)
Omar Bin Haji Abdul Rahim	000595 (Reel 21)
Taha Bin Haji Abdullah	000608 (Reel 1)
Buang Haji Siraj	000715 (Reel 3)
Mohammed Amin Bin Abdul Wahhab	001597 (Reel 22)
Fatimah Binte Ismail	001905 (Reel 7)

Printed Primary Sources

Bidwell, Robin (ed.). *The Arab Bulletin, 1916–1919*. Volumes 1–4. Gerrards Cross: Archive Editions, 1986.

Burdett, Anita (ed.). *The Slave Trade into Arabia, 1820–1973*. Volumes 1–9. Gerrards Cross: Archive Editions, 2006.

Dening, S. L. (ed.). *King Abdul Aziz, Political Correspondence, 1904–1953*. Volumes 1–4. Gerrards Cross: Archive Editions, 1996.

Jarman, Robert (ed.). *The Jedda Diaries, 1919–1940*. Volumes 1–4. Gerrards Cross: Archive Editions, 1990.

Rush, Alan (ed.). *Records of the Hajj: A Documentary History of the Pilgrimage to Mecca*. Volumes 1–10. Gerrards Cross: Archive Editions, 1993.

Acknowledgments

THIS BOOK, LIKE many others, was completed only with the help of a large number of people and institutions. My research would not have been possible without the financial support of the Arts and Humanities Research Council and, at Cambridge, the Smuts Fund. I am grateful to Queens' College for electing me to a Munro Studentship. I was fortunate to work on the British Museum's blockbuster 2012 exhibition *Hajj: Journey to the Heart of Islam*, and I am extremely grateful to Venetia Porter for giving me that opportunity, and grateful to have worked with Qaisra Khan on the same project.

Further work on the book was made possible thanks to the generosity of St. John's College, Cambridge, where I was elected to a Title A Research Fellowship. It is a fantastic position and environment in which to research and write a book. At St. John's, I am grateful for the support and encouragement provided by the Master, Chris Dobson, and Sylvana Tomaselli. At Harvard University Press, I am grateful for the close attention and expertise of my editor, Ian Malcolm, and Joy Deng. At Westchester Publishing Services, I am grateful for the thorough work of Chris Dahlin and the copyeditor Charles Eberline. Thanks to Jeremy Lowe for careful proofreading. I would like to thank the staff and archivists at the following places: in London, the National Archives, the Oriental and India Office Collections at the British Library, and the British Library Reading Rooms; in Oxford, the Rhodes House and Bodleian Libraries and Debbie Usher at the Middle East Archive at St. Anthony's College; in Cambridge, the University Library; in Durham, the Sudan Archive at Durham University; in Egypt, the Dar al-Kutub, Cairo; in India, the National Archives, Delhi, the Maharashtra State Archives, Mumbai, and Dr. Zareena Parveen at the Andhra Pradesh State Archives,

Hyderabad, who gave me permission to access the nizam's government's files; in Malaysia, the Arkib Negara, Kuala Lumpur; and in Singapore, the Oral History Archives.

I am grateful for the hospitality of the following people: Dr. Peter and Christine Gilbert and Dr. David and Eleanor Harte in Newcastle; Professor Tapan and Hashi Raychaudhuri and Eleanor Watts and Chris Jacques in Oxford; Clare and Dr. Greg Mellor in Cambridge; Blair Gibbs, Gillian Hunter, John O'Connor, Frédérique Bendjelloul, Nick Barr, and Dr. Jonathan Silberstein-Loeb in London; Sarah Quill, Ismael Fathi, Fauzia Dawood, Sarah Marrs, and Sebastian in Cairo; Osman Attia in Khartoum; Nikhilesh Sinha and Samrat Chakrabarti in Delhi; Yashodhara Roy and Joy Roy in Mumbai; and Aparajita Sinha in Hyderabad. I am especially grateful to Dr. James Kelly, who allowed me to stay in my Queens' College flat during my final year as a graduate student.

I am grateful to the following people in Hyderabad, who were extremely helpful in my quest for Urdu Hajj *safar namas* and getting access to the Andhra Pradesh State Archives: Salil Kader, Dr. Aminuddin Khan, Dr. Ziauddin Shakeb, Rashid Ali Khan, Dr. Manni Mehdi, and Dr. Vasant Bawa. I am especially grateful to Mohamed Rafeeque Qasmi, a Deobandi-trained scholar, for his valuable assistance with the nizam's government records and Hajj *safar namas.* My research in Hyderabad would not have been possible without the enormous help provided by my mother-in-law, Aparajita Sinha. In Singapore, I am grateful for the kindness and generosity of Hidayah Amin and Ibrahim Tahir, and the assistance of Sufiyan Hanafi with the recordings in the Oral History Archives. The advice provided by Karl Hack regarding the Arkib Negara in Kuala Lumpur was invaluable.

This work has benefited greatly from comments, suggestions, and criticisms from the following scholars: Andrew Arsan, Amira Bennison, John Darwin, Jan-Georg Deutsch, Faisal Devji, Will Facey, Ulrike Freitag, Nile Green, Friedhelm Hartwig, Andrew Jarvis, Jagjeet Lally, Baz Lecocq, Rachel Leow, Kristen Loveland, Andrew Macdonald, Sumit Mandal, David Motadel, Jake Norris, Polly O'Hanlon, Amr Riyad, Sujit Sivasundaram, and Eric Tagliacozzo.

I am especially grateful to William Gervase Clarence-Smith for his close reading and examination of an early version of this book, and to Carl Watkins for his comments on the book's introduction. The three anonymous peer reviewers for Harvard University Press gave extremely constructive comments and suggestions on the manuscript, which helped further shape the project in useful directions. Any errors in the book that remain are mine alone.

Many thanks to John O'Connor for the maps and other technical assistance and to James Roslington for double-checking various things at a late stage. I am grateful to the Mohamed Ali Foundation; the Thomas Cook Archives; the Royal Geographic Society, London; the Imperial War Museum, London; National Portrait Gallery, London; the Science Photo Library, London; the Middle East Centre Archive, St. Anthony's College, Oxford; Corbis Images; Lady Bullard; Mrs. Gillian Kingham; Ibrahim Tahir; Coralie Hepburn of the British Museum Press; and Jane Hogan of the Sudan Archive, Durham University, for assistance and permission to reproduce images.

Chris Bayly has been a peerless adviser, a source of constructive criticism and intellectual generosity. I am greatly indebted to Richard Rex for admitting me to Queens' College, Cambridge, as an undergraduate in 2001, and to Chris Marks, my secondary-school history teacher; my first piece of work for him at age eleven was about the Prophet Muhammad, on which he wrote "Promising."

Special thanks are due to Tim Harper, whose expertise, guidance, dedication, and support have been exemplary. It has been a pleasure and an honor to work with him.

The Cambridge team has supported me in many and various ways since 2001; many thanks to Pete and Laura Baynton, Esther Bintliff, Alex Gezelius, Ed Gilbert, Duncan Harte, Ian Hogarth, Andre Marmot, Clare and Greg Mellor, Lizzie Ostrom, Oliver Rickman, Cynthia Shanmugalingam, Jennifer Singerman, Pete Smith, Dan Sternberg, and Rado Tylecote. I also gratefully acknowledge backing that stretches back to the twentieth century from Blair Gibbs, John O'Connor, and Nick Barr.

My family has been a constant source of love and support: thank you, Nana, Paul, and especially Mum for everything. My Grandad is not alive to read this, but I like to think that he would have enjoyed it. The whole experience has been immeasurably improved in innumerable ways by Mishka Sinha.

Index